Readings in Economic Sociology

BLACKWELL READERS IN SOCIOLOGY

Each volume in this authoritative series aims to provide students and scholars with comprehensive collections of classic and contemporary readings for all the major sub-fields of sociology. They are designed to complement single-authored works, or to be used as stand-alone textbooks for courses. The selected readings sample the most important works that students should read and are framed by informed editorial introductions. The series aims to reflect the state of the discipline by providing collections not only on standard topics but also on cutting-edge subjects in sociology to provide future directions in teaching and research.

Readings in Economic Sociology

Edited by

Nicole Woolsey Biggart

Copyright © Blackwell Publishers Ltd 2002

First published 2002

2 4 6 8 10 9 7 5 3 1

Blackwell Publishers Inc.
350 Main Street
Malden, Massachusetts 02148
USA

Blackwell Publishers Ltd
108 Cowley Road
Oxford OX4 1JF
UK

Library of Congress Cataloging-in-Publication Data has been applied for.
ISBN 0-631-22861-6 (hardback); 0-631-22862-4 (paperback)

British Library Cataloguing in Publication Data
A CIP catalogue record for this book is available from the British Library.

Typeset in 10 on 12pt Sabon
by Graphicraft Limited, Hong Kong

Printed in Great Britain by Antony Rowe Ltd., Chippenham, Wiltshire

This book is printed on acid-free paper.

Contents

The Contributors

Mitchel Y. Abolafia is Associate Professor in the Rockefeller College of Public Affairs at the University at Albany, SUNY. He is the author of *Making Markets: Opportunism and Restraint on Wall Street* (1996). His current work examines decision making at the Federal Reserve Board.

Nicole Woolsey Biggart is Professor of Management and Sociology at the University of California, Davis. She has written about the economic uses of social relations in various settings including direct selling, Asian business groups, and in peer lending groups. She is the author of *Charismatic Capitalism: Direct Selling in America* (1989) and co-author with Marco Orrù and Gary Hamilton of *The Economic Organization of East Asian Capitalism* (1997).

Fred Block is Professor of Sociology at the University of California, Davis. He has written widely in economic and political sociology; his books include *The Vampire State, Postindustrial Possibilities* (1996) and *The Origins of International Economic Disorder* (1977).

Pierre Bourdieu is a French anthropologist and sociologist who worked extensively in Algeria before becoming Professor of Sociology at the Collège de France. Among Bourdieu's many works are *The Algerians* (1962) and *The Logic of Practice* (1990).

Bruce G. Carruthers teaches in the sociology department at Northwestern University. His books include *City of Capital: Politics and Markets in the English Financial Revolution* (1996), *Rescuing Business: The Making of Corporate Bankruptcy Law in England and the United States* (1998), and *Economy/Society: Markets, Meanings, and Social Structure* (1999).

Randall Collins is Professor of Sociology at the University of Pennsylvania. He is a leading social theorist of macro-historical processes of social and economic change. He is the author of *Conflict Sociology* (1975), *Weberian Sociological Theory* (1986), and many other works.

Paula England is Professor of Sociology at the University of Pennsylvania. Her scholarship focuses on gender inequality in the labor market and the family, and she is a leading contributor to dialogue between sociologists, economists, and feminists.

Wendy Nelson Espeland is Associate Professor of Sociology at Northwestern University. Her works, including *The Struggle for Water: Rationality, Politics and Identity in the American Southwest* (1998), address what it means to different groups to be rational, and how this affects politics.

Neil Fligstein is the Class of 1939 Chancellor's Professor in the Department of Sociology at the University of California. He has done important empirical and theoretical work in economic sociology, including *The Transformation of Corporate Control* (1990) and most recently *The Architecture of Markets* (forthcoming).

Mark Granovetter, Professor of Sociology at Stanford University, is a specialist in economic sociology and social networks. His work examines how people and organizations, not only products and technology, influence the structure of industries.

Mauro F. Guillén is Associate Professor of Management and of Sociology at the University of Pennsylvania. His most recent book, *The Limits of Convergence* (2001), compares organizational change and responses to globalization in Argentina, South Korea, and Spain.

Gary G. Hamilton is Professor of Sociology and a member of the International Studies Faculty of the Henry M. Jackson School of International Relations at the University of Washington, Seattle. He has written widely on the economic structure of East Asia and is well known for his Weberian analyses of social and economic life.

Sherryl Kleinman teaches sociology at the University of North Carolina, Chapel Hill. Her most recent book is *Opposing Ambitions: Gender and Identity in an Alternative Organization* (1996). She has published widely on symbolic interactionism, sociology of emotions, fieldwork, gender, and inequality.

Loren Lutzenhiser is Professor of Sociology and Rural Sociology at Washington State University. A leading environmental sociologist, his work focuses at the intersection of technology, culture, and policy.

Karl Marx was a leading nineteenth-century European intellectual whose ideas were the basis for socialist movements around the world. His critical writings on capitalism include his masterwork, *Capital* (1867).

Karl Polanyi was an economic historian who emigrated from Eastern Europe to the US and later Canada. He is best remembered for *The Great Transformation* (1957). Among other works he authored *Trade and Markets in Early Empires* (1957) with K. Conrad, K. Arensburg, and H. W. Pearson; *Primitive, Archaic and Modern Economics: Essays of Karl Polanyi* (1968); and *The Livelihood of Man* (1977) with H. W. Pearson.

Walter W. Powell is Professor of Education and Affiliated Professor of Sociology, Public Policy, and International Studies at Stanford University, where he is also director of SCANCOR. His writings examine the importance of institutions and networks in social and economic life.

Adam Smith was an eighteenth-century Scottish Enlightenment political economist and philosopher. In addition to writing his famous book *An Inquiry into the Nature and Causes of the Wealth of Nations* (1776), he was author of *Theory of Moral*

Sentiments (1761). The latter work was about standards of ethical conduct necessary for social order, with emphasis on the general harmony of human motives and activities under a beneficent providence.

Charles Smith is Professor of Sociology at Queens College and the Graduate Center of the City University of New York. His research for the last 40 years has focused on auctions and financial markets. In addition to *Auctions: The Social Construction of Value* (1989), he is author of *Success and Survival on Wall Street: Understanding the Mind of the Market* (1999) and *Market Values in American Higher Education: The Pitfalls and Promises* (2000).

Max Weber was educated at the universities of Heidelberg, Berlin, and Göttingen. A jurist in Berlin, he subsequently held professorships in economics at the universities of Freiburg (1894), Heidelberg (1897), and Munich (1919). He was editor of the *Archiv für Sozialwissenschaft und Sozialpolitik*, the German sociology journal, and is remembered especially for *The Protestant Ethic and the Spirit of Capitalism* (1905), and his encyclopedic work, *Economy and Society* (1978).

Viviana A. Zelizer, Professor of Sociology at Princeton University since 1988, specializes in the study of economic processes, historical analysis, and childhood. She has published books on the development of life insurance, the changing economic and sentimental value of children in the United States, and the place of money in social life. Recently, she has been examining the interplay between monetary transfers and different sorts of social relations.

Acknowledgments

The editor and publishers wish to thank the following for permission to use copyright material:

American Sociological Association for Neil Fligstein, "Markets as Politics: A Political-Cultural Approach to Market Institutions," *American Sociological Review*, 61 (1996) pp. 656–73; Nicole Woolsey Biggart and Mauro F. Guillen, "Developing Difference: Social Organization and the Rise of the Auto Industries of South Korea, Taiwan, Spain, and Argentina," *American Sociological Review*, (1999) pp. 722–47; and [with Cambridge University Press for modifications included in Randall Collins, *Weberian Sociological Theory* (1986) pp. 19–44] for Randall Collins, "Weber's Last Theory of Capitalism," *American Sociological Review*, 45 (1980).

Fred Block for 'Deconstructing Capitalism as a System'.

The Free Press, a Division of Simon & Schuster, Inc for material from Charles W. Smith, Auctions: *The Social Construction of Value* (1989) pp. 80–107. Copyright © 1989 by Charles W. Smith.

Greenwood Publishing Group, Inc for Pierre Bourdieu, "The Forms of Capital," trs. Richard Nice in *Handbook of Theory and Research for the Sociology of Education*, ed. John G. Richardson (1986) pp. 241–50, 252–3, 255–7. Copyright © 1986 by John G. Richardson.

Harvard University Press for material from Mitchel Y. Abolafia, *Making Markets: Opportunism and Restraint on Wall Street* (1996) pp. 14–37, 197–8. Copyright © 1996 by the President and Fellows of Harvard College.

Henry Holt and Company, LLC for material from Karl Polanyi, *The Great Transformation* (1957) pp. 56–8, 60–3, 65–7, 68–71, footnotes pp. 269–79. Copyright © 1944 by Karl Polanyi. Copyright © 1972 by Marie Polanyi.

Loren Lutzenhiser for "Greening the Economy from the Bottom Up? Lessons in Consumption from the Energy Case."

New Left Review for material from Karl Marx (1973) *Grundrisse – Foundations of the Critique of Political Economy*, trans. Martin Nicolaus, Penguin Books, pp. 239–42, 248, 256–9.

Princeton University Press for material from Viviana Zelizer, *The Social Meaning of Money* (1997) pp. 53–70. Copyright © 1997 by Princeton University Press.

The Regents of the University of California for Walter W. Powell, "Learning from Collaboration: Knowledge and Networks in the Biotechnology and Pharmaceutical Industries," *California Management Review*, 40:3 (1998) pp. 228–40. Copyright © 1998 by The Regents of the University of California.

Sage Publications, Inc for Bruce G. Carruthers and Wendy Nelson Espeland, "Money, Meaning, and Morality," *American Behavioral Scientist*, 41 (1998) pp. 1384–1408. Copyright © 1998 Sage Publications, Inc.

University of California Press and Mohr Siebeck for material from *Max Weber, Economy and Society: An Outline of Interpretive Sociology*, Vols. I and II, trans/eds Guenther Roth and Claus Wittich (1978) Vol. I – pp. 63–5, 583–9, 635–40, Vol. II – 926–7, 932–3, 938–9. Copyright © 1978 The Regents of the University of California.

The University of Chicago Press for Mark Granovetter, "Economic Action and Social Structure: The Problem of Embeddedness," *American Journal of Sociology*, 91:3 (1985) pp. 481–510; Gary G. Hamilton, "The Structural Sources of Adventurism: The Case of the California Gold Rush," *American Journal of Sociology*, 83:6 (1978) pp. 1466–90; Paula England, "The Separative Self: Androcentric Bias in Neoclassical Assumptions" in *Beyond Economic Man: Feminist Theory and Economics*, eds Marianne A. Ferber and Julie A. Nelson (1993) pp. 37–53; and material from Sherryl Kleinman, *Opposing Ambitions: Gender and Identity in an Alternative Organization* (1996) pp. 12–32, 141–4.

Every effort has been made to trace copyright holders and to obtain their permission for the use of copyright material. The authors and publishers will gladly receive any information enabling them to rectify any error or omission in subsequent editions.

Preface

We all experience the economy when making decisions to buy, to sell, to scrimp, or to borrow. When we purchase clothes, pay income tax, sell an old car, save for tuition, or give a gift, we participate in the economy. Economic activity is part of daily life when we shop and save, but also when we donate goods and even when we grow a vegetable garden. The economy is an important part of the social encounters of all people, whether poor or rich, living in an advanced industrial society or a primitive one. While not all people experience daily and directly the force of government, or religion, or educational institutions, they are all involved each day in economic activity of one form or another.

Sociologists have begun to recognize that this important sphere of activity is critical to understand in its own right, and also because it is so caught up with other realms of social life. Indeed, it is hard to have a full understanding of religion, or politics, or family, without understanding how each is connected to the economy. For example, religious ideas may support an ascetic orientation toward material life and encourage an anticonsumption environmentalism. Religious beliefs may require regular tithing, or encourage contributions of time and money to missionaries or nonreligious causes. Political ideas and institutions may be organized to redistribute income through social welfare services and progressive tax policies. Governments typically regulate financial institutions such as banks and securities exchanges, and establish the rules by which corporations are formed and business contracts enforced. In developed countries, families are experienced primarily as consumption units as they buy homes and vacations, but they may also be economic production units when they run businesses and farms. Indeed, it is difficult to imagine any sphere of social life that is not implicated in the economy and, conversely, any part of the economy that is not involved in noneconomic social realms.

The economy has always been a part of society, of course, but it has taken on new importance for sociologists, for at least three reasons.

First, not since the Industrial Revolution of the nineteenth century have technological and economic transformations so dramatically changed the social order for so many people. The last years of the twentieth century saw dramatic shifts in the economic organization of production and distribution in both industrialized and industrializing economies. The development of new technologies had profound and widespread impacts on economic activity. Computer-aided manufacturing lessened the need for skilled labor in the industrialized world in critical industries such as machine tools and automotives. Innovations in information and transportation technologies enabled manufacturers in the West to design and produce their goods in parts of the globe with lower labor costs, changing the worlds of work and business in both developed and less-developed nations. Globalization of financial and commodities markets both enabled and resulted from these shifts, and tied nations together that had previously been separated by time, space, and history.

Increased economic connection between Asian and Western nations particularly made US and European managers and workers aware of alternative forms of capitalist organization at the level of firms, industries, and economies. The 1980s were a period of intense self-doubt for many Western businesses as they experienced competition from rapidly rising Japanese, Korean, Taiwanese, and other Asian firms. Asian businesses were often built on premises such as cooperation between state and business, inter-firm alliances, nepotism, and other practices that challenged the received wisdom of Western economies. Economic sociologists confronted the presumed "necessary" social foundations for successful capitalism such as individualism and arm's-length relations between economic actors. Economic "principles" were increasingly understood to be economic traditions, conventions, and practices rooted in history and society, not universal precepts necessary to market societies assumed by traditional economic thought.

This was also a period of dramatic restructuring of socialist nations such as the USSR, the People's Republic of China, and other command economies. While it became clear that capitalism had numerous varieties, capitalism was also evidently triumphant as the only viable form of national economic organization. Formerly socialist economies attempted to "marketize," producing a wave of economic and political pundits preaching "free markets." Those who believed that becoming a market society required little more than a hands-off state, unfettered individualism, and political freedom to trade were quickly proven wrong as "restructuring" further devastated economies already torn up by years of socialist mismanagement.

Market societies in fact are built on complex sets of social relations and institutions, lessons painfully learned by Eastern European nations, and negotiated sometimes with difficulty among members of emergent regional trading zones such as NAFTA, ASEAN, and the European Market. Individualism is not "natural," a universal state of being, but rather a learned orientation toward self and others. Many societies built on authoritarian and communitarian social structures are not organized on individualistic principles. "Free markets" are in fact held up by a wide array of institutional structures and ideologies, and they vary substantially where they exist. It was impossible for sociologists to ignore the impact of dramatic market transformations, and this was an important spur to economic sociology.

The second and related factor that has promoted economic sociology has consisted in the widespread marketization of social life in the developed world and the development of consumption as a critical cultural force. This has not happened all at once, but has been a quickening process as there are more two-earner families with less time to provide care and services for themselves. While the wealthy have always been able to afford nurses and private tutors for their children, even the large middle class now goes to the market for childcare, and for all sorts of lessons for children, from gymnastics and ballet to football camp and piano lessons. Even a generation ago, many women sewed clothes and regularly cooked family meals. Increasingly, people eat out and purchase prepared foods, and for some of those who still perform these activities, cooking and sewing have become leisure activities requiring specialized skills and equipment. Many households pay for cleaning and gardening.

Indeed, it is difficult to think of any product or service that cannot be bought today, although some, such as biological goods and services like surrogate motherhood and genetically modified foods, and the production of some cultural products, are subject to moral and ethical debates. That such debates are taking place only reinforces the observation that the commoditization of social life is widespread and has extended itself to the most intimate and value-sensitive areas of society.

Market and society are deeply entwined, often in provocative ways, and this is affecting them both. That so much is "for sale" in society represents a qualitative change in the social fabric and the reconstitution of individuals into new personas as consumers; material goods become shapers and reflectors of identities. These trends represent important areas for sociological understanding.

A third and important impulse for the development of economic sociology has been the overwhelming dominance of the discipline of economics in policy debates on social welfare, trade, market formation, environmental regulation, and other socio-economic arenas. Why should sociology attempt to understand the economy and economic action when there are so many economists prepared to do just that? Increasingly, economic sociologists believe that their approach to the economy provides an important alternative perspective, one founded on more realistic understandings of how the economy actually works.

Economists for the most part are interested in the economy apart from other areas of social life. They study economic variables to see what impact they have on other economic variables, for example, the impact of tax rates on investment, or investment on productivity. Economists tend to treat social factors as exogenous when they consider them at all. When economists do study social arenas, such as the family, they assume that actors behave as they would in the economy, for example, by having a calculating orientation toward others.

Economic sociologists differ from economists in important ways. Sociologists are concerned with markets and exchange as elements of empirical social worlds with ongoing and distinctive social relations. They see economies as historically embedded phenomena. Economists are interested in markets as logical models, a set of assumptions that provide a convenient baseline for the analysis of possible relations between variables. Sometimes economists use data, often gathered by official agencies, but many economists use no data at all in econometric analyses, preferring to base their conclusions on a set of assumptions amenable to mathematical manipulation.

Economic sociologists posit that economic relations and actions spring from social relations, or at least are informed by them. For example, economic sociologists assume that market organization and functioning are a result of political structure, ideologies, and even traditional practices rooted in history. In contrast, economists typically assume that an "invisible hand" creates market order from the aggregation of discrete exchanges.

The principal unit of analysis for economists is the individual, who is assumed to be self-regarding and economically rational. Sociologists assume that individuals act, but that their actions may be shaped by social factors such as class, gender, culture, their relations with others, and the historical moment in which they live. "Rationality," for sociologists, is socially constructed. What is rational depends on who you are and when and where you live. Sociologists are concerned with social structure, social order, and meaning. Economists tend to be concerned with the consequences of economic action in the aggregate, for example, the price or demand for a service.

Sociologists use a wide variety of methods depending on their questions of interest. In settings where there is little understanding of the phenomena involved, they

may prefer qualitative methods such as participant observation and open-ended interviews to discover economic actors' critical ways of thinking and doing. Sometimes
they use comparative methods, surveys, and the statistical analysis of large data sets,
often collected specifically for their questions of interest. Economists occasionally
use experimental methods such as laboratory studies, but model building is the central method of most economic studies.

These differences in approach are profound, and to some extent represent different interests. Economics is concerned with prediction and prescription, and sociologists tend to be concerned with a careful and correct description of economic activity,
and with explanation. Sociologists largely have been content to pursue studies of the
economy in ways that suit their intellectual convictions, while leaving the policy arena
to economists.

This is beginning to change, however, as a generation of economic sociologists
see the value of their analyses to areas that have been of traditional interest to them,
such as economic development and labor market dynamics. They have also been
concerned about the effects of traditional economic prescriptions on newly mar-
ketizing nations, debt crises, and trading policies.

This volume collects papers that demonstrate the variety and promise of economic
sociology. I had three main criteria for the selection of works to include. First, I included
a number of works that are empirical analyses of some aspect of the economy.
Second, I chose works that represent a generous interpretation of economic sociology, demonstrating how it offers insights into areas as diverse as market structure,
entrepreneurial adventure, and environmentalism. Finally, I have chosen works that,
while often challenging, are readable by a broad audience.

The first part, "Foundational Statements," consists of excerpts from theorists
including Adam Smith, a founder of classical economics. Along with selections by
Marx, Weber, and Polanyi, these pieces provide a basis for comparing sociological
and economic approaches.

The second part, "Economic Action," demonstrates a variety of ways in which
society shapes the orientation of actors going into the market (and elsewhere) to
conduct economic activity. In contrast to the autonomous rational individual
assumed by economics, these selections show the impact of social networks, gender, organization, and culture on economic action.

The third part, "Capitalist States and Globalizing Markets," deals with the development of the modern state as an institutional foundation for market capitalism,
and the variety of ways in which states create conditions for economic activity.

Part IV, "Economic Culture and the Culture of the Economy," showcases articles that demonstrate the value bases of economic action, and the role of economic
culture as a powerful shaper of social relations.

There are important areas of omission, such as the domestic economy and issues
of economic migration, and this volume has only a cursory representation of non-
Western economies and economic development. It does not include studies that require
an understanding of quantitative methods. Nonetheless, I believe this is an interesting selection from which one can construct an appreciation of the contributions
of sociology to our understanding of economic life. It is a good basis from which
to develop a course, a research interest, and an awareness of the economy in which
we participate every day.

Part I

Foundational Statements

Introduction

There is widespread agreement that Adam Smith was a founder of modern economics and, indeed, many modern economic assumptions can be traced to this eighteenth-century Scottish Enlightenment scholar. Smith's most famous work, *An Inquiry into the Nature and Causes of the Wealth of Nations*, was an ambitious attempt to grasp an emergent economic order, capitalism, as it developed out of traditional European society with its feudal arrangements and aristocratic strata. The first edition of *The Wealth of Nations* appeared in 1776 and its themes very much reflect the revolutionary concerns of the time. One can find his enthusiasm for an economic system based on competition between reasoned individuals under conditions of "liberty," the abolition of monopolies that were often associated with the Crown, and, more generally, *laissez-faire* relations between government and business. For Smith, capitalism was based on the "natural" propensities of human beings to pursue their own interests through exchange.

The selection from *The Wealth of Nations* included as chapter 1 in this volume is concerned with two issues: the division of labor, and commodity prices. Smith saw the division of labor – breaking down economic tasks into constituent parts – as a critical factor in the development of capitalism. In a famous passage, he describes the improved productivity of ordinary workers in a pin factory when pin-making tasks are decomposed into small jobs and workers can become expert at one of them. The rationalization of tasks results in a dramatic increase in production, surplus available for trade, and thus greater wealth for all members of society.

The division of labor changes social welfare not just by providing more, but by changing the character of society, according to Smith. Workers now need to trade with others who make goods that they no longer make for themselves, forcing sociability through exchange. The basis of sociability is not good will, but rather self-interest. Each one exchanges something they do not want, or have too much of, for something they desire. "It is not from the benevolence of the butcher, the brewer, or the baker, that we expect our dinner, but from their regard to their own interest." Individuals pursue their interests separately, but it contributes to general wellbeing as each develops talents and provides goods and services for the whole. Smith sees trading in a market as a "natural" propensity of everyone, a "general disposition to truck, barter, and exchange."

Smith establishes the self-interested motivation for individuals to go to market, and then describes how discrete exchanges establish market prices. "Natural" prices are those that cover the costs of producing the goods and services and over the long run are the floor to which prices will fall and not go lower. "Market" prices may differ, however, depending on the supply of the commodity and the demand for it. When supply is insufficient to meet demand, people will compete in the marketplace and bid higher prices. Prices fall when supply outstrips demand.

These ideas – that individuals pursue their self-interest in a market, that they compete with each other in pursuit of those interests, that supply and demand determine prices, and that social order results from the aggregated acts of competing individuals – continue to be the bases for modern economics. Smith's belief in "natural" propensities and his universalistic framework for market analysis are also part of mainstream economic thought today.

Smith's ideas are the intellectual foundation of liberal Anglo-American economies (although these principles have been selectively appropriated from his writings), while Marx's ideas can be found expressed in socialist and social welfare regimes around the world. Marx, like Smith, was concerned with trying to deduce the principles of the capitalist economic system and, similarly, tried to create an economic science. Moreover, Marx also focused importantly on production as a critical element in capitalism's economic superiority and its triumph over feudalism.

Chapter 2 in this volume is from *Grundrisse: Foundations of the Critique of Political Economy*, a series of notes that Marx wrote in preparation for his grand work, *Capital*. In the selection, Marx is writing about exchange relations, much as Smith did, but his conclusions are radically different. Whereas Smith sees market exchange as creating conditions of equality between self-interested economic actors and providing a foundation for sociability and solidarity, Marx sees exchange relations under capitalism as the root of social divisions. While exchange relations exist between parties who are formally free and equal, the results of the market system are anything but egalitarian.

Exchange relations are a type of social relation, according to Marx, in which people meet each other in an objectified manner, stripped of more complex bases of interaction. Because capitalism is a system in which people relate to each other primarily as exchangers, it creates a shallow, material, and commoditized social order. Money is a critical medium for forging exchange relations and facilitates the appearance of parity in exchange while in fact alienating people from each other.

Both Smith and Marx were economic determinists; that is, they saw the nature of society and social relations as generally determined by economic arrangements (although in other works Smith expressed a more balanced view). Weber's analysis of capitalism sees interdependence between economic arrangements and social arrangements. He argued that ideas, including religious ideas, might support a particular economic orientation. He studied world religions to try to understand why capitalism emerged in the West, but not in societies such as India and China with differing ethical bases. Weber located causal factors in an array of institutional arrangements such as authority relations and ideologies. Capitalism, he argued, depends on supportive social institutions and can only exist where they are found. Capitalist striving and enterprise are not universal orientations.

In chapter 3, Weber argues that economic action is a type of social action; that is, it is action oriented toward others and has meaning. Unlike Smith, who describes exchange as being motivated by unspecified "interests," and assumed that parties to an exchange would or could be "indifferent" to each other, Weber believed that exchange usually takes place between people who have historically developed desires and relations. Understanding how a real economy works requires that one understand the actual motivations of the exchangers and the nature of the relations between them. Even people who never expect to see each other again may act toward each other in ways that are socially shaped.

Karl Polanyi, like Weber, did not believe that economy produces society, but rather "that man's economy, as a rule, is submerged in his social relationships." Moreover, people do not act primarily to preserve their economic interests, but rather their social standing. Economic behavior reflects the pursuit of social, not material gains. Social orders and principles of different types lead to different forms of economic organization in which people are embedded, and which therefore lead to different patterns of economic action. His book *The Great Transformation*, which is excerpted in chapter 4, is his attempt to understand how pre-modern social orders transformed into a "market society," a social order that "subordinate[s] the substance of society itself to the laws of the market." Where Smith saw the pursuit of material gain as "natural," Polanyi sees it as the product of a society that has marketized.

1 An Inquiry into the Nature and Causes of the Wealth of Nations

Adam Smith

Of the Division of Labour[1]

Division of labour is the great cause of its increased powers,
The greatest improvement in the productive powers of labour, and the greater part of the skill, dexterity, and judgment with which it is any where directed, or applied, seem to have been the effects of the division of labour.

as may be better understood from a particular example,
The effects of the division of labour, in the general business of society, will be more easily understood, by considering in what manner it operates in some particular manufactures. It is commonly supposed to be carried furthest in some very trifling ones; not perhaps that it really is carried further in them than in others of more importance: but in those trifling manufactures which are destined to supply the small wants of but a small number of people, the whole number of workmen must necessarily be small; and those employed in every different branch of the work can often be collected into the same workhouse, and placed at once under the view of the spectator. In those great manufactures, on the contrary, which are destined to supply the great wants of the great body of the people, every different branch of the work employs so great a number of workmen, that it is impossible to collect them all into the same workhouse. We can seldom see more, at one time, than those employed in one single branch. Though in such manufactures, therefore, the work may really be divided into a much greater number of parts, than in those of a more trifling nature, the division is not near so obvious, and has accordingly been much less observed.

such as pin-making.
To take an example, therefore, from a very trifling manufacture; but one in which the division of labour has been very often taken notice of, the trade of the pin-maker; a workman not educated to this business (which the division of labour has rendered a distinct trade), nor acquainted with the use of the machinery employed in it (to the invention of which the same division of labour has probably given occasion), could scarce, perhaps, with his utmost industry, make one pin in a day, and certainly could not make twenty. But in the way in which this business is now carried on, not only the whole work is a peculiar trade, but it is divided into a number of branches, of which the greater part are likewise peculiar trades. One man draws out the wire, another straights it, a third cuts it, a fourth points it, a fifth grinds it at the top for receiving the head; to make the head requires

Original publication: Extracts from Smith, Adam, *An Inquiry into the Nature and Causes of the Wealth of Nations*, ed. Edwin Cannan (Methuen, London, 1961).

two or three distinct operations; to put it on, is a peculiar business, to whiten the pins is another; it is even a trade by itself to put them into the paper; and the important business of making a pin is, in this manner, divided into about eighteen distinct operations, which, in some manufactories, are all performed by distinct hands, though in others the same man will sometimes perform two or three of them. I have seen a small manufactory of this kind where ten men only were employed, and where some of them consequently performed two or three distinct operations. But though they were very poor, and therefore but indifferently accommodated with the necessary machinery, they could, when they exerted themselves, make among them about twelve pounds of pins in a day. There are in a pound upwards of four thousand pins of a middling size. Those ten persons, therefore, could make among them upwards of forty-eight thousand pins in a day. Each person, therefore, making a tenth part of forty-eight thousand pins, might be considered as making four thousand eight hundred pins in a day. But if they had all wrought separately and independently, and without any of them having been educated to this peculiar business, they certainly could not each of them have made twenty, perhaps not one pin in a day; that is, certainly, not the two hundred and fortieth, perhaps not the four thousand eight hundredth part of what they are at present capable of performing, in consequence of a proper division and combination of their different operations.

The effect is similar in all trades and also in the division of employments. In every other art and manufacture, the effects of the division of labour are similar to what they are in this very trifling one; though, in many of them, the labour can neither be so much subdivided, nor reduced to so great a simplicity of operation. The division of labour, however, so far as it can be introduced, occasions, in every art, a proportionable increase of the productive powers of labour. The separation of different trades and employments from one another, seems to have taken place, in consequence of this advantage. This separation too is generally carried furthest in those countries which enjoy the highest degree of industry and improvement; what is the work of one man in a rude state of society, being generally that of several in an improved one. In every improved society, the farmer is generally nothing but a farmer; the manufacturer, nothing but a manufacturer. The labour too which is necessary to produce any one complete manufacture, is almost always divided among a great number of hands. How many different trades are employed in each branch of the linen and woollen manufactures, from the growers of the flax and the wool, to the bleachers and smoothers of the linen, or to the dyers and dressers of the cloth! The nature of agriculture, indeed, does not admit of so many subdivisions of labour, nor of so complete a separation of one business from another, as manufactures. It is impossible to separate so entirely, the business of the grazier from that of the corn-farmer, as the trade of the carpenter is commonly separated from that of the smith. The spinner is almost always a distinct person from the weaver; but the ploughman, the harrower, the sower of the seed, and the reaper of the corn, are often the same. The occasions for those different sorts of labour returning with the different seasons of the year, it is impossible that one man should be constantly employed in any one of them. This impossibility of making so complete and entire a separation of all the different branches of labour employed in agriculture, is perhaps the reason why the improvement of the productive powers of labour in this art, does not always keep pace with their improvement in manufactures. The most opulent nations, indeed, generally excel all their neighbours in agriculture as well as in manufactures; but they are commonly more distinguished by their superiority in the latter than in the former. Their lands are in general better cultivated, and having more labour and expence bestowed upon them, produce more in proportion to the extent and natural fertility of the ground. But this superiority of produce is seldom much more than in proportion to the superiority of labour and expence. In agriculture, the labour of the rich country is not always much more productive than that of the poor; or, at least, it is never so much more productive, as it commonly is in manufactures. The corn of the rich country, therefore, will not always, in the same degree of goodness, come cheaper to market than that of the poor. The corn of Poland, in the same degree of goodness, is as cheap as that of France, notwithstanding the superior opulence and improvement of the latter country. The corn of France is, in the corn provinces, fully as good, and in most years nearly about the same price with the corn of England, though, in opulence and improvement, France is perhaps inferior to England. The corn-lands of England, however, are better cultivated than those of France, and the corn-lands of France are said to be much better cultivated than those of Poland. But though the poor country, notwithstanding the inferiority of its cultivation, can, in some measure, rival the rich in the cheapness and goodness of its corn, it can pretend to no such competition in its manufactures; at least if those manufactures suit the soil, climate, and situation of the rich country. The silks of France are better and cheaper than those of England, because the silk manufacture, at least under the present high duties upon the importation of raw silk, does not so well suit the climate of England as that of France. But the hard-ware and the coarse woollens of England are beyond all comparison superior to those of France, and much cheaper too in the same degree of goodness. In Poland there are said to be scarce any manufactures of any kind, a few of those coarser household manufactures excepted, without which no country can well subsist.

The advantage is due to three circumstances,   This great increase of the quantity of work which, in consequence of the division of labour, the same number of people are capable of performing, is owing to three different circumstances; first to the increase of dexterity in every particular workman; secondly, to the saving of the time which is commonly lost in passing from one species of work to another; and lastly, to the invention of a great number of machines which facilitate and abridge labour, and enable one man to do the work of many.

(1) improved dexterity,   First, the improvement of the dexterity of the workman necessarily increases the quantity of the work he can perform; and the division of labour, by reducing every man's business to some one simple operation, and by making this operation the sole employment of his life, necessarily increases very much the dexterity of the workman. A common smith, who, though accustomed to handle the hammer, has never been used to make nails, if upon some particular occasion he is obliged to attempt it, will scarce, I am assured, be able to make above two or three hundred nails in a day, and those too very bad ones. A smith who has been accustomed to make nails, but whose sole or principal business has not been that of a nailer, can seldom with his utmost diligence make more than eight hundred or a thousand nails in a day. I have seen several boys under twenty years of age who had never exercised any other trade but that of making nails, and who, when they exerted themselves, could make, each of them, upwards of two thousand three

hundred nails in a day. The making of a nail, however, is by no means one of the simplest operations. The same person blows the bellows, stirs or mends the fire as there is occasion, heats the iron, and forges every part of the nail: In forging the head too he is obliged to change his tools. The different operations into which the making of a pin, or of a metal button, is subdivided, are all of them much more simple, and the dexterity of the person, of whose life it has been the sole business to perform them, is usually much greater. The rapidity with which some of the operations of those manufactures are performed, exceeds what the human hand could, by those who had never seen them, be supposed capable of acquiring.

(2) saving of time,   Secondly, the advantage which is gained by saving the time commonly lost in passing from one sort of work to another, is much greater than we should at first view be apt to imagine it. It is impossible to pass very quickly from one kind of work to another; that is carried on in a different place, and with quite different tools. A country weaver, who cultivates a small farm, must lose a good deal of time in passing from his loom to the field, and from the field to his loom. When the two trades can be carried on in the same workhouse, the loss of time is no doubt much less. It is even in this case, however, very considerable. A man commonly saunters a little in turning his hand from one sort of employment to another. When he first begins the new work he is seldom very keen and hearty; his mind, as they say, does not go to it, and for some time he rather trifles than applies to good purpose. The habit of sauntering and of indolent careless application, which is naturally, or rather necessarily acquired by every country workman who is obliged to change his work and his tools every half hour, and to apply his hand in twenty different ways almost every day of his life; renders him almost always slothful and lazy, and incapable of any vigorous application even on the most pressing occasions. Independent, therefore, of his deficiency in point of dexterity, this cause alone must always reduce considerably the quantity of work which he is capable of performing.

and (3) application of machinery, invented by workmen,   Thirdly, and lastly, every body must be sensible how much labour is facilitated and abridged by the application of proper machinery. It is unnecessary to give any example. I shall only observe, therefore, that the invention of all those machines by which labour is so much facilitated and abridged, seems to have been originally owing to the division of labour. Men are much more likely to discover easier and readier methods of attaining any object, when the whole attention of their minds is directed towards that single object, than when it is dissipated among a great variety of things. But in consequence of the division of labour, the whole of every man's attention comes naturally to be directed towards some one very simple object. It is naturally to be expected, therefore, that some one or other of those who are employed in each particular branch of labour should soon find out easier and readier methods of performing their own particular work, wherever the nature of it admits of such improvement. A great part of the machines made use of in those manufactures in which labour is most subdivided, were originally the inventions of common workmen, who, being each of them employed in some very simple operation, naturally turned their thoughts towards finding out easier and readier methods of performing it. Whoever has been much accustomed to visit such manufactures, must frequently have been shewn very pretty machines, which were the inventions of such workmen, in order to facilitate and quicken their own particular part of the work. In the first fire-engines, a boy was constantly employed to open and shut alternately the communication between the boiler and the cylinder, according as the piston either ascended or descended. One of those boys, who loved to play with his companions, observed that, by trying a string from the handle of the valve which opened this communication to another part of the machine, the valve would open and shut without his assistance, and leave him at liberty to divert himself with his playfellows. One of the greatest improvements that has been made upon this machine, since it was first invented, was in this manner the discovery of a boy who wanted to save his own labour.

or by machine-makers and philosophers.
　　All the improvements in machinery, however, have by no means been the inventions of those who had occasion to use the machines. Many improvements have been made by the ingenuity of the makers of the machines, when to make them became the business of a peculiar trade; and some by that of those who are called philosophers or men of speculation, whose trade it is not to do any thing, but to observe every thing; and who, upon that account, are often capable of combining together the powers of the most distant and dissimilar objects. In the progress of society, philosophy or speculation becomes, like every other employment, the principal or sole trade and occupation of a particular class of citizens. Like every other employment too, it is subdivided into a great number of different branches, each of which affords occupation to a peculiar tribe or class of philosophers; and this subdivision of employment in philosophy, as well as in every other business, improves dexterity, and saves time. Each individual becomes more expert in his own peculiar branch, more work is done upon the whole, and the quantity of science is considerably increased by it.

Hence the universal opulence of a well-governed society,
　　It is the great multiplication of the productions of all the different arts, in consequence of the division of labour, which occasions, in a well-governed society, that universal opulence which extends itself to the lowest ranks of the people. Every workman has a great quantity of his own work to dispose of beyond what he himself has occasion for; and every other workman being exactly in the same situation, he is enabled to exchange a great quantity of his own goods for a great quantity, or, what comes to the same thing, for the price of a great quantity of theirs. He supplies them abundantly with what they have occasion for, and they accommodate him as amply with what he has occasion for, and a general plenty diffuses itself through all the different ranks of the society.

even the day-labourer's coat being the produce of a vast number of workmen.
　　Observe the accommodation of the most common artificer or day-labourer in a civilized and thriving country, and you will perceive that the number of people of whose industry a part, though but a small part, has been employed in procuring him this accommodation, exceeds all computation. The woollen coat, for example, which covers the day-labourer, as coarse and rough as it may appear, is the produce of the joint labour of a great multitude of workmen. The shepherd, the sorter of the wool, the wool-comber or carder, the dyer, the scribbler, the spinner, the weaver, the fuller, the dresser, with many others, must all join their different arts in order to complete even this homely production. How many merchants and carriers, besides, must have been employed in transporting the materials from some of those workmen to others who often live in a very distant part of the country! how much commerce and navigation in particular, how many ship-builders, sailors, sail-makers,

rope-makers, must have been employed in order to bring together the different drugs made use of by the dyer, which often come from the remotest corners of the world! What a variety of labour too is necessary in order to produce the tools of the meanest of those workmen! To say nothing of such complicated machines as the ship of the sailor, the mill of the fuller, or even the loom of the weaver, let us consider only what a variety of labour is requisite in order to form that very simple machine, the shears with which the shepherd clips the wool. The miner, the builder of the furnace for smelting the ore, the feller of the timber, the burner of the charcoal to be made use of in the smelting-house, the brick-maker, the brick-layer, the workmen who attend the furnace, the mill-wright, the forger, the smith, must all of them join their different arts in order to produce them. Were we to examine, in the same manner, all the different parts of his dress and household furniture, the coarse linen shirt which he wears next his skin, the shoes which cover his feet, the bed which he lies on, and all the different parts which compose it, the kitchen-grate at which he prepares his victuals, the coals which he makes use of for that purpose, dug from the bowels of the earth, and brought to him perhaps by a long sea and a long land carriage, all the other utensils of his kitchen, all the furniture of his table, the knives and forks, the earthen or pewter plates upon which he serves up and divides his victuals, the different hands employed in preparing his bread and his beer, the glass window which lets in the heat and the light, and keeps out the wind and the rain, with all the knowledge and art requisite for preparing that beautiful and happy invention, without which these northern parts of the world could scarce have afforded a very comfortable habitation, together with the tools of all the different workmen employed in producing those different conveniencies; if we examine, I say, all these things, and consider what a variety of labour is employed about each of them, we shall be sensible that without the assistance and co-operation of many thousands, the very meanest person in a civilized country could not be provided, even according to what we very falsely imagine, the easy and simple manner in which he is commonly accommodated. Compared, indeed, with the more extravagant luxury of the great, his accommodation must no doubt appear extremely simple and easy; and yet it may be true, perhaps, that the accommodation of an European prince does not always so much exceed that of an industrious and frugal peasant, as the accommodation of the latter exceeds that of many an African king, the absolute master of the lives and liberties of ten thousand naked savages.

Of the Principle which Gives Occasion to the Division of Labour

The division of labour arises from a propensity in human nature to exchange.

This division of labour, from which so many advantages are derived, is not originally the effect of any human wisdom, which foresees and intends that general opulence to which it gives occasion. It is the necessary, though very slow and gradual, consequence of a certain propensity in human nature which has in view no such extensive utility; the propensity to truck, barter, and exchange one thing for another.

This propensity is found in man alone.

Whether this propensity be one of those original principles in human nature, of which no further account can be given; or whether, as seems more probable, it be the necessary consequence of the faculties of reason and speech, it belongs not to our present subject to enquire. It is common to all men, and to be found in no other race of animals, which seem to know neither this nor any other species of contracts. Two greyhounds, in running down the same hare, have sometimes the appearance of acting in some sort of concert. Each turns her towards his companion, or endeavours to intercept her when his companion turns her towards himself. This, however, is not the effect of any contract, but of the accidental concurrence of their passions in the same object at that particular time. Nobody ever saw a dog make a fair and deliberate exchange of one bone for another with another dog. Nobody ever saw one animal by its gestures and natural cries signify to another, this is mine, that yours; I am willing to give this for that. When an animal wants to obtain something either of a man or of another animal, it has no other means of persuasion but to gain the favour of those whose service it requires. A puppy fawns upon its dam, and a spaniel endeavours by a thousand attractions to engage the attention of its master who is at dinner, when it wants to be fed by him. Man sometimes uses the same arts with his brethren, and when he has no other means of engaging them to act according to his inclinations, endeavours by every servile and fawning attention to obtain their good will. He has not time, however, to do this upon every occasion. In civilized society he stands at all times in need of the co-operation and assistance of great multitudes, while his whole life is scarce sufficient to gain the friendship of a few persons. In almost every other race of animals each individual, when it is grown up to maturity, is entirely independent, and in its natural state has occasion for the assistance of no other living creature. But man has almost constant occasion for the help of his brethren, and it is in vain for him to expect it from their benevolence only. He will be more likely to prevail if he can interest their self-love in his favour, and show them that it is for their own advantage to do for him what he requires of them. Whoever offers to another a bargain of any kind, proposes to do this. Give me that which I want, and you shall have this which you want, is the meaning of every such offer; and it is in this manner that we obtain from one another the far greater part of those good offices which we stand in need of. It is not from the benevolence of the butcher, the brewer, or the baker, that we expect our dinner, but from their regard to their own interest. We address ourselves, not to their humanity but to their self-love, and never talk to them of our own necessities but of their advantages. Nobody but a beggar chuses to depend chiefly upon the benevolence of his fellow-citizens. Even a beggar does not depend upon it entirely. The charity of well-disposed people, indeed, supplies him with the whole fund of his subsistence. But though this principle ultimately provides him with all the necessaries of life which he has occasion for, it neither does nor can provide him with them as he has occasion for them. The greater part of his occasional wants are supplied in the same manner as those of other people, by treaty, by barter, and by purchase. With the money which one man gives him he purchases food. The old cloaths which another bestows upon him he exchanges for other old cloaths which suit him better, or for lodging, or for food, or for money, with which he can buy either food, cloaths, or lodging, as he has occasion.

It is encouraged by self-interest and leads to division of labour,   As it is by treaty, by barter, and by purchase, that we obtain from one another the greater part of those mutual good offices which we stand in need of, so it is this same trucking disposition which originally gives occasion to the division of labour. In a tribe of hunters or shepherds a particular person makes bows and arrows, for example, with more readiness and dexterity than any other. He frequently exchanges them for cattle or for venison with his companions; and he finds at last that he can in this manner get more cattle and venison, than if he himself went to the field to catch them. From a regard to his own interest, therefore, the making of bows and arrows grows to be his chief business, and he becomes a sort of armourer. Another excels in making the frames and covers of their little huts or moveable houses. He is accustomed to be of use in this way to his neighbours, who reward him in the same manner with cattle and with venison, till at last he finds it his interest to dedicate himself entirely to this employment, and to become a sort of house-carpenter. In the same manner a third becomes a smith or a brazier; a fourth a tanner or dresser of hides or skins, the principal part of the clothing of savages. And thus the certainty of being able to exchange all that surplus part of the produce of his own labour, which is over and above his own consumption, for such parts of the produce of other men's labour as he may have occasion for, encourages every man to apply himself to a particular occupation, and to cultivate and bring to perfection whatever talent or genius he may possess for that particular species of business.

thus giving rise to differences of talent more important than the natural differences,   The difference of natural talents in different men is, in reality, much less than we are aware of; and the very different genius which appears to distinguish men of different professions, when grown up to maturity, is not upon many occasions so much the cause, as the effect of the division of labour. The difference between the most dissimilar characters, between a philosopher and a common street porter, for example, seems to arise not so much from nature, as from habit, custom, and education. When they came into the world, and for the first six or eight years of their existence, they were perhaps, very much alike, and neither their parents nor playfellows could perceive any remarkable difference. About that age, or soon after, they come to be employed in very different occupations. The difference of talents comes then to be taken notice of, and widens by degrees, till at last the vanity of the philosopher is willing to acknowledge scarce any resemblance. But without the disposition to truck, barter, and exchange, every man must have procured to himself every necessary and conveniency of life which he wanted. All must have had the same duties to perform, and the same work to do, and there could have been no such difference of employment as could alone give occasion to any great difference of talents.

and rendering those differences useful.   As it is this disposition which forms that difference of talents, so remarkable among men of different professions, so it is this same disposition which renders that difference useful. Many tribes of animals acknowledged to be all of the same species, derive from nature a much more remarkable distinction of genius, than what, antecedent to custom and education, appears to take place among men. By nature a philosopher is not in genius and disposition half so different from a street porter, as a mastiff is from a greyhound, or a greyhound from a spaniel, or this last from a shepherd's dog. Those different tribes of animals, however, though all of the same species, are of scarce any use to one another. The strength of the mastiff is not in the least supported either by the swiftness of the greyhound, or by the sagacity of the spaniel, or by the docility of the shepherd's dog. The effects of those different geniuses and talents, for want of the power or disposition to barter and exchange, cannot be brought into a common stock, and do not in the least contribute to the better accommodation and conveniency of the species. Each animal is still obliged to support and defend itself, separately and independently, and derives no sort of advantage from that variety of talents with which nature has distinguished its fellows. Among men, on the contrary, the most dissimilar geniuses are of use to one another; the different produces of their respective talents, by the general disposition to truck, barter, and exchange, being brought, as it were, into a common stock, where every man may purchase whatever part of the produce of other men's talents he has occasion for.

Of the Natural and Market Price of Commodities

Ordinary or average rates of wages, profit, There is in every society or neighbourhood an ordinary or average rate both of wages and profit in every different employment of labour and stock. This rate is naturally regulated, as I shall show hereafter, partly by the general circumstances of the society, their riches or poverty, their advancing, stationary, or declining condition; and partly by the particular nature of each employment.

and rent There is likewise in every society or neighbourhood an ordinary or average rate of rent, which is regulated too, as I shall show hereafter, partly by the general circumstances of the society or neighbourhood in which the land is situated, and partly by the natural or improved fertility of the land.

may be called natural rates, These ordinary or average rates may be called the natural rates of wages, profit, and rent, at the time and place in which they commonly prevail.

to pay which a commodity is sold at its natural price, When the price of any commodity is neither more nor less than what is sufficient to pay the rent of the land, the wages of the labour, and the profits of the stock employed in raising, preparing, and bringing it to market, according to their natural rates, the commodity is then sold for what may be called its natural price.

or for what it really costs, which includes profit, The commodity is then sold precisely for what it is worth, or for what it really costs the person who brings it to market; for though in common language what is called the prime cost of any commodity does not comprehend the profit of the person who is to sell it again, yet if he sells it at a price which does not allow him the ordinary rate of profit in his neighbourhood, he is evidently a loser by the trade; since by employing his stock in some other way he might have made that profit. His profit, besides, is his revenue, the proper fund of his subsistence. As, while he is preparing and bringing the goods to market, he advances to his workmen their wages, or their subsistence; so he advances to himself, in the same manner, his own subsistence, which is generally suitable to the profit which he may reasonably expect from the sale of his goods. Unless they yield him this profit, therefore, they do not repay him what they may very properly be said to have really cost him.

since no one will go on selling without profit. Though the price, therefore, which leaves him this profit, is not always the lowest at which a dealer may sometimes sell his goods, it is the lowest at which he is likely to sell them for any considerable time; at least where there is perfect liberty, or where he may change his trade as often as he pleases.

Market price   The actual price at which any commodity is commonly sold is called its market price. It may either be above, or below, or exactly the same with its natural price.

is regulated by the quantity brought to market and the effectual demand.   The market price of every particular commodity is regulated by the proportion between the quantity which is actually brought to market, and the demand of those who are willing to pay the natural price of the commodity, or the whole value of the rent, labour, and profit, which must be paid in order to bring it thither. Such people may be called the effectual demanders, and their demand the effectual demand; since it may be sufficient to effectuate the bringing of the commodity to market. It is different from the absolute demand. A very poor man may be said in some sense to have a demand for a coach and six; he might like to have it; but his demand is not an effectual demand, as the commodity can never be brought to market in order to satisfy it.

When the quantity brought falls short of the effectual demand, the market price rises above the natural;   When the quantity of any commodity which is brought to market falls short of the effectual demand, all those who are willing to pay the whole value of the rent, wages, and profit, which must be paid in order to bring it thither, cannot be supplied with the quantity which they want. Rather than want it altogether, some of them will be willing to give more. A competition will immediately begin among them, and the market price will rise more or less above the natural price, according as either the greatness of the deficiency, or the wealth and wanton luxury of the competitors, happen to animate more or less the eagerness of the competition. Among competitors of equal wealth and luxury the same deficiency will generally occasion a more or less eager competition, according as the acquisition of the commodity happens to be of more or less importance to them. Hence the exorbitant price of the necessaries of life during the blockade of a town or in a famine.

when it exceeds the effectual demand the market price falls below the natural;   When the quantity brought to market exceeds the effectual demand, it cannot be all sold to those who are willing to pay the whole value of the rent, wages and profit, which must be paid in order to bring it thither. Some part must be sold to those who are willing to pay less, and the low price which they give for it must reduce the price of the whole. The market price will sink more or less below the natural price, according as the greatness of the excess increases more or less the competition of the sellers, or according as it happens to be more or less important to them to get immediately rid of the commodity. The same excess in the importation of perishable, will occasion a much greater competition than in that of durable commodities; in the importation of oranges, for example, than in that of old iron.

when it is just equal to the effectual demand the market and natural price coincide.   When the quantity brought to market is just sufficient to supply the effectual demand and no more, the market price naturally comes to be either exactly, or as nearly as can be judged of, the same with the natural price. The whole quantity upon hand can be disposed of for this price, and cannot be disposed of for more. The competition of the different dealers obliges them all to accept of this price, but does not oblige them to accept of less.

It naturally suits itself to the effectual demand.   The quantity of every commodity brought to market naturally suits itself to the effectual demand. It is the interest of all those who employ their land, labour, or stock, in bringing any commodity to market, that the quantity never should exceed the effectual demand; and it is the interest of all other people that it never should fall short of that demand.

When it exceeds that demand, some of the component parts of its price are below their natural rate;   If at any time it exceeds the effectual demand, some of the component parts of its price must be paid below their natural rate. If it is rent, the interest of the landlords will immediately prompt them to withdraw a part of their land; and if it is wages or profit, the interest of the labourers in the one case, and of their employers in the other, will prompt them to withdraw a part of their labour or stock from this employment. The quantity brought to market will soon be no more than sufficient to supply the effectual demand. All the different parts of its price will rise to their natural rate, and the whole price to its natural price.

when it falls short, some of the component parts are above their natural rate.   If, on the contrary, the quantity brought to market should at any time fall short of the effectual demand, some of the component parts of its price must rise above their natural rate. If it is rent, the interest of all other landlords will naturally prompt them to prepare more land for the raising of this commodity; if it is wages or profit, the interest of all other labourers and dealers will soon prompt them to employ more labour and stock in preparing and bringing it to market. The quantity brought thither will soon be sufficient to supply the effectual demand. All the different parts of its price will soon sink to their natural rate, and the whole price to its natural price.

Natural price is the central price to which actual prices gravitate.   The natural price, therefore, is, as it were, the central price, to which the prices of all commodities are continually gravitating. Different accidents may sometimes keep them suspended a good deal above it, and sometimes force them down even somewhat below it. But whatever may be the obstacles which hinder them from settling in this center of repose and continuance, they are constantly tending towards it.

Note

1   This phrase, if used at all before this time, was not a familiar one. Its presence here is probably due to a passage in Mandeville, *Fable of the Bees*, pt. ii. (1729), dial. vi., p. 335: "CLEO. . . . When once men come to be governed by written laws, all the rest comes on apace . . . No number of men, when once they enjoy quiet, and no man needs to fear his neighbour, will be long without learning to divide and subdivide their labour. HOR. I don't understand you. CLEO. Man, as I have hinted before, naturally loves to imitate what he sees others do, which is the reason that savage people all do the same thing: this hinders them from meliorating their condition, though they are always wishing for it: but if one will wholly apply himself to the making of bows and arrows, whilst another provides food, a third builds huts, a fourth makes garments, and a fifth utensils, they not only become useful to one another, but the callings and employments themselves will, in the same number of years, receive much greater improvements, than if all had been promiscuously followed by every one of the five. HOR. I believe you are perfectly right there; and the truth of what you say is in nothing so conspicuous as it is in watch-making, which is come to a higher degree of perfection than it would have been arrived at yet, if the whole had always remained the employment of one person; and I am persuaded that even the plenty we have of clocks and watches, as well as the exactness and beauty they may be made of,

are chiefly owing to the division that has been made of that art into many branches." The index contains, "Labour, The usefulness of dividing and subdividing it". Joseph Harris, *Essay upon Money and Coins*, 1757, pt. i., § 12, treats of the "usefulness of distinct trades," or "the advantages accruing to mankind from their betaking themselves severally to different occupations," but does not use the phrase "division of labour".

2 Grundrisse: Foundations of the Critique of Political Economy

Karl Marx

Selections from the Chapter on Capital[1]

> From the beginnings of civilization, men have fixed the exchange value of the products of their labour not by comparison with the *products offered in exchange*, but by comparison with a product they preferred. *(Ganilh, 13,9)*[2]

Simple exchange. *Relations between exchangers.* Harmonies of equality, freedom, etc. (Bastiat, Proudhon)

The special difficulty in grasping money in its fully developed character as money – a difficulty which political economy attempts to evade by forgetting now one, now another aspect, and by appealing to one aspect when confronted with another – is that a social relation, a definite relation between individuals, here appears as a metal, a stone, as a purely physical, external thing which can be found, as such, in nature, and which is indistinguishable in form from its natural existence. Gold and silver, in and of themselves, are not money. Nature does not produce money, any more than it produces a rate of exchange or a banker. In Peru and Mexico gold and silver did not serve as money, although it does appear here as jewellery, and there is a developed system of production. To be money is not a natural attribute of gold and silver, and is therefore quite unknown to the physicist, chemist etc. as such. But money is directly gold and silver. Regarded as a measure, money still predominates in its formal quality; even more so as coin, where this appears externally on its face impression; but in its third aspect, i.e. in its perfection, where to be measure and coinage appear as functions of money alone, there all formal character has vanished, or directly coincides with its metallic existence. It is not at all apparent on its face that its character of being money is merely the result of social processes; it *is* money. This is all the more difficult since its immediate use value for the living individual stands in no relation whatever to this role, and because, in general, the memory of use value, as distinct from exchange value, has become entirely extinguished in this incarnation of pure exchange value. Thus the fundamental contradiction contained in exchange value, and in the social mode of production corresponding to it, here emerges in all its purity. We have already criticized the attempts made to overcome this contradiction by depriving money of its metallic form, by positing it outwardly, as well, as something *posited* by society, as the expression of a social relation, whose

Original publication: Extracts from Marx, *Grundrisse: Foundations of the Critique of Political Economy*, trans. Martin Nicolaus (Vintage Books, New York, 1973).

ultimate form would be that of labour-money. It must by now have become entirely clear that this is a piece of foolishness as long as exchange value is retained as the basis, and that, moreover, the illusion that metallic money allegedly falsifies exchange arises out of total ignorance of its nature. It is equally clear, on the other side, that to the degree to which opposition against the ruling relations of production grows, and these latter themselves push ever more forcibly to cast off their old skin – to that degree, polemics are directed against metallic money or money in general, as the most striking, most contradictory and hardest phenomenon which is presented by the system in a palpable form. One or another kind of artful tinkering with money is then supposed to overcome the contradictions of which money is merely the perceptible appearance. Equally clear that some revolutionary operations can be performed with money, in so far as an attack on it seems to leave everything else as it was, and only to rectify it. Then one strikes a blow at the sack, intending the donkey. However, as long as the donkey does not feel the blows on the sack, one hits in fact only the sack and not the donkey. As soon as he feels it, one strikes the donkey and not the sack. As long as these operations are directed against money as such, they are merely an attack on consequences whose causes remain unaffected; i.e. disturbance of the productive process, whose solid basis then also has the power, by means of a more or less violent reaction, to define and to dominate these as mere passing *disturbances*.

On the other hand, it is in the character of the money relation – as far as it is developed in its purity to this point, and without regard to more highly developed relations of production – that all inherent contradictions of bourgeois society appear extinguished in money relations as conceived in a simple form; and bourgeois democracy even more than the bourgeois economists takes refuge in this aspect (the latter are at least consistent enough to regress to even simpler aspects of exchange value and exchange) in order to construct apologetics for the existing economic relations. Indeed, in so far as the commodity or labour is conceived of only as exchange value, and the relation in which the various commodities are brought into connection with one another is conceived as the exchange of these exchange values with one another, as their equation, then the individuals, the subjects between whom this process goes on, are simply and only conceived of as exchangers. As far as the formal character is concerned, there is absolutely no distinction between them, and this is the economic character, the aspect in which they stand towards one another in the exchange relation; it is the indicator of their social function or social relation towards one another. Each of the subjects is an exchanger; i.e. each has the same social relation towards the other that the other has towards him. As subjects of exchange, their relation is therefore that of *equality*. It is impossible to find any trace of distinction, not to speak of contradiction, between them; not even a difference. Furthermore, the commodities which they exchange are, as exchange values, equivalent, or at least count as such (the most that could happen would be a subjective error in the reciprocal appraisal of values, and if one individual, say, cheated the other, this would *happen not because of the nature of the social function in which they confront one another*, for this is *the same*, in this they are *equal*; but only because of natural cleverness, persuasiveness etc., in short only the purely individual superiority of one individual over another. The difference would be one of natural origin, irrelevant to the nature of the relation as such, and it may be said in anticipation of further development, the difference is even lessened and robbed of its original force by competition etc.). As regards the pure form, the economic side of this relation – the content, outside this form, here still falls entirely outside economics, or is posited as a natural content distinct from the economic, a content about which it may be said that it is still entirely separated from the economic relation because it still directly coincides with it – then only three moments emerge as formally distinct: the subjects of the relation, *the exchangers* (posited in the same character); the objects of their exchange, exchange values, *equivalents*, which not only are equal but are expressly supposed to be equal, and are posited as equal; and finally the act of exchange itself, the mediation by which the subjects are posited as exchangers, equals, and their objects as equivalents, equal. The equivalents are the objectification [*Vergegenständlichung*] of one subject for another; i.e. they themselves are of equal worth, and assert themselves in the act of exchange as equally worthy, and at the same time as mutually indifferent. The subjects in exchange exist for one another only through these equivalents, as of equal worth, and prove themselves to be such through the exchange of the objectivity in which the one exists for the other. Since they only exist for one another in exchange in this way, as equally worthy persons, possessors of equivalent things, who thereby prove their equivalence, they are, as equals, at the same time also indifferent to one another; whatever other individual distinction there may be does not concern them; they are indifferent to all their other individual peculiarities. Now, as regards the content outside the act of exchange (an act which constitutes the positing as well as the proving of the exchange values and of the subjects as exchangers), this content, which falls outside the specifically economic form, can only be: (1) The natural particularity of the commodity being exchanged. (2) The particular natural need of the exchangers, or, both together, the different use values of the commodities being exchanged. The content of the exchange, which lies altogether outside its economic character, far from endangering the social equality of individuals, rather makes their natural difference into the basis of their social equality. If individual A had the same need as individual B, and if both had realized their labour in the same object, then no relation whatever would be present between them; considering only their production, they would not be different individuals at all. Both have the need to breathe; for both the air exists as atmosphere; this brings them into no social contact; as breathing individuals they relate to one another only as natural bodies, not as persons. Only the differences between their needs and between their production gives rise to exchange and to their social equation in exchange; these natural differences are therefore the precondition of their social equality in the act of exchange, and of this relation in general, in which they relate to one another as productive.

Transition from circulation to capitalist production. – Capital objectified labour etc. – Sum of values for production of values

This movement appears in different forms, not only historically, as leading towards value-producing labour, but also within the system of bourgeois production itself, i.e. production for exchange value. With semi-barbarian or completely barbarian peoples, there is at first interposition by trading peoples, or else tribes whose production is different by nature enter into contact and exchange their superfluous products. The former case is a more classical form. Let us therefore dwell on it. The exchange of the overflow is a traffic which posits exchange and exchange value. But it extends only to the overflow and plays an accessory role to production itself. But if the trading peoples who solicit exchange appear repeatedly (the Lombards, Normans etc. play this role towards nearly all European peoples), and if an ongoing commerce develops, although the producing people still engages only in so-called *passive* trade, since the impulse for the activity of positing exchange values comes from the outside and not from the inner structure of its production, then the surplus of production must no longer be something accidental, occasionally present, but must be constantly repeated; and in this way domestic production itself takes on a tendency towards circulation, towards the positing of exchange values. At first the effect is of a more physical kind. The sphere of needs is expanded; the aim is the satisfaction of the new needs, and hence greater regularity and an increase of production. The organization of domestic production itself is already modified by circulation and exchange value; but it has not yet been completely invaded by them, either over the surface or in depth. This is what is called the *civilizing influence* of external trade. The degree to which the movement towards the establishment of exchange value then attacks the whole of production depends partly on the intensity of this external influence, and partly on the degree of development attained by the elements of domestic production – division of labour etc. In England, for example, the import of Netherlands commodities in the sixteenth century and at the beginning of the seventeenth century gave to the surplus of wool which England had to provide in exchange, an essential, decisive role. In order then to produce more wool, cultivated land was transformed into sheep-walks, the system of small tenant-farmers was broken up etc., clearing of estates took place etc. Agriculture thus lost the character of labour for use value, and the exchange of its overflow lost the character of relative indifference in respect to the inner construction of production. At certain points, agriculture itself became purely determined by circulation, transformed into production for exchange value. Not only was the mode of production altered thereby, but also all the old relations of population and of production, the economic relations which corresponded to it, were dissolved. Thus, here was a circulation which presupposed a production in which only the overflow was created as exchange value; but it turned into a production which took place only in connection with circulation, a production which posited exchange values as its exclusive content.

On the other hand, in modern production, where exchange value and developed circulation are presupposed, it is prices which determine production on one side, and production which determines prices on the other.

When it is said that capital "is accumulated (realized) labour (properly, *objectified* [*vergegenständlichte*] labour), which serves as the means for new labour (production)",[3] then this refers to the simple material of capital, without regard to the formal character without which it is not capital. This means nothing more than that capital is an instrument of production, for, in the broadest sense, every object, including those furnished purely by nature, e.g. a stone, must first be appropriated by some sort of activity before it can function as an instrument, as means of production. According to this, capital would have existed in all forms of society, and is something altogether unhistorical. Hence every limb of the body is capital, since each of them not only has to be developed through activity, labour, but also nourished, reproduced, in order to be active as an organ. The arm, and especially the hand, are then capital. Capital would be only a new name for a thing as old as the human race, since every form of labour, including the least developed, hunting, fishing, etc., presupposes that the product of prior labour is used as means for direct, living labour. A further characteristic contained in the above definition is that the material stuff of products is entirely abstracted away, and that antecedent labour itself is regarded as its only content (matter); in the same way, abstraction is made from the particular, special purpose for which the making of this product is in its turn intended to serve as means, and merely production in general is posited as purpose. All these things only seemed a work of abstraction, which is equally valid in all social conditions and which merely leads the analysis further and formulates it more abstractly (generally) than is the usual custom. If, then, the specific form of capital is abstracted away, and only the content is emphasized, *as which it is a necessary moment of all labour, then of course nothing is easier than to demonstrate that capital is a necessary condition for all human production*. The proof of this proceeds precisely by abstraction from the specific aspects which make it the moment of a specifically developed *historic* stage of human production. The catch is that if all capital is objectified labour which serves as means for new production, it is not the case that all objectified labour which serves as means for new production is capital. *Capital is conceived as a thing, not as a relation*.

If it is said on the other hand that capital is a sum of values used for the production of values, then this means: capital is self-reproducing exchange value. But, formally, exchange value reproduces itself even in simple circulation. This explanation, it is true, does contain the form wherein exchange value is the point of departure, but the connection with the content (which, with capital, is not, as in the case of simple exchange value, *irrelevant*) is dropped. If it is said that capital is exchange value which produces profit, or at least has the intention of producing a profit, then capital is already presupposed in its explanation, for profit is a specific relation of capital to itself. Capital is not a simple relation, but a *process*, in whose various moments it is always capital. This process therefore to be developed. Already in *accumulated* labour, something has sneaked in, because, in its essential characteristic, it should be merely *objectified* labour, in which, however, a certain amount of labour is accumulated. But accumulated labour already comprises a quantity of objects in which labour is realized.

"At the beginning everyone was content, since exchange extended only to objects which had no value for each exchanger: no significance was assigned to objects other than those which were without value for each exchanger; no significance was assigned to them, and each was satisfied to receive a useful thing in exchange for a thing without utility. But after the division of labour had made every one into a merchant and society into a commercial society, no one wanted to give up his products except in return for their equivalents; it thus became necessary, in order to determine this equivalent, to know the *value* of the thing received" (Ganilh, 12, b).[4] This means in other words that exchange did not stand still with the formal positing of exchange values, but necessarily advanced towards the subjection of production itself to exchange value.

Notes

1 The first few pages of the Chapter on Capital (pp. 239–50) were entitled by Marx "Chapter on Money as Capital".

2 Charles Ganilh (1758–1836; French neo-Mercantilist economist, an advocate of the Napoleonic Continental System), *Des systèmes d'économie politique, de leurs inconvéniences, de leurs avantages, et de la doctrine la plus favorable aux progrès de la richesse des nations*, Paris, 1809, Vol. II, pp. 64–5.

3 Adam Smith, *Wealth of Nations*, Vol. II, pp. 355–6.

4 The reference is to Marx's own excerpt-book; the quotation is from Ganilh, *Des systèmes d'économie politique*, Vol. II, pp. 11–12.

3 Economy and Society: An Outline of Interpretive Sociology

Max Weber

Economic Action

The concept of economic action

1.   Action will be said to be "economically oriented" so far as, according to its subjective meaning, it is concerned with the satisfaction of a desire for "utilities" (*Nutzleistungen*). "Economic action" (*Wirtschaften*) is any peaceful exercise of an actor's control over resources which is in its main impulse oriented towards economic ends. "Rational economic action" requires instrumental rationality in this orientation, that is, deliberate planning. We will call autocephalous economic action an "economy" (*Wirtschaft*), and an organized system of continuous economic action an "economic establishment" (*Wirtschaftsbetrieb*).

2.   The definition of economic action must be as general as possible and must bring out the fact that all "economic" processes and objects are characterized as such entirely by the *meaning* they have for human action in such roles as ends, means, obstacles, and by-products. It is not, however, permissible to express this by saying, as is sometimes done, that economic action is a "psychic" phenomenon. The production of goods, prices, or even the "subjective valuation" of goods, if they are empirical processes, are far from being merely psychic phenomena. But underlying this misleading phrase is a correct insight. It is a fact that these phenomena have a peculiar type of subjective *meaning*. This alone defines the unity of the corresponding processes, and this alone makes them accessible to subjective interpretation.

The definition of "economic action" must, furthermore, be formulated in such a way as to include the operation of a modern business enterprise run for profit. Hence the definition cannot be based directly on "consumption needs" and the "satisfaction" of these needs, but must, rather, start out on the one hand from the fact that there is a *desire* (demand) for utilities (which is true even in the case of orientation to purely monetary gains), and on the other hand from the fact that *provision* is being made to furnish the supplies to meet this demand (which is true even in the most primitive economy merely "satisfying needs," and regardless of how primitive and frozen in tradition the methods of this provision are).

3.   As distinguished from "economic action" as such, the term "economically oriented action" will be applied to two types: (a) every action which, though primarily oriented to other ends, takes account, in the pursuit of them, of economic

Original publication: Extracts from Weber, Max, *Economy and Society: An Outline of Interpretive Sociology*, eds Guenther Roth and Claus Wittich (University of California Press, Berkeley, CA, 1978).

considerations; that is, of the consciously recognized necessity for economic prudence. Or (b) that which, though primarily oriented to economic ends, makes use of physical force as a means. It thus includes all primarily non-economic action and all non-peaceful action which is influenced by economic considerations. "Economic action" thus is a *conscious, primary* orientation to economic considerations. It must be conscious, for what matters is not the objective necessity of making economic provision, but the belief that it is necessary. Robert Liefmann has rightly laid emphasis on the subjective understandable orientation of action which makes it economic action. He is not, however, correct in attributing the contrary view to all other authors.[1]

4. Every type of action, including the use of violence, may be economically *oriented*. This is true, for instance, of war-like action, such as marauding expeditions and trade wars. Franz Oppenheimer, in particular, has rightly distinguished "economic" means from "political" means.[2] It is essential to distinguish the latter from economic action. The use of force is unquestionably very strongly opposed to the spirit of economic acquisition in the usual sense. Hence the term "economic action" will not be applied to the direct appropriation of goods by force, and the direct coercion of the other party by threats of force. It goes without saying, at the same time, that exchange is not the *only* economic means, though it is one of the most important. Furthermore, the formally peaceful provision for the means and the success of a projected exercise of force, as in the case of armament production and economic organization for war, is just as much economic action as any other.

Every rational course of political action is economically oriented with respect to provision for the necessary means, and it is always possible for political action to serve the interest of economic ends. Similarly, though it is not necessarily true of every economic system, certainly the modern economic order under modern conditions could not continue if its control of resources were not upheld by the legal compulsion of the state; that is, if its formally "legal" rights were not upheld by the threat of force. But the fact that an economic system is thus dependent on protection by force, does not mean that it is itself an example of the use of force.

How entirely untenable it is to maintain that the economy, however defined, is only a *means*, by contrast, for instance, with the state, becomes evident from the fact that it is possible to define the state itself only in terms of the means which it today monopolizes, namely, the use of force. If anything, the most essential aspect of economic action for practical purposes is the prudent choice *between ends*. This choice is, however, oriented to the scarcity of the means which are available or could be procured for these various ends.

5. Not every type of action which is rational in its choice of means will be called "rational economic action," or even "economic action" in any sense; in particular, the term "economy" will be distinguished from that of "technology."[3] The "technique" of an action refers to the means employed as opposed to the meaning or end to which the action is, in the last analysis, oriented. "Rational" technique is a choice of means which is consciously and systematically oriented to the experience and reflection of the actor, which consists, at the highest level of rationality, in scientific knowledge.

Religious Ethics and Economic Rationality

The rejection of usury appears as an emanation of this central religious mood in almost all ethical systems purporting to regulate life. Such a prohibition against usury is completely lacking, outside of Protestantism, only in the religious ethics which have become a mere accommodation to the world, e.g., Confucianism; and in the religious ethics of ancient Babylonia and the Mediterranean littoral in which the urban citizenry (more particularly the nobility residing in the cities and maintaining economic interests in trade) hindered the development of a consistent caritative ethics. The Hindu books of canonical law prohibit the taking of usury, at least for the two highest castes. Among the Jews, collecting usury from "members of the tribe" (*Volksgenossen*) was prohibited. In Islam and in ancient Christianity, the prohibition against usury at first applied only to brothers in faith, but subsequently became unconditional. It seems probable that the proscription of usury in Christianity is not primary in that religion. Jesus justified that biblical injunction to lend to the impecunious on the ground that God will not reward the lender in transactions which present no risk. This verse was then misread and mistranslated in a fashion that resulted in the prohibition of usury: μηδένα ἀπελπίζοντες was mistranslated as μηδὲν, which in the Vulgate became *nihil inde sperantes*.[4]

The original basis for the thoroughgoing rejection of usury was generally the primitive custom of economic assistance to one's fellows, in accordance with which the taking of usury "among brothers" was undoubtedly regarded as a serious breach against the obligation to provide assistance. The fact that the prohibition against usury became increasingly severe in Christianity, under quite different conditions, was due in part to various other motives and factors. The prohibition of usury was not, as the materialist conception of history would represent it, a reflection of the absence of interest on capital under the general conditions of a natural economy. On the contrary, the Christian church and its servants, including the Pope, took interest without any scruples even in the early Middle Ages, i.e., in the very period of a natural economy; even more so, of course, they condoned the taking of interest by others. It is striking that the ecclesiastical persecution of usurious lending arose and became ever more intense virtually as a concomitant of the incipient development of actual capitalist instruments and particularly of acquisitive capital in overseas trade. What is involved, therefore, is a struggle in principle between ethical rationalization and the process of rationalization in the domain of economics. As we have seen, only in the nineteenth century was the church obliged, under the pressure of certain unalterable facts, to remove the prohibition in the manner we have described previously.

The real reason for religious hostility toward usury lies deeper and is connected with the attitude of religious ethics toward the imperatives of rational profitmaking. In early religions, even those which otherwise placed a high positive value on the possession of wealth, purely commercial enterprises were practically always the objects of adverse judgment. Nor is this attitude confined to predominantly agrarian economies under the influence of warrior nobilities. This criticism is usually found when commercial transactions are already relatively advanced, and indeed it arose in conscious protest against them.

We may first note that every economic rationalization of a barter economy has a weakening effect on the traditions which support the authority of the sacred law. For this reason alone the pursuit of money, the typical goal of the rational acquisitive quest, is religiously suspect. Consequently, the priesthood favored the maintenance of a natural economy (as was apparently the case in Egypt) wherever the particular economic interests of the temple as a bank for deposit and loans under divine protection did not militate too much against a natural economy.

But it is above all the impersonal and economically rationalized (but for this very reason ethically irrational) character of purely commercial relationships that evokes the suspicion, never clearly expressed but all the more strongly felt, of ethical religions. For every purely personal relationship of man to man, of whatever sort and even including complete enslavement, may be subjected to ethical requirements and ethically regulated. This is true because the structures of these relationships depend upon the individual wills of the participants, leaving room in such relationships for manifestations of the virtue of charity. But this is not the situation in the realm of economically rationalized relationships, where personal control is exercised in inverse ratio to the degree of rational differentiation of the economic structure. There is no possibility, in practice or even in principle, of any caritative regulation of relationships arising between the holder of a savings and loan bank mortgage and the mortgagee who has obtained a loan from the bank, or between a holder of a federal bond and a citizen taxpayer. Nor can any caritative regulation arise in the relationships between stockholders and factory workers, between tobacco importers and foreign plantation workers, or between industrialists and the miners who have dug from the earth the raw materials used in the plants owned by the industrialists. The growing impersonality of the economy on the basis of association in the market place follows its own rules, disobedience to which entails economic failure and, in the long run, economic ruin.

Rational economic association always brings about depersonalization, and it is impossible to control a universe of instrumentally rational activities by charitable appeals to particular individuals. The functionalized world of capitalism certainly offers no support for any such charitable orientation. In it the claims of religious charity are vitiated not merely because of the refractoriness and weakness of particular individuals, as it happens everywhere, but because they lose their meaning altogether. Religious ethics is confronted by a world of depersonalized relationships which for fundamental reasons cannot submit to its primeval norms. Consequently, in a peculiar duality, priesthoods have time and again protected patriarchalism against impersonal dependency relations, also in the interest of traditionalism, whereas prophetic religion has broken up patriarchal organizations. However, the more a religious commitment becomes conscious of its opposition to economic rationalization as such, the more apt are the religion's virtuosi to end up with an anti-economic rejection of the world.

Of course, the various religious ethics have experienced diverse fates, because in the world of facts the inevitable compromises had to be made. From of old, religious ethics has been directly employed for rational economic purposes, especially the purposes of creditors. This was especially true wherever the state of indebtedness legally involved only the *person* of the debtor, so that the creditor had to appeal to the filial piety of the heirs. An example of this practice is the impounding of the mummy of the deceased in Egypt [to shame his descendants into paying his debts]. Another example is the belief in some Asiatic religions that whoever fails to keep a promise, including a promise to repay a loan and especially a promise guaranteed by an oath, would be tortured in the next world and consequently might disturb the quiet of his descendants by evil magic. In the Middle Ages, as Schulte has pointed out,[5] the credit standing of bishops was particularly high because any breach of obligation on their part, especially of an obligation assumed under oath, might result in their excommunication, which would have ruined a bishop's whole existence. This reminds one of the credit-worthiness of our lieutenants and fraternity students [which was similarly upheld by the efficacy of threats to the future career].

By a peculiar paradox, asceticism actually resulted in the contradictory situation already mentioned on several previous occasions, namely that it was precisely its rationally ascetic character that led to the accumulation of wealth. The cheap labor of ascetic celibates, who underbid the indispensable minimum wage required by married male workers, was primarily responsible for the expansion of monastic businesses in the late Middle Ages. The reaction of the middle classes against the monasteries during this period was based on the "coolie" economic competition offered by the brethren. In the same way, the secular education offered by the cloister was able to underbid the education offered by married teachers. . . .

The inner-worldly asceticism of Protestantism first produced a capitalistic ethics, although unintentionally, for it opened the way to a career in business, especially for the most devout and ethically rigorous people. Above all, Protestantism interpreted success in business as the fruit of a rational mode of life. Indeed, Protestantism, and especially ascetic Protestantism, confined the prohibition against usury to clear cases of complete selfishness. But by this principle it now denounced interest as uncharitable usury in situations which the Roman church itself had, as a matter of practice, tolerated, e.g., in the *montes pietatis*, the extension of credit to the poor. It is worthy of note that Christian business men and the Jews had long since felt to be irksome the competition of these institutions which lent to the poor. Very different was the Protestant justification of interest as a legitimate form of participation by the provider of capital in the business profits accruing from the money he had lent, especially wherever credit had been extended to the wealthy and powerful – e.g., as political credit to the prince. The theoretical justification of this attitude was the achievement of Salmasius [*de usuris*, 1638].

One of the most notable economic effects of Calvinism was its destruction of the traditional forms of charity. First it eliminated unsystematic almsgiving. To be sure, the first steps toward the systematization of charity had been taken with the introduction of fixed rules for the distribution of the bishop's fund in the later medieval church, and with the institution of the medieval hospital – in the same way that the poor tax in Islam had rationalized and centralized almsgiving. Yet random almsgiving had still retained its qualification in Christianity as a "good work." The innumerable charitable institutions of ethical religions have always led in practice to the creation and direct cultivation of mendicancy, and in any case charitable institutions tended to make of charity a purely ritual gesture, as the fixed number of daily meals in the Byzantine monastic establishment or the official soup days of the Chinese. Calvinism put an end to all this, and especially to any benevolent attitude toward the beggar. For Calvinism held that the inscrutable God possessed good reasons for having distributed the gifts of fortune unequally. It never ceased to stress the notion that a man proved himself exclusively in his vocational work. Consequently, begging was explicitly stigmatized as a violation of the injunction to love one's neighbor, in this case the person from whom the beggar solicits.

What is more, all Puritan preachers proceeded from the assumption that the idleness of a person capable of work was inevitably his own fault. But it was felt necessary to organize charity systematically for those incapable of work, such as orphans and cripples, for the greater glory of God. This notion often resulted in such striking phenomena as dressing institutionalized orphans in uniforms reminiscent of fool's attire and parading them through the streets of Amsterdam to divine services with the greatest possible fanfare. Care for the poor was oriented to the goal of discouraging the slothful. This goal was quite apparent in the social welfare program of the English Puritans, in contrast to the Anglican program, so well described by H. Levy.[6] In any case, charity itself became a rationalized "enterprise," and its religious significance was therefore eliminated or even transformed into the opposite significance. This was the situation in consistent ascetic and rationalized religions.

Mystical religions had necessarily to take a diametrically opposite path with regard to the rationalization of economics. The foundering of the postulate of brotherly love in its collision with the loveless realities of the economic domain once it became rationalized led to the expansion of love for one's fellow man until it came to require a completely unselective generosity. Such unselective generosity did not inquire into the reason and outcome of absolute self-surrender, into the worth of the person soliciting help, or into his capacity to help himself. It asked no questions, and quickly gave the shirt when the cloak had been asked for. In mystical religions, the individual for whom the sacrifice is made is regarded in the final analysis as unimportant and exchangeable; his individual value is negated. One's "neighbor" is simply a person whom one happens to encounter along the way; he has significance only because of his need and his solicitation. This results in a distinctively mystical flight from the world which takes the form of a non-specific and loving self-surrender, not for the sake of the man but for the sake of the surrender itself – what Baudelaire has termed "the sacred prostitution of the soul."

The Market: Its Impersonality and Ethic

A market may be said to exist wherever there is competition, even if only unilateral, for opportunities of exchange among a plurality of potential parties. Their physical assemblage in one place, as in the local market square, the fair (the "long distance market"), or the exchange (the merchants' market), only constitutes the most consistent kind of market formation. It is, however, only this physical assemblage which allows the full emergence of the market's most distinctive feature, viz., dickering. Since the discussion of the market phenomena constitutes essentially the content of economics (*Sozialökonomik*), it will not be presented here. From a sociological point of view, the market represents a coexistence and sequence of rational consociations, each of which is specifically ephemeral insofar as it ceases to exist with the act of exchanging the goods, unless a norm has been promulgated which imposes upon the transferors of the exchangeable goods the guaranty of their lawful acquisition as warranty of title or of quiet enjoyment. The completed barter constitutes a consociation only with the immediate partner. The preparatory dickering, however, is always a social action (*Gemeinschaftshandeln*) insofar as the potential partners are guided in their offers by the potential action of an indeterminately large group of real or imaginary competitors rather than by their own actions alone. The more this is true, the more does the market constitute social action. Furthermore, any act of exchange involving the use of money (sale) is a social action simply because the money used derives its value from its relation to the potential action of others. Its acceptability rests exclusively on the expectation that it will continue to be desirable and can be further used as a means of payment. Group formation (*Vergemeinschaftung*) through the use of money is the exact counterpart to any consociation through rationally agreed or imposed norms.

Money creates a group by virtue of material interest relations between actual and potential participants in the market and its payments. At the fully developed stage, the so-called money economy, the resulting situation looks as if it had been created by a set of norms established for the very purpose of bringing it into being. The explanation lies in this: Within the market community every act of exchange, especially monetary exchange, is not directed, in isolation, by the action of the individual partner to the particular transaction, but the more rationally it is considered, the more it is directed by the actions of all parties potentially interested in the exchange. The market community as such is the most impersonal relationship of practical life into which humans can enter with one another. This is not due to that potentiality of struggle among the interested parties which is inherent in the market relationship. Any human relationship, even the most intimate, and even though it be marked by the most unqualified personal devotion, is in some sense relative and may involve a struggle with the partner, for instance, over the salvation of his soul. The reason for the impersonality of the market is its matter-of-factness, its orientation to the commodity and only to that. Where the market is allowed to follow its own autonomous tendencies, its participants do not look toward the persons of each other but only toward the commodity; there are no obligations of brotherliness or reverence, and none of those spontaneous human relations that are sustained by personal unions. They all would just obstruct the free development of the bare market relationship, and its specific interests serve, in their turn, to weaken the sentiments on which these obstructions rest. Market behavior is influenced by rational, purposeful pursuit of interests. The partner to a transaction is expected to behave according to rational legality and, quite particularly, to respect the formal inviolability of a promise once given. These are the qualities which form the content of market ethics. In this latter respect the market inculcates, indeed, particularly rigorous conceptions. Violations of agreements, even though they may be concluded by mere signs, entirely unrecorded, and devoid of evidence, are almost unheard of in the annals of the stock exchange. Such absolute depersonalization is contrary to all the elementary forms of human relationship. Sombart has pointed out this contrast repeatedly and brilliantly.[7]

The "free" market, that is, the market which is not bound by ethical norms, with its exploitation of constellations of interests and monopoly positions and its dickering, is an abomination to every system of fraternal ethics. In sharp contrast to all other groups which always presuppose some measure of personal fraternization or even blood kinship, the market is fundamentally alien to any type of fraternal relationship.

At first, free exchange does not occur but with the world outside of the neighborhood or the personal association. The market is a relationship which transcends the boundaries of neighborhood, kinship group, or tribe. Originally, it is indeed the only peaceful relationship of such kind. At first, fellow members did not trade with one another with the intention of obtaining profit. There was, indeed, no need for such transactions in an age of self-sufficient agrarian units. One of the most characteristic forms of primitive trade, the "silent" trade . . ., dramatically represents the contrast between the market community and the fraternal community. The silent trade is a form of exchange which avoids all face-to-face contact and in which the supply takes the form of a deposit of the commodity at a customary place; the counter-offer takes the same form, and dickering is effected through the increase in the number of objects being offered from both sides, until one party either withdraws dissatisfied or, satisfied, takes the goods left by the other party and departs.

It is normally assumed by both partners to an exchange that each will be interested in the future continuation of the exchange relationship, be it with this particular partner or with some other, and that he will adhere to his promises for this reason and avoid at least striking infringements of the rules of good faith and fair dealing. It is only this assumption which guarantees the law-abidingness of the exchange partners. Insofar as that interest exists, "honesty is the best policy." This proposition, however, is by no means universally applicable, and its empirical validity is irregular; naturally, it is highest in the case of rational enterprises with a stable clientele. For, on the basis of such a stable relationship, which generates the possibility of mutual personal appraisal with regard to market ethics, trading may free itself most successfully from illimited dickering and return, in the interest of the parties, to a relative limitation of fluctuation in prices and exploitation of momentary interest constellations. The consequences, though they are important for price formation, are not relevant here in detail. The fixed price, without preference for any particular buyer, and strict business honesty are highly peculiar features of the regulated local neighborhood markets of the medieval Occident, in contrast to the Near and Far East. They are, moreover, a condition as well as a product of that particular stage of capitalistic economy which is known as Early Capitalism. They are absent where this stage no longer exists. Nor are they practiced by those status and other groups which are not engaged in exchange except occasionally and passively rather than regularly and actively. The maxim of *caveat emptor* obtains, as experience shows, mostly in transactions involving feudal strata or, as every cavalry officer knows, in horse trading among comrades. The specific ethics of the market place is alien to them. Once and for all they conceive of commerce, as does any rural community of neighbors, as an activity in which the sole question is: who will cheat whom.

The freedom of the market is typically limited by sacred taboos or through monopolistic consociations of status groups which render exchange with outsiders impossible. Directed against these limitations we find the continuous onslaught of the market community, whose very existence constitutes a temptation to share in the opportunities for gain. The process of appropriation in a monopolistic group may advance to the point at which it becomes closed toward outsiders, i.e., the land, or the right to share in the commons, may have become vested definitively and hereditarily. As the money economy expands and, with it, both the growing differentiation of needs capable of being satisfied by indirect barter, and the independence from land ownership, such a situation of fixed, hereditary appropriation normally creates a steadily increasing interest of individual parties in the possibility of using their vested property rights for exchange with the highest bidder, even though he be an outsider. This development is quite analogous to that which causes the co-heirs of an industrial enterprise in the long run to establish a corporation so as to be able to sell their shares more freely. In turn, an emerging capitalistic economy, the stronger it becomes, the greater will be its efforts to obtain the means of production and labor services in the market without limitations by sacred or status bonds, and to emancipate the opportunities to sell its products from the restrictions imposed by the sales monopolies of status groups. Capitalistic interests thus favor the continuous extension of the free market, but only up to the point at which some of them succeed, through the purchase of privileges from the political authority or simply through the power of capital, in obtaining for themselves a monopoly for the sale of their products or the acquisition of their means of production, and in thus closing the market on their own part.

The breakup of the monopolies of status groups is thus the typical immediate sequence to the full appropriation of all the material means of production. It occurs where those having a stake in the capitalistic system are in a position to influence, for their own advantage, those communities by which the ownership of goods and the mode of their use are regulated; or where, within a monopolistic status group, the upper hand is gained by those who are interested in the use of their vested property interests in the market. Another consequence is that the scope of those rights which are guaranteed as acquired or acquirable by the coercive apparatus of the property-regulating community becomes limited to rights in material goods and to contractual claims, including claims to contractual labor. All other appropriations, especially those of customers or those of monopolies by status groups, are destroyed. This state of affairs, which we call free competition, lasts until it is replaced by new, this time capitalistic, monopolies which are acquired in the market through the power of property. These capitalistic monopolies differ from monopolies of status groups[8] by their purely economic and rational character. By restricting either the scope of possible sales or the permissible terms, the monopolies of status groups excluded from their field of action the mechanism of the market with its dickering and rational calculation. Those monopolies, on the other hand, which are based solely upon the power of property, rest, on the contrary, upon an entirely rationally calculated mastery of market conditions which may, however, remain formally as free as ever. The sacred, status, and merely traditional bonds, which have gradually come to be eliminated, constituted restrictions on the formation of rational market prices; the purely economically conditioned monopolies are, on the other hand, their ultimate consequence. The beneficiary of a monopoly by a status group restricts, and maintains his power against, the market, while the rational-economic monopolist rules through the market. We shall designate those interest groups which are enabled by formal market freedom to achieve power, as market-interest groups.

A particular market may be subject to a body of norms autonomously agreed upon by the participants or imposed by any one of a great variety of different groups, especially political or religious organizations. Such norms may involve limitations of market freedom, restrictions of dickering or of competition, or they may establish guaranties for the observance of market legality, especially the modes or means of payment or, in periods of interlocal insecurity, the norms may be aimed at guaranteeing the market peace. Since the market was originally a consociation of persons who are not members of the same group and who are, therefore, "enemies," the guaranty of peace, like that of restrictions of permissible modes of warfare, was ordinarily left to divine powers.[9] Very often the peace of the market was placed under the protection of a temple; later on it tended to be made into a source of revenue for the chief or prince. However, while exchange is the specifically peaceful form of acquiring economic power, it can, obviously, be associated with the use of force. The seafarer of Antiquity and the Middle Ages was pleased to take without pay whatever he could acquire by force and had recourse to peaceful dickering only where he was confronted with a power equal to his own or where he regarded it as shrewd to do so for the sake of future exchange opportunities which might be endangered otherwise. But the intensive expansion of exchange relations has always gone together with a process of relative pacification. All of the "public peace" arrangements of the Middle Ages were meant to serve the interests of exchange.[10] The appropriation of goods through free, purely economically rational exchange, as Oppenheimer has said time and again, is the conceptual opposite of appropriation of goods by coercion of any kind, but especially physical coercion, the regulated exercise of which is the very constitutive element of the political community.

Class, Status, Party[11]

Economically Determined Power and the Status Order

The structure of every legal order directly influences the distribution of power, economic or otherwise, within its respective community. This is true of all legal orders and not only that of the state. In general, we understand by "power" the chance of a man or a number of men to realize their own will in a social action even against the resistance of others who are participating in the action.

"Economically conditioned" power is not, of course, identical with "power" as such. On the contrary, the emergence of economic power may be the consequence of power existing on other grounds. Man does not strive for power only in order to enrich himself economically. Power, including economic power, may be valued for its own sake. Very frequently the striving for power is also conditioned by the social honor it entails. Not all power, however, entails social honor: The typical American Boss, as well as the typical big speculator, deliberately relinquishes social honor. Quite generally, "mere economic" power, and especially "naked" money power, is by no means a recognized basis of social honor. Nor is power the only basis of social honor. Indeed, social honor, or prestige, may even be the basis of economic power, and very frequently has been. Power, as well as honor, may be guaranteed by the legal order, but, at least normally, it is not their primary source. The legal order is rather an additional factor that enhances the chance to hold power or honor; but it can not always secure them.

The way in which social honor is distributed in a community between typical groups participating in this distribution we call the "status order." The social order and the economic order are related in a similar manner to the legal order. However, the economic order merely defines the way in which economic goods and services are distributed and used. Of course, the status order is strongly influenced by it, and in turn reacts upon it.

Now: "classes," "status groups," and "parties" are phenomena of the distribution of power within a community.

Determination of Class Situation by Market Situation

In our terminology, "classes" are not communities; they merely represent possible, and frequent, bases for social action. We may speak of a "class" when (1) a number of people have in common a specific causal component of their life chances, insofar as (2) this component is represented exclusively by economic interests in the possession of goods and opportunities for income, and (3) is represented under the conditions of the commodity or labor markets. This is "class situation."

It is the most elemental economic fact that the way in which the disposition over material property is distributed among a plurality of people, meeting competitively in the market for the purpose of exchange, in itself creates specific life chances. The mode of distribution, in accord with the law of marginal utility, excludes the non-wealthy from competing for highly valued goods; it favors the owners and, in fact, gives to them a monopoly to acquire such goods. Other things being equal, the mode of distribution monopolizes the opportunities for profitable deals for all those who, provided with goods, do not necessarily have to exchange them. It increases, at least generally, their power in the price struggle with those who, being propertyless, have nothing to offer but their labor or the resulting products, and who are compelled to get rid of these products in order to subsist at all. The mode of distribution gives to the propertied a monopoly on the possibility of transferring property from the sphere of use as "wealth" to the sphere of "capital," that is, it gives them the entrepreneurial function and all chances to share directly or indirectly in returns on capital. All this holds true within the area in which pure market conditions prevail. "Property" and "lack of property" are, therefore, the basic categories of all class situations. It does not matter whether these two categories become effective in the competitive struggles of the consumers or of the producers. . . .

Status Honor

In contrast to classes, *Stände* (*status groups*) are normally groups. They are, however, often of an amorphous kind. In contrast to the purely economically determined "class situation," we wish to designate as *status situation* every typical component of the life of men that is determined by a specific, positive or negative, social estimation of *honor*. This honor may be connected with any quality shared by a plurality, and, of course, it can be knit to a class situation: class distinctions are linked in the most varied ways with status distinctions. Property as such is not always recognized as a status qualification, but in the long run it is, and with extraordinary regularity. In the subsistence economy of neighborhood associations, it is often simply the richest who is the "chieftain." However, this often is only an honorific preference. For example, in the so-called pure modern democracy, that is, one devoid of any expressly ordered status privileges for individuals, it may be that only the families coming under approximately the same tax class dance with one another. This example is reported of certain smaller Swiss cities. But status honor need not necessarily be linked with a class situation. On the contrary, it normally stands in sharp opposition to the pretensions of sheer property.

Both propertied and propertyless people can belong to the same status group, and frequently they do with very tangible consequences. This equality of social esteem may, however, in the long run become quite precarious. The equality of status among American gentlemen, for instance, is expressed by the fact that outside the subordination determined by the different functions of business, it would be considered strictly repugnant – wherever the old tradition still prevails – if even the richest boss, while playing billiards or cards in his club, would not treat his clerk as in every sense fully his equal in birthright, but would bestow upon him the condescending status-conscious "benevolence" which the German boss can never dissever from his attitude. This is one of the most important reasons why in America the German clubs have never been able to attain the attraction that the American clubs have.

In content, status honor is normally expressed by the fact that above all else a specific *style of life* is expected from all those who wish to belong to the circle. Linked with this expectation are restrictions on social intercourse (that is, intercourse which is not subservient to economic or any other purposes). These restrictions may confine normal marriages to within the status circle and may lead to complete endogamous closure. Whenever this is not a mere individual and socially irrelevant imitation of another style of life, but consensual action of this closing character, the status development is under way.

In its characteristic form, stratification by status groups on the basis of conventional styles of life evolves at the present time in the United States out of the traditional democracy. For example, only the resident of a certain street ("the Street") is considered as belonging to "society," is qualified for social intercourse, and is visited and invited. Above all, this differentiation evolves in such a way as to make for strict submission to the fashion that is dominant at a given time in society. This submission to fashion also exists among men in America to a degree unknown in Germany; it appears as an indication of the fact that a given man puts forward a *claim* to qualify as a gentleman. This submission decides, at least *prima facie*, that he will be treated as such. And this recognition becomes just as important for his employment chances in swank establishments, and above all, for social intercourse and marriage with "esteemed" families, as the qualification for dueling among Germans. As for the rest, status honor is usurped by certain families resident for a long time, and, of course, correspondingly wealthy (e.g. F.F.V., the First Families of Virginia), or by the actual or alleged descendants of the "Indian Princess" Pocahontas, of the Pilgrim fathers, or of the Knickerbockers, the members of almost inaccessible sects and all sorts of circles setting themselves apart by means of any other characteristics and badges. In this case stratification is purely conventional and rests largely on usurpation (as does almost all status honor in its beginning). But the road to legal privilege, positive or negative, is easily traveled as soon as a certain stratification of the social order has in fact been "lived in" and has achieved stability by virtue of a stable distribution of economic power. . . .

Parties

Whereas the genuine place of classes is within the economic order, the place of status groups is within the social order, that is, within the sphere of the distribution of honor. From within these spheres, classes and status groups influence one another and the legal order and are in turn influenced by it. "*Parties*" reside in the sphere of power. Their action is oriented toward the acquisition of social power, that is to say, toward influencing social action no matter what its content may be. In principle, parties may exist in a social club as well as in a state. As over against the actions of classes and status groups, for which this is not necessarily the case, party-oriented social action always involves association. For it is always directed toward a goal which is striven for in a planned manner. This goal may be a cause (the party may aim at realizing a program for ideal or material purposes), or the goal may be personal (sinecures, power, and from these, honor for the leader and the followers of the party). Usually the party aims at all these simultaneously. Parties are, therefore, only possible within groups that have an associational character, that is, some rational order and a staff of persons available who are ready to enforce it. For parties aim precisely at influencing this staff, and if possible, to recruit from it party members.

In any individual case, parties may represent interests determined through class situation or status situation, and they may recruit their following respectively from one or the other. But they need be neither purely class nor purely status parties; in fact, they are more likely to be mixed types, and sometimes they are neither. They may represent ephemeral or enduring structures. Their means of attaining power may be quite varied, ranging from naked violence of any sort to canvassing for votes with coarse or subtle means: money, social influence, the force of speech, suggestion, clumsy hoax, and so on to the rougher or more artful tactics of obstruction in parliamentary bodies.

The sociological structure of parties differs in a basic way according to the kind of social action which they struggle to influence; that means, they differ according to whether or not the community is stratified by status or by classes. Above all else, they vary according to the structure of domination. For their leaders normally deal with its conquest. In our general terminology, parties are not only products of modern forms of domination. We shall also designate as parties the ancient and medieval ones, despite the fact that they differ basically from modern parties. Since a party always struggles for political control (*Herrschaft*), its organization too is frequently strict and "authoritarian." Because of these variations between the forms of domination, it is impossible to say anything about the structure of parties without discussing them first. Therefore, we shall now turn to this central phenomenon of all social organization.

Before we do this, we should add one more general observation about classes, status groups and parties: The fact that they presuppose a larger association, especially the framework of a polity, does not mean that they are confined to it. On the contrary, at all times it has been the order of the day that such association (even when it aims at the use of military force in common) reaches beyond the state boundaries. This can be seen in the [interlocal] solidarity of interests of oligarchs and democrats in Hellas, of Guelphs and Ghibellines in the Middle Ages, and within the Calvinist party during the age of religious struggles; and all the way up to the solidarity of landlords (International Congresses of Agriculture), princes (Holy Alliance, Karlsbad Decrees [of 1819]), socialist workers, conservatives (the longing of Prussian conservatives for Russian intervention in 1850). But their aim is not necessarily the establishment of a new territorial dominion. In the main they aim to influence the existing polity.

Notes

1   Robert Liefmann, *Grundsätze der Volkswirtschaftslehre*, vol. I, 3rd ed. (Stuttgart 1923), p. 74ff. and *passim*.

2   See Franz Oppenheimer, *System der Soziologie*, Part III, *Theorie der reinen und politis-chen Ökonomie*, 5th ed. (Jena 1923), pp. 146–152.

3   The German word *Technik* which Weber uses here covers both the meanings of the English word "technique" and of "technology." Since the distinction is not explicitly made in Weber's terminology, it will have to be introduced according to the context in the translation.

4   "Do not expect anything from it" instead of "Do not deprive anybody of hope." Weber relied on the painstaking analysis of Luke 6:35 by Adalbert Merx, *Die Evangelien des Markus und Lukas* (Berlin: Reimer, 1905), 223ff. Weber mentions Merx below, ch. XV: 10:D; cf. also *Economic History*, ch. 21 and p. 274.

5   See Aloys Schulte, *Geschichte des mittelalterlichen Handels und Verkehrs zwischen Westdeutschland und Italien* (Leipzig: Dunker & Humblot, 1900), I, 263ff.

6   See Hermann Levy, *Economic Liberalism* (London: Macmillan, 1913), ch. VI; first published in German in 1902.

7   *Die Juden und das Wirtschaftsleben* (1911, Epstein tr. 1913, 1951, s.t. *The Jews and Modern Capitalism*); *Der Bourgeois* (1913); *Händler und Helden* (1915); *Der moderne Kapitalismus*, vol. III, Part I, p. 6; see also *Deutscher Sozialismus* (1934) (Geiser tr. s.t. *A New Social Philosophy*, 1937). Revulsion against the so-called "de-humanization" of relationships has constituted an important element in the German neo-romanticism of such groups and movements as the circle around the poet Stefan George, the youth move-ment, the Christian Socialists, etc. Through the tendency to ascribe this capitalistic spirit to the Jews and to hold them responsible for its rise and spread, these sentiments became highly influential in the growth of organized anti-Semitism and, especially, National-Socialism.

8   Such as the monopoly of guild members to sell certain goods within the city, or the monopoly of the lord of a manor to grind the grain of all peasants of the district, or the monopoly of the members of the bar to give legal advice, a monopoly which was abolished in most Continental countries in the nineteenth century.

9   On market peace, cf. S. Rietschel, *Markt und Stadt* (1897); H. Pirenne, *Villes, marchés et marchands au moyen âge* (1898).

10 On such medieval peace arrangements (*Landfrieden*), which were aimed at the elimina-tion of feuds and private wars and which occurred either as non-aggression pacts con-cluded, often with ecclesiastical or royal cooperation, between barons, cities, and other potentates, or were sought to be imposed on his unruly subjects by the king, see Quidde, "Histoire de la paix publique en Allemagne au moyen âge" (1929), 28 *Recueil des cours de l'académie de droit international* 449.

11 The major terminological change in this section is the elimination of the dichotomy of "communal" versus "societal" action and the substitution of "group" for "community."

4 The Great Transformation

Karl Polanyi

Societies and Economic Systems

Before we can proceed to the discussion of the laws governing a market economy, such as the nineteenth century was trying to establish, we must first have a firm grip on the extraordinary assumptions underlying such a system.

Market economy implies a self-regulating system of markets; in slightly more technical terms, it is an economy directed by market prices and nothing but market prices. Such a system capable of organizing the whole of economic life without outside help or interference would certainly deserve to be called self-regulating. These rough indications should suffice to show the entirely unprecedented nature of such a venture in the history of the race.

Let us make our meaning more precise. No society could, naturally, live for any length of time unless it possessed an economy of some sort; but previously to our time no economy has ever existed that, even in principle, was controlled by markets. In spite of the chorus of academic incantations so persistent in the nineteenth century, gain and profit made on exchange never before played an important part in human economy. Though the institution of the market was fairly common since the later Stone Age, its role was no more than incidental to economic life.

We have good reason to insist on this point with all the emphasis at our command. No less a thinker than Adam Smith suggested that the division of labor in society was dependent upon the existence of markets, or, as he put it, upon man's "propensity to barter, truck and exchange one thing for another." This phrase was later to yield the concept of the Economic Man. In retrospect it can be said that no misreading of the past ever proved more prophetic of the future. For while up to Adam Smith's time that propensity had hardly shown up on a considerable scale in the life of any observed community, and had remained, at best, a subordinate feature of economic life, a hundred years later an industrial system was in full swing over the major part of the planet which, practically and theoretically, implied that the human race was swayed in all its economic activities, if not also in its political, intellectual, and spiritual pursuits, by that one particular propensity. Herbert Spencer, in the second half of the nineteenth century, could, without more than a cursory acquaintance with economics, equate the principle of the division of labor with barter and exchange, and another fifty years later, Ludwig von Mises and Walter Lippmann could repeat this same fallacy. By that time there was no need for argument. A host of writers on political economy, social history, political philosophy, and general sociology had followed in Smith's wake and established his paradigm

Original publication: Extracts from Polanyi, Karl, *The Great Transformation* (Beacon Press, Beacon Hill, MA, 1957).

of the bartering savage as an axiom of their respective sciences. In point of fact, Adam Smith's suggestions about the economic psychology of early man were as false as Rousseau's were on the political psychology of the savage. Division of labor, a phenomenon as old as society, springs from differences inherent in the facts of sex, geography, and individual endowment; and the alleged propensity of man to barter, truck, and exchange is almost entirely apocryphal. While history and ethnography know of various kinds of economies, most of them comprising the institution of markets, they know of no economy prior to our own, even approximately controlled and regulated by markets. This will become abundantly clear from a bird's-eye view of the history of economic systems and of markets, presented separately. The role played by markets in the internal economy of the various countries, it will appear, was insignificant up to recent times, and the change-over to an economy dominated by the market pattern will stand out all the more clearly.

To start with, we must discard some nineteenth century prejudices that underlay Adam Smith's hypothesis about primitive man's alleged predilection for gainful occupations. Since his axiom was much more relevant to the immediate future than to the dim past, it induced in his followers a strange attitude toward man's early history. On the face of it, the evidence seemed to indicate that primitive man, far from having a capitalistic psychology, had, in effect, a communistic one (later this also proved to be mistaken). Consequently, economic historians tended to confine their interest to that comparatively recent period of history in which truck and exchange were found on any considerable scale, and primitive economics was relegated to prehistory. Unconsciously, this led to a weighting of the scales in favor of a marketing psychology, for within the relatively short period of the last few centuries everything might be taken to tend towards the establishment of that which was eventually established, i.e., a market system, irrespective of other tendencies which were temporarily submerged. The corrective of such a "short-run" perspective would obviously have been the linking up of economic history with social anthropology, a course which was consistently avoided.

We cannot continue today on these lines. The habit of looking at the last ten thousand years as well as at the array of early societies as a mere prelude to the true history of our civilization which started approximately with the publication of the *Wealth of Nations* in 1776, is, to say the least, out of date. It is this episode which has come to a close in our days, and in trying to gauge the alternatives of the future, we should subdue our natural proneness to follow the proclivities of our fathers. But the same bias which made Adam Smith's generation view primeval man as bent on barter and truck induced their successors to disavow all interest in early man, as he was now known *not* to have indulged in those laudable passions. The tradition of the classical economists, who attempted to base the law of the market on the alleged propensities of man in the state of nature, was replaced by an abandonment of all interest in the cultures of "uncivilized" man as irrelevant to an understanding of the problems of our age.

Such an attitude of subjectivism in regard to earlier civilizations should make no appeal to the scientific mind. The differences existing between civilized and "uncivilized" peoples have been vastly exaggerated, especially in the economic sphere. According to the historians, the forms of industrial life in agricultural Europe were, until recently, not much different from what they had been several thousand years earlier. Ever since the introduction of the plow – essentially a large hoe drawn by animals – the methods of agriculture remained substantially unaltered over the major part of Western and Central Europe until the beginning of the modern age. Indeed, the progress of civilization was, in these regions, mainly political, intellectual, and spiritual; in respect to material conditions, the Western Europe of 1100 AD had hardly caught up with the Roman world of a thousand years before. Even later, change flowed more easily in the channels of statecraft, literature, and the arts, but particularly in those of religion and learning, than in those of industry. In its economics, medieval Europe was largely on a level with ancient Persia, India, or China, and certainly could not rival in riches and culture the New Kingdom of Egypt, two thousand years before. Max Weber was the first among modern economic historians to protest against the brushing aside of primitive economics as irrelevant to the question of the motives and mechanisms of civilized societies. The subsequent work of social anthropology proved him emphatically right. For, if one conclusion stands out more clearly than another from the recent study of early societies it is the changelessness of man as a social being. His natural endowments reappear with a remarkable constancy in societies of all times and places; and the necessary preconditions of the survival of human society appear to be immutably the same.

The outstanding discovery of recent historical and anthropological research is that man's economy, as a rule, is submerged in his social relationships. He does not act so as to safeguard his individual interest in the possession of material goods; he acts so as to safeguard his social standing, his social claims, his social assets. He values material goods only in so far as they serve this end. Neither the process of production nor that of distribution is linked to specific economic interests attached to the possession of goods; but every single step in that process is geared to a number of social interests which eventually ensure that the required step be taken. These interests will be very different in a small hunting or fishing community from those in a vast despotic society, but in either case the economic system will be run on noneconomic motives.

The explanation in terms of survival, is simple. Take the case of a tribal society. The individual's economic interest is rarely paramount, for the community keeps all its members from starving unless it is itself borne down by catastrophe, in which case interests are again threatened collectively, not individually. The maintenance of social ties, on the other hand, is crucial. First, because by disregarding the accepted code of honor, or generosity, the individual cuts himself off from the community and becomes an outcast; second, because, in the long run, all social obligations are reciprocal, and their fulfillment serves also the individual's give-and-take interests best. Such a situation must exert a continuous pressure on the individual to eliminate economic self-interest from his consciousness to the point of making him unable, in many cases (but by no means in all), even to comprehend the implications of his own actions in terms of such an interest. This attitude is reinforced by the frequency of communal activities such as partaking of food from the common catch or sharing in the results of some far-flung and dangerous tribal expedition. The premium set on generosity is so great when measured in terms of social prestige as to make any other behavior than that of utter self-forgetfulness simply not pay. Personal character has little to do with the matter. Man can be as good or evil, as social or asocial, jealous or generous, in respect to one set of values as in respect to another. Not to allow anybody reason for jealousy is, indeed, an accepted principle of ceremonial distribution, just as publicly bestowed praise is the due of the industrious, skillful, or otherwise successful gardener (unless he be *too* successful, in which case he may deservedly be allowed to wither away under the delusion of being the victim of black magic). The human passions, good or bad, are merely directed towards noneconomic ends. Ceremonial display serves to spur emulation to the utmost and the custom of communal labor tends to screw up both quantitative and qualitative standards to the highest pitch. The performance of all acts of exchange as free gifts that are expected to be reciprocated though not necessarily by the same individuals – a procedure minutely articulated and perfectly safeguarded by elaborate methods of publicity, by magic rites, and by the establishment of "dualities" in which groups are linked in mutual obligations – should in itself explain the absence of the notion of gain or even of wealth other than that consisting of objects traditionally enhancing social prestige.

In this sketch of the general traits characteristic of a Western Melanesian community we took no account of its sexual and territorial organization, in reference to which custom, law, magic, and religion exert their influence, as we only intended to show the manner in which so-called economic motives spring from the context of social life. For it is on this one negative point that modern ethnographers agree: the absence of the motive of gain; the absence of the principle of laboring for remuneration; the absence of the principle of least effort; and, especially, the absence of any separate and distinct institution based on economic motives. But how, then, is order in production and distribution ensured?

The answer is provided in the main by two principles of behavior not primarily associated with economics: *reciprocity* and *redistribution*.[1] With the Trobriand Islanders of Western Melanesia, who serve as an illustration of this type of economy, reciprocity works mainly in regard to the sexual organization of society, that is, family and kinship; redistribution is mainly effective in respect to all those who are under a common chief and is, therefore, of a territorial character. Let us take these principles separately.

The sustenance of the family – the female and the children – is the obligation of their matrilineal relatives. The male, who provides for his sister and her family by delivering the finest specimens of his crop, will mainly earn the credit due to his good behavior, but will reap little immediate material benefit in exchange; if he is slack, it is first and foremost his reputation that will suffer. It is for the benefit of his wife and her children that the principle of reciprocity will work, and thus compensate him economically for his acts of civic virtue. Ceremonial display of food both in his own garden and before the recipient's storehouse will ensure that the high quality of his gardening be known to all. It is apparent that the economy of garden and household here forms part of the social relations connected with good husbandry and fine citizenship. The broad principle of reciprocity helps to safeguard both production and family sustenance.

The principle of redistribution is no less effective. A substantial part of all the produce of the island is delivered by the village headmen to the chief who keeps it in storage. But as all communal activity centers around the feasts, dances, and other occasions when the islanders entertain one another as well as their neighbors from other islands (at which the results of long distance trading are handed out, gifts are given and reciprocated according to the rules of etiquette, and the chief distributes the customary presents to all), the overwhelming importance of the storage system becomes apparent. Economically, it is an essential part of the existing system of division of labor, of foreign trading, of taxation for public purposes, of defense provisions. But these functions of an economic system proper are completely absorbed by the intensely vivid experiences which offer superabundant noneconomic motivation for every act performed in the frame of the social system as a whole.

However, principles of behavior such as these cannot become effective unless existing institutional patterns lend themselves to their application. Reciprocity and redistribution are able to ensure the working of an economic system without the help of written records and elaborate administration only because the organization of the societies in question meets the requirements of such a solution with the help of patterns such as *symmetry* and *centricity*.

Reciprocity is enormously facilitated by the institutional pattern of symmetry, a frequent feature of social organization among nonliterate peoples. The striking "duality" which we find in tribal subdivisions lends itself to the pairing out of individual relations and thereby assists the give-and-take of goods and services in the absence of permanent records. The moieties of savage society which tend to create a "pendant" to each subdivision, turned out to result from, as well as help to perform, the acts of reciprocity on which the system rests. Little is known of the origin of "duality"; but each coastal village on the Trobriand Islands appears to have its counterpart in an inland village, so that the important exchange of breadfruits and fish, though disguised as a reciprocal distribution of gifts, and actually disjoint in time, can be organized smoothly. In the Kula trade, too, each individual has his partner on another isle, thus personalizing to a remarkable extent the relationship of reciprocity. But for the frequency of the symmetrical pattern in the subdivisions of the tribe, in the location of settlements, as well as in intertribal relations, a broad reciprocity relying on the long-run working of separated acts of give-and-take would be impracticable.

The institutional pattern of centricity, again, which is present to some extent in all human groups, provides a track for the collection, storage, and redistribution of goods and services. The members of a hunting tribe usually deliver the game to the headman for redistribution. It is in the nature of hunting that the output of game is irregular, besides being the result of a collective input. Under conditions such as these no other method of sharing is practicable if the group is not to break up after every hunt. Yet in all economies of kind a similar need exists, be the group ever so numerous. And the larger the territory and the more varied the produce, the more will redistribution result in an effective division of labor, since it must help to link up geographically differentiated groups of producers.

Symmetry and centricity will meet halfway the needs of reciprocity and redistribution; institutional patterns and principles of behavior are mutually adjusted. As long as social organization runs in its ruts, no individual economic motives need come into play; no shirking of personal effort need be feared; division of labor will automatically be ensured; economic obligations will be duly discharged; and, above all, the material means for an exuberant display of abundance at all public festivals will be provided. In such a community the idea of profit is barred; higgling and haggling is decried; giving freely is acclaimed as a virtue; the supposed propensity to barter, truck, and exchange does not appear. The economic system is, in effect, a mere function of social organization. . . .

The third principle, which was destined to play a big role in history and which we will call the principle of *householding*, consists in production for one's own use. The Greeks called it *oeconomia*, the etymon of the word "economy". As far as ethnographical records are concerned, we should not assume that production for a person's or group's own sake is more ancient than reciprocity or redistribution. On the contrary, orthodox tradition as well as some more recent theories on the subject have been emphatically disproved. The individualistic savage collecting food and hunting on his own or for his family has never existed. Indeed, the practice of catering for the needs of one's household becomes a feature of economic life only on a more advanced level of agriculture; however, even then it has nothing in common either with the motive of gain or with the institution of markets. Its pattern is the closed group. Whether the very different entities of the family or the settlement or the manor formed the self-sufficient unit, the principle was invariably the same, namely, that of production and storing for the satisfaction of the wants of the members of the group. The principle is as broad in its application as either reciprocity or redistribution. The nature of the institutional nucleus is indifferent: it may be sex as with the patriarchal family, locality as with the village settlement, or political power as with the seigneurial manor. Nor does the internal organization of the group matter. It may be as despotic as the Roman *familia* or as democratic as the South Slav *zadruga*; as large as the great domains of the Carolingian magnates or as small as the average peasant holding of Western Europe. The need for trade or markets is no greater than in the case of reciprocity or redistribution.

It is such a condition of affairs which Aristotle tried to establish as a norm more than two thousand years ago. Looking back from the rapidly declining heights of a world-wide market economy we must concede that his famous distinction of householding proper and money-making, in the introductory chapter of his *Politics*, was probably the most prophetic pointer ever made in the realm of the social sciences; it is certainly still the best analysis of the subject we possess. Aristotle insists on production for use as against production for gain as the essence of householding proper; yet accessory production for the market need not, he argues, destroy the self-sufficiency of the household as long as the cash crop would also otherwise be raised on the farm for sustenance, as cattle or grain; the sale of the surpluses need not destroy the basis of householding. Only a genius of common sense could have maintained, as he did, that gain was a motive peculiar to production for the market, and that the money factor introduced a new element into the situation, yet nevertheless, as long as markets and money were mere accessories to an otherwise self-sufficient household, the principle of production for use could operate. Undoubtedly, in this he was right, though he failed to see how impracticable it was to ignore the existence of markets at a time when Greek economy had made itself dependent upon wholesale trading and loaned capital. For this was the century when Delos and Rhodes were developing into emporia of freight insurance, sea-loans, and giro-banking, compared with which the Western Europe of a thousand years later was the very picture of primitivity. Yet Jowett, Master of Balliol, was grievously mistaken when he took it for granted that his Victorian England had a fairer grasp than Aristotle of the nature of the difference between householding and money-making.

He excused Aristotle by conceding that the "subjects of knowledge that are concerned with man run into one another; and in the age of Aristotle were not easily distinguished." Aristotle, it is true, did not recognize clearly the implications of the division of labor and its connection with markets and money; nor did he realize the uses of money as credit and capital. So far Jowett's strictures were justified. But it was the Master of Balliol, not Aristotle, who was impervious to the human implications of money-making. He failed to see that the distinction between the principle of use and that of gain was the key to the utterly different civilization the outlines of which Aristotle accurately forecast two thousand years before its advent out of the bare rudiments of a market economy available to him, while Jowett, with the full-blown specimen before him, overlooked its existence. In denouncing the principle of production for gain "as not natural to man," as boundless and limitless, Aristotle was, in effect, aiming at the crucial point, namely the divorcedness of a separate economic motive from the social relations in which these limitations inhered.

Broadly, the proposition holds that all economic systems known to us up to the end of feudalism in Western Europe were organized either on the principles of reciprocity or redistribution, or householding, or some combination of the three. These principles were institutionalized with the help of a social organization which, *inter alia*, made use of the patterns of symmetry, centricity, and autarchy. In this framework, the orderly production and distribution of goods was secured through a great variety of individual motives disciplined by general principles of behavior. Among these motives gain was not prominent. Custom and law, magic and religion co-operated in inducing the individual to comply with rules of behavior which, eventually, ensured his functioning in the economic system.

The Greco-Roman period, in spite of its highly developed trade, represented no break in this respect; it was characterized by the grand scale on which redistribution of grain was practiced by the Roman administration in an otherwise householding economy, and it formed no exception to the rule that up to the end of the Middle Ages, markets played no important part in the economic system; other institutional patterns prevailed.

From the sixteenth century onwards markets were both numerous and important. Under the mercantile system they became, in effect, a main concern of government; yet there was still no sign of the coming control of markets over human society. On the contrary. Regulation and regimentation were stricter than ever; the very idea of a self-regulating market was absent. To comprehend the sudden change-over to an utterly new type of economy in the nineteenth century, we must now turn to the history of the market, an institution we were able practically to neglect in our review of the economic systems of the past.

Selected references to "Societies and Economic Systems"

The nineteenth century attempted to establish a self-regulating economic system on the motive of individual gain. We maintain that such a venture was in the very nature of things impossible. Here we are merely concerned with the distorted view of life and society implied in such an approach. Nineteenth century thinkers assumed, for instance, that to behave like a trader in the market was "natural," any other mode of behavior being artificial economic behavior – the result of interference with human instincts; that markets would spontaneously arise, if only men were let alone; that whatever the desirability of such a society on moral grounds, its practicability, at least, was founded on the immutable characteristics of the race, and so on. Almost exactly the opposite of these assertions is implied in the testimony of modern research in various fields of social science such as social anthropology, primitive economics, the history of early civilization, and general economic history. Indeed, there is hardly an anthropological or sociological assumption – whether explicit or implicit – contained in the philosophy of economic liberalism that has not been refuted. Some citations follow.

(a) The motive of gain is not "natural" to man

"The characteristic feature of primitive economics is the absence of any desire to make profits from production or exchange" (Thurnwald, *Economics in Primitive Communities*, 1932, p. xiii). "Another notion which must be exploded, once and forever, is that of the Primitive Economic Man of some current economic textbooks" (Malinowski, *Argonauts of the Western Pacific*, 1930, p. 60). "We must reject the *Idealtypen* of Manchester liberalism, which are not only theoretically, but also historically misleading" (Brinkmann, "Das soziale System des Kapitalismus." In *Grundriss der Sozialökonomik*, Abt. IV, p. 11).

(b) To expect payment for labor is not "natural" to man

"Gain, such as is often the stimulus for work in more civilized communities, never acts as an impulse to work under the original native conditions" (Malinowski, op. cit., p. 156). "Nowhere in uninfluenced primitive society do we find labor associated with the idea of payment" (Lowie, "Social Organization," *Encyclopedia of the Social Sciences*, Vol. XIV, p. 14). "*Nowhere* is labor being leased or sold" (Thurnwald, *Die menschliche Gesellschaft*, Bk. III, 1932, p. 169). "The treatment of labor as an obligation, not requiring indemnification . . ." is general (Firth, *Primitive Economics of the New Zealand Maori*, 1929). "Even in the Middle Ages payment for work for strangers is something unheard of." "The stranger has no *personal* tie of duty, and, therefore, he should work for honor and recognition." Minstrels, while being strangers, "accepted payment, and were consequently despised" (Lowie, op. cit.).

(c) To restrict labor to the unavoidable minimum is not "natural" to man

"We can not fail to observe that work is never limited to the unavoidable minimum but exceeds the absolutely necessary amount, owing to a natural or acquired functional urge to activity" (Thurnwald, *Economics*, p. 209). "Labor always tends beyond that which is strictly necessary" (Thurnwald, *Die menschliche Gesellschaft*, p. 163).

(d) The usual incentives to labor are not gain but reciprocity, competition, joy of work, and social approbation

Reciprocity: "Most, if not all economic acts are found to belong to some chain of reciprocal gifts and countergifts, which in the long run balance, benefiting both sides equally. . . . The man who would persistently disobey the rulings of law in his economic dealings would soon find himself outside the social and economic order – and he is perfectly well aware of it" (Malinowski, *Crime and Custom in Savage Society*, 1926, pp. 40–41).

Competition: "Competition is keen, performance, though uniform in aim, is varied in excellence. . . . A scramble for excellence in reproducing patterns" (Goldenweiser, "Loose Ends of Theory on the Individual, Pattern, and Involution in Primitive Society." In *Essays in Anthropology*, 1936, p. 99). "Men vie with one another in their speed, in their thoroughness, and in the weights they can lift, when bringing big poles to the garden, or in carrying away the harvested yams" (Malinowski, *Argonauts*, p. 61).

Joy of work: "Work for its own sake is a constant characteristic of Moari industry" (Firth, "Some Features of Primitive Industry," *E.J.*, Vol. I, p. 17). "Much time and labor is given up to aesthetic purposes, to making the gardens tidy, clean, cleared of all debris; to building fine, solid fences, to providing specially strong and big yam-poles. All these things are, to some extent, required for the growth of the plant; but there can be no doubt that the natives push their conscientiousness far beyond the limit of the purely necessary" (Malinowski, op. cit., p. 59).

Social approbation: "Perfection in gardening is the general index to the social value of a person" (Malinowski, *Coral Gardens and Their Magic*, Vol. II, 1935, p. 124). "Every person in the community is expected to show a normal measure of application" (Firth, *Primitive Polynesian Economy*, 1939, p. 161). "The Andaman Islanders regard laziness as an antisocial behavior" (Ratcliffe-Brown, *The Andaman Islanders*). "To put one's labor at the command of another is a social service, not merely an economic service" (Firth, op. cit., p. 303).

(e) Man the same down the ages

Linton in his *Study of Man* advises caution against the psychological theories of personality determination, and asserts that "general observations lead to the conclusion that the total range of these types is much the same in all societies. . . . In other words, as soon as he [the observer] penetrates the screen of cultural difference, he finds that these people are fundamentally like ourselves" (p. 484). Thurnwald stresses the similarity of men at all stages of their development: "Primitive economics as studied in the preceding pages is not distinguished from any other form of economics, as far as human relations are concerned, and rests on the same general principles of social life" (*Economics*, p. 288). "Some collective emotions of an elemental nature are essentially the same with all human beings and account for the recurrence of similar configurations in their social existence" ("Sozialpsychische Abläufe im Völkerleben." In *Essays in Anthropology*, p. 383). Ruth Benedict's *Patterns of Culture* ultimately is based on a similar assumption: "I have spoken as if human temperament were fairly constant in the world, as if in every society a roughly similar distribution were potentially available, and, as if the culture selected from these, according to its traditional patterns, had moulded the vast majority of individuals into conformity. Trance experience, for example, according to this interpretation, is a potentiality of a certain number of individuals in any population. When it is honored and rewarded, a considerable proportion will achieve or simulate it . . ." (p. 233). Malinowksi consistently maintained the same position in his works.

(f) Economic systems, as a rule, are embedded in social relations; distribution of material goods is ensured by noneconomic motives

Primitive economy is "a social affair, dealing with a number of persons as parts of an interlocking whole" (Thurnwald, *Economics*, p. xii). This is equally true of wealth, work, and barter. "Primitive wealth is not of an economic but of a social nature" (ibid.). Labor is capable of "effective work," because it is *integrated into an organized effort by social forces*" (Malinowski, *Argonauts*, p. 157). "Barter of goods and services is carried on mostly within a standing partnership, or associated with definite social ties or coupled with a mutuality in non-economic matters" (Malinowski, *Crime and Custom*, p. 39).

The two main principles which govern economic behavior appear to be reciprocity and *storage-cum-redistribution*:

"The whole tribal life is permeated by a constant give and take" (Malinowski, *Argonauts*, p. 167). "Today's giving will be recompensed by tomorrow's taking. This is the outcome of the principle of reciprocity which pervades every relation of primitive life . . ." (Thurnwald, *Economics*, p. 106). In order to make such reciprocity possible, a certain "duality" of institutions or "symmetry of structure will be found in every savage society, as the indispensable basis of reciprocal obligations" (Malinowski, *Crime and Custom*, p. 25). "The symmetrical partition of their chambers of spirits is based with the Banaro on the structure of their society, which is similarly symmetrical" (Thurnwald, *Die Gemeinde der Bánaro*, 1921, p. 378).

Thurnwald discovered that apart from, and sometimes combined with, such reciprocating behavior, the practice of storage and redistribution was of the most general application from the primitive hunting tribe to the largest of empires. Goods were centrally collected and then distributed to the members of the community, in a great variety of ways. Among Micronesian and Polynesian peoples, for instance, "the kings as the representatives of the first clan, receive the revenue, redistributing it later in the form of largesse among the population" (Thurnwald, *Economics*, p. xii). This distributive function is a prime source of the political power of central agencies (ibid., p. 107).

(g) Individual food collection for the use of his own person and family does not form part of early man's life

The classics assumed the pre-economic man had to take care of himself and his family. This assumption was revived by Carl Buecher in his pioneering work around the turn of the century and gained wide currency. Recent research has unanimously corrected Buecher on this point. (Firth, *Primitive Economics of the New Zealand Maori*, pp. 12, 206, 350; Thurnwald, *Economics*, pp. 170, 268, and *Die menschliche Gesellschaft*, Vol. III, p. 146; Herskovits, *The Economic Life of Primitive Peoples*, 1940, p. 34; Malinowski, *Argonauts*, p. 167, footnote).

(h) Reciprocity and redistribution are principles of economic behavior which apply not only to small primitive communities, but also to large and wealthy empires

"Distribution has its own particular history, starting from the most primitive life of the hunting tribes." ". . . The case is different with societies with a more recent and more pronounced stratification. . . ." "The most impressive example is furnished by the contact of herdsmen with agricultural people." ". . . The conditions in these societies differ considerably. But the distributive function increases with the growing political power of a few families and the rise of despots. The chief receives the gifts of the peasant, which have now become 'taxes,' and distributes them among his officials, especially those attached to his court."

"This development involved more complicated systems of distribution. . . . All archaic states – ancient China, the Empire of the Incas, the Indian kingdoms, Egypt, Babylonia – made use of a metal currency for taxes and salaries but relied mainly on payments in kind stored in granaries and warehouses . . . and distributed to officials, warriors, and the leisured classes, that is, to the non-producing part of the population. In this case distribution fulfills an essentially economic function" (Thurnwald, *Economics*, pp. 106–8).

"When we speak of feudalism, we are usually thinking of the Middle Ages in Europe. . . . However, it is an institution, which very soon makes its appearance in stratified communities. The fact that most transactions are in kind and that the upper stratum claims all the land or cattle, are the economic causes of feudalism . . ." (ibid., p. 195).

Evolution of the Market Pattern

The dominating part played by markets in capitalist economy together with the basic significance of the principle of barter or exchange in this economy calls for a careful inquiry into the nature and origin of markets, if the economic superstitions of the nineteenth century are to be discarded.[2]

Barter, truck, and exchange is a principle of economic behavior dependent for its effectiveness upon the market pattern. A market is a meeting place for the purpose of barter or buying and selling. Unless such a pattern is present, at least in patches, the propensity to barter will find but insufficient scope: it cannot produce prices.[3] For just as reciprocity is aided by a symmetrical pattern of organization, as redistribution is made easier by some measure of centralization, and householding must be based on autarchy, so also the principle of barter depends for its effectiveness on the market pattern. But in the same manner in which either reciprocity, redistribution, or householding may occur in a society without being prevalent in it, the principle of barter also may take a subordinate place in a society in which other principles are in the ascendant.

However, in some other respects the principle of barter is not on a strict parity with the three other principles. The market pattern, with which it is associated, is more specific than either symmetry, centricity or autarchy – which, in contrast to the market pattern, are mere "traits," and do not create institutions designed for one function only. Symmetry is no more than a sociological arrangement, which gives rise to no separate institutions, but merely patterns out existing ones (whether a tribe or a village is symmetrically patterned or not involves no distinctive institution). Centricity, though frequently creating distinctive institutions, implies no motive that would single out the resulting institution for a single specific function (the headman of a village or another central official might assume, for instance, a variety of political, military, religious, or economic functions, indiscriminately). Economic autarchy, finally, is only an accessory trait of an existing closed group.

The market pattern, on the other hand, being related to a peculiar motive of its own, the motive of truck or barter, is capable of creating a specific institution, namely, the market. Ultimately, that is why the control of the economic system by the market is of overwhelming consequence to the whole organization of society: it means no less than the running of society as an adjunct to the market. Instead of economy being embedded in social relations, social relations are embedded in the economic system. The vital importance of the economic factor to the existence of society precludes any other result. For once the economic system is organized in separate institutions, based on specific motives and conferring a special status, society must be shaped in such a manner as to allow that system to function according to its own laws. This is the meaning of the familiar assertion that a market economy can function only in a market society.

The step which makes isolated markets into a market economy, regulated markets into a self-regulating market, is indeed crucial. The nineteenth century – whether hailing the fact as the apex of civilization or deploring it as a cancerous growth – naïvely imagined that such a development was the natural outcome of the spreading of markets. It was not realized that the gearing of markets into a self-regulating system of tremendous power was not the result of any inherent tendency of markets towards excrescence, but rather the effect of highly artificial stimulants administered to the body social in order to meet a situation which was created by the no less artificial phenomenon of the machine. The limited and unexpansive nature of the market pattern, as such, was not recognized; and yet it is this fact which emerges with convincing clarity from modern research.

"Markets are not found everywhere; their absence, while indicating a certain isolation and a tendency to seclusion, is not associated with any particular development any more than can be inferred from their presence." This colorless sentence from Thurnwald's *Economics in Primitive Communities* sums up the significant results of modern research on the subject. Another author repeats in respect to money what Thurnwald says of markets: "The mere fact, that a tribe used money differentiated it very little economically from other tribes on the same cultural level, who did not." We need hardly do more than point to some of the more startling implications of these statements.

The presence or absence of markets or money does not necessarily affect the economic system of a primitive society – this refutes the nineteenth century myth that money was an invention the appearance of which inevitably transformed a society by creating markets, forcing the pace of the division of labor, and releasing man's natural propensity to barter, truck, and exchange. Orthodox economic history, in effect, was based on an immensely exaggerated view of the significance of markets as such. A "certain isolation," or, perhaps, a "tendency to seclusion" is the only economic trait that can be correctly inferred from their absence; in respect to the internal organization of an economy, their presence or absence need make no difference.

The reasons are simple. Markets are not institutions functioning mainly within an economy, but without. They are meeting places of long-distance trade. Local markets proper are of little consequence. Moreover, neither long-distance nor local markets are essentially competitive, and consequently there is, in either case, but little pressure to create territorial trade, a so-called internal or national market. Every one of these assertions strikes at some axiomatically held assumption of the classical economists, yet they follow closely from the facts as they appear in the light of modern research.

The logic of the case is, indeed, almost the opposite of that underlying the classical doctrine. The orthodox teaching started from the individual's propensity to barter; deduced from it the necessity of local markets, as well as of division of labor; and inferred, finally, the necessity of trade, eventually of foreign trade, including even long-distance trade. In the light of our present knowledge we should almost reverse the sequence of the argument: the true starting point is long-distance trade, a result of the geographical location of goods, and of the "division of labor" given by location. Long-distance trade often engenders markets, an institution which involves acts of barter, and, if money is used, of buying and selling, thus, eventually, but by no means necessarily, offering to some individuals an occasion to indulge in their alleged propensity for bargaining and haggling. . . .

It might seem natural to assume that, given individual acts of barter, these would in the course of time lead to the development of local markets, and that such markets, once in existence, would just as naturally lead to the establishment of internal or national markets. However, neither the one nor the other is the case. Individual acts of barter or exchange – this is the bare fact – do not, as a rule, lead to the establishment of markets in societies where other principles of economic behavior prevail. Such acts are common in almost all types of primitive society, but they are considered as incidental since they do not provide for the necessaries of life. In the vast ancient systems of redistribution, acts of barter as well as local markets were a usual, but no more than a subordinate trait. The same is true where reciprocity rules: acts of barter are here usually embedded in long-range relations implying trust and confidence, a situation which tends to obliterate the bilateral character of the transaction. The limiting factors arise from all points of the sociological compass: custom and law, religion and magic equally contribute to the result, which is to restrict acts of exchange in respect to persons and objects, time and occasion. As a rule, he who barters merely enters into a ready-made type of transaction in which both the objects and their equivalent amounts are given. *Utu* in the language of the Tikopia[4] denotes such a traditional equivalent as part of reciprocal exchange. That which appeared as the essential feature of exchange to eighteenth century thought, the voluntaristic element of bargain, and the higgling so expressive of the assumed motive of truck, finds but little scope in the actual transaction; in so far as this motive underlies the procedure, it is seldom allowed to rise to the surface.

The customary way to behave is, rather, to give vent to the opposite motivation. The giver may simply drop the object on the ground and the receiver will pretend to pick it up accidentally, or even leave it to one of his hangers-on to do so for him. Nothing could be more contrary to accepted behavior than to have a good look at the counterpart received. As we have every reason to believe that this sophisticated attitude is not the outcome of a genuine lack of interest in the material side of the transaction, we might describe the etiquette of barter as a counteracting development designed to limit the scope of the trait.

Indeed, on the evidence available it would be rash to assert that local markets ever developed from individual acts of barter. Obscure as the beginnings of local markets are, this much can be asserted: that from the start this institution was surrounded by a number of safeguards designed to protect the prevailing economic organization of society from interference on the part of market practices. The peace of the market was secured at the price of rituals and ceremonies which restricted its scope while ensuring its ability to function within the given narrow limits. The most significant result of markets – the birth of towns and urban civilization – was, in effect, the outcome of a paradoxical development. Because the towns, the offspring of the markets, were not only their protectors, but also the means of preventing them from expanding into the countryside and thus encroaching on the prevailing economic organization of society. The two meanings of the word "contain" express perhaps best this double function of the towns, in respect to the markets which they both enveloped and prevented from developing.

If barter was surrounded by taboos devised to keep this type of human relationship from abusing the functions of the economic organization proper, the discipline of the market was even stricter. Here is an example from the Chaga country: "The market must be regularly visited on market days. If any occurrence should prevent the holding of the market on one or more days, business cannot be resumed until the market-place has been purified. . . . Every injury occurring on the market-place and involving the shedding of blood necessitated immediate expiation. From that moment no woman was allowed to leave the market-place and no goods might be touched; they had to be cleansed before they could be carried away and used for food. At the very least a goat had to be sacrificed at once. A more expensive and more serious expiation was necessary if a woman bore a child or had a miscarriage on the market-place. In that case a milch animal was necessary. In addition to this, the homestead of the chief had to be purified by means of sacrificial blood of a milch-cow. All the women in the country were thus sprinkled, district by district."[5] Rules such as these would not make the spreading of markets easier.

The typical local market at which housewives procure some of their daily needs, and growers of grain or vegetables as well as local craftsmen offer their wares for sale, shows an amazing indifference to time and place. Gatherings of this kind are not only fairly general in primitive societies, but remain almost unchanged right up to the middle of the eighteenth century in the most advanced countries of Western Europe. They are an adjunct of local existence and differ but little whether they form part of Central African tribal life, or a *cité* of Merovingian France, or a Scottish village of Adam Smith's time. But what is true of the village is also true of the town. Local markets are, essentially, neighborhood markets, and, though important to the life of the community, they nowhere showed any sign of reducing the prevailing economic system to their pattern. They were not starting points of internal or national trade.

Internal trade in Western Europe was actually created by the intervention of the state. Right up to the time of the Commercial Revolution what may appear to us as national trade was not national, but municipal. The Hanse were not German merchants; they were a corporation of trading oligarchs, hailing from a number of North Sea and Baltic towns. Far from "nationalizing" German economic life, the Hanse deliberately cut off the hinterland from trade. The trade of Antwerp or Hamburg, Venice or Lyons, was in no way Dutch or German, Italian or French. London was no exception: it was as little "English" as Luebeck was "German." The trade map of Europe in this period should rightly show only towns, and leave blank the countryside – it might as well have not existed as far as organized trade was concerned. So-called nations were merely political units, and very loose ones at that, consisting economically of innumerable smaller and bigger self-sufficing households and insignificant local markets in the villages. Trade was limited to organized townships which carried it on either locally as neighborhood trade or as long-distance trade – the two were strictly separated, and neither was allowed to infiltrate the countryside indiscriminately.

Such a permanent severance of local trade and long-distance trade within the organization of the town must come as another shock to the evolutionist, with whom things always seem so easily to grow into one another. And yet this peculiar fact forms the key to the social history of urban life in Western Europe. It strongly tends to support our assertion in respect to the origin of markets which we inferred from conditions in primitive economies. The sharp distinction drawn between local and long-distance trade might have seemed too rigid, especially as it led us to the somewhat surprising conclusion that neither long-distance trade nor local trade was the parent of the internal trade of modern times – thus apparently leaving no alternative but to turn for an explanation to the *deus ex machina* of state intervention. We will see presently that in this respect also recent investigations bear out our conclusions. But let us first give a bare outline of the history of urban civilization as it was shaped by the peculiar severance of local and long-distance trade within the confines of the medieval town. . . .

Deliberate action of the state in the fifteenth and sixteenth centuries foisted the mercantile system on the fiercely protectionist towns and principalities. Mercantilism destroyed the outworn particularism of local and intermunicipal trading by breaking down the barriers separating these two types of noncompetitive commerce and thus clearing the way for a national market which increasingly ignored the distinction between town and countryside as well as that between the various towns and provinces.

The mercantile system was, in effect, a response to many challenges. Politically, the centralized state was a new creation called forth by the Commercial Revolution which had shifted the center of gravity of the Western world from the Mediterranean to the Atlantic seaboard and thus compelled the backward peoples of larger agrarian countries to organize for commerce and trade. In external politics, the setting up of sovereign power was the need of the day; accordingly, mercantilist statecraft involved the marshaling of the resources of the whole national territory to the purposes of power in foreign affairs. In internal politics, unification of the countries fragmented by feudal and municipal particularism was the necessary by-product of such an endeavor. Economically, the instrument of unification was capital, i.e., private resources available in form of money hoards and thus peculiarly suitable for the development of commerce. Finally the administrative technique underlying the economic policy of the central government was supplied by the extension of the traditional municipal system to the larger territory of the state. In France, where the craft gilds tended to become state organs, the gild system was simply extended over the whole territory of the country; in England, where the decay of the walled towns had weakened that system fatally, the countryside was industrialized without the supervision of the gilds, while in both countries trade and commerce spread over the whole territory of the nation and became the dominating form of economic activity. In this situation lie the origins of the internal trade policy of mercantilism.

State intervention, which had freed trade from the confines of the privileged town, was now called to deal with two closely connected dangers which the town had successfully met, namely, monopoly and competition. That competition must ultimately lead to monopoly was a truth well understood at the time, while monopoly was feared even more than later as it often concerned the necessaries of life and thus easily waxed into a peril to the community. All-round regulation of economic life, only this time on a national, no more on a merely municipal, scale was the given remedy. What to the modern mind may easily appear as a shortsighted exclusion of competition was in reality the means of safeguarding the functioning of markets under the given conditions. For any temporary intrusion of buyers or sellers in the market must destroy the balance and disappoint regular buyers or sellers, with the result that the market will cease to function. The former purveyors will cease to offer their goods as they cannot be sure that their goods will fetch a price, and the market left without sufficient supply will become a prey to the monopolist. To a lesser degree, the same dangers were present on the demand side, where a rapid falling off might be followed by a monopoly of demand. With every step that the state took to rid the market of particularist restrictions, of tolls and prohibitions, it imperiled the organized system of production and distribution which was now threatened by unregulated competition and the intrusion of the interloper who "scooped" the market but offered no guarantee of permanency. Thus it came that although the new national markets were, inevitably, to some degree competitive, it was the traditional feature of regulation, not the new element of competition, which prevailed.[6] The self-sufficing household of the peasant laboring for his subsistence remained the broad basis of the economic system, which was being integrated into large national units through the formation of the internal market. This national market now took its place alongside, and partly overlapping, the local and foreign markets. Agriculture was now being supplemented by internal commerce – a system of relatively isolated markets, which was entirely compatible with the principle of householding still dominant in the countryside.

This concludes our synopsis of the history of the market up to the time of the Industrial Revolution. The next stage in mankind's history brought, as we know, an attempt to set up one big self-regulating market. There was nothing in mercantilism, this distinctive policy of the Western nation-state, to presage such a unique development. The "freeing" of trade performed by mercantilism merely liberated trade from particularism, but at the same time extended the scope of regulation. The economic system was submerged in general social relations; markets were merely an accessory feature of an institutional setting controlled and regulated more than ever by social authority.

Selected references to "Evolution of the Market Pattern"

Economic liberalism labored under the delusion that its practices and methods were the natural outgrowth of a general law of progress. To make them fit the pattern, the principles underlying a self-regulating market were projected backward into the whole history of human civilization. As a result the true nature and origins of trade, markets, and money, of town life and national states were distorted almost beyond recognition.

(a) Individual acts of "truck, barter, and exchange" are only exceptionally practiced in primitive society

"Barter is originally completely unknown. Far from being possessed with a craving for barter primitive man has an aversion to it" (Buecher, *Die Entstehung der Volkswirtschaft*, 1904, p. 109). "It is impossible, for example, to express the value of a bonito-hook in terms of a quantity of food, since no such exchange is ever made and would be regarded by the Tikopia as fantastic. . . . Each kind of object is appropriate to a particular kind of social situation" (Firth, op. cit., p. 340).

(b) Trade does not arise within a community; it is an external affair involving different communities

"In its beginnings commerce is a transaction between ethnic groups; it does not take place between members of the same tribe or of the same community, but it is, in the oldest social communities an external phenomenon, being directed only towards foreign tribes" (Max Weber, *General Economic History*, p. 195). "Strange though it may seem, medieval commerce developed from the beginnings under the influence, not of local, but of export trade" (Pirenne, *Economic and Social History of Medieval Europe*, p. 142). "Trade over long distances was responsible for the economic revival of the Middle Ages (Pirenne, *Medieval Cities*, p. 125).

(c) Trade does not rely on markets; it springs from one-sided carrying, peaceful or otherwise

Thurnwald established the fact that the earliest forms of trade simply consisted in procuring and carrying objects from a distance. Essentially it is a hunting expedition. Whether the expedition is warlike as in a slave hunt or as in piracy, depends mainly on the resistance that is encountered (op. cit., pp. 145, 146). "Piracy was the initiator of maritime trade among the Greeks of the Homeric era, as among the Norse Vikings; for a long time the two vocations developed in concert" (Pirenne, *Economic and Social History*, p. 109).

(d) The presence or absence of markets not an essential characteristic; local markets have no tendency to grow

"Economic systems, possessing no markets, need not on this account have any other characteristics in common" (Thurnwald, *Die menschliche Gesellschaft*, Vol. III,

p. 137). On the early markets "only definite quantities of definite objects could be bartered for one another" (ibid., p. 137). "Thurnwald deserves special praise for his observation that primitive money and trade are essentially of social rather than of economic significance" (Loeb, "The Distribution and Function of Money in Early Society." In *Essays in Anthropology*, p. 153). Local markets did not develop out of "armed trade" or "silent barter" or other forms of foreign trade, but out of the "peace" maintained on a meeting place for the limited purpose of neighborhood exchange. "The aim of the local market was to supply the provisions necessary for daily life to the population settled in the districts. This explains their being held weekly, the very limited circle of attraction and the restriction of their activity to small retail operations" (Pirenne, op. cit., Ch. 4, "Commerce to the End of the Twentieth Century," p. 97). Even at a later stage local markets, in contrast to fairs, showed no tendency to grow: The market supplied the wants of the locality and was attended only by the inhabitants of the neighborhood; its commodities were country produce and the wares of every-day life" (Lipson, *The Economic History of England*, 1935, Vol. I, p. 221). Local trade "usually developed to begin with as an auxiliary occupation of peasants and persons engaged in house industry, and in general as a seasonal occupation . . ." (Weber, op. cit., p. 195). "It would be natural to suppose, at first glance, that a merchant class grew up little by little in the midst of the agricultural population. Nothing, however, gives credence to this story" (Pirenne, *Medieval Cities*, p. 111).

(e) Division of labor does not originate in trade or exchange, but in geographical, biological, and other noneconomic facts

"The division of labor is by no means the result of complicated economics, as rationalistic theory will have it. It is principally due to physiological differences of sex and age" (Thurnwald, *Economics*, p. 212). "Almost the only division of labor is between men and women" (Herskovits, op. cit., p. 13). Another way in which division of labor may spring from biological facts is the case of the symbiosis of different ethnic groups. "The ethnic groups are transformed into professional-social ones" through the formation of "an upper layer" in society. "There is thus created an organization based, on the one hand, on the contributions and services of the dependent class, and, on the other, on the power of distribution possessed by the heads of families in the leading stratum" (Thurnwald, *Economics*, p. 86). Herein we meet one of the origins of the state (Thurnwald, *Sozialpsyschische Abläufe*, p. 387).

(f) Money is not a decisive invention; its presence or absence need not make an essential difference to the type of economy

"The mere fact that a tribe used money differentiated it very little economically from other tribes who did not" (Loeb, op. cit., p. 154). "If money is used at all, its function is quite different from that fulfilled in our civilization. It never ceases to be concrete material, and it never becomes an entirely abstract representation of value" (Thurnwald, *Economics*, p. 107). The hardships of barter played no role in the "invention" of money. "This old view of the classical economists runs counter to ethnological investigations" (Loeb, op. cit., p. 167, footnote 6). On account of the specific utilities of the commodities which function as money as well as their symbolic significance as attributes of power, it is not possible to regard "economic possession from a one-sided rationalistic point of view" (Thurnwald, *Economics*). Money may, for instance, be in use for the payment of salaries and taxes only (ibid., p. 108) or it may be used to pay for a wife, for blood money, or for fines. "We can thus see that in these examples of pre-state conditions the evalution of objects of value results from the amount of the customary contributions, from the position held by the leading personages, and from the concrete relationship in which they stand to the commoners of their several communities" (Thurnwald, *Economics*, p. 263).

Money, like markets, is in the main an external phenomenon, the significance of which to the community is determined primarily by trade relations. "The idea of money [is] usually introduced from outside" (Loeb, op. cit., p. 156). "The function of money as a general medium of exchange originated in foreign trade" (Weber, op. cit., p. 238).

(g) Foreign trade originally not trade between individuals but between collectivities

Trade is a "group undertaking"; it concerns "articles obtained collectively." Its origin lies in "collective trading journeys." "In the arrangements for these expeditions which often bear the character of foreign trade the principle of collectivity makes its appearance" (Thurnwald, *Economics*, p. 145). "In any case the oldest commerce is an exchange relation between alien tribes" (Weber, op. cit., p. 195). Medieval trade was emphatically not trade between individuals. It was a "trade between certain towns, an *inter-communal* or *inter-municipal* commerce" (Ashley, *An Introduction to English Economic History and Theory*, Part I, "The Middle Ages," p. 102).

(h) The countryside was cut out of trade in the Middle Ages

"Up to and during the course of the fifteenth century the towns were the sole centers of commerce and industry to such an extent that none of it was allowed to escape into the open country" (Pirenne, *Economic and Social History*, p. 169). "The struggle against rural trading and against rural handicrafts lasted at least seven or eight hundred years" (Heckscher, *Mercantilism*, 1935, Vol. I, p. 129). "The severity of these measures increased with the growth of 'democratic government'. . . ." "All through the fourteenth century regular armed expeditions were sent out against all the villages in the neighborhood and looms or fulling-vats were broken or carried away" (Pirenne, op. cit., p. 211).

(i) No indiscriminate trading between town and town was practiced in the Middle Ages

Intermunicipal trading implied preferential relationships between particular towns or groups of towns, such as, for instance, the Hanse of London and the Teutonic Hanse. Reciprocity and retaliation were the principles governing the relationships between such towns. In case of nonpayment of debts, for instance, the magistrates of the creditor's town might turn to those of the debtor's and request that justice be done in such manner as they would wish their folk to be treated "and threaten that, if the debt is not paid, reprisal will be taken upon the folk of that town" (Ashley, op. cit., Part I, p. 109).

(j) National protectionism was unknown

"For economic purposes it is scarcely necessary to distinguish different countries from one another in the thirteenth century for there were fewer barriers to social intercourse within the limits of Christendom than we meet today" (Cunningham, *Western Civilization in Its Economic Aspects*, Vol. I, p. 3). Not until the fifteenth century are there tariffs on the political frontiers. "Before that there is no evidence of the slightest desire to favor national trade by protecting it from foreign competition" (Pirenne, *Economic and Social History*, p. 92). "International" trading was free in all trades (Power and Postan, *Studies in English Trade in the Fifteenth Century*).

(k) Mercantilism forced freer trade upon towns and provinces within the national boundaries

The first volume of Heckscher's *Mercantilism* (1935) bears the title *Mercantilism as a Unifying System*. As such, mercantilism "opposed everything that bound down economic life to a particular place and obstructed trade within the boundaries of the state" (Heckscher, op. cit., Vol. II, p. 273). "Both aspects of municipal policy, the suppression of the rural countryside and the struggle against the competition of foreign cities, were in conflict with the economic aims of the state" (ibid., Vol. I, p. 131). "Mercantilism 'nationalized' the countries through the action of commerce which extended local practices to the whole territory of the state" (Pantlen, "Handel." In *Handwörterbuch der Staatswissenschaften*, Vol. VI, p. 281). "Competition was often artificially fostered by mercantilism, in order to organize markets with automatic regulation of supply and demand" (Heckscher). The first modern author to recognize the liberalizing tendency of the mercantile system was Schmoller (1884).

(l) Medieval regulationism was highly successful

"The policy of the towns in the Middle Ages was probably the first attempt in Western Europe, after the decline of the ancient world, to regulate society on its economic side according to consistent principles. The attempt was crowned with unusual success. . . . Economic liberalism or *laissez-faire*, at the time of its unchallenged supremacy, is, perhaps, such an instance, but in regard to duration, liberalism was a small, evanescent episode in comparison with the persistent tenacity of the policy of the towns" (Heckscher, op. cit., p. 139). "They accomplished it by a system of regulations, so marvellously adapted to its purpose that it may be considered a masterpiece of its kind. . . . The city economy was worthy of the Gothic architecture with which it was contemporaneous" (Pirenne, *Medieval Cities*, p. 217).

(m) Mercantilism extended municipal practices to the national territory

"The result would be a city policy, extended over a wider area – a kind of municipal policy, superimposed on a state basis" (Heckscher, op. cit., Vol. I, p. 131).

(n) Mercantilism, a most successful policy

"Mercantilism created a masterful system of complex and elaborate want-satisfaction" (Buecher, op. cit., p. 159). The achievement of Colbert's *Règlements*, which worked for high quality in production as an end in itself, was "tremendous" (Heckscher, op. cit., Vol. I, p. 166). "Economic life on a national scale was mainly the result of political centralization" (Buecher, op. cit., p. 157). The regulative system of mercantilism must be credited "with the creation of a labor code and a labor discipline, much stricter than anything that the narrow particularism of medieval town governments was able to produce with their moral and technological limitations" (Brinkmann, "Das soziale System des Kapitalismus." In *Grundriss der Sozialökonomik*, Abt. IV).

The Self-Regulating Market and the Fictitious Commodities: Labor, Land, and Money

This cursory outline of the economic system and markets, taken separately, shows that never before our own time were markets more than accessories of economic life. As a rule, the economic system was absorbed in the social system, and whatever principle of behavior predominated in the economy, the presence of the market pattern was found to be compatible with it. The principle of barter or exchange, which underlies this pattern, revealed no tendency to expand at the expense of the rest. Where markets were most highly developed, as under the mercantile system, they throve under the control of a centralized administration which fostered autarchy both in the households of the peasantry and in respect to national life. Regulation and markets, in effect, grew up together. The self-regulating market was unknown; indeed the emergence of the idea of self-regulation was a complete reversal of the trend of development. It is in the light of these facts that the extraordinary assumptions underlying a market economy can alone be fully comprehended.

A market economy is an economic system controlled, regulated, and directed by markets alone; order in the production and distribution of goods is entrusted to this self-regulating mechanism. An economy of this kind derives from the expectation that human beings behave in such a way as to achieve maximum money gains. It assumes markets in which the supply of goods (including services) available at a definite price will equal the demand at that price. It assumes the presence of money, which functions as purchasing power in the hands of its owners. Production will then be controlled by prices, for the profits of those who direct production will depend upon them; the distribution of the goods also will depend upon prices, for prices form incomes, and it is with the help of these incomes that the goods produced are distributed amongst the members of society. Under these assumptions order in the production and distribution of goods is ensured by prices alone.

Self-regulation implies that all production is for sale on the market and that all incomes derive from such sales. Accordingly, there are markets for all elements of industry, not only for goods (always including services) but also for labor, land, and money, their prices being called respectively commodity prices, wages, rent, and interest. The very terms indicate that prices form incomes: interest is the price for the use of money and forms the income of those who are in the position to provide it; rent is the price for the use of land and forms the income of those who supply it;

wages are the price for the use of labor power, and form the income of those who sell it; commodity prices, finally, contribute to the incomes of those who sell their entrepreneurial services, the income called profit being actually the difference between two sets of prices, the price of the goods produced and their costs, i.e., the price of the goods necessary to produce them. If these conditions are fulfilled, all incomes will derive from sales on the market, and incomes will be just sufficient to buy all the goods produced.

A further group of assumptions follows in respect to the state and its policy. Nothing must be allowed to inhibit the formation of markets, nor must incomes be permitted to be formed otherwise than through sales. Neither must there be any interference with the adjustment of prices to changed market conditions – whether the prices are those of goods, labor, land, or money. Hence there must not only be markets for all elements of industry,[7] but no measure or policy must be countenanced that would influence the action of these markets. Neither price, nor supply, nor demand must be fixed or regulated; only such policies and measures are in order which help to ensure the self-regulation of the market by creating conditions which make the market the only organizing power in the economic sphere.

To realize fully what this means, let us return for a moment to the mercantile system and the national markets which it did so much to develop. Under feudalism and the gild system land and labor formed part of the social organization itself (money had yet hardly developed into a major element of industry). Land, the pivotal element in the feudal order, was the basis of the military, judicial, administrative, and political system; its status and function were determined by legal and customary rules. Whether its possession was transferable or not, and if so, to whom and under what restrictions; what the rights of property entailed; to what uses some types of land might be put – all these questions were removed from the organization of buying and selling, and subjected to an entirely different set of institutional regulations.

The same was true of the organization of labor. Under the gild system, as under every other economic system in previous history, the motives and circumstances of productive activities were embedded in the general organization of society. The relations of master, journeyman, and apprentice; the terms of the craft; the number of apprentices; the wages of the workers were all regulated by the custom and rule of the gild and the town. What the mercantile system did was merely to unify these conditions either through statute as in England, or through the "nationalization" of the gilds as in France. As to land, its feudal status was abolished only in so far as it was linked with provincial privileges; for the rest, land remained *extra commercium*, in England as in France. Up to the time of the Great Revolution of 1789, landed estate remained the source of social privilege in France, and even after that time in England Common Law on land was essentially medieval. Mercantilism, with all its tendency towards commercialization, never attacked the safeguards which protected these two basic elements of production – labor and land – from becoming the objects of commerce. In England the "nationalization" of labor legislation through the Statute of Artificers (1563) and the Poor Law (1601), removed labor from the danger zone, and the anti-enclosure policy of the Tudors and early Stuarts was one consistent protest against the principle of the gainful use of landed property.

That mercantilism, however emphatically it insisted on commercialization as a national policy, thought of markets in a way exactly contrary to market economy, is best shown by its vast extension of state intervention in industry. On this point there was no difference between mercantilists and feudalists, between crowned planners and vested interests, between centralizing bureaucrats and conservative particularists. They disagreed only on the methods of regulation: gilds, towns, and provinces appealed to the force of custom and tradition, while the new state authority favored statute and ordinance. But they were all equally averse to the idea of commercializing labor and land – the precondition of market economy. Craft gilds and feudal privileges were abolished in France only in 1790; in England the Statute of Artificers was repealed only in 1813–14, the Elizabethan Poor Law in 1834. Not before the last decade of the eighteenth century was, in either country, the establishment of a free labor market even discussed; and the idea of the self-regulation of economic life was utterly beyond the horizon of the age. The mercantilist was concerned with the development of the resources of the country, including full employment, through trade and commerce; the traditional organization of land and labor he took for granted. He was in this respect as far removed from modern concepts as he was in the realm of politics, where his belief in the absolute powers of an enlightened despot was tempered by no intimations of democracy. And just as the transition to a democratic system and representative politics involved a complete reversal of the trend of the age, the change from regulated to self-regulating markets at the end of the eighteenth century represented a complete transformation in the structure of society.

A self-regulating market demands nothing less than the institutional separation of society into an economic and political sphere. Such a dichotomy is, in effect, merely the restatement, from the point of view of society as a whole, of the existence of a self-regulating market. It might be argued that the separateness of the two spheres obtains in every type of society at all times. Such an inference, however, would be based on a fallacy. True, no society can exist without a system of some kind which ensures order in the production and distribution of goods. But that does not imply the existence of separate economic institutions; normally, the economic order is merely a function of the social, in which it is contained. Neither under tribal, nor feudal, nor mercantile conditions was there, as we have shown, a separate economic system in society. Nineteenth century society, in which economic activity was isolated and imputed to a distinctive economic motive, was, indeed, a singular departure.

Such an institutional pattern could not function unless society was somehow subordinated to its requirements. A market economy can exist only in a market society. We reached this conclusion on general grounds in our analysis of the market pattern. We can now specify the reasons for this assertion. A market economy must comprise all elements of industry, including labor, land, and money. (In a market economy the last also is an essential element of industrial life and its inclusion in the market mechanism has, as we will see, far-reaching institutional consequences.) But labor and land are no other than the human beings themselves of which every society consists and the natural surroundings in which it exists. To include them in the market mechanism means to subordinate the substance of society itself to the laws of the market.

Notes

1 Cf. Notes on Sources, page 274. The works of Malinowski and Thurnwald have been extensively used in this chapter.
2 Cf. Notes on Sources, page 347.
3 Hawtrey, G. R., *The Economic Problem*, 1925, p. 13. "The practical application of the principle of individualism is entirely dependent on the practice of exchange." Hawtrey, however, was mistaken in assuming that the existence of markets simply followed from the practice of exchange.
4 Firth, R., *Primitive Polynesian Economics*, 1939, p. 347.
5 Thurnwald, R. C., *Economics in Primitive Communities*, 1932, pp. 162–164.
6 Montesquieu, *L'Esprit des lois*, 1748. "The English constrain the merchant, but it is in favor of commerce."
7 Henderson, H. D., *Supply and Demand*, 1922. The practice of the market is twofold: the apportionment of factors between different uses, and the organizing of the forces influencing aggregate supplies of factors.

Part II

Economic Action

Introduction

Why do individuals act economically in the ways that they do? Are they motivated by greed? Do they consider others when they buy and sell? Are people economically rational? If so, does this mean that all people would do the same thing if faced with the same circumstances? These are all questions that deal with the issue of economic action: the way people actually behave, or at least are assumed to behave, when contemplating economic activities such as seeking one's fortune, bidding on an antique, or making investment decisions.

This part includes five chapters that deal in different ways with the important subject of economic action. Chapter 5, by Mark Granovetter, takes up the issues discussed by the classical theories in Part I, but seen through the perspective of modern economic and sociological studies. This work was a critical programmatic statement for economic sociology at the end of the twentieth century. Chapter 6, by Mitchel Abolafia, looks at economic action in the competitive Wall Street bond market and asks if this is the "natural" behavior posited by economic theory. Chapter 7 is an except from Charles Smith's study of auctions, places where people come to haggle over commodities. Gary Hamilton's historical research on those who came to California's gold fields in the nineteenth century, chapter 8, asks "Who wants to go on an economic adventure?" Finally, in chapter 9, Paula England criticizes as androcentric the economic actor assumed by neoclassical theory.

In the 1980s when Mark Granovetter's article first appeared prominently in the *American Journal of Sociology*, economic sociology was just beginning its resurgence. Sociologists had been increasingly displeased that economic concerns such as firm behavior, economic development, and poverty were only being understood from the perspective of the neoclassic tradition, but there was no theoretical rejoinder coming from sociology. This article created a platform around which sociologists began to consider a distinctively social approach, one not rooted in individualistic premises, to understanding economic action.

Granovetter begins by asking the enduring question, "How is economic behavior shaped by social relations?" He argues that, ironically, both traditional sociology and economics have been unable to answer this question. Sociologists have given so much credibility to the idea of socialization, the overwhelming influence of "society" on individuals, that there is no room for individual action to emerge apart from socially determined roles. On the other hand, economics has postulated a rational actor and leaves no room for the influence of social factors. In the economic perspective people are not influenced by society at all; rather, they are unaware of and uninfluenced by each other. While most sociologists and economists would accept that these extreme positions are not the way that economic action really takes place, they had assumed that their assumptions are reasonable starting points for analysis.

Granovetter takes up Polanyi's position, arguing that a better assumption is that individuals are embedded in social relations. It is the character of those relations that will influence how people behave in the economy. Granovetter posits that by examining the distinctive character of an actor's social relations, one can see the influence of society without assuming an undifferentiated social effect. Much of this chapter is devoted to a critique of transaction cost economics, an attempt by institutional economists to allow "social factors" to enter into their studies of markets and firms. Granovetter argues that this approach avoids truly social and historical factors in an attempt to preserve the assumption that economic organization is the result of efficiency attempts. Sociologists argue that efficiency is only one possible motivation for action.

The next two chapters are empirical studies of markets that attempt to understand how economic actors actually behave in different settings. Mitchel Abolafia spent 18 months in the New York bond markets and found that traders in fact exhibited many of the behaviors assumed by economists. These Wall Street players are brokers and dealers who try to match buyers and sellers, but who also trade on their own accounts in order to amass great personal wealth. Abolafia found the bond traders to be highly competitive, individualistic, self-interested, and economically calculating. They show few restraints on aggressive behavior, little loyalty to their firms, and take advantage of others when the opportunity arises. One would imagine that this is strong evidence for the *Homo economicus* model assumed by economists. Abolafia, however, shows that this sort of behavior is the outcome of the organizational structure and culture of the bond traders' world, not a state of nature. The social structure of the bond market creates the conditions for these behaviors.

Charles Smith's study of auctions is likewise an attempt to understand a fundamental economic assumption, one traceable to Adam Smith. Smith argued that market prices would reflect supply and demand, and according to economists today the price of a good would be the place at which supply and demand curves meet. Another way of thinking about the price of a good is the notion of a "fair" price. This is a social determination of what something is worth and reflects the judgment of a community according to criteria that the community values. Historically, prices could reflect religious judgments about the worth of a good, the status of the purchaser, or other social factors. These sorts of conventions are not assumed to be important today, however, where market factors are expected to dominate price setting.

Charles Smith studied price setting in auctions, perhaps the "purest" market conditions in the sense that they emulate economists' assumed market of strangers coming together to compete for goods. Smith studied a wide variety of auctions, from country auctions of household products and auctions of cars confiscated by a city, to auctions for diverse animal commodities such as fresh fish, thoroughbred horses, and cattle. Smith found that auctions vary, but in all cases are strongly subject to underlying social arrangements that function to assure a sense of fairness.

He distinguishes between two main auction types. In exchange auctions, such as elite art and antique auctions, where the competitors are primarily dealers or members of a community of bidders who are likely to know each other, the community itself legitimates the auction. The workings of the auction and its outcomes are presumed legitimate because the auction took place among people who know each other and trust that they will obey community norms about representing the goods as authentic, for example. To fail to accede to social standards is self-limiting in the longer term, because the actors will be cut out of future exchanges, and they understand this.

On the other hand, commodity auctions that bring together strangers establish explicit rules and regulations in an attempt to guarantee fairness and legitimate the auction. Third parties, such as the auction house, may act to guarantee the provenance of an antique, for example. When the economic actors have weak ties, other parties intervene to assure everyone that the auction and the resulting price are in fact "fair." Smith reviews a number of other price-setting practices in auctions, such as the use of reserves, floor bidding, and pools, and shows how each economic practice can be related back to the social structure of the auction community.

Are we all equally motivated to become rich? Would we all do the same thing to achieve wealth given the opportunity? Gary Hamilton's fascinating historical study attempts to answer these questions by examining who went to the California Gold Rush in the mid-1800s. He argues that adventurism, the taking of great risks in hopes of great gain, is a socially patterned activity. People become adventurers seeking their fortunes not only because of personality characteristics, but also because of the type of society from which they come.

The California Gold Rush was a phenomenon that appealed worldwide. People, mostly men, came from the East Coast, Asia, Europe, and South America hoping to strike it rich. Hamilton examined the historical record and found that the "argonauts" varied considerably by place of origin. Some countries caught "gold fever," but in others a collective economic hysteria did not form. The historical record shows that Chileans came in vast numbers, but Peruvians were not moved to migrate. The Chinese, Western Europeans, and Northeastern Americans were caught up in the frenzy, but the Japanese and Americans from the South did not participate in gold mania.

Chile, China, England, and New England are all very different societies, so no cultural explanation could account for their producing so many economic adventurers. Hamilton argues, however, that societies that produced Gold Rush migrants all had a "particularistic-achievement" orientation. These are all social orders where individuals' bonds with others in their society are strong, and where they orient themselves to status achievement within these affiliations. Hamilton gives the example of an impoverished noble who feels entitled to a noble lifestyle in his society, but who has no wealth to maintain this way of life. For this person, adventurism is a low-risk strategy because getting the money in any way is the object; the social status has already been achieved. People who came to California to seek their fortune were more likely to be those who had secure places in a social structure such as a community, family, or ethnic group. They could go abroad, knowing they could always return home at little or no social cost, and perhaps with great fortunes.

This study, which pre-dates Granovetter's call for examining "embeddedness," is a marvelous example of how the character of social ties shapes economic orientation. People may have made rational calculations about whether or not to seek their fortunes in California, but what was rational for a Chilean was not rational for a Peruvian who had to remain in place in order to protect a status climb.

The chapters by Abolafia, Smith, and Hamilton all question the precepts of modern economics by examining empirical cases. Paula England critiques economic assumptions, which see the autonomous economic actor model as both universal and "good," for having androcentric biases. She argues that the assumed "separative self" is empirically wrong and based on Western notions of the importance of individualism. The model denies the reality of empathy as a tool in making utility comparisons; that is, judging who benefits most from exchanges and economic relations. It assumes that tastes or preferences are exogenous to social relations, that social relations cannot shape and form our preferences. England argues that the separative self assumes selfish actors and cannot account for men and women's altruism, or for the ways in which those actors' altruism may discriminate in favor of some and not others in a marketplace. Finally, she argues that economists' assumption of altruism in the family, but selfishness in the market, is based on gendered notions of family construction. Assuming the separative self is not only theoretically flawed but has important negative consequences for gender equity in economic policies regarding labor markets and other public and private settings.

5 Economic Action and Social Structure: The Problem of Embeddedness

Mark Granovetter

How behavior and institutions are affected by social relations is one of the classic questions of social theory. This paper concerns the extent to which economic action is embedded in structures of social relations, in modern industrial society. Although the usual neoclassical accounts provide an "undersocialized" or atomized-actor explanation of such action, reformist economists who attempt to bring social structure back in do so in the "oversocialized" way criticized by Dennis Wrong. Under- and oversocialized accounts are paradoxically similar in their neglect of ongoing structures of social relations, and a sophisticated account of economic action must consider its embeddedness in such structures. The argument is illustrated by a critique of Oliver Williamson's "markets and hierarchies" research program.

Introduction: The Problem of Embeddedness

How behavior and institutions are affected by social relations is one of the classic questions of social theory. Since such relations are always present, the situation that would arise in their absence can be imagined only through a thought experiment like Thomas Hobbes's "state of nature" or John Rawls's "original position." Much of the utilitarian tradition, including classical and neoclassical economics, assumes rational, self-interested behavior affected minimally by social relations, thus invoking an idealized state not far from that of these thought experiments. At the other extreme lies what I call the argument of "embeddedness": the argument that the behavior and institutions to be analyzed are so constrained by ongoing social relations that to construe them as independent is a grievous misunderstanding.

This article concerns the embeddedness of economic behavior. It has long been the majority view among sociologists, anthropologists, political scientists, and historians that such behavior was heavily embedded in social relations in premarket societies but became much more autonomous with modernization. This view sees the economy as an increasingly separate, differentiated sphere in modern society, with economic transactions defined no longer by the social or kinship obligations of those transacting but by rational calculations of individual gain. It is sometimes further argued that the traditional situation is reversed: instead of economic life being

Original publication: Granovetter, Mark, "Economic Action and Social Structure: The Problem of Embeddedness," *American Journal of Sociology*, 91, no. 3 (November 1985): 481–510.

submerged in social relations, these relations become an epiphenomenon of the market. The embeddedness position is associated with the "substantivist" school in anthropology, identified especially with Karl Polanyi (1944; Polanyi, Arensberg, and Pearson, 1957) and with the idea of "moral economy" in history and political science (Thompson, 1971; Scott, 1976). It has also some obvious relation to Marxist thought.

Few economists, however, have accepted this conception of a break in embeddedness with modernization; most of them assert instead that embeddedness in earlier societies was not substantially greater than the low level found in modern markets. The tone was set by Adam Smith, who postulated a "certain propensity in human nature . . . to truck, barter and exchange one thing for another" ([1776] 1979, book 1, chap. 2) and assumed that since labor was the only factor of production in primitive society, goods must have exchanged in proportion to their labor costs – as in the general classical theory of exchange ([1776] 1979, book 1, chap. 6). From the 1920s on, certain anthropologists took a similar position, which came to be called the "formalist" one: even in tribal societies, economic behavior was sufficiently independent of social relations for standard neoclassical analysis to be useful (Schneider, 1974). This position has recently received a new infusion as economists and fellow travelers in history and political science have developed a new interest in the economic analysis of social institutions – much of which falls into what is called the "new institutional economics" – and have argued that behavior and institutions previously interpreted as embedded in earlier societies, as well as in our own, can be better understood as resulting from the pursuit of self-interest by rational, more or less atomized individuals (e.g., North and Thomas, 1973; Williamson, 1975; Popkin, 1979).

My own view diverges from both schools of thought. I assert that the level of embeddedness of economic behavior is lower in nonmarket societies than is claimed by substantivists and development theorists, and it has changed less with "modernization" than they believe; but I argue also that this level has always been and continues to be more substantial than is allowed for by formalists and economists. I do not attempt here to treat the issues posed by nonmarket societies. I proceed instead by a theoretical elaboration of the concept of embeddedness, whose value is then illustrated with a problem from modern society, currently important in the new institutional economics: which transactions in modern capitalist society are carried out in the market, and which subsumed within hierarchically organized firms? This question has been raised to prominence by the "markets and hierarchies" program of research initiated by Oliver Williamson (1975).

Over- and Undersocialized Conceptions of Human Action in Sociology and Economics

I begin by recalling Dennis Wrong's (1961) complaint about an "oversocialized conception of man in modern sociology" – a conception of people as overwhelmingly sensitive to the opinions of others and hence obedient to the dictates of consensually developed systems of norms and values, internalized through socialization, so that obedience is not perceived as a burden. To the extent that such a conception was prominent in 1961, it resulted in large part from Talcott Parsons's recognition of the problem of order as posed by Hobbes and his own attempt to resolve it by transcending the atomized, *undersocialized* conception of man in the utilitarian tradition of which Hobbes was part (Parsons, 1937, pp. 89–94). Wrong approved the break with atomized utilitarianism and the emphasis on actors' embeddedness in social context – the crucial factor absent from Hobbes's thinking – but warned of exaggerating the degree of this embeddedness and the extent to which it might eliminate conflict:

> It is frequently the task of the sociologist to call attention to the intensity with which men desire and strive for the good opinion of their immediate associates in a variety of situations, particularly those where received theories or ideologies have unduly emphasized other motives. . . . Thus sociologists have shown that factory workers are more sensitive to the attitudes of their fellow workers than to purely economic incentives. . . . It is certainly not my intention to criticize the findings of such studies. My objection is that . . . [a]lthough sociologists have criticized past effort to single out one fundamental motive in human conduct, the desire to achieve a favorable self-image by winning approval from others frequently occupies such a position in their own thinking.
>
> *(1961, pp. 188–89)*

Classical and neoclassical economics operates, in contrast, with an atomized, *undersocialized* conception of human action, continuing in the utilitarian tradition. The theoretical arguments disallow by hypothesis any impact of social structure and social relations on production, distribution, or consumption. In competitive markets, no producer or consumer noticeably influences aggregate supply or demand or, therefore, prices or other terms of trade. As Albert Hirschman has noted, such idealized markets, involving as they do "large numbers of price-taking anonymous buyers and sellers supplied with perfect information . . . function without any prolonged human or social contact between the parties. Under perfect competition there is no room for bargaining, negotiation, remonstration or mutual adjustment and the various operators that contract together need not enter into recurrent or continuing relationships as a result of which they would get to know each other well" (1982, p. 1473).

It has long been recognized that the idealized markets of perfect competition have survived intellectual attack in part because self-regulating economic structures are politically attractive to many. Another reason for this survival, less clearly understood, is that the elimination of social relations from economic analysis removes the problem of order from the intellectual agenda, at least in the economic sphere. In Hobbes's argument, disorder arises because conflict-free social and economic transactions depend on trust and the absence of malfeasance. But these are unlikely when individuals are conceived to have neither social relationships nor institutional context – as in the "state of nature." Hobbes contains the difficulty by superimposing a structure of autocratic authority. The solution of classical liberalism, and correspondingly of classical economics, is antithetical: repressive political structures are rendered unnecessary by competitive markets that make force or fraud unavailing. Competition determines the terms of trade in a way that individual traders cannot manipulate. If traders encounter complex or difficult relationships, characterized by mistrust or malfeasance, they can simply move on to the legion of other traders willing to do business on market terms; social relations and their details thus become frictional matters.

In classical and neoclassical economics, therefore, the fact that actors may have social relations with one another has been treated, if at all, as a frictional drag that impedes competitive markets. In a much-quoted line, Adam Smith complained that "people of the same trade seldom meet together, even for merriment and diversion, but the conversation ends in a conspiracy against the public, or in some contrivance to raise prices." His laissez-faire politics allowed few solutions to this problem, but he did suggest repeal of regulations requiring all those in the same trade to sign a public register; the public existence of such information "connects individuals who might never otherwise be known to one another and gives every man of the trade a direction where to find every other man of it." Noteworthy here is not the rather lame policy prescription but the recognition that *social atomization is prerequisite to perfect competition* (Smith [1776] 1979, pp. 232–33).

More recent comments by economists on "social influences" construe these as processes in which actors acquire customs, habits, or norms that are followed mechanically and automatically, irrespective of their bearing on rational choice. This view, close to Wrong's "oversocialized conception," is reflected in James Duesenberry's quip that "economics is all about how people make choices; sociology is all about how they don't have any choices to make" (1960, p. 233) and in E. H. Phelps Brown's description of the "sociologists' approach to pay determination" as deriving from the assumption that people act in "certain ways because to do so is customary, or an obligation, or the 'natural thing to do,' or right and proper, or just and fair" (1977, p. 17).

But despite the apparent contrast between under- and oversocialized views, we should note an irony of great theoretical importance: both have in common a conception of action and decision carried out by atomized actors. In the undersocialized account, atomization results from narrow utilitarian pursuit of self-interest; in the oversocialized one, from the fact that behavioral patterns have been internalized and ongoing social relations thus have only peripheral effects on behavior. That the internalized rules of behavior are social in origin does not differentiate this argument decisively from a utilitarian one, in which the source of utility functions is left open, leaving room for behavior guided entirely by consensually determined norms and values – as in the oversocialized view. Under- and oversocialized resolutions of the problem of order thus merge in their atomization of actors from immediate social context. This ironic merger is already visible in Hobbes's *Leviathan*, in which the unfortunate denizens of the state of nature, overwhelmed by the disorder consequent to their atomization, cheerfully surrender all their rights to an authoritarian power and subsequently behave in a docile and honorable manner; by the artifice of a social contract, they lurch directly from an undersocialized to an oversocialized state.

When modern economists do attempt to take account of social influences, they typically represent them in the oversocialized manner represented in the quotations above. In so doing, they reverse the judgment that social influences are frictional but sustain the conception of how such influences operate. In the theory of segmented labor markets, for example, Michael Piore has argued that members of each labor market segment are characterized by different styles of decision making and that the making of decisions by rational choice, custom, or command in upper-primary, lower-primary, and secondary labor markets respectively corresponds to the origins of workers in middle-, working-, and lower-class subcultures (Piore, 1975). Similarly, Samuel Bowles and Herbert Gintis, in their account of the consequences of

American education, argue that different social classes display different cognitive processes because of differences in the education provided to each. Those destined for lower-level jobs are trained to be dependable followers of rules, while those who will be channeled into elite positions attend "elite four-year colleges" that "emphasize social relationships conformable with the higher levels in the production hierarchy. . . . As they 'master' one type of behavioral regulation they are either allowed to progress to the next or are channeled into the corresponding level in the hierarchy of production" (Bowles and Gintis, 1975, p. 132).

But these oversocialized conceptions of how society influences individual behavior are rather mechanical: once we know the individual's social class or labor market sector, everything else in behavior is automatic, since they are so well socialized. Social influence here is an external force that, like the deists' God, sets things in motion and has no further effects – a force that insinuates itself into the minds and bodies of individuals (as in the movie *Invasion of the Body Snatchers*), altering their way of making decisions. Once we know in just what way an individual has been affected, ongoing social relations and structures are irrelevant. Social influences are all contained inside an individual's head, so, in actual decision situations, he or she can be atomized as any *Homo economicus*, though perhaps with different rules for decisions. More sophisticated (and thus less oversocialized) analyses of cultural influences (e.g., Fine and Kleinman, 1979; Cole, 1979, chap. 1) make it clear that culture is not a once-for-all influence but an ongoing process, continuously constructed and reconstructed during interaction. It not only shapes its members but also is shaped by them, in part for their own strategic reasons.

Even when economists do take social relationships seriously, as do such diverse figures as Harvey Leibenstein (1976) and Gary Becker (1976), they invariably abstract away from the history of relations and their position with respect to other relations – what might be called the historical and structural embeddedness of relations. The interpersonal ties described in their arguments are extremely stylized, average, "typical" – devoid of specific content, history, or structural location. Actors' behavior results from their named role positions and role sets; thus we have arguments on how workers and supervisors, husbands and wives, or criminals and law enforcers will interact with one another, but these relations are not assumed to have individualized content beyond that given by the named roles. This procedure is exactly what structural sociologists have criticized in Parsonian sociology – the relegation of the specifics of individual relations to a minor role in the overall conceptual scheme, epiphenomenal in comparison with enduring structures of normative role prescriptions deriving from ultimate value orientations. In economic models, this treatment of social relations has the paradoxical effect of preserving atomized decision making even when decisions are seen to involve more than one individual. Because the analyzed set of individuals – usually dyads, occasionally larger groups – is abstracted out of social context, it is atomized in its behavior from that of other groups and from the history of its own relations. Atomization has not been eliminated, merely transferred to the dyadic or higher level of analysis. Note the use of an oversocialized conception – that of actors behaving exclusively in accord with their prescribed roles – to implement an atomized, undersocialized view.

A fruitful analysis of human action requires us to avoid the atomization implicit in the theoretical extremes of under- and oversocialized conceptions. Actors do not behave or decide as atoms outside a social context, nor do they adhere slavishly to a script written for them by the particular intersection of social categories that they happen to occupy. Their attempts at purposive action are instead embedded in concrete, ongoing systems of social relations. In the remainder of this article I illustrate how this view of embeddedness alters our theoretical and empirical approach to the study of economic behavior. I first narrow the focus to the question of trust and malfeasance in economic life and then use the "markets and hierarchies" problem to illustrate the use of embeddedness ideas in analyzing this question.[1]

Embeddedness, Trust, and Malfeasance in Economic Life

Since about 1970, there has been a flurry of interest among economists in the previously neglected issues of trust and malfeasance. Oliver Williamson has noted that real economic actors engage not merely in the pursuit of self-interest but also in "opportunism" – "self-interest seeking with guile; agents who are skilled at dissembling realize transactional advantages.[2] Economic man . . . is thus a more subtle and devious creature than the usual self-interest seeking assumption reveals" (1975, p. 255).

But this points out a peculiar assumption of modern economic theory, that one's economic interest is pursued only by comparatively gentlemanly means. The Hobbesian question – how it can be that those who pursue their own interest do not do so mainly by force and fraud – is finessed by this conception. Yet, as Hobbes saw so clearly, there is nothing in the intrinsic meaning of "self-interest" that excludes force or fraud.

In part, this assumption persisted because competitive forces, in a self-regulating market, could be imagined to suppress force and fraud. But the idea is also embedded in the intellectual history of the discipline. In *The Passions and the Interests*, Albert Hirschman (1977) shows that an important strand of intellectual history from the time of *Leviathan* to that of *The Wealth of Nations* consisted of the watering down of Hobbes's problem of order by arguing that certain human motivations kept others under control and that, in particular, the pursuit of economic self-interest was typically not an uncontrollable "passion" but a civilized, gentle activity. The wide though implicit acceptance of such an idea is a powerful example of how under- and oversocialized conceptions complement one another: atomized actors in competitive markets so thoroughly internalize these normative standards of behavior as to guarantee orderly transactions.[3]

What has eroded this confidence in recent years has been increased attention to the micro-level details of imperfectly competitive markets, characterized by small numbers of participants with sunk costs and "specific human capital" investments. In such situations, the alleged discipline of competitive markets cannot be called on to mitigate deceit, so the classical problem of how it can be that daily economic life is not riddled with mistrust and malfeasance has resurfaced.

In the economic literature, I see two fundamental answers to this problem and argue that one is linked to an undersocialized, and the other to an oversocialized, conception of human action. The undersocialized account is found mainly in the new institutional economics – a loosely defined confederation of economists with an interest in explaining social institutions from a neoclassical viewpoint. (See, e.g., Furubotn and Pejovich, 1972; Alchian and Demsetz, 1973; Lazear, 1979; Rosen, 1982; Williamson, 1975, 1979, 1981; Williamson and Ouchi, 1981.) The general story told by members of this school is that social institutions and arrangements previously thought to be the adventitious result of legal, historical, social, or political forces are better viewed as the efficient solution to certain economic problems. The tone is similar to that of structural-functional sociology of the 1940s to the 1960s, and much of the argumentation fails the elementary tests of a sound functional explanation laid down by Robert Merton in 1947. Consider, for example, Schotter's view that to understand any observed economic institution requires only that we "infer the evolutionary problem that must have existed for the institution as we see it to have developed. Every evolutionary economic problem requires a social institution to solve it" (1981, p. 2).

Malfeasance is here seen to be averted because clever institutional arrangements make it too costly to engage in, and these arrangements – many previously interpreted as serving no economic function – are now seen as having evolved to discourage malfeasance. Note, however, that they do not produce trust but instead are a functional substitute for it. The main such arrangements are elaborate explicit and implicit contracts (Okun, 1981), including deferred compensation plans and mandatory retirement – seen to reduce the incentives for "shirking" on the job or absconding with proprietary secrets (Lazear, 1979; Pakes and Nitzan, 1982) – and authority structures that deflect opportunism by making potentially divisive decisions by fiat (Williamson, 1975). These conceptions are undersocialized in that they do not allow for the extent to which concrete personal relations and the obligations inherent in them discourage malfeasance, quite apart from institutional arrangements. *Substituting* these arrangements for trust results actually in a Hobbesian situation, in which any rational individual would be motivated to develop clever ways to evade them; it is then hard to imagine that everyday economic life would not be poisoned by ever more ingenious attempts at deceit.

Other economists have recognized that some degree of trust *must* be assumed to operate, since institutional arrangements alone could not entirely stem force or fraud. But it remains to explain the source of this trust, and appeal is sometimes made to the existence of a "generalized morality." Kenneth Arrow, for example, suggests that societies, "in their evolution have developed implicit agreements to certain kinds of regard for others, agreements which are essential to the survival of the society or at least contribute greatly to the efficiency of its working" (1974, p. 26; see also Akerlof [1983] on the origins of "honesty").

Now one can hardly doubt the existence of some such generalized morality; without it, you would be afraid to give the gas station attendant a 20-dollar bill when you had bought only five dollars' worth of gas. But this conception has the oversocialized characteristic of calling on a generalized and automatic response, even though moral action in economic life is hardly automatic or universal (as is well known at gas stations that demand exact change after dark).

Consider a case where generalized morality does indeed seem to be at work: the legendary (I hesitate to say apocryphal) economist who, against all economic rationality, leaves a tip in a roadside restaurant far from home. Note that this transaction has three characteristics that make it somewhat unusual: (1) the transactors are previously unacquainted, (2) they are unlikely to transact again, and (3) information about the activities of either is unlikely to reach others with whom they might transact in the future. I argue that it is only in situations of this kind that the absence of force and fraud can mainly be explained by generalized morality. Even there, one might wonder how effective this morality would be if large costs were incurred.

The embeddedness argument stresses instead the role of concrete personal relations and structures (or "networks") of such relations in generating trust and discouraging malfeasance. The widespread preference for transacting with individuals of known reputation implies that few are actually content to rely on either generalized morality *or* institutional arrangements to guard against trouble. Economists *have* pointed out that one incentive not to cheat is the cost of damage to one's reputation; but this is an undersocialized conception of reputation as a generalized commodity, a ratio of cheating to opportunities for doing so. In practice, we settle for such generalized information when nothing better is available, but ordinarily we seek better information. Better than the statement that someone is known to be reliable is information from a trusted informant that he has dealt with that individual and found him so. Even better is information from one's own past dealings with that person. This is better information for four reasons: (1) it is cheap; (2) one trusts one's own information best – it is richer, more detailed, and known to be accurate; (3) individuals with whom one has a continuing relation have an economic motivation to be trustworthy, so as not to discourage future transactions; and (4) departing from pure economic motives, continuing economic relations often become overlaid with social content that carries strong expectations of trust and abstention from opportunism.

It would never occur to us to doubt this last point in more intimate relations, which make behavior more predictable and thus close off some of the fears that create difficulties among strangers. Consider, for example, why individuals in a burning theater panic and stampede to the door, leading to desperate results. Analysts of collective behavior long considered this to be prototypically irrational behavior, but Roger Brown (1965, chap. 14) points out that the situation is essentially an *n*-person Prisoner's Dilemma: each stampeder is actually being quite rational given the absence of a guarantee that anyone else will walk out calmly, even though all would be better off if everyone did so. Note, however, that in the case of the burning houses featured on the 11:00 P.M. news, we never hear that everyone stampeded out and that family members trampled one another. In the family, there is no Prisoner's Dilemma because each is confident that the others can be counted on.

In business relations the degree of confidence must be more variable, but Prisoner's Dilemmas are nevertheless often obviated by the strength of personal relations, and this strength is a property not of the transactors but of their concrete relations. Standard economic analysis neglects the identity and past relations of individual transactors, but rational individuals know better, relying on their knowledge of these relations. They are less interested in *general* reputations than in whether a particular other may be expected to deal honestly with *them* – mainly a function of whether they or their own contacts have had satisfactory past dealings with the other. One sees this pattern even in situations that appear, at first glance, to approximate the classic higgling of a competitive market, as in the Moroccan bazaar analyzed by Geertz (1979).

Up to this point, I have argued that social relations, rather than institutional arrangements or generalized morality, are mainly responsible for the production of trust in economic life. But I then risk rejecting one kind or optimistic functionalism for another, in which networks of relations, rather than morality or arrangements, are the structure that fulfills the function of sustaining order. There are two ways to reduce this risk. One is to recognize that as a solution to the problem of order, the embeddedness position is less sweeping than either alternative argument, since networks of social relations penetrate irregularly and in differing degrees in different sectors of economic life, thus allowing for what we already know: distrust, opportunism, and disorder are by no means absent.

The second is to insist that while social relations may indeed often be a necessary condition for trust and trustworthy behavior, they are not sufficient to guarantee these and may even provide occasion and means for malfeasance and conflict on a scale larger than in their absence. There are three reasons for this.

1. The trust engendered by personal relations presents, by its very existence, enhanced opportunity for malfeasance. In personal relations it is common knowledge that "you always hurt the one you love"; that person's trust in you results in a position far more vulnerable than that of a stranger. (In the Prisoner's Dilemma, knowledge that one's coconspirator is certain to deny the crime is all the more rational motive to confess, and personal relations that abrogate this dilemma may be less symmetrical than is believed by the party to be deceived.) This elementary fact of social life is the bread and butter of "confidence" rackets that simulate certain relationships, sometimes for long periods, for concealed purposes. In the business world, certain crimes, such as embezzling, are simply impossible for those who have not built up relationships of trust that permit the opportunity to manipulate accounts. The more complete the trust, the greater the potential gain from malfeasance. That such instances are statistically infrequent is a tribute to the force of personal relations and reputation; that they do occur with regularity, however infrequently, shows the limits of this force.

2. Force and fraud are most efficiently pursued by teams, and the structure of these teams requires a level of internal trust – "honor among thieves" – that usually follows preexisting lines of relationship. Elaborate schemes for kickbacks and bid rigging, for example, can hardly be executed by individuals working alone, and when such activity is exposed it is often remarkable that it could have been kept secret given the large numbers involved. Law-enforcement efforts consist of finding an entry point to the network of malfeasance – an individual whose confession implicates others who will, in snowball-sample fashion, "finger" still others until the entire picture is fitted together.

Both enormous trust and enormous malfeasance, then, may follow from personal relations. Yoram Ben-Porath, in the functionalist style of the new institutional economics, emphasizes the positive side, noting that "continuity of relationships can generate behavior on the part of shrewd, self-seeking, or even unscrupulous individuals that could otherwise be interpreted as foolish or purely altruistic. Valuable diamonds change hands on the diamond exchange, and the deals are sealed by a handshake" (1980, p. 6). I might add, continuing in this positive vein, that this transaction is possible in part because it is not atomized from other transactions but embedded in a close-knit community of diamond merchants who monitor one another's behavior closely. Like other densely knit networks of actors, they generate clearly defined standards of behavior easily policed by the quick spread of information about instances of malfeasance. But the temptations posed by this level of trust are considerable, and the diamond trade has also been the scene of numerous well-publicized "insider job" thefts and of the notorious "CBS murders" of April 1982. In this case, the owner of a diamond company was defrauding a factoring concern by submitting invoices from fictitious sales. The scheme required cooperation from his accounting personnel, one of whom was approached by investigators and turned state's evidence. The owner then contracted for the murder of the disloyal employee and her assistant; three CBS technicians who came to their aid were also gunned down (Shenon, 1984).

3.   The extent of disorder resulting from force and fraud depends very much on how the network of social relations is structured. Hobbes exaggerated the extent of disorder likely in his atomized state of nature where, in the absence of sustained social relations, one could expect only desultory dyadic conflicts. More extended and large-scale disorder results from coalitions of combatants, impossible without prior relations. We do not generally speak of "war" unless actors have arranged themselves into two sides, as the end result of various coalitions. This occurs only if there are insufficient crosscutting ties, held by actors with enough links to both main potential combatants to have a strong interest in forestalling conflict. The same is true in the business world, where conflicts are relatively tame unless each side can escalate by calling on substantial numbers of allies in other firms, as sometimes happens in attempts to implement or forestall takeovers.

Disorder and malfeasance do of course occur also when social relations are absent. This possibility is already entailed in my earlier claim that the presence of such relations inhibits malfeasance. But the *level* of malfeasance available in a truly atomized social situation is fairly low; instances can only be episodic, unconnected, small scale. The Hobbesian problem is truly a problem, but in transcending it by the smoothing effect of social structure, we also introduce the possibility of disruptions on a larger scale than those available in the "state of nature."

The embeddedness approach to the problem of trust and order in economic life, then, threads its way between the oversocialized approach of generalized morality and the undersocialized one of impersonal, institutional arrangements by following and analyzing concrete patterns of social relations. Unlike either alternative, or the Hobbesian position, it makes no sweeping (and thus unlikely) predictions of universal order or disorder but rather assumes that the details of social structure will determine which is found.

The Problem of Markets and Hierarchies

As a concrete application of the embeddedness approach to economic life, I offer a critique of the influential argument of Oliver Williamson in *Markets and Hierarchies* (1975) and later articles (1979, 1981; Williamson and Ouchi, 1981). Williamson asked under what circumstances economic functions are performed within the boundaries of hierarchical firms rather than by market processes that cross these boundaries. His answer, consistent with the general emphasis of the new institutional economics, is that the organizational form observed in any situation is that which deals most efficiently with the cost of economic transactions. Those that are uncertain in outcome, recur frequently, and require substantial "transaction-specific investments" – for example, money, time, or energy that cannot be easily transferred to interaction with others on different matters – are more likely to take place within hierarchically organized firms. Those that are straightforward, nonrepetitive, and require no transaction-specific investment – such as the one-time purchase of standard equipment – will more likely take place between firms, that is, across a market interface.

In this account, the former set of transactions is internalized within hierarchies for two reasons. The first is "bounded rationality," the inability of economic actors to anticipate properly the complex chain of contingencies that might be relevant to long-term contracts. When transactions are internalized, it is unnecessary to anticipate all such contingencies; they can be handled within the firm's "governance structure" instead of leading to complex negotiations. The second reason is "opportunism," the rational pursuit by economic actors of their own advantage, with all means at their command, including guile and deceit. Opportunism is mitigated and constrained by authority relations and by the greater identification with transaction partners that one allegedly has when both are contained within one corporate entity than when they face one another across the chasm of a market boundary.

The appeal to authority relations in order to tame opportunism constitutes a rediscovery of Hobbesian analysis, though confined here to the economic sphere. The Hobbesian flavor of Williamson's argument is suggested by such statements as the following: "Internal organization is not beset with the same kinds of difficulties that autonomous contracting [among independent firms] experiences when disputes arise between the parties. Although interfirm disputes are often settled out of court . . . this resolution is sometimes difficult and interfirm relations are often strained. Costly litigation is sometimes unavoidable. Internal organization, by contrast . . . is able to settle many such disputes by appeal to fiat – an enormously efficient way to settle instrumental differences" (1975, p. 30). He notes that complex, recurring transactions require long-term relations between identified individuals but that opportunism jeopardizes these relations. The adaptations to changing market circumstances required over the course of a relationship are too complex and unpredictable to be encompassed in some initial contact, and promises of good faith are unenforceable in the absence of an overarching authority:

> A general clause . . . that "I will behave responsibly rather than seek individual advantage when an occasion to adapt arises," would, in the absence of opportunism, suffice. Given, however, the unenforceability of general clauses and the proclivity of human agents to make false and misleading (self-disbelieved) statements, . . . both buyer and seller are strategically situated to bargain over the disposition of any incremental gain whenever a proposal to adapt is made by the other party. . . . Efficient adaptations which would otherwise be made thus result in costly haggling or even go unmentioned, lest the gains be dissipated by costly subgoal pursuit. *Governance structures* which attenuate opportunism and otherwise infuse confidence are evidently needed.
>
> *(1979, pp. 241–42, emphasis mine)*

This analysis entails the same mixture of under- and oversocialized assumptions found in *Leviathan*. The efficacy of hierarchical power within the firm is overplayed, as with Hobbes's oversocialized sovereign state.[4] The "market" resembles Hobbes's state of nature. It is the atomized and anonymous market of classical political economy, minus the discipline brought by fully competitive conditions – an undersocialized conception that neglects the role of social relations among individuals in different firms in bringing order to economic life. Williamson does acknowledge that this picture of the market is not always appropriate: "Norms of trustworthy behavior sometimes extend to markets and are enforced, in some degree, by group pressures. . . . Repeated personal contacts across organizational boundaries support some minimum level of courtesy and consideration between the parties. . . . In addition, expectations of repeat business discourage efforts to seek a narrow advantage in any particular transaction. . . . Individual aggressiveness is curbed by the prospect of ostracism among peers, in both trade and social circumstances. The reputation of a firm for fairness is also a business asset not to be dissipated" (1975, pp. 106–8).

A wedge is opened here for analysis of social structural influences on market behavior. But Williamson treats these examples as exceptions and also fails to appreciate the extent to which the dyadic relations he describes are themselves embedded in broader systems of social relations. I argue that the anonymous market of neoclassical models is virtually nonexistent in economic life and that transactions of all kinds are rife with the social connections described. This is not necessarily more the case in transactions between firms than within – it seems plausible, on the contrary, that the network of social relations within the firm might be more dense and long-lasting on the average than that existing between – but all I need show here is that there is sufficient social overlay in economic transactions across firms (in the "market," to use the term as in Williamson's dichotomy) to render dubious the assertion that complex market transactions approximate a Hobbesian state of nature that can only be resolved by internalization within a hierarchical structure.

In a general way, there is evidence all around us of the extent to which business relations are mixed up with social ones. The trade associations deplored by Adam Smith remain of great importance. It is well known that many firms, small and large, are linked by interlocking directorates so that relationships among directors of firms are many and densely knit. That business relations spill over into sociability and vice versa, especially among business elites, is one of the best-documented facts in the sociological study of business (e.g., Domhoff, 1971; Useem, 1979). In his study of the extent to which litigation was used to settle disputes between firms, Macaulay notes that disputes are "frequently settled without reference to the contract or potential or actual legal sanctions. There is a hesitancy to speak of legal rights or to threaten to sue in these negotiations. . . . Or as one businessman put it, 'You can settle any dispute if you keep the lawyers and accountants out of it. They just do not understand the give-and-take needed in business.' . . . Law suits for breach of contract appear to be rare" (1963, p. 61). He goes on to explain that the

> top executives of the two firms may know each other. They may sit together on government or trade committees. They may know each other socially and even belong to the same country club. . . . Even where agreement can be reached at the negotiation stage, carefully planned arrangements may create undesirable exchange relationships between business units. Some businessmen object that in such a carefully worked out relationship one gets performance only to the letter of the contract. Such planning indicates a lack of trust and blunts the demands of friendship, turning a cooperative venture into an antagonistic horse trade. . . . Threatening to turn matters over to an attorney may cost no more money than postage or a telephone call; yet few are so skilled in making such a threat that it will not cost some deterioration of the relationship between the firms.   (1963, pp. 63–4)

It is not only at top levels that firms are connected by networks of personal relations, but at all levels where transactions must take place. It is, for example, a commonplace in the literature on industrial purchasing that buying and selling relationships rarely approximate the spot-market model of classical theory. One source indicates that the "evidence consistently suggests that it takes some kind of 'shock' to jolt the organizational buying out of a pattern of placing repeat orders with a favored supplier or to extend the constrained set of feasible suppliers. A moment's reflection will suggest several reasons for this behavior, including the costs associated with searching for new suppliers and establishing new relationships, the fact that users are likely to prefer sources, the relatively low risk involved in dealing with known vendors, and the likelihood that the buyer has established personal relationships that he values with representatives of the supplying firm" (Webster and Wind, 1972, p. 15).

In a similar vein, Macaulay notes that salesmen "often know purchasing agents well. The same two individuals may have dealt with each other from five to 25 years. Each has something to give the other. Salesmen have gossip about competitors, shortages and price increases to give purchasing agents who treat them well" (1963, p. 63). Sellers who do not satisfy their customers "become the subject of discussion in the gossip exchanged by purchasing agents and salesmen, at meetings of purchasing agents' associations and trade associations or even at country clubs or social gatherings . . ." (p. 64). Settlement of disputes is eased by this embeddedness of business in social relations: "Even where the parties have a detailed and carefully planned agreement which indicates what is to happen if, say, the seller fails to deliver on time, often they will never refer to the agreement but will negotiate a solution when the problem arises as if there never had been any original contract. One purchasing agent expressed a common business attitude when he said, 'If something comes up, you get the other man on the telephone and deal with the problem. You don't read legalistic contract clauses at each other if you ever want to do business again. One doesn't run to lawyers if he wants to stay in business because one must behave decently'" (Macaulay, 1963, p. 61).

Such patterns may be more easily noted in other countries, where they are supposedly explained by "cultural" peculiarities. Thus, one journalist recently asserted,

> Friendships and longstanding personal connections affect business connections everywhere. But that seems to be especially true in Japan. . . . The after-hours sessions in the bars and nightclubs are where the vital personal contacts are established and nurtured slowly. Once these ties are set, they are not easily undone. . . . The resulting tight-knit nature of Japanese business society has long been a source of frustration to foreign companies trying to sell products in Japan. . . . Chalmers Johnson, a professor at . . . Berkeley, believes that . . . the exclusive dealing within the Japanese industrial groups, buying and selling to and from each other based on decades-old relationships rather than economic competitiveness . . . is . . . a real nontariff barrier [to trade between the United States and Japan].
> *(Lohr, 1982)*

The extensive use of subcontracting in many industries also presents opportunities for sustained relationships among firms that are not organized hierarchically within one corporate unit. For example, Eccles cites evidence from many countries that in construction, when projects "are not subject to institutional regulations which require competitive bidding . . . relations between the general contractor and his subcontractors are stable and continuous over fairly long periods of time and only infrequently established through competitive bidding. This type of 'quasi-integration' results in what I call the 'quasifirm.' It is a preferred mode to either pure market transactions or formal vertical integration" (1981, pp. 339–40). Eccles describes this "quasifirm" arrangement of extensive and long-term relationships among contractors and subcontractors as an organizational form logically intermediate between the pure market and the vertically integrated firm. I would argue, however, that it is not *empirically* intermediate, since the former situation is so rare. The case of construction is closer to vertical integration than some other situations where firms interact, such as buying and selling relations, since subcontractors are physically located on the same site as the contractor and are under his general supervision. Furthermore, under the usual fixed-price contracts, there are "obvious incentives for shirking performance requirements" (Eccles, 1981, p. 340).

Yet a hierarchical structure associated with the vertically integrated firm does not arise to meet this "problem." I argue this is because the long-term relations of contractors and subcontractors, as well as the embeddedness of those relations in a community of construction personnel, generate standards of expected behavior that not only obviate the need for but are superior to pure authority relations in discouraging malfeasance. Eccles's own empirical study of residential construction in Massachusetts shows not only that subcontracting relationships are long term in nature but also that it is very rare for a general contractor to employ more than two or three subcontractors in a given trade, whatever number of projects is handled in the course of a year (1981, pp. 349–51). This is true despite the availability of large numbers of alternative subcontractors. This phenomenon can be explained in part in investment terms – through a "continuing association both parties can benefit from the somewhat idiosyncratic investment of learning to work together" (Eccles, 1981, p. 340) – but also must be related to the desire of individuals to derive pleasure from the social interaction that accompanies their daily work, a pleasure that would be considerably blunted by spot-market procedures requiring entirely new and strange work partners each day. As in other parts of economic life, the overlay of social relations on what may begin in purely economic transactions plays a crucial role.

Some comments on labor markets are also relevant here. One advantage that Williamson asserts for hierarchically structured firms over market transactions is the ability to transmit accurate information about employees. "The principal impediment to effective interfirm experience-rating," he argues, "is one of communication. By comparison with the firm, markets lack a rich and common rating language. The language problem is particularly severe where the judgments to be made are highly subjective. The advantages of hierarchy in these circumstances are especially great if those persons who are most familiar with a worker's characteristics, usually his immediate supervisor, also do the experience-rating" (1975, p. 78). But the notion that good information about the characteristics of an employee can be transmitted only within firms and not between can be sustained only by neglecting the widely variegated social network of interaction that spans firms. Information about employees travels among firms not only because personal relations exist between those in each firm who do business with each other but also, as I have shown in detail (Granovetter, 1974), because the relatively high levels of interfirm mobility in the

United States guarantee that many workers will be reasonably well known to employees of numerous other firms that might require and solicit their services. Furthermore, the idea that internal information is necessarily accurate and acted on dispassionately by promotion procedures keyed to it seems naive. To say, as Williamson does, that reliance "on internal promotion has affirmative incentive properties because workers can anticipate that differential talent and degrees of cooperativeness will be rewarded" (1975, p. 78) invokes an ideal type of promotion as reward-for-achievement that can readily be shown to have only limited correspondence to existing internal labor markets (see Granovetter, 1983, pp. 40–51, for an extended analysis).

The other side of my critique is to argue that Williamson vastly overestimates the efficacy of hierarchical power ("fiat," in his terminology) within organizations. He asserts, for example, that internal organizations have a great auditing advantage: "An external auditor is typically constrained to review written records. . . . An internal auditor, by contrast, has greater freedom of action. . . . Whereas an internal auditor is not a partisan but regards himself and is regarded by others in mainly instrumental terms, the external auditor is associated with the 'other side' and his motives are regarded suspiciously. The degree of cooperation received by the auditor from the audited party varies accordingly. The external auditor can expect to receive only perfunctory cooperation" (1975, pp. 29–30). The literature on intrafirm audits is sparse, but one thorough account is that of Dalton, in *Men Who Manage*, for a large chemical plant. Audits of parts by the central office were supposed to be conducted on a surprise basis, but warning was typically surreptitiously given. The high level of cooperation shown in these internal audits is suggested by the following account: "Notice that a count of parts was to begin provoked a flurry among the executives to hide certain parts and equipment . . . materials *not* to be counted were moved to: 1) little-known and inaccessible spots; 2) basements and pits that were dirty and therefore unlikely to be examined; 3) departments that had already been inspected and that could be approached circuitously while the counters were en route between official storage areas and 4) places where materials and supplies might be used as a camouflage for parts. . . . As the practice developed, cooperation among the [department] chiefs to use each other's storage areas and available pits became well organized and smoothly functioning" (Dalton, 1959, pp. 48–49).

Dalton's work shows brilliantly that cost accounting of all kinds is a highly arbitrary and therefore easily politicized process rather than a technical procedure decided on grounds of efficiency. He details this especially for the relationship between the maintenance department and various production departments in the chemical plant; the department to which maintenance work was charged had less to do with any strict time accounting than with the relative political and social standing of department executives in their relation to maintenance personnel. Furthermore, the more aggressive department heads expedited their maintenance work "by the use of friendships, by bullying and implied threats. As all the heads had the same formal rank, one could say that an inverse relation existed between a given officer's personal influence and his volume of uncompleted repairs" (1959, p. 34). Questioned about how such practices could escape the attention of auditors, one informant told Dalton, "If Auditing got to snooping around, what the hell could they find out? And if they did find anything, they'd know a damn sight better than to say anything about it. . . . All those guys [department heads] have got lines through Cost Accounting. That's a lot of bunk about Auditing being independent" (1959, p. 32).

Accounts as detailed and perceptive as Dalton's are sadly lacking for a representative sample of firms and so are open to the argument that they are exceptional. But similar points can be made for the problem of transfer pricing – the determination of prices for products traded between divisions of a single firm. Here Williamson argues that though the trading divisions "may have profit-center standing, this is apt to be exercised in a restrained way. . . . Cost-plus pricing rules, and variants thereof, preclude supplier divisions from seeking the monopolistic prices [to] which their sole source supply position might otherwise entitle them. In addition, the managements of the trading divisions are more susceptible to appeals for cooperation" (1975, p. 29). But in an intensive empirical study of transfer-pricing practices, Eccles, having interviewed nearly 150 managers in 13 companies, concluded that no cost-based methods could be carried out in a technically neutral way, since there is "no universal criterion for what is cost. . . . Problems often exist with cost-based methods when the buying division does not have access to the information by which the costs are generated. . . . Market prices are especially difficult to determine when internal purchasing is mandated and no external purchases are made of the intermediate good. . . . There is no obvious answer to what is a markup for profit . . ." (1982, p. 21). The political element in transfer-pricing conflicts strongly affects whose definition of "cost" is accepted: "In general, when transfer pricing practices are seen to enhance one's power and status they will be viewed favorably. When they do not, a countless number of strategic and other sound business reasons will be found to argue for their inadequacy" (1982, p. 21; see also Eccles, 1983, esp. pp. 26–32). Eccles notes the "somewhat ironic fact that many managers consider internal transactions to be more difficult than external ones, even though vertical integration is pursued for presumed advantages" (1983, p. 28).

Thus, the oversocialized view that orders within a hierarchy elicit easy obedience and that employees internalize the interests of the firm, suppressing any conflict with their own, cannot stand scrutiny against these empirical studies (or, for that matter, against the experience of many of us in actual organizations). Note further that, as shown especially well in Dalton's detailed ethnographic study, resistance to the encroachment of organizational interests on personal or divisional ones requires an extensive network of coalitions. From the viewpoint of management, these coalitions represent malfeasance generated by teams; it could not be managed at all by atomized individuals. Indeed, Dalton asserted that the level of cooperation achieved by divisional chiefs in evading central audits involved joint action "of a kind rarely, if ever, shown in carrying on official activities . . ." (1959, p. 49).

In addition, the generally lower turnover of personnel characteristic of large hierarchical firms, with their well-defined internal labor markets and elaborate promotion ladders, may make such cooperative evasion more likely. When many employees have long tenures, the conditions are met for a dense and stable network of relations, shared understandings, and political coalitions to be constructed. (See Homans, 1950, 1974, for the relevant social psychological discussions; and Pfeffer, 1983, for a treatment of the "demography of organizations.") James Lincoln notes, in this connection, that in the ideal-typical Weberian bureaucracy, organizations are "designed to function independently of the collective actions which can be mobilized through [internal] interpersonal networks. Bureaucracy prescribes fixed relationships among positions through which incumbents flow, without, in theory, affecting organizational operations" (1982, p. 26). He goes on to summarize studies showing, however, that "when turnover is low, relations take on additional contents of an expressive and personal sort which may ultimately transform the network and change the directions of the organization" (1982, p. 26).

To this point I have argued that social relations between firms are more important, and authority within firms less so, in bringing order to economic life than is supposed in the markets and hierarchies line of thought. A balanced and symmetrical argument requires attention to power in "market" relations and social connections within firms. Attention to power relations is needed lest my emphasis on the smoothing role of social relations in the market leads me to neglect the role of these relations in the conduct of conflict. Conflict is an obvious reality, ranging from well-publicized litigation between firms to the occasional cases of "cutthroat competition" gleefully reported by the business press. Since the effective exercise of power between firms will prevent bloody public battles, we can assume that such battles represent only a small proportion of actual conflicts of interest. Conflicts probably become public only when the two sides are fairly equally matched; recall that this rough equality was precisely one of Hobbes's arguments for a probable "war of all against all" in the "state of nature." But when the power position of one firm is obviously dominant, the other is apt to capitulate early so as to cut its losses. Such capitulation may require not even explicit confrontation but only a clear understanding of what the other side requires (as in the recent Marxist literature on "hegemony" in business life; see, e.g., Mintz and Schwartz, 1985).

Though the exact extent to which firms dominate other firms can be debated, the voluminous literature on interlocking directorates, on the role of financial institutions vis-à-vis industrial corporations, and on dual economy surely provides enough evidence to conclude that power relations cannot be neglected. This provides still another reason to doubt that the complexities that arise when formally equal agents negotiate with one another can be resolved only by the subsumption of all parties under a single hierarchy; in fact, many of these complexities are resolved by implicit or explicit power relations *among* firms.

Finally, a brief comment is in order on the webs of social relations that are well known from industrial and organizational sociology to be important within firms. The distinction between the "formal" and the "informal" organization of the firm is one of the oldest in the literature, and it hardly needs repeating that observers who assume firms to be structured in fact by the official organization chart are sociological babes in the woods. The connection of this to the present discussion is that insofar as internalization within firms does result in a better handling of complex and idiosyncratic transactions, it is by no means apparent that hierarchical organization is the best explanation. It may be, instead, that the effect of internalization is to provide a focus (see Feld, 1981) for an even denser web of social relations than had occurred between previously independent market entities. Perhaps this web of interaction is mainly what explains the level of efficiency, be it high or low, of the new organizational form.

It is now useful to summarize the differences in explanation and prediction between Williamson's markets and hierarchies approach and the embeddedness view offered here. Williamson explains the inhibition of "opportunism" or malfeasance in economic life and the general existence of cooperation and order by the subsumption of complex economic activity in hierarchically integrated firms. The empirical evidence that I cite shows, rather, that even with complex transactions, a high level of order can often be found in the "market" – that is, across firm boundaries – and a correspondingly high level of disorder within the firm. Whether these occur, instead of what Williamson expects, depends on the nature of personal relations and networks of relations between and within firms. I claim that both order *and* disorder, honesty *and* malfeasance have more to do with structures of such relations than they do with organizational form.

Certain implications follow for the conditions under which one may expect to see vertical integration rather than transactions between firms in a market. Other things being equal, for example, we should expect pressures toward vertical integration in a market where transacting firms lack a network of personal relations that connects them or where such a network eventuates in conflict, disorder, opportunism, or malfeasance. On the other hand, where a stable network of relations mediates complex transactions and generates standards of behavior between firms, such pressures should be absent.

I use the word "pressures" rather than predict that vertical integration will always follow the pattern described in order to avoid the functionalism implicit in Williamson's assumption that whatever organizational form is most efficient will be the one observed. Before we can make this assumption, two further conditions must be satisfied: (i) well-defined and powerful selection pressures toward efficiency must be operating, and (ii) some actors must have the ability and resources to "solve" the efficiency problem by constructing a vertically integrated firm.

The selection pressures that guarantee efficient organization of transactions are nowhere clearly described by Williamson. As in much of the new institutional economics, the need to make such matters explicit is obviated by an implicit Darwinian argument that efficient solutions, however they may originate, have a staying power akin to that enforced by natural selection in the biological world. Thus it is granted that not all business executives "accurately perceive their business opportunities and faultlessly respond. Over time, however, those [vertical] integration moves that have better rationality properties (in transaction cost and scale-economy terms) tend to have better survival properties" (Williamson and Ouchi, 1981, p. 389; see also Williamson, 1981, pp. 573–74). But Darwinian arguments, invoked in this cavalier fashion, careen toward a Panglossian view of whatever institution is analyzed. The operation of alleged selection pressures is here neither an object of study nor even a falsifiable proposition but rather an article of faith.

Even if one could document selection pressures that made survival of certain organizational forms more likely, it would remain to show how such forms could be implemented. To treat them implicitly as mutations, by analogy to biological evolution, merely evades the issue. As in other functionalist explanations, it cannot be automatically assumed that the solution to some problem is feasible. Among the resources required to implement vertical integration might be some measure of market power, access to capital through retained earnings or capital markets, and appropriate connections to legal or regulatory authorities.

Where selection pressures are weak (especially likely in the imperfect markets claimed by Williamson to produce vertical integration) and resources problematic, the social-structural configurations that I have outlined are still related to the efficiency of transaction costs, but no guarantee can be given that an efficient solution will occur. Motives for integration unrelated to efficiency, such as personal aggrandizement of CEOs in acquiring firms, may in such settings become important.

What the viewpoint proposed here requires is that future research on the markets-hierarchies question pay careful and systematic attention to the actual patterns of personal relations by which economic transactions are carried out. Such attention will not only better sort out the motives for vertical integration but also make it easier to comprehend the various complex intermediate forms between idealized atomized markets and completely integrated firms, such as the quasi firm discussed above for the construction industry. Intermediate forms of this kind are so intimately bound up with networks of personal relations that any perspective that considers these relations peripheral will fail to see clearly what "organizational form" has been effected. Existing empirical studies of industrial organization pay little attention to patterns of relations, in part because relevant data are harder to find than those on technology and market structure but also because the dominant economic framework remains one of atomized actors, so personal relations are perceived as frictional in effect.

Discussion

In this article, I have argued that most behavior is closely embedded in networks of interpersonal relations and that such an argument avoids the extremes of under- and oversocialized views of human action. Though I believe this to be so for all behavior, I concentrate here on economic behavior for two reasons: (i) it is the type-case of behavior inadequately interpreted because those who study it professionally are so strongly committed to atomized theories of action; and (ii) with few exceptions, sociologists have refrained from serious study of any subject already claimed by neo-classical economics. They have implicitly accepted the presumption of economists that "market processes" are not suitable objects of sociological study because social relations play only a frictional and disruptive role, not a central one, in modern societies. (Recent exceptions are Baker, 1983; Burt, 1983; and White, 1981.) In those instances in which sociologists study processes where markets are central, they usually still manage to avoid their analysis. Until recently, for example, the large sociological literature on wages was cast in terms of "income attainment," obscuring the labor market context in which wages are set and focusing instead on the background and attainment of individuals (see Granovetter, 1981 for an extended critique). Or, as Stearns has pointed out, the literature on who controls corporations has implicitly assumed that analysis must be at the level of political relations and broad assumptions about the nature of capitalism. Even though it is widely admitted that how corporations acquire capital is a major determinant of control, most relevant research "since the turn of the century has eliminated that [capital] market as an objective of investigation" (1982, pp. 5–6). Even in organization theory, where considerable literature implements the limits placed on economic decisions by social structural complexity, little attempt has been made to demonstrate the implications of this for the neoclassical theory of the firm or for a general understanding of production or such macroeconomic outcomes as growth, inflation, and unemployment.

In trying to demonstrate that all market processes are amenable to sociological analysis and that such analysis reveals central, not peripheral, features of these processes, I have narrowed my focus to problems of trust and malfeasance. I have also used the "market and hierarchies" argument of Oliver Williamson as an illustration of how the embeddedness perspective generates different understandings and predictions from that implemented by economists. Williamson's perspective is itself "revisionist" within economics, diverging from the neglect of institutional and transactional considerations typical of neoclassical work. In this sense, it may appear to have more kinship to a sociological perspective than the usual economic arguments. But the main thrust of the "new institutional economists" is to deflect the analysis of institutions from sociological, historical, and legal argumentation and show instead that they arise as the efficient solution to economic problems. This mission and the pervasive functionalism it implies discourage the detailed analysis of social structure that I argue here is the key to understanding how existing institutions arrived at their present state.

Insofar as rational choice arguments are narrowly construed as referring to atomized individuals and economic goals, they are inconsistent with the embeddedness position presented here. In a broader formulation of rational choice, however, the two views have much in common. Much of the revisionist work by economists that I criticize above in my discussion of over- and undersocialized conceptions of action relies on a strategy that might be called "psychological revisionism" – an attempt to reform economic theory by abandoning an absolute assumption of rational decision making. This strategy has led to Leibenstein's "selective rationality" in his arguments on "X-inefficiency" (1976), for example, and to the claims of segmented labor-market theorists that workers in different market segments have different kinds of decision-making rules, rational choice being only for upper-primary (i.e., professional, managerial, technical) workers (Piore, 1979).

I suggest, in contrast, that while the assumption of rational action must always be problematic, it is a good working hypothesis that should not easily be abandoned. What looks to the analyst like nonrational behavior may be quite sensible when situational constraints, especially those of embeddedness, are fully appreciated. When the social situation of those in nonprofessional labor markets is fully analyzed, their behavior looks less like the automatic application of "cultural" rules and more like a reasonable response to their present situation (as, e.g., in the discussion of Liebow, 1966). Managers who evade audits and fight over transfer pricing are acting nonrationally in some strict economic sense, in terms of a firm's profit maximization; but when their position and ambitions in intrafirm networks and political coalitions are analyzed, the behavior is easily interpreted.

That such behavior is rational or instrumental is more readily seen, moreover, if we note that it aims not only at economic goals but also at sociability, approval, status, and power. Economists rarely see such goals as rational, in part on account of the arbitrary separation that arose historically, as Albert Hirschman (1977) points out, in the 17th and 18th centuries, between the "passions" and the "interests," the latter connoting economic motives only. This way of putting the matter has led economists to specialize in analysis of behavior motivated only by "interest" and to assume that other motives occur in separate and nonrationally organized spheres; hence Samuelson's much-quoted comment that "many economists would separate economics from sociology upon the basis of rational or irrational behavior" (1947, p. 90). The notion that rational choice is derailed by social influences has long discouraged detailed sociological analysis of economic life and led revisionist economists to reform economic theory by focusing on its naive psychology. My claim here is that however naive that psychology may be, this is not where the main difficulty lies – it is rather in the neglect of social structure.

Finally, I should add that the level of causal analysis adopted in the embeddedness argument is a rather proximate one. I have had little to say about what broad historical or macrostructural circumstances have led systems to display the social-structural characteristics they have, so I make no claims for this analysis to answer large-scale questions about the nature of modern society or the sources of economic and political change. But the focus on proximate causes is intentional, for these broader questions cannot be satisfactorily addressed without more detailed understanding of the mechanisms by which sweeping change has its effects. My claim is that one of the most important and least analyzed of such mechanisms is the impact of such change on the social relations in which economic life is embedded. If this is so, no adequate link between macro- and micro-level theories can be established without a much fuller understanding of these relations.

The use of embeddedness analysis in explicating proximate causes of patterns of macro-level interest is well illustrated by the markets and hierarchies question. The extent of vertical integration and the reasons for the persistence of small firms operating through the market are not only narrow concerns of industrial organization; they are of interest to all students of the institutions of advanced capitalism. Similar issues arise in the analysis of "dual economy," dependent development, and the nature of modern corporate elites. But whether small firms are indeed eclipsed by giant corporations is usually analyzed in broad and sweeping macropolitical or macro-economic terms, with little appreciation of proximate social structural causes.

Analysts of dual economy have often suggested, for example, that the persistence of large numbers of small firms in the "periphery" is explained by large corporations' need to shift the risks of cyclical fluctuations in demand or of uncertain R & D activities; failures of these small units will not adversely affect the larger firms' earnings. I suggest here that small firms in a market setting may persist instead because a dense network of social relations is overlaid on the business relations connecting such firms and reduces pressures for integration. This does not rule out risk shifting as an explanation with a certain face validity. But the embeddedness account may be more useful in explaining the large number of small establishments not characterized by satellite or peripheral status. (For a discussion of the surprising extent of employment in small establishments, see Granovetter, 1984.) This account is restricted to proximate causes: it logically leads to but does not answer the questions why, when, and in what sectors does the market display various types of social structure. But those questions, which link to a more macro level of analysis, would themselves not arise without a prior appreciation of the importance of social structure in the market.

The markets and hierarchies analysis, important as it may be, is presented here mainly as an illustration. I believe the embeddedness argument to have very general applicability and to demonstrate not only that there is a place for sociologists in the study of economic life but that their perspective is urgently required there. In avoiding the analysis of phenomena at the center of standard economic theory, sociologists have unnecessarily cut themselves off from a large and important aspect of social life and from the European tradition – stemming especially from Max Weber – in which economic action is seen only as a special, if important, category of social action. I hope to have shown here that this Weberian program is consistent with and furthered by some of the insights of modern structural sociology.

Notes

1 There are many parallels between what are referred to here as the "undersocialized" and "oversocialized" views of action and what Burt (1982, chap. 9) calls the "atomistic" and "normative" approaches. Similarly, the embeddedness approach proposed here as a middle ground between under- and oversocialized views has an obvious family resemblance to Burt's "structural" approach to action. My distinctions and approach also differ from Burt's in many ways that cannot be quickly summarized; these can be best appreciated by comparison of this article with his useful summary (1982, chap. 9) and with the formal models that implement his conception (1982, 1983). Another approach that resembles mine in its emphasis on how social connections affect purposive action is Marsden's extension of James Coleman's theories of collective action and decision to situations where such connections modify results that would occur in a purely atomistic situation (Marsden, 1981, 1983).
2 Students of the sociology of sport will note that this proposition had been put forward previously, in slightly different form, by Leo Durocher.
3 I am indebted to an anonymous referee for pointing this out.
4 Williamson's confidence in the efficacy of hierarchy leads him, in discussing Chester Barnard's "zone of indifference" – that realm within which employees obey orders simply because they are indifferent about whether or not they do what is ordered – to speak instead of a "zone of acceptance" (1975, p. 77), thus undercutting Barnard's emphasis on the problematic nature of obedience. This transformation of Barnard's usage appears to have originated with Herbert Simon, who does not justify it, noting only that he "prefer[s] the term 'acceptance'" (Simon, 1957, p. 12).

References

Akerlof, George (1983) "Loyalty Filters," *American Economic Review* 73 (1): 54–63.
Alchian, Armen and Demsetz, Harold (1973) "The Property Rights Paradigm," *Journal of Economic History* 33 (March): 16–27.
Arrow, Kenneth (1974) *The Limits of Organization*, New York: Norton.
Baker, Wayne (1983) "Floor Trading and Crowd Dynamics," in Patricia Adler and Peter Adler (eds), *Social Dynamics of Financial Markets*, Greenwich, CN: JAI.
Becker, Gary (1976) *The Economic Approach to Human Behavior*, Chicago, IL: University of Chicago Press.
Ben-Porath, Yoram (1980) "The F-Connection: Families, Friends and Firms in the Organization of Exchange," *Population and Development Review* 6 (1): 1–30.
Bowles, Samuel and Gintis, Herbert (1975) *Schooling in Capitalist America*, New York: Basic.
Brown, Roger (1965) *Social Psychology*, New York: Free Press.
Burt, Ronald (1982) *Toward a Structural Theory of Action*, New York: Academic Press.
Burt, Ronald (1983) *Corporate Profits and Cooptation*, New York: Academic Press.

Cole, Robert (1979) *Work, Mobility and Participation: A Comparative Study of American and Japanese Industry*, Berkeley and Los Angeles, CA: University of California Press.

Dalton, Melville (1959) *Men Who Manage*, New York: Wiley.

Doeringer, Peter and Piore, Michael (1971) *Internal Labor Markets and Manpower Analysis*, Lexington, MA: Heath.

Domhoff, G. William (1971) *The Higher Circles*, New York: Random House.

Duesenberry, James (1960) Comment on "An Economic Analysis of Fertility," in Universities–National Bureau Committee for Economic Research (eds), *Demographic and Economic Change in Developed Countries*, Princeton, NJ: Princeton University Press.

Eccles, Robert (1981) "The Quasifirm in the Construction Industry," *Journal of Economic Behavior and Organization* 2 (December): 335–57.

Eccles, Robert (1982) "A Synopsis of *Transfer Pricing: An Analysis and Action Plan*," mimeographed, Cambridge, MA: Harvard Business School.

Eccles, Robert (1983) "Transfer Pricing, Fairness and Control," Working Paper no. HBS 83-167, Cambridge, MA: Harvard Business School.

Feld, Scott (1981) "The Focused Organization of Social Ties," *American Journal of Sociology* 86 (5): 1015–35.

Fine, Gary and Kleinman, Sherryl (1979) "Rethinking Subculture: An Interactionist Analysis," *American Journal of Sociology* 85 (July): 1–20.

Furubotn, E. and Pejovich, S. (1972) "Property Rights and Economic Theory: A Survey of Recent Literature," *Journal of Economic Literature* 10 (3): 1137–62.

Geertz, Clifford (1979) "Suq: The Bazaar Economy in Sefrou," pp. 123–225 in C. Geertz, H. Geertz and L. Rosen (eds), *Meaning and Order in Moroccan Society*, New York: Cambridge University Press.

Granovetter, Mark (1974) *Getting a Job: A Study of Contacts and Careers*, Cambridge, MA: Harvard University Press.

Granovetter, Mark (1981) "Toward a Sociological Theory of Income Differences," pp. 11–47 in Ivar Berg (ed.), *Sociological Perspectives on Labor Markets*, New York: Academic Press.

Granovetter, Mark (1983) "Labor Mobility, Internal Markets and Job-Matching: A Comparison of the Sociological and Economic Approaches," mimeographed.

Granovetter, Mark (1984) "Small Is Bountiful: Labor Markets and Establishment Size," *American Sociological Review* 49 (3): 323–34.

Hirschman, Albert (1977) *The Passions and the Interests*, Princeton, NJ: Princeton University Press.

Hirschman, Albert (1982) "Rival Interpretations of Market Society: Civilizing, Destructive or Feeble?," *Journal of Economic Literature* 20 (4): 1463–84.

Homans, George (1950) *The Human Group*, New York: Harcourt Brace & Co.

Homans, George (1974) *Social Behavior*, New York: Harcourt Brace Jovanovich.

Lazear, Edward (1979) "Why Is There Mandatory Retirement?," *Journal of Political Economy* 87 (6): 1261–84.

Leibenstein, Harvey (1976) *Beyond Economic Man*, Cambridge, MA: Harvard University Press.

Liebow, Elliot (1966) *Tally's Corner*, Boston, MA: Little, Brown.

Lincoln, James (1982) "Intra- (and Inter-) Organizational Networks," pp. 1–38 in S. Bacharach (ed.), *Research in the Sociology of Organizations*, vol. 1, Greenwich, CN: JAI.

Lohr, Steve (1982) "When Money Doesn't Matter in Japan," *New York Times* (December 30).

Macaulay, Stewart (1963) "Non-Contractual Relations in Business: A Preliminary Study," *American Sociological Review* 28 (1): 55–67.

Marsden, Peter (1981) "Introducing Influence Processes into a System of Collective Decisions," *American Journal of Sociology* 86 (May): 1203–35.

Marsden, Peter (1983) "Restricted Access in Networks and Models of Power," *American Journal of Sociology* 88 (January): 686–17.

Merton, Robert (1947) "Manifest and Latent Functions," pp. 19–84 in *Social Theory and Social Structure*, New York: Free Press.

Mintz, Beth and Schwartz, Michael (1985) *The Power Structure of American Business*, Chicago: University of Chicago Press.

North, D. and Thomas, R. (1973) *The Rise of the Western World*, Cambridge: Cambridge University Press.

Okun, Arthur (1981) *Prices and Quantities*, Washington, DC: Brookings.

Pakes, Ariel and Nitzan S. (1982) "Optimum Contracts for Research Personnel, Research Employment and the Establishment of 'Rival' Enterprises," NBER Working Paper no. 871, Cambridge, MA: National Bureau of Economic Research.

Parsons, Talcott (1937) *The Structure of Social Action*, New York: Macmillan.

Pfeffer, Jeffrey (1983) "Organizational Demography," in L. L. Cummings and B. Staw (eds), *Research in Organizational Behavior*, vol. 5, Greenwich, CN: JAI.

Phelps Brown, Ernest Henry (1977) *The Inequality of Pay*, Berkeley, CA: University of California Press.

Piore, Michael (1975) "Notes for a Theory of Labor Market Stratification," pp. 125–50 in R. Edwards, M. Reich and D. Gordon (eds), *Labor Market Segmentation*, Lexington, MA: Heath.

Piore, Michael (ed.) (1979) *Unemployment and Inflation*, White Plains, NY: Sharpe.

Polanyi, Karl (1944) *The Great Transformation*, New York: Holt, Rinehart.

Polanyi, Karl, Arensberg, C. and Pearson, H. (1957) *Trade and Market in the Early Empires*, New York: Free Press.

Popkin, Samuel (1979) *The Rational Peasant*, Berkeley and Los Angeles, CA: University of California Press.

Rosen, Sherwin (1982) "Authority, Control and the Distribution of Earnings," *Bell Journal of Economics* 13 (2): 311–23.

Samuelson, Paul (1947) *Foundations of Economic Analysis*, Cambridge, MA: Harvard University Press.

Schneider, Harold (1974) *Economic Man: The Anthropology of Economics*, New York: Free Press.

Schotter, Andrew (1981) *The Economic Theory of Social Institutions*, New York: Cambridge University Press.

Scott, James (1976) *The Moral Economy of the Peasant*, New Haven, CN: Yale University Press.

Shenon, Philip (1984) "Margolies Is Found Guilty of Murdering Two Women," *New York Times* (June 1).

Simon, Herbert (1957) *Administrative Behavior*, Glencoe, IL: Free Press.

Smith, Adam [1776] (1979) *The Wealth of Nations*, Andrew Skinner (ed.), Baltimore: Penguin.

Stearns, Linda (1982) "Corporate Dependency and the Structure of the Capital Market: 1880–1980," PhD dissertation, State University of New York at Stony Brook.

Thompson, E. P. (1971) "The Moral Economy of the English Crowd in the Eighteenth Century," *Past and Present* 50 (February): 76–136.

Useem, Michael (1979) "The Social Organization of the American Business Elite and Participation of Corporation Directors in the Governance of American Institutions," *American Sociological Review* 44: 553–72.

Webster, Frederick and Wind, Yoram (1972) *Organizational Buying Behavior*, Englewood Cliffs, NJ: Prentice-Hall.

White, Harrison C. (1981) "Where Do Markets Come From?," *American Journal of Sociology* 87 (November): 517–47.

Williamson, Oliver (1975) *Markets and Hierarchies*, New York: Free Press.

Williamson, Oliver (1979) "Transaction-Cost Economics: The Governance of Contractual Relations," *Journal of Law and Economics* 22 (2): 233–61.

Williamson, Oliver (1981) "The Economics of Organization: The Transaction Cost Approach," *American Journal of Sociology* 87 (November): 548–77.

Williamson, Oliver and Ouchi, William (1981) "The Markets and Hierarchies and Visible Hand Perspectives," pp. 347–70 in Andrew Van de Ven and William Joyce (eds) *Perspectives on Organizational Design and Behavior*, New York: Wiley.

Wrong, Dennis (1961) "The Oversocialized Conception of Man in Modern Sociology," *American Sociological Review* 26 (2): 183–93.

6 Making Markets: Opportunism and Restraint on Wall Street

Mitchel Y. Abolafia

Homo Economicus Unbound: Bond Traders on Wall Street

Bond trader (looking out across the trading floor): Traders are dying to make money. That's all they care about. Most traders don't care about the diplomacy that you see in the corporate environment. They don't care about titles. They are here to make money. They live in a four-by-four foot space and put up with all the bullshit that goes on around them. They put up with a lot, but the money is worth it.

Mitch: What else is different from the corporate environment?

Bond trader: Wall Street salaries are so much higher that you are comparing apples and oranges. The typical guy that walks in the door on Wall Street is probably making what a senior V.P. is making in corporate America. And this guy is younger and cockier. A lot of guys under thirty making big bucks. You don't find that too much in corporate America . . . On Wall Street there is no "working your way up." You have a good year, make a million dollars. You're a hot shot.

Mitch: What happens to the guy who has a bad year?

Bond trader: There's always someone waiting to take your chair. Lose a few hundred thousand in a week or over six months and you're out. You see winners and you see losers. It's best not to get too excited for the winners and it's best not to get too close to the losers.

I began my fieldwork on bond markets in early October of 1987. I did not know then that I was observing the peak of a speculative mania in financial markets. Bond markets had experienced explosive growth since October 1979, when the Federal Reserve Board decided to let interest rates float. The mania came to an end on October 19, 1987 when the Dow Jones Industrial Average crashed 508 points. Just four days before the crash a managing director in bond trading at a major investment bank explained the firm's strategy for growth: "The strategy is simple. You fill up one trading room, and you open a new one. You go out and hire the talent. A guy's making a million dollars a year . . . you can give him two million. He's making two you give him . . . [w]hatever the numbers are. Simple." After the crash, the heady optimism and bravado of the pre-crash era never totally evaporated, but the trading community was chastened. My fieldwork in the bond market continued for another year and a half after the crash. Market growth receded during this time, but salaries remained high and trading continued to be a profitable business for the firms.

Original publication: Chapter 1 of Abolafia, Mitchel Y., *Making Markets: Opportunism and Restraint on Wall Street* (Harvard University Press, Cambridge, MA, 1996).

My first day on a bond trading floor left a strong impression. My field notes recorded the youth, intensity, and pace: "There is almost no gray hair to be seen. Most traders are white men between twenty-five and thirty-five years old. They wear short hair and dark business suits with the suit jacket slung over the back of a chair. There are a few women, most of them clerks or analysts,[1] and a few older men . . . The people on the trading floor are highly focused. They stare intently at computer screens, hold several phones at once or shout information to nearby colleagues in staccato bursts. Their concentration on the immediate transaction is all-consuming. We are on the fortieth floor with windows all around offering spectacular views of New York harbor. No one is distracted . . . All of this activity is performed at a dizzying pace. Deals are begun and finished in less than a minute. Market fluctuations generate flurries of activity. Money, though invisible here, is in constant motion. The energy of the market infects everyone, myself included."

As the weeks went by the market slowed down and it became more difficult for traders to find profitable trades. Some of the energy began to dissipate. This gave the traders more time to talk with me. Behavior that had at first seemed like explosions of chaotic aggression began, instead, to look like a highly organized, even ritualized, game. Firms offered huge incentives to aggressive young people willing and able to play a game of deep concentration and discipline. The game required that they gather endless amounts of information to be applied in periodic bursts of risk-taking.

Based on their youth and incomes, bond traders looked like a fairly exotic group to study. But there was something familiar about them. This resemblance was not to any person or group but to an academic idea. Bond traders bore a striking resemblance to *Homo economicus*: the highly rational and self-interested decision maker portrayed in economists' models. Bond traders' behavior appeared to come closer than I expected to the economists' assumptions of perfect rationality and unambiguous self-interest.

The Study

The subjects in this study are fifty-four bond traders employed at four of the ten largest investment banks on Wall Street. They perform the dual roles of broker and dealer. As brokers, they match buyers with sellers, thereby earning commissions for the firm. As dealers, they trade bonds for the firm's account, either buying or selling, to create profits for the firm. Traders are paid a salary plus a bonus that often exceeds their salaries. The work consists of a continuous stream of transactions each worth millions of dollars. The pace, which is often frantic, is dictated by the activity and volatility in the market.

The traders in this study work on large trading floors surrounded by one hundred to two hundred other traders, salespeople, and support staff. They work at desks that are typically four feet across and are piled with three or four quote screens, a personal computer, and two or three telephones. These desks are attached to other traders' desks on three sides. Traders can be seen standing by their desks, holding several phones at once on long extension cords, and simultaneously carrying on a conversation with a nearby salesperson or clerk. The air vibrates with the low roar of voices punctuated by an occasional effort to be heard above the tumult.

The data consist of formal interviews and extensive field notes based on observation. Interviews and observation were completed between October 1987 and March

1989. Formal interviews were conducted on the trading floor or in adjacent offices. All interviews were taped, transcribed, and coded. Less formal conversations took place through follow-up phone calls and meetings with informants.

Economic Man: A Grounded Model

Although the Wall Street bond traders interviewed differed in age, education, and personal style, certain common concerns predominated. The limits and variations of these concerns were explored in successive interviews. Taken together these concerns constitute a skeletal script for membership on the trading floor. The inductive model of economic man constructed from these interviews is based on the primary goals of traders, their strategies for attaining those goals, and the institutional rules that define both the actors and the action.

Economic behavior is pursued for more than one reason. The primary purpose of economic behavior in market societies is the accumulation of wealth. Extraordinary personal wealth is the dominant goal among bond traders. The trading floor of investment banks provides an organized and legitimate institutional context for turning undirected desires into viable strategies of action. It is a context in which a certain amount of specialized and focused self-interest is considered a very good thing. Self-interest is the raw material from which the local version of economic man is constructed and legitimated.

Even the drive for extraordinary personal wealth has a subsidiary meaning, a meaning given by the related but subordinate goals of the bond trader. Trading is construed as a source of both excitement and mastery among bond traders. Bond trading is a form of what anthropologist Clifford Geertz, writing of Balinese cockfighters, calls "deep play." In such games, successful play confers high prestige. As Geertz writes, "In deep (play), where the amounts of money are great, much more is at stake than material gain: namely, esteem, honor, dignity, respect – in a word . . . status."[2] Among bond traders, trading is often described as an ordeal that, if successfully mastered, confers status. A typical story told repeatedly on the trading floor involves the first time a trader goes home for the night having purchased a large block of bonds for the firm, especially when the market is particularly volatile. "Until you've taken your first position home and tried to go to sleep at night and woken up with a loss staring you in the face, you'll never know if you can make it." Like other games, the process of playing and winning is the reward. "It's not just the money. It's the excitement, the chance to test yourself every day," one trader commented.

The dominant metaphor on the trading floor is the game. Bond traders compare themselves to gunfighters, fighter pilots, and professional athletes. The comparison is not to team-based games but rather to one-on-one challenges. Traders also compare trading to such betting games as poker and shooting dice. Each transaction is a one time gamble in which there is no room for complacency or compromise. The trading floor is not understood as a place to footdrag or merely survive, as are other organizational settings. It is a place to win. As one trader expressed it, "The sheer raw enjoyment of winning . . . you'll never find anything like it in any other business."

The money, the heightened materialism, is not the only goal in this game. For a significant share of veteran traders the ultimate goal is the excitement and status incumbent in winning. As one senior trader explained, "There is a tremendous feeling every day when you roll down here and you come onto the Manhattan Bridge and see the Wall Street skyline. This could be the day I win it all." "Testing" and the "raw joy of winning" are powerful seductions to professional athletes, fighter pilots, and professional crooks, as well as bond traders. Success in these forms of deep play results in immediate, visible status. Bond trading is the practical method available to these MBA graduates by their social position.

If the trading floor is a context that attracts those with a pressing desire for extreme wealth, it is because it is constructed to do just that. Unlike most of corporate America, there is no career ladder for traders. There are only traders who make more and traders who make less in a continuous contest for wealth. Traders refer to themselves as entrepreneurs in the sense of being self-reliant. Ironically, it is a self-reliance framed by the organizational structure in which they operate. "You trade for your own account," one trader explained. "You have the ability to hang yourself here. They're giving you a framework in what you should do and that framework is pretty loose. Each individual is making his own market . . . Profit and loss is what the trader is all about."

The means for achieving entrepreneurial success are provided by the investment banks that employ the traders. These means must then combine with the individual characteristics ascribed to economic man: self-interest and rationality. They become visible as strategies that traders enact on Wall Street: opportunism and hyper-rationality. Bond traders construct their own version of entrepreneurial behavior, becoming local and somewhat stylized versions of economic man.

Strategies

The economist Oliver Williamson defines opportunism as "self-interest seeking with guile." We will use the term to refer to those actions in which a trader uses his advantage to deceive his trading partner. Among opportunism's most significant forms is the selective or distorted disclosure of information in a transaction. Not surprisingly, none of the subjects in this study voluntarily described their own behavior as opportunistic. As J. Van Maanen notes, few informants in an ethnographic study are likely to reveal their hidden techniques, but informants freely offered that deceptive practices were part of their business, that they had seen instances of deception, and that one had to be wary. In this sense, opportunism is part of the script in terms of what *other* people are likely to do to *you*. The trading floor is understood as a dog-eat-dog world, one in which individualism is a survival strategy. Thus, while traders would reject the label of "opportunist," they were quite comfortable describing incidents in which their own behavior had been particularly "aggressive" or "entrepreneurial." Such aggression often turned out to involve locally approved forms of opportunism.

Bond traders are at the center of the market-making process, yet they never deal directly with their transaction partner. They have two options. They may trade "in the Street" or with the investment bank's customers through its institutional salesforce. "In the Street" trading is based on bids or offers that are publicly available through computer screens or "broker's brokers" who cover specific sectors of the market. Trading through the salesforce involves dealing with a salesperson, usually on the same trading floor, who manages an average of four or five institutional customers that want to buy from the firm or sell to it. Trading through the salesforce is preferred in that it services the firm's customers and carries a higher return for the firm. It also affords most of the possibilities for opportunism.

Opportunism among bond traders takes the form of culturally scripted strategies. The first and simplest form of opportunism is "laying off" bonds. It involves offering incomplete information and taking advantage of a transaction partner's ignorance. Traders may communicate incomplete or misleading information to the salesperson when selling bonds out of the firm's inventory. As one trader admitted, "The trader will know the true story on a bond and sell it anyway, where they know they shouldn't sell it for as much." Although the trader knows that the bond is not worth that much, he also knows that such behavior is acceptable in this context. As Michael Lewis, a former salesman at Salomon Brothers explained, "The trader can pressure one of his salesmen to persuade insurance company Y that IBM bonds are worth more than pension fund X paid for them initially. Whether it is true is irrelevant. The trader buys the bonds from X and sells them to Y and takes out another eighth" (i.e. he charges Y a commission of an eighth of a point).[3] The belief that this happens frequently leads institutional customers, such as mutual funds and insurance companies, to resent and mistrust bond traders. This mistrust is reflected in the fact that institutional customers often seek information from four or five different firms before transacting. "There are a lot of accounts that feel that Wall Street is a conniving, calculating institution that would rip the eyes out of anyone they can," one trader commented.

A second, more deceptive form of opportunism is the use of false information. Traders not only conceal information, they may actively distort it by "showing a bid." This refers to posting a false, but highly visible bid on a computer network in order to support the price of bonds you already own. As a trader explained, "Frequently, if you own bonds you show a bid on the Street to support your position. If I own bonds and I think they are worth 65 I'm going to show a bid on the Street so that when an account comes in and wants to know what the market is, another trader in another shop will say, 'Well there's a bid on the Street for them . . .'" Traders may post a deceptively high bid on the Street and then strategically withdraw it. In the following instance my informant was lured into buying bonds cheap that he intended to sell to a high "bid in the Street." The high bidder withdrew his bid, leaving my informant stuck with the bonds he bought. He expects that he will still sell the bonds to that bidder, but at a considerably lower price, just as his adversary intended.

> I bought some bonds the other day based on a bid that was in the Street. The bid was very rich. When I turned around to sell those bonds to that bid in the Street the bid was no longer there. The guy who was bidding needed the bonds. He was probably short, but he wanted to smoke me out and make me panic. I think he needs the bonds but is just not showing his hand. So his bid is ridiculous now. Ten points below his bid before. It's just a waiting game. At first I thought I'd gotten raped and was going to get buried. Fortunately, it wasn't a large block.

The two strategies discussed above represent relatively mild forms of opportunism. They are considered a routine part of playing the game. As one trader put it, "You can be too honest and you'll go nowhere." The selective use of information is a taken-for-granted part of the local repertoire of strategies. At more extreme levels of deception are the third and fourth forms of opportunism: agent opportunism and insider opportunism. They involve the theft of proprietary information and are considered significant violations of the securities laws. The most common script for agent opportunism is front-running. In front-running a trader becomes aware that a customer is going to place an order. The trader then buys the bonds, marks them up, and sells them to the customer through one of the firm's salespeople. This form of opportunism is very hard to catch, although bond traders agree that it is fairly common. Insider trading is the use of information about the economic condition or intentions of a bond issuer that is not available to the public. It is sometimes referred to as "trading a leak" and is still considered a rare occurrence. Both of these are very clear violations, although traders believe that the former is more common and less egregious than the latter.

Much opportunism occurs in what traders themselves refer to as the gray areas: instances in which a particular formal market regulation is widely ignored. At such points traders bend the rules. "If an account [a pension fund, mutual fund, etc.] had given bonds to another broker/dealer for the bid and that broker/dealer goes to a broker's broker and you just happen to find out what account it is that has the bonds out for bid, now you're getting into one of the gray areas. You're not supposed to go direct (to the account), but more times than not you'll go direct and save the broker's commission."

Young traders acquire a working knowledge of these "gray areas," learning which forms of opportunism are part of the local script. Older informants suggest that the script in the bond markets became more opportunistic in the 1980s. "A lot of things that are OK now, we thought of and dismissed. Nice people wouldn't do such trashy things." In the eighties, following the floating of interest rates by the Federal Reserve Board, the bond markets grew in volume and volatility. There was much more trading and many new traders. The firms expanded their trading floor operations so rapidly that it became increasingly difficult to socialize trainees to the unwritten scripts and the institutional rules defining the limits of opportunism. In addition, the Reagan administration sent clear signals that regulatory oversight was being reduced. Noting the changes, one informant in his mid-forties explained, "It began to occur to me that I was playing some old game that is no longer. The rules have changed. To play ball, you really have to get in there and root around." Another said, "It used to be 'My word is my bond.' That was all you needed to know."

Opportunism, particularly in the first two forms discussed, was a common strategy among the subjects in this study. The strategies existed prior to the action – part of the tool kit available to every trader. Opportunism is one of the forms of rationality accessible to traders. In the next section I discuss the dominant mode of rationality on the trading floor: hyper-rationality.

Just as self-interest is constructed as opportunism on the trading floor, rationality appears as hyper-rationality. The question is not whether alternative forms of rationality exist, but rather the conditions under which they make their appearance and the resulting forms that they take. In recent years, economists have shown an increasing recognition that rationality is not a simple fact of nature. In the ideal type of economic man, the actor has fully ordered preferences, perfect information, and immaculate computing power. All of these assumptions have been called into question recently by economists[4] as well as non-economists.[5] The ideal type of rationality has been replaced by cognitive biases and heuristics,[6] rational foolishness,[7] and anomalies.[8] All are alternative forms of bounded rationality.

Bond traders exhibit a form of bounded rationality that might be called hyper-rationality. Hyper-rational decision makers are those who make the greatest use of analytic techniques, but still include elements of intuitive judgment in their decision process. Among bond traders, hyper-rationality is manifested in habits or ritualized customs that are tacitly but continuously invoked throughout the trading day. The most important elements in hyper-rationality involve context-dependent versions of vigilance and intuitive judgment.

Vigilance involves the ability to search and assimilate a broad range of information that one expects may be useful in decision making. Trading floors are continuously deluged by economic indicators and interpretations of those indicators. During their internships, novice traders learn which indicators and modes of analysis are most culturally valued on the Street and in the firm. Hyper-rationality involves dealing with continuous information overload using prescribed modes of vigilance. "Everybody is inundated with information," a trader noted. "Every machine in the world is spewing out technical information, fundamental information, news releases, everything. You have to be very agile, very focused."

Bond traders engage in a continuous and aggressive search using a variety of electronic, print, and interpersonal information sources. There is a sense that indicators must be assessed because they are available. Each represents a potential resource for reducing the uncertainty of highly consequential buy and sell decisions. Such indicators come in a wide variety of forms, from government statistics to experts' predictions and local rumors. Specific strategies of vigilance vary from market to market. Vigilance in corporate bond trading is slightly different than it is in government bond trading: the most valued specific indicators are different for each.

Vigilance consists of several related elements: sorting, checking, and establishing value. The first step in vigilance is sorting. The volume of information available is so overwhelming that a subsidiary industry has grown up to supply information and analysis of market trends to traders. Most traders depend primarily on statistics and the highly regarded interpreters of such statistics who publish newsletters and have columns in the trade papers. These interpretations are important because all traders are presumably looking at the same numbers. The interpretation of such numbers is somewhat equivocal. Every trading floor has an adjacent research department offering interpretations of the behavior of the Federal Reserve Board, as well as the latest government reports and statistics. Every trader must sort through both the numbers and their multiple interpretations. Most develop a routinized sorting procedure to cover their favored sources. This procedure is enacted daily prior to the start of trading and continues throughout the day.

New information often interrupts the routinized sorting. The trading community grabs at new pieces of information. Stories on the newswire occasionally require immediate consideration. At the moment when a key indicator is about to be released by a government agency, traders all over Wall Street stand poised at their phones. When enough people with significant trading power share the same belief about the meaning of this information, the collective effect may be a self-fulfilling prophecy. This is particularly evident when the government releases indicators like the Producer Price Index or retail sales figures. If the news is surprising, it will often move the market. If it fails to move the market, traders will say that it has already been discounted.

Once information has been gathered and sorted, traders employ a checking strategy to see how others are perceiving the same or different information. They are in contact with an assortment of brokers, salespeople, economists, and informants in government agencies. Traders are generally aware that it is not the correctness of the interpretation that counts, but rather the degree to which others will read the same information the same way. As one trader explained it: "A lot of smart people don't do very well at trading because they know what information means. When you trade you need to know what people *think* the information means. You don't have to be smart, you just have to be perceptive. You have to have a sense of what motivates people – to be a good listener to what people think."

The same point is made by John Maynard Keynes. "[Professional investors] are concerned, not with what an investment is really worth . . . but with what the market will value it at . . ."[9] In keeping with this, most traders do little analysis themselves. Rather, they work hard, through sorting and checking, to stay apprised of what others are hearing and thinking. This is shown by their constant recharting of the yield curve, an indicator that reflects what others have most recently been willing to pay for bonds at a range of interest rates and maturities. Market rivals make buy and sell decisions by watching each other.[10]

Establishing value is the final step in the script for vigilance. It is the local term for making an estimate of where a bond "ought to be" in terms of price. It is at this point that traders focus on a particular bond. The most important rituals in establishing value are called "taking the runs," in which a trader finds out what's available in the Street from an intermediary known as a broker's broker and through the "inquiry" from the salesforce. These are ritualized morning activities that provide the trader with price information on past transactions and ongoing bids and offers. Both of these rituals allow the traders to begin to array their alternatives. In this kind of highly liquid market, recent transactions are among the most important sources of information for establishing value.[11] There are also norms about appropriate price movement over time and the influence of movement in one instrument on another that influence the process of establishing value. One trader explains his ritual: "Each morning I call my broker's broker to take what is called a run. This is a list of bonds I trade. These [pointing to long pages of handwritten price quotes] are the very active issues. On Friday I used five brokers. They gave me a whole run of issues and the size of those offerings or bids. Then the inquiry from the salesforce begins."

The post-modern trading floor is a setting that elicits vigilance. Every major investment bank reproduces this context for vigilance. All over the Street investment firms provide a nearly identical set of resources. They create the setting for vigilance activities in the form of daily strategy meetings, internal economic reports, and informal interaction that defines the meaning of various types of information. But in the end, a firm cannot make the individual, split second decisions required in bond trading. "The key thing is judgment," a trader explained. "It's the toughest thing about being here, not the mechanics (of trading). Those things are simple; very easy to follow and not a big deal. But that split second judgment that you have to make. (It) probably comes from some subliminal input you don't even recognize. That's what makes the difference. You can't be trained to do that. You just have to be exposed."

Traders often say that they did a trade because it felt right or felt good. Asked to explain this, one trader said, "It's a visceral thing. The brain to mouth reflex. Traders cannot put into words what they've done, even though they may be great money-makers. They have a knack. They can't describe it." Intuitive judgment involves the use of tacit knowledge in an unconscious process to arrive at a decision. Jerome Bruner suggests, "Intuition implies the act of grasping the meaning or significance or structure of a problem without explicit reliance upon the analytic apparatus of one's craft. It is the intuitive mode that yields hypotheses quickly . . ."[12] Intuitive processes are built up through trial and error experience, independent of any conscious effort to learn. Intuitive judgment is most often contrasted with "analytic thinking" and is considered a critical decision tool by bond traders.

Although vigilance is a cultural capacity that may be developed through training and access to information resources, intuitive judgment about bond prices is a craft that is learned through practice. The bond trader develops an abstract sense of how the raw material, in this case the market, reacts under various conditions. These abstractions or images are developed through watching others trade, "paper" trading, and ultimately, the direct experience of trading for one's own account. The novice engages in a lengthy internship during which he is first exposed to the market and ultimately thrown in for a "baptism by fire."

Traders often say that successful trading is an art. "If you have to know how to trade you will never be any good. That's sort of a certainty here. It's not a science, it's an art. People who have to know never make money. You can't learn it. We don't teach it. We just sort of expose people." As Michael Polanyi explained, "An art which cannot be specified in detail cannot be transmitted by prescription, since no prescription for it exists. It can be passed on only by example from master to apprentice."[13] Recruits compete to apprentice themselves to the best traders. These traders do not reveal their "trading secrets," rather the recruits watch and listen as the trader connects disparate facts to arrive at successful choices.

The last steps in the trader's vigilance routine, "taking the runs" and "inquiry," are the precipitants to arriving at particular buy and sell decisions. Traders are faced with a series of immediate opportunities by their brokers and salespeople. They must assess this information in light of other information derived from sorting and checking. This assessment of disparate facts occurs instantaneously as the broker or salesperson waits for a response. It is the flow of bids and offers in the market that stops the vigilant search and precipitates choice. This "flow" forces decisions about whether to act or not.

At this point, the trader takes a leap, hoping that his interpretation is correct and that a particular bond will respond to the forces as expected. This is the point where most traders acknowledge such non-analytic tools as experience and "feel for the market." The technology of trading changes dramatically at this point. It is less like the continuous processing of information and more like custom craftsmanship. One trader explained, "Experience is the next step. You find over time that each issue trades a bit differently. You can only get it (experience) by being on the desk and trading. Just sitting on the desk and watching trades occur in your own positions. Seeing where they trade."

The uncertainty and ambiguity of the decisions described come from the nature of the information being gathered, the time constraints set by the rapid flow of bids and orders in the market, and the cognitive limits of humans as information processors. The flow of information about the market cannot be fully assimilated. As one trader explained, "The market is a nebulous type of animal that you can't get your arms around. It is always right. It is never wrong. It is something you spend countless hours trying to second guess, trying to interpret." Recruits learn that they must develop "the knack" or fail. Although judgment itself may not be easily taught, the belief in its efficacy has become an important cultural script in the decision process.

Institutional Rules

Recruits to the trading floor seeking extraordinary wealth do not arrive on Wall Street and create the world anew. They arrive to find an established institutional order. This order, most evident in its rules, is the result of traders' habituation to existing strategies, e.g. opportunism and hyper-rationality. These rules have come to have external force in the lives of traders. They are experienced as objective standards of behavior, even though they are derived from habituation to the most salient strategies. The recruit encounters an ordered social world that must be learned before he will be allowed to sit at a trading desk. "The institutions must and do claim authority over the individual, independently of the subjective meanings he may attach to any particular situation."[14] I begin this section with a discussion of the institutional rules on the bond trading floor and then turn to the socialization process through which these rules are learned.

The trading floor, as a social setting, is constituted by both general and specific institutional rules that define the identities of the traders and the patterns of appropriate action. There are historical rules legitimating the form of exchange (over-the-counter), the form of securities being traded (bonds), and the modes of rational calculation employed (yield curves, inflation rates). They reflect not only the local setting but more widely accepted strategies of finance capitalism. These rules are really accounts of how this part of the economic world works.

At deeper and more specific levels, institutional rules define both the identity of individuals and the patterns of appropriate action. They operate as vocabularies of motive, explaining to the trader and others the reasons for action. The institutional rules of the trading floor are, not surprisingly, caricatures of the "spirit of capitalism" identified by Weber.[15] Among the most significant are those relating to self-reliance, risk, and money – key elements in this version of the spirit of capitalism.

Self-reliance

Traders are very clear that they are expected to be self-reliant. "It's a very entrepreneurial business. No one is going to help you make money. They're too busy helping themselves." Traders sitting in a room full of other traders feel atomized and alone. In the words of another trader, "I don't really feel like I can rely on anybody here. *That's the way this business is.* You've got to rely on yourself." Such statements define both actors and action, revealing the rules of the game. They describe an impersonal environment in which trust and cooperation are nearly absent. One of the oldest informants stated, "There is an adversarial relationship in that the trader is not a fraternity type of brother. It is you against him. You would love to make money at his expense and that's all over the Street." In this context, trust is minimal, one's only obligation is to oneself, and opportunism is understood as an appropriate form of action.

Risk

Another institutional rule is that traders should excel at *calculated* risks. Money supplies the incentive, and rationality is the means linking money and risk. "Trading is taking calculated risks using the capital of the firm. We just went to an [Treasury] auction. I spent $200 million on seven year notes. They're ours. I have to do something with them. If I keep them and the market goes down, I've lost money." Traders are aware that the stakes are very high. "There is a high roller mentality ingrained in the job description. There are big dollars on the line." Although such commitments of capital are risky, "with risk comes reward." As another trader puts it, "You are rewarded for the risks you are incurring." Implicit is the understanding that the pursuit of extraordinary wealth requires some worthwhile risk.

At the same time that traders see themselves as risk-seeking, they also see the risk as highly calculated and rational. "You've got to keep your position balanced. You've got to be in a situation so that no one trade can take you out." A trader does not trade randomly; he tries to predict market direction. "You are trying to lower the odds against you. I mean, obviously it's a crap shoot. If we had all the answers we'd all trade our own accounts. You try to get a good feeling for the market." It is a game of chance with an extraordinary incentive to win attached. As one trader explained, "You have to make a rational game out of it." Many of the traders from high status MBA programs grudgingly admire the small but visible group of locally bred risk-takers who seem to balance calculation with risk-taking intuitively: "You have to have a lot of street smarts to do trading, so some of the boys from Brooklyn have done very well for themselves."

Money is everything

It is nearly a cliche to say that the pursuit of money is at the heart of Wall Street culture. As one trader put it, "It's a money business. People are very focused on it and that's across the board." Like self-reliance and calculated risk, heightened materialism is one of the key elements in the contemporary spirit of capitalism. But on the bond trading floor that spirit is magnified and sanctified.

Money is more than just the medium of exchange; it is a measure of one's "winnings." It provides an identity that prevails over charisma, physical attractiveness, or sociability as the arbiter of success and power on the bond trading floor. The top-earning trader is king of the mountain. Consumption is often immediate and conspicuous. A young and aspiring trader explained, "It's about how much you made this year or what you bought with it. How many cars, where you go on vacation, where your apartment is or how big your house is. A lot of money goes into things that are just smoke: clothes, dinners. Nobody knows where it goes. There are a lot of status symbols in this business." This penchant for squandering reinforces the idea that it is not the accumulation of money that is important, but its symbolic ability to convey status. Money defines who you are and what you ought to be doing. Another trader put the rule more succinctly, "Money is everything in this business. Whatever money you make is what you're worth."

Self-reliance, risk-taking, and materialism are part of the culture of entrepreneurship that defines the contemporary spirit of capitalism. But the interpretation on the trading floor seems narrower and more extreme than that which is in general use. Self-reliance is enacted as aggressive opportunism, and calculated risk becomes hyper-rational gaming. These local interpretations or scripts are constructed in the process of interaction by traders and learned during the extended training programs with which every trader begins his career.

The initial socialization experiences of subjects in this study ran from six months to two years. These training programs included a short period of classroom work to learn the technicalities of bond trading, and a much longer period of internship on the floor. During this extended internship the recently graduated MBAs were rotated from desk to desk, mostly doing clerical tasks and trying to fit in. "You were supposed to go around from desk to desk in different departments. If they liked you they would offer you a job. If they didn't they'd send you on your merry way." During this time they are in an extended limbo, having low status, and are not yet guaranteed a space on the trading floor. Trainees are expected to ingratiate themselves with the traders. This "stripping down" of the self, common to a variety of socialization experiences such as boot camp, builds commitment to the role of trader and signals this commitment to others. The trainees are often left to fend for themselves on the trading floor, learning self-reliance. The training program ends when the recruit is awarded a trading desk and the opportunity to succeed or fail. As one recent graduate of such a program explained, the status degradation often continues until the trainee has made his first big win or behaved opportunistically with abandon.[16]

It is during this long internship that trainees become aware of the repertoire of strategies available. They observe senior traders, overhear conversations, and receive explicit communication about what it takes to survive. "You watch the guys around you . . . I got my post-doctorate degree in the bars, mostly after work, hanging around with the older guys, letting them beat me up and tell stories. Then you begin to see how things work." It is during this time that they acquire role-specific vocabularies and tacit knowledge about the rules of self-reliance and risk by which all traders live. Self-reliance and calculated risk are institutional rules that define the relationship of the trader to his actions. Traders can both draw their identity from these rules and define appropriate modes of action.

The significance of socialization in determining trader behavior was confirmed by the few traders in their late thirties and forties I was able to interview. The feeling among these senior traders was that the moral climate had changed. As one trader put it, "The kids coming in now are smarter . . . more educated really, but something's missing." The rapid growth in bond trading created pressure to bring in new recruits. Along with the increased competition among traders, this meant that each recruit received less attention from a senior colleague and the attention he did receive was focused on rapid return on the firm's growing investment.

Structure and Culture

Traders' construction of their culture does not occur in a vacuum. There are important structural conditions that shape traders' strategies and are, in turn, shaped by the continued use of those strategies. These structural conditions are significant characteristics of traders' environments. They are the variables most likely to cause changes in the strategies and rules on the trading floor. In the absence of these conditions, or the presence of others, we should expect to find different strategies and, ultimately, different forms of competitive capitalism.

The structural conditions of opportunism

The key structural conditions underlying the probability of opportunistic action are extraordinary incentives, opportunity, and low levels of informal and formal restraint.

Extraordinary short-term incentives

The compensation system for bond traders is structured by the firm to inspire maximum individual performance. Informants believed that average traders, who were predominantly between 25 and 35 years old, made between $250,000 and $750,000 a year. The best traders were paid into the millions of dollars. More important than the size of these rewards is the fact that bonuses are known to fluctuate widely based on individual contribution to the bottom line. Several older traders pointed out that the association between contributions and rewards was not linear. Some of it was based on what you were paid last year and what it might take to keep you from jumping ship, as well as on profits in the department and the firm. Regardless of the actual explanation for compensation calculations, traders believed that the organization gave them strong incentive to maximize their individual performance through "aggressive" behavior.

Investment banking firms have given their traders unquestionable incentive to maximize personal income and firm profits as quickly as possible. This is heightened by the fact that there is no career ladder for a trader. There are few incentives for loyalty. Informants volunteered that they had no desire to move into management. Managers frequently earn less than their best traders. Traders move easily and frequently to other firms in search of higher rewards. In fact, there is considerable disincentive to delay proving one's financial worth to the firm given the competition for the best trading desk assignments. Failure to compete effectively leads to transfer off the floor or dismissal.

Opportunities for information impactedness

Opportunism requires a situation in which the opportunist has some potential advantage. Most opportunistic actions are based on the opportunity traders have to know more than their exchange partner or to offer incomplete or misleading information to a salesperson or customer. Traders' knowledge of the firm's inventory and of the placement of particular bonds gives them information not generally available in the Street. Like the used car dealer or antiques dealer who can hide the current market value of a commodity from the customer, traders are able to take advantage of their position in the marketplace.

Traders may also use knowledge of a customer's intentions to trade ahead of that customer without the customer knowing. The limited ability of customers to monitor traders' behavior enhances the impactedness of information, even when customers suspect that someone has traded ahead or taken advantage of them. Customers must choose their trading firms based on the firm's reputation and the alternatives available in the market. They are caught between the desire for aggressive agents who offer profit opportunities and the fear that this aggression will shade into opportunism against them. The resolution of this dilemma requires close monitoring of the trading process, which even the institutional investor is not in a position to design or enforce.

Limited informal restraint

Bond trading in this setting requires relatively little cooperative behavior or even interaction between the buyers and the sellers. Traders are anonymous to other professional traders, trading through brokers' brokers. They are buffered from customers by salespeople. There is little sense of obligation in this most fleeting of relationships. Traders talk about trading "for their own account" although it is the firm's money with which they trade. Under these conditions, there is very limited opportunity for restraint based on continuing relationships or trust. In contrast, market makers at the stock exchange and futures markets transact primarily with known participants in daily face-to-face interactive cliques, thereby developing bonds of trust and a reputational network. On the floors of these exchanges the participants constitute a trading community.[17]

Limited formal restraint

The de-regulation movement during the Reagan administration sent clear signals to the financial community about the level of formal restraint from government. Many of the older traders in this study remarked on the changed regulatory environment. Among Reagan's earliest actions was the appointment of John Shad, an executive from the brokerage firm E. F. Hutton rather than a securities lawyer, to head the Securities and Exchange Commission (SEC). Aggressive enforcement at the SEC was reined in.[18] This, in turn, took pressure off the National Association of Securities Dealers (NASD), the self-regulatory association in the bond market studied here. The self-regulatory system is most active in regulating the interface between retail brokers and the general public.[19] It is here that complaints from vulnerable retail clients, or what traders refer to as "widows and orphans," are most likely to attract intervention from Congress and the Securities and Exchange Commission.

The self-regulatory system is more passive and susceptible to politics when regulating the trading floor, an arena where traders trade only with other trading professionals.[20] The system seems to wink at the strategies of opportunism common to the trading floor. The rules of the NASD and the government oversight agencies seemed distant to my informants in the bond market between 1987 and 1989. When

I mentioned them informants were mostly either ignorant or indifferent.[21] The manipulation of the Treasury bond market by traders at Salomon Brothers, discussed in the Introduction, is perhaps the most egregious example of the casual attitude toward self-regulation common on bond trading floors.

This, when combined with the bond trader data presented in this study, suggests a pattern of passive self-regulation and a culture of tolerance that is inadequate to inhibit opportunism on the trading floor. Self-regulation functions as a system of cooperation among firms to maintain a market that offers optimum benefits to the market makers. It has little impact on the day-to-day actions of traders whose opportunism is aimed at other traders and at large financial institutions such as insurance companies and mutual funds. The trading floor is thereby maintained as a stage on which economic man may play his part in a relatively unimpeded fashion and self-interest may be turned to aggressive opportunism.

The structural conditions of hyper-rationality

A rich and continuous flow of information

Trading floors are designed to provide a steady flow of information to the trader in addition to the information he more actively searches out. There are also commercially available predictive models and interpretations by a network of associates. Another source of information for the trader is the continuous and immediate feedback on performance. Traders are provided with a daily profit and loss statement by which they assess their contribution. This feedback is an additional goad to hyper-rationality. The trader is reminded of his progress in the competition for high bonuses. He may also be reminded of specific bonds that are losing value. With computerization of the daily trading record of every trader, short-term profits and losses are closely tracked, visible, and salient.

High outcome uncertainty

The strategy of hyper-rationality is most likely to be employed under conditions of high market volatility. In highly volatile markets price is changing rapidly and in unpredictable directions, a common feature of the bond markets of the late 1980s. Volatility has several consequences. First, traders are uncertain of the appropriate market price for a bond thereby eliciting increased search. Second, bids and offers may disappear at any moment, forcing rapid action. Third, volatility enhances the potential for asymmetric information. Traders with better information, born of exhaustive search or better access, can take advantage of those with less information. The trader must increase his vigilance. Ultimately, the flow of information cannot be assimilated and the direction of the market remains uncertain. Predictive models and expert opinions are not definitive, and traders must make intuitive leaps.

High stakes outcomes

Hyper-rational decision making is most likely when the outcome is highly consequential. Like the fighter pilots and the surgeons to whom my informants compared themselves, bond traders perceive themselves as taking relatively large risks. Despite the fact that they are employees of large investment banks, the hazard is experienced as personal. "I commit my own capital, it's completely my own risk," remarked one trader. The result is exhaustive search behavior that is only interrupted by the unpredictable flow of transactional opportunities that force a rapid choice.

These structural conditions cannot stand alone as explanations of economic action. Actors must create a meaning system of personal strategies and rules. The strategies are themselves embedded in cultural idioms like "entrepreneurship" and "risk-taking" that interact with structural conditions to enable and constrain economic action. The structural conditions and cultural forms identified here are themselves social constructions. They are shaped and reshaped by the creative action of economic actors over time.

Discussion

The analysis of self-interest in this chapter and the scandals in financial markets in recent years suggest that there is a culture of opportunism in the bond market. It seems reasonable to wonder why customers tolerate such opportunism. Why doesn't a market for fair-dealing firms develop? In fact, reputation does operate in the bond market, but to a more limited degree than in the stock and futures markets discussed later in this book. First, in stock and futures markets trading is centralized on a single trading floor, like the New York Stock Exchange or the New York Mercantile Exchange, where market makers transact face to face, day in and day out. The bond market is "over-the-counter," meaning that trading, even among market makers, is over the phone and often buffered through intermediaries. The personal relations so important in reputation are mediated by distance, technology, and the rapid growth in the number of institutional investors.

Second, traders' relations with their firm's customers are mediated through the salesforce. Traders feel little obligation to the customer or the salesperson. Institutional customers are faced with a dilemma in that it is the most "aggressive" firms, like Salomon Brothers and Drexel Burnham, that also provide the deepest markets and the greatest profit opportunities. In most bond markets, the number of primary dealers is limited and dominated by a few. While reputation is important, reputation for providing profit opportunities may take precedence over reputation for opportunism, especially if the uncertain cost of opportunism is less than the presumed or real profit opportunities afforded by a relationship with a top firm. Finally, traders and salespeople reported that institutional customers expect traders to use opportunistic strategies, but could not predict which of the many transactions conducted would involve opportunistic strategies. Even after Salomon Brothers admitted manipulating the Treasury securities market, most of their customers continued to trade government securities with them.

Bond traders in Wall Street investment banks in the 1980s produced their own version of *Homo economicus*. He was hyper-rational, highly self-interested and relatively free of social control as he traded in the debt of corporations and governments. More specifically, he engaged in both opportunistic and hyper-rational strategies and was guided by rules of self-reliance, calculated risk, and extreme materialism. These characteristics are products of a unique environment in which new entrants to the labor force soon find themselves trading in millions of dollars of government or corporate debt. Tom Wolfe captured the ego inflation and cockiness inherent in this situation in his novel, *Bonfire of the Vanities*, referring to bond traders at investment banks as "masters of the universe."

But this version of *Homo economicus* is not universal. While most economic actors exist in dense webs of trust, obligation, and reputation, investment banks in the 1980s constructed an environment with minimal interdependence, extraordinary incentives for self-interest and limited constraints on behavior: a poor prescription for a legitimate or stable economic system. Other financial markets that had high historic levels of opportunism responded by constructing systems of restraint.

Notes

1   Because I was accustomed to teaching women MBAs, it was surprising to see that there are still occupations, even in major banks, where women are so under-represented. Male pronouns are used to maintain realism.
2   C. Geertz, *The Interpretation of Cultures* (New York: Basic Books, 1973), p. 433.
3   M. Lewis, *Liar's Poker: Rising through the Wreckage on Wall Street* (New York: Norton, 1989), p. 34.
4   See Oliver Williamson, *Markets and Hierarchies* (New York: Free Press, 1975); Williamson, *The Economic Institutions of Capitalism* (New York: Free Press, 1985); A. Sen, "Rational Fools," *Philosophy and Public Affairs* 6 (1977), pp. 317–34; T. Scitovsky, *The Joyless Economy* (New York: Oxford, 1976); H. Leibenstein, "Allocative Efficiency vs. 'X-Efficiency,'" *American Economic Review* 56 (1966), pp. 392–415.
5   See H. Simon, *Administrative Behavior*, 3rd ed. (New York: Free Press, 1976); J. March and H. Simon, *Organizations* (New York: Wiley, 1958); J. March and J. Olsen, *Ambiguity and Choice in Organizations* (Bergen, Norway: Universitetsforlaget, 1976); and A. Etzioni, *The Moral Dimension: Toward a New Economics* (New York: Free Press, 1988).
6   A. Tversky and D. Kahneman, "Judgment under Uncertainty," *Science* 185 (27 September 1974), pp. 1124–31.
7   Sen, "Rational Fools."
8   R. Thaler, *The Winner's Curse* (New York: Free Press, 1992).
9   J. M. Keynes, *The General Theory of Employment, Interest, and Money* (New York: Harcourt, Brace, 1964), p. 154.
10   For a model of how this works, see H. White, "Where Do Markets Come From?," *American Journal of Sociology* 87 (March 1981), pp. 517–47.
11   For a discussion of establishing value in other markets, see C. W. Smith, *Auctions: The Social Construction of Value* (Berkeley, CA: University of California Press), 1989.
12   Jerome Bruner, *On Knowing* (Cambridge, MA: Harvard University Press, 1962).
13   M. Polanyi, *Personal Knowledge* (Chicago, IL: University of Chicago Press, 1958).
14   P. L. Berger and T. Luckmann, *The Social Construction of Reality: A Treatise in the Sociology of Knowledge* (New York: Anchor Books, 1966), p. 62.
15   Max Weber, *The Protestant Ethic and the Spirit of Capitalism*, trans. Talcott Parsons (New York: Charles Scribner's, 1958). The spirit of capitalism may be thought of as a typification of the strategies of the early Calvinists. These Calvinists would likely be shocked by the behavior of the bond traders, particularly their materialism.
16   Lewis, *Liar's Poker*.
17   W. Baker, "The Social Structure of a National Securities Market," *American Journal of Sociology* 89 (January 1984), pp. 775–811; and M. Y. Abolafia, "Self-Regulation as

Market Maintenance," in R. Noll (ed.), *Regulatory Policy and the Social Sciences*, (Berkeley: University of California Press, 1985).

18   D. A. Vise and S. Coll, *Eagle on the Street* (New York: Charles Scribner's, 1991).

19   D. P. McCaffrey and S. Faerman, "Shared Regulation in the United States Securities Industry," *Administration and Society* 26 (August 1994), pp. 204–35.

20   Abolafia, "Self-Regulation."

21   In contrast, a study of specialists on the floor of the New York Stock Exchange found that the specialists were conscious of regulation, easily citing three regulations that constrained their trading on a daily basis.

7 Auctions: The Social Construction of Value

Charles Smith

The Search for a Fair Price

To many people, including most economists, the idea that auctions function to establish a "fair" price is incontrovertible; by their definition, the auction price is both correct and fair since it is the price at which market supply and demand curves cross. This particular view of fair value, however, only has meaning within the economic paradigm. "Fairness" for most people connotes something more; it implies a governing principle of legitimacy grounded within the community. It is not merely the product of rational individual decision makers, it is a social goal.

Social goals and norms are not part of the economic model. The only pertinent rules are those contractually accepted by individuals to serve their own self-interests; rational self-interest not only explains what people do but what they should do. According to the broader sociological view, this is not the way things happen. Practices are judged proper insofar as they conform to communal standards rather than rationally calculated individual self-interest. Auction practices are no exception. Fairness is not an unintended consequence of numerous individual auction decisions, but it is an explicit, if not always conscious, objective of the auction community.

Although legitimacy is a central concern of all auctions, both its form and means of implementation vary depending on the structure of the community. Of decisive importance is the relative cohesiveness of the auction community; the more cohesive the community, the less manifest the concern for legitimacy. The reason for this is that legitimacy and community are not only mutually dependent upon each other, but given their intrinsic connection, substitutive for each other. The more salient the one, the less pressing the explicit need for the other. When the sense of community is strong and decisions are seen as embodying communal judgment, the question of the legitimacy of the decision generally does not explicitly arise because it is implicitly assumed. In relatively tight communities, such as those found in most commodity-exchange auctions, for example, the members feel no need to justify the price or the allocation of goods. The fact that it is an exchange decision is sufficient. The legitimacy of the price is taken for granted.

When the sense of community is diffuse, however, there is commonly a felt need for explicit rules and regulations in whose terms auction decisions can be judged.[1] Participants are more apprehensive and seek greater assurance that auction determinations are properly and fairly executed. The auction itself, rather than the community that supports it, becomes the perceived means for establishing legitimacy. This is most commonly the case in sales auctions in which the sense of community

Original publication: Chapter 4 of Smith, Charles, *Auctions: The Social Construction of Value* (Free Press, New York, 1989).

tends to be most attenuated because of the relatively high percent of nonprofessional participants and fewer extra-auction business ties among the professionals who do attend. At a typical summer weekend country auction in New England, over half those in attendance are likely to be tourists and another quarter nonprofessional locals. Most of the collectors and dealers will know each other from past auctions, but few will have had specific business relationships with each other. Everyone will be monitoring what happens to ensure that all rules are followed.

Further support for the inverse relationship between community cohesiveness and concern with legitimacy is offered by dealer-dominated auctions. The more closed to outside buyers a dealer-dominated auction is, the more it operates like an exchange auction; the more open it is, the more it resembles a sales auction. While dealers attending a jewelry auction in a suite at the Waldorf-Astoria accept their mutual evaluations without question, a jewelry auction at Doyle's or Christie's requires estimates and extensive information on size and quality of the stones. Similarly when third parties – individuals who do not actively participate in an auction but have some economic, legal, or fiduciary interest in the process – are significant to an auction, be it a publisher critiquing the performance of a subsidiary rights manager, a bank officer reevaluating repossession practices, or a judge reviewing an estate liquidation, legitimacy concerns tend to increase as compared to similar auctions without third parties.

Auctions of subsidiary rights of literary works, for example, are normally confined to a tight-knit group of rights managers and editors. The primary purpose of such auctions is to ensure that everyone in the community has an equal opportunity to acquire these rights. There is also a desire to establish a consensual evaluation, especially when the author has no established track record. (The subsidiary rights of established authors are more often sold privately, since there is often a communal understanding, if not a legally binding contract, that the previous purchaser of this author's subsidiary rights has an option on such future rights.)

While such auctions satisfy the need to ascertain value and allow equal access to all, these are not always their most important function. In many cases, there is a high degree of consensus regarding the value of the property; in other cases, there may be little or no interest in the work; while in yet other cases, the rights may have been sold informally based on a special relationship between editors. Nevertheless, an auction will be held. In part, this posturing serves to ensure that communal rights are maintained even though no one seems interested in exerting them. Often more important is the need to legitimate the price and choice of paperback publisher to the author, the author's agent, and even the directors of the buying and selling publishing houses.

The rights managers and editors seldom have a need for such justification. The determination of the final price as well as the eventual purchaser of the subsidiary rights is accepted as fair by those involved insofar as it reflects their communal judgment as ratified by auction. Participants in such auctions often discuss whether the price was high or low, whether one house or another would have been better for the book, whether one assessed the dynamics accurately, but they don't normally talk about whether it was fair. Having followed their own established procedures for making such decisions, they accept the decision as reflecting their best collective judgment. The auction is valued as a means for verifying this consensus.

Authors, literary agents, and publishing executives do not usually participate directly in either the pricing or allocation of subsidiary rights. They are not part of that literary community and consequently not ready to trust its decisions. But they do trust the auction process. Even if the price realized through the auction proves to have been low – the book becomes a best-seller – the publisher is not likely to blame the rights director providing he or she went through the proper auction procedures. Even if the auction produced only one bidder, the publisher can defend the legitimacy of the transaction. "An auction was held and that was the top price." Authors and literary agents usually accept this view.

Third parties accept auctions as means for establishing a legitimate price rather than merely as reflecting a communal judgment in other auctions. In New York as in a number of other cities, if an automobile gets a sufficient number of parking tickets that are not paid, a default judgment may be made against the car. When this happens, a city marshal can take possession of the car and tow it away if he or she can find it. There are a number of marshals who, working from lists of default cars, with addresses, will scour different neighborhoods looking for cars, especially late-model expensive cars, with numerous tickets. Once such a car is spotted, the marshal will call a tow-truck operator who will pull the car in; most marshals work with specific tow-truck operators. The city runs a similar, though less picky, operation of its own. Once a car is taken, the owner is informed and given the opportunity to pay the fines plus the towing and storage fees to reacquire the car. If the owner fails to do this, the car can be auctioned to pay off the charges. In either case, the marshal gets a percentage of the moneys, and the tow operator gets his towing and storage fees. The city meanwhile gets its fines paid. (Sometimes, especially with older cars with many fines, there may not be enough money to cover all of these charges. In these cases, it is usually the city that ends up not getting its full share.)

In a given week in New York City, there will be an average of six such auctions. Most buyers tend to be mechanics and persons interested in using the cars as sources of auto parts; there are also small dealers who buy and sell inexpensive cars and trucks. There are also a good number of persons interested in buying one of the better cars for themselves. While prices can vary considerably, most cars sell for less than they could be bought for elsewhere. In fact, it is probable that more money would be realized if the garage–tow-truck owner were allowed to set a price on each car and to sell it off by private treaty. Clearly other considerations are involved. As a major tow-truck operator revealed:

> Sure, the city would probably end up with ten to fifteen percent more if the cars were sold one on one. But you couldn't do it. There'd be too many problems. There are a lot of regulars here. If I sold a car to one guy, another guy might come in the next day and say "Hey, I hear you've got a 1983 red Caddie." I'd answer "No more. Vinie bought it yesterday." Right away he would start to bitch. "What did you sell it to him for?" "A grand." "A grand?" he'd answer. "Hell, I would have given you that much. You know I have a thing for Caddies. It's not right, you should have given me a call."
>
> It is just not worth it. The next thing, someone from downtown would be calling to find out if there was monkey business going on and if I was selling cars for less than they were worth.

The quote reveals some of the subtle differences in the attitudes of the various participants. The garage owner clearly feels that there is a sufficient consensus among dealers and mechanics to enable him to determine a reasonable price on most cars. He isn't concerned that dealers will complain about the prices he would set, but about being denied access to cars they might fancy. On the other hand, he sees the auction as protecting him from accusations of unfair pricing from government officials responsible for impounding the cars to pay off tickets. Concern with legitimacy is seen as coming from auction outsiders, "someone downtown"; the regulars are perceived as interested in maintaining their communal rights. The auction achieves both ends.

Bank-automobile-repossession auctions serve a similar purpose, though the participants are slightly different. The bank takes possession of the car in an attempt to recapture the money owed on an unpaid loan. The cars in repossession auctions tend to be newer, with the result that more of the buyers are private individuals looking for a personal car; there are fewer auto strippers – mechanics and dealers interested in the cars for their parts – than at police auctions. The dealers present are primarily interested in buying the most expensive cars for resale. Often they have come to buy one or two specific cars that have been advertised. This mix of buyers is much less cohesive than that found at most police auctions. The auctioneer, consequently, spends more time attempting to establish a sense of trust. The rules are more explicitly stated; often there is a printed copy of the rules.[2]

Because the cars are newer, the auctioneer, dealers, and banks actually have a more specific idea of the value of each car. Most of the buyers, in contrast, being non-professionals and not part of any community of buyers tend to be highly uncertain of the value of the cars. Such a situation would seem to favor a system whereby the banks in collaboration with dealers and auctioneers would simply set minimum prices for all cars. Nevertheless, banks still favor auctioning repossessed cars because the process insulates them from disgruntled ex-owners. As an auctioneer who sells these automobiles almost exclusively puts it:

> The banks could probably get more money for their cars if they sold them privately through a dealer, but then they would be exposing themselves for all sorts of trouble. Here they pick up a year-old Buick with an outstanding loan of seven thousand bucks. The blue-book value on the car is eleven thousand, but that is a retail price. There is no way that a dealer will give more than eight and a half grand for that car. At auction it may bring only seven and a half. If the bank takes the eight and a half, however, the guy who they took the car from will start to bitch that the bank did him out of two and a half grand because the blue-book value of the car is eleven thousand dollars. If he takes the bank to court, they may have a hell of a time convincing the judge that they really got the best price, especially if they have regular dealings with this dealer. If they auction it, they have no problems. They simply tell the judge that they put the car up for auction with a recognized auctioneer who advertised the auction, and that is the price that the car brought.

In both types of car auctions there is no question on the part of most participants that the cars are worth more than they will bring at auction. The auction is not seen as maximizing the return. The sense of legitimacy attributed to the price in each case, therefore, is clearly not due to the fact that the auction reveals the true economic value of the cars. Rather the legitimacy in each case is due to the public manner in which the price is determined. The price is legitimized by the community of active participants much as punishment is legitimized by a jury.[3]

The similarity between auctions and juries runs deep. In both situations there is a properly constituted group that has the ability to establish communal guidelines and to determine a final outcome be it a price or a sentence. An especially revealing story that illustrates the commonalities between the auction and the jury is told by auctioneer Tom Caldwell:

> One day Tom's father received a call from a judge he knew. The judge had been presiding over a divorce case involving one of the richest men in town, who was married to a woman of considerable wealth in her own right. The divorce proceedings had moved ahead quite easily until it had come to the division of the joint property. It had been agreed to divide the property evenly, but all attempts to work out an equitable division had failed. The judge had brought in a whole range of different experts to value this and that, but sooner or later both husband and wife refused to accept the evaluations offered by the various experts. Only they knew the true value of what they owned, and they couldn't agree.
>
> The judge proposed that Tom's father hold a two-person auction at which he would auction off everything they jointly owned, and when it was over they could settle up the difference. If one bought $10,000 more worth of goods in the auction than the other, that person would have to give the other $5,000 to even things out. Everyone agreed to this plan and the next week, after going through all the items as he would have in a normal sale, Tom's father set up his stand in the courtroom and proceeded to auction off the joint property. It took the whole day, but the commission was sizable. The auction had been used to establish fair prices when the distrust of the people involved made other more established means for assigning value unacceptable. What is particularly poignant about this particular auction is that it functioned as a marriage substitute, enabling the couple to reclaim their ability to make mutually acceptable joint decisions in order to dissolve their marriage.

In most marriages or families, if disagreement or simple uncertainty regarding the value of some item occurs, the interested parties will normally discuss the matter. In effect, this means that a joint effort to define the item correctly and from this definition to deduce its value is being made by all interested participants. If this cannot be done, due to a failure to agree on criteria of value or a lack of trust, outside experts are likely to be called in.[4] In the case of a divorce, signifying the breakdown of the family and hence normally the end of the family consensual base, reliance on outside experts to resolve disagreements and uncertainties is common. Tom Caldwell's story is so arresting because even though the divorcing couple has elected to dissolve their own particular "community," that is, their marriage, they will only accept this community's (their own) judgment regarding the value of their joint property. They rely on the judgment of exactly the community they are dissolving. It is nevertheless a communal judgment on which they are willing to rely rather than their individual self-interests, which are seen as suspect.

If the purpose of the auction were to reveal the "true" value of each item, there would be no need to restrict the auction to the couple. The more interested parties the better for arriving at an objective estimation of value. If, on the other hand, the auction served only to reveal the particular subjective value of the items to each of them, it could not work, since many items with a high market value might go for relatively little (if only one of the two were interested in it) providing grounds for later controversy and thereby further complicating the final division of goods.

The success of this auction was that it revealed the value of items as they related to the two of them as a couple. In the case of some items, one or the other of them drove the price up even though they had no interest in the item. They did so knowing that the other really wanted it. In other cases, items went for a tenth of what they were worth. It is important to realize that while this process clearly was influenced by the preferences of the parties involved, the prices reached did not reflect these preferences in any logical way. The prices rather revealed the complex joint values of the items in question, determined by the couple's collective evaluation. This collective evaluation was not a simple composite of their individual evaluations, but a unique product of their respective evaluations and expectations concerning each other. The final evaluation and outcome was not an aggregate phenomenon but a product of their psychological and social interaction.

The above example demonstrates that auctions are capable of generating a sense of legitimacy normally associated with collective decisions, even when those participating in the auction may not feel as if they are part of a communal process. Admittedly, in many auctions, including most exchange auctions, the legitimacy of auction determinations is quite clearly linked to an explicit awareness that such decisions reflect the consensus of the group. In others, including not only the couple just described but most sales auctions, acceptance is dependent on following auction procedures. Participants accept as fair the highest bid for a specific item, be it a horse or painting, often unaware of its consensual character. To them it is simply the winning bid according to the auction rules. The fact that these procedures have become institutionalized specifically because they insure that the decision will be a consensual decision is often not realized. It is a case of people believing in specific rules even though they no longer grasp the reason for the rules. The more manifest the community, the more likely its decision will be accepted at face value. The more attenuated the community, the more likely the need to establish the legitimacy of the auction process separately.

Despite these differences, there are also similarities in the way participants interrelate within both types of auctions. In both cases, there tends to be a high degree of apprehension associated with the interpersonal relationships. In sales auctions, this apprehension is commonly due to ignorance about the intentions and resources of other participants. In exchange auctions and other auctions where there exists a cohesive community, the anxiety is linked to the awareness that while the members of the exchange are united in certain respects, they are also in direct competition with each other. Trust is consequently always limited. Participants may be willing to take each other's word, but they would prefer it if the word was spoken publicly. It is such interpersonal uncertainty – as much as uncertainty of value, price, and allocation – that promotes and supports auctions.

This uncertainty is reflected in the response of the director of a major art museum when questioned about the relative value of auctions as compared to private transactions in acquiring and dispersing museum works. He said that while he had made and would continue to make selective purchases for the museum at auctions, he normally sold museum property privately. He admitted that auctions could bring very high prices for some items, but that he dealt almost exclusively with items of known value and in such situations auctions tended to bring slightly less than he could arrange privately. It was specifically because the types of items he was interested in tended to bring slightly lower prices at auction that he would buy at auctions.[5] The only exceptions to this policy were situations when he had to sell through an auction for interpersonal rasons:

> Some years ago I discovered that we were overloaded with paintings by a good but fairly minor late-nineteenth-century painter. I, with my board's approval, elected to sell half of our holdings. I knew a very reputable dealer who was interested in this man's work and felt I could get top dollar from him for two of the paintings. For the third, I had arranged an exchange with another museum.
>
> Unfortunately, in the middle of my negotiations, I received a telephone call from the son of the gentleman who had originally donated the painting to the museum. In discussing the matter with him, he became very upset, not with the fact that we were going to sell the painting, but with the price I had negotiated. He felt that the painting was worth considerably more and ever so gently questioned my relationship with this particular dealer. I called the dealer as soon as I hung up and withdrew the painting. Next, I called Sotheby's and arranged to have the painting auctioned. It was sold three months later for significantly less than I had been offered by, I believe, the same dealer. There was no way I was going to get involved in that sort of mess. Since then, I have probably sold a half dozen objects at auction and all but one were sold that way for the same reason. Someone, somewhere was questioning the legitimacy of a private sale I had arranged.[6]

In auctioning a particular painting this museum director sought to legitimate and justify the transaction to a donor's son, an outside interested party. He knew the auction process would protect him from the ire and criticism of the donor's son much in the same way that the subsidiary rights director was able to protect herself from the ire and criticism of her publisher. The rights director, however, chose the auction mode not only to protect herself from her boss, but to maintain group cohesiveness by ensuring access for all, and to resolve any uncertainty surrounding the value of the particular rights being offered. If not for the donor's son, the museum director would probably have arranged a private sale because he felt that the value of the painting was known. It was this interpersonal uncertainty rather than value uncertainty which required the legitimating powers of an auction.

The legitimating power of auctions is evidenced in other situations, including charity auctions. It is specifically the ability of auctions to legitimate prices that explains their popularity at charity functions. As in the museum director case, fairness in most charity auctions is more tied up with interpersonal relationships than the items themselves. The question often is not what a particular item should sell for, but rather how much should different individuals pay. In these cases, it is often third parties who use the auction format to legitimate their price to the actual bidders rather than vice versa. Where the museum director used the auction to justify the price he received for the painting to the donor's son, the members of charitable groups often use the format to legitimate the comparatively inflated prices they expect from donors. Not only can they urge prospective bidders on, they can join in the bidding themselves, simultaneously raising and legitimating the higher price.[7] Just the fact that someone else made a ninety-five-dollar bid can be used to justify a hundred-dollar bid.

An important ramification of this process is that it serves to produce self-legitimation. If one buys through an auction, one can always rationalize a high price by observing that others were willing to pay almost as much. The same justification can be made selling through an auction; the price may be low, but that was all that anyone would offer. Even such self-legitimation is grounded in a social context, since the process is totally dependent on the social interactions intrinsic to the auction and cannot be explained in terms of individual self-interest or rationality.

This need to establish the legitimacy of price and allocation informs auctions from top to bottom. The significance of fairness is surprising given the common belief that auctions are places where the buyer must beware. In reality, the buyer probably is better protected at most auctions than in many department stores, to say nothing of most flea markets. The continual warnings associated with auctions are, in fact, often the result of attempts on the part of auctioneers to ensure that the highest degree of fairness will be attained.

The effort to ensure that the price paid is fair starts before the auction actually begins. In nearly all auctions, items are sold under strict conditions concerning faults, returns, and refunds. In most cases things are sold "as is." In most commodity-exchange auctions this fact is simply assumed; it doesn't have to be spelled out because everyone knows the rules. In sale and dealer auctions, where such knowledge of rules and practices cannot be assumed, it is presented continually in various ways. They are not only printed in the catalogue but announced at the beginning of most auctions and at regular intervals. There is, in addition, generally a preview where the items can be inspected. Despite all these safeguards, most professional auctioneers will ensure that items are held and shown with defects apparent and will more often than not indicate the defect before starting the bidding. If it is a car auction, liens and known defects will be announced. At horse auctions, a special light on the tote board, where the bids are shown, flashes on to indicate whether the horse is a "cribber,"[8] while past operations, broken bones, bleeding, and other illnesses are announced. Even at Luther's – where the sums of money tend to be minimal – the rabbit's blind eye and the pony's skin rash are noted. Admittedly, some things may not be noticed or reported, but such omissions are more the exception than the rule.

The extent to which the search for a "fair" price governs most auctions is revealed by a number of other practices. Despite the rule that all items are sold as is, and the previews scheduled before the auction, if a bidder changes his or her mind immediately after purchasing an item because the item isn't what he or she thought it was (or it is more damaged), most auctioneers will take it back. (Such a situation is only likely to occur in sales or dealer auctions and is unlikely to involve a regular. If it does, the auctioneer is not as likely to be so understanding.) The auctioneer may refuse to accept a bid from that person for the rest of the auction, but he will nevertheless normally take back the item. In short, professional auctioneers are seldom guilty of the type of "sharp" practices that are commonly attributed to them.

To say that auctioneers are not generally guilty of sharp practices does not mean that such practices do not occur. More often than not, however, the guilty party/parties (normally such sharp practices are carried out by teams) are sellers and buyers.[9] Perhaps the most common practice of this sort is "pool" buying by dealer rings noted earlier, in which a number of dealers agree that they will not bid against each other. In this way they hope to keep the bid down. Afterwards they hold a private auction among themselves, with the difference between the price paid at the formal auction and the price finally paid in their private auction divided among the pool members. Here again, however, we find a situation in which an apparent breach of a principle proves otherwise.

At one level, pools would seem to be a violation of fairness. By refusing to bid against each other the members of the pool are supporting a practice that would seemingly lead to unfairly low prices. Auctioneers obviously do not commonly approve of this type of activity. On the other hand, they often tolerate it, providing the item is sold at a price that the auctioneer feels is fair. This may seem to be an impossibility by definition. How can such pools and fair prices exist side by side?

The apparent paradox rests on the fact that in such situations we are often dealing with both an established community and outsiders. If the price set by the pool is seen to be a fair dealer's price, and the number of outsiders is few and they are not regulars, an auctioneer is unlikely to make a big fuss. Most of the items are going to be bought by the dealers, and provided they give the auctioneer their fair price, he or she will not complain. A private agreement between a few dealers, in fact, may be experienced as less disturbing than a bidding war among two or three dealers, which results in a highly inflated final price for one item, which serves in turn to make other items seem underpriced.[10]

Moreover, an auctioneer may actually make use of such a pool to get rid of some items that would otherwise be difficult to sell. He or she may actually address the members of the pool directly and ask them to buy the item. "Hey, come on guys. You know this is worth more than I have here. One of you give me a bid and take it off my hands." If the auctioneer has treated the pool fairly, more often than not they will cooperate when so propositioned.

Sometimes when nearly all the buyers are dealers, "agreements" among buyers are sufficiently open and spontaneous that it is questionable if they really constitute a pool, even when items bought at the auction may be exchanged and resold afterwards. In some midrange jewelry auctions, for example, which are often held in hotel suites and attended only by dealers, it is not unusual for the auctioneer to suggest a single bid and have it met by one or another dealer with no other bids. Dealers openly remark to one another, "I know, you like that sort of stuff. Remember though, the next item is mine." On the other hand, one dealer may approach another after the auction and purchase the item at a price that gives the first buyer a small profit. If questioned about the equity of such actions, these dealers would be taken aback. As one commented:

> I'm not sure I know what you mean. We know what the items are worth and we are paying good money for these items. No one is going to steal anything here. We won't let anyone do it, and even if we wanted to the auctioneer wouldn't let us. He has his own responsibilities. On the other hand, we aren't going to run the price up on an item just because two of us like it.

In more open auctions, such cooperation is not as spontaneous. Pools, when they exist, tend to be more formally organized. The particular form of the pool can vary. It can be organized as either a round robin, where the payoff is equal for all members, or an English knockout where payoff is proportional to bids made in the knockout auction. This difference has nothing to do with the relationship of the pool to the formal auction. It is a purely internal matter and is a reflection of the inverse relationship between group cohesiveness and the need for explicit rules to ensure legitimacy. When the members of the pool constitute a strong community with a high degree of mutual trust, most are willing to use the round-robin method, which assumes equality of members. When the pool is less cohesive there is more likely to be a move on the part of some members to use the English knockout, where the rules explicitly recognize differences in the members' bids in the distribution of profits.

Provided pools function to ensure stable prices within an acceptable range, they tend not only to be tolerated but are often quite inconspicuous. Things get slightly more complicated when there is a sizable group of outsiders and the pool acts to inhibit the emergence of a new consensus. In these cases auctioneers may become more than a little testy, no matter how well they know the members of the pool.

The acceptance-nonacceptance of auction rings, both formal and informal, is just one example of the various types of accommodations and adjustments common to auctions. The social flux and context of auctions requires flexibility from its participants. In practice, different types of auctions give assorted advantages to distinct players. Sometimes the auctioneer is allowed to maintain a reserve against which he or she may bid, which normally favors sellers. Sometimes sellers and buyers are permitted to enter into such preauction arrangements as the use of floor bids in publishing or similar agreements in which buyer and seller negotiate a price subject to modification in the auction. Sometimes sellers are able to withdraw their goods after the auction is over such as the right of fishermen to take back their entire catch if they feel the total price received for the catch is too low. Varied situations require giving the parties different handicaps if a "legitimate" price is to be determined; no single set of rules can do this in all situations. Nowhere is this better demonstrated than in the way split bids – that is, bids that offer a smaller increase over the last one than normal or requested by the auctioneer – are handled.[11]

Split bids force auctioneers to earn their keep. Judging the acceptability of a bid lower than what was called for presents two potentially conflicting principles: On the one hand, it is the auctioneer's responsibility to get the most he or she can for any item; even if the split bid offers less than was requested, it is higher. If no other bids are forthcoming, it may well be the highest bid. On the other hand, it is the auctioneer's responsibility to run an orderly auction in which everyone feels fairly treated; this generally entails the use of standard increments, since a bidder who has been required to increase the bid by one hundred dollars in order to acquire the bid will feel cheated if another bidder is able to take the bid back with an increase of only ten dollars. The specific increments used vary from auction to auction, but the common practice is to use increments of between 5 and 10 percent of the last bid, adjusting such increments to "round" figures.[12] These percentages will vary at very low and very high prices, with larger increases normal in the former and smaller percentage increases in the latter.

The bidding on an antique chest of drawers at Sotheby's, New York, for example, could well go as follows: "Will someone start it off at $2,000? $2,000? $1,800? $1,500? $1,300? I have a bid of $1,200. Will someone say 1,300? I have 1,300! 1,400?" The bids may then go 1,500, 1,600, 1,700, 1,800, 1,900, 2,000 but then jump to increments of 200: 2,200, 2,400, 2,600, 2,800, 3,000.[13] If the bidding is brisk, the increments may be jumped more rapidly. The following sequence of bids on a yearling colt at a Keeneland select sale is an example of this. "$100,000, I have 100,000! 120,000! 130,000! I have 140,000 out back, and 150,000! Will you give 175? 175! 200? 200! 250? Will you give me 250?"

With used cars, bric-a-brac, jewelry, and real estate, the rhythm is very similar. The question is what happens if someone offers $145,000, $142,000, or $141,000 when the auctioneer is asking for $150,000? There is no fast rule on this; it will depend on the type of auction, whose bid it is, where in the bidding the split bid occurs, and the particular mood and judgment of the auctioneer at that moment. In some cases, the auctioneer him- or herself may introduce such a bid. Having increased the bid by increments of a thousand dollars, for example, an auctioneer may ask for an increase of only five hundred dollars if he or she cannot get a thousand and the bidding has dried up. In nearly all cases, however, the practice selected appears to make the process fairer to all concerned.

In commodity-exchange auctions, for example, where split bids are so common as to be the norm rather than the exception, they provide the fine tuning required to ensure that goods are allocated in accordance with communal needs. Since all buyers end up paying the same price, such bids do not serve to give one buyer an advantage over another. They may serve to benefit the sellers somewhat, but given the overall disadvantage of sellers in most commodity-exchange auctions, this is not considered unfair. On the other hand, it is sometimes difficult to label a bid as a split bid in such auctions even if it is technically less than would be expected, because normal increments tend to be quite small. The bids on many commodities increase by a cent or less per bid.

This, of course, is not the case when dealing with prize livestock, be it an Angus bull or a thoroughbred yearling colt. In these cases, the increments may be sizable. Although such commodity auctions are more correctly seen as sales auctions rather than exchange auctions, split bids will in most cases also be accepted. The bidding at Keeneland, for example, may commonly drop to the minimum thousand-dollar increment[14] after reaching a quarter of a million dollars by jumps of twenty-five thousand dollars. The auctioneer may take the opportunity to poke fun at a bidder making such a bid, but he will take it. "Oh, come on now. What are you doing to me? You're offering me a thousand more? Daddy told me there'd be days like this. Okay, I've got 251,000, anyone offer me 275,000? I'll take 260 if it will make it any easier on anybody." This is not likely to happen at Sotheby's or Christie's, or any other major art-antique auction house. The response is much more likely to be, "The bid is $250,000. Will anyone say 260?"

This does not mean that split bids are never accepted at Sotheby's or Christie's. A half bid, that is, an increment of $5,000 when a $10,000 was requested, which still represents a 5 percent increase will normally be taken if the auctioneer feels that the bidding is reaching its upper limits. A $1,000 increment to a $300,000 bid, however, would not be accepted. In this respect, Sotheby's and Christie's are more representative of auctions in general than are Keeneland and Fasig-Tipton. Even at the end, Sotheby's and Christie's are not likely to take increments of less than 5 percent, whereas many smaller art and antique, "country," estate, and liquidation auctions will.

In many instances these differences seem to be a matter of past practices and tradition. Horse auctioneers often say that though they don't like taking split bids, they have always been allowed – providing they meet the minimum – in horse auctions. Liquidation auctioneers describe their auctions as similar in this respect. In contrast, auctioneers for Sotheby's, Christie's, and other high-market art-antique auction houses have indicated that such bids are demeaning to the whole process and have traditionally been avoided.

While tradition and related practices clearly are significant in determining what is acceptable – the practice of accepting split bids in select livestock auctions is in part a carryover from the more conventional agricultural commodity auctions – there are other factors at work. Horse auctioneers, for example, will commonly add that their job is to get the most they can even if it is only another thousand dollars on a quarter of a million. In contrast, art-antique auctioneers, especially at the more select houses, defend their policy of not taking split bids by arguing that it would not be fair to the other buyers who have been playing by the "rules."[15]

The policy of attempting to get the last dollar in auctions of prize livestock, even at the risk of irritating buyers who may feel that they are being nickled and dimed by the process, is not surprising when it is remembered that these auctions are organized and run primarily by the sellers. Keeneland and Fasig-Tipton are sales organizations. The same thing can be said for many liquidation, estate auctions, and most real estate auctions, which are also organized to benefit the seller. In some cases, such as farm liquidations, there may be additional communal sympathy for the seller. In these situations, anything which can bring in a little more for the seller is legitimate and tolerated by the auction community.

In contrast to these auctions, the dominant community in most collectible/dealer auctions is constituted by the buyers. This is also often the case in regular liquidation and estate auctions run by an auctioneer with a significant following of professional buyers. The same can be said for many if not most mid-range art and antique auctions. It is the community of dealers and collectors that makes these auctions possible. The sellers tend to be liquidating individual holdings and are unrelated to each other. They tend to be neither auction regulars nor well known to the auctioneer.

The buyers, in contrast, are regulars and are known. They have their own rules that govern who gets what. To allow one of them, much worse an outsider, to "steal" a particular item with a split bid is seen as illegitimate. In addition, such bids introduce an element of haggling that can work to the detriment of the auctioneer. They not only can serve to "cheapen" the process but can take a good deal of time for little substantial increase. In these cases split bids serve the interests of neither the auctioneer nor the more important members of the auction community. It is not surprising, consequently, that they are seldom tolerated.

There are, of course, always exceptions. Auctioneers will themselves sometimes ask for a split bid toward the apparent end of a bidding sequence. This is quite common when the increments have been substantial but are petering out and the auctioneer believes a drop in increments may help extend the bidding. There are other times when a sensitive auctioneer will keep the increments below their normal level because he or she senses that bidding may cease if the increments are jumped in a normal fashion.

In the case of John Lennon's Rolls-Royce, at two hundred thousand dollars, when the increment would normally have jumped from ten thousand dollars to twenty-five thousand, it was decided to stick with the ten-thousand-dollar increment. This remained the increment all the way up to the final bid of two million three hundred thousand dollars. Under normal conditions the increments would have been minimally a hundred thousand dollars.[16]

To summarize, split bids are routinely accepted in commodity-exchange auctions, but the small increments common to these auctions, coupled with the fact that all buyers generally end up paying the same price, tend to make them a nonissue. In contrast, they are an issue of major importance in most dealer-dominated auctions, where they are commonly seen as illegitimate, especially if they are used against the dealers. (If the bid has been increasing by increments of ten dollars and the bid is presently held by a dealer, the auctioneer is not supposed to accept an increase of two dollars from a chance buyer. On the other hand, if the present bid is held by such a chance buyer, the auctioneer may accept such a split bid from a dealer.) The situation in sales auctions will depend on the relative powers and rights of buyers and sellers. In art and antique auctions, in which buyers tend to dominate, they are discouraged. In most select livestock, real estate, and liquidation auctions, in which sellers are in charge, they are commonly not only accepted but encouraged, especially near the end of a bidding sequence.

Attitudes toward split bids relate in an interesting way to attitudes toward pools. In many cases, tolerance of buyer cooperation, if not collusion, is seen as offsetting the relative advantages of buyers and sellers as reflected in the use of split bids. Cooperation among buyers at select livestock sales, for example, is not only common but quite open. It is almost as if the sellers' advantage is understood and the buyers are given an offsetting right. In contrast, pooling is not allowed in most art and antique auctions. When, in fact, it does occur, it is often justified by those in the pool as being necessary because the auctioneer is refusing to respect their rights as buyers.

There are a number of variations concerning the acceptability of split bids related to other bidding practices. In Dutch auctions, for example, the issue really doesn't come up because the decreasing bid is usually tied to some mechanism that moves down in a continuous fashion. This is consistent with the nature of Dutch auctions, which are nearly always commodity-exchange auctions. In silent auctions – that is, auctions in which bidders write their bids on a bidding pad attached to each item on display – which are commonly used in charity auctions, minimum increments are built into the rules; each new bid must be so much more than the preceding one. Most charity auctions are run by an in-group of sponsors-buyers who prefer not to lose an item to a guest for a penny or two.[17]

Auctions that use sealed written bids are slightly more difficult to locate on a buyer-seller-favored auction spectrum. The fact that only one bid is allowed would seem to place them more with buyer-dominated auctions, since there is no way for the auctioneer to "milk" the buyers for just a little bit more. On the other hand, bids that are only slightly higher than others may be submitted, resulting in a higher price for the seller. In some cases, such as bond auctions, the whole issue becomes academic, since bidders that are close together are both likely to "win" – that is, to receive their share of bonds, or lose. (In this respect, they are very much like commodity-exchange auctions, which, of course, is exactly what they are.) Moreover, they will end up with rates very close to each other or actually the same if that is the form of the auction.[18] It is difficult to see how such minor differences favor either buyers or sellers.

When such bidding is used to award contracts, in contrast to bond or other high-multiple items, there is usually only one winner. Theoretically, this should put additional pressure on buyers to increase their bids, since it is not sufficient, as it is when there are multiple winners, to have one of the higher bids. This is not surprising, given that sellers tend to control such auctions as in the letting of government contracts. In actuality, if the bids are very close, the rules may allow the auctioning party to treat them as identical and to enter into further negotiations. This relaxes somewhat the pressure to be the high bidder, but it also gives the seller an additional opportunity to increase the bids.

All of these factors would indicate that such a system in the long run favors the seller. Often, however, buyer-bidders in such auctions are organized since they are commonly fellow professionals – for example, building contractors, suppliers, or maintenance companies. If they perceive the auction as favoring the seller, it is not unusual for them to engage in collusive practices. The seller is unlikely to feel that this is legitimate and may well retaliate by claiming that buyers are engaging in price-fixing. What commonly emerges from such disputes is a system of checks and balances which both parties feel protect their interests.

The use and acceptance of reserves raises many issues similar to those raised by the question of legitimate increments. Again, there are differences among auctions, and the deciding factor seems to be the relative rights and responsibilities of those involved. When strong communities exist, the particular practice, whatever it might be, is commonly accepted. When such communities do not exist, there is more concern with legitimating the practice.

In most commodity-exchange auctions, for example, sellers normally retain the right to reject any final bid, though they seldom employ formal reserves. If the last bid is not acceptable to the sellers, they can in some cases simply withdraw their goods. This is the dominant practice in most fish auctions, where it is known as "scratching." In other commodity situations, especially those where buyers have more control, the seller may be allowed to buy back his or her offering. This technique is quite common in horse sales where it is called simply a "buy-back." The seller who withdraws goods is normally still liable for a commission or equivalent charge, though there are often discounts for such scratches and buy-backs. Restrictions may also be placed on the future sale of the withdrawn goods, such as not being able to reauction them for a period of time.

At the higher end of livestock auctions, the auctioneer usually knows what minimum price will be accepted; moreover, he will usually act as the seller's agent in supporting such a reserve. He will generally not bid against the reserve himself, which is common practice in most art and antique auctions; that is, though he will not sell for less than the reserve, he will not continue to enter his own bids in order to reach the level of the reserve. If the last real bid is not sufficiently high, he will put in his own bid and, in effect, buy the item back. In scratches and buy-backs, the auctioneer normally does not know ahead of time what the seller's minimum acceptable bid will be. In most such cases, even the seller often hasn't thought out ahead of time what this minimum will be. The decision to scratch a fish catch may be made up to a half hour after the auction. Many buy-backs are quite spontaneous and more than a few are unintentional; the seller makes a bid intending to push the bid just a little higher and ends up buying his own horse.

These situations entail a range of compromises between buyers and sellers. The buyers would prefer not to give the seller the added leverage offered by a flexible reserve. On the other hand, they realize that they have to provide the option of withdrawing from the process altogether. This is the situation that holds in most exchange-type auctions. In those cases, however, where sellers have more power, they normally preserve their option of controlling the minimum bid by bidding directly on their goods. When this happens, however, the seller is normally also part of the community that is buying. It is a situation in which buyers and sellers overlap. When this is not the case, and buyers are in control, it is important for the auctioneer to develop a special relationship with the sellers to ensure their trust. This is clearly what happens in tobacco auctions and many local commodity auctions; in fact, the need to protect the sellers – or at least to be seen as doing so – was stressed by auctioneers from the New England Fish Exchange to the tobacco floors of Kentucky.

Reserves are not common in distress and liquidation sales. Again we have a situation where the buyers are normally in control; the sellers, as liquidating owners or as agents for such owners, in fact, may have no alternative but to sell. The professional buyers, who tend to be dealers, are consequently much less tolerant of reserves of any sort. In commodity auctions there is a sense in which the buyers realize that the sellers are also professionals and need some protection. In liquidation and distress sales, the buyers' attitude tends to be that they are there as a service to the seller and the goods should be sold to the highest bidder.

In commodity auctions, in which basically identical goods are sold on a regular basis, it is possible for auctioneers to work with flexible, unstated reserves. What commonly happens is that the auctioneer will buy for his or her own account anything that seems to be going for much less than it is worth – and then attempt to sell it at a later auction. This option is normally not available in liquidation auctions. What the auctioneer can do, however, is attempt to solicit the cooperation of specific buyers to offer equivalent minimum bids by accepting them when offered in response to a direct appeal. In doing this, it is not uncommon for the auctioneer to address the buyers by name and literally tell them to up their bids:

> Come on now, men, you know that this press is worth a lot more money than that. [Bidding has stopped at a price which the auctioneer feels is too low.] John, you paid five hundred more for one not nearly as good last week. Someone give me $2,000. John? Okay, thank you. $2,000 sold to number 158. Sorry, too late. [John responds to the request and makes a bid, and then others elect to bid also, since the price is on the low side, but the auctioneer ignores their bids and takes John's solicited bid of $2,000.] You had your chance.

This dialogue aptly reflects what often happens in these situations. At the request of the auctioneer, a dealer puts in a higher bid. Then, after some hesitation, another buyer makes a higher bid. In part as a reward to the first bidder for responding to his request, the auctioneer sells the item out for the two-thousand-dollar bid although he could have kept things going. If the winning bidder really doesn't want the item, he or she may be able to sell it privately for a profit to the late bidder. That is a reward for helping out the auctioneer.

The seller's preference for a reserve and the buyer's disapproval carries over to the more common country and art and antique auctions. Buyers have come to buy, and they feel that items should be sold without reserves. This also tends to be the view of most auctioneers. Auctioneers realize, however, that there will be no auction without sellers and that the sellers will normally want some sort of protection. The question is whether the seller is in a position to demand such protection. Over the last few years it appears that those auction houses dealing with more expensive items have begun to switch the balance more toward the sellers. For one thing, the practice of officially charging the seller only half the commission and the buyer the other half is fast becoming standard.[19] The other practice that has become common is the reserve. Moreover, in these auctions, it is quite normal for the auctioneer to aid the seller by bidding against the reserve throughout the auction in an attempt to raise the bid, moving through a series of artificial bids below the reserve price before taking a real bid just at the reserve level.

The increased use of reserves has produced its own counter-reaction from buyers. There is growing concern among buyers that they have been misled. It is one thing, they will argue, for an auctioneer to enter a single bid above their bid if a previously determined reserve has not been met. It is something else to bid above the reserve or to orchestrate a series of bids. In many cases buyers' concern with this has led to a new practice of announcing the underbidder – the last bidder below the winning bidder.

In a further attempt to balance the rights and privileges of buyers and sellers, a variety of practices has sprung up to inform the public when an item has not sold. These practices range from announcing the fact at the moment – "$350? Will someone say $350? I'm sorry, $325 is not good enough. The item is withdrawn" – to noting the fact in a follow-up auction report. The former practice is becoming more common at art and antique auctions; the latter practice is standard in horse auctions where the sales summary published soon after the auction notes which horses were not sold. The practice is to put either a "Not Sold" or an "RNA" (reserve not attained) notation next to the horse's hip number where the sales price would normally be. These practices serve to ensure that buyers are not misled into believing that items have been sold for prices higher than they were able to bring. It also protects other potential sellers from overestimating the value of their own goods, though it can hurt them in deflating inflationary expectations that drive prices up.

Other practices used to disclose to all or to a specific subgroup whether an item has been sold or not include knocking or not knocking the auction hammer on the lectern, specific statements such as "sold," or code words known only to the regulars. In horse auctions, for example, the practice is not to announce nonsales at the auction, since it is felt that nonsales may prove contagious, depressing future sales. The people working the auction, however, need to know immediately in order to determine whether they need the signature of the buyer, which not only legally commits him for the money involved, but also transfers ownership and all associated liabilities. If the horse drops dead on the way back to the barn, it is the buyer's loss, not the seller's. Changeable codes, consequently, such as repeating the name of the "spotter," the auctioneer assistant, who has apparently taken the winning bid, are used by the auctioneer to indicate a nonsale.

One of the most interesting and idiosyncratic systems of reserves, increments, and disclosures is the use of floor bids common in literary auctions. A floor bid is an initial bid by a potential buyer made and announced before the auction begins; it is, in short, a guaranteed minimum bid. In return for making an acceptable floor bid – to be acceptable it must be sufficiently high to start the bidding at a level that would be judged a reasonable final bid – this bidder gets the option to top the final bid by 10 percent. If, for example, the floor bidder makes an opening bid of $100,000 and the bidding then goes up to $250,000, the opening bidder will have the option of acquiring the rights for a bid of $275,000 (the last bid of $250,000 plus a 10 percent increase of $25,000). The floor bidder does not participate in the bidding except for the first and the last bid. Before going back to the floor bidder, however, the seller will normally ask the high bidder among the other auction participants if he or she wishes to increase the bid. The present high bidder might raise the bid in an attempt to discourage the floor bidder from exercising the topping privilege.

The high bidder may feel that the floor bidder is willing to go up to $300,000 but no more. He or she may, therefore, put in a bid of $275,000, knowing that the floor would have to counter with a bid of $302,500. This will be the high bidder's last chance to enter a bid. There will be no opportunity to enter a higher bid if the floor bidder chooses to execute his or her option.

On the surface this seems like an overly complex system. But it makes perfectly good sense when we remember that in literary auctions buyers and sellers are part of a very close-knit community. It is a community in which private treaty transactions are as normal as auction transactions. This particular system allows a type of private treaty within an auction framework. It allows the seller to establish a minimum and buyers to know ahead of time what that minimum is. It further protects buyers from having a book in which they are interested "stolen away," since they know the winning bid must be at least 10 percent higher. The floor bidder, meanwhile, receives certain privileges for making the first bid and allowing the seller to publicize it before the auction. Such bids are extremely valuable to the seller as an expression of confidence in a relatively unknown commodity. A reasonably high floor bid from one publisher will generally attract the attention of other publishers and get them to take a closer look at the book.

Floor bids highlight the fact that different types of auctions occur within specific contexts rich in their own meaning. The rules of a literary auction only make sense within the framework of that particular community, with its particular relationships and history. The same can be said about most other auctions. In one major standardbred auction in Pennsylvania, for example, problems arose because the seller was not only a breeder but also a trainer and racer of horses. Buyers were suspicious that he was selling his less promising horses and keeping the best for himself. To deal with this problem, the seller instituted a practice of bringing two horses into the ring simultaneously. When the bidding ended, the winning bidder could choose either horse. The other horse would be kept and raced by the seller. In this way the breeder-trainer was able to reassure his buyers and yet offer only half of his yearlings for sale, keeping the other half to be trained and raced by him. His adaptation, like that of the literary auction, was aimed at demonstrating his fairness while protecting his own self-interest.

All these practices and decisions concerning reserves, split bids, buy-backs, disclosures, scratches, and nonsales are continually subject to review and modification according to relative fairness toward buyers and sellers. In all instances, their existence testifies to the ongoing awareness and need to sustain the community's faith in the fairness of the process. This is not to deny that buyers and sellers are apt to press their advantage. Even here, however, they are likely to do so only insofar as they feel it is appropriate and acceptable to the community. A recent series of laboratory experiments confirmed this.[20] In simulated auctions, student subjects did not utilize their advantages in a bargaining situation when they saw such advantages as being arbitrarily conferred. They only pressed their advantages when they believed that they had been earned based on their earlier performances. Their sense of community fairness took priority over their individual self-interests.

The sense of fairness operative in an auction can be quite particularistic, reflecting similarly particularistic conditions that pertain to the specific situation. Such idiosyncrasies underscore the communal character of fairness in auctions. In thoroughbred auctions, for example, it is considered perfectly fair for sellers to do all sorts of things to make their horses look better and sounder. This is crucial since the most important quality of a yearling horse, besides its bloodlines, is its soundness. A thoroughbred that stays healthy normally makes its owner money; unfortunately for owners, many of them go lame or break down some other way.[21] In buying a yearling horse that has never raced, it is most important to try to determine if there are any signs that the horse may not prove sound. Buyers carefully watch the way a horse walks and stands in order to detect any misalignments in the legs which could create the type of extra pressures that would lead to lameness.

Sellers are, of course, aware of this practice and will often doctor up a horse to correct for any such misalignments. One way to do this is to carve the front hoofs of the horse in such a way that a leg that is actually slightly twisted in or out looks as if it is facing directly forward. Another more radical technique, especially if such misalignments are caught early, is to operate on the horse and put in splints which will straighten the leg. Both of these practices are considered fair and it is up to the buyer to detect them. (Here we again see the relative power of the sellers in these types of auctions. In fish auctions and many types of commodity auctions, where sellers are in a much weaker position, the buyer may very well refuse to accept goods that are later shown to have been doctored in a similar manner.)

It is not legitimate, however, for the seller to dye the front legs of an animal that has had splints in order to cover up the small telltale white marks caused by the splint operation. Although this may in part represent a communal compromise on the use of splints (they can be used, but the telltale signs must remain), it is more likely related to the very strict rules bearing on markings to ensure that racehorses are not switched, enforced by the Jockey Club. In contrast, in auctioning an antique chair, the use of a small amount of stain to cover up a slight crack in a leg would be acceptable, whereas replacing the leg with a new leg would not be acceptable. In car auctions, it is considered legitimate to change all the oils to cover up mechanical difficulties, but cheating to change the odometer. An argument could be made in each case that there is something wrong with what is considered fair and unfair. What is evident is that much that is considered fair in an auction reflects the traditions and history of the specific auction community.

The fact that a number of auction practices considered fair within specific auctions appear on reflection to be ethically questionable, reveals a somewhat paradoxical facet to the way community cohesiveness and explicit legitimacy concerns complement each other. The more manifest the need to establish an aura of legitimacy and fairness, the greater the possibility of exploitation.

Deliberate exploitation, in contrast simply to profiting more from a transaction, requires that the manipulating party know the value of the items exchanged. Given that auctions occur primarily in situations characterized by value uncertainty, it follows that auctions would be insusceptible to such practices. The greater the uncertainty, the greater the immunity. All auctions are not subject to the same degree of uncertainty, however. There are auctions – for example, automobile, jewelry, and estate – in which many of the regular participants have quite definite knowledge of the value of the goods being auctioned. It is often the need to satisfy interested third parties that prohibits them from entering into private treaty transactions.

It is specifically these auctions in which, because of the interest of third parties, the aura of legitimacy is most consciously developed. Where there is true uncertainty and ambiguity, coupled with community cohesiveness, legitimacy and fairness are taken for granted as ingrained in the auction process. The primary concern among participants is to resolve both the price and the allocation uncertainties. It is assumed that the auction process, especially as it is embedded in the community, does so in as fair a way as possible. When the rules seem peculiar and no one appears particularly concerned about fairness, the probabilities are high that no one is taking advantage of anyone else. On the other hand, it is when everything makes sense, and great effort has been taken to assure everyone that everything is above board, that the buyer should truly beware.

In auctions things are often not as they appear. Economic, psychological, and social concerns combine in a myriad of ways, both producing and reflecting the complex social context of the auction processes: the show itself.

Notes

1   Such a relationship is consistent with Durkheim's classical analysis of the relationship between social solidarity and moral order, Durkheim, Emile, *The Division of Labor in Society* (Free Press, New York, 1956). In homogeneous, simple societies, social solidarity is evident to all and the moral order assumed; in modern complex, more diffuse societies, the moral order must be explicitly promulgated.

2   The typical set of rules found at these auctions will take up a single mimeographed page and emphasize that there are no guarantees or warranties. Most of the page will then be used to spell out the charges and commissions for different-price cars, storage charges, as well as the types of payments acceptable – normally only cash or certified check.

3   There are occasions, of course, such as John Lennon's Rolls-Royce, or the 250 GTO Ferrari racing car confiscated from an accused drug dealer and auctioned in November 1987 for $1,600,000, when the auction price, due to the uniqueness of the automobile and the attending hype, may be in excess of either the fixed price or expected private treaty

price. There is also less concern with the legitimacy of the values so generated, since they apply to little if anything else. In auctioning most used automobiles, the legitimacy of the process tends to take precedence over maximizing return.

4   If the meaning system of the family proves inadequate, the members will rely on the meaning system of the encompassing society, which normally means the experts of this society.

5   I should note that this conversation occurred sometime in 1983, when the art auction market was less volatile.

6   The one exception was a very unusual and rare piece of sculpture whose value could really not be determined.

7   This technique is used quite often in charity auctions. Friends will often pressure one of their group to bid up on an item they know he or she is interested in by bidding against him or her to the level they think is appropriate. This is often done in good spirit, with the intended winner telling them when he or she isn't about to go any higher.

8   A cribber is a horse that chews on wood, which some believe can produce breathing problems. Many horsemen think it means nothing, however.

9   Those instances where auctioneers are guilty of questionable practices are usually cases where the auctioneer is selling his or her own goods.

10   Two dealers may both be willing to overpay for an item if each believes that there is a buyer for the item who is willing to pay whatever is asked.

11   If the bidding has been going up by a hundred dollars a bid – two hundred, three hundred, four hundred, for example – and then someone offers four hundred and fifty, the four-hundred-and-fifty bid would be a split bid.

12   In some auctions the rules stipulate minimum increments. Select thoroughbred auctions, for example, have an "upset," that is, starting, price of $1,000. If a horse doesn't bring that quite quickly, it will be passed over. The minimum increment up to $25,000 is then $100, and $500 after $25,000. At select standardbred auctions the upset price is the same, but the minimum up to $25,000 is $500 and $1,000 over that. In practice the normal increments are much larger and only come down to these limits when someone offers a split bid. The size of increments in most other auctions is at the discretion of the auctioneer, who can, by the rules, ignore any bid he or she chooses.

13   In England, the sequence is more likely to be 2,000, 2,200, 2,500, 2,800, 3,000; for some reason, the 2, 5, 8, 10 sequence is used extensively in England, while in the United States increments tend to be consistent.

14   At most select auctions, a thousand dollars is set as the minimum increment. In practice most increments are considerably higher.

15   The issue of fairness does not normally arise in more traditional commodity auctions, since there tend not to be any winners and losers, and where consequently the acceptance of split bids is really a nonissue. Legitimacy per se, however, tends to be of secondary importance in such auctions, given that community tends to overshadow the question of legitimacy.

16   In this particular case, a junior person was actually running the auction. The car was expected to sell for around two hundred thousand dollars. When the bid passed two hundred thousand, the young auctioneer looked around for some help and was told to keep the increment at ten thousand dollars – which, following orders, he did all the way up to the final bid. My guess is that a more experienced auctioneer would have increased the increment at the half-million and million-dollar levels, with perhaps negative results.

17   Most charity auctions are built around a core group of organizers who are generally the big spenders, with a looser group of friends and acquaintances appended.

18   In sealed bid bond auctions two systems are commonly used. One is to pay out at the rates bid until all bonds are placed. If one hundred million dollars' worth of bonds are

offered and the highest bid is 8.5 percent for five million, 8.45 for five million, 8.4 for twenty million, 8.35 for thirty million, 8.3 for twenty-five million, 8.2 for forty-five million, 8.15 for thirty-five million, and 8.1 for fifty million, those bidding 8.3 percent or higher would get their full allotment at the rate bid since their total request is for 8.5 million with those bidding 8.2 percent receiving one-third of what they had asked for at the 8.2 rate, since the request at 8.2 is for 45 million and only 15 million are left. Everyone else would get nothing. The second system would allocate the bonds to the same bidders but at the single rate of 8.3375, which is the average rate of the winning bids. In both cases, when government bonds are auctioned, a sizable portion of the offering will be offered to the public after the auction at this average rate regardless of the rate paid to those actually participating in the auction.

19   Ten years ago, most country and art and antique auctions charged the seller a 20 percent commission with discounts for very desirable lots. Today the practice, brought in by Christie's from England, of charging sellers and buyers each a 10 percent commission is becoming the norm. In many cases in which very valuable estates are concerned, the seller's commission may be forfeited.

20   See Elizabeth Hoffman and Mathew L. Spitzer, "Entitlements, Rights, and Fairness: An Experimental Examination of Subjects' Concepts of Distributive Justice," *Journal of Legal Studies* 14 (June 1985): 259–97.

21   Racing, especially track racing – as compared to turf and jumping – takes a tremendous toll on a horse. Any aberration in anatomy is likely to create problems and lead to a breakdown of one sort or another.

8 The Structural Sources of Adventurism: The Case of the California Gold Rush

Gary G. Hamilton

This paper attempts to analyze sociologically the actions of a type of individual called the "adventurer."[1] In learned parlance this label is applied to a variety of people whose circumstances differ considerably. Participants in the "Age of Discovery," as well as modern historians, have found this an apt title for the European explorers of the New World and for the maritime merchants traveling to the Spice Islands and beyond to Cathay. These adventurers are a distinctive type of migrants who seek wealth and fame beyond the geographical, but not the social, confines of their own society. But "adventurer" is also an appellation applied to persons who seek rapid social advancement without migrating. The courtier, the courtesan, the politician, the commercial speculator, and a variety of other types are occasionally called adventurers. Thus the factor determining the appropriateness of the label is not the occupancy of a particular role or even the performance of a general set of actions. Instead, it is the combination of the act and the motivation behind the act. For the purposes of this study, the combination of the act and the motivation will be termed "adventurism."

Adventurism, accordingly, has two definitional components. First, it refers to the adventure, the act of taking great risks whose outcomes are not calculable in advance. Second, it signifies that such actions are undertaken for sizable social, political, or economic gains that might occur if the venture is successful. Because of the nature of the odds involved as well as the nature of what is being gambled (one's personal safety), risk taking of this type differs qualitatively from the risk taking associated with bourgeois capitalism. Max Weber (1958, pp. 20–21, 58), in particular, has shown this distinction to be of major historical importance by linking rational risk taking to the "spirit of capitalism" and adventurism to plunder (booty capitalism). By concentrating his efforts on the analysis of capitalism, however, Weber provided only few insights into adventurism. This paper can be seen as an attempt to augment somewhat our understanding of this type of high-risk behavior.

Defined in this way, adventurism is a historically common, sociologically important form of social action. At first glance, however, it is a type of action that defies sociological understanding, primarily because it blends two characteristics not often associated with one another: charisma and worldly gain.[2] Like the charismatic, the adventurer departs from the routine expectations of everyday life, appeals to chance to guide his way in the face of uncertainty, and engages in concerted though often sporadic activity. He is often a tradition breaker. But, like the entrepreneur, the

Original publication: Hamilton, Gary G., "The Structural Sources of Adventurism: The Case of the California Gold Rush," *American Journal of Sociology* (vol. 83, no. 6, 1978), pp. 1466–90.

adventurer is oriented to this world – to the attainment of worldly goods and accolades and to the manipulation of people and circumstances insofar as conditions permit. The active search for sudden wealth or recognition, perhaps the most common forms of adventurism, simultaneously circumvents the established modes of upward mobility and substantiates the importance of the social climb. To undertake such risks requires audacity – a foolhardiness or courage, depending on one's perspective – that is not found in every individual or even in every stratum of society. Because this behavior can be considered marginal and, at times, antagonistic to normative social activity, adventurism is an important source of social change. Yet, as a social phenomenon, adventurism is little understood, a fact perhaps indicating the diversity of the actions that could be called adventurous, of the outcomes that result from such actions, and of the individuals who attempt them.

This study is an exploratory investigation of adventurism in the context of a single historical event, the California gold rush. The purpose of examining this event is to arrive at some preliminary understanding of the social factors influencing individuals to engage in adventurism and hence of the underlying sociological dimensions of adventurism. The following essay will be structured with this purpose in mind. First, the gold rush is examined as an instance of what will be termed adventure migration. The effort here is to show that adventurism is a patterned activity with individuals from some class positions and from some societies being more likely to be adventurers than individuals from other origins. Second, an attempt is made to explain why particular types of people or people in particular types of societies are more inclined toward adventurism than other types. To fashion such an explanation, adventurism is viewed as a mobility strategy, a course of action designed to alter one's social standing. The explanation then revolves around what stratificational conditions influence the use of this strategy as opposed to less adventurous strategies. The study concludes with a comparison between adventurism and bourgeois capitalism as types of rational calculated risk taking.

The Setting: Migration to the Gold Fields, 1849–51

The first great surge of worldwide migration to the United States during the 19th century came as a direct result of the discovery of gold in California (Thomas, 1973, p. 94). As compared with the waves of migration that followed later in the century, the initial years of the gold rush (1849–51) are not typical. In fact, in the history of world migrations, the California gold rush is quite unusual. Seldom has a more rapid accumulation of a more ethnically diverse or more totally male population converged on a location where so few facilities existed for newcomers, each of whom was intent upon achieving the same goal – to strike it rich (Paul, 1947, 1967; Caughey, 1975).

There are other characteristics that further separate this migration from the typical one. For the majority of the early arrivals, it was a temporary sojourn, often lasting only one or two years. This was a "focused" migration, based more on the chance for sudden wealth than on the undesirability of the place of origin. Perhaps its most unusual characteristic was the suddenness of the rush to California. Tens of thousands of individuals almost simultaneously made the decision to migrate without the benefit of preexisting migration chains to organize their movements and with only minimal information of conditions to be encountered upon arrival.

Given the distance and conditions of travel, the migration was rapid, massive, and temporary. At the time of the discovery, the population of California totaled around 15,000, excluding the native Indians (Wright, 1940, p. 323). By the end of 1849, after the international gold rush had been under way for nearly six months, the total population had passed 90,000. By 1852, it had reached well over 220,000 (Loosley, 1971). Of these migrants, most were between 20 and 40 years of age, and over 90% were male. By 1850, the second year of the gold rush, individuals from over 40 different nations and from every state and territory in the Union had landed in California (Wright, 1940, pp. 338–41). During the initial years the great majority of these migrants were concentrated in the gold fields, mostly mountainous terrain inhabited before 1848 only by the native Indians. And approximately 70% of the numbers arriving in San Francisco by sea (over 175,000) between 1849 and 1853 had left California by the same means before the end of 1853 (Wright, 1940, p. 341). No figures are available for those who left California overland or who – by accident, disease, or design – perished there during these years.

The singularity of this migration, as compared with other migrations of comparable size, stems from its being almost totally composed of adventurers – individuals who had made the decision to quit temporarily their affairs in their places of origin in order to search for sudden wealth in California. According to W. Petersen (1970, p. 63), the "free migration of individuals," a type similar to that which is here termed adventurer migration, is "always rather small." Because the gold rush is one of the few exceptions to this rule, it illustrates on a large scale that which usually occurs on a small one. For this reason, the California gold rush provides one of the best contexts in which to study adventurism.

Social and Geographical Characteristics of the Argonauts

What sorts of individuals are able to adopt adventurism as a means to attain their worldly ambitions? In what type of society is adventurism likely to be adopted as a strategy of upward mobility? In other words, if one views adventurism as a means to an end, then what social factors influence the use of this strategy as opposed to alternative and less adventurous strategies? Consider, more concretely, the rush to the California gold fields. What made the possibility of discovering gold and becoming rich so attractive to some individuals that they knowingly took several years out of their lives in the society of their aspirations to pursue the venture? Although these questions cannot be easily answered, they seem to be central to a sociological understanding of adventurism.

The data that can be teased out of the voluminous primary and secondary materials on the gold rush do not permit definitive answers. Although these materials record life in the gold fields in considerable detail, they offer little on the argonauts' motivations for migrating and on their plans for using their anticipated wealth. Nevertheless, census data and other primary sources permit descriptions of the demographic characteristics of the argonauts,[3] from which one can approach the questions indirectly.

Most eyewitness accounts of the gold rush suggest that the migration to California was more likely to be undertaken by certain types of individuals and by individuals from certain societies than by others. First of all, there was an upper-class bias to the migration; those who came by sea (80% of the total) usually had to pay for their own passage in advance. Said one observer in 1850 (Nasatir, 1964, p. 122):

> This mining population is well worthy of interest. In it all levels of civilized society are represented, intermixed, and it is not at all those on the lowest rung of the social ladder who are the most numerous; on the contrary they are the fewest because everyone cannot afford such a trip. . . . Engineers are in good company with scholars, professors, artists, men of letters, doctors, captains who have left their ships, officers who have abandoned their rank, and lawyers their cases. Everyone has rushed here: merchants, workmen, clerks, women, old men, children, everyone, from the peasant to the man of the world and even (who would believe it?) the *rentier*, who hoped to triple his income and who is eating it up.

The fact that most accounts of the gold rush were written by fairly well-educated people probably exaggerates the impression of the argonauts' upper- and middle-class origins. Nonetheless, such empirical data as exist on the class origins of the migrants substantiate this impression (Bancroft, 1888, pp. 227, 248–50; Read and Gaines, 1949, pp. xxxix–xl). For instance, some of the early accounts of the gold rush list the members of companies traveling to California. In 1849 from Ohio, one "company going to the promised land . . . consisted of a son of the Hon. Thomas Ewing, Secretary of the Interior . . . a constable . . . a State Attorney . . . a shrewd lawyer . . . a farmer . . . a merchant . . . a druggist . . . a potter" (Morgan and Scobie, 1964, pp. 2–3). In the most extensive studies of gold mining companies, O. T. Howe (1923, p. 5) notes that "of professional men there were always an abundance." Most companies included physicians, lawyers, and clergymen in addition to skilled craftsmen.

Precise information on the class origins of foreign-born migrants is not available. A number of observers, however, did comment on the types of upper- and middle-class individuals found in California. From France came many of noble birth (Nasatir, 1964, p. 20); from England, many "gentlemen"; from Chile, many upper-class *mestizos* (Monaghan, 1973, pp. 42–53; Faugsted, 1973, p. 20; Giacobbi, 1974, pp. 7–8); from Germany and America, many professionals (Howe, 1923, pp. 4, 180; Read and Gaines, 1949, p. xxxii); and from all these places, many artisans and merchants.

Individuals from lower-class origins were also present in California, but the poor who did not come overland often traveled at the expense and for the benefit of others. Upper-class Chileans brought paid laborers with them to mine their gold (Giacobbi, 1974, pp. 18–23; Monaghan, 1973, pp. 74, 173). Although not peons in the sense that they were bound to their master by ties of patronage, such paid laborers formed a sizable percentage of the Chilean argonauts.[4] Some sea captains even booked these laborers without passage money in order to sell them as bond servants in San Francisco (Monaghan, 1973, p. 53). Once in California, Chilean masters formed associations designed to prevent desertions of their laborers, though often to no avail (Monaghan, 1973, pp. 61, 127).

France, like Chile, contributed many poor argonauts whose passage was primarily for the benefit of the rich (Shepard, 1955). When the gold mania seized the rich

Parisians, they often bought shares in joint stock companies, some of which paid passage or extended credit to poor Frenchmen in exchange for a percentage of the gold they might discover in California. At least 83 such companies formed, some dangling the phrase "millions for a sou" before wealth speculators (Nasatir, 1964, pp. 20–24). The most ignoble French effort to supply California with miners was initiated by the French government of Louis-Napoleon Bonaparte.[5] Under the direction of Bonaparte, the government organized an immigration company, Société des Lingots d'Or, and a lottery to finance the passage of impoverished Frenchmen to California. In addition to lesser prizes, the government offered as grand prize a golden ingot worth 400,000 francs. This attempt to "rid France of her undesirables" (Nasatir, 1964, p. 20) sent almost 4,000 paupers to California, a fact bemoaned by Karl Marx (1969, p. 84) in his well-known phrase that "golden dreams were to supplant the socialist dreams of the Paris proletariat." All of the 83 companies organized in France disbanded upon docking in California. Former members, both rich and poor, went their own way.

The largest number of lower-class sea arrivals came from China. Most of these Chinese argonauts were from peasant backgrounds. They generally financed their passage to California in one of two ways (Williams, 1971): Some obtained passage money from their families, lineages, or villages, which would pool their resources in order for one of their members to try their luck in California. However, the majority appear to have used the credit-ticket system: The migrant received his passage on credit, which obliged him to pay off the debt with a portion of the gold he found.

Except for Chinese migrants and poorer Americans who traveled overland, adventurers from lower-class rural origins were the exception. Moreover, the poor who did migrate from Latin America and France were not peasants, but rather urban poor. In Chile, according to Monaghan (1973, p. 5), most of the poor migrants were *rotos*, "landless vagabonds," and not *inquilinos*, "sharecroppers, serfs, peons . . . [who were] too poor and closely attached to the land to leave their ancestral allotments." For France, Marx's analysis (1969, pp. 84, 125) seems to hold true: Poor emigrants were "Parisian vagabonds," who made up the city's vast lumpenproletariat, and not peasants, who lived in "stupefied seclusion." By contrast, Chinese peasants, whose attachment to the land is legendary, left their ancestral plots with relative ease, a characteristic, as it will be shown, that favors adventurism.

If the California sojourn was more likely an adventure for upper- than lower-class individuals, it is even more the case that it was an adventure undertaken by people from only some societies. Here the evidence is more clear.[6] Migration from Chile outnumbered many times the combined total from all of the rest of South and Central America. China alone supplied over 95% of all migrants from the Far East and the Pacific. About 90% of European migrants came from countries in western Europe (Great Britain, France, and Germany), 4% from southern Europe (Portugal, Spain, and Italy), 1% from eastern Europe and the Baltic region, and the remaining 5% from northern and central Europe (Scandinavia, Switzerland, Belgium, and Holland).

The majority of all migrants to California came, of course, from the United States (somewhere around 65% of the total), but even from the United States there are significant sectional differences.[7] In 1850, 46% of the U.S. argonauts came from the Northeast (particularly New York, Pennsylvania, and Massachusetts), 28% from the border states (particularly Kentucky, Missouri, and Tennessee), 18% from the

Midwest (particularly from Ohio), and only 8% from the South. Based on the 1850 census totals, about 0.4% of the total population of the border states had joined the gold rush, 0.31% of that of the Northeast, 0.24% of that of the Midwest, and 0.11% of that of the South.

The vast majority of the argonauts were young rather than old, had middle- to upper- rather than lower-class origins, and (except for American and Chinese argonauts) came from urban rather than rural settings. Most came from the United States, western Europe, Chile, and China. One other characteristic stands out. Those who came left families, friends, and jobs in order to seek their fortune in the gold fields.[8] With the exception of the French and Chilean poor, it would seem difficult to describe these migrants as coming from socially marginal groups. Instead they aspired to or occupied relatively high-status (often professional) positions and were thus, by all indications, well integrated into their respective societies.

This portrait of the argonauts matches the typical description of particular adventurers presented by historians. According to Petersen (1970, p. 62), the early migrants from 19th-century Sweden were "men with a good cultural and social background, mostly young and of a romantic disposition. Since the risks in emigration were great and difficult to calculate, those who left tended to be adventurers or intellectuals motivated by their ideals. . . ." The Spanish adventurers who conquered the Americas, the *conquistadores*, were predominantly young, male, and drawn from the lower aristocracy and the gentry class. "*Hidalgos* in particular were well represented in the conquista – men such as Cortes himself, who came from noble but impoverished families, and were prepared to try their luck in an unknown world" (Elliott, 1966, p. 62). Likewise, the first British colonizers in the West Indies and America (e.g., Jamestown) were adventurers – "penniless younger sons of gentility desirous of amassing means sufficient to become landed proprietors in the homeland" (Ragatz, 1928, p. 3). The information on the California gold rush, while revealing considerable variation in the social origins of adventurers and with the important exception of American and Chinese argonauts, is consistent with this characterization.

Push and Pull Factors in the Gold Rush

Was the lure of gold sufficient to cause such a widespread migration? If it were only the promise of easy riches that prompted individuals to join the gold rush, then why did the majority come from only a few widely dispersed societies?

Given the social and geographical origins of the argonauts, one might account for the geographical dispersion by showing the influence of accidental circumstances upon individual decisions to migrate. For instance, in each of the principal contributing societies, circumstantial events that coincided with the discovery of gold might have precipitated the migration to California. In western Europe, massive social movements, economic depressions, and revolutions occurring around 1848 contributed to a feeling of social unrest and insecurity. In China, the Taiping Rebellion and widespread famine paralyzed much of central and south China. Because Valparaiso was the principal port of call for most ships going around the Horn, Chile had a fortuitous location on the world trading routes. And not long before 1848 Chile had had its own political unrest, culminating in its political independence from Spanish rule. In America, the end of the Mexican-American war in 1848 brought the release of a large number of soldiers, some of whom supposedly sought further excitement in California (Caughey, 1975, p. 44).

Most historians of the gold rush (as well as sociologists discussing migration more generally) explain the migration in terms of these calamitous or fortuitous events. Closer examination shows, however, that the distribution of these events is far more widespread than the actual geographical origins of the migrants. Revolutions in 1848–49 occurred throughout Europe, but the vast majority of the European migrants came only from western Europe. The rebellion and famine in China were concentrated in a broad area of central China, but Chinese argonauts migrated only from south China. Other Latin American countries besides Chile were well situated on the world trading routes and had had their own revolutions, most more disruptive than the one in Chile. Thus all these "push factors" had only an indirect bearing on the causes for this instance of adventure migration.

For adventure migration, push factors are more complex than simply individual misfortune, and they should be seen in a very different light from push factors motivating people to migrate permanently.[9] When people decide to make a permanent move, they presumably evaluate their native society as less desirable in important respects than their potential destination. By contrast, when adventurers migrate, they do so only to return to their native society at a later date, hopefully with the wherewithal to partake more fully in those things they most desire in their homelands. To adventurers the relative desirability of their native society far outweighs that of their destination, or at least initially. Thus the calamitous aspects of revolution in Europe or rebellion in China do not in themselves seem to be sufficient causes to explain gold seeking in California. Something more is at work here, and that something is not misfortune, but dreams of great fortune, regardless of the misery required to obtain it. Thus, whereas most push factors are usually seen as negative, push factors for adventure migration are viewed as positive,[10] a point I will describe in detail below.

Besides disruptive push factors, historians and sociologists often view migration in terms of pull factors. In this sense, one of the most important precipitating causes for the gold rush was something that might be called gold fever – a collective hysteria caused by the discovery of gold (Bieber, 1948; Caughey, 1975, pp. 38–55). In each of the societies that contributed in a major way to the argonauts, documentary evidence suggests that the gold rush had an important collective component, so much so that the gold rush can be seen as a competitive race to the gold fields. Rumor piled upon rumor, supplemented by eyewitness accounts appearing in newspapers, produced the promise of great wealth for the first ones to arrive at the gold fields. The urge to be first in the race to California created a gold mania.[11]

In the Northeast as well as in areas west of the Appalachian Mountains, the California gold mania was intense. "People of all classes succumbed to the fever" (Bieber, 1948, pp. 20–22). People became "California mad." Declared the *Boston Courier*, "adventurers were 'starting off for California by the dozen, the score, and the hundred, hardly allowing themselves time to pull on their boots, and put bread and cheese in their pockets.'" Another newspaper asserted that "the coming of the Messiah, or the dawn of the Millennium would not have excited anything like the interest" caused by the discovery of gold. By 1850, about a year after the discovery of gold became widely known in the eastern half of the United States, almost 70,000 Americans had already arrived in California.

Similar gold manias occurred in all the countries producing large numbers of argonauts. Proclaimed one Liverpool observer (Wright, 1941, p. 66) in January 1849, "The gold excitement here and in London exceeds anything ever before known or heard of. . . . Nothing is heard or talked about but the new El Dorado." According to A. P. Nasatir (1964), the best historian on the French in California, gold mania seized Parisians. French newspapers reported every detail that could be found about California, often erroneously; hysteria sparked a movement of about 20,000 Frenchmen to California in the first two years of the gold rush. In China, where most argonauts were from rural areas, the news of the discovery traveled more slowly. First posted on placards in the main cities, the news spread to outlying marketing towns and from there to villages. Though not as rapid or widespread as in other locations, the response still constituted a collective movement; between 1850 and 1855, as many as 50,000 Chinese sought wealth in California. Another 40,000 set out for Australia, where gold had been discovered in 1851 (Choi, 1975). Over 90% of these gold seekers came from Kwangtung Province in south China (Choi, 1975; Speer, 1856). And in Chile, as one skeptic observed in 1848 (Monaghan, 1973, pp. 53–55), "The reports of riches in California which have caused such a stir in Valparaiso have also created much agitation in the habitually sedate Santiago. The spirit of adventure, like the tides on the beaches of Valparaiso, draws [Chileans] away to California. All wish only to be the first in the land of a portentous future. They go arming themselves with only a pick, or shovel, or even a knife to dig gold by handfuls."

Despite widespread excitement, gold fever did not stir all parts of the world equally. Outside of western Europe, Chile, China, and the United States, there were few symptoms. This differential reaction to the news of the discovery is illustrated by the contrast between southern and northeastern United States. According to Bieber (1948, p. 24), "Along the South Atlantic coast the excitement was less intense, though a few ships departed for California from Norfolk, Wilmington, and Charleston. However, no vessel cleared from Savannah for California in 1849. North Carolina was probably the least affected of any of the South Atlantic states; the gold fever, according to the Raleigh *Times*, 'has hardly disturbed the snooze of our quiet old State.'" Although the southern newspapers printed the same stories about the discovery of gold, there was no mania.[12]

The same outcome occurred in Peru, where the absence of a gold mania forced would-be promoters to fill ships bound for California with freight instead of passengers (Monaghan, 1973, pp. 94–110). As in the South, Peruvian newspapers reported the discovery of gold in full, the first announcement coming one day before it appeared in Chilean newspapers. But no gold fever developed, either among the rich or among the poor. Monaghan (1973, pp. 103–4) puts it mildly: The "gold-rush excitement in Peru . . . lacked the keen aggressiveness displayed in Valparaiso."

Why should people in some societies or a part of a society be so little inspired to join the gold rush? Or, conversely, why should so many people in other areas be so greatly influenced by the discovery? Even though mass movements swept into the rush to California many who would not ordinarily have been influenced by a vision of sudden wealth, these differential patterns of behavior seem symptomatic of the presence of some more fundamental factors influencing individual actions.

Structural Sources of Adventurism among the Argonauts

Although a great many people undoubtedly found the idea of California's wealth attractive, only very few acted on the basis of this idea. To be sure, calamitous events and gold manias were precipitating causes for the gold rush; but to understand this instance of adventurism – the motivation behind it as well as the act – is to uncover those secondary causes, as de Tocqueville (1971, p. 78) once called them, that prepare the ground in advance and shape the course of events without actually causing their occurrence. In other words, motivational factors are not so much ideas in the minds of individuals as structural arrangements in society that give salience to ideas and instill in them a force beyond the content of the ideas themselves. In this sense, ideas are socially grounded in the circumstances of people's lives; individuals act on the basis of the world they see before them; they espouse and manipulate those ideas that make sense to them – the same ideas that, at times, consume them. The secondary causes of the California gold rush have little to do with calamities or gold fever and have much to do with individual interpretations of how one could profit from the wealth that California's gold fields promised. At the risk of considerable oversimplification, the secondary causes of adventurism are to be found in a society's social structure.[13]

The following comparative analysis does little more than outline a hypothesis about what types of structures seem to be conducive to adventurism. Moreover, such comments as I offer result primarily from an ex post facto examination of adventurism in the gold rush and may not apply to adventurism in general. My reason for presenting such a provisional approach, however, is grounded in my belief that risk taking is an important form of behavior in modern as well as historical times. Thus the tentativeness of this effort is to be balanced by the need to open discussion on this neglected feature of social life.

On the surface, the social structures of western Europe, Chile, China, and the United States would seem to be very different from one another, as in fact they are. But they shared in 1848 at least one characteristic: a "particularistic-achievement" orientation, to borrow a concept from Talcott Parsons's discussion of the principal types of stratification.

As Parsons (1951, pp. 195–98) defines it, a particularistic-achievement pattern is a particular type of social structure in which individuals orient their lives toward the attainment of social objects within "the relational system." Universalism is weak; individuals' particularistic bonds are strong. An achievement orientation within this system takes the form of individuals striving for "a *proper* pattern of adaptation . . . which can be maintained only by continuous effort and if not maintained must be re-achieved." Although couched in very general terms, the thrust of Parsons's description depicts the individual actor as having both particularistic affiliations and the obligation to achieve his status within these affiliations.

The concept is suggestive of the conditions that confront would-be adventurers. Consider, for instance, a common sort of adventurer, the impoverished noble. A person may be born noble and feel entitled to practice an aristocratic style of life, but that in itself is insufficient to be of the nobility. To occupy that position is to have enough wealth to live as a noble lives. In this situation the goal of one's orientation is quite specific – to achieve the wealth necessary to practice a style of life to which one already feels entitled. The means to achieve this goal (the mobility strategies) are diverse; any number of different courses of action enable the individual to reach the same goal. The crucial factor is the acquisition of wealth and not the means by which wealth is obtained, though presumably some means would be more honorable than others.

To an individual in this sort of situation, adventurism is a low-risk strategy; the possible gains of an adventure far outweigh the possible losses. One does not lose one's ascribed status (e.g., a noble birth) by engaging in adventurism. One may, however, gain the material goods to play a particular role more fully. A strategy of adventurism holds special gains to such individuals because one need have no commitment to the means by which wealth is obtained. The adventure itself can be undertaken for one's own personal and perhaps secret purposes rather than for society's benefit; and it holds the promise of a rapid, if not an easy, road to achieve one's particularistic goals.

Two components of this structural orientation seem most important. First, one's ambitions are directed toward attaining particularistic goals, which are typically defined in relation to established groups such as the lineage, community, ethnic group, or more generally status group. Membership in these sodalities can be easily claimed, in the case of the community, or is ascribed, in the case of the lineage. Thus membership itself is not problematic. What is problematic is the individual's standing and esteem within the group of which he claims membership. Intragroup status rankings are ambiguous, informal, but important. Second, one's status within the group is achieved, in part, through the accumulation of objects highly valued by the group. Combining these two components, one can characterize this structural framework as one which favors individuated action taken to satisfy particularistic goals.

One can suggest that this type of orientation is found in many different social settings. In fact, it probably exists to an extent in all societies. The important point and the appropriate focus of analysis is, however, to show that some social settings favor it, while others do not. This hypothesis can be illustrated by comparing societies which did and did not contribute argonauts to the gold rush.

The contrast between Chilean and Peruvian society is a good place to begin. The former supplied California with many adventurers, the latter very few. Two features of Chilean society seem particularly important in explaining this difference: (1) the lack of a system of patronage linking the members of lower and middle classes to the upper class, and (2) the cohesiveness of an upper class into which upward mobility could be achieved by people who were not indigenes, who had wealth, and who could emulate upper-class standards.

In Chile, the absence of an interclass patronage system occurred, in part, because there was no need to bind peasants to the soil. Chile's vast arable terrain, large mestizo population, and concentrated landownership provided a surplus of laborers. Although service tenancy was widespread, landlord/tenant relations lacked the coercive features of debt peonage and the moral features of the *compadrazgo* (patron-client) system (Bauer, 1975, pp. 48–52). The decisive characteristic here is that the stability of the landowning elite was largely independent of its ties to the peasantry. In contrast, Peru's mountainous terrain, desert coastal regions, and large Indian population made it difficult for large landowners to maintain a labor force that was not a dependent one. Debt peonage and the *compadrazgo* system, both in widespread use, formed the basis for interclass ties that helped to ensure a stable labor force and to fix a person in a network of interclass relations. Because these ties cut across class lines, they also provided a source of patronage and conflict within the upper class, members of which varied in the amount of resources they could mobilize (Orlove, 1977; van den Berghe and Primov, 1977).

In Chile, the lack of interclass patronage helped produce a cohesive yet relatively open upper class. In fact, Chile's revolution against Spanish rule reinforced its cohesiveness as well as its openness. According to Arnold Bauer (1975, p. 18), in an excellent study of Chilean society, "The cohesive and class-conscious creole elite moved smoothly, compared with other former Spanish colonies, to control the machinery of republican government." Although relatively small and primarily composed of titled families, the upper class was not closed. There "was a steady and welcome intrusion of new faces. . . . Money and distinguished military service permitted entry into the best circles" (Bauer, 1975, p. 36). And for those who could qualify – people with a European heritage – admittance to the upper class was a goal to be desired. Upper-class status allowed individuals access to secure position in the government as well as prestige and a cultivated style of life. In discussing the most frequently used strategies to enter the upper class, Bauer (1975, p. 40) says that "mining offered the fastest road to wealth and social prominence," a conclusion also reached by Chile's newspapers in 1848 (Monaghan, 1973, p. 45). In contrast, Peru's revolution against Spain accentuated cleavages within the upper class (Dobyns and Doughty, 1976; Monaghan, 1973, pp. 79–93). The elite itself became divided into political factions; an individual's place in the upper class was in large part determined by his ties of patronage to other and more powerful political figures. Access to money-making opportunities, such as the very lucrative guano trade, likewise depended on patronage. Thus one's social mobility in the Peruvian context was a matter requiring constant negotiation, a lapse in which might cause a loss of power, access, and prestige.

Thus, in comparison, Chile's social structure favored adventurism more than did Peru's. In Chile, acceptance in the upper class was based largely on emulation and consumption, both of which required wealth. Hence adventurism was a viable strategy of upward mobility for those who had the pedigree for membership in the upper class but lacked the wealth. In Peru, however, upwardly mobile individuals had to protect their vested interests against factional disputes and had to oversee and, to a certain extent, fulfill their *compadrazgo* obligations, lest they lose their dependent laborers. All these things required constant and personal attention, thus precluding the use of adventurism as a mobility strategy.

Very different conditions facilitated adventurism in western Europe. The revolutions in western Europe, beginning with the French Revolution and continuing through the revolutions of 1848, overturned the old order. Except for Britain, the hereditary aristocracy lost its secure hold over upper-class positions and had to vie with the wealthy from all backgrounds for high social prestige. As de Tocqueville (1969, p. 628) makes clear, however, aristocratic social conventions – the customs, the manners, the accoutrements – did not die out, but rather became the standards for all groups to emulate. Accordingly, observes de Tocqueville, a consequence of revolution, long after the revolution itself is over, is an impression that "nothing seems impossible" for those having money. "The passions roused by revolution by no means vanished at its close. . . . Longings on a vast scale remain, though the means to satisfy them become daily less. The taste for huge fortunes persists, though such fortunes in fact become rare, and on all sides there are those who eat out their hearts in secret, consumed by inordinate and frustrated ambition." Marx (1969), who on this point agrees with de Tocqueville, chided the adventurism of Parisians in 1848, condemned their lack of commitment, and ridiculed their selection, as president and later emperor, of Louis Bonaparte, "an adventurer blown in from abroad."

In 1848–49, adventurism in western Europe was a strategy of the moment; the gains seemed great, the losses few, because for a time previously established routes to success had vanished and new, more certain routes had not yet become institutionalized. Little by little, predicted de Tocqueville (1969, p. 628), "Longings once more become proportionate to the available means. Wants, ideas, and feelings again learn their limits."

By contrast, the revolutions of 1848–49 in eastern and southern Europe did not cause the social transformations that they did in western Europe. Though shaken, the Austro-Hungarian Empire held firm against the revolutionary tides of 1848–49. Newly emancipated serfs did not immediately migrate, nor did the aristocracy lose its hold over them. In Italy, the revolutions degenerated into wars between competing states; factionalism within the elite was omnipresent. And by mid-1849, throughout the area conservatism and repression gained the upper hand. One observer (Palmer, 1961, p. 485) said of the Austrian-Hungarian Empire that the society became "a standing army of soldiers, a sitting army of officials, a kneeling army of priests, and a creeping army of informers." As a consequence, the few adventurers from these areas who did take part in the gold rush tended to be expatriates – the radicals and the exiled aristocrats, such as those from Poland – whose adventurism had become a way of life rather than a means to an end.

In both western Europe and Chile, adventurism was a strategy used as a means to gain entrance into the upper class. These upper classes were national ones. Paris, London, Santiago – all were the central cities in a national culture and the only locations in which upper-class recognition could be gained. The trappings of the upper classes – the proper accent, manners, and material goods – were established at the center. And it was in these cities that gold fever fired the imagination of those whose ambitions were directed toward this particularistic goal. In these locations, virtually by definition, adventurers were not provincials.

In China and the United States, it was otherwise. Both societies lacked a unified upper class and had cohesive, yet highly competitive local communities. Here adventurism, stemmed from local concerns, aimed at less grandiose ends, involved greater numbers, but was no less consuming than adventurism elsewhere. Accordingly, adventurism in these two societies provides a source of variation important in understanding the phenomenon.

Among 19th-century Asian societies, China had no parallel in terms of the openness of its class structure. At the time of the gold rush, Japan's feudalistic social structure circumscribed individual aspirations, despite the influence of widespread commercialization (Rozman, 1974). Moreover, as Chie Nakane (1970) makes clear, even in modern Japanese society mobility strategies continue to be plotted through carefully made and constantly maintained ties with one's superior. Thailand's patrimonial state hierarchically arranged and linked everyone, from the peasantry to the nobility, in an extensive system of clientage (Rabibhadana, 1969). A similar system existed in parts of Indonesia, a modern-day version of which is reported by Geertz (1963). And in India, castes (*jati*) constrained the visions of their members, resulting, paradoxically, in attention being paid to both the minutiae of daily life and other-worldliness (Schluchter, 1976). Of course, social mobility was possible in all these places, but adventurism was hardly a viable strategy in any of them, except China.

Adventurism in China stemmed from a convergence of factors: the centrality of the patrilineal, patrilocal kinship structure; the absence of interclass clientage systems; a bureaucracy recruited through achievement criteria; and a class structure labeled by the eminent authority on social mobility in late Imperial China, Ho Ping-ti (1964), as not only open but "fluid."[14] An understanding of the patrilineage is most important.[15] No group in Chinese society gave the individual a more long-lasting or stable identity than the lineage. Lineages in south China sometimes numbered several thousand living members; they claimed extensive territory and controlled local affairs; their members often lived together in exclusive single-lineage villages. Unlike the clan or super lineage, which had mythical ancestors, the lineage had actual and acknowledged founders who were objects of veneration. Members had their names and accomplishments recorded in the lineage genealogy and plots reserved for them in the lineage cemetery.

Lineages, however, were not peaceful or cooperative communities. Lineage membership was ascribed; but lineage rank, power, and prestige were gained through competition and conspicuous consumption. One of the most important factors in this status competition was the possession of wealth. Through wealth one could become a landowning member of the local gentry, purchase a literary degree, and obtain the fineries that were so important in revealing to others that a high station had been reached. And finally, wealth allowed its possessor the possibility of becoming a lineage founder – and an object of veneration in his own right – through the establishment of an independent-lineage segment with its own corporate property holdings, ancestral shrine, and burial plot (Freedman, 1958, 1966, 1970).

Obtaining wealth in most rural areas was highly problematic. Because of the scarce resources, overpopulation, and intense competition, the ambitious left their native place in search of riches. By the time of the gold rush, temporary migration from rural to urban areas had long been an established strategy to obtain the material means to become influential in local affairs (Skinner, 1976). In one of the better analyses of a south China village, Daniel Kulp (1925, p. 48) notes that the "fundamental motivation of emigration" is security – the desire for wealth which would enable the migrant to return to his native village and assume a secure position. Although the Chinese peasant was bound by no tie of patronage to a landowner (tenancy was contractual), he was tied to his immediate family and more generally to his lineage. Though this tie may have been socially and emotionally binding, it was not geographically binding. If anything, it forced him into adventurism (Kulp, 1925, p. 49). "Sometimes the young farmer, himself unaffected by the stories [of wealth] becomes a victim of filial piety. The aged parents, lacking the comforts they see others enjoy, urge or sometimes compel him to seek their support where it is more sure. The ideals of forty centuries are the very core of his being; he cannot refuse. He leaves to take up the struggle; and the parents watch for the captain of the ferry to bring them news and money from their son." As Kulp (1925, pp. 48–49) observes, however, the Chinese peasant had relatively little to lose and much to gain by his sojourning. He could expect assistance from other Chinese wherever he traveled; and if he failed, he would return to his native village no worse off than when he left. But if he succeeded, he would "return the object of envy and emulation, and in every respect [would] enjoy superiority over the 'ricepot-keeping-turtles' who lacked the courage to break away." So great was the desire for local success and so strong the structural sources of adventurism that the Chinese peasant is the prototype of the sojourner (Siu, 1952). No society has supplied the world with more adventurers.[16]

As in China, adventurism in the United States seems to be a response to one's involvement in local society. The foremost observer of early 19th-century America, Alexis de Tocqueville (1969, pp. 62–87, 520–38), found the most distinctive feature of American society to be the township. The community encompassed the individual, limited his vision of the world, and instilled in him a restless ambition to possess those things that others around him had. The ambiguousness of rankings in democratic society and the intensity with which Americans invested their ambition and future in local communities created, thought de Tocqueville, a peculiarly American mentality: constant status competition and the use of material goods to signify success. Weber (1968, p. 933) reached the same conclusion about status stratification in the United States, as have most sociologists who study social mobility in the context of local communities. A portion of de Tocqueville's (1969, pp. 536, 548) masterful analysis follows: "It is odd to watch with what feverish ardor the Americans pursue prosperity and how they are ever tormented by the shadowy suspicion that they may not have chosen the shortest route to get it. . . . When everyone is constantly striving to change his position . . . men think in terms of sudden and easy fortunes, of great possessions easily won and lost, and chance in every shape and form. Amid all these perpetual fluctuations of fate the present looms large and hides the future, so that men do not want to think beyond tomorrow."

The discovery of gold in California must have seemed to a great many the shortest route. The letters and journals of American argonauts, in fact, repeat in specific terms what de Tocqueville said in general ones. As Samuel McNeil of Lancaster, Ohio, wrote (Morgan and Scobie, 1964, pp. 2–3), "Being a shoemaker, and ambitious to rise somewhat over the bench, it is no wonder that the discovery of gold in California excited my fancy and hopes." To Enos Christman (1930, pp. 225–26), a printer's apprentice from West Chester, Pennsylvania, the promise of gold meant money to marry his fiancée: "At home there is little chance for a mechanic without capital to rise very fast." Both McNeil and Christman joined companies organized within their local communities, as did thousands of other Americans who journeyed to California. From Massachusetts alone, at least 124 companies set out for California in 1849, each company representing a specific locality (Howe, 1923, pp. 171–72, 187–213). Thus, in contrast to western European and Chilean argonauts, American migrants were provincials and organized as such.[17]

Rural areas in the South, unlike those in other parts of the United States, lacked autonomous townships and status ambiguity (Cash, 1941, p. 35). The plantation rather than the community as the center of social organization encompassed even those who did not live on them, the poor whites. According to W. J. Cash (1941, pp. 36–39), the plantation system tended to make the division between the successful and unsuccessful rigid. The former thought of society as "a division . . . into Big Men and Little Men, with reference to property, power, and the claim to gentility." The latter were "those whose vague ambition, though it might surge up in dreams now and then, was too weak ever to rise to a consistent lust for plantations and slaves, or anything else requiring an extended exercise of will – those who, sensing their own inadequacy, expected and were content with little." Adventurism in the South was constrained by the framework of its society. Though many adventurers came out of the South, its social structure did not favor adventurism on so widespread a scale as that in the rest of the country.

In summary, an analysis of the gold rush suggests that adventurism is an outcome of a particularistic achievement orientation with a structural component: identity-bestowing collectivities in which one's relative standing must be achieved. In the societies examined above, these collectivities include cohesive upper-class status groups, communities, and kinship organizations. Theoretically, other types of collectivities (e.g., ethnic groups) should provide similar bases for adventurism. It should be noted, however, that the nature of the collectivity, its size and location, is a determining factor in the extensiveness and probably the outcome of adventurism.

By contrast, in those societies examined that did not exhibit adventurism, an individual's social mobility was constrained, channeled, or intertwined with that of others in such a fashion as to exclude alternative courses of action. In each, adventurism would appear to have been an unlikely form of action for any but the most socially marginal individual to take. In these settings, one's personal aspirations as well as less subjective factors limited one's choices and increased the likelihood of one's conformity to a normative order. To violate these norms of conduct in this context, as adventuring would do, would have led to dishonor, failure, or disenfranchisement.

Adventurism is thus most likely in those societies composed of individuals who are ascribed or who claim an identity without having the means to fulfill the particularistic demands of that identity. Adventurism can be seen as a response to particularistic demands and as an attempt to achieve particularistic goals. Traditionalistic loyalties – such as those to a family, an ethnic group, or a community – are the types of particularistic affiliations that compel individuals to seek adventure while at the same time making their adventure temporary and their commitment personal. It is the brevity of their intended sojourn and the intensity of their status involvement that paradoxically lead adventurers to maximize their endeavors in the short run without giving full regard to the social consequences of their actions.

Conclusion

The above analysis demonstrates that social structure contributes differentially to the amount and to the kind of risk individuals are willing to take. In other words, some structural conditions nurture attitudes favorable to risk taking, while others favor "playing it safe."

Now, in conclusion, I want to expand my original definition of adventurism by addressing the contrast Weber (1958) makes between types of risk taking: Long-term calculated risks, such as those methodically and routinely taken in the course of modern business, qualitatively differ, says Weber (1958, p. 20), from the "irrational" short-term recklessness associated with adventurism. Although Weber's discussion of adventurism is very brief, he (1958, p. 58) draws a sharp distinction between adventurers and bourgeois capitalists. "The inner attitude of the adventurer, which laughs at all ethical limitations, has been universal. . . . This attitude was one of the strongest inner obstacles which the adaptation of men to the conditions of an ordered bourgeois-capitalistic economy has encountered everywhere." Thus Weber seemingly implies that the motivational posture of the adventurer undermines rational calculation, that the adventurer does not make a capitalist.

This investigation alters Weber's findings. The analysis shows that adventurism, as a form of risk taking, may well be a relatively calculated, even a logical way to achieve individual goals. The important factors determining the use of this strategy are the actors' perceptions of their situation and their recognition of available alternatives to achieve their situationally specific ambitions. Acting on conditions of uncertainty, as does the adventurer, is a reasonable alternative for people who find other options blocked or distasteful or falling short of the gains needed. Although it may be a reasonable response in specific social contexts, adventurism nonetheless differs from capitalist risk taking in terms of the two definitional components given at the beginning of this essay – namely, (1) in the nature of the risks being taken (the act) and (2) in the nature of the goals being sought (the motivation).

With adventurism, the odds for success cannot be calculated as they can in capitalist enterprises. In fact, the thrust of capitalist risk taking is cautiously balancing the minimization of risk with the maximization of profit. Beyond caring for superficial details, adventurers, however, are unable to minimize systematically the uncertainty they will be facing or to maximize their potential gains, simply because both are unknown or uncalculable prior to the venture itself. For this reason, associations of adventurers emphasize not the minimization but rather the equalization of risks; the uncertainties of the venture will be shared more or less equally. This emphasis limits the use of hierarchical forms of group organization, particularly bureaucratic forms, which Weber saw as an important feature of capitalist enterprise. The kinds of organizations spawned by adventurism do not lend themselves to capitalist adaptation, or for that matter to any complexly organized endeavors.

The actions of the argonauts clearly illustrate this inability to form complex organizations. Of the companies organized to mine gold together, few survived the journey to California; once in California almost none survived the frantic search for gold. Only the Chinese were able to organize their numbers to mine gold cooperatively, and even they did so with difficulty. But once gold deposits that allowed for the systematic balancing of risks and profits were discovered, capitalist enterprises (e.g., hard-rock and hydraulic mining companies) began to form and then to predominate in the gold fields. Thus, it can be suggested that adventurers do act logically, according to the type of risks they are facing, but that the nature of their risks qualitatively differs from that of the risks encountered in routine business.[18]

Second, adventurism differs from capitalism in terms of the "inner attitudes" of the participants. Capitalist ethos, as Weber defines it, subordinates personal desires and happiness to the demands of routine, continuous work, which from the individual's point of view, notes Weber (1958, p. 70), is "so irrational." Adventurism, on the other hand, is a form of action that gives full rein to one's personal ambitions, often at the expense of one's obligation to submit to routine expectations of every-day life. From an individual perspective, adventurism can be seen as a calculated, if not a calculable, strategy to achieve personal goals rapidly by circumventing established modes of upward mobility. From a societal perspective, which Weber takes in this instance, adventurism can be seen as irrational, as a hedonistic response that, if universally practiced, would threaten, if not destroy, the stability of routine economic activity.

But these two ideal-typical forms of action – subordination versus attainment of personal goals – are not neatly separated into discrete categories of behavior. Rather, as Weber clearly recognizes, they are part of an often ambiguous internal tension, an inner struggle between meeting social obligations and attaining personal happiness that is felt by all individuals and that resolves itself differently in different situations. This study indicates that those deciding to pursue personal goals by breaking with established routines are those having the least to lose socially; adventurers gamble their persons – their health, even their lives – more than their social memberships. It is thus not surprising that some social contexts favor adventurism more than others. Nor is it surprising that the entrepreneurial breakthrough that laid the technological foundation for routine bourgeois capitalism should have occurred in many of the same locations from which the argonauts came; for, as Schumpeter notes (1962, p. 132), the entrepreneur, like the adventurer, travels "beyond the range of familiar beacons." Thus, the inner attitudes of the adventurer perhaps do not differ from those of the capitalist as much as Weber would suggest. Nonetheless, I believe the main point of Weber's argument is correct. The individuation inherent in adventurism and the intensely personal goals sought from adventures threaten the orderliness of routine social and economic activity. It is this inner conflict between meeting "the demands of the day" and finding personal satisfaction that "the spirit of capitalism" tries always to subdue by making the two seem to coincide.

Notes

1 Insofar as I am aware, no attempt has been made to conceptualize the adventurer as a sociological type, other than Weber's (1958, p. 58) brief characterization. Numerous concepts have been developed which directly relate to the adventurer. This is particularly the case with the "sojourner" (Siu, 1952; Bonacich, 1973) and the "stranger" (Simmel, 1950).

2 In several locations, Weber (1951, pp. 86, 104; 1958, pp. 20–21, 58; 1968, pp. 244–45) briefly mentions this association in the context of booty (adventure) capitalism. Also see Bendix (1962, p. 306).

3 It should be noted that the 1850 U.S. census data for California are judged unreliable (Bancroft, 1888, p. 158; Loosley, 1971) and thus can be used only to give indications of patterns.

4 William Perkins (Morgan and Scobie, 1964, p. 222), an argonaut whose journal provides much of what is known about Latin Americans in the gold rush, writes as follows: "[As compared to other Latin American countries] the immigration of Chile is much more of a mixed character. Men of all classes have come from there; for Chile is not only a seaboard country, but its people are infinitely more enterprising than any other of the Spanish Republic of South America."

5 In his analysis of this government's first years, Karl Marx (1969, pp. 84–85) has an excellent description of this effort to send "Parisian vagabonds to California."

6 DeBow (1854, p. 118) and Wright (1940, 1941) give the 1850 census figures upon which this evidence is based. Other records concerning the migration of specific groups are probably more accurate. Based on Chinese associational records, Speer (1856) estimates the number of Chinese in California in 1855 to be 48,000. Based on consul registers and passenger lists, Nasatir (1964, p. 26) estimates the French in California in 1851 at 20,000. Based on passport applications, Giacobbi (1974, p. 22) estimates the Chileans in California in 1850 to be between 5,000 and 8,000.

7 Based on the 1850 census figures (DeBow, 1854, pp. 116–17; Wright, 1940, 1941), the total migration from the Northeast (Connecticut, Delaware, Maine, Maryland, Massachusetts, New Hampshire, New Jersey, New York, Pennsylvania, Rhode Island, Vermont) was 28,893; from the border states (Arkansas, Kentucky, Missouri, Tennessee, Texas, Virginia), 17,738; from the Midwest (Illinois, Indiana, Iowa, Michigan, Ohio, Wisconsin), 11,172; and from the South (Alabama, Florida, Georgia, Louisiana, Mississippi, North Carolina, South Carolina), 4,808.

8 Comments to this effect are frequent, especially in journals of American argonauts. Typical in this regard is a journal entry made in 1849 by Enos Christman (1930, p. 11) on his first day of travel to California. "My feelings and emotions on leaving my friends and my native land on such an expedition, I cannot describe. I have left all that is near and dear and turned my face towards a strange land, expecting to be absent two or three years, hoping in that time to realize a fortune; and then return and be greeted by kind friends."

9 The research on "temporary migration," which in theory would include adventure migration, is not large. For a survey of this research see Bovenkerk (1974).

10 Neil Smelser (1962, p. 171) also makes this point in a slightly different context when he defines "crazes as mobilization for action based on a positive wish-fulfillment belief."

11 Gold mania can be profitably categorized, according to the typology developed by Smelser (1962), as a craze. It should, however, be noted that, as it is analyzed here, adventurism is a form of action undertaken by individuals who may or may not be responding to a collective movement. Historically, most examples of adventurism have not been associated with collective movements that could be confidently labeled as crazes. Thus crazes do not cause adventurism.

12 A striking illustration of the difference between the Northeast and the South in response to the discovery of gold is found in the autobiographical account of Howard Gardiner (Morgan, 1970, pp. 7–8). Gardiner, a northeastern merchant traveling in North Carolina a short time after the discovery became known, reported that the news of the discovery provided "an interesting topic of conversation" for the local inhabitants. At about the same time he received a letter from his home on Long Island informing him "that the exodus from that vicinity seemed likely to depopulate the village, as almost all the able-bodied men had either gone or were preparing to go" to California.

13 I should note here that this attempt to specify the stratificational conditions which favor adventurism differs from Smelser's (1962, pp. 175–80) more general attempt to define the structural conduciveness for crazes.

14 This following discussion on China is drawn from a variety of sources, particularly Freedman (1958, 1966), Ahern (1976), Skinner (1976), Chen (1940), and Hamilton (1977). It should also be noted that Chinese society was the prototype for Parsons' discussion of particularistic-achievement orientation.

15 For a general theory of patriliny that is applicable to Chinese society, see Paige (1974).

16 The scale of temporary migration from China exceeds that of any other society. Based on the figures given by Ta Chen (1923), between 1850 and 1925 an estimated 13,500,000 Chinese had migrated to Southeast Asia from two provinces in south China. One of the

best descriptions of temporary migration from 19th-century China is found in China
Imperial Maritime Customs (1870).
17 Chinese argonauts also organized according to their native locality. See Speer (1856) and
Williams (1971) for their discussions on this point.
18 For an excellent general discussion of different strategies of action in conditions of varying amounts of risk, see Heath (1976). His discussion of the "theory of choice under
uncertainty" has some bearing on the choices made by adventurers.

References

Ahern, Emily (1976) "Segmentation in Chinese Lineages: A View through Written Genea-
logies," *American Ethnologist* 3 (February): 1–16.
Bancroft, Hubert H. (1888) *History of California*, vol. 6, San Francisco, CA: History Co.
Bauer, Arnold (1975) *Chilean Rural Society*, Cambridge: Cambridge University Press.
Bendix, Reinhard (1962) *Max Weber: An Intellectual Portrait*, New York: Anchor.
Bieber, Ralph (1948) "California Gold Mania," *Mississippi Valley Historical Review* 35 (June):
3–28.
Bonacich, Edna (1973) "A Theory of Middlemen Minorities," *American Sociological Review*
38 (October): 583–94.
Bovenkerk, Frank (1974) *The Sociology of Return Migration: A Bibliographic Essay*, The
Hague: Nijhoff.
Cash, W. J. (1941) *The Mind of the South*, New York: Vintage.
Caughey, John W. (1975) *The California Gold Rush*, Berkeley, CA: University of California Press.
Chen, Ta (1923) "Chinese Migrations, with Special Reference to Labor Conditions," *U.S.
Bureau of Labor Statistics Bulletin*, misc. ser., vol. 340.
Chen, Ta (1940) *Emigrant Communities in South China*, New York: Institute of Pacific
Relations.
China Imperial Maritime Customs (1870) *Annual Reports*, Shanghai: Statistical Department
of the Inspectorate General of Customs.
Choi, C. Y. (1975) *Chinese Migration and Settlement in Australia*, Sydney: Sydney University
Press.
Christman, Enos (1930) *One Man's Gold*, New York: McGraw-Hill.
DeBow, J. D. B. (1854) *Statistical View of the United States*, Washington, D.C.: Government
Printing Office.
Dobyns, Henry and Doughty, Paul (1976) *Peru: A Cultural History*, Oxford: Oxford
University Press.
Elliott, J. H. (1966) *Imperial Spain 1469–1716*, New York: Mentor.
Faugsted, George (1973) *The Chilenos in the California Gold Rush*, San Francisco, CA:
R & E Research.
Freedman, Maurice (1958) *Lineage Organization in Southeastern China*, London: Athlone.
Freedman, Maurice (1966) *Chinese Lineage and Society: Fukien and Kwangtung*, London:
Athlone.
Freedman, Maurice (ed.) (1970) *Family and Kinship in Chinese Society*, Stanford, CA:
Stanford University Press.
Geertz, Clifford (1963) *Peddlers and Princes*, Chicago, IL: University of Chicago Press.
Giacobbi, Steve (1974) *Chile and Her Argonauts in the Gold Rush*, San Francisco, CA: R &
E Research.
Hamilton, Gary (1977) "Chinese Consumption of Foreign Commodities: A Comparative
Perspective," *American Sociological Review* 42 (December): 877–91.
Heath, Anthony (1976) *Rational Choice and Social Exchange*, Cambridge: Cambridge
University Press.

Ho, Ping-ti (1964) *The Ladder of Success in Imperial China*, New York: Wiley.

Howe, D. T. (1923) *Argonauts of '49, History and Adventurers of the Emigrant Companies from Massachusetts 1849–1850*, Cambridge, MA: Harvard University Press.

Kulp, Daniel (1925) *Country Life in South China*, New York: Teachers College, Columbia University.

Loosley, Allyn (1971) *Foreign Born Population of California, 1848–1920*, San Francisco, CA: R & E Research.

Marx, Karl (1969) *The Eighteenth Brumaire of Louis Bonaparte*, New York: International.

Monaghan, Jay (1973) *Chile, Peru, and the California Gold Rush of 1849*, Berkeley, CA: University of California Press.

Morgan, Dale (ed.) (1970) *In Pursuit of the Golden Dream*, Stoughton, MA: Western Hemisphere.

Morgan, Dale L. and Scobie, James (eds) (1964) *Three Years in California: William Perkins' Journal of Life at Sonora, 1848–1852*, Berkeley, CA: University of California Press.

Nakane, Chie (1970) *Japanese Society*, Berkeley, CA: University of California Press.

Nasatir, A. P. (ed.) (1964) *A French Journalist in the California Gold Rush*, Georgetown, CA: Talisman.

Orlove, Benjamin (1977) *Alpacas, Sheep, and Men: The Wool Export Economy and Regional Society in Southern Peru*, New York: Academic Press.

Paige, Jeffery (1974) "Kinship and Polity in Stateless Societies," *American Journal of Sociology* 80 (September): 301–20.

Palmer, R. R. (1961) *A History of the Modern World*, New York: Knopf.

Parsons, Talcott (1951) *The Social System*, New York: Free Press.

Paul, Rodman (1947) *California Gold*, Cambridge, MA: Harvard University Press.

Paul, Rodman (1967) *The California Gold Discovery*, Georgetown, CA: Talisman.

Petersen, W. (1970) "A General Typology of Migration," pp. 49–68 in Clifford J. Jansen (ed.), *Readings in the Sociology of Migration*, London: Pergamon.

Rabibhadana, Akin (1969) *The Organization of Thai Society in the Early Bangkok Period, 1782–1873*, Ithaca, NY: Cornell University, Cornell Thailand Project.

Ragatz, L. S. (1928) *The Fall of the Planter Class in the British Caribbean*, New York: Octagon.

Read, Georgia and Gaines, Ruth (eds) (1949) *Gold Rush, the Journal, Drawings and Other Papers of J. Goldsborough Bruff*, New York: Columbia University Press.

Rozman, Gilbert (1974) "Edo's Importance in the Changing Tokugawa Society," *Journal of Japanese Studies* 1 (Autumn): 91–112.

Schluchter, Wolfgang (1976) "The Paradox of Rationalizations: On the Relation between 'Ethics' and 'World,'" paper presented at the annual meeting of the International Society for the Comparative Study of Civilizations, Philadelphia.

Schumpeter, Joseph (1962) *Capitalism, Socialism, and Democracy*, New York: Harper Torchbooks.

Shepard, W. F. (1955) "Parisian Paupers in the Gold Rush," pp. 31–45 in R. Coke Wood (ed.), *Proceedings of the First Annual Meeting of the Conference of California Historical Societies*, Stockton, CA: College of the Pacific.

Simmel, Georg (1950) *The Sociology of Georg Simmel*, New York: Free Press.

Siu, Paul C. P. (1952) "The Sojourner," *American Journal of Sociology* 58 (July): 34–44.

Skinner, G. William (1976) "Mobility Strategies in Late Imperial China: A Regional-Systems Analysis," pp. 327–64 in Carol A. Smith (ed.), *Regional Analysis*, vol. 1, New York: Academic Press.

Smelser, Neil (1962) *Theory of Collective Behavior*, New York: Free Press.

Speer, William (1856) *An Humble Plea Addressed to the Legislature of California in Behalf of the Immigrants from the Empire of China to This State*, San Francisco, CA: Sterett.

Thomas, Brinley (1973) *Migration and Economic Growth*, Cambridge: Cambridge University Press.

Tocqueville, Alexis de (1969) *Democracy in America*, Garden City, NY: Anchor.

Tocqueville, Alexis de (1971) *Recollections*, Garden City, NY: Anchor.

Van den Berghe, Pierre and Primov, George (1977) *Inequality in the Peruvian Andes*, Columbia, MS: University of Missouri Press.

Weber, Max (1951) *The Religion of China*, New York: Macmillan.

Weber, Max (1958) *The Protestant Ethic and the Spirit of Capitalism*, New York: Scribner's.

Weber, Max (1968) *Economy and Society*, New York: Bedminster.

Williams, Stephen (1971) *The Chinese in the California Mines, 1848–1860*, San Francisco, CA: R & E Research.

Wright, Doris (1940) "The Making of Cosmopolitan California. I," *California Historical Society Quarterly* 19 (December): 323–43.

Wright, Doris (1941) "The Making of Cosmopolitan California. II," *California Historical Society Quarterly* 20 (March): 65–79.

9 The Separative Self: Androcentric Bias in Neoclassical Assumptions

Paula England

There are androcentric biases in the deep theoretical structure of neoclassical economics. Three of the most basic assumptions underlying economic theory are that interpersonal utility comparisons are impossible, that tastes are exogenous to economic models and unchanging, and that actors are selfish (have independent utilities) in markets. I argue that each of these assumptions flows from a separative model of human nature that has become a focus of criticism by feminists across a number of disciplines. I call the model "separative" because it presumes that humans are autonomous, impervious to social influences, and lack sufficient emotional connection to each other to make empathy possible. This is how they are presumed to behave in "the economy" or the "market."

A fourth, often more implicit, assumption in many neoclassical models is that individuals do *not* behave according to the separative model vis-à-vis their families. In the family, individuals (particularly men) are presumed to be altruistic. Thus, empathic emotional connections between individuals are emphasized in the family whereas they are denied in analyzing markets. I will argue that these assumptions exaggerate both the atomistic, separative nature of behavior in markets and the connective empathy and altruism within families.

These assumptions may be called "androcentric," or male-centered, in part because had the existing system of gender relations not been seen as the only possible or desirable arrangement, these particular assumptions would not have been chosen. In particular, such sharp contrasts between the assumptions thought appropriate to analyze households and those thought appropriate to analyze markets would not have seemed appropriate. These assumptions are also androcentric in the sense of being biased in favor of men's interests. Men's interests are furthered because analyses proceeding from these assumptions direct our attention away from the ways in which typical arrangements between men and women perpetuate women's disadvantage both in their families and in labor markets.

It is quite possible to criticize the major assumptions of neoclassical theory without making reference to feminist scholarship. Many economists and other social scientists have done so.[1] This paper draws upon many of their insights, but it emphasizes something that many criticisms of economic theory ignore: that the way gender has been socially organized has much to do with *which* parts of human experience have been left out of neoclassical models.[2] Contributions typically made

Original publication: England, Paula, "The Separative Self: Androcentric Bias in Neoclassical Assumptions," in Marianne A. Farker and Julie A. Nelson (eds), *Beyond Economic Man: Feminist Theory and Economics* (University of Chicago Press, Chicago, IL, 1993).

by women are often rendered invisible by the theory; men's advantages and power are often rendered invisible as well. Ignoring women's contributions and men's power are important parts of what may be called "androcentric" bias. The reader should bear in mind, however, that all sexism in economic writing cannot be reduced to these criticisms of gender bias in the deep theoretical assumptions of economics. Some analyses suffer from gender bias in the auxiliary assumptions of their particular applications rather than in the most basic assumptions discussed here.

Feminist Critiques of Theoretical Biases

Before applying a feminist critique to economic theory, it is first necessary to clarify what I mean by feminist theory. One result of the entry of women, often feminists, into the academy in the last twenty years has been the allegation that theories in every discipline have been affected by gender bias. Over time, feminist thought has become increasingly diverse and today contains much healthy controversy.[3] What is common to virtually all feminist views, however, is the belief that women are subordinated to men to a degree that is morally wrong and unnecessary. Beyond this, views differ as to the sources of women's disadvantage and the proper remedy.

Two major, though not mutually exclusive, emphases within feminist thinking can be discerned: One body of thought emphasizes the exclusion of women from traditionally male activities and institutions. For example, laws, cultural beliefs, and other discriminatory practices have excluded most women from politics, religious leadership, military positions, and traditionally male crafts and professions within paid employment. These exclusions are significant for women since activities traditionally regarded as male are those associated with the largest rewards of honor, power, and money. The mechanisms of exclusion are sometimes so effective that most women do not choose to enter "male" domains, although a minority have always attempted to do so. Here feminists see the corrective to be allowing women to participate in these spheres on an equal basis with men.

A second body of feminist thought emphasizes the devaluation of and low material rewards accorded to activities and traits that traditionally have been deemed appropriate for women. The sexism here is in failing to see how much traditionally female activities or dispositions contribute to the economy, society, or polity. Examples include failing to see how much child rearing, household work, and volunteer work contribute to "the wealth of nations." Another example is failing to see the extent to which work in predominantly female occupations contributes to firms' profits, the issue raised by the movement for "comparable worth" in wage setting (England, 1992). Feminists who emphasize this sort of sexism see the remedy to include changing values that deprecate traditionally female activities as well as allocating higher rewards to such activities.[4]

Sometimes these two feminist positions are read as being in conflict: the first is seen as advocating that women enter traditionally male activities while the second is seen to advocate women's continued attention to traditionally female activities. In fact, however, the second position is not inconsistent with a commitment to opening all valued activities to both men and women on an equal basis. It is possible to believe that we should acknowledge the value of traditionally female activities and reward them accordingly without believing that women should continue to do a disproportionate share of these activities. Indeed, a culture that really valorized traditionally female activities would undoubtedly encourage men as well as women to learn these skills and values. In this sense the two feminist positions can be seen as compatible, since together they would encourage that activities traditionally associated with both men and women be open to both men and women, while simultaneously encouraging a more equal valuing and rewarding of both kinds of activities. However, the second feminist emphasis *does* entail disagreement with those feminists who glorify a self for either men or women modeled upon the unconnected, nonempathic self that classical liberalism evoked for men. The second feminist position sees this as a mistaken value for either men or women.

I draw upon the second feminist emphasis here to distinguish between a "separative" self and a self that is emotionally connected to others. Emotional connections, and the skills and work entailed in honoring connections, are an important part of the activities traditionally assigned to women. The focus in this essay is on the theoretical consequences of deprecating and thus ignoring emotional connections. The feminist objection here is as much to the glorification of the separative self as to its link to gender.

The feminist critique of the separative self model has been applied in a number of disciplines other than economics. Seyla Benhabib (1987) traces the ideal of separative autonomy through liberalism in political philosophy. This tradition (whether the version of Hobbes, Locke, Rousseau, Kant, or Rawles) discusses moving from a "state of nature" to the metaphorical "contract" to set up the state. Both before and after the contract, men are presumed to be separative and autonomous; what changes with the contract is the degree of civility or justice achieved by these separative individuals. As these ideas evolved from the seventeenth to the nineteenth century, authors presumed that women would continue to do child-rearing and household work as well as provide emotional comfort and sexual satisfaction for men. They never seriously considered that men would do this sort of work. Nor did they recognize that men are *not* entirely autonomous – that no man would have survived to adulthood but for the altruistic work of a woman, and that every man continues to benefit from such work as an adult. This women's work was taken for granted, seldom discussed, and excluded from political theory, because these authors viewed women and their work as "part of nature" within a metaphysic that denigrated nature. Moreover, women's activities did not count as "moral," since only exercising "autonomy" in the public sphere counted as "moral." Thus the separative self was valued while nurturant connection was either ignored or deprecated.

The emphasis on separation also can be seen in developmental psychology (Keller, 1986; Chodorow, 1978; Gilligan, 1982). Carol Gilligan points out that Freud, Jung, Erikson, Piaget, and Kohlberg, despite their differences, all viewed individuation as synonymous with maturation but viewed connection to others as developmentally regressive. Their views are deeply sexist in that they assumed women would do the emotional work of child-rearing and would provide emotional comfort for men, yet they did not acknowledge learning the capacity for intimacy and nurturance as part of maturation. They presented their theories as generic theories of the human developmental process rather than theories of male development under certain social arrangements.

The separative self is glorified in the philosophy of science as well. Evelyn Fox Keller (1983, 1985) argues that objectivity has been defined in terms of the separation of the subject (the scientist) from the object of study. She believes it is more than coincidental that the men developing science conceived their methodology in terms of what was emphasized as "masculine" – separative autonomy. Emotional connections with one's subject matter were seen as contaminating knowledge. Keller insists, however, that these connections sometimes yield useful insights. Some of our deepest insights come from the ability to empathize with those whose behavior we study. Under the current norms of science, such connections are permitted within the "context of discovery" but not within the "context of justification." Yet scientific articles are written in the language of the context of justification, rendering the context of discovery invisible, rather like housework and child-rearing. As a result, any traces of how empathic connection to the subject provided insights are written out of the record of science, and we do not see how having a connected self in this phase of the research process might contribute to the recognized goals of science. Scientific texts thus deprecate the connective part of the enterprise.

Applying the Feminist Critique of Separative Self Models to Neoclassical Economics

How does the feminist critique of the separative self model apply to neoclassical economic theory? The assumptions to be criticized are: (1) that interpersonal utility comparisons are impossible; (2) that tastes are exogenous and unchanging; and (3) that actors are selfish. These three assumptions are applied to behavior in market transactions – the primary focus of economics. Then, in a dramatic switch, a fourth assumption is invoked when analyzing the family: that altruism is the rule between family members. I will argue that each of the first three assumptions embodies a view of the self that is separative and hence vulnerable to the feminist critique discussed above. The fourth assumption is not discussed in most textbooks, but it is explicit in the one area of economics that has emphasized the household, the "new home economics" (Backer, 1981; Pollak, 1985). The contrast between the behavior assumed for the family and for markets will reveal how steeped in notions of gender roles these assumptions are.

Interpersonal utility comparisons

Neoclassical economists assume that interpersonal utility comparisons are impossible. Since the 1930s, utility has been conceived as the satisfaction of an individual's subjective desires; the concept lacks any dimension of objective, measurable welfare that might form the basis for interpersonal comparison (Cooter and Rappoport, 1984). As a result, neoclassical theory tells us that we cannot know which of two persons gained more from a given exchange because the relevant "currency" in which gain or advantage is measured is utility, and utility is conceived as being radically subjective. This is so basic an assumption that it is generally mentioned in undergraduate microeconomic textbooks (e.g., Hirshleifer, 1984, p. 476).

Using Pareto-optimality as the criterion of efficiency derives at least in part from the assumption that interpersonal utility comparisons are impossible. A distributional change is defined as Pareto-superior if at least one party gains utility and no one loses any. For example, voluntary exchange between self-interested individuals produces a Pareto-superior distribution. Each party must have felt that s/he would be made better off by the exchange than by foregoing it or s/he would not have made it. When no more Pareto-superior changes can be made through exchange, the distribution is said to be Pareto-optimal. Thus redistribution requiring some affluent persons to lose utility for the sake of a gain by the poor cannot be Pareto-superior by definition.

How does the feminist critique of separation/connection relate to interpersonal utility comparisons? The assumption that interpersonal utility comparisons are impossible flows from assuming a separative self. To see how this is true, imagine that we started by assuming the sort of emotional connection that facilitates empathy. Such empathy would facilitate making interpersonal utility comparisons, since being able to imagine how someone else feels in a given situation implies the possibility of translating between one's own and another person's metric for utility. Assuming that interpersonal utility comparisons are impossible amounts to assuming a separative self, and to denying the possibility of an empathic, emotionally connected self. But if we assume instead that individuals *can* make interpersonal utility comparisons, then surely we would conclude that as scholars we, too, are capable of making such comparisons. These comparisons would provide information about the relative advantage and disadvantage of individuals under study. We then would view such comparisons as practical measurement problems (analogous to calculating "shadow prices") rather than as impossible in principle.

As long as we accept the principle that utility comparisons between individuals are impossible, we find that the same principle applies to comparisons between groups. To answer questions about groups requires not only measuring utility but also averaging utilities across persons. While some applied economists study inequalities in wealth or income between groups, and discuss their findings in language that seems to imply something about unequal utility between the groups, such interpretations are in fundamental conflict with the theoretical core of neoclassical economics. Hence generalizations such as that women in a particular society are disadvantaged relative to men or that the poor are disadvantaged relative to the rich are moved to the margin of serious research and seldom discussed.

These beliefs also explain why positive neoclassical theories harmonize so well with conservative normative positions on distributional issues. The paradigm denies one the possibility of stating that those at the bottom of hierarchies average less utility than others, which otherwise might provide a basis for questioning the justice of initial unequal distributions of endowments and their consequences. The paradigm also implies that virtually all collectivistic redistribution is non-Pareto-optimal. In sum, it permits no assessments of inequal utility that otherwise might serve as grounds for advocating egalitarian redistribution; rather it criticizes such a redistribution on the grounds of efficiency, To take only one example, this assumption leads one to question the merit of assistance to the large proportion of female-headed families who live in poverty. More generally, it denies us a theoretical basis for saying existing arrangements benefit men more than women.

Tastes: exogenous and unchanging

What the utility maximizer of economic theory will do is often indeterminate unless one knows the individual's tastes. Tastes (also called preferences) determine the amount of utility provided by different combinations of goods, services, leisure, working conditions, children, and so forth. They are an input to economic models. Economists do not attempt to explain the origin of these tastes. In a now famous article, George Stigler and Gary Becker (1977) argued that there is little variation in tastes between individuals, so most behavior can be explained by prices or endowments. Other economists disagree and see a role for disciplines such as sociology and psychology in explaining variations in tastes (Hirshleifer, 1984). But whether or not they believe that tastes vary across individuals, economists typically see tastes as exogenous to their models.[5] Further, tastes are not expected to change as individuals interact with others in markets or as they experience the consequences of market interaction.

Economists have recently also moved onto the "turf" of other social sciences with models purporting to explain seemingly "nonmarket" areas such as crime (Becker, 1968; Witte, 1980) and family behavior (Becker, 1981; Pollak, 1985). But as they enlarge the scope of their theories and claim that their paradigms can explain not only behavior in what we usually think of as markets but all human behavior, the assumption that tastes are exogenous becomes even more heroic. For example, to retain the assumption in the "new home economics," one must be prepared to argue that tastes are exogenous even to interactions in one's family of origin. But if tastes don't come, at least in part, from the family in which one was raised, where do they come from? Is the implicit assumption that they are freely chosen or biologically determined? Either proposition is highly questionable as a complete explanation.

There is no doubt that assuming fixed and exogenous rather than changing and endogenous preferences radically simplifies neoclassical models. But is the assumption reasonable? To see that it is not, consider the following questions. Are most individuals really so impervious to their surroundings that they can hold a job for years without their preferences being affected by the routines they get used to in this job? Are preferences never influenced by interactions with coworkers? If they are, then results of events in a labor market are affecting tastes. Are consumer tastes never altered by interactions with neighbors? If they are, then events in the housing market (which determine the identity of one's neighbors) are affecting tastes. One needs to assume a misleading degree of emotional separation and atomism to deny the possibility of these effects of market exchanges upon tastes. A model that does not help to elucidate how tastes change through such interactions leaves out too much of human experience. Further, as economists enlarge their scope, the implausibility of the assumption becomes ever clearer. Does anyone really believe that the choice of a spouse in the "marriage market" has no effects on later tastes?

One additional problem with ignoring the endogeneity of tastes is that it obscures some of the processes through which gender inequality is perpetuated. In some of these processes, economic outcomes affect tastes. For example, according to cognitive-developmental psychologists such as Lawrence Kohlberg (1966), childhood socialization is largely a matter of watching what same-sex adults do and forming one's own tastes and values accordingly. Thus, at the societal level discrimination may affect the tastes of the next generation. To take an example from somewhat later in the life cycle, if schools or employers discriminate against women who start out wanting to enter "male" fields, women may adjust their tastes to the available options. In these ways, either market outcomes result from premarket discrimination or market discrimination may create gender-related tastes, thus perpetuating women's lower earnings.[6]

Selfishness in markets

Neoclassical theory assumes self-interested actors. Since it says nothing explicit about what gives people utility, it is not inconsistent with neoclassical assumptions for some individuals to derive satisfaction from being altruistic (Friedman and Diem, 1990). That is, self-interest need not imply selfishness in the sense of failing to care for others. Nonetheless, in practice, most economists *do* assume selfishness in markets, as Robert Frank (1988) has pointed out. Sometimes auxiliary assumptions preclude altruism, for instance, the assumption that utilities are independent (Folbre, 1993). Since economists generally define A's altruism toward B as the case where whatever gives B utility contributes to A's utility, altruism is precluded by the assumption that actors' utilities are independent.[7]

The assumption that individuals are selfish is related to the separative model of self. Emotional connection often creates empathy, altruism, and a subjective sense of social solidarity. For example, the experience of attending to the needs of a child or of mentoring a student often makes us care more about others' well-being. (Note that this is also an example of changing tastes.) Separative selves would have little basis on which to develop the necessary empathy to practice altruism.[8]

Most labor economists assume selfishness of employers toward employees and vice versa. If employers were altruistic toward some or all of their employees, they might pay them above-market wages, foregoing some profit. Of course, the *strategic* payment of above-market wages in the new "shirking" models of efficiency wages (Katz, 1986; Bulow and Summers, 1986) does not violate the assumption of selfishness. In these models, employers are profit maximizing, and thus they pay above-market wages only when such wages increase the productivity of workers, and thus revenue, enough to more than compensate for the costs of the higher wage.[9]

Assuming selfishness in markets is not merely a "male" model of self that may fit women less well; it also fails to account for men's altruism in market behavior, altruism that may work to the disadvantage of women. When people engage in collective action, a kind of *selective* altruism may be at work, at least in the initial stages (Elster, 1979; Sen, 1987). For example, when male employees collude in order to try to keep women out of "their" jobs, they are exhibiting within-sex altruism.[10]

Sometimes selective within-sex altruism also exists between male employers and employees, so that employers are willing to pay male workers more than the contribution of the marginal worker to revenue product. This may be termed pro-male altruistic discrimination as opposed to the more common form of anti-female discrimination in which women are paid less than the (two-sex) market-clearing wage. Matthew Goldberg (1982) has shown that this pro-male altruistic discrimination will not necessarily erode in competitive markets as anti-female discrimination presumably will.[11] The essence of his argument is that a nondiscriminator cannot buy out an altruistic discriminator for a price consistent with the present value of the business to the nondiscriminator. This is because the nonpecuniary utility the pro-male discriminator is getting from indulging his taste for altruism toward male workers makes the business worth more to the discriminator than to the nondiscriminator. By contrast, a nondiscriminator's offer to buy out an anti-female discriminator (who is hiring men for more than he could hire women) will be compelling because the nondiscriminator can make more money than the anti-female discriminator with no sacrifice of nonpecuniary utility. If we assume the absence of altruism in markets, then we cannot recognize the possibility that this selective altruism is a source of sex discrimination that *can* endure in competitive markets. Thus, recognizing selective altruism would revise neoclassical economists' usual assumption that discrimination cannot endure in competitive markets.

Altruism at home

When it comes to the family, economists generally assume a single family utility function in which the "head" is an altruist. This is clearest in the "new home economics," the application of the neoclassical model to the household, an effort for which Gary Becker (1981) has become famous. From a feminist perspective, the acknowledgment of the importance to the economy of work that goes on in the household must be applauded. However, Becker's assumptions about altruism are in need of a feminist critique. (These same criticisms apply to the more recent 1988 version of Becker's *Treatise on the Family* as well as the 1981 edition.)

Becker's well-known "rotten kid" theorem posits an altruistic family head who takes the utility functions of family members as arguments of "his" own utility function. Becker argues that even a selfish "rotten" spouse or child will be induced to "behave" because of the reinforcement mechanism set up by the altruist. This "rotten kid" theorem doesn't hold without the assumption that the family member who is an altruist *also* controls the resources to be distributed (Ben-Porath, 1982; Pollak, 1985). Becker refers to the altruistic head as male and to the beneficiaries as women and children, although he claims that he used masculine and feminine pronouns only to distinguish the altruist from the beneficiary (Becker, 1981, p. 173). Since Becker certainly knows that it is generally men who have greater access to money, we must be suspicious of his claim that his choice of the male pronoun to denote the altruist was arbitrary. Yet Becker never discusses the effects of such differential power in the family (England and Farkas, 1986, ch. 3), although he does discuss the efficiencies of a division of labor in which men are the primary earners (Becker, 1981, ch. 2). Thus his discussion shows us the advantages but none of the disadvantages for women of the conventional sex division of labor. Becker ignores male power and its potentially harmful effects on women while exaggerating male altruism. It is particularly ironic that altruism, in which women seem to specialize more than men (England and Farkas, 1986, ch. 3 and 4; England, 1989), gets credited to men!

My disagreement is not with the notion that altruism exists in the family, or even with the notion that, on average, people are more altruistic toward family members than toward others. It is rather with the extreme bifurcation of the assumptions about the two spheres.[12] If economic man or woman is so altruistic in the family, might not some altruism be present in market behavior as well? Doesn't this altruism imply an ability to empathize with others that might permit making at least rough interpersonal utility comparisons? Doesn't the susceptibility of an altruist to being influenced by another's joy or pain suggest that s/he also might modify certain tastes through the process of interaction with others? If the answers to these questions are yes, as may well be the case, then the altruistic self assumed for the household is inconsistent with the separative self assumed for market behavior. It is simply not plausible that the altruist who displays an emotionally connective self in the family is the same person who marches out into the market selfish, unable to empathize with others, with utterly rigid tastes.

A second objection to the assumption of extreme altruism in the family is that it conceals the harmful effects of men's selfishness when combined with their greater power within the family. In one of the theoretical traditions within sociology most consistent with neoclassical economic assumptions, exchange theory (Cook, 1987), practitioners chose to model the family by characterizing each actor as selfish, or at least as less than completely altruistic. Empirical research in this tradition has examined how relative earnings of husbands and wives affect marital decision-making. The game-theoretic logic of exchange theory suggests that since earnings are resources the earner could withdraw from his/her spouse if the relationship were terminated, we would expect earnings to affect marital power.[13]

When individuals were surveyed, asked to identify areas of disagreement with their spouses, and asked whose wishes prevailed, the general findings showed that men's wishes prevail more often than women's wishes, but that this disparity is less pronounced when women are employed and least pronounced when women's earnings are high relative to their husbands' earnings. (For a review of such studies and a theoretical interpretation, see England and Kilbourne, 1990c.) This research makes it clear that men do not use the power they derive from earnings entirely altruistically, as Becker's (1981) model assumes. It also demonstrates that the sex division of labor in the typical household disadvantages women in bargaining within marriage by leaving them with less (or no) earnings to take with them if they left the relationship.[14]

The new home economics ignores issues of power when considering consequences of the traditional division of labor and the attendant loss of equity, and instead emphasizes only the efficiency gains from specialization according to comparative advantage (England and Farkas, 1986, ch. 4). It also obscures the fact that market discrimination against women results in women's inferior bargaining power within the family.

Conclusion

I have criticized economists' assumptions that, in market behavior, interpersonal utility comparisons are impossible, tastes are exogenous and unchanging, and individuals are selfish (i.e., utilities are independent), but that altruism is the rule in the family. The first three of these assumptions of neoclassical theory contain the "separative-self" bias that feminist theorists have traced in many disciplines. Taken together, this view glorifies men's autonomy outside the family while giving them credit for altruism within the family. Two specific aspects of gender bias were emphasized: unexamined assumptions about gender roles lead to a sharp disjuncture of views about the household and the market, and these assumptions result in an inability to see how conventional arrangements perpetuate women's systematic subordination to men.

But I have not challenged the most "sacred" neoclassical assumption of all, rationality. Clearly, this term has a variety of meanings. Some feminist philosophers argue that the concept of rationality in Western thought has been constructed to be inconsistent with anything associated with traits and activities presumed to be "feminine"

– nature, the body, passion, change, emotion – and that this has distorted the concept of rationality (Schott, 1988; Bordo, 1986; Lloyd, 1984). Yet rationality has a rather limited meaning in neoclassical theory. The rational actor has preferences that are both transitive (if I prefer A to B and B to C, I will prefer A to C) and complete (any two outcomes can be compared), and s/he acts on the basis of correct calculations about what means will best maximize utility given these preferences (Varian, 1984; Sen, 1987). Perhaps this neoclassical concept of rationality is relatively free from gender bias, including the assumption that rationality entails a separative self; perhaps it is not.[15] Resolving this question is beyond the scope of this paper. However, even if we retain the rationality assumption, the neoclassical model needs to be changed substantially in the directions I have indicated above. Relaxing the three assumptions discussed as problematic assertions of a separative self will severely blunt the predictive power of the rationality assumption, even if it is retained. For example, when it comes to wages and discrimination, it is harder to predict what a rational, selectively altruistic employer will do than to predict what a rational, profit-maximizing employer will do. Similarly, it is harder to predict how a rational husband who earns more than his wife will behave in a model of marriage that admits the possibility of both altruism and selfishness than in a model that assumes only one or the other.

Correcting the biases discussed in this paper will generate models in which separation and connection are variable; this variation needs to be explained within both households and markets. Although these new models may entail a loss of deductive certainty, they will illuminate rather than ignore gender inequality in the social and economic world.

Notes

1   For critical discussions of the neoclassical assumptions of self-interest, exogenous tastes, and impossibility of interpersonal utility comparisons that do not draw upon feminist theory, see Mansbridge (1990), Etzioni (1988), Sen (1982, 1987), Piore (1974), Hahnel and Albert (1990), Pollak (1976), Frank (1988), and Granovetter (1985, 1988). For critical discussions of the neoclassical rationality assumption (an assumption I do not examine in this paper) that do not draw upon feminist theory, see Hogarth and Reder (1987) and Elster (1979).
2   For other criticisms of economic theory that *do* link the omissions to gender bias, see Folbre and Hartmann (1988) and Nelson (1992) as well as the other papers in this volume.
3   For one excellent review of feminist positions, see Jaggar (1983).
4   Nelson (1992) points out that traditionally female and traditionally male qualities each have both a positive and a negative aspect, but our culture has tended to see only the positive side of supposedly masculine qualities and the negative side of supposedly feminine qualities. Consider, for example, the oppositional terms "hard" and "soft" often metaphorically associated with men and women respectively. At least in intellectual or business life, "hard" is seen as positive and "soft" as negative. But Nelson points out that it is more telling to see "hard" as having a positive aspect, strength, and a negative aspect, rigidity, while "soft" has a negative aspect, weakness, as well as a positive aspect, flexibility. The tendency to see the hard-soft distinction as a matter of strong versus weak and to ignore the fact that it is also a matter of flexible versus rigid is an instance of androcentric bias. Nelson's discussion shows that the second feminist emphasis I am

discussing here is most defensible when it argues for valorization of the *positive aspects* of traditionally female activities and traits, and when its criticism of androcentric values focuses on the *negative aspects* of traditionally male activities and traits.

5   Becker's recent work on addiction is sometimes interpreted as endogenizing tastes (Becker and Murphy, 1988). I believe this is a misinterpretation. In Becker's model, called "rational addiction," the actor is presumed to calculate the present value of the future utility that will result from using the drug as well as the future disutility that will ensue from addiction. Then the actor makes a decision based on his/her present tastes about whether or not to begin use of the addictive drug. I see this work as an attempt to show that a model assuming rationality and exogenous tastes can be used to analyze even those phenomena noneconomists see as *most* obviously irrational and *most* obviously involving changes in tastes.

6   There is, however, one sense in which assuming endogenous tastes militates against recognizing gender inequalities in *utilities*. In the extreme, if we believe that people come to desire whatever they are limited to, then no disutility results from discrimination or other types of oppression. I believe that this extreme view distorts reality as much as the view that tastes never change as a result of the constraints one encounters.

7   The assumption that each actor's utility is independent of the utility of other actors is distinct from the assumption that one cannot make interpersonal utility comparisons. The assumption of independent utilities is about whether A's utility affects B's; the assumption that interpersonal utility comparisons are impossible concerns whether either the actors or the scientist can measure the amount by which total utilities increased from a particular distributional change. It is the assumption of independent utilities that implies selfishness. One could have a model in which people are capable of making interpersonal utility comparisons but are selfish (i.e., have independent utilities). Even so, the assumptions are related. It is difficult to imagine a model in which people are altruistic (i.e., utilities are not independent) that does not feature actors making interpersonal utility comparisons. To see this, consider how my choice to spend twenty dollars on a gift for my spouse, toward whom I am altruistic, affects my utility. If I buy the gift I forego the utility I would have gained from spending the money on myself, but I gain the utility that comes from seeing my spouse's utility increase upon receiving the gift. A fully specified utility function of the sort economists assume must be able to determine which gain is greater, requiring some common metric. In sum, to assume interdependent utilities may require admitting interpersonal utility comparisons, but admitting the possibility of interpersonal utility comparisons does not necessarily imply interdependent utilities.

8   Of course, empathy can also be used selfishly. As people who have gone through a painful divorce can attest, it is often those who know their utility functions the best who can hurt them the most should they cease to feel altruism (Friedman and Diem, 1990).

9   By contrast, Akerloff's (1982, 1984) "gift exchange" model of efficiency wages does presume a sort of altruism on the part of employers. In this sense, it is a radical departure from the usual neoclassical assumption of selfishness in markets.

10   Such behavior is documented by Reskin and Roos (1990).

11   For a nontechnical elaboration of Goldberg's argument as well as an explanation of why economists believe most discrimination will eventually disappear in competitive markets, see England (1992, ch. 2). I have taken quite a few liberties in translating Goldberg's technical argument into words. For example, his discussion is about race rather than sex discrimination, and he uses the term "nepotism" rather than "altruism." However, he has stated in a personal communication that he considers my elaboration consistent with the intent of his paper. One qualification is in order: I have characterized "pro-male" discrimination as altruistic toward men because it entails a willingness to pay more than marginal revenue product. It could also be seen as altruistic toward men in the

willingness to pay them more than necessary to employ equally productive workers. However, on this latter criterion, anti-female discrimination (paying women less than marginal revenue product) could also be seen as altruistic toward men since it, too, leads to paying men more than the wage for which equally productive women could be employed. Thus, I have not considered discrimination to be altruistic unless it involves a willingness to pay more than marginal revenue product.

12 Folbre and Hartmann (1988) also make this point.

13 Not all exchange theorists assume that each party is maximizing selfish gain. Some exchange theorists presume that actors also follow norms of equity. Yet those taking the latter view often presume that any existing distribution will tend to acquire an aura of legitimacy and equity over time, regardless of the actual equity of its origins.

14 For a discussion of why a woman's domestic services, which also could be withdrawn if the marriage broke up, seem not to "count" as heavily in exchange as earnings, see England and Kilbourne (1990c).

15 I have argued elsewhere (England, 1989; England and Kilbourne, 1990a, 1990b) that the rationality assumption, *in combination with the assumption of exogenous tastes*, does entail an androcentric bias in that it considers emotion and reason to be radically separate phenomena, an idea tied to notions of gender differentiation in the history of Western thought.

References

Akerloff, George A. (1982) "Labor Contracts as Partial Gift Exchange," *Quarterly Journal of Economics*, 47: 543–69.

Akerloff, George A. (1984) "Gift Exchange and Efficiency-Wage Theory: Four Views," *American Economic Review* 74: 79–83.

Becker, Gary (1968) "Crime and Punishment: An Economic Approach," *Journal of Political Economy* 76: 169–217.

Becker, Gary (1981) *A Treatise on the Family*, Cambridge, MA: Harvard University Press.

Becker, Gary and Murphy, K. M. (1988) "A Theory of Rational Addiction," *Journal of Political Economy* 96(4): 675–700.

Benhabib, Seyla (1987) "The Generalized and the Concrete Other: The Kohlbert-Gilligan Controversy and Feminist Theory," Seyla Benhabib and Drucilla Cornell (eds), in pp. 77–95 *Feminism as Critique: On the Politics of Gender*, Minneapolis, MN: University of Minnesota Press.

Ben-Porath, Yoram (1982) "Economics and the Family – Match or Mismatch? A Review of Becker's *A Treatise on the Family*," *Journal of Economic Literature* 20: 52–64.

Bordo, Susan (1986) "The Cartesian Masculinization of Thought," *Signs* 11: 439–56.

Bulow, Jeremy I. and Summers, Lawrence H. (1986) "A Theory of Dual Labor Markets with Application to Industrial Policy, Discrimination, and Keynesian Unemployment," *Journal of Labor Economics* 4: 376–414.

Chodorow, Nancy (1978) *The Reproduction of Mothering*, Berkeley, CA: University of California Press.

Cook, Karen (ed.) (1987) *Social Exchange Theory*, Newbury Park, CA: Sage.

Cooter, Robert and Rappoport, Peter (1984) "Were the Ordinalists Wrong about Welfare Economics?," *Journal of Economic Literature* 22: 507–30.

Elster, Jon (1979) *Ulysses and the Sirens: Studies in Rationality and Irrationality*, Cambridge, MA: Cambridge University Press.

England, Paula (1989) "A Feminist Critique of Rational-Choice Theories: Implications for Sociology," *American Sociologist* 20: 14–28.

England, Paula (1992) *Comparable Worth: Theory and Evidence*, New York: Aldine de Gruyter.

England, Paula and Farkas, George (1986) *Households, Employment, and Gender: A Social, Economic, and Demographic View*, New York: Aldine de Gruyter.

England, Paula and Kilbourne, Barbara Stanek (1990a) "Feminist Critiques of the Separative Model of Self: Implications for Rational Choice Theory," *Rationality and Society* 2: 156–72.

England, Paula and Kilbourne, Barbara Stanek (1990b) "Does Rational Choice Theory Assume a Separative Self?," *Rationality and Society* 2: 522–26.

England, Paula and Kilbourne, Barbara Stanek (1990c) "Markets, Marriages, and Other Mates: The Problem of Power," pp. 163–88 in Roger Friedland and A. F. Robertson (eds), *Beyond the Marketplace: Rethinking Economy and Society*, New York: Aldine de Gruyter.

Etzioni, Amatai (1988) *The Moral Dimension*, New York: Free Press.

Folbre, Nancy (1993) "Micro, Macro, Choice and Structure," pp. 329–37 in Paula England (ed.) *Theory on Gender/Feminism on Theory*, New York: Aldine de Gruyter.

Folbre, Nancy and Hartmann, Heidi (1988) "The Rhetoric of Self Interest: Ideology and Gender in Economic Theory," pp. 184–203 in Arjo Klamer, Donald N. McCloskey and Robert M. Solow (eds), *The Consequences of Economic Rhetoric*, New York: Cambridge University Press.

Frank, Robert (1988) *Passions within Reason: The Strategic Role of the Emotions*, New York: W. W. Norton.

Friedman, Debra and Diem, Carol (1990) "Comments on England and Kilbourne," *Rationality and Society* 2: 517–21.

Gilligan, Carol (1982) *In a Different Voice: Psychological Theory and Women's Development*, Cambridge, MA: Harvard University Press.

Goldberg, Matthew S. (1982) "Discrimination, Nepotism, and Long-Run Wage Differentials," *Quarterly Journal of Economics* 97: 308–19.

Granovetter, Mark (1985) "Economic Action and Social Structure: The Problem of Embeddedness," *American Journal of Sociology* 91: 481–510.

Granovetter, Mark (1988) "The Sociological and Economic Approaches to Labor Market Analysis: A Social Structural View," pp. 187–216 in George Farkas and Paula England (eds), *Industries, Firms, and Jobs: Sociological and Economic Approaches*, New York: Plenum.

Hahnel, Robin and Albert, Michael (1990) *Quiet Revolution in Welfare Economics*, Princeton, NJ: Princeton University Press.

Hirshleifer, Jack (1984) *Price Theory and Applications*, 3rd edn, Englewood Cliffs, NJ: Prentice-Hall.

Hogarth, Robin M. and Reder, Melvin W. (eds) (1987) *Rational Choice: The Contrast between Economics and Psychology*, Chicago, IL: University of Chicago Press.

Jaggar, Alison M. (1983) *Feminist Politics and Human Nature*, Totowa, NJ: Rowman & Allanheld.

Katz, Lawrence (1986) "Efficiency Wage Theories: A Partial Evaluation," *Macroeconomic Annual*, Cambridge, MA: National Bureau of Economic Research.

Keller, Catherine (1986) *From a Broken Web: Separation, Sexism, and Self*, Boston, MA: Beacon Press.

Keller, Evelyn Fox (1983) *A Feeling for the Organism: The Life and Work of Barbara McClintock*, New York: Freeman.

Keller, Evelyn Fox (1985) *Reflections on Gender and Science*, New Haven, CN: Yale University Press.

Kohlberg, Lawrence (1966) "A Cognitive Developmental Analysis of Children's Sex-Role Concepts and Attitudes," pp. 82–173 in E. E. Maccoby (ed.), *The Development of Sex Differences*, Stanford, CA: Stanford University Press.

Lloyd, Genevieve (1984) *The Man of Reason: "Male" and "Female" in Western Philosophy*, Minneapolis, MN: University of Minnesota Press.

Mansbridge, Jane J. (ed.) (1990) *Beyond Self-Interest*, Chicago, IL: University of Chicago Press.

Nelson, Julie A. (1992) "Gender, Metaphor, and the Definition of Economics," *Economics and Philosophy* 8: 103–25.

Piore, Michael J. (1974) "Comment on Wachter," *Brookings Papers on Economic Activity* 3: 684–88.

Pollak, Robert A. (1976) "Habit Formation and Long-Run Utility Functions," *Journal of Economic Theory* 13: 272–97.

Pollak, Robert A. (1985) "A Transaction Cost Approach to Families and Households," *Journal of Economic Literature* 23: 581–608.

Reskin, Barbara F. and Roos, Patricia (1990) *Job Queues, Gender Queues: Explaining Women's Inroads into Male Occupations*, Philadelphia, PA: Temple University Press.

Schott, Robin May (1988) *Cognition and Eros: A Critique of the Kantian Paradigm*, Boston, MA: Beacon Press.

Sen, Amartya K. (1982) *Choice, Welfare and Measurement*, Cambridge, MA: MIT Press.

Sen, Amartya K. (1987) *On Ethics and Economics*, New York: Basil Blackwell.

Stigler, George and Becker, Gary (1977) "De Gustibus Non Est Disputandum," *American Economic Review* 67: 76–90.

Varian, Hal (1984) *Microeconomic Analysis*, 2nd edn, New York: W. W. Norton.

Witte, Ann (1980) "Estimating the Economic Model of Crime with Individual Data," *Quarterly Journal of Economics* 94: 57–84.

Part III

Capitalist States and Globalizing Markets

Introduction

There are many possible ways to organize economies, and if one looks historically, many types of economies are visible. Economic orders range from simple barter systems and household-based economies such as manorial plantations, to elaborate mercantilist systems with far-flung colonies, and large state-socialist economies. Each economic element such as production, consumption, exchange, and ownership can be arranged differently, and combined with each other element in numerous ways to form qualitatively distinctive economic orders.

Economic sociology, like economics, has been concerned almost exclusively with the origins and dynamics of one type of economy – capitalism – the characteristically modern economic system prevailing in the developed world. Indeed, for many "modern" means "capitalist." Other kinds of economic organization can be found today, for example, religious communes and inner-city patrilineal ethnic enclaves, but they are often seen as residuals of traditional society or as pre-capitalist structures on their way toward modern capitalism. Whether or not they will change, these alternative economic settings remind us that capitalism is only one way to organize economically, and that capitalism is a particular type of economic system.

What is capitalism? Capitalism is an economic system where the means of production are privately owned, and exchange is conducted in a marketplace. This means that land, machines, even one's own labor and creative works are private property and may be used to create private wealth. In other kinds of economic systems, an aristocracy may own the means of production, and in yet others property is communally held. Under slave and feudal systems people are not free to sell even their own labor power, which is under the control of others. In a capitalist system, goods are allocated by means of exchange in a formally free market. Other kinds of allocation systems include centralized redistribution systems, or allocation according to principles of heritage, need, might, or some other rule. Capitalism, then, differs from other systems by having both private ownership and allocation by exchange in a market.

Although capitalism is now found in various expressions worldwide, it rose in Western Europe. Why did capitalism, so critical to the transformation of traditional society, rise in the West, and not in China, or India, or some other place? Many have attempted to answer this question, including Smith, Marx, Polanyi, and Weber. Most scholars have given causal precedence to either the development of markets in the West, or to the development of the Western state. Both economic (market) factors and political (state) factors accompanied and certainly support capitalism. The five chapters in this part are concerned with the origins, social bases, varieties, and global dispersion of capitalism as an economic system.

Adam Smith and Karl Marx both saw the emerging markets of Western Europe as a "natural" or "inevitable" evolution of economic activity, one that was superior to feudalism and therefore destined to triumph. Polanyi, too, saw the market as the critical factor in the development of capitalist modernity. He argued that although markets existed in many pre-modern societies, it is only under capitalism that the market comes to dominate social and political order.

Other scholars have claimed that it was the rise of the nation state that made capitalism possible. In the early modern period kings were able to consolidate military and financial power under their control, and large bureaucratic organizations developed to administer royal military and financial institutions. Although the locus of power was to switch to the people under democratic revolutions, the apparatus of a state was well under development. States were able to create the legal and regulatory systems required by capitalism.

Weber's argument about the rise of capitalism in the West favors neither the economic nor the political as an explanation. Rather, he argues that it was the particular historical combination of factors that created the conditions fertile for a new capitalist economic order to emerge. Capitalism rose in the West, and not elsewhere, because of the combination of conditions that took hold there. Chapter 10 by Randall Collins is a concise summary of Weber's thesis that is found in bits and parts throughout his writings. Weber's extraordinary erudition in history and legal studies, as well as contemporary social science, enabled him to marshal a wide variety of evidence to create a complex causal explanation for the development of Western capitalism.

Weber's argument focuses, first, on the impediments to capitalism that were eliminated in the West, particularly the "freeing" of labor, land, and goods. These elements, which had often been restricted geographically and socially under feudalism, became untethered from traditional restrictions and available for exchange in markets in Europe. Secondly, Weber discusses the conditions that supported an emergent capitalist system, particularly institutions that stabilized markets and created an environment for predictable risk taking by capitalists. These institutions included the rise of an individualist ethic in citizenship, calculable law, rational accounting and record keeping, and state regimes that created social order, transportation security, and monetary systems. These, and other supportive conditions, were historically unique to the West. In India, for example, a caste system functioned to limit the flow of people and goods, and in China bureaucratic officials sustained local clan control of the economy. Neither India nor China developed an individualistic ethic, an ethic Weber traced to the West's Judeo-Christian religious heritage.

Neil Fligstein's work in chapter 11 further extends our understanding of market structure. Rather than ask where markets come from, Fligstein asks why they take the forms that they do. Economists and sociologists both recognize that markets are not all alike. Economists assume that there is, at least analytically, a "perfect" market and real markets are seen as deviations from this assumed ideal. Markets differ insofar as they exhibit different "imperfections" that influence their functioning, the primary concern of economic analysis. Fligstein, however, focuses on a somewhat different issue: according to him, markets are not all alike because powerful economic actors have been able to shape markets to their advantage in different settings. Power and culture are the reasons that markets differ, and ultimately that is why markets function differently.

Powerful economic actors want to control the conditions of the market in which they operate in order to create stability and mitigate risk. Fligstein sees that actors have two fundamental problems: preventing unbridled competition with other firms who might undercut them, and maintaining internal control over their firms. Market control strategies include cooperating with competitors through joint ventures and alliances and encouraging favorable state regulation of markets. Indeed, Fligstein sees state building as a critical project for capitalists. Only the state and its agencies can set and enforce rules of exchange, contracts, and property rights that create stable economic conditions. Some political processes have resulted in interventionist states – for example, France – while other states have developed into regulatory regimes, such as in the United States. The second problem, control of firms, is managed by constructing ideological "conceptions of control," which explain and justify dominant firm actions, and thwart alternative conceptions of "correct" market arrangements. Markets are arenas for ideological as well as material contest.

In chapter 12, Fred Block also has a political-ideological view of markets and market discourse. According to Block, it is ironic that both neoclassical economics and Marxian perspectives have treated capitalism as a "natural" system. Many people, including policy makers and the general public, now assume that capitalism takes the form and functions it does because it is in the nature of capitalism to do so. When the Japanese, for example, resist US or IMF conceptions of a market, they are seen as thwarting the "proper" and "inevitable" dynamics of capitalism.

The "varieties of capitalism" movement in economic sociology has demonstrated, in fact, that now there are diverse capitalisms around the globe, and that each can be traced back to social and political factors in the society. Block argues that this conceptualization of capitalism as a social-political project needs to be pushed further, and that it is critical that people more generally understand capitalism to be socially constructed. Varieties of capitalism are the outcome of historical events, and not an inevitable force of nature. Block argues that the construction of capitalism as a system becomes obvious when one begins to examine contradictions in the capitalist order that must be "welded" together to make the system appear naturally coherent.

Chapter 13, which I have co-written with Mauro Guillén, begins by asking what difference the organization of a society makes in economic development. If societies are not all alike, and economies differ as a result, can all nations develop equally well in the global marketplace? What difference does the institutional structure of a society make to economic development? Our chapter reports on the results of a comparative analysis of four countries, which varied in important ways and which all tried to develop automotive assembly and components industries at about the same time. Cars are a favorite industry for developing nations because they provide needed transportation, they keep hard currency at home by lessening import of an expensive commodity, they stimulate other industries such as electronics and glass, and they are symbolic of being "modern."

The four countries we studied, South Korea, Taiwan, Spain, and Argentina, had considerable involvement by their states in industry development and pursued many of the same policies. Nonetheless, each country developed differently. South Korea and Spain build cars, Taiwan and Spain build components, and Argentina builds relatively little of either. Why couldn't Korea make the parts for its auto assembly industry? Why could Taiwan make the parts, but not put the cars together? Why could Spain do both, and Argentina neither? The answers, we argue, have to do with the relationship of the social structure to the economic structure, and that of both to world markets.

Chapter 14 examines the development of market structure from the perspective of a particular industry, biotechnology. The economic production and exchange about which Adam Smith and the other classical theorists wrote was largely based in agrarian and factory production of relatively simple commodities. The economy of the twenty-first century, at least in developed nations, has shifted substantially toward being service based and knowledge based. Even the production of everyday commodities, such as washing machines and tomatoes, includes large components of intellectual labor. Washing machines may have electronic parts and tomatoes are often hybridized and even genetically engineered by scientists. Today's production process includes knowledge and services, not just material inputs and outputs.

No industry better exemplifies this economic transformation than biotechnology. Walter Powell discusses how profitability in high-tech fields is less about keeping costs down and more about competing to generate new knowledge. In seeking critical new knowledge, biotech firms have created new collaborative arrangements that position firms at the hub of knowledge-creating networks. The arrangements sometimes bring competitors together, and often transform the partners in unexpected ways. Powell's research takes Polanyi's idea of embeddedness, and Granovetter's emphasis on economic networks, to gain new insights on how this dynamic market forms and reforms with the development of scientific breakthroughs.

This part begins with trying to understand why capitalism rose in the West. It is clear now, however, that capitalism is not confined to Western civilization, even if it was nurtured there. Capitalism is globalizing. A global economy is distinctive in that it is not just about trade between nations – which has taken place for centuries – but rather about the ability of integrated production to take place all over the globe at the same time. Information and communication technologies have made geography increasingly unimportant. The very states that made capitalism possible paradoxically are now hindrances to its spread globally. Institutional differences and varieties of capitalism create social and political barriers to globalization. Nonetheless, transnational corporations, new technological capabilities, and supranational institutions are creating conditions for the wide spread of capitalist economic order.

10 Weber's Last Theory of Capitalism

Randall Collins

Max Weber had many intellectual interests, and there has been considerable debate over the question of what constitutes the central theme of his life work. Besides treating the origins of capitalism, Weber dealt extensively with the nature of modernity and of rationality (Tenbruck, 1975; Kalberg, 1979, 1980; Seidman, 1980), and with politics, methodology, and various substantive areas of sociology. Amid all the attention which has been paid to these concerns, one of Weber's most significant contributions has been largely ignored. This is his mature theory of the development of capitalism, found in his last work (1961), *General Economic History*.

This is ironic because Weber's (1930) first major work, *The Protestant Ethic and the Spirit of Capitalism*, has long been the most famous of all. The argument that the Calvinist doctrine of predestination gave the psychological impetus for rationalized, entrepreneurial capitalism is only a fragment of Weber's full theory. But many scholars have treated it as Weber's distinctive contribution, or Weber's distinctive fallacy, on the origins of capitalism (e.g., Tawney, 1938; McClelland, 1961; Samuelsson, 1961; Cohen, 1980). Debate about the validity of this part of Weber's theory has tended to obscure the more fundamental historical and institutional theory which he presented in his later works.

The so-called "Weber thesis," as thus isolated, has been taken to be essentially idealist. Weber (1930, p. 90) defines his purpose in *The Protestant Ethic* as "a contribution to the manner in which ideas become effective forces in history." He (1930, p. 183) polemically remarks against the Marxists that he does not intend to replace a one-sided materialism with its opposite, but his correcting of the balance sheet in this work concentrates largely on ideal factors. The germ of Weber's institutional theory of capitalism can also be found in *The Protestant Ethic* (1930, pp. 58, 76).[1] But it remained an undeveloped backdrop for his main focus on the role of religious ideas. The same may be said about his (1951, 1952, 1958b) comparative studies of the world religions. These broadened considerably the amount of material on social, economic, and political conditions, but the main theme still stressed that divergent ideas made an autonomous contribution to the emergence of world-transforming capitalism in the Christian West rather than elsewhere in the world.[2] Thus, Parsons (1963, 1967) treats these works as extending the early Weber thesis from Protestantism to Christianity in general, describing an evolution of religious ideas and their accompanying motivational propensities from ancient Judaism up through the secularized achievement culture of the modern United States.

Original publication: Chapter 2 of Collins, Randall, *Weberian Sociological Theory* (Cambridge University Press, Cambridge, 1986).

From these works, and from (1968) Part II of *Economy and Society*, it is possible to pull out an extensive picture of institutional factors which Weber includes in his overall theory of capitalism. But *Economy and Society* is organized encyclopedically, by analytically defined topics, and does not pull together the theory as a whole. There is only one place in Weber's works where he brings together the full theory of capitalism as a historical dynamic. This is in the *General Economic History*, and, especially, in the 70-page section comprising Part IV of that work. These lectures, delivered in the winter and spring of 1919–20, before Weber's death that summer, are Weber's last word on the subject of capitalism. They are also the most neglected of his works; *General Economic History* is the only one of Weber's major works that remains out of print today, both in English and in German.

One important change in the *General Economic History* is that Weber pays a good deal more attention to Marxian themes than previously. This is a significant difference from the anti-Marxist comments scattered through *The Protestant Ethic* (e.g., pp. 55–56, 61, 90–91, 183). In the *General Economic History*, Weber reduces the ideal factor to a relatively small place in his overall scheme. During this same period, to be sure, Weber was preparing a new introduction and footnotes for the reissue of *The Protestant Ethic* among his collected religious writings, in which he defended his original thesis about Calvinism. But his claims for its importance in the overall scheme of things were not large, and the well-rounded model which he presents in *General Economic History* does not even mention the doctrine of predestination. Instead, what we find is a predominantly institutional theory, in which religious *organization* plays a key role in the rise of modern capitalism but especially in conjunction with particular forms of political organization.

In what follows, I will attempt to state systematically Weber's mature theory of capitalism, as it appears in the *General Economic History*, bolstered where appropriate by the building blocks presented in *Economy and Society*. This argument involves a series of causes, which we will trace backward, from the most recent to the most remote. This model, I would suggest, is the most comprehensive general theory of the origins of capitalism that is yet available. It continues to stand up well in comparison with recent theories, including Wallerstein's (1974) historical theory of the capitalist and world-system.

Weber himself was primarily concerned with the sensitizing concepts necessary for an interpretation of the unique pattern of history and, in his methodological writings, he disavowed statements in the form of general causal principles (cf. Burger, 1976). Nevertheless, Weber's typologies contain implicit generalizations about the effects of institutional arrangements upon each other, and statements of cause-and-effect abound in his substantive writings. There is nothing to prevent us from stating his historical picture of changing institutional forms in a more abstract and generalized manner than Weber did himself.

Weber's model continues to offer a more sophisticated basis for a theory of capitalism than any of the rival theories of today. I put forward this formalization of Weber's mature theory, not merely as an appreciation of one of the classic works of the past, but to make clear the high-water mark of sociological theory about capitalism. Weber's last theory is not the last word on the subject of the rise of capitalism, but if we are to surpass it, it is the high point from which we ought to build.

The Components of Rationalized Capitalism

Capitalism, says Weber (1961, pp. 207–8, 260) is the provision of human needs by the method of enterprise, which is to say, by private businesses seeking profit. It is exchange carried out for positive gain, rather than forced contributions or traditionally fixed gifts or trades. Like all of Weber's categories, capitalism is an analytical concept: capitalism can be found as part of many historical economies, as far back as ancient Babylon. It became the indispensable form for the provision of everyday wants only in Western Europe around the middle of the nineteenth century. For this large-scale and economically predominant capitalism, the key is the "rational permanent enterprise" characterized by "rational capital accounting."

The concept of "rationality" which appears so often in Weber's works has been the subject of much debate. Marxist critics of capitalism, as well as critics of bureaucracy, have attacked Weber's alleged glorification of these social forms (e.g., Hirst, 1976). On the other hand, Parsons (1947), in his long introduction to the definitional section of *Economy and Society*, gives "rationalization" both an idealist and an evolutionary bent, as the master trend of world history, involving an inevitable upgrading of human cognitive and organizational capacities. Tenbruck (1975) claims the key to Weber's works is an inner logic of rational development found within the realm of religious solutions to the problem of suffering.

It is clear that Weber himself used the term "rationalism" in a number of different senses.[3] But for his *institutional* theory of capitalist development, there is only one sense that need concern us. The "rational capitalistic establishment," says Weber (1961, p. 207), "is one with capital accounting, that is, an establishment which determines its income yielding power by calculation according to the methods of modern bookkeeping and the striking of a balance." The key term is *calculability*; it occurs over and over again in those pages. What is distinctive about modern, large-scale, "rational" capitalism – in contrast to earlier, partial forms – is that it is methodical and predictable, reducing all areas of production and distribution as much as possible to a routine. This is also Weber's criterion for calling bureaucracy the most "rational" form of organization.[4]

For a capitalist economy to have a high degree of predictability, it must have certain characteristics. The logic of Weber's argument is first to describe these characteristics; then to show the obstacles to them that were prevalent in virtually all societies of world history until recent centuries in the West; and, finally, by the method of comparative analysis, to show the social conditions responsible for their emergence.

According to his argument, the components of "rationalized" capitalism are as follows:

There must be *private appropriation of all the means of production*, and their concentration under the control of entrepreneurs. Land, buildings, machinery, and materials must all be assembled under a common management, so that decisions about their acquisition and use can be calculated with maximal efficiency. All these factors must be subject to sale as private goods on an open market. This development reaches its maximal scope when all such property rights are represented by commercial instruments, especially shares in ownership which are themselves negotiable in a stock market.

Within this enterprise, capital accounting is optimized by a *technology which is "reduced to calculation to the largest possible degree"* (1961, p. 208). It is in this sense that mechanization is most significant for the organization of large-scale capitalism.

Labor must be free to move about to any work in response to conditions of demand. Weber notes that this is a formal and legal freedom, and that it goes along with the economic compulsion of workers to sell their labor on the market. Capitalism is impossible without a propertyless stratum selling its services "under the compulsion of the whip of hunger" (1961, p. 209), for only this completes a mass market system for the factors of production which makes it possible to clearly calculate the costs of products in advance.

Trading in the market must not be limited by irrational restrictions. That is to say, noneconomic restrictions on the movement of goods or of any of the factors of production must be minimized. Such restrictions include class monopolies upon particular items of consumption (such as sumptuary laws regulating dress), or upon ownership or work (such as prohibitions on townspeople owning land, or on knights or peasants carrying on trade; more extensively, caste systems in general). Other obstacles under this heading include transportation difficulties, warfare, and robbery – which make long-distance trading hazardous and unreliable.

Finally, there must be *calculable law, both in adjudication and in public administration.* Laws must be couched in general terms applicable to all persons, and administered in such a way as to make the enforcement of economic contracts and rights highly predictable. Such a legal system is implicated in most of the above characteristics of rational capitalism: the extension of private property rights over the factors of production; the subdivision and easy transferability of such rights through financial instruments and banking operations; formal freedom for laborers; and legally protected markets.

The picture that Weber gives us, then, is of the institutional foundations of the market as viewed by neoclassical economics. He sees the market as providing the maximal amount of calculability for the individual entrepreneur. Goods, labor, and capital flow continuously to the areas of maximal return; at the same time, competition in all markets reduces costs to their minimum. Thus, prices serve to summarize all the necessary information about the optimal allocation of resources for maximizing profit; on this basis, entrepreneurs can most reliably make calculations for long-term production of large amounts of goods. "To sum up," says Weber (1961, p. 209), "it must be possible to conduct the provision for needs exclusively on the basis of market opportunities and the calculation of net income."

It is, of course, the model of the laissez-faire capitalist economy that Weber wishes to ground. At the extreme, this is an unrealistic view of any economy that has ever existed. Weber treats it as an ideal type and, hence, in a fuller exposition would doubtless have been prepared to see it as only partially realized even in the great capitalist takeoff period of the nineteenth century. But it is worth noting that a critique of Weber along these lines could certainly not be a classical Marxian one. The central dynamic of capitalism in Marx's theory, in fact, depends even more immediately than Weber's on the unrestricted competitiveness of the open market for all factors of production (cf. Sweezy, 1942). And Weber and Marx agree in claiming that the initial breakthrough to an industrial society had to occur in the form of capitalism.

Thus, although Weber may have a personal bias toward the neoclassical market economy, both as analytical model and as political preference, this would give no grounds for a critique of the adequacy of his explanation of this phase of world history. Even for a later period, Weber is hardly dogmatic. As we shall see, he recognizes the possibility of socialism emerging, once capitalism has matured – although he does not admire the prospect – and he even gives some indications of the forces that might produce it. Like German and Austrian non-Marxist economists of his generation, Weber includes socialism within his analytical scheme.

Weber's model of the modern economy is particularly striking with regard to the concept of the "industrial revolution." For it is not mechanization per se that is the key to the economic transformation, despite the far-reaching consequences of shifts from agrarian to inanimate-energy-based technologies (cf. Lenski, 1966). In Weber's scheme, technology is essentially a dependent variable. The key *economic* characteristic of mechanization is that it is feasible only with mass production (Weber, 1961, pp. 129, 247). The costs of even simpler machines such as steam-powered looms would make them worthless without a large-scale consumers' market for cloth, as well as a large-scale producers' market in wool or cotton. Similar considerations apply a fortiori to machinery on the scale of a steel rolling mill. But large-scale production is impossible without a high degree of predictability that markets will exist for the products, and that all the factors of production will be forthcoming at a reasonable cost. Thus, mechanization depends on the prior emergence of all the institutional factors described above.

Weber does not elaborate a systematic theory of technological innovation, but it would be possible to construct one along these lines. He does note that all the crucial inventions of the period of industrial takeoff were the result of deliberate efforts to cheapen the costs of production (1961, pp. 225–6, 231). These efforts took place because previous conditions had intensified the capitalist pursuit of profits. The same argument could be made, although Weber did not make it, in regard to the search for methods to improve agricultural production that took place in the seventeenth and eighteenth centuries. The "green revolution" which preceded (and made possible) the industrial revolution was not a process of mechanization (agricultural mechanization took place only in the late nineteenth century) but was, more simply, the application of capitalist methods of cost accounting to hitherto traditional agriculture. Thus, it is the shift to the calculating practices of the capitalist market economy which makes technological innovation itself predictable, rather than, as previously, an accidental factor in economic life (1961, p. 231).[5]

The Causal Chain

What are the social preconditions for the emergence of capitalism as thus described?

Note, first of all, that economic life, even in the most prosperous of agrarian societies, generally lacked most of these traits. Property systems frequently tied land ownership to aristocratic status, while commercial occupations were often prohibited to certain groups and monopolized by others. The labor force was generally unfree – being either slaves or tied to the land as serfs. Technologies of mass production hardly existed. The market was generally limited either to local areas or to long-distance trade in luxuries, due to numerous near-confiscatory tax barriers, unreliable and

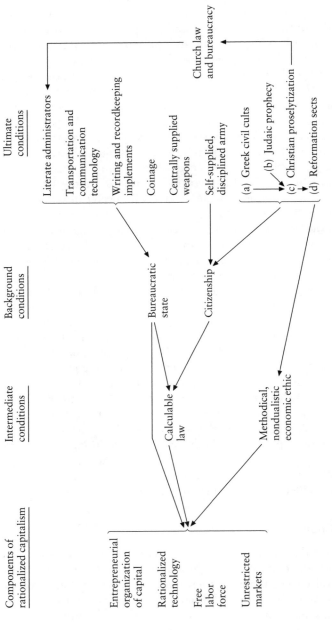

Figure 10.1 The Weberian causal chain.

varying coinage, warfare, robbery, and poor transportation. And legal systems, even in literate states, tended to be characterized by patrimonial or magical-religious procedures, by differential application to different social groups and by different localities, and by the practices of officials seeking private gain. Reliable financial transactions, including the operation of a banking system relatively free from political interference and plundering, were particularly handicapped by these conditions.

The social preconditions for large-scale capitalism, then, involved the destruction of the obstacles to the free movement or economic transfer of labor, land, and goods. Other preconditions were the creation of the institutional supports for large-scale markets, especially the appropriate systems of property, law, and finance.

These are not the only preconditions of capitalism, but, specifically, Weber is seeking the organizational forms that made capitalism a world-transforming force in the West but not elsewhere. By a series of comparisons, Weber shows that a number of other factors that have been advanced to account for the Western takeoff cannot have been crucial. Against Sombart, he points out that standardized mass production for war cannot have been decisive, for although a good deal of this existed in Europe in the seventeenth century, and thereafter, it also existed in the Mogul Empire and in China without giving an impetus to capitalism (1961, p. 229). Similarly, the enormous expenditures for court luxury found in both Orient and Occident were incapable of generating a mass market (1961, pp. 229–30). Against the simpler arguments of Adam Smith, which attribute the industrial division of labor to the extension of trade, Weber points out that trade can be found everywhere, even in the Stone Age. In ancient Babylon, for example, trade was such as to disintegrate "primitive economic fixity" to a considerable degree (1961, p. 232). On the other hand, politically determined agrarian economies show how "specialization takes place without exchange" (1961, p. 103). Nor is the pursuit of profit per se the crucial motive for mass capitalism: the "ruthlessness" and "unscrupulousness" of the traditional foreign trader were incapable of transforming the economy at large (1961, p. 232). Nor can population growth have been the cause of Western capitalism, for the same trend occurred in China without the same result (1961, pp. 258–9). Neither, finally, can the price revolution of the sixteenth century, due to the influx of precious metals from the Americas, have been decisive (see the later discussion on Wallerstein).[6]

The features that Weber finds unique to the West constitute a causal chain.[7] I have represented this schematically in Figure 10.1. The characteristics of rational capitalism itself are the entrepreneurial organization of capital, rational technology, free labor, unrestricted markets, and calculable law. These make up a complex: the markets for goods, labor, and capital all mesh around entrepreneurial property using mass production technology; the operation of all of these factors together creates further pressures to both rationalize technology and expand each factor market – while yet distributing wealth in such a way as to further the demand. The legal system is both an ongoing prop for all of these features and a causal link backward to their social preconditions. At this intermediate causal level there is a second crucial factor which, like the law, is essentially cultural, although not in the sense of disembodied ideas, but, rather, in the sense of beliefs expressed in institutionalized behavior. This is the "lifting of the barrier . . . between internal and external ethics" (1961, p. 232).

In virtually all premodern societies there are two sharply divergent sets of ethical beliefs and practices. Within a social group, economic transactions are strictly controlled by rules of fairness, status, and tradition: in tribal societies, by ritualized exchanges with prescribed kin; in India, by rules of caste; in medieval Europe, by required contributions on the manor or to the great church properties. The prohibition on usury reflected this internal ethic, requiring an ethic of charity and the avoidance of calculation of gain from loans within the community (cf. Nelson, 1949).[8] In regard to outsiders, however, economic ethics were at the opposite extreme: cheating, price gouging, and loans at exorbitant interest were the rule. Both forms of ethic were obstacles to rational, large-scale capitalism: the internal ethic because it prevented the commercialization of economic life, the external ethic because it made trading relations too episodic and distrustful. The lifting of this barrier and the overcoming of this ethical dualism were crucial for the development of any extensive capitalism. Only this could make loans available regularly and promote the buying and selling of all services and commodities for moderate gain. Through innumerable daily repetitions, such small (but regular) profits could add up to much more massive economic transactions than could either the custom-bound or the predatory economic ethics of traditional societies.

What, then, produced the calculable legal system of saleable private property and free labor and the universal ethic of the pursuit of moderate economic profit? The next links in the causal chain are political and religious. The bureaucratic state is a crucial background determinant for all legal and institutional underpinnings of capitalism. Moreover, its legal system must be based on a concept of universal citizenship, which requires yet further political preconditions. The religious factor operates both as a direct influence on the creation of an economic ethic and as a final level of causality implicated in the rise of the rational-legal state and of legal citizenship.

The state is the factor most often overlooked in Weber's theory of capitalism. Yet it is the factor to which he gave the most attention; in *Economy and Society*, he devoted eight chapters of 680 pages to it, as opposed to one chapter of 235 pages to religion, with yet another chapter – the neglected but very important chap. XV of Part II – to the relations between politics and religion. In the *General Economic History*, he gives the state the two penultimate chapters, religion the final chapter. For Weber, this political material was not an extraneous interest but, instead, the key to all of the *institutional* structures of rational capitalism. Only the West developed the highly bureaucratized state, based on specialized professional administrators and on a law made and applied by full-time professional jurists for a populace characterized by rights of citizenship. It is this bureaucratic-legal state that broke down feudalism and patrimonialism, freeing land and labor for the capitalist market. It is this state that pacified large territories, eliminated internal market barriers, standardized taxation and currencies. It is this state that provided the basis for a reliable system of banking, investment, property, and contracts, through a rationally calculable and universally applied system of law courts. One may even argue that the bureaucratic state was the proximate cause of the impulse to rationalization, generally – above all, via the late seventeenth- and eighteenth-century spirit of enlightened absolutism, which set the stage for the industrial revolution.

There are three causal questions about the rational/legal state. Why did it rise to predominance? Where did its structural characteristics come from? How did its legal system take the special form of conceiving of its subjects as holding the rights of citizenship?

The first question is easily answered. The bureaucratic state rose to predominance because it is the most efficient means of pacifying a large territory. It is effective externally in that it can supply a larger military, with better weapons, than can non-bureaucratic states; and it is effective, internally, as it tends to be relatively safe against disintegration by civil war or political *coup*.[9]

The sources of the bureaucratic state are, to a degree, quite familiar. In the widely reprinted section on bureaucracy from *Economy and Society* (1968, pp. 956–1005), Weber outlines the prerequisites: literate administrators, a technology of long-distance transportation and communication, writing and record-keeping materials, monetary coinage. The extent to which these could be put into effect, however, depended on a number of other factors. Geographical conditions such as easy transportation in river valleys, or favorable situations for state-controlled irrigation (1961, p. 237), fostered bureaucratic centralization, as did intense military competition among adjacent heartlands. Types of weapons which are centrally (rather than individually) supplied also favor bureaucratization. If such conditions make central control easy, however, bureaucratization need not proceed very deeply, and the society may be ruled by a thin stratum of officials above a local structure which remains patrimonial. In China, for example, this superficial bureaucratization constituted a long-term obstacle to capitalism, as it froze the economy under the patrimonial control of local clans.

The most thorough bureaucratization, as well as that uniquely favorable to capitalism, is that which incorporates a formalistic legal code based on citizenship. Citizenship meant, first of all, membership in a city; by extension, membership in a state and hence holding political rights within it. This was an alien concept throughout most of history. In the patrimonial state, political office was a form of private property or personal delegation, and even in most premodern quasi-bureaucratic states the populace at large was only subject to the state, not holders of rights within it. The latter condition arose only in the West. In both Mediterranean antiquity and the European Middle Ages, cities came under the control of brotherhoods of warriors banded together for mutual protection. Such cities had their own laws and courts, administered by the citizens themselves, all of whom stood under it in relation of formal equality. Such citizenship rights remained historically significant after the original civic forms changed or disappeared. The formal rights and legal procedures originally applied only to a local elite, but when cities were incorporated into large-scale bureaucratic states, they provided the basis for a much more widely inclusive system of adjudication. This was the case when Rome, originally one of these military-fraternity cities, became an empire and, again, in the Middle Ages, when cities in alliance with kings lost their independence but contributed their legal structures to the larger states.[10]

Nearing the end of our chain of causality, we ask: What factors enabled this distinctive type of city to arise in the West? Weber gives two conditions: one military, the other religious.

The military condition is that in the West the city consisted of "an organization of those economically competent to bear arms, to equip and train themselves" (1961, p. 237). This was the case in the formative period of the ancient Greek and Italian cities and, again, in the medieval cities with their disciplined infantries fielded by the guilds. In both cases, the money power of the cities bolstered their military power and, hence, democratization and concomitant legal citizenship. In the Orient and in ancient Egypt, on the contrary, the military princes with their armies were older than the cities and, hence, legally independent cities did not arise; Weber attributed this pattern to the impetus to early centralization given by irrigation.

The second condition is that in the East, magical taboos prevented the organization of military alliances among strangers and, hence, did not allow formation of independent cities. In India, for example, the ritual exclusion of castes had this effect. More generally, in Asia and the Middle East, the traditional priests held monopolies over communion with the gods, whereas in Western antiquity it was the officials of the city who themselves performed the rites (1961, p. 238). In the one case, the boundaries of religious communion reinforced preexisting group divisions; in the other, religious boundaries were an explicit political tool by which civic alliances could be established and enlarged. It is at this point that the two main lines of Weber's chain of causality converge.

We have been tracing the causal links behind the emergence of the rational/legal state, which is one of the two great intermediate conditions of the emergence of an open market economy. The other great intermediate condition (noted earlier) is an economic ethic which breaks the barrier between internal and external economies. Now we see that the religious factors that produced the citizenship revolution and those that produced the economic ethic are essentially the same.

Our last question, then, is: What brought about this religious transformation? Weber gives a series of reasons, each intensifying the effects of the last (1961, p. 238). Ethical prophecy within ancient Judaism was important, even though it did not break down ritual barriers between Jews and Gentiles, because it established a tradition of hostility to magic, the main ethos within which barriers flourished. The transformation of Christianity from a Jewish sect into a proselytizing universal religion gave this tradition widespread currency, while the pentecostal spirit of Christian proselytization set aside the ritual barriers among clans and tribes, which still characterized the ancient Hellenistic cities to some degree. The Judeo-Christian innovations are not the whole story, however; the earlier development of Greek religion into the civic cults had already done much to make universalistic legal membership possible.

The religious factors, as we have seen, entwine with political ones, and their influence in the direction of legal citizenship and upon an economic ethic have fluctuated historically. There is no steady nor inevitable trend toward increasing rationalization of these spheres, but Western history does contain a series of episodes which happen to have built up these effects at particular points in time so that, eventually, a whole new economic dynamic was unleashed. On the political side, the Christian cities of the Middle Ages, drawing upon the institutional legacies of the ancient world, were able to establish religiously sworn confraternities which reestablished a legal system based on citizenship. A second political factor was fostered by religion: the Christian church provided the literate administrators, the educational system, and the example of its own bureaucratic organization as bases upon which the bureaucratic states of the West could emerge. And, on the strictly motivational side, the development of European Christianity gave a decisive ethical push toward rationalized capitalism.

Here, at last, we seem to touch base with Weber's original Protestant Ethic thesis. But in the mature Weber, the thesis is greatly transformed. Protestantism is only the last intensification of one of the chains of factors leading to rational capitalism. Moreover, its effect now is conceived to be largely negative, in the sense that it removes one of the last institutional obstacles diverting the motivational impetus of Christianity away from economic rationalization. For, in medieval Christianity, the methodical, disciplined organization of life was epitomized by the monastic communities.[11] Although the monasteries contributed to economic development by rationalizing agriculture and promoting their own industries, Weber generally saw them as obstacles to the full capitalist development of the secular economy. As long as the strongest religious motivation was siphoned off for essentially otherworldly ends, capitalism in general could not take off (1961, pp. 267–9). Hence, the Reformation was most significant because it abolished the monasteries. The most advanced section of the economy would, henceforth, be secular. Moreover, the highest ethics of a religious life could no longer be confined to monks but had to apply to ordinary citizens living in the world. Calvinism and the other voluntary sects were the most intense version of this motivation, not because of the idea of predestination (which no longer receives any mention in Weber's last text) but only because they required a specific religious calling for admission into their ranks, rather than automatic and compulsory membership in the politically more conservative churches. Weber's (1961, pp. 269–70) last word on the subject of Protestantism was simply this:

> The development of the concept of the calling quickly gave to the modern entrepreneur a fabulously clear conscience – and also industrious workers; he gave to his employees as the wages of their ascetic devotion to the calling and of co-operation in his ruthless exploitation of them through capitalism the prospect of eternal salvation, which in an age when ecclesiastical discipline took control of the whole life to an extent inconceivable to us now, represented a reality quite different from any it has today. The Catholic and Lutheran churches also recognized and practiced ecclesiastical discipline. But in the Protestant ascetic communities admission to the Lord's Supper was conditioned on ethical fitness, which again was identified with business honor, while into the content of one's faith no one inquired. Such a powerful, unconsciously refined organization for the production of capitalistic individuals has never existed in any other church or religion.

Weber's General Theory of History

Is there an overall pattern in Weber's argument? It is not a picture of a linear trend toward ever-increasing rationality. Nor is it an evolutionary model of natural selection, in the sense of random selection of the more advanced forms, accumulating through a series of stages. For Weber's constant theme is that the *pattern of relations among the various factors* is crucial in determining their effect upon economic rationalization. Any one factor occurring by itself tends to have opposite effects, overall, to those which it has in combination with the other factors.

For example, self-supplied military coalitions produce civic organizations and legal systems which are favorable to capitalism. But if the self-armed civic groups are too strong, the result is a series of guild monopolies which stifle capitalism by overcontrolling markets. Cities, on the other hand, have to be balanced by the bureaucratic state. But when the state is too strong by itself, it, too, tends to stifle capitalism. This can happen by bolstering the immobility of labor (as in the case of "the second serfdom" produced in Russia and eastern Europe as absolutist states developed in the seventeenth and eighteenth centuries); or by directly controlling the division of labor by forced contributions instead of allowing a market to develop. In the areas of the world where bureaucratization was relatively easy, as in ancient Egypt or China, or the Byzantine Empire, the unrestrained power of the state stereotyped economic life and did not allow the dynamics of capitalism to unfold.

The same is true of the religious variables. The creation of the great world religions, with their universalism and their specialized priesthoods, was crucial for the possibility of breaking the ritual barriers among localized groups, with all the consequences this might have for subsequent developments. But, in the absence of other factors, this could actually bolster the obstacles to capitalism. This happened in India, where the development of Hinduism fostered the caste system: the universalistic religion set an external seal upon the lineup of particularistic groups that happened to exist at the time. Even in Christianity, where moral prophecy had a much more barrier-breaking and world-transforming effect, the Church (in the period when it was predominant) created another obstacle against its capitalist implications. This was the period of the High Middle Ages in Europe, when monasticism proliferated and, thus, channeled all the energy of religious motivation into a specialized role and away from the economic concerns of ordinary life.[12]

Weber saw the rise of large-scale capitalism, then, as the result of a series of combinations of conditions which had to occur together. This makes world history look like the result of configurations of events so rare as to appear accidental. Weber's position might well be characterized as historicist, in the sense of seeing history as a concatenation of unique events and unrepeatable complexities. Once a crucial conjuncture occurs, its results transform everything else – and not just locally but also in the larger world of competing states. This was true of the great charismatic revelations of the world religions, which shut off China, India, or the West from alternative lines of development as well as determined the ways that states upon these territories would interact with the rest of the world. Similarly, the full-scale capitalist breakthrough itself was a once-only event, radiating outward to transform all other institutions and societies. Hence, the original conditions necessary for the emergence of capitalism were not necessary for its continuation. The original religious ethic could fade, once the calculability of massive economic transactions had become a matter of routine. Hence, late-industrializing states need not follow the route of classic capitalism. In the advanced societies, the skeleton of the economic structure might even be taken over by socialism.

Weber's account of the rise of capitalism, then, is in a sense not a theory at all, in that it is not a set of universal generalizations about economic change. Nevertheless, on a more abstract level, Weber is at least implicitly proposing such a theory. On one level, he may be read as a collection of separate hypotheses about specific processes and their effects.[13] The foregoing caveat about the necessary balance among factors may be incorporated by specifying that the causal variables must operate at a given strength – that is, by turning them into quantitative generalizations specified to a given range of variation.

On a second level, one may say that the fundamental generalizations in Weber's theory of capitalism concern the crucial role of balances and tensions between opposing elements. "All in all," says Weber in a little-known passage (1968, pp. 1192–3), "the specific roots of Occidental culture must be sought in the tension and peculiar balance, on the one hand, between office charisma and monasticism, and on the other between the contractual character of the feudal state and the autonomous bureaucratic hierocracy."[14] No one element must predominate if rationalization is to increase. More concretely, since each "element" is composed of real people struggling for precedence, the creation of a calculable, open-market economy depends upon a continuous balance of power among differently organized groups. The formal egalitarianism of the law depends upon balances among competing citizens and among competing jurisdictions. The nondualistic economic ethic of moderated avarice depends upon a compromise between the claims of in-group charity and the vicious circle of out-group rapaciousness.

The capitalist economy depends on this balance. The open-market system is a situation of institutionalized strife. Its essence is struggle, in an expanded version of the Marxian sense, but with the qualification that this could go on continuously, and indeed must, if the system is to survive.[15] Hence, if there is any generalization implicit in Weber's theory applicable to economic history after the initial rise of capitalism, it is this: The possibility for the follower-societies of the non-Western world to acquire the dynamism of industrial capitalism depends on there being a balance among class forces, and among competing political forces and cultural forces as well. In the highly industrialized societies also, the continuation of capitalism depends on continuation of the same conflicts. The victory of any one side would spell the doom of the system. In this respect, as in others, Weber's theory is a conflict theory indeed.

An Assessment: Weber's Confrontation with Marxism

How valid is Weber's theory? To fully answer this question would require extensive comparative analyses and a good deal of explication of principles on different levels of abstraction. These tasks are beyond the scope of what is intended here. What I can present is a confrontation between Weber's theory and the one rival theory of capitalism which claims a comparable degree of historical and theoretical comprehensiveness, Marxism. This is especially appropriate because Weber himself devoted a great deal of attention in the *General Economic History* to the points at which his analysis impinges on Marxist theories.

The book begins and ends on Marxian themes. The first chapter deals with the question of primitive agrarian communism. Characteristically, Weber finds it to be only one variant of primitive agriculture; where it does exist, it is usually the result of fiscal organization imposed from above (1961, pp. 121–36). The closing words of the book speak of the threat of working class revolution which appears once capitalism matures and work discipline loses its religious legitimation (1961, p. 270). In between, there are numerous references to Marxism, far more than in any other of Weber's works. His attitude is critically respectful, as in his comment on the Engels-Bebel theory of the origins of the family: "although it is untenable in detail it forms, taken as a whole, a valuable contribution to the solution of the problem. Here again is the old truth exemplified that an ingenious error is more fruitful for science than stupid accuracy" (1961, p. 40).[16]

Weber's intellectual maturity coincides with a period of high-level debate in Germany and Austria between Marxian and non-Marxian economists. In the years between 1885 and 1920 appeared Engels's editions of the later volumes of *Capital*, as well as the principal works of Kautsky, Hilferding, and Luxemburg. On the other side, Sombart, Bortkiewitz, and Tugan-Baranowski provided what they considered to be revisions in the spirit of Marxian economics, while Böhm-Bawerk (1896) and Schumpeter (1911) launched explicit efforts to shore up the weaknesses of neo-classical economics vis-à-vis Marxism, and attacked the technical weaknesses of Marxian theory.[17] This period was in many ways the high-water mark in political economy, for an atmosphere of balanced debate is beneficial for intellectual advance. Weber in particular was concerned to meet the Marxian challenge on its own grounds, leaving out nothing that must be conceded, but also turning up what-ever factors the Marxists left out. Moreover, the German Marxists had suddenly become stronger with the end of the World War and the downfall of the German monarchy. Weber delivered his lectures in Munich just after the short-lived Com-munist commune of 1919, and his lecture room contained many radical students. It is not surprising that Weber was so much more explicitly concerned with Marxism in his last work than in the religious studies he published while the war was going on.

Weber had one great advantage over the Marxists. The discipline of historical scholarship reached its maturity around the end of the nineteenth century. Not only had political and military history reached a high degree of comprehensiveness and accuracy, but so had the history of law, religion, and economic institutions not only for Europe and the ancient Mediterranean but for the Orient as well. The histor-ical researches of the twentieth century have not brought to light any great body of facts about the past that has radically changed our view of world history since Weber's day. Weber was perhaps the first great master of the major institutional facts of world history. By contrast, Marx, pursuing his assiduous researches in the 1840s and 50s, had much narrower materials at his disposal (Hobsbawm, 1964, pp. 20–7). The histories of India, China, Japan, or Islam had scarcely begun to be available; the permeation of the ancient Greco-Roman world by religious institutions was only beginning to be analyzed; and the complex civilization of the European High Middle Ages was hidden beneath what Marx considered the "feudal rubbish" of the *Ancien Régime* of the eighteenth century. Marx wrote before the great coming-of-age of historical scholarship; Weber, just as it reached its peak. Weber thus rep-resents for us the first and in many ways still the only effort to make a truly informed comparative analysis of major historical developments.

It should be borne in mind that Marx and most of his followers have devoted their attention primarily to showing the dynamics of capitalism, not to the precon-ditions for its emergence. Weber's concerns were almost entirely the reverse. Hence, it is possible that the two analyses could be complementary, Marx's taking up where Weber's leaves off. Only in the 1970s have there been efforts comparable to Weber's from within the Marxian tradition, notably that of Wallerstein (1974). Interestingly enough, Weber anticipated Wallerstein's major points in the *General Economic History*. On the other side, Wallerstein's revision of Marxism is in many ways a movement toward a more Weberian mode of analysis, stressing the import-ance of external relations among states.

The classical Marxian model of the preconditions for capitalism covers only a few points (Marx, 1967, pp. I, 336–70, 713–64; II, 323–37, 593–613; 1973, pp. 459–514). Some of these are a subset of Weber's model, while two of them are distinctive to Marx. Weber and Marx both stressed that capitalism requires a pool of formally free but economically propertyless labor; the sale of all factors of production on the market; and the concentration of all factors in the hands of capitalist entrepreneurs. Marx did not see the importance of the *calculable* aspect of technology; at times, he seemed to make the sheer productive power of techno-logy the central moving force in economic changes, while at others, he downplayed this as part of a larger economic system – much in the way Weber did. Unlike Weber, Marx gave no causal importance at all to calculable law, nor did he see the earlier links in Weber's causal chain: economic ethics, citizenship, bureaucratization, and their antecedents.[18]

The uniqueness of Marx's discussion is in two factors: primitive accumulation and revolution. About the latter, Marx had surprisingly little to say beyond the dramatic imagery of revolution breaking the bonds imposed by the property system upon the growing engines of production (Marx, 1959, pp. 43–4). Primitive accumulation takes up nearly the whole of his historical discussion. It means the accumulation of enough raw materials, tools, and food for laborers to live on before subsequent pro-duction was completed; hence, it is the quantitative prerequisite for any takeoff into expanded economic production. Such accumulation took place historically in two ways. One was by the expropriation of peasants from their land, which simultan-eously concentrated wealth in the hands of the capitalists who received the lands and required the expropriated masses to sell their labor on the market. The other means of primitive accumulation was by usury and merchants' capital. Marx down-played the importance of monetary factors by themselves, as they operated only in the realm of circulation and did nothing to productive relations; but he did assert that the growth of money capital furthered the dissolution of the feudal economy once it was already under way (1967, pp. III, 596–7).

Of these two factors, Weber says almost nothing explicitly about primitive accu-mulation. However, the entire earlier sections of the *General Economic History* (1961, pp. 21–203) deal with the various forms of appropriation of material and financial means, which have made up, among other things, the capitalism that has been omnipresent throughout history, although not in a rationalized form. The idea that there must be a specific accumulation of surplus for the purpose of a capitalist take-off, I suspect, is one that Weber would reject. The assumption ought to be subjected to proof. After all, agrarian societies already have the most extreme concentration of wealth at the top of the social hierarchy of any type of society in world history (Lenski, 1966); the industrial takeoff need only have been fueled by a shift in the use of this wealth, not by a further extraction process. As Weber understood, and as subsequent research has shown, capitalists do not have to rise "from below," having amassed their own wealth; it has been far more typical for the aristocracy themselves to go into capitalist production (Stone, 1967; Moore, 1966).[19]

Weber is somewhat more sympathetic to the importance of revolutions. Perhaps the final conditions for the capitalist takeoff in England were the revolutions of 1640 and 1688. These put the state under the control of political groups favorable to capitalism, thus fulfilling the condition of keeping markets and finances free of "irrational" and predatory state policies. Of more fundamental institutional con-sequence were the revolutions within the cities of ancient Greece and of medieval

Italy. The latter Weber lists among "the five great revolutions that decided the destiny of the occident" (1951, p. 62).[20] For it was the uprising of the plebeians which replaced the charismatic law of the older patrician class with the universalistic and "rationally instituted" law upon which so much of the institutional development of capitalism was to depend (Weber, 1968, pp. 1312–13, 1325). In effect, this was a revolution in a system of property, but not in the gross sense of a replacement of one form of appropriation with another. For Weber, a system of property is a complex of daily actions – above all, the making of transfers and contracts and the adjudication of disputes. Hence, political revolutions are most crucial where they set the pattern for ongoing legal actions in a highly calculable form, with all the consequences noted above.

Wallerstein's (1974) theory, as developed in volume I, emphasizes two conditions in the origins of capitalism. One is the influx of bullion from the European colonies, which caused the price inflation of the 16th century. During this period, wages remained approximately constant. The gap between prices and wages constituted a vast extraction of surplus which could be invested in expanding capitalist enterprises (Wallerstein, 1974, pp. 77–84).[21] This is Wallerstein's version of the primitive accumulation factor.

Wallerstein's (1974, p. 348) second condition also emerges from the international situation. "[C]apitalism as an economic system is based on the fact that economic factors operate within an arena larger than that which any political entity can totally control. This gives capitalists a freedom of maneuver that is structurally based." He (1974, p. 355) goes on to say that the different states must be of different strengths, so that not all states "would be in the position of blocking the effective operation of transnational economic entities whose locus were in another state." Capitalists in effect must have opportunities to shift their grounds among varied political climates to wherever the situation is most favorable.

Weber (1961, p. 259) was generally aware of both conditions. Regarding the effects of gold and silver influx, however, he was largely unfavorable.

> It is certainly true that in a given situation an increase in the supply of precious metals may give rise to price revolutions, such as that which took place after 1530 in Europe, and when other favorable conditions are present, as when a certain form of labor organization is in the process of development, the progress may be stimulated by the fact that large stocks of cash come into the hands of certain groups. But the case of India proves that such an importation of metal will not alone bring about capitalism. In India in the period of the Roman power, an enormous mass of precious metal – some twenty-five million sestertii annually – came in exchange for domestic goods, but this inflow gave rise to commercial capitalism only to a slight extent. The greater part of this precious metal disappeared into the hoards of the rajahs instead of being converted into cash and applied in the establishment of enterprises of a rational capitalistic character. This fact proves that it depends entirely upon the nature of the labor system what tendency will result from an inflow of precious metal.

In another passage, Weber (1961, p. 231) does say that the price revolution of the sixteenth and seventeenth centuries "provided a powerful lever for the specifically capitalistic tendencies of seeking profit through cheapening production and lowering the price." This came about for industrial (but not agricultural) products, because the quickened economic tempo put on pressures toward further rationalizing economic relations and inventing cheaper technologies of production. Weber thus gives the influx of precious metals a place as a contributory factor, though apparently not an indispensable one, *within* the framework of economic institutions which had already appeared in Europe at the time.[22]

Weber (1961, p. 249) largely agrees, however, with Wallerstein's argument about the international character of capitalism. Modern cities, he points out,

> came under the power of competing national states in a condition of perpetual struggle for power in peace or war. This competitive struggle created the largest opportunities for modern Western capitalism. The separate states had to compete for mobile capital, which dictated to them the conditions under which it would assist them to power. Out of this alliance of the state with capital, dictated by necessity, arose the national citizen class, the bourgeoisie in the modern sense of the word. Hence it is the closed national state which afforded to capitalism its chance for development – and as long as the national state does not give place to a world empire capitalism will also endure.

Here the coincidence with Wallerstein is remarkable. Weber does not emphasize the contours of Wallerstein's world system, with its tiers of core, semiperiphery, and periphery, but Weber does show the central importance of mobile capital among military competing states, and he gives a more specific analysis than Wallerstein of the mechanism by which this is transformed into an advantage for capitalism.

In general, there is considerable convergence, as well as complementarity, between Weber's last theory of the origins of capitalism, and the mature Marxian theory which is only now emerging. Weber largely rejects Marxian theories of primitive accumulation, or at least relegates them to minor factors. On the other side, Wallerstein, as well as modern Marxism in general, has moved the state into the center of the analysis. Weber had already gone much further in that direction, so that the main Weberian criticism of the Marxian tradition, even in its present form, is that it does not yet recognize the set of institutional forms, especially as grounded in the legal system, upon which capitalism has rested.

For Weber, the state and the legal system are by no means a superstructure of ideas determining the material organization of society. Rather, his theory of the development of the state is to a considerable extent an analogy to the Marxian theory of the economy. The key factor is the form of appropriation of the material conditions of domination. We have seen the significance of the organization of weapons for Weber's chain of causes of capitalism. In this connection, Weber (1961, p. 237) remarks:

> Whether the military organization is based on the principle of self-equipment or on that of military equipment by an overlord who furnishes horses, arms and provisions, is a distinction quite as fundamental for social history as the question whether the means of economic production are the property of the worker or of a capitalistic entrepreneur . . . [T]he army equipped by the war lord, and the separation of the soldier from the paraphernalia of war, [is] in a way analogous to the separation of the worker from the means of production. . . .

Similarly, state bureaucracy depends upon a set of material conditions, and upon the separation of the administrator from treating the office and its incomes as private property (1968, pp. 980–3). Weber diverges from the Marxian analogy by being a more thoroughgoing conflict theorist. As we have seen, and as the quotation given above on the international basis of capitalism bears out, for Weber the conditions of rationalized organization, in political and economic spheres alike, depend upon a continuous open struggle.[23]

The main disagreements between Marx and Weber have less to do with the origins of capitalism than with its future. Weber thought that capitalism could endure indefinitely as an economic system, although political factors could bring it down. As we have seen, he thought that the disappearance of religious legitimation in mature capitalism opened the way for workers to express their discontents in the form of a political movement for socialism. Ironically, it is the rationalized world view promoted by the underlying conditions of capitalism that gave birth to rational socialism, a doctrine that proclaims that the social order itself, rather than the gods, is to blame for economic distress; and that having been deliberately instituted, that order is capable of being consciously changed (1961, pp. 217–18). For Weber, however, economic crises may be endemic to modern capitalism, but they are not caused by a fundamental contradiction in it, nor is there any necessary tendency for them to worsen toward an ultimate breakdown. He attributes crises to overspeculation and the resulting overproduction of producers' (but not consumers') goods (1961, p. 217). To decide who is right on these points requires further consideration than can be given here.

Conclusion

Weber's last theory is still today the only comprehensive theory of the origins of capitalism. It is virtually alone in accounting for the emergence of the full range of institutional and motivational conditions for large-scale, world-transforming capitalism. Even so, it is incomplete. It needs to be supplemented by a theory of the operation of mature capitalism, and of its possible demise. And even on the home territory of Weber's theory, there remain to be carried out the comprehensive tests that would provide adequate proof. But sociological science, like any other, advances by successive approximations. The theory expressed in Weber's *General Economic History* constitutes a base line from which subsequent investigations should depart.

Notes

1   The list of institutional characteristics given on pp. 21–25 of the English-language edition of *The Protestant Ethic* (1930), however, are not in the 1904–5 original, but are from an introduction written in 1920 (1930: ix–x).

2   Cf. the closing words of *The Religion of China*: "To be sure the basic characteristics of the 'mentality,' in this case practical attitudes towards the world, were deeply codetermined by political and economic destinies. Yet, in view of their autonomous laws, one can hardly fail to ascribe to these attitudes effects strongly counteractive to capitalist development" (1951, p. 249), and of *The Religion of India*: "However, for the plebeian strata no ethic of everyday life derived from its rationally formed missionary prophecy. The appearance of such in the Occident, however – above all, in the Near East – with the extensive consequences borne with it, was conditioned by highly particular historical

constellations without which, despite differences of natural conditions, development there could easily have taken the course typical of Asia, particularly of India" (1958b, p. 343).

3   In Part I of *Economy and Society* (written 1918–20), Weber distinguishes formal and substantive rationality of economic action (1968, pp. 85–6). In "The Social Psychology of the World Religions" (written 1913), Weber (1946, pp. 293–4) defines three different types of rationalism: (1) a systematic world view based on precise, abstract concepts; (2) practical means-ends calculations; (3) a systematic method, including that of magic or prayer. In *The Protestant Ethic* (1904–5), Weber (1930, pp. 76–78) attacks the notion that the spirit of capitalism is "part of the development of rationalism as a whole," and says he is interested in "the origin of precisely the irrational element which lies in this, as in every conception of a calling." Kalberg (1980) points out that under one or another of Weber's types of rationality, *every* action, even the most superstitious, might be called "rational." Kalberg argues that only one type of rationality is relevant for the methodical conduct of affairs.

4   It is plain that Weber (1968, pp. 85–6) is referring to what in *Economy and Society* he calls "formal" rationality, efficiency based on quantitative calculation of means, rather than "substantive" rationality, the adequacy of actions for meeting ultimate values. Such values could be criteria of economic welfare, whether maximal production, quality of life, or a socialist economic distribution, or they could be ethical or religious values. Weber makes it clear that formal and substantive rationality can diverge widely, especially in his late political writings about the dangers of bureaucracy (1946, pp. 77–128; 1968, pp. 1393–1415). Weber himself tended to defend the formal rationality of modern capitalism as coinciding to a fair degree with substantive rationality in meeting the value of maximizing the economic welfare of the population at large (1968, pp. 108–9). It goes without saying that this is an empirical, not an analytical judgment.

5   Weber does mention "rational science and in connection with it a rational technology" (1961, p. 232) as one of the features of the West important for modern capitalism. On the other hand he says: "It is true that most of the inventions of the 18th century were not made in a scientific manner. . . . The connection of industry with modern science, especially the systematic work of the laboratories, beginning with Justus von Liebig [i.e., *Circa* 1830], enabled industry to become what it is today and so brought capitalism to its full development." On the balance, I think science comes out as a secondary factor in the model.

6   Weber (1961, p. 260) also mentions geographical conditions as more favorable to capitalism in Europe than in China or India, due to transportation advantages in the former via the Mediterranean Sea and the interconnecting rivers. But he goes on (p. 261) to discount this, in that no capitalism arose in Mediterranean antiquity, when civilization was predominantly coastal, whereas early modern capitalism in Europe was born in the cities of the interior.

7   Weber does not clearly describe a chain, and sometimes he lumps characteristics of rational capitalism with its preconditions. Although some of these preconditions continue into the operation of modern capitalism, a logical chain of explanation, I believe, requires something like the separation I have given. It should be understood that Weber gives a highly condensed summary in these lectures.

8   Hence the role of "guest peoples" such as the Jews and the Caursines in Christian Europe, or the Christians in Islamic societies, or the Parsees in India, as groups of tolerated outsiders who were available for making loans, which otherwise would not be forthcoming within the controlled internal economy (1961, p. 267).

9   The main exception is that revolutions can occur after the military breakdown of the state itself due to foreign wars.

10   Contractual forms of feudalism also contributed somewhat to legal citizenship. Weber neglected this in the *General Economic History*, but considered it in *Economy and Society* (1968, p. 1101). The earlier preconditions (military and religious) for contractual feudalism and for independent cities, however, are essentially the same.

11   Weber did not live to write his planned volume on medieval Christianity. If he had, I believe he would have found that the High Middle Ages were the most significant institutional turning point of all on the road to the capitalist takeoff. His commitment to the vestiges of his Protestantism argument may have kept him from recognizing this earlier.

12   This was also the time when the church took the offensive against incipient capitalism, in the form of pronouncements against usury (Weber, 1968, pp. 584–6).

13   One clearly formulated proposition, for example, is that armies based on coalitions of self-supplied individuals produce citizenship rights. (For a series of such propositions, see Collins, 1975, pp. 356–64.)

14   In other words, the main features of the West depend on a tension between the routinization of religious charisma in the church and the participatory communities of monks, and on a tension between the democratizing tendencies of self-supplied armies and the centralized bureaucratic state. These give us Weber's two great intermediate factors, a nondualistic religious ethic and calculable law, respectively.

15   "The formal rationality of money calculation is dependent on certain quite specific substantive conditions. Those which are of a particular sociological importance for present purposes are the following: (1) Market struggle of economic units which are at least relatively autonomous. Money prices are the product of conflicts of interest and of compromises: they thus result from power constellations. Money is not a mere 'voucher for unspecified utilities,' which could be altered at will without any fundamental effect on the character of the price system as a struggle of man against man. 'Money' is, rather, primarily a weapon in this struggle, and prices are expressions of the struggle: they are instruments of calculation only as estimated quantifications of relative chances in this struggle of interests" (Weber, 1968, pp. 107–8).

16   Weber goes on to say, "A criticism of the theory leads to consideration first of the evolution of prostitution, in which connection, it goes without saying, no ethical evaluation is involved." There follows (1961, pp. 40–53) a brilliant outline of a theory of the organization of the family as one set of variants on sexual property relations, in which material transactions and appropriations are fundamentally involved. Later versions of this line of theory are found in Lévi-Strauss (1949/1969) and in Collins (1975, pp. 228–59).

17   Böhm-Bawerk also made an analysis of socialist economies. He regarded these as possible *politically* (as did Schumpeter and Weber), but denied that production would be organized differently than in capitalism. Socialism could affect only the distribution of capitalist profits among the populace. For the economic thought of this period, see Schumpeter (1954, pp. 800–20, 843–55, 877–85) and Sweezy (1942, pp. 190–213).

18   Marx (1973, pp. 459–514) gave a very general outline of early forms of property as based on family and tribal membership, and he recognized that the ancient cities were military coalitions. He missed the central organizing role of religion in these developments, and failed to see the crucial effect of the revolutions within the ancient cities upon the uniquely Western legal tradition. For Marx, the rise of cities simply meant the growing separation of town and country, an instance of dialectical antithesis, and of the progress of the division of labor (1967, pp. I, 352). For the period immediately preceding the capitalist takeoff, Marx noted that the state had hastened the transition from feudalism to capitalism by creating public finance and conquering foreign markets. These effects Marx subsumed under his concept of "primitive accumulation."

19   Weber also anticipated Barrington Moore's (1966) theory of the political consequences of different property modes in the commercialization of agriculture (1961, pp. 81–94).

20   The others were "the Netherland revolution of the sixteenth century, the English revolution of the seventeenth century, and the American and French revolutions of the eighteenth century."

21   To this, Wallerstein adds the argument that surplus is further extracted by coerced labor on the periphery, to be consumed in the core, where however (somewhat contrary to the point about the price revolution) labor is well enough paid to constitute a potential consumers' market for capitalist production.

22   Weber's (1961, p. 223) comment on the economic benefits of the colonies is even more negative: "This accumulation of wealth brought about through colonial trade has been of little significance for the development of modern capitalism – a fact which must be emphasized in opposition to Werner Sombart. It is true that the colonial trade made possible the accumulation of wealth to an enormous extent, but this did not further the specifically occidental form of the organization of labor, since colonial trade itself rested on the principle of exploitation and not that of securing an income through market operations. Furthermore, we know that in Bengal for example, the English garrison cost five times as much as the money value of all goods carried thither. It follows that the markets for domestic industry furnished by the colonies under the conditions of the time were relatively unimportant, and that the main profit was derived from the transport business."

23   It is true that Weber continues to leave more room for religious conditions than any of the Marxians. Yet even here, military conditions play a key role in the ultimate determinants of religions. The earliest Greek civic cults were war coalitions; and the this-worldly, antimagical character of Judaism derives from the cult of Yahwe, the war god of the coalition of Jewish tribes.

References

Böhm-Bawerk, Eugen von (1896/1949) *Karl Marx and the Close of his System*, New York: Augustus Kelley.

Burger, Thomas (1976) *Max Weber's Theory of Concept Formation*, Durham, NC: Duke University Press.

Cohen, Jere (1980) "Rational Capitalism in Renaissance Italy," *American Journal of Sociology* 85: 1340–55.

Collins, Randall (1975) *Conflict Sociology*, New York: Academic Press.

Hirst, Paul Q. (1976) *Evolution and Social Categories*, London: Allen & Unwin.

Hobsbawm, E. J. (1964) "Introduction," in Karl Marx, *Precapitalist Economic Formations*, New York: International Publishers.

Kalberg, Stephen (1979) "The Search for Thematic Orientations in a Fragmented Oeuvre: The Discussion of Max Weber in Recent German Sociological Literature," *Sociology* 13: 127–39.

Kalberg, Stephen (1980) "Max Weber's Types of Rationality," *American Journal of Sociology* 85: 1145–79.

Lenski, Gerhard E. (1966) *Power and Privilege: A Theory of Stratification*, New York: McGraw-Hill.

Lévi-Strauss, Claude (1949/1969) *The Elementary Structures of Kinship*, Boston, MA: Beacon Press.

McClelland, David C. (1961) *The Achieving Society*, New York: Van Nostrand.

Marx, Karl (1856/1959) "Preface to a Contribution to the Critique of Political Economy," in L. Feuer (ed.), *Marx and Engels: Basic Writings on Politics and Philosophy*, New York: Doubleday.

Marx, Karl (1857–8/1973) *Grundrisse*, New York: Random House.

Marx, Karl (1867, 1885, 1894/1967) *Capital*, New York: International Publishers.

Moore, Barrington, Jr. (1965) *Soviet Politics*, New York: Harper & Row.

Moore, Barrington (1966) *Social Origins of Dictatorship and Democracy*, Boston, MA: Beacon Press.

Nelson, Benjamin (1949) *The Idea of Usury*, Princeton, NJ: Princeton University Press.

Parsons, Talcott (1947) "Introduction," in Max Weber, *The Theory of Social and Economic Organization*, trans. A. M. Henderson and Talcott Parsons, New York: Oxford University Press.

Parsons, Talcott (1963) "Introduction," in Max Weber, *The Sociology of Religion*, Boston, MA: Beacon Press.

Parsons, Talcott (1967) *Societies: Comparative and Evolutionary Perspectives*, Englewood Cliffs, NJ: Prentice-Hall.

Samuelsson, Kurt (1961) *Religion and Economic Action*, New York: Basic Books.

Schumpeter, Joseph A. (1911/1961) *The Theory of Economic Development*, New York: Oxford University Press.

Schumpeter, Joseph A. (1954) *History of Economic Analysis*, New York: Oxford University Press.

Seidman, Steven (1980) "Enlightenment and Reaction: Aspects of the Enlightenment Origins of Marxism and Sociology," unpublished dissertation, University of Virginia.

Stone, Lawrence (1967) *The Crisis of the Aristocracy, 1558–1641*, New York: Oxford University Press.

Sweezy, Paul M. (1942) *The Theory of Capitalist Development*, New York: Oxford University Press.

Tawney, R. H. (1938) *Religion and the Rise of Capitalism*, New York: Penguin Books.

Tenbruck, F. H. (1975) "Das Werk Max Webers," *Kölner Zeitschrift für Soziologie und Sozialpsychologie* 27: 663–702.

Wallerstein, Immanuel (1974) *The Modern World-System: Capitalist Agriculture and the Origins of the European World-Economy in the Sixteenth Century*, New York: Academic Press.

Weber, Max (1904–5/1930) *The Protestant Ethic and the Spirit of Capitalism*, trans. Talcott Parsons, New York: Scribner.

Weber, Max (1916/1951) *The Religion of China*, trans. Hans H. Gerth, New York: Free Press. Originally published in *Archiv für Sozialwissenschaft und Sozialforschung*.

Weber, Max (1917–19/1952) *Ancient Judaism*, trans. Hans H. Gerth and Don Martindale, New York: Free Press. Originally published in *Archiv für Sozialwissenschaft und Sozialforschung*.

Weber, Max (1922/1958b) *The City*, trans. Don Martindale and Gertrud Neuworth, Glencoe, IL: Free Press.

Weber, Max (1922/1968) *Economy and Society*, Guenter Roth and Klaus Wittich (eds), New York: Bedminster Press.

Weber, Max (1923/1961) *General Economic History*, trans. Frank H. Knight, New York: Collier-Macmillan. Original from 1919–20 lectures.

Weber, Max (1946) *From Max Weber: Essays in Sociology*, trans. and eds Hans H. Gerth and C. Wright Mills, New York: Oxford University Press.

11 Markets as Politics: A Political-Cultural Approach to Market Institutions

Neil Fligstein

Most key insights of the sociology of markets have been framed as reactions to neoclassical economic views of the functioning of markets. White (1981) suggested that stable production markets were only possible if actors took one another into account in their behavior, contrary to the basic assumption of the neoclassical economic view, which stresses anonymity of actors. Granovetter (1985) extended this argument, suggesting that all forms of economic interaction were centered in social relations, what he called the embeddedness of markets. Various scholars have presented evidence that market embeddedness produced effects that economic models could not predict (Burt, 1983; Zelizar, 1983; Baker, 1984; Fligstein, 1990).

The empirical literature has failed to clarify the precise nature of the social embeddedness of markets. Granovetter (1985) argued that network relatedness is the most important construct. Burt (1983) proposed that networks stand in for resource dependence. Podolny (1993) has used networks as a cause and consequence of the creation of a status hierarchy. Fligstein (1990) and Fligstein and Brantley (1992) argued that the social relations within and across firms and their more formal relations to the state are pivotal to understanding how stable markets emerge. Campbell and Lindberg (1990) and Campbell, Hollingsworth, and Lindberg (1991) took a similar approach and focused on the emergence of what they call governance structures in industries. Institutional theory in the organizational literature has argued that institutional entrepreneurs create new sets of social arrangements in organizational fields with the aid of powerful organized interests, both inside and outside of the state (DiMaggio, 1989; DiMaggio and Powell, 1991).

These latter perspectives have been buttressed by studies on comparative industrial organization (Hamilton and Biggart, 1988; Chandler, 1990; Gerlach, 1992) that show how state–firm interactions in various societies have produced unique cultures of production. Industrial countries are not converging toward a single form (Fligstein and Freeland, 1995). Instead a plurality of social relations have been observed that structure markets within and across societies. These observations have challenged the neoclassical economists' view that markets select efficient forms which, over time, converge to a single form.[1]

Original publication: Fligstein, Neil, "Markets as Politics: A Political-Cultural Approach to Market Institutions," *American Sociological Review* (vol. 61, August, 1996): 656–73.

To push this debate forward, sociologists must go beyond documenting the shortcomings of the neoclassical model. Thus, in this paper, I begin to structure a new view from the existing literature. The basic insight is that the social structures of markets and the internal organization of firms are best viewed as attempts to mitigate the effects of competition with other firms. I outline a political-cultural approach, and I use the metaphor "markets as politics" to discuss how these social structures come into existence, produce stable worlds, and are transformed.

The "markets as politics" metaphor has two dimensions. First, I view the formation of markets as part of state-building. Modern states with capitalist economies create the institutional conditions for markets to be stable. I identify what institutions are contested and view their construction as a political project undertaken by powerful actors. Great societal crises, such as war, depression, or the entry of a nation into modern development, are pivotal to understanding a society's economic development. Once in place, these "rules" of market-building and market intervention are keys to understanding how new markets develop in a society.

Second, I argue that processes within a market reflect two types of political projects: the internal firm power struggle and the power struggle across firms to control markets. These are related "control" projects (White, 1992). The internal power struggle is about who will control the organization, how it will be organized, and how situations will be analyzed and responded to. The winners of the internal power struggle will be those with a compelling vision of how to make the firm work internally and how to interact with the firm's main competitors. I use a social movement metaphor to characterize action in markets during market creation or crisis.

The production of market institutions is a cultural project in several ways. Property rights, governance structures, conceptions of control, and rules of exchange define the social institutions necessary to make markets. Economic worlds are social worlds; therefore, they operate according to principles like other social worlds. Actors engage in political actions vis-à-vis one another and construct local cultures to guide that interaction (Geertz, 1983).

An important purpose of this paper is to bring together the versions of economic sociology that stress institutions with those that stress networks and population ecology. I use the metaphor of "markets as politics" as the unifying construct which focuses on how social structures are produced to control competition and organize the firm. My approach combines key features of the other perspectives, but fills in what I consider to be important shortcomings of those theories. Institutional theory in the organizational literature is concerned with the construction of rules, but it lacks a theory of politics and agency. Networks are at the core of markets to the degree that they reflect social relations between actors. The major limitation of the network approaches is that networks are sparse social structures, and it is difficult to see how they can account for what we observe in markets. Put another way, they contain no model of politics, no social preconditions for the economic institutions in question, and no way to conceptualize how actors construct their worlds (Powell and Smith-Doerr, 1994). Population ecology has usually taken the existence of niches or markets as a given, which would seem to be antithetical to a more social constructionist approach. However, Hannan and Freeman (1985) have argued that niches are social and political constructions, and they discussed how boundaries are formed. I elaborate on such a perspective, but with a more explicitly political model.

Market Institutions: Some Definitions

My focus is on the organization of modern production markets (White, 1981). *Markets* refer to situations in which some good or service is sold to customers for a price that is paid in money (a generalized medium of exchange). The first problem for developing a sociology of markets is to propose theoretically the social institutions necessary as preconditions to the existence of such markets. *Institutions* refer to shared rules, which can be laws or collective understandings, held in place by custom, explicit agreement, or tacit agreement. These institutions – what can be called property rights, governance structures, conceptions of control, and rules of exchange – enable actors in markets to organize themselves, to compete and cooperate, and to exchange.

Property rights are social relations that define who has claims on the profits of firms (akin to what agency theorists call "residual claims" on the free cash flow of firms – Jensen and Meckling, 1974; Fama, 1980). This leaves open the issues of legal forms; the relationships between shareholders and employees, local communities, suppliers, and customers; and the role of the state in directing investment, owning firms, and protecting workers. Unlike agency theorists, I argue that the constitution of property rights is a continuous and contestable political process, not the outcome of an efficient process (Roe, 1994). Organized groups from business, labor, government agencies, and political parties will try to affect the constitution of property rights.

Governance structures refer to the general rules in a society that define relations of competition, cooperation, and market-specific definitions of how firms should be organized. These rules define the legal and illegal forms of how firms can control competition. They take two forms: (1) laws and (2) informal institutional practices.

Laws, called antitrust, competition, or anticartel laws, exist in all advanced industrial societies. The passage, enforcement, and judicial interpretation of these laws is contested (Fligstein, 1990), and the content of such laws varies widely across societies from allowing cooperation or mergers between competitors to enforcing competition.

Market societies also develop more informal institutional practices which are embedded in existing organizations as routines and are available to actors in other organizations. Some mechanisms of transmission are professional associations, management consultants, and the exchange of professional managers (DiMaggio and Powell, 1983). These informal practices include how to arrange a work organization (such as the multidivisional form), how to write labor and management contracts, and where to draw the boundaries of the firm. They also include current views of what constitutes legal and illegal behavior of firms.

The purpose of action in a given market is to create and maintain stable worlds within and across firms that allow firms to survive. *Conceptions of control* refer to understandings that structure perceptions of how a market works and that allow actors to interpret their world and act to control situations. A conception of control is simultaneously a worldview that allows actors to interpret the actions of others and a reflection of how the market is structured. Conceptions of control reflect market specific agreements between actors in firms on principles of internal organization (i.e., forms of hierarchy), tactics for competition or cooperation, and the hierarchy or status ordering of firms in a given market. A conception of control can be thought of as "local knowledge" (Geertz, 1983). The state must ratify, help create, or at the very least, not oppose a conception of control.

Rules of exchange define who can transact with whom and the conditions under which transactions are carried out. Rules must be established regarding shipping, billing, insurance, the exchange of money (i.e., banks). and the enforcement of contracts. These rules become even more important across societies. As with property rights, governance structures, and conceptions of control, states are essential to the creation and enforcement of rules of exchange.

The Model of Action

The key insight of the perspective I propose here is that there are two forms of potential sources of instability in markets: (1) the tendency of firms to undercut one another's prices, and (2) the problem of keeping the firm together as a political coalition (March, 1961). Market actors try to control both sources of instability to promote the survival of their firm. The goal of a conception of control is to erect social understandings whereby firms can avoid direct price competition and can solve their internal political problems.[2] These problems are related, and the solution to one will be part of the solution to the other.

The potential of price competition to undermine market structures is always there. Stable markets may last from a few years to decades. In some classically competitive markets, such as restaurants and barber shops, stability has never emerged. Even in these markets, actors try to differentiate their products to form niches to protect themselves from price competition (for example, restaurants serving high-priced California cuisine). My claim is not that actors in firms are always successful at creating stable shelters from price competition, but that the politics of markets and the social organization of markets involve attempts to do so.

Market actors live in murky worlds where it is never clear which actions will have which consequences. Yet, actors must construct an account of the world that interprets the murkiness, motivates and determines courses of action, and justifies the action decided upon. In markets, the goal of action is to ensure the survival of the firm. No actor can determine which behaviors will maximize profits (either a priori or post hoc), and action is therefore directed toward the creation of stable worlds.

Issues of internal organization revolve around producing stable (reproducible) social relations. The intraorganizational power struggle is about actors within the organization making claims to solve the "critical" organizational problems (March, 1961; Pfeffer, 1981). Actors need to have a coherent view of organizing that allows them to simplify their decision-making processes. Those actors that convince or defeat others will be able to define, analyze, and solve problems in their own terms. They will also be the leaders of the organization (Fligstein, 1987). Once in place, a firm-specific conception of control operates as a corporate culture.

What are some of the common competitor-oriented strategies used to control price competition? Actors often try to cooperate with competitors to share markets. Cartels, price controls, creating barriers to entry, limiting production, patents, licensing agreements, and joint ownership of production facilities are all tactics that firms use to divide markets. A related tactic is to involve the state in regulation or protective legislation that increases the odds of firm survival.

Actors simultaneously use two internal principles of organization to indirectly control competition: (1) integration and (2) diversification, which is often accompanied by producing multiple divisions in the organization. Integration can be vertical (the merger of suppliers or customers) or horizontal (the merger with competitors). Vertical integration prevents others from threatening valued inputs or outputs. The integration or merger of a large share of an industry means that a few firms can control the market by tacitly agreeing not to threaten one another's position through a price war. They often publicly announce pricing and production decisions so that other firms can follow suit.

Diversification implies entering new markets to increase the probability of firm survival. It begins with the differentiation of a single product on the basis of quality or price (White, 1981). To the degree that firms are not competing because their products differ, price competition will not threaten firm existence.[3] Through diversification, a firm that produces multiple products can reduce its dependence on any one product, and hence, increase the likelihood that the firm will survive. This allows the firm to grow larger, which increases firm stability as well. Firms search for new markets because there can be huge gains to the first mover. Such gains help stabilize the firm. If markets fail to materialize or market conditions deteriorate, a diversified firm can exit a failed market without threatening the larger corporate entity. The production of multiple products introduces internal control problems, and actors are constantly reorganizing around variations of the holding company and multidivisional form (Fligstein, 1985; Prechel, 1994).

Actions to control competition can be thought of as a cultural tool kit (Swidler, 1986). Actors are prepared to take what they can get and work toward a more stable market situation. In this way, conceptions of control are inspired solutions based in the pragmatics of experience (Padgett and Ansell, 1992).

Conceptions of control refer to broader cultural conceptions in which these "tool kit" tactics are embedded. Actors in two different markets might use product diversification, but one might view it as diversifying the financial portfolio (a financial perspective), while the other might see it as carrying a full line of goods (a marketing perspective) (Fligstein, 1990). Conceptions of control also allow actors to interpret what a particular strategic move by competitors might mean.

Actors stick with the conception they believe works. After some period of time, others will recognize some key set of factors and begin to imitate them. But these factors are rarely articulated before the fact; they become accepted or common knowledge only after they operate to produce stability for some firms. Such tactics and conceptions create cultural stories that can be used over and over again to justify an action or produce a new one.

State-Building as Market-Building

One implication of my metaphor, "markets as politics," is that states play an important role in the construction of market institutions. Why are states so important? The organizations, groups, and institutions that comprise the state in modern capitalist society claim to make and enforce the rules governing economic interaction in a given geographic area (Krasner, 1988).[4] Capitalist firms could not operate without collective sets of rules governing interaction. While most modern discussions of state-building have focused on welfare and warfare, modern capitalist states have been constructed in interaction with the development of their economies, and the governance of economies is part of the core of state-building (Fligstein, 1990; Hooks, 1990; Campbell, Hollingsworth, and Lindberg, 1991; Dobbin, 1994; Evans, 1995).[5]

Property rights, governance structures, and rules of exchange are arenas in which modern states establish rules for economic actors. States provide stable and reliable conditions under which firms organize, compete, cooperate, and exchange. The enforcement of these laws affects what conceptions of control can produce stable markets. There are political contests over the content of laws, their applicability to given firms and markets, and the extent and direction of state intervention into the economy. Such laws are never neutral. They favor certain groups of firms.

My argument is that it is likely that states are important to the formation and ongoing stability of markets. How they will be important and to what degree is a matter of context. Some states have greater capacities for intervention than others, and the likelihood of intervention depends on the nature of the situation and the institutional history of the state (Evans, Skocpol, and Rueschmeyer, 1985; Laumann and Knoke 1989).[6]

Property rights define the relation between an economic elite and the state. Business elites struggle to keep states from owning property, but they want states to enforce property rights. States differ with regard to their rules for cooperation and competition. Some allow extensive cooperation between firms, particularly in export markets (e.g., Germany), while others restrict the ability of firms in similar industries to cooperate (e.g., the United States). All states restrict competition to some degree by not allowing certain forms of predatory competition or by restricting entry into certain industries by using trade barriers (either tariff or nontariff) and regulation. The political processes that generate these rules often reflect the organized interests of a given set of firms in one market. A good working hypothesis is: One way to produce stable markets is to get the state to intervene to restrict competition. This is a "normal" firm strategy.

An important dimension of state involvement into markets is captured by the distinction between direct intervention and regulation. Interventionist states (e.g., France) are involved in making substantive decisions for many markets. They may own firms, direct investment, and heavily regulate firm entries, exits, and competition in markets. In contrast, regulatory states (e.g., the United States) create agencies to enforce general rules in markets, but do not decide who can own what and how investments proceed. Both strategies of intervention can be captured by firms. States can either intentionally or unintentionally upset the status quo of a given market by changing rules.

Below I advance some propositions about the interactions between states and other organized societal groups under different social conditions. These propositions imply research agendas that have been only partially exploited.

Proposition 1: The entry of countries into capitalism pushes states to develop rules about property rights, governance structures, and rules of exchange in order to stabilize markets for the largest firms.

The timing of entry of countries into capitalism has had huge effects on societal trajectories (Westney, 1980; Chandler, 1990; Fligstein, 1990; Dobbin, 1994). For countries just establishing modern capitalist markets, creating stable conceptions of control is more difficult precisely because property rights, governance structures, and rules of exchange are not well specified. Firms are exposed to the ravages of cutthroat competition and demand that the state establish rules about property rights, governance structures, and rules of exchange. Creating these new institutions requires the interaction of firms, political parties, states, and newly invented conceptions of regulation.

Proposition 2: Initial regulatory institutions shape the development of new markets because they produce cultural templates that affect how to organize.

The shape of these initial regulatory institutions has a profound effect on subsequent capitalist development. Indeed, any new markets that come into existence do so under a given set of institutions. One can observe that as countries industrialize, the demand for laws or enforceable understandings is high, and that once they are produced, they are stable, and demand for laws lessens.

As new industries emerge or old ones are transformed, new rules are made in the context of the old rules. Dobbin (1994) has argued that societies create "regulatory styles." These styles are embedded in regulatory organizations and in the statutes that support them. New rules follow the contours of old ones. States are often the focus of market crises, but actors continue to use an existing set of laws and practices to resolve crises.

Proposition 3: State actors are constantly attending to some form of market crisis or another. This is because markets are always being organized or destabilized, and firms are lobbying for state intervention.

In normal times, change in markets will be incremental and dependent upon the construction of interests of actors in and around the state.[7] Having stable rules is often more important than the content of the rules. However, rules do embody the interests of dominant groups, and state actors will not intentionally transform rules unless dominant groups are in crisis. Because of their central place in the creation and enforcement of market institutions, states will become the focus of crisis in any important market. Given the constant turmoil inherent in markets, one can expect the state to be constantly attending to some form of market crisis.

Pressure on states can come from two sources: other states (and by implication, their firms), and existing markets that can be constructed either locally (within the geography of the state) or globally (across states). As economic interdependence across societies has increased, there has been an explosion of cross-state agreements about property rights, governance structures, and rules of exchange.

Proposition 4: Laws and accepted practices often reflect the interests of the most organized forces in society. These groups support wholesale transformation of institutions only under crisis circumstances like war, depression, or state collapse.

The possibility for wholesale transformation occurs when there is an economy-wide failure of existing rules. Wars, depression, and possibly international economic competition can undermine society-wide arrangements. Massive economic crises will bring about political demands for changes in the rules.

These propositions illuminate the kinds of problems confronting the late-comers to capitalist social relations in Eastern Europe. The international organization of markets means that firms in developed product markets are poised to invade these societies and take over the local product markets. Moreover, there exist few market institutions, such as property rights, governance structures, or rules of exchange, to guide actors in new firms (Stark, 1992, 1996; Burawoy and Krotov, 1992).

It is interesting to consider Hungary. Stark (1992, 1996) has found that state actors in Hungary have turned state owned ministries into corporations. The government holds the bulk of stock in these corporations, although control appears to have devolved to managers. Eventually, state actors appear willing to have firms sold off to private interests. Complicated patterns of shareholding have developed whereby the state owns all of some firms and parts of others. What is particularly interesting is how managers have responded to the problem of competition.

Stark (1996) documents that managers have reorganized firms into complex structures in which large firms incorporate satellites of smaller firms in which the large firms hold equity shares. Finns have taken up two tactics. First, they have taken ownership stakes in firms producing similar products and have tried to control both the inputs and outputs of production. Second, groups of firms with related and unrelated products have joined together. These two tactics, integration and diversification, are tactics described earlier as used by firms to avoid direct competition.

A number of problems are engendered by this particular combination of nascent property rights and conceptions of control. State actors have recently forced Western-style accounting standards to attract Western investment, which has resulted in many bankruptcies (Stark, 1996). As a result, the state is pressured to prop firms up. Moreover, the state is the holder of equity and debt, and making the financial situation more precarious makes it harder to appeal to Western investors. It is not clear whether integration and diversification will produce stable outcomes. The problem is that these strategies may not be able to stand up to invasion by Western firms, particularly given the financial problems firms face.

While my approach cannot say how these transformations in Eastern Europe will turn out, it suggests how to study these processes. One begins by locating a set of policy changes in property rights, governance structures, or rules of exchange, and then tracking how these policies restructure social relations in markets. This would include detecting emerging conceptions of control and whether or not they produce successful outcomes for firms. If firms fail, there will be demands for new institutional changes.

One potential objection to my focus on states is that it fails to deal with the fact that the world economy is now truly global. But I believe that this state-centered approach is quite useful in analyzing so-called global markets. A market is "globalized" if there are a small number of participants who know one another and operate across countries with a common conception of control. Firms producing automobiles, computers, software, and pharmaceuticals may fit this definition. The emergence of these markets depends on cooperation between firms and states to produce rules of exchange and provide guarantees that firms can compete and expropriate profits.

One hypothesis is that the increases in world trade produce demand for more of these agreements and greater extensiveness of these agreements. The European

Union, the North American Free Trade Agreement, and the recently completed GATT Treaty can all be analyzed according to whether or not they consider issues around property rights, governance structures, and rules of exchange. They can also be broken down by sectors that do or do not involve exporters to see if rules tend to apply more or less exclusively to those sectors (Fligstein and Mara-Drita, 1996).

One arena in which agreements have not occurred is the creation of a world market for corporate control. It is very difficult to engage in hostile takeovers in any society, except in the United States and Great Britain. Earlier I suggested that property rights were at the core of the relations between national elites and states. Most national elites have resisted having property rights transferred to the highest bidder because they would lose power. States remain players in the creation of the global economy because their elites depend on them to preserve their power and guarantee entry to global markets.

The Problem of Change and Stability in Markets

There are three phases in market formation: emergence, stability, and crisis.[8] My concern is to specify how actors' perceptions of the current social structure affects the tactics they use to seek stability for their firms. It is here that the second part of my metaphor, "markets as politics," comes into play.

In any market, participants can be usefully distinguished in terms of their size relative to their market. Large firms control more external resources than small firms, including pricing from suppliers, financial assistance, and legitimacy, and they may possess control over key technologies or large customers (Pfeffer and Salancik, 1978; Burt, 1983). As a result, it makes sense to distinguish market participants as incumbents and challengers (Gamson, 1975). Incumbent firms are large, and actors in those firms know their major competitors and frame their actions on other large competitors. Challenger firms are smaller and frame their actions in terms of the largest firms. But, they will experience the world as a given – one out of their control.

Differing conditions of market stability produce different kinds of politics. A stable market is defined as a market in which the identities and status hierarchy of firms (the incumbents and the challengers) are well known and a conception of control that guides actors who lead firms is shared. Firms resemble one another in tactics and organizational structure. Politics will reproduce the position of the advantaged groups.

In new markets, the politics resemble social movements. Actors in different firms are trying to convince other firms to go along with their conception of the market. If they are powerful enough, they try to force their view. If there are many different firms of equivalent size, then alliances around conceptions of control are possible. Conceptions of control may become political compromises that bring market stability to firms.

Markets in crisis are susceptible to transformation. On rare occasions, the push for change may come from within the firms in a market. More frequently, firms invade the market and transform the conception of control. This can look like a social movement in the sense that the invading firms are trying to establish a new conception of control, and in doing so they are likely to ally themselves with some of the challengers or existing incumbents.

The most fluid period in a market is during its emergence. The roles of challengers and incumbents have yet to be defined, and there is no accepted set of social relations. It is useful to explore the metaphor of a social movement and its application to an emerging market. The ability of groups in a social movement to attain success depends on factors similar to firms trying to produce a stable market: the size of groups, their resources, the existence of a political opportunity to act, state actors willing to negotiate grievances, and the ability to build a political coalition around a collective identity (Snow et al., 1986; McAdam, 1982; Tarrow, 1994).

A new market spawns the growth of new firms as well as the entrance of firms operating in other markets, just as a political opportunity creates new social movement organizations. Firms try to take advantage of a market opening in the same way that organizations in social movements try to take advantage of a political opportunity. In a new market, the situation is fluid and is characterized by multiple conceptions of control proposed by actors from various firms. A stable market requires the construction of a conception of control to promote non-cutthroat ways to compete that all can live with and that state actors can accept. A conception of control operates as a kind of collective identity that many groups can attach to in order to produce a successful market.

Proposition 5: At the beginning of a new market, the largest firms are the most likely to be able to create a conception of control and a political coalition to control competition.

At the origination of a market, all interorganizational relations must be constructed. Markets are the outcome of an institutionalization project which is the equivalent of discovering a conception of control (DiMaggio, 1989). In this way, markets are social constructions. Making these institutional projects successful is inherently a political project. Actors need to find conceptions of control to signal to other firms in the moment of market formation what one's intentions are. One can predict that the largest firms in an emerging market are likely to create a conception of control and persuade others to go along with it because of the perceived advantages that size entails.

Proposition 6: Power struggles within firms are over who can solve the problem of how to best organize the firm to deal with competition. The winners of the struggle will impose their organizational culture and design on the firm.

A firm's internal power struggle depends on actors coming up with coherent conceptions of control that they can impose on others within the firm. The internal power struggle is likely to be most intense during the emergence of markets. Different groups believe they hold the solution to the problem of how to organize the firm to best deal with competition. Those actors that win impose their organizational design and culture on the firm. Internal firm structure and who controls the firm result from the conception of control that deals with the problem of market competition. These conceptions of control are available to other firms and help produce a stable status hierarchy of firms.

Proposition 7: Through intended and unintended actions, states can thwart the actions of firms to create stable conceptions of control.

All conceptions of control are built around current understandings of legal and illegal market behavior. Firms avoid conceptions of control that are illegal, but occasionally find themselves scrutinized by government officials. More frequently, state regulation of economic activities changes the balance of power in a market away from one conception of control and towards another. This occurs in regulated markets such as drugs, food, telecommunications, utilities, banks, and media.

Proposition 8: The "liability of newness" in a new market reflects, in part, the market's lack of social structure or conception of control (i.e., it reflects participants' inability to control competition).

It is at the emergence of markets that competition and price mechanisms exact their greatest toll. With no established conception of control to structure nonpredatory forms of competition, price has its strongest effect (Stinchcombe, 1965; Hannan and Freeman, 1977). There is a tendency to blame business failures on a lack of resources or the inability of managers to construct organizations that reliably deliver products. I argue that part of what is going on is the lack of a social structure to control competition. Markets in which a conception of control never emerges continue to have relatively high rates of firm death, while markets that are able to produce conceptions of control stabilize at lower death rates.

Proposition 9: New markets borrow conceptions of control from nearby markets, particularly when firms from other markets choose to enter the new market.

New markets are born in close social proximity to existing markets. Earlier, I argued that diversifying products is a way to produce more stable firms. Entering new markets does not require confronting entrenched interests and does not directly threaten the stability of the firm. If new markets succeed, then firm stability is enhanced. The differentiation and creation of new products is most frequently the spinoff of existing products. The start of a new market is not random, but is shaped by existing conceptions of control, legal conceptions of property and competition, and the existing organization of related markets.

To illustrate these principles, it is useful to consider examples. The creation of the U.S. steel industry is a clear case of firms struggling to create a social structure to control competition.[9] In the nineteenth century, the steel industry was susceptible to huge price swings because of its role in the railroad industry and building trades. These price swings were devastating to firms in the industry because they had invested large amounts of fixed capital. Thus, there was a great deal of incentive to find legal mechanisms to stabilize prices (Hogan, 1970).

The basic problem for the steel industry was to discover a conception of control that controlled competition. Cartels and monopolies were illegal in the United States (Thorelli, 1955). The choice that remained was to integrate firms to control the market. My proposition that the largest firms in the market are the leaders in such efforts is historically accurate in this case (Hogan, 1970).

During the turn of the century merger movement, the largest industrial corporation in the world emerged: the U.S. Steel Corporation. The merger created a large corporation that controlled inputs into the steel-making process as well as divisions that produced outputs for every segment of the market. The company controlled more than 65 percent of the market for steel and 75 percent of the industry's iron ore reserves (Hogan, 1970). In spite of being in a strong position, the firm found itself confronted by wild swings in product demand and unstable prices well into the twentieth century. It faced a dilemma in enforcing its position against its competitors. If the firm vigorously pursued price-cutting to gain monopoly control over the industry, it would find itself a target of antitrust authorities; if it did nothing, it would find its large investment threatened.

U.S. Steel began to pursue an alternative tactic. It posted its prices and production schedules and defended them by decreasing production in the face of aggressive competitors (Fligstein, 1990). U.S. Steel tried to cajole others into going along with its prices by threatening to use its control over inputs and its huge capacity to produce. If all behaved "reasonably," then some price stability could result. This strategy worked to stabilize steel prices from 1904 until the depression in 1929 (Kolko, 1963).

U.S. Steel's strategy of integrating production, setting prices, and daring others to undercut them was ratified as a legal way to control competition when it won its antitrust lawsuit in 1920. This conception of control spread in social-movement-like fashion during the 1920s merger movement, when oligopoly structures emerged in all of the core metal-making and petroleum industries (Eis, 1978). This structure proved durable in the U.S. steel industry and lasted until the 1960s (Hogan, 1970).

It is useful to examine an emerging industry where there is not yet a conception of control and apply the perspective advanced here to predict an outcome. The biotechnology industry has sprung up from common technologies that developed at major universities. To figure out which conceptions of control are contenders for organizing the industry, one asks: "What problem of competition would a social structure need to resolve?" One way to control competition is patent laws. Firms who discover a product first can extract monopoly rents from their investment in that product, thereby avoiding competition. The game is to find new products that can be patented. Two competing conceptions of control can be identified to take advantage of patent laws.

Powell and Brantley (1992) have argued that the critical problem for biotechnology firms is to control the supply of scientists who have the knowledge about the products. They view a network organization as a stable conception of control because it is a political compromise in which scientists may be able to leave a firm with knowledge of products, but firms have extensive organizational ties so that they will not have to depend on just one or two scientists for information or products. If the arrangements one firm has with other firms are alliances, then the collapse of any given alliance will not necessarily lead to a collapse of a given firm, by denying it either products or information. If a given scientist leaves, firms will presumably have a number of other scientists or alliances who can take up the slack. In this way, a networked firm oriented toward producing patents to control competition might prove stable.

Two other features of the biotechnology industry imply an alternative conception of control (Barley, Freeman, and Hybels, 1992; Powell and Brantley, 1992). Most biotechnology products must undergo extensive testing by the Food and Drug

Administration. Firms need money to survive this period of testing before bringing products to market. Thus, the state, through FDA regulation of the market, shifts the competitive conditions in the market from the discovery of new products to the ability to survive the testing and approval process. Once through the testing phase, firms will have to reliably produce, market, and distribute the product. This creates a second arena of competition that relies on poduction and marketing expertise.

These two competition problems imply that a different conception of control might emerge. I suggested earlier that one source of conceptions of control was nearby markets. The drug industry has extensive experience with the same testing and production processes used by the biotechnology industry, and is built on the creation, production, and control of proprietary drugs. I predict that to the degree that surviving the testing process and producing and marketing the product are pivotal, biotechnology firms will be tempted to form alliances with drug companies. Moreover, drug companies would be tempted to buy out the most successful of the biotechnology firms. The drug companies' conception of control (integrated firms that produce drugs with monopoly patent rights to eliminate competition to gain back the cost of producing the drug) would dominate.

A more hybrid form could emerge that would focus on maintaining the network organizations by keeping the discovery of products separate from the production and distribution of those products. This has advantages for both drug companies and biotechnology firms. The biotechnology firms maintain some control, while the drug companies lower their risk.

There is evidence that all three conceptions of control are practiced (Barley, Freeman, and Hybels, 1992; Powell and Brantley, 1992). The earlier discussion might predict that the most likely outcome is a merger between the two industries, whereby large biotechnology companies become drug companies or divisions thereof. The largest players in the market are the drug companies; their conception of control solves competition problems in the pharmaceutical industry; they already have negotiated the legitimacy of that solution with states. The problem of controlling the defection of scientists would be more ephemeral to solving the problem of getting products through the patent process.

Proposition 10: In markets with stable conceptions of control, there is a great deal of agreement by market participants on the conception of control and the status hierarchies and strategies it implies.

Once a stable market emerges, the roles of incumbents and challengers are defined and the power structure of the market becomes apparent. Actors in firms throughout the market will be able to tell observers who occupies what position and what their central tactics are. They will be able to make their actions contingent on their interpretation of those tactics.

Proposition 11: Incumbent firms pay attention to the actions of other incumbent firms, not challenger firms, while challenger firms focus on incumbent behavior.

A stable world depends on social relations between the largest firms. The central players will generally ignore challenger organizations under most circumstances because they pose little threat to the overall stability of the market. If these organizations live up to their name and begin to challenge the existing order, incumbent organizations will confront them and attempt to reinforce the governing conception of control.

Proposition 12: Firms in stable markets continue to use the governing conception of control, even when confronted with outside invasion or general economic crisis.

The major force that holds a market together over a period of time is the ability of the incumbent firms to continue to enforce a conception of control vis-à-vis one another. Incumbents are constantly trying to edge one another (and challengers) out for market share, but they refrain from direct confrontation that might prove the ruin of all. These actions will be guided by the existing conception of control (i.e., the conception of what is a reasonable action). This requires actors to frame action for their firm against their competitors and to have the resources (power) to make it stick. They know the identity of the important firms in the market, they try and make sense of their moves, and they respond to those moves.

This accounts for the relative stability of established markets, both in the identities of the participants and their tactics. To produce a stable order where firms survive is a relatively difficult problem. Once stability is attained, actors in firms are loath to engage in actions that undermine their incumbency. If challengers shift tactics or invaders come into the market, incumbent firms continue to engage in the same kinds of actions that produced the stable order in the first place. Incumbent firms may allow some redefinition of who is an incumbent and who is a challenger, but they will remain committed to the overall conception of control that lessens competition. To break down the stable order could potentially bring more chaos than would enforcing the "way things are done." Actors are also cognitively constrained by a conception of control. Their analysis of a crisis will be framed by the current conception of control and their attempts to alleviate the crisis by applying "the conventional wisdom."

The case of the Japanese *keiretsu* illustrates how a stable conception of control has withstood both political and economic assaults. Japanese *keiretsu* are families of firms in different industries that share ownership ties. The overall structure of the *keiretsu* is to cement important interdependencies and allow various *keiretsu* members to survive economic downturns. Often banks are at the center of *keiretsu* and they function as an internal capital market for the firms.

The *keiretsu* show high growth, high investment, and relatively low, but stable profits (Aoki, 1988). In economic downturns, *keiretsu* structures allow workers to be transferred across firms rather than being laid off (Lincoln, Gerlach, and Takahashi, 1992). This exerts downward pressure on profits, but secures employee loyalty. When firms within the structure are experiencing economic troubles, managers in other firms respond by helping to reorganize the troubled firm (Gerlach, 1992).

After World War II, *keiretsu* were reformed from prewar economic conglomerates (*zaibatsu*) that were family controlled. The *zaibatsu* were broken up during the American occupation, but began slowly to reform in a looser manner (Hadley, 1970). Since World War II, they have been directed by state actors to enter new markets, and they have proved adept at producing new products (Johnson, 1981).

The *keiretsu* structure contains firms with activities spread across a wide spectrum of industries and markets. The *keiretsu* structure, as a conception of control, does not directly control competition in a given market. Its advantage is how it stabilizes competition across markets. It has been noted that within given product markets, the firms from different *keiretsu* compete quite vigorously (Aoki, 1988).

The *keiretsu* structures operate to mitigate competition across markets in a number of ways. First, firms tend to purchase goods and services from inside the *keiretsu*. This means that some markets are captive and price competition is held down. Second, if a given firm faces an economic crisis, the other firms will attempt to support it. Management expertise, capital, and the ability to place workers with other firms during slumps, mitigate short-run competitive processes. Third, the focus on market share implies that firms invest for the long run and expectations for short-run profits are not high which gives managers latitude in dealing with competitive conditions. Fourth, because of the ownership relations between firms and banks, the cost of capital tends to be lower (see Gerlach, 1992 for a review of the literature). One can see the intimate connection between the problem of trying to control competition externally and the internal social organization working to solve that problem.

Recently, two forces began to close in on the *keiretsu*. First, the U.S. government applied pressure to open up Japanese markets, part of which was directed against the *keiretsu* structures (Gerlach, 1992). The U.S. wanted to break open the procurement arrangements of the *keiretsu* and demanded that the Japanese open their financial markets and allow a market for corporate control to develop. Second, the economic downturn of the early 1990s has put pressure on the permanent employment system of the *keiretsu*. It has been more difficult to pass workers onto other firms in the *keiretsu*. The managers who controlled the *keiretsu* have been able to use their traditional methods to fight off these attacks. They were politically connected enough to fight off reforms within Japan and economically able to endure a long recession (Gerlach, 1992).

Proposition 13: Market crisis is observed when incumbent organizations begin to fail.

Crisis comes to markets when the largest firms are unable to reproduce themselves from period to period. This can be caused by three kinds of events: (1) decrease in demand for the firm's products can result from bad economic conditions or a shift in buyers' preferences, (2) an invasion by other firms can upset the conception of control and introduce procedures which force a reorganization of the market, or (3) the state can intentionally or unintentionally undermine the market by changing rules.

Incumbents rarely become innovators because they are busy defending the status quo; market transformation is precipitated by invaders. The reorganization of a market around a new conception of control resembles a social movement and is very much like what occurs at the formation of markets. Invading firms can form alliances with existing firms around a new conception of control or a compromise conception of control, and this makes the reorganization of the market more predictable than it was at market formation.[10]

Proposition 14: Transformation of existing markets results from exogenous forces: invasion, economic crisis, or political intervention by states.

One of the key features of capitalist society is the dynamic interplay of markets, whereby some markets are emerging, others are stable, and still others are in crisis and undergoing transformation. I propose an exogenous theory of market transformation that views the basic cause of changes in market structure as resulting from forces outside the control of producers, due either to shifts in demand, invasion by other firms, or actions of the state. Incumbent firms will respond to these destabilizing forces by trying to reinforce the status quo. Markets are connected in a wide variety of ways. Firms rely on suppliers, capital markets, labor markets, and customers as well as on states for their stability. It follows that these market and state forces are always interacting and thereby producing potential problems for an existing conception of control in a given market. Crises in relations across markets can undermine existing agreements by threatening the well-being of all firms, either by withholding key resources or through the direct invasion of firms from nearby markets.

Proposition 15: Invaders are more likely to come from nearby rather than distant markets.

This argument parallels the argument about where new markets come from. Firms seek stability by finding new markets. The invasion of an existing market can occur in a couple of ways. First, firms in closely related markets enter existing markets where they can successfully introduce a new conception of control to increase their advantage. Second, firms might enter into the same product market in different geographic areas, thereby undermining a local stable order.

Proposition 16: When firms begin to fail, the intraorganizational power struggle heats up, leading to higher turnover of top personnel and greater activism by boards of directors and nonmanagement shareholders. New sets of organizational actors attempt to reconstruct the firm along the lines of the invaders.

Conceptions of control are used by actors in incumbent firms to ward off market crises. The internal firm power struggle will become more intense as market crises become more pronounced and the reigning conception of control proves to be inadequate to deal with the crisis.

Consider the example of the transformation of the finance conception of control as the guiding principle in the market for corporate control in the U.S. during the 1980s. The financial conception of control dominated the actions of many large U.S. firms between 1950 and 1970 (Fligstein, 1990). This view held that firms were composed of assets that could be deployed and redeployed by financial actors within firms in order to promote firm growth. The major tactics of this conception were the use of financial tools to internally monitor divisional performance and the use of mergers to buy and sell divisions that produced diversification for firms (Fligstein, 1990). These tactics solved the competition problems of large firms by allowing them to exit and enter businesses and stabilize the overall corporate structure. Firms were the principal actors in the market for corporate control as they sought to use the stock market to add to or subtract from their "portfolios."

What crisis made this conception of control no longer viable for large corporations? The high inflation rates during the 1970s meant that interest rates were high, stock prices were low, and the values of assets were inflated, thereby making returns on investments poor (Friedman, 1985). The financial conception of the firm, with its focus on the profitability of product lines and market diversification, suggested that "good" managers would deal with these problems by keeping debt low and funding investments from cash generated internally. The market for corporate control was in crisis because managers were not reorganizing their assets, even though corporate profits were low. This presented a new opportunity for actors to seek a new rationale to reorganize the market for corporate control.

What was this "new" conception of control, and who were its proponents? Davis and Thompson (1994) have argued that the language of "shareholder value" and the discourse that blamed managers for being ineffective spread amongst institutional investors in a social movement fashion in the early 1980s. The financial strategy of holding undervalued assets, funding investment internally, and keeping debt low was viewed as a problem. This language was allied with "agency theory" from economics (Jensen, 1989) to emphasize that if managers were not going to maximize shareholder value, then they should be replaced by management teams who would.

Institutional investors were a heterogeneous group and included investment bankers and representatives from pension funds, mutual funds, and insurance companies. They were from a closely related industry, financial services, and they invaded the turf of financial managers who controlled the largest U.S. corporations. Their goal was to force these managers to redeploy their assets to reflect how the 1970s had affected their balance sheets. They wanted managers to sell off overvalued assets, assume debt to keep firms disciplined, and to remove layers of management to save money. They also forced managers to focus their business by buying up competitors and selling off their most diversified assets (Davis, Diekmann, and Tinsley, 1994). They, of course, benefited by making money on organizing and executing mergers.

Research shows that firms that were merger targets tended to ignore financial reorganization to increase "shareholder value" (Davis and Stout, 1992; Fligstein and Markowitz, 1993). Useem (1993) showed how managers adopted this language and the behaviors it prescribed. The merger movement of the 1980s resembled a social movement whereby some financial executives and the various actors within the financial services industry discovered a common language and produced a conception of control to reorganize the market for corporate control.

The federal government played both direct and indirect roles. The Reagan Administration passed a huge tax cut that produced windfalls for corporate America in 1981. The Administration expected firms to reinvest that capital in new plants and equipment, but instead firms bought other firms. The Administration also announced that they would not vigorously enforce the antitrust laws (Fligstein and Markowitz, 1993). Davis and Stout (1992) argue that the Reagan Administration became a cheerleader for the shareholder value conception of control. The shareholder value conception of control is related to the finance conception of the firm, but it uses a stark discourse that only recognizes the rights of one group: those who own stock. All other concerns are subordinated to maximizing the returns for owners. The attention of top managers is focused on evaluating their product markets, but more importantly how the financial markets evaluate their stock price.

How does this new conception of control affect competition in the market for corporate control? If managers are paying attention to shareholder value in a narrow sense, they will be less likely to become merger targets. To the degree that the "game" is to avoid becoming the object of acquisition from outsiders (i.e., mergers), managers with a narrow focus are likely to maintain control. I hypothesize that the managers who win the internal power struggle will be those who can claim to maximize shareholder value. This process explains the spread of these tactics to most large firms during the 1980s.

Conclusions

Markets are social constructions that reflect the unique political-cultural construction of their firms and nations. The creation of markets implies societal solutions to the problems of property rights, governance structures, conceptions of control, and rules of exchange. There are many paths to those solutions, each of which might promote the survival of firms. I have sketched how states and markets are interconnected and what actions produce various outcomes. I have extracted general principles by which these outcomes can be understood. I now relate this framework back to current perspectives in economic sociology: networks, population ecology, institutional theory, and the problem of constructing action. While these perspectives differ, I believe that the political-cultural approach I have advanced here unites many of the positive features of each.

Network perspectives have been used to document a large number of social relationships in markets. They have indexed resource dependence, status hierarchies, brokering, channels of information, and trust relations. I have argued that stable markets reflect status hierarchies that define incumbents and challengers and that market leaders enforce the market social order and signal how crises are to be handled. These complex role structures in markets operate through networks. My view of markets takes seriously the problem of how states interact with markets to produce general rules by which social structures can be formed. It also makes market structures easier to observe, takes into account the role of actors' intentions in the production of market structures, and makes more sense of how firms are likely to behave under different market conditions.

Ecological approaches have focussed on the problem of how firms establish a niche, the population dynamics of firms, and the process of legitimation of firms in a niche. A political reading of these processes is consistent with the approach I developed here. The liability of newness results, at least partially, from the lack of social structure in a market and the social-movement-like search for such a structure. Legitimacy is bestowed by states on markets. A "stable" market for an ecologist resembles one in which a conception of control is shared. Similarly, as in ecology, the transformation of markets results from external sources of change.

Much of the perspective developed here is latent in institutional theories and the organizational theories they rely on. My approach focuses more than most institutional theories on political processes, both in the formal structuring of institutions by the state, and in the formation, stability, and transformation of markets. But the goal of action is to build stable markets, a view I have adopted from institutional and organizational theory.

I have tried to take the problem of agency quite seriously and to predict how actors' choices depend upon market structures and sets of rules. I have argued that what goes into these choices is more open to contestation during fluid market conditions, and that Padgett and Ansell's conception of robust action (1992) captures how actors come to take advantage of such situations. To this, I have added the broader notion that conceptions of control capture an important aspect of how actors frame action vis-à-vis one another. Conceptions of control are shared cognitive structures within and across organizations that have profound effects on organizational design and competition.

The metaphor of "markets as politics" is the theme used to unite these ideas. I have shown how this view makes possible a unified approach to the study of markets – an approach that focuses on the political processes that underlie market interactions. Ultimately, however, the usefulness of any metaphor is in the research it generates and the intuitive and counterintuitive insights it creates.

Notes

1   Finance economics, agency theory, and transaction cost theory are all attempts to specify how profit maximizing social relations evolve to govern firms and industries. Some proponents argue that all firms in every market (defined in product or geographic terms) will ultimately converge (Jensen, 1989), but others are prepared to recognize that pre-existing social relations might provide additional efficiencies (Williamson, 1985, 1991). Evolutionary theory (Nelson and Winter, 1982) and path dependence arguments (Arthur, 1989) can be used in a very similar way to account for the dynamics of real markets.

2   In White's (1981) model, this is done by firms watching one another's pricing and production behavior and then deciding to differentiate their product from their competitors. The main difference between White's argument and the argument proposed here is that I want to view this process as a political process as opposed to an economic one.

3   White's (1981) model is very close to what the population ecologists would call firms trying to create a "niche." The search for a niche is an attempt to avoid direct competition by differentiating your product from those of your competitors.

4   One could argue that markets for illegal goods develop and that this negates the arguments about the role of states in markets. My view is that illegal markets depend on states in a great many ways as well. For instance, illegal markets use many of the commercial channels that were set up by legal markets (e.g., shipping and banking). The definition of a market as illegal implies much about how it is likely to be organized. Hence, the conception of control governing illegal markets will not be ratified by states, but will be a reaction against them.

5   Much of this discussion is inspired by the recent literature in political science that defines itself as historical institutionalism (March and Olsen, 1989; Hall, 1989; Steinmo, Thelen, and Longstreth, 1992).

6   This perspective does not imply that the state is pivotal for every economic process. Even in societies where states have a history of intervention, state involvement is variable, and its effects are variable as well. The state's role depends on which market is being discussed and the current conditions in that or related markets.

7   The purpose here is not to develop a theory of the *forms* of states, but only to note their potential influence on market formation through their power to make the rules that govern all forms of social activity in a given geographic area.

8   My view of markets is roughly consistent with the idea of organizational fields, in that a market consists of firms who orient their actions toward one another (DiMaggio and Powell, 1983). I have elaborated this view by considering how markets are constructed and the roles that conceptions of control and politics play in this process.

9 I do not mean to imply that markets and industries are the same thing. Markets involve buyers and sellers of a commodity whereby industries refer to producers of similar commodities. Another issue is that most large firms participate in many markets. For instance, there are a number of markets where steel is sold. The firms who produce the product often sell into different markets. Since the basic product is similar across the markets (although its end use may be different, i.e., rails, automobiles, bridges) and the participants in these markets take one another into account in their actions, it is useful to speak of the steel industry. The general abstract dynamics discussed within markets can be played out across producers of some product or set of related products.

10 Invader organizations or new actions by challenger organizations do not necessarily produce a new conception of control. Actions can be oriented toward shifting the identities of challengers and incumbents within a market, and thereby preserving the basis of the noncompetitive order. It is only when the situation is fluid (i.e., the market is in crisis) that it is possible to create a "social movement" around a new conception of control.

References

Aoki, Mashiko (1988) *Information, Incentives, and Bargaining in the Japanese Economy*, Cambridge: Cambridge University Press.

Arthur, Brian (1989) "Competing Technologies and Lock-In by Historical Events: The Dynamics of Allocation Under Increasing Returns," *Economic Journal* 99: 116–31.

Baker, Wayne (1984) "The Social Structure of a Securities Market," *American Journal of Sociology* 89: 775–881.

Barley, Stephen, Freeman, John, and Hybels, Richard (1992) "Strategic Alliances in Biotechnology," pp. 311–47 in N. Nohria and R. Eccles (eds), *Networks and Organizations*, Boston, MA: Harvard Business School Press.

Burt, Ronald (1983) *Corporate Profits and Cooptation*, New York: Academic Press.

Burawoy, Michael and Krotov, Pavel (1992) "The Soviet Transition from Socialism to Capitalism: Worker Control and Economic Bargaining in the Wood Industry," *American Sociological Review* 57: 16–38.

Campbell, John and Lindberg, Leon (1990) "Property Rights and the Organization of Economic Activity by the State," *American Sociological Review* 55: 3–14.

Campbell, John, Hollingsworth, J. Rogers, and Lindberg, Leon (1991) *Governance in the American Economy*, Cambridge: Cambridge University Press.

Chandler, Alfred (1990) *Scale and Scope*, Cambridge, MA: Harvard University Press.

Davis, Gerald and Stout, Susan (1992) "Organization Theory and the Market for Corporate Control," *Administrative Science Quarterly* 37: 605–33.

Davis, Gerald and Thompson, Suzanne (1994) "A Social Movement Perspective on Corporate Control," *Administrative Science Quarterly* 39: 141–73.

Davis, Gerald, Diekmann, Kristina, and Tinsley, Catherine (1994) "The Deinstitutionalization of the Conglomerate Firms in the 1980s," *American Sociological Review* 59: 547–70.

DiMaggio, Paul (1989) "Interest and Agency in Institutional Theory," pp. 3–21 in L. Zucker (ed.), *Research on Institutional Patterns: Environment and Culture*, Cambridge, MA: Ballinger Press.

DiMaggio, Paul and Powell, Walter (1983) "The Iron Cage Revisited: Institutional Isomorphism and Collective Rationality in Organizational Fields," *American Sociological Review* 48: 147–60.

DiMaggio, Paul and Powell, Walter (1991) "Introduction," pp. 3–45 in W. Powell and P. DiMaggio (eds), *The New Institutionalism in Organizational Theory*, Chicago, IL: University of Chicago Press.

Dobbin, Frank (1994) *Forging Industrial Policy*, Cambridge: Cambridge University Press.

Eis, Carl (1978) *The 1919–30 Merger Movement in American Industry*, New York: Arno Press.

Evans, Peter (1995) *Embedded Autonomy*, Princeton, NJ: Princeton University Press.

Evans, Peter, Skocpol, Theda, and Rueschemeyer, Dietrich (1985) "On the Road Toward a More Adequate Understanding of the State," pp. 347–66 in P. Evans, D. Rueschmeyer, and T. Skocpol (eds), *Bringing the State Back In*, New York: Cambridge University Press.

Fama, Eugene (1980) "Agency Problems and the Theory of the Firm," *Journal of Political Economy* 88: 288–307.

Fligstein, Neil (1985) "The Spread of the Multidivisional Form," *American Sociological Review* 50: 377–91.

Fligstein, Neil (1987) "The Intraorganizational Power Struggle: The Rise of Finance Presidents in Large Corporations," *American Sociological Review* 52: 44–58.

Fligstein, Neil (1990) *The Transformation of Corporate Control*, Cambridge, MA: Harvard University Press.

Fligstein, Neil and Brantley, Peter (1992) "Bank Control, Owner Control or Organizational Dynamics: Who Controls the Modern Corporation," *American Journal of Sociology* 98: 280–307.

Fligstein, Neil and Freeland, Robert (1995) "Theoretical and Comparative Perspectives on Corporate Organization," *Annual Review of Sociology* 21: 21–43.

Fligstein, Neil and Mara-Drita, Iona (1996) "How to Make a Market: Reflections on the European Community's Single Market Program," *American Journal of Sociology*, 102(1): 1–33.

Fligstein, Neil and Markowitz, Linda (1993) "The Finance Conception of the Corporation and the Financial Reorganization of Large American Corporations, 1979–1988," pp. 185–206 in W. J. Wilson (ed.), *Sociology and the Public Agenda*, Beverly Hills, CA: Sage.

Friedman, Benjamin (1985) "The Substitutability of Debt and Equity Structures," pp. 23–39 in Benjamin Friedman (ed.), *Corporate Capital Structures in the United States*, Chicago, IL: University of Chicago Press.

Gamson, William (1975) *The Strategy of Social Protest*, Homewood, IL: Dorsey Press.

Geertz, Clifford (1983) *Local Knowledge*, New York: Basic Books.

Gerlach, Michael (1992) *Alliance Capitalism*, Berkeley, CA: University of California Press.

Granovetter, Mark (1985) "Economic Action, Social Structure, and Embeddedness," *American Journal of Sociology* 91: 481–510.

Hadley, Eleanor (1970) *Antitrust in Japan*, Princeton, NJ: Princeton University Press.

Hall, Peter (1989) *The Political Power of Economic Ideas*, Princeton, NJ: Princeton University Press.

Hamilton, Gary and Biggart, Nicole (1988) "Market Culture and Authority: a Comparative Analysis of Management and Organization in the Far East," *American Journal of Sociology* 94 (supp.): S52–S94.

Hannan, Michael and Freeman, John (1977) "The Population Ecology of Organizations," *American Journal of Sociology* 82: 929–64.

Hannan, Michael and Freeman, John (1985) "Where Do Organizations Come From?," *Sociological Forum* 1: 50–72.

Hogan, William (1970) *Economic History of the Iron and Steel Industry*, Lexington, MA: D. C. Heath.

Hooks, Greg (1990) "The Rise of the Pentagon and U.S. State Building," *American Journal of Sociology* 96: 358–404.

Jensen, Michael (1989) "Eclipse of the Public Corporation," *Harvard Business Review*, September: 61–73.

Jensen, Michael and Meckling, Paul (1974) "Theory of the Firm: Managerial Behavior, Agency Costs, and Ownership Structure," *Journal of Financial Economics* 3: 305–60.

Johnson, Chalmers (1981) *MITI and the Japanese Miracle*, Stanford, CA: Stanford University Press.

Kolko, Gabriel (1963) *The Triumph of Conservatism*, New York: Free Press.

Krasner, Stephen (1988) "Sovereignty: An Institutional Perspective," *Comparative Political Studies* 21: 66–94.

Laumann, Edward and Knoke, David (1989) *The Organizational State*, Chicago, IL: University of Chicago Press.

Lincoln, James, Gerlach, Michael, and Takahashi, Peggy (1992) "Keiretsu Networks in Japan," *American Sociological Review* 57: 561–85.

McAdam, Doug (1982) *Political Process and the Development of Black Insurgency*, Chicago, IL: University of Chicago Press.

March, James (1961) "The Firm as a Political Coalition," *Administrative Science Quarterly* 2: 23–41.

March, James and Olsen, Johan (1989) *Rediscovering Institutions*, New York: Free Press.

Nelson, Richard and Winter, Sidney (1982) *An Evolutionary Theory of Economic Change*, Cambridge, MA: Harvard University Press.

Padgett, John and Ansell, Chris (1992) "Robust Action and the Rise of the Medici," *American Journal of Sociology* 98: 1259–1320.

Pfeffer, Jeffrey (1981) *Power in Organizations*, Marshfield, MA: Pittman.

Pfeffer, Jeffrey and Salancik, Gerald (1978) *The External Control of Organizations*, New York: Harper Row.

Podolny, Joel (1993) "A Status Based Model of Market Competition," *American Journal of Sociology* 98: 829–72.

Powell, Walter and Brantley, Peter (1992) "Competitive Cooperation in Biotechnology: Learning Through Networks?," pp. 366–94 in N. Nohria and R. Eccles (eds), *Networks and Organizations*, Boston, MA: Harvard Business School Press.

Powell, Walter and Smith-Doerr, Laurel (1994) "Networks and Economic Life," pp. 368–403 in N. Smelser and R. Swedburg (eds), *The Handbook of Economic Sociology*, New York: Russell Sage.

Prechel, Harland (1994) "Economic Crisis and the Centralization of Control," *American Sociological Review* 59: 723–45.

Roe, Mark (1994) *Strong Owners, Weak Managers*, Princeton, NJ: Princeton University Press.

Snow, David, Rochford, E. Burke, Worden, Steven, and Benford, Robert (1986) "Frame Alignment and Mobilization," *American Sociological Review* 51: 464–81.

Stark, David (1992) "Path Dependence and Privatization Strategies in East Central Europe," *Eastern European Politics and Societies* 6: 17–51.

Stark, David (1996) "Recombinant Property in East European Capitalism," *American Journal of Sociology* 101: 993–1028.

Steinmo, Svein, Thelen, Katherine, and Longstreth, Frederick (1992) *Structuring Politics*, Cambridge: Cambridge University Press.

Stinchcombe, Arthur (1965) "Social Structure and Organization," pp. 142–93 in J. March (ed.), *The Handbook of Organizations*, Chicago, IL: Rand McNally.

Swidler, Ann (1986) "Culture in Action," *American Sociological Review* 51: 273–86.

Tarrow, Sidney (1994) *Power in Movement*, Cambridge: Cambridge University Press.

Thorelli, Hans (1995) *Federal Antitrust Policy*, Baltimore, MD: Johns Hopkins Press.

Useem, Michael (1993) *Executive Defense*, Cambridge, MA: Harvard University Press.

Westney, Eleanor (1980) *Innovation and Imitation: The Transfer of Western Organizational Patterns to Meiji Japan*, Cambridge, MA: Harvard University Press.

White, Harrison (1981) "Where Do Markets Come From?," *American Journal of Sociology* 87: 517–47.

White, Harrison (1992) *Identity and Control*, Princeton, NJ: Princeton University Press.

Williamson, Oliver (1985) *The Economic Institutions of Capitalism*, New York: Free Press.

Williamson, Oliver (1991) "Comparative Economic Organization," *Administrative Science Quarterly* 36: 269–96.

Zelizar, Viviana (1983) *Markets and Morals*, Princeton, NJ: Princeton University Press.

12 Rethinking Capitalism

Fred Block

One of the key tasks of sociology is to explain the nature of the society in which we currently live. C. Wright Mills argued that sociology must provide answers to such questions as:

> What is the structure of this particular society as a whole? What are its essential components, and how are they related to one another? How does it differ from other varieties of social order? *(Mills, 1959, p. 6)*

Answers to these questions are vital because our fundamental understandings about how we should live our lives depend upon grasping the nature and dynamics of the particular social order in which we are situated. In recent years, most sociologists have provided the same answers to these questions as journalists and business leaders – that we live in a "capitalist" society organized around the systematic pursuit of profit in the marketplace. This essay, however, builds on a body of recent work to argue that our inherited notions of capitalism need to be modified if we are to understand the social order in which we live.

The Great Reversal in Terminology

This shared definition of US society as capitalist is of relatively recent origin; as late as the 1960s, the term was not used in polite company because of its political associations. The concept of capitalism had been elaborated by socialists in the nineteenth century as part of their critique of the existing social order. Karl Marx entitled his masterwork *Capital*, since he saw the accumulation of capital as the central activity of the emerging bourgeois society. Marx's followers from the middle of the nineteenth century onwards denounced capitalism and capitalists for placing profits over human needs and for believing that a society should be organized around individual greed. Defenders of market society in the nineteenth century rejected this entire terminology; they viewed the concept of capitalism as polemical and misleading.

In the twentieth century, this definitional battle intensified, particularly once Communist parties had seized power in Russia, China, and other nations. From the late 1940s on, Soviet and Communist Chinese spokespersons denounced Western capitalism for extreme inequalities between rich and poor, for the subordination of all other activities to money making, and for imperialist exploitation of the poor in the developing world. Defenders of the West responded to these attacks by insisting that

This chapter was specifically commissioned for this volume.

the system that Marxists were attacking no longer existed. They argued that the fiercely competitive free-market economy of the nineteenth century, with its severe cycles of boom and bust, had been replaced in the twentieth century by a managed economy with social welfare policies designed to protect the poor. In place of capitalism, these defenders preferred to speak about the West having a "mixed economy" or "a free enterprise system."

This was still the situation through the first half of the 1960s. Most academics avoided reference to capitalism to avoid any association with ideas that belonged to the Russian and Chinese Communists. Even more fundamentally, the core Marxist idea that the economic organization of society sets the basic frame for the larger society was considered objectionable; it was rejected as "vulgar materialism." The wisdom of that era was that the economy was no more important in shaping the society than were cultural beliefs or the political system.

The change over the intervening 35 years is incredible. Capitalism is now the name that the business press uses to describe both the US and the global economies and the term has lost any hint of connection to a critical discourse. Moreover, the idea that the structure of the economy determines the basic frame of the larger society has been transformed from "vulgar materialism" to common sense. Most importantly, the fundamentally Marxian claim that capitalism as a system is global, unified, and coherent was embraced by Margaret Thatcher, Ronald Reagan, and other apostles of neoliberalism in the belief that the world economy should maximize the role of market forces. This is their foundation for arguing that each nation must engage in the same processes of privatization, deregulation, and public-sector retrenchment if it is to prosper in an increasingly competitive global capitalist system. In other words, Marx has become the chief theorist of the global bourgeoisie. How did such a conceptual transformation occur?

Back to Marx

We have to go back to Marx to understand how we reached the current situation. In Marx's more theoretical works, he takes great pains to engage in a process of "denaturalizing" capitalism by showing how it emerged historically, how it contrasts with other ways of organizing society's productive forces, and how it can be transcended. But in many of his more political pieces Marx takes a different tack: he treats capitalism as being similar to a force of nature, like a flood or a hurricane that transforms everything in its path. One of the most striking of these natural images occurs in *The Eighteenth Brumaire of Louis Bonaparte* (Marx, 1963, p. 19), when he contrasts bourgeois revolutions with proletarian revolutions. While the bourgeois revolution "storms swiftly from success to success,"

> proletarian revolutions, like those of the nineteenth century, criticize themselves constantly, interrupt themselves continually in their own course, come back to the apparently accomplished in order to begin it afresh, deride with unmerciful thoroughness the inadequacies, weaknesses and paltrinesses of their first attempts, seem to throw down their adversary only in order that he may draw new strength from the earth and rise again, more gigantic, before them, recoil ever and anon from the indefinite prodigiousness of their own aims, until a situation has been created which makes all turning back impossible . . .

The passage invokes the struggle of Hercules with the giant Antaeus, whose strength was renewed each time he was thrown down to the earth. For Marx, capitalism is like Antaeus, a superhuman natural force that derives energy and sustenance from the efforts of its opponents to defeat it. This is a surprising image, since it makes the defeat of capitalism appear impossibly difficult.

Marx's rhetorical moves to depict capitalism as a natural system had a very specific intent. His argument that capitalism was pervasive and systematic in its dominance over society was designed to preclude reformist strategies that left the basic economic structures of society intact. Marx saw the workers' movement as continually facing the temptation to settle for reforms and he was constantly trying to reinforce the message that only a radical revolution – a root and branch transformation – would accomplish the goals of the workers' movement. The imagery of capitalism as a natural system was, therefore, necessary to make the point that only a more massive counterforce – the force of a proletarian revolution – could suffice to dislodge capitalist dominance.

Moreover, Marx was not worried that emphasizing the monumental nature of the task would disempower the working class. For Marx, there was little risk in emphasizing the difficulty of overthrowing capitalism, because capitalist development was continually expanding the ranks of the proletariat. Capitalism was like a force of nature, but it was part of that nature constantly to increase the population of its own gravediggers. In fact, the sheer quantitative growth, year after year, in the number of industrial workers was the critical empowering factor for the socialist movement.

But in the second half of the twentieth century, the industrial working class started to decline as a percentage of the total population in all of the developed nations. This decline, by itself, does not preclude the possibility of a viable anticapitalist politics. Industrial workers in alliance with other social groups are still capable of dominating electoral outcomes in a range of different countries. The point, rather, is that when the industrial working class was on a trajectory to become the majority of society, the political dominance of working-class parties appeared inevitable and natural. It did not seem to require much political effort to bring together a winning coalition; one could easily imagine that capitalist development would do that automatically. However, once that numerical growth stopped, the political task became more complex because now different social groups, with competing interests, would have to be fused into a unified political force.[1] Class solidarity operated as a powerful lubricant that made these efforts at reconciliation easier.

In the absence of a comparable solidaristic identity, it is harder to build durable alliances between industrial workers and other social groups. In this changed historical circumstance, the political impact of Marxian imagery began to change. The old imagery of capitalism as a natural system became less and less radical in its effects.

One irony is that it was the student movement of the 1960s that took the first critical steps to reintroduce Marx's natural imagery of capitalism into US political debates. In its opposition to the Vietnam War, the student movement started tentatively and then more assertively to find the roots of the war in the structures of capitalism.[2] By the late 1960s, both Marxist ideas and the word "capitalism" had gained wide circulation. There was a rapid shift in scholarly debate as a new generation of intellectuals began to explore the implications of Marxist ideas for the social and historical sciences. One small indicator was that in 1974, Immanuel Wallerstein's work on *The Modern Capitalist World System* received a major award from the American Sociological Association.

However, conservative intellectuals did not stand idly by as this leftward shift in political language occurred in the late 1960s and early 1970s. Instead, following the lead of Irving Kristol, an important neoconservative theorist, they began to insist that they were procapitalist and proud. This rhetorical move by the right was more than the equivalent of "black is beautiful," attempting to inject new meaning into a once derogatory term. The right went further and freely embraced the full Marxian imagery of capitalism as a natural system with its own logic and rhythms. Whereas earlier in the century the octopus – the many-tentacled monstrosity – had served as a powerful anticapitalist image, the right openly embraced this same idea of the capitalist tentacles reaching into every corner of social life and every corner of the globe. When conservative political leaders such as Margaret Thatcher and Ronald Reagan came to power in the late 1970s and early 1980s, they deliberately deployed this imagery of capitalism as a natural system to reinforce the argument that "there is no alternative" for people throughout the globe but to obey the logic of this all-powerful system.

Varieties of Capitalism

In the 1990s, a number of scholars adopted a new approach as they recognized that neoliberals were now using recycled Marxist imagery. These analysts insisted that there are many different varieties of capitalism, so that the claim that there is a single system with one uniform logic is mistaken. Drawing particularly on the experiences of the Japanese and the "Rhine model" of capitalism, a large and impressive body of evidence has been amassed to establish the significant institutional variations across the developed market societies (Albert, 1993; Berger and Dore, 1996; Crouch and Streeck, 1997; Hollingsworth and Boyer, 1997; Orru, Biggart, and Hamilton, 1997). But while this has been an important movement in deepening our theoretical understanding, its effectiveness as a challenge to neoliberal claims has been limited.

The first difficulty is the problem that Gray (1998) has identified as "bad capitalisms driving out good." The Anglo-American variety of capitalism has exercised disproportionate power in shaping the international rules of the game governing financial and trade transactions. For some time, the US has been self-consciously using these rules to reduce the extent of variation among different types of capitalism. This is most obvious in the sustained effort by the US to force Japan to liberalize its financial markets, and in the efforts by the US and the IMF to challenge the high debt model of East Asian capitalism (Wade and Veneroso, 1998). However, part of this process also works through continuing market pressures on Europe and Japan to adopt the same kind of economic practices as in the US.

The second difficulty is that the varieties-of-capitalism approach has generally been silent on the critical issue of capitalism as a natural system. Most particularly, there have been few attempts to explain how these different varieties of capitalism articulate together into some kind of larger system. To be sure, it is implicit in the varieties-of-capitalism argument that there is no single system that operates like a force of nature. But, given the weight and force of the Marxist imagery that is now shamelessly recirculated as neoliberal imagery, implicit arguments quickly get swept away. For this reason, the varieties-of-capitalism argument has had great difficulty in influencing political debates.

An Alternative: Capitalism as a Constructed System

The way to deepen and push forward the varieties-of-capitalism perspective is to reconceptualize capitalism as a constructed system and to reject explicitly the imagery of it as a natural system. When conceived as a natural system, international capitalism integrates different societies into a unified and coherent transnational mechanism that operates according to its own powerful logic. As elaborated in the work of Immanuel Wallerstein, for example, there is an extraordinarily high level of continuity in the way in which this systemic logic has played itself out over the last 300 years. After all, the capitalist world system is like an organism that grows and develops through certain cycles, but its fundamental nature is unchanging over time. Once the system is in place, the only important change can be the system's death – when it gives way to another kind of system. It is for this reason that change is all or nothing; either the entire system is overthrown or its logic will continue to prevail. To be sure, antisystemic movements can win important victories, but these victories do not alter the basic logic of the system and they remain highly vulnerable to reversals.

The alternative standpoint is to insist that both within societies and as an international system, capitalist arrangements are not natural but need to be constantly constructed and reconstructed. Capitalism cannot rely on simple continuity over time because it is continually generating new conflicts and contradictions that have to be resolved or contained through conscious activity. The logic underlying this argument is developed in Karl Polanyi's (1957) discussion of fictitious commodities. The market system is based on the illusion that all factors of production – including land, labor, and money – are commodities that are produced for sale on a market. This commodity status must be assumed because otherwise there is no assurance that the price mechanism will equilibrate supply and demand. However, land, labor, and money are not true commodities; they were not really produced for sale on a market. The constant work of "constructing capitalism" is the effort needed to paper over this yawning gap between reality and the market model. It is not just a question of obscuring the gap; it is also a question of modifying institutional arrangements to make them work despite the discrepancy between theory and reality.

One important arena for this activity of construction is the vexed issue of monetary policy. Within societies, there is no way to rely on market mechanisms – by themselves – to determine the supply of money and credit. Yet, when growth of the money supply is either too rapid or too slow, the results can be disastrous. Hence, there is a continuous need for a political practice of money supply management to make market societies work, and these practices must change and evolve over time as financial innovations and other changes create a continually moving target. But the very existence of this political practice of monetary management, in turn, creates new sets of problems, since there is a conflict between the system's need for political management and its basic ideology that markets should be left alone to regulate themselves. It is in this context that societies develop complex mythologies about central bankers to obscure the fact that money supply management is a political act. At the international level, the problem of monetary policy is even more vexing, since there are the interlocking issues of setting the growth rate for the global money supply, facilitating international payments, and assuring adjustment between national economies and the world economy. As we know from the history of international bailouts and debt renegotiations over the past 20 years, the management of the global monetary system requires sustained political effort to avoid ruinous defaults and escalating financial crises.

In this view of capitalism as a constructed system, it follows that there are many varieties of capitalism and there are many different ways that these varieties can be articulated together into a global system. Some systems of articulation – like the ones favored by neoliberals – operate to reduce the varieties of capitalism that are possible at the national or regional level; but other systems of articulation are consistent with much greater variety at the national or regional level. It also follows that just as different varieties of capitalism can have dramatically differing levels of inequality or of economic insecurity for poor and working people, different systems of international articulation might be more or less consistent with reforms favoring subordinate classes.

It follows logically that whereas capitalism as a natural system has an unchanging essence that can only be altered through a root-and-branch transformation, capitalism as a constructed system can be reformed or reconstructed in piecemeal ways. To be sure, such reform efforts are likely to meet stiff resistance, and even when victories are won, there is no guarantee of their durability. Defenders of the status quo can always be relied on to insist that the reforms will be inconsistent with the system's fundamental logic, and efforts to reverse the reforms are likely to persist for decades. Nevertheless, the very nature of a constructed system is that it is continually being reconstructed, and this means that scenarios in which the reconstruction efforts consistently move the system in a different direction are imaginable.

Understanding the System

It is not enough to say that capitalism is a constructed system. The task is to illuminate how it is constructed: to see how a diverse and often contradictory set of practices are welded together to produce something that has the appearance of being a natural and unified entity. Here, I will focus on three of these welds or connective mechanisms that help to give capitalism the appearance of coherence and naturalness. This is not intended as an exhaustive accounting; there might well be critically important connective mechanisms that I have not discussed. Nor do I want to claim that all three of the mechanisms I am describing are of equal importance: some of them might carry more of the weight of the overall structure than do others.

However, the point of the welds is to show that at any moment, notwithstanding the claims of neoliberals, there are many different ways in which capitalist societies can be structured. How much pollution we tolerate or how much social and economic inequality we need to have are not dictated by the inevitable logic of market forces. They can and should be shaped by choices made in the arena of politics.

Combining market and nonmarket elements

In the standard view, capitalist societies are unitary; all social institutions are organized around the pursuit of profit and individuals are socialized to pursue their economic self-interest over all other considerations. But it is easy to show that a society organized entirely around the individual pursuit of self-interest would quickly dissolve (Block, 1990, ch. 3). We see this even in advertising campaigns. Mastercard has been running a series of television ads that suggest that the most important experiences in life – such as bonding with children – are priceless, while for everything else one can use a credit card. The advertising takes advantage of the popular understanding that not everything is for sale: that our most important relationships such as family and friendships are based on suspending – at least momentarily – the conscious pursuit of economic self-interest (Zelizer, 1985).

Moreover, it is not just the family and intimate relations; other social institutions also rely on the subordination of immediate self-interest to higher considerations. For example, we expect professionals such as doctors, lawyers, and architects not simply to maximize their incomes, but to obey a series of ethical injunctions. Of course, professionals sometimes ignore these ethical considerations: journalists slant their coverage in exchange for personal favors or gifts, or surgeons recommend the same lucrative operation to patients whether they need it or not. The point, however, is that the effective functioning of these institutions is compromised when these ethical injunctions are completely disregarded. If, for example, accountants simply charged a little extra to approve a firm's balance sheet no matter how much financial fraud was involved, economic activity would quickly grind to a halt because investors would no longer be able to trust the financial information they were receiving.

One analyst has captured this complexity with the concept of "blocked exchanges" (Walzer, 1983). While capitalist societies encourage the sale of a variety of things on the market, they simultaneously block other types of exchanges. Hence, there are norms and sometimes laws that prohibit the sale of political offices, fundamental rights, defective merchandise, friendship, and body parts. Moreover, many of our most intense political debates are over whether certain exchanges should or should not be blocked. Many conservatives want to outlaw the purchase of abortion services and cultural products with sexual themes, while liberals often favor stricter rules governing gun sales and tighter controls over campaign contributions. Debates over decriminalizing drugs and prostitution are also issues of what exchanges should or should not be blocked.

The point, quite simply, is that there is no natural procapitalist position – a market economy needs a complex mixture of blocked and unblocked exchanges. Capitalism rests on what Geoffrey Hodgson (1984) has called "the impurity principle" – it requires a mix of market and nonmarket institutions and motivations to operate, and there is room for considerable variation in establishing where these lines are drawn. But this reality has been largely obscured by the second weld: the ideology of market self-regulation.

The theory of self-regulating markets

The theory of self-regulating markets insists that markets should be left alone to find their own equilibria; it views all government action with extreme suspicion. But this theory is not some superstructural element that emerged out of intellectual efforts to make sense of already existing market societies. From the beginning, the theory of self-regulating markets has played a central role in constituting capitalism and in giving it the appearance of coherence. This is one of the central points of Polanyi's

Great Transformation (1957): that the historical trajectory from 1795 to 1933 would have been profoundly different had economic liberalism not played such a central role in Anglo-American thought.

However, acknowledging the extraordinary importance of this theory tends only to increase our perplexity. If capitalist societies need to block a variety of specific types of exchanges, then market self-regulation is obviously not a sufficient foundation for organizing a society. So why should a way of looking at the world that is so profoundly wrong exert such extraordinary influence over such a long historical period? We need only look at the disastrous experience of "shock therapy" in the former Soviet bloc to reinforce our belief that the theory of self-regulating markets is utterly inadequate as a way of understanding the world. The Russian experience shows that the theory of market self-regulation gave policymakers the confidence to pursue bold policy directions in complete disregard of multiple warning signs that those policies were unlikely to achieve the desired results. My own favorite example is a quote in the *New York Times* from a finance professor discussing the near collapse of Long Term Capital Management, the hedge fund that made huge financial bets based on extremely sophisticated mathematical models: "A series of events occurred that were outside the norm. These catastrophes happen. The fault isn't with the models" (Morgenson and Weinstein, 1998). The logic is unassailable: the models used by LTCM's rocket scientists based on the theory of self-regulating markets were obviously correct; it was reality that was at fault for producing unanticipated catastrophes.

The theory of self-regulating markets derives its power from two sources. First, it is not just a theory about how markets work, but a theory of human nature and human freedom. At its core is a view that can be termed "social naturalism," which identifies the market with that which is natural and the state with the arbitrary realm of culture (Somers, 1995a, 1995b, 1999). Hence, the ability of markets to be self-regulating is derived from nature's obedience to laws that humans are powerless to change. The logic of social naturalism was played out in Malthus's (1985 [1798]) classic critique of welfare. Providing assistance to the poor, he argued, interfered with the natural processes through which the threat or reality of starvation served to regulate population growth, so that is was bound to make the poor worse off than they would have been without assistance. The fact that this argument continues to have powerful resonance in shaping welfare policies in the US and the UK is testimony to the continuing influence of social naturalism in shaping perceptions of reality.

Second, social naturalism has been almost continually reinforced by the strategic use of market self-regulation rhetoric by business interests. The use of the rhetoric tends to be highly selective, since some business interests are continually demanding state support in a variety of different forms. Nevertheless, the invocation of the rhetoric of market self-regulation is still tremendously useful, because it limits the possibility of establishing a system of reciprocity between the state and business interests. It would be logical, for example, for political leaders to offer to provide generous subsidies for corporate research in exchange for such things as greater business efforts to upgrade wages and working conditions of low-wage workers. However, by using the rhetoric of market self-regulation, it is possible for business interests to simultaneously demand the former and resist the latter.

From these two sources, the theory of market self-regulation became a central part of both classical and neoclassical economics and has exerted extraordinary influence over political debates. Today, any proposal for social reform – environmental regulations, more equitable treatment of the poor, changes in the rules governing the global economy, and so on – will be met by arguments that the proposed measure will not meet its intended objectives because it will interfere with the proper functioning of the self-regulating market. It is for this reason that a frontal assault on the idea of market self-regulation is central to any effort to expand the range of political debate within developed market societies.

Class power and efficiency

Neoliberals insist that the concentration of political and economic power in the hands of the wealthy is optimal for economic efficiency. We are frequently told, for example, that if the rich are forced to pay too high a rate of taxation, they will have no incentive to invest and we will all be worse off. Marx insisted, on the contrary, that at a certain stage of capitalist development there would be a deep and profound contradiction between the efficient organization of economic activity and the existing property relations. It was at the point when capitalism had become a fetter on the further development of the productive forces that he anticipated a proletarian revolution.

While Marx's expectations were not realized, the idea of a tension between economic efficiency and class power can be useful when it is thought of in institutional terms. This is the third weld line that this paper will explore. The problem is clearest in thinking about the role of the large corporation in society. Our general expectation is that the people who run large corporations will share the political agenda of the wealthy, but this might mean sacrificing efficiency for class power. So, for example, while the wealthy generally resist progressivity in the tax system and favor limitations on the growth of state spending, some corporations might benefit from tax progressivity that puts more spending power in the hands of ordinary consumers, or from expanding state budgets that increase research and infrastructure spending.

These tensions could be intensified by structural reforms designed to increase the autonomy of the large corporation from wealthy shareholders. Work in the "varieties of capitalism" literature has consistently emphasized that Japanese corporations are managed more in the interests of stakeholders – including employees – than in the interests of shareholders (Dore, 1997). Why not try to achieve the same end in the United States by legal reforms? Elsewhere (Block, 1992, 1996), I have elaborated a proposal for restructuring how large corporations are legally organized. This would require that all corporations above a certain size would be federally chartered. The rules on federal chartering would then specify that the shareholders would elect 35 percent of the members of the corporate board, and another 35 percent would be elected by employees in a process that gave them full free speech rights to wage vigorous campaigns. The last 30 percent of the board could be elected by diverse constituencies including community representatives, consumers, suppliers, and bondholders. Since no single group would have an automatic majority on the board of directors, there would be strong pressure for compromises between the interests of shareholders and the interests of employees.

This kind of reform rests on the idea that the corporation is a social construction whose pursuit of profits is structured by specific financial and legal rules. Since both neoliberalism and Marxism envision capitalism as a natural system, they lack the ability to see the corporation as a constructed institution that is capable of being reconstructed.

Conclusion

What follows from this alternative conceptual framework is a renewed awareness that we are nowhere near the "end of history" that some commentators announced after the collapse of the Soviet Union. The idea that the "triumph of capitalism" would produce an end to international conflicts rests on the imagery of capitalism as a natural system that would automatically dissolve national boundaries and make governments increasingly irrelevant. The reality is quite different: capitalism as a constructed system is heavily dependent upon both national governments and inter-governmental cooperation to manage the world economy. And because there are significant differences in the institutional arrangements and cultural patterns of different capitalist societies, there is no certainty that governments of these different nations will always cooperate.

Within national societies, we can expect that there will be continuing conflicts over which economic exchanges will be allowed and which will be blocked or tightly controlled. Similar conflicts will also increasingly dominate the international arena. Should countries be able to export goods produced by child labor, by prison labor, or by laborers forced to work in dangerous and degrading "sweatshops"? Will there be global environmental standards or will some nations be able to gain economic advantage by giving firms the freedom to degrade the environment? Should corporations have free rein to sell prescription drugs or genetically modified food products in whatever way they deem appropriate? Should global investors be free to move vast quantities of liquid funds into and out of small economies without regard to the consequences?

All of these issues will be debated with growing intensity, and the future of capitalism as a constructed system depends on both the rules that are decided for governing these different transactions and the mechanisms for determining those rules. Most importantly, will there be increased global cooperation to resolve these kinds of questions, or will there be growing conflict as different groups struggle to advance their own interests?

Notes

1   In building working-class movements, effort was required to reconcile the conflicting inter-ests of different sectors of the industrial working class, such as the more skilled and the less skilled and workers from different regions and different ethnic groups. However, the idea of class solidarity operated as a powerful lubricant that made these efforts at recon-ciliation easier. In the absence of a comparable solidaristic identity, it is harder to build durable alliances between industrial groups and other social groups.

2   The taboo against Marxist language is indicated by the fact that at the first Washington march against the Vietnam War, the leader of Students for a Democratic Society emphas-ized the need to "name the system" that had produced the war, but he actually did not use

the word capitalism. SDS leaders feared that the word would signal their movement's links to the old left (Miller, 1987).

References

Albert, Michel (1993) *Capitalism against Capitalism*, trans. Paul Haviland, New York: Four Walls Eight Windows.

Berger, Suzanne and Dore, Ronald (eds) (1996) *National Diversity and Global Capitalism*, Ithaca, NY: Cornell University Press.

Bhagwati, Jagdish (1998) "The Capital Myth," *Foreign Affairs*, May–June: 7–12.

Blair, Margaret (1995) *Ownership and Control: Rethinking Corporate Governance for the Twenty-First Century*, Washington: Brookings.

Block, Fred (1990) *Postindustrial Possibilities: A Critique of Economic Discourse*, Berkeley, CA: University of California Press.

Block, Fred (1992) "Capitalism without Class Power," *Politics and Society*, 20(3, September): 277–303.

Block, Fred (1996) *The Vampire State*, New York: New Press.

Callon, Michel (1998) "Introduction," in Michel Callon (ed.), *The Laws of the Market*, Oxford: Blackwell.

Crouch, Colin and Streeck, Wolfgang (eds) (1997) *Political Economy of Modern Capitalism: Mapping Convergence and Diversity*, Thousand Oaks, CA: Sage.

Dore, Ronald (1997) "The Distinctiveness of Japan," pp. 19–32 in Colin Crouch and Wolfgang Streeck (eds), *Political Economy of Modern Capitalism: Mapping Convergence and Diversity*, Thousand Oaks, CA: Sage.

Gibson-Graham, J. K. (1996) *The End of Capitalism (As We Knew It)*, Cambridge, MA: Blackwell.

Gray, John (1998) *False Dawn: The Delusions of Global Capitalism*, London: Granta.

Hayek, Friedrich (1994) *The Road to Serfdom*, Chicago, IL: University of Chicago Press.

Hodgson, Geoffrey M. (1984) *The Democratic Economy: A New Look at Planning, Markets and Power*, Harmondsworth: Penguin.

Hollingsworth, J. Rogers and Boyer, Robert (eds) (1997) *Contemporary Capitalism: The Embeddedness of Institutions*, Cambridge: Cambridge University Press.

Kristol, Irving (1978) *Two Cheers for Capitalism*, New York: Basic Books.

Malthus, Thomas Robert (1985 [1798]) *An Essay on the Principle of Population*, London: Penguin.

Marx, Karl (1963 [1869]) *The Eighteenth Brumaire of Louis Bonaparte*, New York: International Publishers.

Miller, James (1987) *Democracy Is in the Streets: From Port Huron to the Siege of Chicago*, New York: Simon and Schuster.

Mills, C. Wright (1959) *The Sociological Imagination*, New York: Oxford University Press.

Morgenson, Gretchen and Weinstein, Michael M. (1998) "Two Nobel Economists Get a Lesson in Real Economics," *New York Times*, November 14.

Orru, Marco, Biggart, Nicole Woolsey and Hamilton, Gary G. (1997) *The Economic Organization of East Asian capitalism*, Thousand Oaks, CA: Sage.

Polanyi, Karl (1957 [1994]) *The Great Transformation*, Boston, MA: Beacon Press.

Somers, Margaret (1995a) "What's Political or Cultural about Political Culture and the Public Sphere? Toward an Historical Sociology of Concept Formation," *Sociological Theory* 13(2, July): 113–44.

Somers, Margaret (1995b) "Narrating and Naturalizing Civil Society and Citizenship Theory: The Place of Political Culture and the Public Sphere," *Sociological Theory* 13(3, November): 221–65.

Somers, Margaret (1999) "The Privatization of Citizenship: How to Unthink a Knowledge Culture," pp. 121–61 in Victoria E. Bonnell and Lynn Hunt (eds), *Beyond the Cultural Turn*, Berkeley, CA: University of California Press.

Twentieth Century Fund Task Force (1992) *The Report of the Twentieth Century Fund Task Force on Market Speculation and Corporate Governance*, New York: Twentieth Century Fund.

Wade, Robert and Veneroso, Frank (1998) "The Asian Crisis: the High Debt Model versus the Wall Street–Treasury–IMF Complex," *New Left Review* 228(Mar–Apr): 3–22.

Wallerstein, Immanuel (1974) *The Modern World-System: Capitalist Agriculture and the Origins of the European World-Economy in the Sixteenth Century*, New York: Academic Press.

Walzer, Michael (1983) *Spheres of Justice*, New York: Basic Books.

Zelizer, Viviana A. (1985) *Pricing the Priceless Child: The Changing Social Value of Children*, New York: Basic Books.

13 Developing Difference: Social Organization and the Rise of the Auto Industries of South Korea, Taiwan, Spain, and Argentina

Nicole Woolsey Biggart and Mauro F. Guillén

Great inequalities in economic development have been an enduring issue of interest in the social sciences. Theorists have been concerned with diagnosing the causes of underdevelopment, and practitioners with formulating prescriptions for elevating countries economically. Although many theories point helpfully to causal factors in underdevelopment, no single theory has proved adequate to the considerable task of explaining, retrospectively and prospectively, the routes to successful development. Yet many developing countries in Latin America, East Asia, and Southern Europe managed to increase their real per capita incomes three-, four-, and even fivefold between the 1950s and the 1990s (Maddison, 1995, p. 228).

We accomplish three tasks in this paper. First, we briefly review the most influential theories of economic development, suggesting how each of them posits a different critical factor as necessary to development success. Second, we propose an institutional perspective on development, one rooted in organization and management scholarship. We argue that *development depends on successfully linking a country's historical patterns of social organization with opportunities made available by global markets*. A country's economic actors are most able to succeed when they pursue courses of action that take advantage not only of material and human capital resources, but also of social resources inherent in indigenous patterns of authority relations and social organization. We also describe how our approach represents a sociological reformulation of the theory of cross-national comparative advantage first developed by the classic political economists (Ricardo, 1951 [1817]; Smith, 1976 [1776]). Third, we illustrate the merits of our approach with a comparative analysis of four emerging countries during the post-World War II period; each of these countries attempted to create automobile assembly and component manufacturing industries with no regard for their social organization. Although the four countries

Original publication: Biggart, Nicole Woolsey and Guillén, Mauro F., "Developing Difference: Social Organization and the Rise of the Auto Industries of South Korea, Taiwan, Spain, and Argentina," *American Sociological Review* (vol. 64, October, 1999): 722–47.

held a common aim and employed similar economic policies, their development outcomes differed dramatically because policies were filtered through social orders that were institutionally very different.

Our institutional approach focuses on the importance of social organization in economic development. We ask two key questions: (1) Which actors – the state, families, large firms, small firms, business networks, or foreign multinationals – are legitimate players in the economy? (2) What is the pattern of social organization that binds actors to one another? Thus we focus our analysis on which social units are able to act economically in a society, and how these actors relate to each other and to the global economy. The answers to these questions are not the same for all societies and emerge from unique historical experience. Patterns of social organization constrain and facilitate the range of roles that firms and other actors may play domestically and in the global economy, enabling or discouraging the development of different economic resources.

Our empirical design is both longitudinal and cross-sectional. Methodologically we pursue an historical analysis of four countries' experiences. Countries were chosen according to the variation-finding comparative approach (Skocpol, 1984, pp. 368–74; Tilly, 1984, pp. 116–24). We examine how South Korea, Taiwan, Spain, and Argentina attempted to develop automobile assembly and component manufacturing industries during the post-World War II period. We then compare those experiences and observe that each country gravitated over time toward a configuration of component manufacturing and automobile assembly made possible by indigenous institutional arrangements. Taiwan has succeeded in auto component exports, while Korea is a large exporter of assembled vehicles. Spain, in contrast, makes large exports of both assembled vehicles and components, but Argentina has failed to export either. We develop an institutional explanation for these observations, drawing on social-organizational logics to account for such divergent outcomes. Although we aim at explaining development outcomes in these four cases, our primary intent is theoretical: We hope to suggest an alternative and more complete way of understanding development outcomes generally.

Development Theories

Modern development scholarship arose in response to major political and economic changes at the end of World War II, including the need to reconstruct economies and to provide financial and political infrastructure for increasing international trade (McMichael, 1996). Initially, scholars adopted a "developmentalist" approach toward former European colonies in Africa and Asia. At the conclusion of independence efforts, former colonies (many of which were impoverished) attempted to gain both political and economic stability through national growth strategies. The models for these "third-world" countries were the developed American and European "first-world" countries; Soviet-bloc "second-world" countries provided an alternative, socialist model. Fundamental to both models was the nation-state, a political institution based in territorial sovereignty that developed from European historical experience and materialized as either the liberal capitalist state or the socialist state. Development policies, as proposed and interpreted by elites, were the instruments aimed at improving nation-states' economic performance.

Table 13.1   A comparison of theories of development.

Features	Theory				
	Modernization	Dependency	World-System	Market Reform	Institutional
Obstacle to development	Traditionalism	Neocolonialism	Peripheral status	Wrong prices	Institutional disregard
Solution	Gradual change of values	Import substitution	Radical social and political change	Free markets, property rights	Contingent match of organizing logics with world markets
Agents or actors	Modernizing elites foster gradual change in stages	Autonomous state imposes its logic on actors	Internal contradictions trigger change	Autonomous technocracy imposes its logic	Different actors and relationships allowed and enabled
Representative scholars	Rostow (1960), Apter (1965)	Frank (1967), Cardoso and Faletto (1979), Evans (1979)	Wallerstein (1974), Evans (1979)	Sachs (1993)	Bendix (1974 [1956]), Dore (1973)

Two developmentalist theories dominated until the 1970s. In modernization theory, famously expressed by Rostow (1960), it was argued that countries, provided the right conditions, progress from "undeveloped" to "developed" in five predictable stages. At each stage a country forms political, economic, and social institutions that make possible more economically advanced activities. Political scientists (e.g., Apter, 1965) further argued that the primary engine of change tended to be a gradual shift from traditional to modern values, or a transformation of authority structures by a modernizing elite. As reflected in table 13.1, modernization theorists identified traditionalism as the main obstacle to economic growth and equated development with a transformation, however piecemeal, of prevailing ideologies.

Writing at about the same time as modernization scholars, dependency theorists protested that it is illusory to see national economies as independent entities. Rather, they claimed that developing countries depend on more advanced countries, often former colonizers, for economic opportunities, finance, technology, and access to markets. In some instances, multinational enterprises were described as the agents for structuring dependent economic relations between first- and third-world countries. In these theorists' view, only an autonomous state capable of imposing a logic of import-substitution industrialization could offer a feasible solution to dependency (Cardoso and Faletto, 1979; Cumings, 1987; Frank, 1967; also see table 13.1). Other state-centered development theories did not emphasize dependent status so strongly, but still argued in favor of economic policies that encouraged indigenous production and discouraged consumption of imported goods (Hirschman, 1968).

By the 1970s it was clear that capitalism was not an exchange structure between nation-states, but a global economic system with its own independent logic. Globalism is expressed in world-system theory, most closely associated with Wallerstein (1974). Wallerstein and his affiliates have attempted to understand underdevelopment in terms of the systemic and political character of global capitalist forces. With clear intellectual connections to dependency theory, world-system analysis is based on the argument that countries are not autonomous players, but rather are embedded in a structure of exchange relations that make up the world capitalist system. The political economy of relations shapes countries' possibilities differentially: Advanced "core" nation-states are able to determine the alternatives available to nation-states at the "periphery" of global capitalism.

A politically very different globalism is at the foundation of recent economic approaches to development. Market-based theorists presume that a global marketplace exists and that it should be organized according to an ideal of free competition (e.g., Sachs, 1993). Formerly socialist economies, for example, are encouraged to develop legal, political, and economic institutions that emulate a laissez-faire model in order to increase investment and establish trade relations in the global economy. As in the case of dependency theory, market-based reform demands an autonomous technocracy in the state willing and able to impose its logic on the society (table 13.1).

It is not our intent here to assess the empirical strengths and weaknesses of the considerable body of research that we have outlined (for detailed reviews, see Gilpin, 1987; Haggard, 1990; McMichael, 1996). This scholarship has been the basis for many important analyses of individual countries. We wish to point out, however, what we view as a limitation to much of the development scholarship of recent decades: *the search for a unified theory of development* applicable to *all* countries. Theorists have posited a proper sequence of institution building, correct economic policies, nonexploitative trading relations, and, most recently, adherence to what Evans has characterized as the "market as magic bullet" view of economic development (Evans, 1997, p. 2). Development theories as well as empirical studies typically have been attempts to identify the *one critical factor* that explains economic success or failure. Yet consistent evidence demonstrating that such obstacles actually preclude or retard development has not been forthcoming (Portes and Kincaid, 1989). In contrast, research on organizations and management demonstrates that *variety and diversity* of economic action and form provide multiple solutions to the complex problem of economic performance.

Development and Theories of Organization and Management

Although their intellectual and political origins are very different, development theory and organization and management scholarship now often explore much the same intellectual and geographic terrain – the global economy and economic units within it – with the common intent of understanding and improving economic performance. Development theories, however, have not been informed by an important and productive trend in organization and management research: the understanding that firms are phenomenological accomplishments embedded in institutional "logics" that shape possible strategies of action.

Institutional theorists, although they differ in some respects (Powell and DiMaggio, 1991), tend to agree that organizations are "sites of situated social action" in the process of being socially constructed rather than realist structures with fixed properties (Clegg and Hardy, 1996, p. 4). The subjectivist approach to organization has abandoned rational-actor conceptions of workers and managers (Nord and Fox, 1996) in favor of a view of organization as a routinized or "institutionalized" orientation toward action by knowledgeable actors. These institutional logics are sense-making constructs expressed as conventionalized understandings of what is appropriate, normal, and reasonable (Barley and Tolbert, 1997; Scott, 1995). Institutional logics are more than beliefs and normative pressures, however: They find social and material expression in concrete practices and taken-for-granted organizational arrangements that both prompt and constrain economic actors at multiple levels, from individual actors to the state as actor, and help to determine which social roles and strategies are conceivable, efficacious, and legitimate in a given setting. Persons or organizations acting outside institutionalized frames or in disregard of acceptable roles signal that they are not legitimate or not knowledgeable.

Organizing logics vary substantially in different social milieus. For example, in some settings it is "normal" to raise business capital through family ties; in others, this is an "inappropriate" imposition and fostering ties to banks or to foreign investors might be a more successful or legitimate fund-raising strategy. Logics are the product of historical development, are deeply rooted in collective understandings and cultural practices, and are resilient in the face of changing circumstances. Culture and social organization provide not only ideas and values, but also strategies of action (Swidler, 1986).

A variety of organization and management theorists have used a phenomenological framework to understand the development of organizational forms and management practices over time and across countries (Fligstein, 1990; Guillén, 1994; Kenney and Florida, 1993; Oliver, Delbridge, and Lowe, 1996; Orrù, Biggart, and Hamilton, 1997; Westney, 1987). This literature documents that even countries wishing to adopt the practices presumed to be most efficient or effective can incorporate only those that "make sense" to the actors being organized – that is only practices that are consistent with the prevailing institutional logic. This theoretical and empirical tradition has its roots in the classic comparative analyses of industrialization by Bendix (1974 [1956]) and Dore (1973) – the fifth approach listed in table 13.1. This perspective highlights that practices are to be understood in their historical, social, and political contexts. Although an institutional approach has been used to understand advanced countries' responses to economic restructuring (see Hollingsworth, Schmitter, and Streeck, 1994; Katzenstein, 1985; Lindberg, Campbell, and Hollingsworth, 1991; Streeck, 1991), and more recently to analyze the transition from plan to market (Stark and Bruszt, 1998), it has rarely been applied to developing countries.

The institutional research tradition suggests three important points for development theory and for our empirical analysis. First, *institutional arenas – whether the firm, the industry, or the society – are internally coherent and are based on organizing logics that inform action and meaning.* Firms and interfirm constellations, such as business groups or networks, no less than the family or the state, are expressions of social order and imply an array of possible legitimate actions. Economic organizations are imbued with the patterns of meaning of the larger society in which they find themselves. This is not to suggest, however, that institutional arenas do not change, are not contested, or do not coexist with alternative institutionalized worlds (Collins, 1997; Fligstein, 1990; Guillén, 1994).

Second, *economic and managerial practices and actions not consistent with the institutional logic of society, even if they are abstractly "better" or "more efficient," are not readily recognized and incorporated.* The comparative and historical literature on organization and management shows clearly that industrial "best practices" can be emulated only if they are consistent with the institutional logic of the firm or country and do not impose illegitimate roles or practices on actors. Gain-seeking entrepreneurs and managers have no alternative but to work within institutionalized structures of meaning if they hope to succeed (Collins, 1997; Guillén, 1994; Orrù, Biggart, and Hamilton, 1997; Westney, 1987).

Third, *organizing logics are not merely constraints on the unfolding of otherwise unimpeded social action, but rather are repositories of distinctive capabilities that allow firms and other economic actors to pursue some activities in the global economy more successfully than others.* Organization and management theorists studying firms' performance from a resource-based perspective have long advanced this idea (Nelson, 1995; Nelson and Winter, 1982; Peteraf, 1993; Wernerfelt, 1984). Development scholars, however, have not been sensitive to the importance of difference and variation in accounting for countries' economic performance; they prefer to highlight "critical factors" that supposedly apply to all societies and economies. In fact, in the earlier theories outlined in table 13.1, it is assumed that the social organization pattern typical of developing countries stands in the way of economic growth. For development to occur, a modernizing elite, an autonomous state bureaucracy, a revolutionary movement, or a cadre of economic experts – depending on the theory – must change indigenous patterns of social organization and impose a certain logic of behavior on economic actors ("society"). In an institutional approach, by contrast, social organization is taken as a foundation for economic growth under the assumption that paths to development vary. Thus development actually may be blocked or retarded when policymakers neglect social organization and do not design policies that match the country's underlying strengths with the opportunities available in global markets. The institutional approach to development departs from previous theories in its *contingent* nature, emphasizing that there is no single best path, process, or pattern of development or of social organization. Rather, institutional patterns of social organization enable countries to take different approaches to development.

Our institutional perspective on development represents a sociological reformulation of classical economic thinking on the comparative advantage of nations. Smith (1976 [1776]) believed that economic actors would prosper by specializing in certain production activities. Specialization allows individuals or firms to gain "absolute advantages" of skill and scale over similar others and leads to interdependence because actors are required to trade for products that they do not produce, or produce less efficiently than others. Smith envisioned specialization as leading to increases in overall output and hence to the general well-being of all parties to the exchange. Ricardo (1951 [1817]), however, argued that trade across national boundaries differs fundamentally from exchange between individuals and firms. An efficient international division of labor is hindered by political and social institutions that limit the movement of capital, labor, and other resources to their most efficient utilization in specialized production. Hence the goods that a nation produces for trade are not those that it can produce most efficiently in the global economy in an "absolute" sense, but rather those that it can produce at the least cost in comparison with other domestic goods it produces. Nations will prosper most when they produce goods in which they can develop a "comparative advantage" – that is, in comparison with other goods they can produce for exchange. According to the theory of comparative advantage, nations or regions do best when they produce goods with the lowest relative costs of production, namely, goods associated with relatively generous endowments of factors such as labor, capital, natural resources, and stocks of knowledge.

Comparative advantage is an important concept that helps to explain the existence of an international and interregional division of production and trade, but institutional economists and sociologists have criticized it as static and ignoring sociological factors. Tied to equilibrium models, comparative advantage typically is conceptualized in a way that does not allow for historical processes or change (but see Amsden's [1989, p. 244] discussion and critique of Balassa's [1981] stage theory of comparative advantage). Moreover, the factor endowments believed to contribute to comparative advantage are usually limited by economic theorists to material factors of production; Ricardian theory (Ricardo, 1951 [1817]), excludes even technology and capital endowments. In the agrarian and early manufacturing era in which Ricardo and other classical theorists wrote, material factors of production were the critical inputs, and geographic distance to markets was an important determinant of the final cost of goods. In today's global economy, however, factors of production not only are locally endowed but also are shaped by networks of international firms that diffuse product, process, and distribution technologies. Today "almost any developed country can become as efficient as the next country in a technologically stable manufacturing sector" (Storper and Salais, 1997, p. 6).

In global manufacturing, where international commodity chains link producers to consumers and where knowledge-based services and information technology have increased as a percentage of production, location near material factor endowments has become a smaller part of the cost and significance of inputs. Increasingly important is the ability of countries and regions to organize rapidly and effectively in response to changes in demand and changes in technology, and to use production, distribution, and financial networks as leverage.

These latter "factors" are social endowments, and not all societies are equally capable, or capable in the same ways, of organizing for economic growth under technologically advanced global capitalism. Social theorists are just beginning to understand the growing importance of social organization for economic development, what Sorge (1991) called the "societal effect" and Biggart and Orrù (1997) called "societal strategic advantage." Here we trace the institutional sources and the social constitution of comparative advantage (and disadvantage) for four developing nations to show the critical role of patterns of authority and social organization for economic development.

Patterns of Institutional Variation

For the sake of analysis, an institutional theory of development must include the understanding that logics of social organization favor different categories of actors and render certain types of relationships among them appropriate or legitimate: large versus small firms, foreign versus domestic ownership, and vertical versus horizontal or competitive versus cooperative relationships. Variation in actors and relationship types shapes what a country is best equipped to do in the global economy. The actors and relationships enabled by social organization are as important for development as are material endowments.

Consider three ideal-typical configurations of actors and the relationships among those actors. First, an organizing logic that favors large firms and vertical relationships, organized either by the state or by powerful private interests, will be more likely to excel at large-scale undertakings emphasizing heavy capital investment and economies of scale and scope. This logic leads to "producer-driven" or "push links" to the global economy, wherein actors make a product and then offer it for sale in the global marketplace (Gereffi, 1993). Some scholars have identified this pattern of development for the United States and Great Britain (Chandler, 1990), as well as for South Korea (Orrù, Biggart, and Hamilton, 1997).

Second, small-firm economies with horizontal networks may be more adept at developing nimble, responsive, "buyer-driven" or "pull links" to the global economy (Gereffi, 1993; Greenhalgh, 1988; Redding, 1989). Buyer-driven economies respond to orders from customers – for example, retailers such as Sears, Auto Mart, and Wal-Mart, or large manufacturing companies. When changes occur in consumers' tastes in clothing and other low-capital-intensive goods, these economies can respond quickly to orders for new styles. Some scholars have found this pattern in Italy and Taiwan as well as in certain industrial districts of Japan and Germany (Gerlach, 1992; Hollingsworth, Schmitter, and Streeck, 1994; Orrù, 1996; Piore and Sabel, 1984; Streeck, 1991).

Third, countries may be linked to the global economy via foreign ownership of production assets. A country whose social organization fosters (or at least is not opposed to) extensive foreign ownership may be linked to foreign owners' established technology resources and market channels, and may be shaped, where socially possible, by alien organizational arrangements. This pattern is observed, for example, in Singapore, Ireland, and Spain, and more recently in Mexico (Guillén, 1997, 2000; Haggard, 1990). Our point is not that one type of link or another will lead to better performance, but rather that different kinds of activities, and even different industries, will develop more easily depending on the links facilitated by social organization.

Given that historical patterns of social organization affect the types, availability, and legitimacy of actors for industrial development, our approach presents an important corrective to recent sociological theorizing on development, which is based primarily on the nature of state–society relations. For example, Evans (1995) argues that successful industrial transformation occurs only when an autonomous and capable state can establish a collaborative relationship with business actors. This approach is an important step toward an institutional and contingent analysis of development insofar as it allows one to analyze feasible state capacities and roles under various patterns of state–business relations. It does so, however, at the expense of holding constant the nature of business actors and the relationships among them (Campbell, 1998; Stark and Bruszt, 1998, pp. 124–29). Thus, in Evans's model of "embedded autonomy," it is assumed that business actors are a given and that they do not vary across societies. By contrast, in our approach we do not take for granted that business actors exist or that, if they do, they are equally capable, legitimate, or embedded in networks of relationships among themselves. Rather, we take account of differences in the characteristics, legitimacy, and (perhaps most important) *social organization* of business and other actors, including the state.

Difference Illustrated

Categories of actors and of relationships among them form the conceptual core of an institutional perspective on development. This approach highlights the diversity of links between countries and the global economy, as opposed to a single path to continued economic growth. To examine the empirical usefulness of our approach, and to avoid falling into the trap of universal explanations, we focus on automobile production, an industry that has the potential to generate both producer-driven and buyer-driven links to the global economy.

Automobile production is a complex endeavor that requires not only the ability to establish and conduct capital-intensive assembly operations, but also the development of an extensive sector of smaller firms devoted to component manufacturing. Assembly operations organized as a large-scale undertaking usually create producer-driven links to the global economy, whereas component manufacturing for high-volume auto assembly tends to be a buyer-driven activity because of the responsiveness requirements imposed by large-scale assembly. There is no guarantee, however, that a single pattern of social organization can support successful development in both auto assembly and component manufacturing. Thus the auto industry provides a superb empirical setting for assessing the value of an institutional theory of development. It allows one (1) to explore whether a single pattern of social organization characteristic of a particular country leads to differences in economic performance between auto assembly and component manufacturing; and (2) to analyze how different countries' patterns of social organization compare with each other in their effects on the performance of auto assembly and component manufacturing.

Policymakers in South Korea, Taiwan, Spain, and Argentina all have recognized the importance of automobile manufacturing as a strategy for development, for several reasons. First, autos are expensive goods that send crucial capital offshore if purchased from abroad. Second, autos and other forms of transportation are important infrastructural elements needed for moving goods and people around a developing economy; they are also crucial to any military buildup. Third, and perhaps most important, developing countries wish to establish auto production because the industry can create backward links to numerous small firms that manufacture components such as machined goods (e.g., brakes and jacks, textiles for seat coverings, plastic for knobs and dashboards, electrical and electronic gauges, and safety glass for windshields). A vibrant auto assembly sector creates employment and encourages technological skills. Finally, more than any other product, the

Table 13.2   Social-organizational structures, state policies, and outcomes in the auto assembly and auto components industries of four emerging countries.

Auto Assembly	Auto Components	
	Inward-Looking	Export-Oriented
Export-Oriented	**South Korea: Patrimonialism** • 1960s–1970s: Import-substitution benefits large *chaebol* in assembly • 1980s: Export push forces *chaebol* to integrate or control the supply chain • Domestic control dominates • Focus on lower-end auto parts • World quality standards not met	**Spain: Internationalism** • 1940s–1950s: Import substitution chokes private initiatives in assembly • 1970s–1980s: Liberalization forces auto parts firms out of business • Foreign control dominates • Focus on lower-end auto parts • World quality and cost standards met
Inward-Looking	**Argentina: Populism** • 1960s: Too-high local content requirements force to integrate • 1970s: Liberalization and currency overvaluation produce bankruptcies • Mixed pattern of control • Lack of focus or specialization • World quality and cost standards not met	**Taiwan: Flexible Networks** • 1970s–1980s: Failure to promote export-oriented assembly • 1980s–1990s: Firm networks respond to global demand for cheap auto parts • Domestic control dominates • Focus on lower- and medium-end parts • World quality and cost standards met

automobile signals entry into the industrialized world, and its manufacture is prized as a symbol of development success.

We chose these four countries after taking a variation-finding approach (Tilly, 1984, pp. 116–24). All four possible combinations of success and failure in auto assembly and component manufacturing were represented in our sample (see table 13.2). Two of our cases – South Korea and Spain – rank among the top six auto-assembling countries in the world. The other two – Taiwan and Argentina – are low-volume assemblers mostly devoted to catering to the needs of the domestic market. Figure 13.1 shows the evolution, between 1970 and 1995, of each country's exports of assembled passenger cars and of auto components, expressed as a percentage of the GDP. Since the early 1980s, Spain has rapidly grown its exports of both cars and components, while Korea has achieved growth only in exports of cars. In Taiwan exports of components increased swiftly between 1975 and 1985, but declined relative to GDP (and total exports) between 1985 and 1990, when currency curbs were

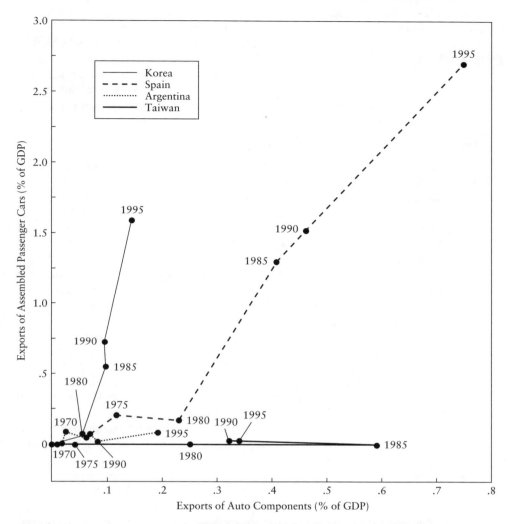

Figure 13.1 Exports of assembled passenger cars and of automobile components: Argentina, Korea, Spain, and Taiwan, 1970 to 1995
Sources: Feenstra, Lipsey, and Bowen (1997); Executive Yuan (1996).

lifted and some component manufacturing moved to the People's Republic of China. Finally, Argentina has never attained high levels of exports of automotive products. Exports of components increased in the early 1990s, however, mostly as a result of the implementation of bilateral balanced-trade arrangements with Brazil.

In the 2 × 4 matched-case empirical design – auto assembly and components manufacturing in four countries with different combinations of success and failure – we seek to assess the impact of state policies and of patterns of social organization on development. We propose a meaningful historical understanding of development success and failure, and present the evidence in narrative form for each case (Skocpol, 1984, pp. 368–74). In focusing our analysis on state and business actors' motives

and struggles to become legitimate, we advance an interpretive sociology addressing how economic development occurs (Collins, 1997; Weber, 1978 [1922]). Our
comparative study achieves two goals. First, it exposes the limitations of previous
approaches to development, which centered on applying general theory to explain
historical instances (Portes and Kincaid, 1989). Second, it provides comparative historical evidence supporting the argument that patterns of social organization enable
and facilitate some economic activities and development efforts but not others.

South Korea: Strong on assembly, weak on components

Despite a concerted effort by the state to promote an automobile industry, South
Korea has an economically and technologically limited auto components sector, which
supplies the needs of domestic car manufacturers but is not significant in the global
market. Most Korean-made components are low-end mechanical parts, such as brakes
and exhausts, and electrical parts, such as batteries and wiring systems. And Korea
has been forced to rely on foreign partners for technology and components crucial
to the assembly of its cars.

How could a country that assembles more than 2 million automobiles and that
ranks fifth in the world fail to develop a thriving and innovative components sector
that matches the assemblers' export prowess? One might even expect that components manufacturers in Korea would have reached the global marketplace before the
assemblers, as small auto repair shops, engine rebuilders, and components manufacturers actually predate the establishment of the country's assemblers. In the early
1950s, during the Korean War, dozens of small enterprises were established to meet
the vehicle maintenance and repair needs of the U.S. and Korean militaries. Only
later, in 1962, did Korea begin assembling vehicles from complete knocked-down
kits purchased from Ford and from Japanese manufacturers. Despite this head start,
at least three interrelated factors have contributed to a weak auto components industry in South Korea: counterproductive state policies, dominance by big business, and
failure to improve quality standards.

First, the backwardness of Korean auto component firms is a consequence of state
policies. The Korean state targeted auto production as a key industry for development. Programs such as the Automobile Industry Protection Law (1962) and the
Automobile Industry Basic Promotion Plan (1969) prohibited imports of assembled
cars but allowed for tariff-free imports of components. Assembly operations oriented
to a small, though growing, domestic market blossomed, but local parts producers
suffered. The Long-Term Automobile Promotion Plan of 1974 provided some
incentives for export, but it focused on increasing local content requirements. These
were raised from 20 to 90 percent by the late 1970s, too late for the small component suppliers to catch up (Green, 1992).

Second, development policies in South Korea have always targeted the large
chaebol, or business groups – Hyundai, Daewoo, and KIA, or their predecessors
– which responded by creating huge assembly operations and their own, tightly
controlled suppliers (Dyer, Cho, and Chu, 1998). After 1980, when the government
shifted its policy toward export promotion, only the *chaebol* were in a position to
play a role. Big business received cheap loans, export facilities, and assistance in
opening markets (Amsden, 1989, p. 181). Focus on the development of these large,

increasingly wealthy, family-owned businesses to the exclusion of the small firms that could contribute to them resulted in both economic and political distortions, including chronic labor unrest.

Although the Korean state belatedly recognized that much of the innovation by Japan's large exporters comes from the many subcontracting networks with whom they interact, Korean manufacturing industries have failed to develop network links with small- and medium-sized independent but affiliated firms: "The first key difference is that South Korean [assemblers] have not yet put in place the 'tiered' arrangement prevalent in Japan, in which a smaller number of first-tier (direct) suppliers manage the larger number of second- and third-tier suppliers on behalf of the [assembler]" (McKinsey and Co., 1996, p. 112). Japanese assemblers produced more than 10,000 cars per purchasing staff, five times more than Korea's 2,000.

Unlike their Japanese counterparts, Korean component manufacturers generally have not developed economically or technologically significant long-term, mutually beneficial relations with assemblers. When components form a crucial part of the production process, Korean assemblers have attempted to buy up firms or otherwise to control them authoritatively. Because key suppliers are controlled by assemblers, suppliers have few opportunities to seek export markets independently or to learn from connections with higher-quality manufacturers (Amsden, 1989, p. 184; McKinsey and Co., 1996, p. 109). In 1997, when the KIA *chaebol* faced bankruptcy, more than a dozen of its large suppliers went out of business, having failed to establish any independent market ties (*Korea Times*, 1997).

The third factor in Korea's difficulties in auto components is that small- and medium-sized auto parts suppliers have been incapable of producing high-quality, latest-technology components, unlike the Japanese subcontractors with whom they are often compared. Purchasers of low-cost, low-quality cars for domestic consumption might tolerate shoddy components, but exporters to the developed world must meet international standards. Component quality may be poor because Korean assemblers have not been high-quality producers themselves, at least in part because of oppressive labor relations; they have been forced to focus strategically on high volume and low price. In a 1995 survey of new car owners, J. D. Power & Associates found that the quality of all four Korean export models ranked at the bottom, with an average of 193 problems per 100 cars, in contrast to the industry average of 110. Only Alfa Romeo ranked lower (Clifford, 1991, p. 42; Kraar, 1995, p. 152). More recently, Korean manufacturers, recognizing their inability to compete head-to-head with high-quality Japanese, European, and U.S. producers, have targeted new emerging markets such as India, China, and Russia; together with Latin America, Africa, and the Middle East, these markets now account for half of Korean auto exports (Kraar, 1995, pp. 152–60). Parts manufacturers thus have not seen leadership by domestic assemblers in a drive for quality. In an attempt to upgrade quality, Korean manufacturers have been forced to form alliances with foreign firms or to purchase components from abroad (Clifford, 1991, p. 40).

One can point to government policy, dominance by large firms, and failure to raise quality as contributors to Korea's successful automotive assembly sector and weak components industry. Why, however, did these factors come into play at all? It was not necessary to focus on large-scale production at low prices and low quality, on subordination of small business interests to those of a few elite-owned businesses, or on oppressive labor relations. Indeed, the organizing pattern of the Japanese, Korea's former colonizer and close neighbor, is different from the Korean pattern in important ways: most notably, in the dense networks that connect firms of all sizes, both horizontally and vertically (Gerlach, 1992). Organizationally the Korean economy is dominated by vertically integrated *chaebol* with few ties outside each group, and with no significant ties between them.

The institutional context of the Korean auto industry is best understood as an expression of Korean patrimonialism, a pattern of political and economic organization that has deep roots in Korean society. Patrimonialism is a form of social organization in which the country, firm, or other social unit is regarded as a "household" under the unilateral domination of a patrimonial figurehead or leader (Weber, 1978 [1922]). All members of the household must submit to the whims of the patriarch, to whom they owe obedience and personal loyalty. This form of organization tends to develop unequal, vertically integrated units under the command of centralized authority (Biggart, 1990; Orrù, Biggart, and Hamilton, 1997). Korean patrimonialism can be traced to a preindustrial era in which rule was implemented by an autocratic emperor; he oversaw competing elite families that had their roots in regional spheres of authority (Henderson, 1968; Jacobs, 1985). Although the actors certainly have changed, modern Korean economic order reproduces in important ways the organizational logic of patrimonial authority. It is an indigenous form of organization possessing widespread understanding and legitimacy (Biggart, 1990).

The powerful *chaebol* are the private economic empires of elite families with strong regional roots, acting much like preindustrial elite clans. *Chaebol* operate at the whims of their founders and descendants; unlike Japanese business groups, they do not cooperate or hold shares in each other's firms. Indeed, the state has been unable to induce Korean assemblers to cooperate even on the purchase of parts unrelated to product distinctiveness, such as oil filters and ashtrays: "Progress on this front is very slow, as assemblers find it hard to give up control over any part of design, however trivial" (McKinsey and Co., 1996, p. 116). It is in the logic of patrimonial economic organization to incorporate crucial elements of production into the household, where they can be controlled by the chairman's personal staff. *Chaebol* also compete fiercely with each other for state favors such as the right to enter industries or privileged financing. The state has encouraged competition between the business groups, rewarding or punishing them according to their willingness to meet state objectives. Indeed, Samsung, one of the largest *chaebol*, gained permission to found an auto company at a time when there was a world oversupply of assembly capacity.

The Korean institutional logic legitimates centralized control by competing elites, and patrimonialism confers on the state the legitimate right to target industries for development. This institutional logic supports the development of shipbuilding, steelmaking, and automobile production, industries that are capital- and technology-intensive and in which single-minded concern with output is a priority. It supports a Fordist economic strategy of large-scale, vertically integrated mass production and standardization. This organizing logic, however, does not promote connections between groups for synergy or innovation. Nor does it promote responsiveness to world markets or quality production. Patrimonialism has favored the assembly of reasonably priced, second-quality cars but small producers in the auto components industry have been forced to fend (unsuccessfully) for themselves. The organizing logic of patrimonialism has proved conducive to one kind of industrial activity but not to another; this point suggests that there is no single route to development, even within a single economy.

Taiwan: State failures and responsive networks

In 1972 Taiwan manufactured 22,102 motor vehicles, more than twice as many as South Korea's 9,525. By 1993 that relationship was reversed: South Korea produced 2,050,058 vehicles, more than four times as many as Taiwan's 408,409. Moreover, in 1994 Korea exported 635,000 vehicles and became the world's fifth largest manufacturer. Korea's three primary producers each had a large share of the market; the smallest, Daewoo, produced more than 300,000 vehicles for an 18.7 percent share. Industry experts believe that a minimum of 200,000 cars is required to achieve economies of scale sufficient for a viable export business. Also in 1993, Taiwan's vehicle manufacturing was divided among 16 assemblers, mostly in joint ventures with foreign manufacturers. The largest by far, Ford Lio-Ho, assembled only 96,067 vehicles (a 23.9 percent market share), well below the minimum for an efficient scale. An industry guide described 1993 as a "difficult year, with most [assemblers] reporting falling sales and operating losses" (Ward's, 1994, p. 57). Taiwan, however, is known for its prowess as an exporter in the global economy, producing not only electronics and machine tools but also a variety of auto components.

Why, despite a substantial head start over Korea, did Taiwan fail as a producer and exporter of assembled automobiles? Conversely, how did Taiwan develop a world-class export market for components in the absence of a substantial assembly sector? As in South Korea, three important contextual factors played a part in the outcome of these sectors: the role of the state, the dominance of small- and medium-sized businesses in the economy, and the ability of Taiwanese businesses to meet global quality standards.

Development scholars often categorize Taiwan as a "strong state" able to impose its will on major groups in society (Amsden, 1985; Gold, 1986; Haggard and Cheng, 1987; Wade, 1990). Certainly Taiwan's leaders after World War II, the nationalist forces that had fled mainland China, had a strong, even a repressive, grip on the polity for years. Using Taiwan as a base for continued political struggle, the government initially was more preoccupied with military matters than with economic affairs. Indeed, until recently, native Taiwanese led Taiwan's economic development, and mainland refugees dominated the government. Although the Taiwanese state has been "strong" politically, it is less obviously the case that the bureaucracy has directed the economy authoritatively.

From 1953 to 1977 the state protected the tiny automotive assembly industry from foreign imports by imposing high tariffs, but allowed foreign manufacturers to serve as partners to local companies. In fact, Generalissimo Chiang Kai-shek invited Henry Ford Jr. to establish a factory in Taiwan. The tax incentives and a steep tariff were very attractive, and Ford built a factory with local partner Lio-Ho. Only later did Ford realize that Chiang hardly understood the economics of car manufacturing: He offered the same deal to virtually everyone, thus flooding the tiny market (Moore, 1990, p. 76). The foreign partners – including Nissan, Willys, General Motors, Fuji, and Toyota – did little more than assemble kit cars in Taiwan;

they failed to transfer the technology. High tariffs protected the domestic industry, making it uneconomical and inefficient. Despite the policy failure, the industry received little attention from the state, which was concerned with developing infrastructure and basic industries such as chemicals, steel, and plastics: "Taiwan policy toward autos wobbled and drifted" (Wade, 1990, p. 101).

State revival of interest in automotive products began in the late 1970s with a strategic shift away from import substitution and toward exports. Government officials proposed a "Big Auto Plant" project that would produce 200,000 low-cost cars for export, and sought a major foreign partner to participate in a joint venture (Arnold, 1989). A few Japanese and American companies were interested, but the protracted process was bumbling and politicized, very different from the targeted economic implementation conducted by the Korean state. Toyota finally was selected as a partner for China Steel, a state-owned company. In 1984, after several years of bureaucratic machinations and flipflops in policy, Toyota withdrew. As Arnold (1989) summarized the situation, "[I]t was clear that the state's capacity to define and implement an industrial policy for Taiwan's automobile industry had been afflicted by serious problems" (p. 202).

In the 1980s the state tried a third time to promote an auto assembly industry, dramatically lowering tariffs on imports and reducing local content requirements. Local manufacturers were pushed either to grow large enough to become mass producers or to transform themselves into offshore producers of low-end Japanese models. The rapid appreciation of the Taiwanese dollar, however, turned the Japanese toward the less costly Southeast Asia. Also, imports of foreign cars increased quickly in Taiwan, further damaging the local assemblers. In comparison with South Korea, the Taiwanese state was inept at creating and implementing a workable strategy for developing an automotive assembly sector (Gold, 1986, p. 105). Taiwan's focus on political factors and its inability to administer economic policies in partnership with the private sector doomed its attempts to lead the country into the ranks of automobile exporters. Indeed, the number of cars that Taiwan assembled for export declined from 6,002 in 1986 to only *nine* in 1997 (Taiwan Transportation Vehicle Manufacturers Association, personal correspondence).

The organization of the economy is a second important factor in Taiwan's failure to establish a viable auto assembly industry, and in its success in producing components. Neighboring South Korea is dominated by large private business groups; Taiwan is a country of relatively small family firms (Orrù, 1996, p. 348). A small-firm economy is difficult to control from above: There are simply too many firms, few of which are individually significant. Automotive manufacturers require large amounts of capital concentrated in a single substantial organization, even one that uses many suppliers. Very few such plants exist in Taiwan, and most of these are state-owned producers of intermediate goods, not of finished consumer products. Taiwanese networked firms historically have grown, not by enlarging, but by spinning off additional small firms. Large-scale manufacturing organizations, while not unknown in Taiwan, are an unusual form of enterprise. Export prosperity has been impelled by small firms linked to each other in horizontal networks based on personal relationships between owners and their families.

This economy of densely networked family firms is ill suited to a capital-intensive enterprise such as auto assembly. It is ideal, however, for producing capital-light but knowledge-intensive products. Taiwan's nimble networks have incurred few sunken costs, and their many connections to Chinese entrepreneurs both domestically and globally allow them to respond quickly to changes in taste and technology. Taiwan has succeeded in producing easily assembled consumer goods such as lawn furniture and bicycles, and knowledge-intensive products such as custom software.

While South Korea has established "producer-driven" links to the global economy, Taiwan has developed mostly demand-responsive connections (Hamilton, 1997, p. 241). Firms do not determine the goods they will produce; they take orders from foreign retailers and manufacturers, responding to shifts in market demands. As one observer remarked, "Taiwan is simply a collection of international subcontractors serving the American market" (Sease, 1987, p. 1). As such, it does not design or establish quality standards for the products it makes. Taiwanese manufacturers often collaborate on an order: Networked firms each produce part of the product and rely on personal relations, which are powerful in family networks, to assure quality control. This form of "cooperative" economic organization is ideally suited to the production of high-quality aftermarket components such as brakes, mufflers, and other auto supplies retailed by Grand Auto, Wal-Mart, and Sears. In fact, Taiwan is a leading exporter of such goods.

The proximate causes for the failure of auto assembly and the success of component manufacturing in Taiwan are misguided state policies, a small-firm economy, and the ability of demand-responsive firms to meet the quality standards of the global marketplace. Although these are important contemporary business conditions, they have roots in the institutional structure of Chinese society. Hamilton (1997, p. 245) argues that the Taiwanese state has assumed a principle of imperial Chinese statecraft: "allowing the people to prosper" without directing the economy in authoritarian ways. In contemporary industrial Taiwan, state enterprises provide infrastructure and intermediate goods such as the steel, transportation, energy, and raw materials necessary to the small businesses that make up the rest of the Taiwanese economy. The state, however, has directed the course of the economy half-heartedly and ineffectively. It engages in economic planning, but its implementation function is weak, certainly in comparison with the Korean bureaucracy. The legitimate role of the Taiwanese state is to help families but to remain aloof, in what Western observers mistakenly perceive as a laissez-faire policy (Wu, 1978, p. 9).

Taiwan is unlikely to ever develop large, capital-intensive private businesses. The local pattern of small family firms is rooted in the patrilineal institutional logic of Chinese families. To build large family businesses, as is possible in Korea and Japan, the enterprise must be passed on intact from generation to generation. In Chinese societies, however, partible inheritance rules demand division of the family fortunes at the patriarch's death so that each son will receive an equal share. Hence Chinese families favor horizontal growth through investment in new businesses rather than vertical integration (Wong, 1985).

Spain: Competitiveness via internationalization

Spain is the world's sixth largest auto assembler, after the United States, Japan, Germany, France, and South Korea. Because three-fourths of Spain's automotive products are exports, the country ranks as the fourth largest exporter of motor vehicles, surpassed only by Japan, Germany, and France. The auto assembly and components industry is Spain's largest, accounting for 6 percent of GDP and 24 percent of total exports. The components sector comprises over 1,100 firms with 200,000 employees, and exports about half of its production as nonassembled components for the original and replacement markets. All auto assembly and more than three-fourths of component manufacturing are presently conducted by foreign-owned companies, which have specialized their Spanish operations in the European marketplace.

The institutional history of the Spanish auto industry has been shaped by the direct involvement of two key actors: the state and foreign multinationals. This path, however, was not the only possibility. Private domestic entrepreneurs in both auto assembly and auto components were willing to develop a domestic industry. As in Taiwan, the origin of modern auto assembly in Spain was marked by a lack of indigenous technology and by the confusion of military aims with purely economic goals. The first high-volume assembly line became operational in the mid-1950s as a joint venture (SEAT) involving the state's enterprise holding (INI), the Italian auto manufacturer, FIAT, and six domestic banks. As in Korea, however, policymakers ignored the rudimentary assembly operations of small workshops and disregarded several private initiatives. Students of economic development later identified the Spanish state during the late 1940s and 1950s as "relatively autonomous": Between 1945 and 1951 an officer in the navy and a personal friend of the dictator was both Minister of Industry and President of the INI enterprise holding. Privileged freedom of action allowed the minister to directly influence how the emerging auto industry would be organized (San Román López, 1995).

Between 1939 and 1946 the INI opposed and defeated one attempt by General Motors, in association with the March banking family, and two attempts by the Urquijo banking group and Italy's FIAT to establish auto companies with mass-production capabilities. Hispano-Suiza, a small-scale but prestigious domestic auto manufacturer, also participated in the Urquijo-FIAT joint ventures. Another small firm, Eucort, attempted in 1945 to obtain credit and permission from the state to transform itself into a large-scale assembler, based on its relatively modest operations: Eucort employed 900 workers who assembled an average of two automobiles per day (San Román López, 1995, pp. 104–24). The INI, however, had other plans for the industry, which included its own truck and auto companies (ENASA and SEAT) as well as entries by Renault and Citroën in the early 1950s. SEAT was guaranteed the lion's share of the domestic market.

The stiff protection of the domestic market through tariffs, quotas, and a stringent local content requirement of 90 percent, in combination with the favorable financing terms awarded to the state company and the multinationals during the 1950s and 1960s, choked the development of private domestic initiatives in auto assembly. The small assembly workshops that had developed from the 1920s to the 1940s went under. The myriad repair workshops and auto components manufacturers that had flourished in the shadow of the domestic assembly operations and the formerly burgeoning import business languished during the 1950s and 1960s as the three large-scale assemblers pursued vertically integrated strategies or persuaded some of their foreign suppliers to co-locate in Spain. In addition, two of the three assemblers were forced to set up their lines in relatively backward and sparsely populated areas, far from the traditional enclaves of automobile-related activity. Both the assemblers and the auto components producers focused on the domestic market; exports did not rise above 10 percent of total production until the mid-1970s.

Given the presence of three auto makers in a protected though relatively narrow market, plants did not meet minimum standards for efficient scale, and model production runs were relatively short. Inflated prices were the result. Protectionism bred complacency, and profitability in auto assembly was the highest among all Spanish industries (Banco Urquijo, 1970). The status quo created during the 1950s was not upset by the entries of Authi, Talbot, and Chrysler during the late 1960s; all of these operations failed in the 1970s. The heavy involvement by an autonomous state had resulted in the destruction of the flourishing, though small-scale, auto assembly and components workshops, and in the creation of a backward industry protected by steep barriers (Auto-Revista, 1987; Bolsa de Madrid, 1981; Hawkesworth, 1981).

Although output continued to rise through the first oil crisis of 1973–76 thanks to subsidized export growth, the shock of 1979 hit the industry hard after years of lagging investment, sluggish growth in productivity, and technological backwardness. At this time the new democratic governments broadened the liberalization measures first introduced in the early 1970s. Old and new assemblers now were allowed to expand capacity or to set up new plants, to wholly own their operations, to source components from abroad almost freely, and to specialize in the European marketplace. In compensation, foreign assemblers were required to invest heavily, to create jobs, and to increase exports to at least two-thirds of output. Attracted by the new conditions, Ford, General Motors, Volkswagen, and Nissan established new production facilities or acquired existing plants, specializing in low-end vehicles for export, while the older plants of Renault and Citroën were expanded and retooled (Bolsa de Madrid, 1981).

The shift from import-substitution policies in keeping with dependency theory to liberal local content requirements took the auto components sector by storm. More than 20 percent of the jobs in auto components were lost during the years of crisis and restructuring. Although the policies were diametrically opposed, the liberal policies of the 1980s achieved a result similar to that of the protectionist policies initiated in the late 1940s: a debacle among existing components manufacturers. In the 1940s and 1950s a relatively autonomous state had strangled private initiatives in auto assembly; as a side effect of the liberalization reforms of the 1970s and 1980s, hundreds of auto components firms were driven out of business, and the industry was placed under heavy foreign control. In 1979 the government approved the first major foreign acquisition: Robert Bosch's takeover of Femsa, the largest domestic components manufacturer at that time. Between 1979 and 1994 – when Exide Corporation of the United States acquired the battery maker Tudor, one of the world's largest – dozens of Spanish components firms were bought by foreigners. Overall the proportion of foreign-controlled auto parts companies, weighted by sales, grew from 37 percent in 1973 to 56 percent in 1983, and to a staggering 71 percent in 1990. By the late 1980s, after Volkswagen took over the state-owned SEAT factories, all assembly operations were under foreign control (Auto-Revista, 1986, pp. 83, 130, 166–72, 179, 219; Bolsa de Madrid, 1986; MICT, 1991; EIU, 1996).

As a member of the European Union since 1986, Spain has become a world center for subcompact automobile and auto parts manufacturing (Bolsa de Madrid, 1986). The components industry has attained world standards of competitiveness, unlike Korea's. According to the OECD, auto parts and other transportation equipment are one of Spain's areas of comparative technological strength, as measured by the number and specialization of patents (Archibugi and Pianta, 1992, pp. 76–77). In a study by Andersen Consulting (1994), Spain's labor productivity in auto components manufacturing was ranked the highest in the world, topping even Japan's (Economist, 1994; EIU, 1996; Sernauto, 1996, pp. 37, 45). Clearly, however, these favorable aspects of the auto components industry in Spain are not the result of local entrepreneurial initiatives, but rather the outcome of heavy involvement by foreign capital and technology.

The evolution of the auto components industry in Spain illustrates a more general trend. The country has transformed itself from one of the most isolated economies in Europe to one of the most integrated, becoming a favorite destination for multinationals. The subsidiaries of foreign multinationals account for roughly 55 percent of manufacturing value-added and 75 percent of merchandise exports.

Traditionally, analyses of Spanish society and economy have emphasized the lack of local entrepreneurial activities, often with an undertone of national inferiority. This anxiety prompted the government to experiment with state-owned firms during the 1940s and 1950s. Because local enterprises, whether private or state-owned, were regarded as not contributing sufficiently to development, the state invited foreign multinational involvement, especially during the 1980s and 1990s. In searching for alternatives to the presumed lack of private entrepreneurship, the state contributed to a self-fulfilling prophecy by stifling initiatives emerging from the private sector. Both the inward-looking statism of the 1940s and the liberal policies of the 1980s stymied local entrepreneurial initiatives, although the latter succeeded in attracting foreign investors.

Spain's social organization is distinguished most easily from Korea's and Taiwan's by its strong corporatist character: quasi-stable arrangements for resolving conflicts between hierarchically organized and functionally differentiated interest groups such as labor, business, banks, and the professions, with the state acting as arbiter (Linz, 1981). Whereas Asian authoritarian regimes remarkably avoided making concessions to interest groups, Southern European – and later Latin American – regimes found in corporatism a formula for promoting their own continuity without engaging in wholesale repression. Though not always successful, corporatist institution building and policymaking became the rule rather than the exception between the turn of the century and the 1970s. Spanish industrialization proceeded slowly and unevenly by region and by industry, with many ups and downs. Financial capital – either state- or bank-controlled – played a key role in the establishment of new industries. The acute political problems generated by unbalanced industrial growth were usually contained by negotiated agreements between labor, banks, and big business; the state assumed a coordinating role, often repressive though sometimes conciliatory. Frequently such arrangements implied a tit-for-tat among groups under the state's protective umbrella. As a result, interest groups gradually became entrenched in their positions within the polity, a situation that undermined entrepreneurial initiatives.

Internationalization as an ideology and a policy prescription has provided a solution to the inflexibility of corporatist arrangements. Only foreign multinationals, as outsiders, were acceptable to all parties as key actors in development, and only multinationals, thanks to their credible threat to exit, could impose their own logic on the system of entrenched interest groups. To make the multinationals acceptable to all interest groups, however, required consensus about internationalization. Such a consensus was forged in the context of European integration, a goal shared by political parties, labor unions, and other social forces of the left, center, and moderate right (Álvarez-Miranda, 1996; Guillén, 1997, 2000). Spain can boast high exports of both cars and components because its social organization has been conducive to the arrival of foreign multinationals, which would compete among themselves for skilled workers, component supplies, and the domestic and international market share.

As we discuss below, Argentina is also characterized by deeply entrenched interest groups. Internationalization, however, has not yet proved to be a viable solution there because the pervasive influence of populist attitudes legitimized a different set of actors and relationships among those actors.

Argentina: Populism and backwardness

The auto industry in Argentina is only beginning to change as a result of economic liberalization and integration with Brazil since the late 1980s. Currently, the assembly sector includes Volkswagen, CIADEA (Renault), Sevel (Peugeot), Ford, General Motors, FIAT, and Toyota. Total output reached a record high of just over 300,000 autos in 1994, declined to 225,000 in 1995 as a result of the recession, and recovered to reach 270,000 in 1996, only to fall again in 1998. Exports are small but growing (Auto-Revista, 1997; Nofal, 1989).

As in the other three countries studied here, the first high-volume assembly operations were established some 40 years ago when the state erected high protectionist walls and introduced import-substitution incentives for both assembled autos and parts. As in Taiwan, the state allowed as many as 21 different assemblers to operate, frequently in joint ventures between large local business groups and a foreign automotive company. Their production costs were four times as high as in the United States or Europe; output per worker averaged three vehicles a year. The 13 principal assemblers made as many as 68 models during the 1960s, and shared a total market never exceeding 200,000 units (Nofal, 1989).

The developmentalist state of the 1960s made a critical mistake that proved devastating to the auto components sector. Over a mere five years, local content requirements were raised from 55 percent to 90 to 95 percent. This import-substitution policy was established without the recognition that Argentina – unlike Taiwan or Spain – had no local firms able to serve as auto parts suppliers. Thus the government's impatience forced assemblers to integrate vertically, even into areas such as forging, castings, axles, transmissions, and suspensions; sometimes they acquired local firms. By 1972, over half of auto parts production was controlled by foreign capital (Bisang, Burachik, and Katz, 1995, p. 248; Dorfman, 1983, pp. 200–1; Montero, 1996, p. 34; Nofal, 1989; Sourrouille, 1980, pp. 158–67). Later the government provided incentives to encourage auto components production and exports, but they tended to benefit the vertically integrated assemblers rather than the small and medium-sized firms (Nofal, 1989, pp. 167–97). Thus the Argentine auto components sector has never been internationally competitive.

After peaking in 1973 at 293,000 units, auto assembly declined until the early 1990s to annual volumes as low as 100,000. This trend was exacerbated between

1979 and 1982, when the military dictatorship experimented with a set of mutually inconsistent neoliberal policies at industry and macroeconomic levels. The juntas reduced both local content requirements and tariffs on assembled cars (the outright prohibition of imports had been lifted in 1976). The combination of an overvalued currency and freer trade, however, made it impossible for domestic producers to compete. Moreover, the attempt to stabilize the economy by cutting domestic demand was especially damaging to the inward-looking auto industry (Nofal, 1989, pp. 216–17). Disillusioned by stagnant demand and political turmoil, GM left Argentina in 1978; Citroën and Chrysler exited in 1979. The state-owned firm (IME) abandoned auto production a year later. Neoliberalism had cut automotive-related employment and output by 25 percent, while the trade deficit skyrocketed. The incipient exports of components or finished autos dwindled (Montero, 1996; Nofal, 1989). Thus the import-substitution policy of the 1960s and the neoliberal program of the late 1970s contained the same error: ignoring the strengths and weaknesses in the underlying industrial structure. In both cases, the government encouraged the development of an inefficient and inward-looking auto industry.

The 1990s have witnessed a rapid transformation. Trade liberalization in the context of the Mercosur customs union with Brazil has produced more international specialization and integration, a trend that was initiated in 1988 with the Argentina–Brazil Automotive Free Trade Agreement. Currently, the auto components sector is highly fragmented for the size of the industry: It includes 400 firms and 35,700 employees, and contributes a mere 0.45 percent to GDP. Exports account for 16 percent of the industry's output, but they represent only 4.4 percent of total Argentine exports. Trade with Brazil in autos and components has increased quickly since the creation of Mercosur. The seven existing assemblers dominate this trade, however, because they are required to balance their imports of components with exports if they want to avoid tariffs. Small and medium-sized components companies are not active exporters (Auto-Revista, 1997). Therefore it appears that the mistake made in the 1960s and the 1970s is being repeated.

In spite of liberalization, the Argentine economy is still suffering from a lack of export-capable firms (Toulan and Guillén, 1997). The populist policies of many of Argentina's 45 economy ministers over the last 50 years were anchored deeply in widely held social and political myths. Many Argentinians believed that their country was inherently rich, and that labor and business did not need to exert themselves in the global economy in order to prosper. Populism led to numerous regulations aimed at promoting a false sense of security and at keeping interest groups satisfied. Such policies undermined efforts geared toward making Argentina into an export platform linked to the global economy. The distrust of foreign multinationals runs so deep that a Spanish-type solution to the rigidities of corporatism has not been found easily in Argentina. In fact, until recently the attempts to bring in foreign investment have proved counterproductive because significant segments of the business community and the labor movement regarded foreign multinationals as "illegitimate" actors (Guillén, 2000). As a result, foreign multinationals came in halfheartedly, teamed up with local partners to reduce risks, and hardly competed against each other. Although this populist social organization of the economy is changing, the auto assembly and components industries in Argentina have not yet recovered from its influence.

Table 13.3 The development of the auto assembly and components industries in four emerging countries.

Variable	South Korea	Taiwan	Spain	Argentina
Auto Assembly				
Volume	High	Low	High	Low
Exports	High	Low	High	Low
Foreign markets	USA, LDCs	None	Europe	Mercosur
Ownership	Domestic	Mixed	Foreign	Mixed
Auto Parts				
Volume	High	High	High	Low
Exports	Low	High	High	Low
Foreign markets	None	USA, Japan, Europe	Europe, USA, Latin America	Brazil (Mercosur balanced trade)
Ownership	Domestic, some foreign	Domestic	Foreign, some domestic	Domestic, increasingly foreign
Institutional Context				
State policies	Focus on final assembly for domestic market (pre-1980), and for export (post-1980); belated encouragement of domestic component manufacturing	Support of upstream supply of materials; failed attempts to develop auto assembly for domestic market	Distrust of private local initiatives; attraction of export-oriented MNEs since 1970s; promotion of supply links	Focus on final assembly for domestic market; import substitution; noncompetitive, balanced-trade arrangements with Brazil
Legitimate categories of actors	Large *chaebol*	Small family businesses	Foreign MNEs, local families, worker cooperatives	Business groups and local families, foreign MNEs
Legitimate relationships	Vertical, competitive, exclusive	Horizontal, cooperative, flexible	Competitive, cross-border	Noncompetitive, domestic
Underlying social organization logic	Institutionalized patrimonialism	Flexible networks	Corporatism cum internationalism	Corporatism cum populism

Lessons for development

These four case studies suggest the importance of historically developed institutional factors in shaping – though not necessarily limiting – economic growth, as summarized in table 13.3. At various points, the four states experimented with import-substitution and export-oriented policies, drawing on different mixtures of modernization, dependency, world-system, or free-market models and prescriptions. The policies interacted with existing categories of actors and relationships in unexpected ways, rendering state action partially ineffective. Ultimately each country gravitated toward a link to the global economy consistent with the strengths and weaknesses embedded in its social organization, although only after partially destroying or disabling some of the resources rooted in that organization.

In Korea and Spain the emphasis had shifted from import substitution to exports by the late 1970s, but without allowing for full development of an indigenous auto components sector. By creating new patterns of industrialization without considering preexisting ones, those states thwarted possibilities for innovation and growth by existing local firms. Thus state policies benefited large business groups at the expense of small and medium-sized suppliers in Korea, and favored state-owned or foreign firms to the detriment of local entrepreneurs in Spain. The three major passenger car assemblers in Korea integrated vertically on the basis of state protection, subsidized credit, and duty-free imports of certain components, a move that impeded the development of an innovative components sector. When incentives shifted toward exports, the only viable component-supply strategy for the *chaebol* was to continue building vertical, exclusive relationships with tightly controlled firms.

In Spain, an autonomous state twice assumed that domestic entrepreneurs were unprepared, unsuitable, or hopeless prospects, first in the 1950s and then in the 1980s. State technocrats thought that the traditionalism of local private entrepreneurs rendered them incapable of succeeding in the automobile industry. This assumption – combined with an entrenched corporatist system – left only one feasible alternative in the long run: recourse to massive foreign investment. Liberalization of trade and freedom of establishment during the industrial crises of the 1970s forced many local auto suppliers into bankruptcy, paving the way for foreign multinationals in both assembly and components to make the country into an export platform for subcompact cars. In contrast to the situation in Argentina, however, the arrival of foreign multinationals was tied to export incentives and competitive relationships between parts suppliers and assemblers in a European market undergoing integration.

In Taiwan and Argentina the state allowed the proliferation of small-scale auto assemblers, protected them with steep tariffs, and did not encourage export-oriented growth. In Argentina the scarcity of entrepreneurial activities created an inefficient pattern of backward vertical integration into auto parts. In Taiwan the extreme vitality of a family-firm sector barely linked to the state transformed the country into an important exporter of a variety of auto components, regardless of the fortunes of the assembly sector. Clearly, similar sets of import-substitution policies in Argentina and in Taiwan produced thoroughly dissimilar results in component manufacturing because of the differing characteristics of their small-firm sectors. Ultimately, however, auto assemblers in both countries were inefficient because neither Taiwan's nor Argentina's social organization could make good the policies promoted by the government.

Both Korea's social pattern of patrimonialism (Biggart, 1990) and Argentina's populism (Guillén, 1997, 2000) have made it very difficult for small and medium-sized firms to succeed in auto components. By contrast, Taiwan's flexible networks (Hamilton and Biggart, 1988) and Spain's internationalism (Guillén, 1997, 2000) enabled the rise of competitive components manufacturers, although with different characteristics. Thus, although no single pattern of social organization is absolutely necessary for achieving development in a particular industry, not all patterns make success possible. As shown in table 13.3, different categories of social actors and different relationships between actors have produced different links of each country's assembly and components industries to the global economy. No single critical factor accounts for the successes, and the absence of no single factor explains the failures.

Conclusion: Toward an Institutional Theory of Development

Our discussion of the comparative organization and management literature suggests that development scholarship, in looking at the "autonomy and capacity" of key actors such as states or elites, or at economic arrangements such as "perfect" markets, may be seeking illusory causal factors in development success. Recent research on organization and management, we believe, suggests that this is both an impossible and a wrong-headed approach to understanding economic development and performance. Rather, institutional theory proposes that social and economic organization is informed by historically developed logics, which are changed only with difficulty. Institutional blueprints guide which actors are constituted as legitimate economic participants, and how they relate to each other as well as to the state. States also are a product of history and may have different legitimate roles in economic decision making across societies. Institutionalized differences may become the very source of economic advantage, as various resources allow countries and firms to follow various pursuits in the global economy. Identifying such differences is the key to understanding how countries find their place in the global economy by using their unique capabilities as leverage.

In our institutional perspective on development, we argue three main points. First, economies are organized institutional arenas. Their organizing logics create a framework for meaningful economic action at the level of individual actors, firms, interfirm networks, and business–state relations. These logics are historically developed, causally complex, and difficult to change in fundamental ways. Thus, big private firms with close ties to the state became the rule in Korea, as did networks of small firms in Taiwan, foreign multinationals linked to international technology and marketing channels in Spain, and inward-looking coalitions of foreign multinationals and domestic business groups in Argentina.

Second, the internal coherence of such organizing logics limits countries' abilities to copy each other's development strategies, at least at the level of organization. Try as it might, Korea could not emulate Taiwan's success in demand-responsive auto components manufacturing; that achievement was built on the flexibility of networks of family firms. Conversely, Taiwan was unable to replicate Korea's large assembly operations. Argentina, unlike Spain, so far has found it difficult to thrive on the basis of foreign investment, given the populist ideology prevailing there.

Third, the social organization of the economy affects patterns of success in the global marketplace because it acts as a repository of useful resources or capabilities. Social organization influences a country's ability to produce efficiently and effectively certain types of goods – for example, mass-produced versus customized, or capital-intensive versus knowledge-intensive. Production systems are fundamentally social technologies: Social patterns may promote or constrain the ability to innovate and to be a leader in new products and processes. Social structures that enable actors to forge interpersonal, interfirm, and other types of alliances domestically (as in Taiwan) or to establish alliances with partners outside their own institutional arena (as in Spain) are more likely to succeed in demand-driven activities such as auto component manufacturing, which depend on the ability to respond and adapt flexibly to changing market circumstances. Other types of social structures may make such flexible links difficult to establish or sustain, but instead may promote producer-driven relationships to the global economy. The large Korean business groups, for example, are highly adept at mobilizing huge amounts of capital and labor, which are required for success in large-scale auto assembly.

Economic success, once achieved, is not to be taken for granted. Markets and opportunities change, and past sources of success may become liabilities in the future. For example, the global consolidation of automobile assembly in the late 1990s poses a challenge to Taiwan's small and medium-sized components manufacturers. Large assemblers prefer components manufacturers to provide parts and subassemblies wherever in the world they produce cars; this preference has prompted a wave of mergers between components companies. Taiwan's small firms will find it difficult to participate in original equipment manufacture, and will remain confined to the aftermarket, if they cannot organize for global manufacture and distribution.

Our primary intent has been to critique previous theories of development and to generate renewed interest in them. An *institutional perspective* on development includes, with *modernization theory*, the assumption that values or ideologies are of central importance as explanatory variables. Such a perspective differs from modernization theory, however, in rejecting the proposition that countries must make a transition from traditionalism to modernity as a precondition for development. *Dependency theory* and *world-system analysis* call attention to the inequality of structural relationships between advanced and underdeveloped countries. In an institutional perspective, however, it is not assumed that global power structures necessarily stand in the way of development. Nor is it assumed that an autonomous and capable state can resolve underdevelopment with an abstractly ideal solution such as import substitution. Finally, *free market approaches* to development contribute a set of ideas about economic fundamentals in the global economy to which countries must attend, but proposes nothing except a "one-size-fits-all" set of universal prescriptions specifying how to organize the economy.

Our institutional perspective differs most importantly from other development theories in one respect: Whereas previous approaches viewed differences in social organization as obstacles or constraints, we regard them as the very *engine* of development. Countries are socially organized to do some things better than others, which may become a source of comparative advantage. Development theories and practices that act against such institutional logics frustrate genuine entrepreneurial initiatives. If development policies imposed from above by elites, by the state, or by international agencies disregard the society's organizational arrangements and capabilities, outcomes may not build on existing strengths. Indeed, development policies insensitive to institutional resources may even eradicate the social bases of a country's comparative advantage in the world economy. Our four case studies of automobile assembly and component manufacturing illustrate that successful development occurs in keeping with underlying patterns of social organization, not in spite of them or at their expense. Development is about finding a place in the global economy, not about convergence or the suppression of difference.

References

Álvarez-Miranda, Berta (1996) *El Sur de Europa y la Adhesión a la Comunidad: Los Debates Políticos* (Southern Europe and European Community Membership: The Political Debates), Madrid, Spain: CIS and Siglo XXI.

Amsden, Alice H. (1985) "The State and Taiwan's Economic Development," pp. 78–106 in P. B. Evans, D. Rueschemeyer, and T. Skocpol (eds), *Bringing the State Back in*, Cambridge: Cambridge University Press.

Amsden, Alice H. (1989) *Asia's Next Giant: South Korea and Late Industrialization*, New York: Oxford University Press.

Andersen Consulting (1994) *Worldwide Manufacturing Competitiveness Study: The Second Lean Enterprise Report*, London: Andersen Consulting.

Apter, David (1965) *The Politics of Modernization*, Chicago, IL: University of Chicago Press.

Archibugi, Daniele and Pianta, Mario (1992) *The Technological Specialization of Advanced Countries*, London: Kluwer.

Arnold, Walter (1989) "Bureaucratic Politics, State Capacity, and Taiwan's Automotive Industry Policy," *Modern China* 15: 178–214.

Auto-Revista (1986) "25 Años de Automoción en España" (Twenty-Five Years of Automobile Manufacturing in Spain), *Auto-Revista* 1455: 19–401.

Auto-Revista (1987) "Asociación Española de Fabricantes de Equipos y Componentes para Automoción 1967–1987" (Spanish Association of Automobile Parts Manufacturers 1967–1987), *Auto-Revista* (special issue): 1–147.

Auto-Revista (1997) "Mercosur: La Mayor Fuerza Emergente" (Mercosur: The Mightiest Emerging Force), *Auto-Revista* 1976: 33–55.

Balassa, B. (1981) "A Stages Approach to Comparative Advantage," pp. 149–67 in B. Balassa (ed.), *The Newly Industrializing Countries in the World Economy*, New York: Pergamon.

Banco Urquijo (1970) *Evolución a Largo Plazo de la Industria del Automóvil en España* (Long-Term Evolution of Automobile Manufacturing in Spain), Madrid: Banco Urquijo.

Barley, Stephen R. and Tolbert, Pamela S. (1997) "Institutionalization and Structuration: Studying the Links between Action and Institution," *Organization Studies* 18: 93–117.

Bendix, Reinhard (1974 [1956]) *Work and Authority in Industry*, Berkeley, CA: University of California Press.

Biggart, Nicole Woolsey (1990) "Institutionalized Patrimonialism in Korean Business," *Comparative Social Research* 12: 113–33.

Biggart, Nicole Woolsey and Orrù, Marco (1997) "Societal Strategic Advantage: Institutional Structure and Path Dependence in the Automotive and Electronics Industries of East Asia," pp. 201–39 in A. Bugra and B. Usdiken (eds), *State, Market and Organizational Form*, Berlin: Walter de Gruyter.

Bisang, Roberto, Burachik, Gustavo, and Katz, Jorge (1995) "La Reestructuración del Aparato Productivo en la Industria Automotriz (Restructuring in the Automobile Industry)," pp. 243–68 in R. Bisang, G. Burachik, and J. Katz (eds), *Hacia un Nuevo Modelo de Organización Industrial: El Sector Manufacturero Argentino en Los Años 90*, Buenos Aires: Alianza Editorial.

Bolsa de Madrid (1981) *La Industria del Automóvil en España* (The Automobile Industry in Spain), Madrid: Bolsa de Madrid.

Bolsa de Madrid (1986) *La Industria de Equipos y Componentes Para Automoción en España* (The Automobile Equipment and Components Industry in Spain), Madrid: Bolsa de Madrid.

Campbell, John L. (1998) "Peter Evans, *Embedded Autonomy: States and Industrial Transformation*," *Theory and Society* 27: 103–8.

Cardoso, Fernando Henrique and Faletto, Enzo (1979) *Dependency and Development in Latin America*, Berkeley, CA: University of California Press.

Chandler, Alfred D. (1990) *Scale and Scope*, Cambridge, MA: Harvard University Press.

Clegg, Stewart and Hardy, Cynthia (1996) "Organizations, Organization and Organizing," pp. 1–28 in S. Clegg, C. Hardy, and W. Nord (eds), *Handbook of Organization Studies*, London: Sage.

Clifford, Mark (1991) "Model of Paradox," *Far Eastern Economic Review*, January 31: 40–42.

Collins, Randall (1997) "An Asian Route to Capitalism: Religious Economy and the Origins of Self-Transforming Growth in Japan," *American Sociological Review* 62: 843–65.

Cumings, Bruce (1987) "The Origins and Development of the Northeast Asian Political Economy," pp. 44–83 in F. Deyo (ed.), *The Political Economy of the New Asian Industrialism*, Ithaca, NY: Cornell University Press.

Dore, Ronald (1973) *British Factory – Japanese Factory*, Berkeley, CA: University of California Press.

Dorfman, Adolfo (1983) *Ciencuenta Años de Industrialización en la Argentina, 1930–1980* (Fifty Years of Industrialization in Argentina, 1930–1980), Buenos Aires: Ediciones Solar.

Dyer, Jeffrey H., Cho, Dong Sung, and Chu, Wujin (1998) "Strategic Supplier Segmentation: The Next 'Best Practice' in Supply Chain Management," *California Management Review* 40: 57–77.

Economist (1994) "The Gain in Spain Falls Mainly in Parts," *The Economist* 333: 67.

EIU (1996) "The Automotive Components Industry in Spain: Foreign Companies Drive Sector Growth," *Europe's Automotive Components Business* (1st quarter): 71–86.

Evans, Peter (1979) *Dependent Development*, Berkeley, CA: University of California Press.

Evans, Peter (1995) *Embedded Autonomy: States and Industrial Transformation*, Princeton, NJ: Princeton University Press.

Evans, Peter (ed.) (1997) *State-Society Synergy: Government and Social Capital in Development*, International and Area Studies No. 94, Berkeley, CA: University of California at Berkeley.

Executive Yuan (1996) *National Income in Taiwan Area of the Republic of China*, Taipei, Taiwan: Executive Yuan, Republic of China.

Feenstra, Robert C., Lipsey, Robert E. and Bowen, Harry P. (1997) "World Trade Flows, 1970–1992, with Production and Tariff Data," NBER Working Paper 5910, Cambridge, MA: National Bureau of Economic Research.

Fligstein, Neil (1990) *The Transformation of Corporate Control*, Cambridge, MA: Harvard University Press.

Frank, André G. (1967) *Capitalism and Underdevelopment in Latin America*, New York: Monthly Review Press.

Gereffi, Gary (1993) "The Organization of Buyer-Driven Global Commodity Chains," pp. 95–122 in G. Gereffi and M. Korzeniewicz (eds), *Commodity Chains and Global Capitalism*, Westport, CT: Greenwood.

Gerlach, Michael L. (1992) *Alliance Capitalism: The Social Organization of Japanese Business*, Berkeley, CA: University of California Press.

Gilpin, Robert (1987) *The Political Economy of International Relations*, Princeton, NJ: Princeton University Press.

Gold, Thomas B. (1986) *State and Society in the Taiwan Miracle*, Armonk, NY: M. E. Sharpe.

Green, Andrew E. (1992) "South Korea's Automobile Industry," *Asian Survey* 32: 411–28.

Greenhalgh, Susan (1988) "Families and Networks in Taiwan's Economic Development," pp. 224–45 in S. Cohen and S. L. Syme (eds), *Contending Approaches to the Political Economy of Taiwan*, New York: Academic Press.

Guillén, Mauro F. (1994) *Models of Management: Work, Authority, and Organization in a Comparative Perspective*, Chicago, IL: University of Chicago Press.

Guillén, Mauro F. (1997) "Business Groups in Economic Development," pp. 170–174 in *Best Paper Proceedings*, Statesboro, GA: Academy of Management.

Guillén, Mauro F. (2000) "Organized Labor's Images of Multinational Enterprise: Divergent Foreign Investment Ideologies in Argentina, South Korea, and Spain," *Industrial and Labor Relations Review*, 53(3): 419.

Haggard, Stephan (1990) *Pathways from the Periphery: The Politics of Growth in the Newly Industrializing Countries*, Ithaca, NY: Cornell University Press.

Haggard, Stephan and Cheng, Tun-jen (1987) "State and Foreign Capital in the East Asian NICs," pp. 84–135 in F. Deyo (ed.), *The Political Economy of the New Asian Industrialism*, Ithaca, NY: Cornell University Press.

Hamilton, Gary G. (1997) "Organization and Market Processes in Taiwan's Capitalist Economy," pp. 237–96 in M. Orrù, N. W. Biggart, and G. G. Hamilton (eds), *The Economic Organization of East Asian Capitalism*, Thousand Oaks, CA: Sage.

Hamilton, Gary G. and Biggart, Nicole Woolsey (1988) "Market, Culture, and Authority: A Comparative Analysis of Management and Organization in the Far East," *American Journal of Sociology* 94(supp.): S52–S94.

Hawkesworth, Richard E. (1981) "The Rise of Spain's Automobile Industry," *National Westminster Bank Quarterly Review* (February): 37–48.

Henderson, Gregory (1968) *Korea: The Politics of the Vortex*, Cambridge, MA: Harvard University Press.

Hirschman, Albert O. (1968) "The Political Economy of Import-Substituting Industrialization in Latin America," *Quarterly Journal of Economics* 82: 2–32.

Hollingsworth, J. Rogers, Schmitter, Philippe C., and Streeck, Wolfgang (1994) "Capitalism, Sectors, Institutions, and Performance," pp. 3–16 in J. Hollingsworth, P. Schmitter, and W. Streeck (eds), *Governing Capitalist Economies: Performane and Control of Economic Sectors*, New York: Oxford University Press.

Jacobs, Norman (1985) *The Korean Road to Modernization and Development*, Urbana, IL: University of Illinois Press.

Katzenstein, Peter J. (1985) *Small States in World Markets: Industrial Policy in Europe*, Ithaca, NY: Cornell University Press.

Kenney, Martin and Florida, Richard (1993) *Beyond Mass Production: The Japanese System and its Transfer to the U.S.*, Oxford: Oxford University Press.

Korea Times (1997) "Government Determined to Demolish Kia," *Korean Times*, August 30: 18.

Kraar, Louis (1995) "Korea's Automakers Take on the World," *Fortune*, vol. 131 (March 6): 152–58.

Lindberg, Leon N., Campbell, John L., and Hollingsworth, J. Rogers (1991) "Economic Governance and the Analysis of Structural Change in the American Economy," pp. 3–34 in J. L. Campbell, J. R. Hollingsworth, and L. N. Lindberg (eds), *Governance of the American Economy*, New York: Cambridge University Press.

Linz, Juan J. (1981) "A Century of Politics and Interests in Spain," pp. 365–415 in S. Berger (ed.), *Organizing Interests in Western Europe*, New York: Cambridge University Press.

McKinsey and Co. (1996) "The Automotive Supply Base of South Korea: Achievements and Challenges," pp. 104–24 in *Motor Business Asia-Pacific*, London: Economist Intelligence Unit.

McMichael, Philip. (1996) *Development and Social Change: A Global Perspective*, Thousand Oaks, CA: Pine Forge.

Maddison, Angus (1995) *Monitoring the World Economy 1820–1992*, Paris: OECD.

MICT (Ministerio de Industria, Comercio y Turismo) (1991) *Análisis de la Situación y Perspectivas Competitivas del Subsector de Componentes de Automoción* (An Analysis of the Competitive Status and Prospects of the Automotive Components' Sector), Madrid: MICT.

Montero, Oscar (1996) "Supplier Relationships within the Argentine Automotive Industry: Stamping Strategies and the Role of the Steel Industry," master's thesis, Sloan School of Management, Massachusetts Institute of Technology, Cambridge, MA.

Moore, Jonathan (1990) "Traffic Jam," *Far Eastern Economic Review*, June 21: 76–77.

Nelson, Richard R. (1995) "Recent Evolutionary Theorizing about Economic Change," *Journal of Economic Literature* 33: 48–90.

Nelson, Richard R. and Winter, Sidney (1982) *An Evolutionary Theory of Economic Change*, Cambridge, MA: Harvard University Press.

Nofal, Maria Beatriz (1989) *Absentee Entrepreneurship and the Dynamics of the Motor Vehicle Industry in Argentina*, New York: Praeger.

Nord, Walter W. and Fox, Suzy (1996) "The Individual in Organization Studies: The Great Disappearing Act?," pp. 148–74 in S. Clegg, C. Hardy, and W. Nord (eds), *Handbook of Organization Studies*, London: Sage.

Oliver, Nick, Delbridge, Rick, and Lowe, James (1996) "Lean Production Practices: International Comparisons in the Auto Components Industry," *British Journal of Management* 7 (supp.): S29–S44.

Orrù, Marco (1996) "The Institutional Logic of Small-Firm Economies in Italy and Taiwan," *Studies in Comparative International Development* 26: 3–28.

Orrù, Marco, Biggart, Nicole Woolsey, and Hamilton, Gary G. (1997) *The Economic Organization of East Asian Capitalism*, Thousand Oaks, CA: Sage.

Peteraf, Margaret A. (1993) "The Cornerstones of Competitive Advantage: A Resource-Based View," *Strategic Management Journal* 14: 179–91.

Piore, Michael J. and Sabel, Charles F. (1984) *The Second Industrial Divide*, New York: Basic Books.

Portes, Alejandro and Kincaid, A. Douglas (1989) "Sociology and Development in the 1990s: Critical Challenges and Empirical Trends," *Sociological Forum* 4: 479–503.

Powell, Walter W. and DiMaggio, Paul (1991) "Introduction," pp. 1–39 in W. W. Powell and P. DiMaggio (eds), *The New Institutionalism in Organizational Analysis*, Chicago, IL: University of Chicago Press.

Redding, Gordon (1989) *The Spirit of Chinese Capitalism*, Berlin: Walter de Gruyter.

Ricardo, David (1951 [1817]) *On the Principals of Political Economy and Taxation*, P. Sraffa (ed.), London: G. Bell and Sons.

Rostow, Walt W. (1960) *The Stages of Economic Growth: A Non-Communist Manifesto*, Cambridge: Cambridge University Press.

Sachs, Jeffrey (1993) *Poland's Jump to the Market Economy*, Cambridge, MA: MIT Press.

San Román López, Elena (1995) "La Industria del Automóvil en España: El Nacimiento de la SEAT" (The Automobile Industry in Spain: The Birth of the SEAT Company), Working Paper No. 9503, Economic History Program, Fundación Empresa Pública, Madrid, Spain.

Scott, W. Richard (1995) *Institutions and Organizations*, Thousand Oaks, CA: Sage.

Sease, Douglas R. (1987) "Taiwan's Export Boom to U.S. Owes Much to American Firms," *Wall Street Journal*, May 27: 1, 21.

Sernauto (1996) *La Industria Española de Equipos y Componentes para Automoción en 1995* (The Spanish Automobile Parts Industry in 1995), Madrid: Sernauto.

Skocpol, Theda (1984) "Emerging Agendas and Recurrent Strategies in Historical Sociology," pp. 356–91 in T. Skocpol (ed.), *Vision and Method in Historical Sociology*, New York: Cambridge University Press.

Smith, Adam (1976 [1776]) *An Inquiry into the Nature and Causes of the Wealth of Nations*, Oxford: Clarendon.

Sorge, Arndt (1991) "Strategic Fit and the Societal Effect in International Cross-National Comparisons of Technology, Organizations and Human Resources," *Organization Studies* 12: 161–90.

Sourrouille, Juan V. (1980) *Transnacionales en América Latina: El Complejo Automotor en Argentina* (Transnationals in Latin America: The Automobile Complex in Argentina), Mexico City: Editorial Nueva Imagen.

Stark, David and Bruszt, László (1998) *Postsocialist Pathways: Transforming Politics and Property in East Central Europe*, New York: Cambridge University Press.

Storper, Michael and Salais, Robert (1997) *Worlds of Production: The Action Frameworks of the Economy*, Cambridge, MA: Harvard University Press.

Streeck, Wolfgang (1991) "On the Institutional Conditions of Diversified Quality Production," pp. 21–61 in E. Matzner and W. Streeck (eds), *Beyond Keynesianism: The Socio-Economics of Production and Full Employment*, Aldershot: Edward Elgar.

Swidler, Ann (1986) "Culture in Action," *American Sociological Review* 51: 273–86.

Tilly, Charles (1984) *Big Structures, Large Processes, Huge Comparisons*, New York: Russell Sage.

Toulan, Omar and Guillén, Mauro F. (1997) "Beneath the Surface: The Impact of Radical Economic Reforms on the Outward Orientation of Argentine and Mendozan Firms, 1989–1995," *Journal of Latin American Studies* 29: 395–418.

Wade, Robert (1990) *Governing the Market: Economic Theory and the Role of Government in East Asian Industrialization*, Princeton, NJ: Princeton University Press.

Wallerstein, Immanuel (1974) *The Modern World-System: Capitalist Agriculture and the Origins of the European World-Economy in the Sixteenth Century*, New York: Academic.

Ward's (various years) *Ward's Automotive Yearbook*, Southfield, MI: Ward's.

Weber, Max (1978 [1922]) *Economy and Society*, reprint, Berkeley, CA: University of California Press.

Wernerfelt, Birger (1984) "A Resource-Based View of the Firm," *Strategic Management Journal* 5: 171–80.

Westney, D. Eleanor (1987) *Imitation and Innovation: The Transfer of Western Organizational Patterns to Meiji Japan*, Cambridge, MA: Harvard University Press.

Wong, Siu-Lun (1985) "The Chinese Family Firm: A Model," *British Journal of Sociology* 36: 58–72.

Wu, Yuan-li (1978) "Economic Growth: An Introduction," pp. 5–10 in Y. Wu and K. Yeh (eds), *Growth, Distribution and Social Change: Essays on the Republic of China*, Occasional Papers/Reprints Series in Contemporary Asian Studies, vol. 3, Baltimore, MD: University of Maryland Law School.

14 Learning from Collaboration: Knowledge and Networks in the Biotechnology and Pharmaceutical Industries

Walter W. Powell

In a number of technologically advanced industries, a new logic of organizing is developing. Rather than viewing firms as vehicles for processing information, making decisions, and solving problems, the core capabilities of organizations are based increasingly on knowledge-seeking and knowledge-creation. In technologically intensive fields, where there are large gains from innovation and steep losses from obsolescence, competition is best regarded as a learning race. The ability to learn about new opportunities requires participation in them, thus a wide range of interorganizational linkages is critical to knowledge diffusion, learning, and technology development. These connections may be formal contractual relationships, as in a research and development partnership or a joint venture, or informal, involving participation in technical communities. Both mechanisms are highly salient for the transfer of knowledge and are reinforcing. Yet even though the awareness of the importance of both external sources of knowledge and external participation has grown, we know much less about how knowledge is generated, transferred, and acted upon in these new contexts.

The Twin Faces of Collaboration

By a variety of accounts, the number and scope of interorganizational collaborations have grown rapidly in many industries, most notably in the field of biotechnology.[1] In the world of practice, this heightened interest is captured in discussions of the "virtual firm," and evidenced in all manner of cooperative relationships that join two or more organizations in some form of common undertaking.[2] In the world of theory, research on various forms of collaboration has two principle foci: on the transaction and the mutual exchange of rights; and on the relationship and the

Original publication: Powell, Walter W., "Learning from Collaboration: Knowledge and Networks in the Biotechnology and Pharmaceutical Industries," *California Management Review* (vol. 40, no. 3, Spring 1998): 228–40.

mechanisms through which information flows and mutual adjustments take place. Typically, the more exchange-oriented analysis treats collaboration as a variant of the make or buy decision and analyzes key features of the transaction: how it is negotiated and which party retains what control rights.[3] Thus, it matters a great deal whether common assets are being pooled or different resources traded, what stage of development a project is at, and whether some form of ownership is involved.[4] This strand of research, based primarily in the fields of industrial organization economics and business strategy, focuses more on the contractual mechanisms for coordinating interorganizational relations.

The second line of inquiry, stemming more from sociology and organization theory, adopts a processual focus, analyzing whether features of the task require continuous communication and organization learning, and the extent to which the collaboration is embedded in multiple, ongoing relationships.[5] This approach focuses on the relational capability of organizations, how and when organizations are able to combine their existing competencies with the abilities of others. These capabilities are not viewed as static, but rather emerge and deepen over time as firms both develop existing relationships and explore new ones.

These two perspectives are, at times, viewed as competing explanations, but since they involve different units of analysis – the transaction and the relationship, respectively – they need not be. Key structural features of an industry may determine the relative weight that contractual and processual elements play in interorganizational collaborations.[6] Large-scale reliance on interorganizational linkages reflects a fundamental and pervasive concern with access to knowledge. In the rapidly developing field of biotechnology, the knowledge base is both complex and expanding and the sources of expertise are widely dispersed. When uncertainty is high, organizations interact more, not less, with external parties in order to access both knowledge and resources. Hence, the locus of innovation is found in networks of learning, rather than in individual firms. How contracts are structured is not unimportant; in fact, getting the intellectual property rights specified clearly is critical. But focusing too closely on the transactional details of an exchange risks missing the boat as the larger field rides the waves of rapid technological change. Moreover, current work on contractual aspects of collaboration between biotech and pharmaceutical firms suggests that as the relationships unfold, many of the specific covenants contained in contracts are not invoked.[7] In short, process matters, and firms differ in their ability to do relational contracting.

In several key respects, arguments about the learning and strategic aspects of collaboration converge to produce new questions about the pivotal role of learning and interfirm relationships in rapidly developing industries. Firms in technologically intensive fields rely on collaborative relationships to access, survey, and exploit emerging technological opportunities. As the structure of an industry becomes shaped by interorganizational relations, the nature of competition is altered, but the direction of change is very much open. First, collaboration raises entry barriers. To the extent that the capabilities of organizations are based in part on the qualities or capabilities of those with whom they are allied, collaboration increases the price of admission to a field. If parties act either opportunistically or restrictively, collaborating only with a narrow range of partners whose behavior they can influence, then collaboration can exclude admission to many. But if the participants interact broadly and engage in mutual learning with the organizations they are affiliated with, the effects of collaboration are expansive, mobilizing resources throughout a field, with collaboration serving as an inclusive entry pass. Second, interfirm cooperation accelerates the rate of technological innovation. In our earlier work, we demonstrated a ladder effect, in which firms with experienced partners competed more effectively in high-speed learning races.[8] Rather than seeking to monopolize the returns from innovative activity and forming exclusive partnerships with only a narrow set of organizations, successful firms positioned themselves as the hubs at the center of overlapping networks, stimulating rewarding research collaborations among the various organizations to which they were aligned, and profiting from having multiple projects in various stages of development.

Third, reliance on collaboration has potentially transformative effects on all participants. Those positioned in a network of external relations adopt more administrative innovations, and do so earlier.[9] The presence of a dense network of collaborative ties may even alter participants' perceptions of competition. Inside a densely connected field, organizations must adjust to a novel perspective in which it is no longer necessary to have exclusive, proprietary ownership of an asset in order to extract value from it. Moreover, since a competitor on one project may become a partner on another, the playing field resembles less a horse race and more a rugby match, in which players frequently change their uniforms.[10] Seen from this perspective, decisions that were initially framed as strategic have cumulative consequences that alter the economic calculus, while choices motivated by learning and experimentation remake the institutional landscape.

Finally, collaboration may itself become a dimension of competition. As firms turn to outside parties for a variety of resources, they develop a network profile, or portfolio of ties to specific partners for certain activities. Thus, for example, an emerging biotech company may have a research grant from a branch of the National Institutes of Health, a research collaboration with a leading university, licensing agreements with other universities or nonprofit research institutes, clinical studies underway with a research hospital, and sales or distribution arrangements with a large pharmaceutical corporation. Others may have only one such relationship, or may hook up with the same partners for different activities, or with disparate partners for similar activities, or have complex relationships involving multiple activities with each partner. Analytically, each combination of partnership and business activity represents a distinct collaborative relationship. A firm's portfolio of collaborations is both a resource and a signal to markets, as well as to other potential partners, of the quality of the firm's activities and products. Whether firms in a field are constrained to a narrow set of relationships or have broad options in determining their portfolios has profound consequences for competition. To draw on the language of political sociology, heterogeneity and interdependence are greater spurs to collective action than homogeneity and discipline.[11] If the members of an industry are constrained in their choice of partners to a small set of potential partners, competition is increased, but within a narrow sphere. The effect is like a tournament, in which the "winners" receive exclusive sponsorship in order to compete against each other in ever-fiercer rounds. On the other hand, if there is a broad and growing set of nonexclusive partners, then the participants will evince heterogeneous collaborations, and the avenues of rivalry are widened.

In sum, regardless of whether collaboration is driven by strategic motives, such as filling in missing pieces of the value chain, or by learning considerations to gain access to new knowledge, or by embeddedness in a community of practice, connectivity to an inter-organizational network and competence at managing collaborations have become key drivers of a new logic of organizing. This view of organizations and networks as vehicles for producing, synthesizing, and distributing ideas recognizes that the success of firms is increasingly linked to the depth of their ties to organizations in diverse fields. Learning in these circumstances is a complex, multi-level process, involving learning from and with partners under conditions of uncertainty, learning about partners' behavior and developing routines and norms that can mitigate the risks of opportunism, and learning how to distribute newly acquired knowledge across different projects and functions. But learning is also closely linked to the conditions under which knowledge is gained, and in this sense the motives that drive collaboration can shape what can be learned. Much sophisticated technical knowledge is tacit in character – an indissoluble mix of design, process, and expertise. Such information is not easily transferred by license or purchase. Passive recipients of new knowledge are less likely to fully appreciate its value or be able to respond rapidly. In fields such as biotechnology, firms must have the ability to absorb knowledge.[12] In short, internal capability and external collaborations are complementary. Internal capability is indispensable in evaluating ideas or skills developed externally, while collaboration with outside parties provides access to news and resources that cannot be generated internally. A network serves as the locus of innovation in many high-tech fields because it provides timely access to knowledge and resources that are otherwise unavailable, while also testing internal expertise and learning capabilities.

The Network Structure of the Biotechnology Field

The science underlying the field of biotechnology had its origins in discoveries made in university laboratories in the early 1970s. These promising breakthroughs were initially exploited by science-based start-up firms (DBFs, or dedicated biotechnology firms, in industry parlance) founded in the mid to late 1970s. The year 1980 marked a sea change with the U.S. Supreme Court ruling in the Diamond vs. Chakrabaty case that genetically engineered life forms were patentable. And Genentech, which along with Cetus was the most visible biotech company, had its initial public offering, drawing astonishing interest on Wall Street. Over the next two decades, hundreds of DBFs have been founded, mostly in the U.S. but more recently in Canada, Australia, Britain, and Europe.

The initial research – most notably Herbert Boyer and Stanley Cohen's discovery of recombinant DNA methods and Georges Köhler and Cesar Milstein's cell infusion technology that creates monoclonal antibodies – drew primarily on molecular biology and immunology. The early discoveries were so path-breaking that they had a kind of natural excludability, that is, without interaction with those involved in the research, the knowledge was slow to transfer. But what was considered a radical innovation then has changed considerably as the science diffused rapidly. Genetic engineering, monoclonal antibodies, polymerase chain reaction amplification, and gene sequencing are now part of the standard toolkit of microbiology graduate students. To stay on top of the field, one has to be at the forefront of knowledge-seeking and technology development. Moreover, many new areas of science have become inextricably involved, ranging from genetics, biochemistry, cell biology, general medicine, computer science, to even physics and optical sciences. Modern biotechnology, then, is not a discipline or an industry per se, but a set of technologies relevant to a wide range of disciplines and industries.

The commercial potential of biotechnology appealed to many scientists and entrepreneurs even at its embryonic stage. In the early years, the principal efforts were directed at making existing proteins in new ways, then the field evolved to use the new methods to make new proteins, and now today the race is on to design entirely new medicines. The firms that translated the science into feasible technologies and new medical products faced a host of challenges. Alongside the usual difficulties of start-up firms, the DBFs needed huge amounts of capital to fund costly research, assistance in managing themselves and in conducting clinical trials, and eventually experience with the regulatory approval process, manufacturing, marketing, distribution, and sales. In time, established pharmaceutical firms were attracted to the field, initially allying with DBFs in research partnerships and in providing a set of organizational capabilities that DBFs were lacking. Eventually, the considerable promise of biotechnology led nearly every established pharmaceutical corporation to develop, to varying degrees of success, both in-house capacity in the new science and a portfolio of collaborations with DBFs.

Thus the field is not only multi-disciplinary, it is multi-institutional as well. In addition to research universities and both start-up and established firms, government agencies, nonprofit research institutes, and leading research hospitals have played key roles in conducting and funding research, while venture capitalists and law firms have played essential parts as talent scouts, advisors, consultants, and financiers. Two factors are highly salient. One, all the necessary skills and organizational capabilities needed to compete in biotechnology are not readily found under a single roof. Two, in fields such as biotech, where knowledge is advancing rapidly and the sources of knowledge are widely dispersed, organizations enter into a wide array of alliances to gain access to different competencies and knowledge. Progress with the technology goes hand-in-hand with the evolution of the industry and its supporting institutions. The science, the organizations, and the associated institutions' practices are co-evolving. Universities are more attentive to the commercial development of research, DBFs are active participants in basic science inquiry, and pharmaceuticals more keyed into developments at DBFs and universities.

Nevertheless, organizations vary in their abilities to access knowledge and skills located beyond their boundaries. Organizations develop very different profiles of collaboration, turning to partners for divergent combinations of skills, funding, experience, access, and status. Biotech firms have not supplanted pharmaceutical companies, and large pharmaceuticals have not absorbed the biotechnology field. Nor has the basic science component of the industry receded in its importance. Consequently, DBFs, research universities, pharmaceutical companies, research institutions, and leading medical centers are continually seeking partners who can help them stay abreast of, or in front of, this fast-moving field. But organizations vary considerably in their approaches to collaboration. Put differently, some organizations reap more from the network seeds they sow than do others. Despite the efforts of nearly every DBF to strengthen its collaborative capacity, not all of them cultivate similar profiles of relationships, nor are all able to harvest their networks to comparable advantage. Similarly, not every pharmaceutical firm is positioned comparably to exploit the latest breakthroughs in genomics, gene therapy, and a host of other novel methodologies for drug discovery. A key challenge, then, for both small biotechnology firms and large global pharmaceutical corporations is in learning from collaborations with external parties, and in constructing a portfolio of collaborators that provides access to both the emerging science and technology and the necessary organizational capabilities.

Collaborative Portfolios

The various key participants in the biotechnology and pharmaceutical industries pursue different avenues of collaboration. A cursory study of the portfolios of key firms reveals distinctive mixes of alliances for different business functions. For example, in biotech, Amgen, a Los Angeles-based firm founded in 1980, is often regarded as a bellwether for the industry. Amgen has extensive R&D and marketing collaborations with numerous small biotech companies, among them ARRIS, Envirogen, Glycomex, Guilford, Interneuron, Regeneron, and Zynaxis. These are relationships based on a division of labor in which the smaller firm develops promising technology with Amgen's financial and scientific assistance, and Amgen will market the eventual product. Amgen also holds several key licensing agreements with Sloan-Kettering Hospital (for a cell growth factor), the Ontario Cancer Institute (for knockout mice), and Rockefeller University (for an obesity gene). In contrast, Cambridge-based Biogen, founded in 1978 but with only 750 employees, adopted a strategy of licensing its initial research discoveries to such established firms as Abbott, Lilly, Pharmacia Upjohn, Merck, Organon Teknika, and Schering Plough. By 1996, Biogen's royalty stream had grown to $150 million annually. Biogen also outsourced the costly and time-consuming task of analyzing clinical trial data on its medicines in development to contract research organizations, but monitored the work with in-house experts.[13] Chiron, the largest biotech with more than 7,500 employees, and 9 subsidiaries, is also partially owned by Novartis (49.9%) and Johnson and Johnson (4.6%). Chiron, founded in 1981, has the most extensive array of collaborations of any biotech with numerous R&D ties with smaller biotechs and universities, licensing agreements with large pharmaceutical and animal health companies, partnerships with larger biotechs, and manufacturing and marketing alliances with other large firms as well. Indeed, in a January, 1997 news release, Chiron reported that it now has more than 1,400 (informal) agreements with universities and research institutions and 64 (formal) collaborations with other companies. "This network is a core strength of Chiron," the release proclaims.

These different collaborative profiles reflect, in important respects, the mixed motives of strategy and exigency in the early years of building a company. Amgen works with younger, early-stage biotechs, but eschews close affiliations with many established pharmaceuticals. Biogen licensed out some of its initial research discoveries, and the substantial royalties it takes in now fund the development, sales, and distribution of Avonex, its successful drug for multiple sclerosis. Chiron has a spider-webbed universe of affiliations with basic scientists in universities, and it maintains ongoing ties with diverse biotechs and health-care companies. The partial "parent" owner, Novartis of Switzerland, appears to use Chiron as its window into this rapidly developing field.

Similarly, in the pharmaceutical industry, divergent approaches to collaboration are pursued. By the accounting of Recombinant Capital, a San Francisco company that tracks high tech, the big pharmaceutical firms poured $4.5 billion into deals with biotech companies in 1996.[14] Their aim is to capitalize on promising technology and the skills of the nimbler small companies in doing more rapid development. But dominant firms pursue these aims in quite different ways. Industry giant Merck, for example, spreads its search efforts globally, working with research institutes in France, Canada, China, Japan, Costa Rica, and the United States, while pursuing research partnerships with but a few biotechs such as Affymetrix and Transcell to access new technologies. In addition, Merck has innumerable licensing agreements, as well as arrangements to do manufacturing, marketing, and sales for smaller companies. Eli Lilly, another big pharmaceutical player, but about two-thirds the size of Merck, has both more focused and more extensive collaborations. Pursuing a strategy of "discovery without walls," Lilly has several dozen research alliances with a wide variety of U.S. biotech firms, ranging from new startups to more established companies. In addition to these extensive external discovery efforts, Lilly also has licensing and joint sales and distribution agreements with biotechs, but the clear emphasis has been on the research side. The Swiss firm Hoffman LaRoche, one of the largest firms in the industry, has an even more focused approach, owning 66% of the stock in the U.S. biotech firm Genentech, in addition to multiple research, development, and marketing collaborations with Genentech. Roche counts Amgen, Affymetrix, and several other biotechs as partners also, but it utilizes Genentech as its primary talent scout to stay abreast of the field.

At a more micro level, however, these collaborative profiles have their origins in myriad small decisions, stemming from different purposes and initiated by different parties. At one of the larger U.S. pharmaceutical firms, I was involved in a multi-year internal executive development program. During this time, I had regular contact with senior managers on the science side, in the finance and strategy groups, and those in charge of the different therapeutic product lines. I used our conversations to informally trace the origins of the more than twenty R&D partnerships the firm has with various small biotechs. In following these different "stories," it became apparent that collaborations emerged from very different routes. Some were brought forward by business development staff who had "found" young biotechs in financial trouble and in need of cash. Thus, promising technology could be "had" inexpensively. In other circumstances, however, breakthrough technologies triggered great interest throughout the pharmaceutical industry, and all the major players were part of the gold rush, bidding for the new discovery. In still other cases, long-standing personal ties among scientists, sometimes forged decades earlier at universities, led to formal collaborations. Other partnerships were driven by a pressing need to fill out a product portfolio or to replenish the product pipeline in a particular therapeutic category. And still other connections literally fell into their laps, as biotech firms approached the company with proposals that proved viable.

I use these examples of very different starting points not to suggest that the process of deciding which parties to collaborate with is random or haphazard, but to illustrate that there are, especially in a larger company, multiple inputs and opportunities and many decision makers involved. Except in the smallest companies, the same people rarely review all the relevant information and make decisions about whom to ally with and under what terms and for what period of time. Nor should such decisions necessarily be made by the same people or units. But what is necessary is the ability to negotiate two hurdles, the first leaping from information to knowledge, and the second jumping from individual-level learning and expertise to organizational-level learning and routines. In any technology-intensive field, information is abundant and accumulates rapidly. Long ago, Herbert Simon alerted us to the fact that, increasingly, attention is the scarcest commodity in organizations. As firms embark on different combinations of formal and informal collaborations and divergent mixes of external sourcing and internal production, the parties who are most closely involved with outsiders develop skills at relational contracting: How much of an agreement needs to be specified in a contract? How much should rest on a handshake or good faith? What role should the "entangling strings" of friendship or reputation play? What kinds of milestones or interventions are needed to insure a project stays on course?[15] In short, knowledge of how to collaborate means that information is filtered by a specific context and an ongoing relationship, by experience and reflection, and by interpretation. When multiple participants are involved, and their availability varies, making knowledgeable decisions is a challenge.

But even more daunting is moving from individual learning (which is embodied in experienced personnel) to organization-level learning (in which the skills of relational contracting become embedded in organizational routines and procedures) without rendering those competencies lifeless and inert. As an illustration, Richard Di Marchi, Vice President for Endocrine Research at Eli Lilly and Company, remarks that one of the bigger challenges his company faces in managing research partnerships with small firms is in not treating them as "one-offs," that is, independent relationships pursued separately. On the other hand, it is ineffective to force all decisions about collaboration to go forward only after the decision has been vetted by a key committee, composed of staff from different business functions. Such a move can result in a needless delay, which is fatal in a fast-moving field, and can also dampen initiative. Another side-effect of formalizing the approval process is to force external relationships underground, into subterranean linkages, as savvy managers opt to pursue relationships without risking going through the rigmarole of formal approval. But covert efforts may run the risk that key intellectual property or process issues are not aired at the outset. The challenge, then, is to develop routines for cooperation that are widely shared, that apply across decisions, and allow for lessons to be transferred from project to project. In the biotechnology and pharmaceutical fields, firms vary enormously in their capacity to learn across projects.

Learning How and What to Learn

My claim that learning from collaboration is both a function of access to knowledge and possession of capabilities for utilizing and building on such knowledge is not a claim that individuals and organizations are exceedingly calculating or far-sighted. In making the argument that knowledge facilitates the acquisition of more knowledge, I am building on research that stresses that skills are embedded in the exercise of routines. The development of these routines is a key feature in explaining the variability of organizations' capacity for learning. Only by building these skills can knowledge be transferred from one project to another, from one unit to another, in a manner that allows insights gained from one set of experiences to shape subsequent activities.

Most firms in biotech and pharmaceuticals have key individuals who function as network managers, "marriage counselors," and honest brokers. These individuals provide the glue that sustains relationships between parties who have ample opportunities to question one another's intentions or efforts. The participants in a collaboration often learn at very different speeds, prompting one side to wonder if it is benefitting equally. Moreover, the wealthier party is sometimes regarded as a "sugar daddy," present only to write checks. So there are numerous situations where monitoring and interventions are needed to maintain balance in a collaboration. A critical task for the participants enmeshed in a web of many such relationships is to take lessons learned on one project and make them systemic, that is, portable across multiple relationships.

Finding solutions to the problem of learning how to learn is critical for both small and large firms. Biotech companies have created organizational capabilities well out of proportion to their relatively small size by building on relationships with external parties to gain access to resources, knowledge, and skills to support every organizational function from R&D to distribution. And given the huge sums that pharmaceuticals are pouring into biotech, these large firms have had to find methods to harmonize and coordinate their far-flung partnerships. The steps involved range widely, and it is probably too early to pronounce some efforts most efficacious. Clearly not all firms maneuver with equal ease, have comparable access, or utilize high-quality partners with similar results. But some methods do hold promise for facilitating learning.

An enormous amount of information and knowledge resides in the minds and electronic mail of key people, but this material is rarely organized in a fashion that allows for its transmission to others. Some firms build repositories, where contracts, milestone agreements, working papers, publications, press releases, and overheads are stored. These data banks are primarily useful for novices and new hires. A few firms have set up discussion databases in which archival material and reports are enlivened with notes and chat-room-like interactions about lessons learned. These more active sources, where key participants record their experiences as well as respond to others, are potentially quite valuable. Nevertheless they have, according to some informants, a somewhat sterile feel to them, like critiquing others' critiques of a performance, rather than engaging the performance itself. And, to many people, there simply is not sufficient time to join in these discussions. They are too busy with the press of daily activities.

Informal seminars on lessons learned from a partnership, particularly when staff from multiple functions are involved, are a good way to transmit experience across projects. Only limited effort needs to be made to organize such presentations, so they have the advantage of freshness and a hands-on feel. Nevertheless, these seminars, unless performed on a more or less regular basis, are much more valuable in a smaller company than a larger one because the information diffuses more extensively. I have not personally encountered any case where participants from both sides of a collaboration made a joint presentation, although almost every time I suggest such an approach, I am met with a comment, "That would be interesting!" Talking about failures, shortcomings, and rough spots in a relationship would be equally as valuable as discussions of successes and lessons learned. But I have rarely seen presentations where such difficulties are openly discussed. To be sure, these conversations are often pursued, heatedly, but off-stage, again the closed nature of the discussion inhibits the transfer of information. Moreover, problematic points are often dismissed as idiosyncratic to a particular party and not felt to be generalizable. While there is, of course, truth to such claims, a large part of building a reputation as a preferred partner is learning how to broker unexpected disputes.

Many biotech and pharmaceutical firms turn to multi-functional teams to supervise collaborative activities, building on the popular idea of the heavyweight teams used in product development efforts. The more thoughtful teams opt to disseminate their discussions either through electronic posting of minutes of their meetings or by having different participants act as scribes to send out short summaries of meetings.

In all these activities, there is a persistent tension between those activities done informally and on an ad hoc basis and those efforts that are more formalized and structured. Clearly, there are tradeoffs with both approaches. The insight appreciated by only a minority of the firms that we have had contact with is that developing routines for the transmission of information and experience does not necessarily entail formalization. Information can be conveyed routinely through informal means. While formal repositories and powerful task forces can be useful, they are too often not a forum in which outside input is allowed. Building routines for regular contact without formalization allows for the possibility that participants not only contribute ideas, they will take lessons learned and spread them in unexpected and unobtrusive ways.

Conclusion

In innovation-driven fields, firms are engaged in learning races. These contests proceed on parallel tracks, one involving learning *from* collaborations, the other concerns learning *how* to collaborate. Both contests require the development of skills to facilitate the transfer of information and knowledge and their subsequent deployment in other situations. In some respects, the task of learning from outside parties is more difficult. But perhaps because of the importance of the task and/or its considerable expense, organizations in the biotechnology and pharmaceutical fields are rapidly developing the capability to collaborate with a diverse array of partners to speed the timely development of new medicines. Much less refined is the more mundane but difficult and vital task of transferring information and knowledge obtained from external parties throughout the organization. This is done in order that subsequent actions are informed by, and strategic thinking based on, these experiences. A variety of efforts at learning are underway, ranging from electronic discussions to data depositories to seminars to regular meetings of heavyweight teams. All these activities reflect efforts to see that information becomes more widely diffused, and that, with reflection and interpretation, becomes "thickened" into knowledge. But developing routines for knowledge dissemination is always a double-edged sword: informal mechanisms may preclude wide dissemination, while formal procedures can inhibit learning. The challenge is to develop regular venues for the informal transmission of information, such that the process itself becomes tied to knowledge seeking and creation.

Notes

1   See data presented in National Science Board, *Science and Technology Indicators – 1996* (Washington, DC: U.S. Government Printing Office, 1996).

2   A good discussion is found in H. Chesbrough and D. J. Teece, "When Is Virtual Virtuous: Organizing for Innovation," *Harvard Business Review* 74/1 (January/February 1996): 65–73.

3   See O. Williamson, "Comparative Economic Organization," *Administrative Science Quarterly* 36 (1996): 269–96; O. Hart, *Firms, Contracts, and Financial Structure* (New York, NY: Oxford University Press, 1995).

4   Representative examples include Paul Joskow, "Contract Duration and Relation-Specific Investments," *American Economic Review*, 77 (1987): 168–95; Gary Pisano and P. Y. Mang, "Collaborative Product Development and the Market for Know-How," *Research on Technological Innovation, Management, and Policy* 5 (1993): 109–36; Phillipe Aghion and Jean Tirole, "On the Management of Innovation," *Quarterly Journal of Economics* 109 (1994): 361–79.

5   See, for example, Mark Granovetter, "Economic Action and Social Structure: The Problem of Embeddedness," *American Journal of Sociology* 91 (1985): 481–510; Charles Sabel, "Learning by Monitoring," in N. Smelser and R. Swedberg (eds), *Handbook of Economic Sociology* (Princeton, NJ: Princeton University Press, 1994): 137–65; Brian Uzzi, "The Sources and Consequences of Embeddedness for the Economic Performance of Organizations," *American Sociological Review* 61 (1996): 624–48.

6   Walter W. Powell, Kenneth Koput, and Laurel Smith-Doerr, "Interorganizational Collaboration and the Locus of Innovation: Networks of Learning in Biotechnology," *Administrative Science Quarterly* 41 (1996): 116–45; Peter Grindley and David Teece, "Managing Intellectual Capital: Licensing and Cross-Licensing in Semiconductors and Electronics," *California Management Review* 38/2 (Winter 1997): 8–41.

7   Josh Lerner and Robert P. Merges, "The Control of Strategic Alliances: An Empirical Analysis of Biotechnology Collaborations," unpublished manuscript, Harvard Business School.

8   Powell et al., op. cit.

9   On the diffusion of matrix management, see L. R. Burns and D. R. Wholey, "Adoption and Abandonment of Matrix Management Programs," *Academy of Management Journal* 36 (1993): 106–38; on the spread of the "poison pill," see G. Davis, "Agents Without Principles?," *Administrative Science Quarterly* 36 (1991): 583–613; on the multidivisional form, see D. Palmer, P. D. Jennings, and X. Zhan, "Late Adoption of the Multidivisional Form by Large U.S. Corporations," *Administrative Science Quarterly* 38 (1993): 100–31; on the diffusion of total quality management, see J. D. Westphal, R. Gulati, and S. Shortell, "Customization or Conformity," *Administrative Science Quarterly* 42 (1997): 366–94.

10 Walter W. Powell and Laurel Smith-Doerr, "Networks and Economic Life," in N. Smelser and R. Swedberg (eds), *Handbook of Economic Sociology* (Princeton, NJ: Princeton University Press, 1994): 368–402; Richard S. Rosenbloom and Williams J. Spencer, "The Transformation of Industrial Research," *Issues in Science and Technology* 12/3 (1996): 68–74.

11 For introductions to the political sociology literature, see Gerald Maxwell and Pamela Oliver, *The Critical Mass in Collective Action* (Cambridge: Cambridge University Press, 1993); Sidney Tarrow, *Power in Movement: Social Movements, Collective Action, and Politics* (Cambridge: Cambridge University Press, 1994).

12 This argument draws freely on Cohen and Levinthal's ideas about absorptive capacity, Nelson and Winter's work on developing routines for learning, and Brown and Duguid's ideas on situated learning. See Wesley Cohen and Daniel Levinthal, "Absorptive Capacity: A New Perspective on Learning and Innovation," *Administrative Science Quarterly* 35 (1990): 128–52; Richard Nelson and Sidney Winter, *An Evolutionary Theory of Economic Change* (Cambridge, MA: Harvard University Press, 1982); John Seeley Brown and Paul Duguid, "Organizational Learning and Communities-of-Practice," *Organization Science* 2 (1991): 40–57.

13 Lawrence M. Fisher, "Biogen's Triumph against the Odds," *Strategy and Business* 8 (3rd Quarter 1997): 55–63.

14 See Erick Schonfield, "Merck vs. the Biotech Industry: Which One Is More Potent?," *Fortune* March 31 (1997): 161–62.

15 See Ian Macneil, "Relational Contracting: What We Do and Do Not Know," *Wisconsin Law Review* 3 (1985): 483–526.

Part IV

Economic Culture and the Culture of the Economy

Introduction

Economists – and Marx – conceptualize society as the outcome of economic transactions. Conversely, many sociologists see the economy as a subset of society, along with political and religious spheres, for example. Rather than assume that either economy or society is prior and determining, I think that a better way of understanding their relationship is to examine connections empirically. How do social relations and ideologies influence economic relations? How do the need and desire to pursue material gain shape social relations and actions?

The last part of this volume includes five selections concerned with one aspect of the interpenetration of economy and society, the ways in which social and cultural factors are interpreted through economic activities, and the ways in which economic activities incorporate or reflect social understandings. Although there are some economic processes that both sociologists and economists study, such as firm behavior and the labor market, economists rarely examine the cultural aspects of the economy. Cultural studies, by dint of their focus on interpretation, meaning, cognitive categories, and values, do not lend themselves to the parsimonious models favored by economics. Cultural factors are usually reduced to "preferences" in econometrics. Economic sociology and anthropology have important contributions to make to understanding how values, economic practices, the impact of community, and other culturally constitutive and expressive factors contribute to economic choices and processes.

Chapter 15 is from a classic piece by French economic and cultural sociologist Pierre Bourdieu. Bourdieu expands the concept of "capital" to include assets formed by access to culturally valuable symbols, ways of life, and social networks. Chapters 16–19 are all about some aspect of money. Money would seem to be inherently economic, a store of material value with no social substance: A dollar is a dollar, and a pound is a pound – or are they? In fact, money in a capitalist society has powerful symbolic properties. Bruce Carruthers and Wendy Espeland, in "Money, Meaning, and Morality," demonstrate the ways in which currency is not anonymous, fungible, or homogenous as is generally assumed. Rather, money signifies through its use as symbol or marker for a range of socially constructed meanings. Viviana Zelizer similarly argues that currency can have a range of meanings depending on how it is received and controlled. Chapter 18 examines social values and how they shape economic action. Sherryl Kleinman's insights from a fieldwork study among activists in a free clinic reveal, ironically, that people who denigrate a capitalist orientation use money as a marker of moral worth. In chapter 19, Loren Lutzenhiser also talks about the influence of social values on economic practice, in this case consumption. He shows how people trying to save energy (and money) may be thwarted by the institutional structure of the economy.

Money is not the only form of capital. Pierre Bourdieu's "The Forms of Capital" argues against an overly restrictive view of valuable assets. Economic capital, assets easily converted into currency, are merely one store of value. By thinking of worth so narrowly, one misses other important measures of wealth and overlooks other economically important types of exchange. In addition to economic capital, Bourdieu discusses cultural capital and social capital.

Cultural capital is associated with social class. It is the ability to act "cultured" by embodying the language, accents, and mannerisms of elites. It can be "objectified" in cultural goods such as art and literature that only those with cultural capital can understand. Cultural capital can also be institutionalized as diplomas and other sorts of credentials that confer status on those who hold them. Bourdieu argues that not all can accumulate cultural capital equally. Those born into a high social status may have the social skills to benefit from an education, while capable people of lower classes may not be able to profit equally from the same schooling. An important means of the transfer of cultural capital is via inheritance.

Social capital is the value that one gains from personal connections such as membership in a family, an ethnic association, elite clubs, or other solidarity groups. Social connections can lead to jobs, loans, valuable information, and investment opportunities. These connections are sustained through an exchange of both material and symbolic goods, for example, gifts and mutual recognition as members. "Networking" in current parlance is the active attempt to build up social capital and is a form of investment. Social capital, as Bourdieu uses the term, differs somewhat from its usage by many contemporary network theorists. For them, the network is an egocentric web of relations with no necessary bounds, but Bourdieu stresses that social capital is as much about exclusion from the group as about inclusion in it.

Bruce Carruthers and Wendy Espeland explore the ways in which money becomes inscribed with meanings. Money is more than a measure of economic value. It can be used to create meaning, and it is itself given meaning through use. They argue against the view that money has a universal property, and for the idea that money's full value only becomes apparent when one examines how it is used, by whom, and for what purposes. Money can assume meanings depending on where it comes from (e.g., earned, inherited, and stolen), who uses it (e.g., crooks, charities), and how it will be used (e.g., donation to poor, to buy illegal drugs). Money also may take on meanings when it is not used, or is used "inappropriately." The use of money may be restricted in some exchanges where it would be "improper"; for example, to buy votes. Carruthers and Espeland reveal numerous ways in which that most economic of substances, money, has critical symbolic value.

Viviana Zelizer also explores the meaning of money, this time by examining how class and gender influence its perceived social value. When a woman gets an "allowance" from her husband, it can reflect gendered inequality in the home, whereas equal access to the family income (even if the same amount of money) reflects an egalitarian domestic partnership. Money takes on meaning as it comes to be categorized as an allowance, a dole, and a salary. How money is organized reflects social and economic power in society, and Zelizer uses "domestic money" to gain important insights into the structure of family power relations over time.

Sherryl Kleinman studied Renewal, a countercultural free clinic whose staff was largely composed of volunteers and workers paid below-market wages. Kleinman was struck by how much the staff, committed anticapitalists, spoke about money. Topics such as raising fees, fundraisers, poverty, and income equality were part of the daily discourse of Renewal. Kleinman thoughtfully shows how "money talk" was actually less about the need to maintain services than it was a way of constructing an identity around which they could rally. Money became a sort of moral currency that helped to justify Renewal's existence and the shared sacrifice of the members. Unexpectedly, the market value of sacrifice was used to justify the gender inequality that Kleinman found in an organization ostensibly committed to fairness.

Despite the increasing embrace of environmentalist values in the United States, there has been relatively little change in energy consumption practice, even when people want to conserve. Loren Lutzenhiser, in a charming but ultimately sorrowful tale of a man trying to conserve energy, shows how social values do not always translate into economic action when the institutions of society get in the way.

15 The Forms of Capital

Pierre Bourdieu

The social world is accumulated history, and if it is not to be reduced to a discontinuous series of instantaneous mechanical equilibria between agents who are treated as interchangeable particles, one must reintroduce into it the notion of capital and with it, accumulation and all its effects. Capital is accumulated labor (in its materialized form or its "incorporated," embodied form) which, when appropriated on a private, i.e., exclusive, basis by agents or groups of agents, enables them to appropriate social energy in the form of reified or living labor. It is a *vis insita*, a force inscribed in objective or subjective structures, but it is also a *lex insita*, the principle underlying the immanent regularities of the social world. It is what makes the games of society – not least, the economic game – something other than simple games of chance offering at every moment the possibility of a miracle. Roulette, which holds out the opportunity of winning a lot of money in a short space of time, and therefore of changing one's social status quasi-instantaneously, and in which the winning of the previous spin of the wheel can be staked and lost at every new spin, gives a fairly accurate image of this imaginary universe of perfect competition or perfect equality of opportunity, a world without inertia, without accumulation, without heredity or acquired properties, in which every moment is perfectly independent of the previous one, every soldier has a marshal's baton in his knapsack, and every prize can be attained, instantaneously, by everyone, so that at each moment anyone can become anything. Capital, which, in its objectified or embodied forms, takes time to accumulate and which, as a potential capacity to produce profits and to reproduce itself in identical or expanded form, contains a tendency to persist in its being, is a force inscribed in the objectivity of things so that everything is not equally possible or impossible.[1] And the structure of the distribution of the different types and subtypes of capital at a given moment in time represents the immanent structure of the social world, i.e., the set of constraints, inscribed in the very reality of that world, which govern its functioning in a durable way, determining the chances of success for practices.

It is in fact impossible to account for the structure and functioning of the social world unless one reintroduces capital in all its forms and not solely in the one form recognized by economic theory. Economic theory has allowed to be foisted upon it a definition of the economy of practices which is the historical invention of capitalism; and by reducing the universe of exchanges to mercantile exchange, which

Original publication: Bourdieu, Pierre, "The Forms of Capital," trans. Richard Nice, chapter 9 in John G. Richardson (ed.), *Handbook of Theory and Research for the Sociology of Education* (Greenwood Press, Westport, CN, 1986).

is objectively and subjectively oriented toward the maximization of profit, i.e., (economically) *self-interested*, it has implicitly defined the other forms of exchange as noneconomic, and therefore *disinterested*. In particular, it defines as disinterested those forms of exchange which ensure the *transubstantiation* whereby the most material types of capital – those which are economic in the restricted sense – can present themselves in the immaterial form of cultural capital or social capital and vice versa. Interest, in the restricted sense it is given in economic theory, cannot be produced without producing its negative counterpart, disinterestedness. The class of practices whose explicit purpose is to maximize monetary profit cannot be defined as such without producing the purposeless finality of cultural or artistic practices and their products; the world of bourgeois man, with his double-entry accounting, cannot be invented without producing the pure, perfect universe of the artist and the intellectual and the gratuitous activities of art-for-art's sake and pure theory. In other words, the constitution of a science of mercantile relationships which, inasmuch as it takes for granted the very foundations of the order it claims to analyze – private property, profit, wage labor, etc. – is not even a science of the field of economic production, has prevented the constitution of a general science of the economy of practices, which would treat mercantile exchange as a particular case of exchange in all its forms.

It is remarkable that the practices and assets thus salvaged from the "icy water of egotistical calculation" (and from science) are the virtual monopoly of the dominant class – as if economism had been able to reduce everything to economics only because the reduction on which that discipline is based protects from sacrilegious reduction everything which needs to be protected. If economics deals only with practices that have narrowly economic interest as their principle and only with goods that are directly and immediately convertible into money (which makes them quantifiable), then the universe of bourgeois production and exchange becomes an exception and can see itself and present itself as a realm of disinterestedness. As everyone knows, priceless things have their price, and the extreme difficulty of converting certain practices and certain objects into money is only due to the fact that this conversion is refused in the very intention that produces them, which is nothing other than the denial (*Verneinung*) of the economy. A general science of the economy of practices, capable of reappropriating the totality of the practices which, although objectively economic, are not and cannot be socially recognized as economic, and which can be performed only at the cost of a whole labor of dissimulation or, more precisely, *euphemization*, must endeavor to grasp capital and profit in all their forms and to establish the laws whereby the different types of capital (or power, which amounts to the same thing) change into one another.[2]

Depending on the field in which it functions, and at the cost of the more or less expensive transformations which are the precondition for its efficacy in the field in question, capital can present itself in three fundamental guises: as *economic capital*, which is immediately and directly convertible into money and may be institutionalized in the form of property rights; as *cultural capital*, which is convertible, on certain conditions, into economic capital and may be institutionalized in the form of educational qualifications; and as *social capital*, made up of social obligations ("connections"), which is convertible, in certain conditions, into economic capital and may be institutionalized in the form of a title of nobility.[3]

Cultural Capital

Cultural capital can exist in three forms: in the *embodied* state, i.e., in the form of long-lasting dispositions of the mind and body; in the *objectified* state, in the form of cultural goods (pictures, books, dictionaries, instruments, machines, etc.), which are the trace or realization of theories or critiques of these theories, problematics, etc.; and in the *institutionalized* state, a form of objectification which must be set apart because, as will be seen in the case of educational qualifications, it confers entirely original properties on the cultural capital which it is presumed to guarantee.

The reader should not be misled by the somewhat peremptory air which the effort at axiomization may give to my argument.[4] The notion of cultural capital initially presented itself to me, in the course of research, as a theoretical hypothesis which made it possible to explain the unequal scholastic achievement of children originating from the different social classes by relating academic success, i.e., the specific profits which children from the different classes and class fractions can obtain in the academic market, to the distribution of cultural capital between the classes and class fractions. This starting point implies a break with the presuppositions inherent both in the commonsense view, which sees academic success or failure as an effect of natural aptitudes, and in human capital theories. Economists might seem to deserve credit for explicitly raising the question of the relationship between the rates of profit on educational investment and on economic investment (and its evolution). But their measurement of the yield from scholastic investment takes account only of *monetary* investments and profits, or those directly convertible into money, such as the costs of schooling and the cash equivalent of time devoted to study; they are unable to explain the different proportions of their resources which different agents or different social classes allocate to economic investment and cultural investment because they fail to take systematic account of the structure of the differential chances of profit which the various markets offer these agents or classes as a function of the volume and the composition of their assets (see esp. Becker, 1964b). Furthermore, because they neglect to relate scholastic investment strategies to the whole set of educational strategies and to the system of reproduction strategies, they inevitably, by a necessary paradox, let slip the best hidden and socially most determinant educational investment, namely, the domestic transmission of cultural capital. Their studies of the relationship between academic ability and academic investment show that they are unaware that ability or talent is itself the product of an investment of time and cultural capital (Becker, 1964a, pp. 63–66). Not surprisingly, when endeavoring to evaluate the profits of scholastic investment, they can only consider the profitability of educational expenditure for society as a whole, the "social rate of return," or the "social gain of education as measured by its effects on national productivity" (Becker, 1964b, pp. 121, 155). This typically functionalist definition of the functions of education ignores the contribution which the educational system makes to the reproduction of the social structure by sanctioning the hereditary transmission of cultural capital. From the very beginning, a definition of human capital, despite its humanistic connotations, does not move beyond economism and ignores, *inter alia*, the fact that the scholastic yield from educational action depends on the cultural capital previously invested by the family. Moreover, the economic and social yield of the educational qualification depends on the social capital, again inherited, which can be used to back it up.

The embodied state

Most of the properties of cultural capital can be deduced from the fact that, in its fundamental state, it is linked to the body and presupposes embodiment. The accumulation of cultural capital in the embodied state, i.e., in the form of what is called culture, cultivation, *Bildung*, presupposes a process of em-bodiment, incorporation, which, insofar as it implies a labor of inculcation and assimilation, costs time, time which must be invested personally by the investor. Like the acquisition of a muscular physique or a suntan, it cannot be done at second hand (so that all effects of delegation are ruled out).

The work of acquisition is work on oneself (self-improvement), an effort that presupposes a personal cost (*on paie de sa personne*, as we say in French), an investment, above all of time, but also of that socially constituted form of libido, *libido sciendi*, with all the privation, renunciation, and sacrifice that it may entail. It follows that the least inexact of all the measurements of cultural capital are those which take as their standard the length of acquisition – so long, of course, as this is not reduced to length of schooling and allowance is made for early domestic education by giving it a positive value (a gain in time, a head start) or a negative value (wasted time, and doubly so because more time must be spent correcting its effects), according to its distance from the demands of the scholastic market.[5]

This embodied capital, external wealth converted into an integral part of the person, into a habitus, cannot be transmitted instantaneously (unlike money, property rights, or even titles of nobility) by gift or bequest, purchase or exchange. It follows that the use or exploitation of cultural capital presents particular problems for the holders of economic or political capital, whether they be private patrons or, at the other extreme, entrepreneurs employing executives endowed with a specific cultural competence (not to mention the new state patrons). How can this capital, so closely linked to the person, be bought without buying the person and so losing the very effect of legitimation which presupposes the dissimulation of dependence? How can this capital be concentrated – as some undertakings demand – without concentrating the possessors of the capital, which can have all sorts of unwanted consequences?

Cultural capital can be acquired, to a varying extent, depending on the period, the society, and the social class, in the absence of any deliberate inculcation, and therefore quite unconsciously. It always remains marked by its earliest conditions of acquisition which, through the more or less visible marks they leave (such as the pronunciations characteristic of a class or region), help to determine its distinctive value. It cannot be accumulated beyond the appropriating capacities of an individual agent; it declines and dies with its bearer (with his biological capacity, his memory, etc.). Because it is thus linked in numerous ways to the person in his biological singularity and is subject to a hereditary transmission which is always heavily disguised, or even invisible, it defies the old, deep-rooted distinction the Greek jurists made between inherited properties (*ta patroa*) and acquired properties (*epikteta*), i.e., those which an individual adds to his heritage. It thus manages to combine the prestige of innate property with the merits of acquisition. Because the social conditions of its transmission and acquisition are more disguised than those of economic capital, it is predisposed to function as symbolic capital, i.e., to be unrecognized as capital and recognized as legitimate competence, as authority exerting an effect of (mis)recognition, e.g., in the matrimonial market and in all the markets in which economic capital is not fully recognized, whether in matters of culture, with the great art collections or great cultural foundations, or in social welfare, with the economy of generosity and the gift. Furthermore, the specifically symbolic logic of distinction additionally secures material and symbolic profits for the possessors of a large cultural capital: any given cultural competence (e.g., being able to read in a world of illiterates) derives a scarcity value from its position in the distribution of cultural capital and yields profits of distinction for its owner. In other words, the share in profits which scarce cultural capital secures in class-divided societies is based, in the last analysis, on the fact that all agents do not have the economic and cultural means for prolonging their children's education beyond the minimum necessary for the reproduction of the labor-power least valorized at a given moment.[6]

Thus the capital, in the sense of the means of appropriating the product of accumulated labor in the objectified state which is held by a given agent, depends for its real efficacy on the form of the distribution of the means of appropriating the accumulated and objectively available resources; and the relationship of appropriation between an agent and the resources objectively available, and hence the profits they produce, is mediated by the relationship of (objective and/or subjective) competition between himself and the other possessors of capital competing for the same goods, in which scarcity – and through it social value – is generated. The structure of the field, i.e., the unequal distribution of capital, is the source of the specific effects of capital, i.e., the appropriation of profits and the power to impose the laws of functioning of the field most favorable to capital and its reproduction.

But the most powerful principle of the symbolic efficacy of cultural capital no doubt lies in the logic of its transmission. On the one hand, the process of appropriating objectified cultural capital and the time necessary for it to take place mainly depend on the cultural capital embodied in the whole family – through (among other things) the generalized Arrow effect and all forms of implicit transmission.[7] On the other hand, the initial accumulation of cultural capital, the precondition for the fast, easy accumulation of every kind of useful cultural capital, starts at the outset, without delay, without wasted time, only for the offspring of families endowed with strong cultural capital; in this case, the accumulation period covers the whole period of socialization. It follows that the transmission of cultural capital is no doubt the best hidden form of hereditary transmission of capital, and it therefore receives proportionately greater weight in the system of reproduction strategies, as the direct, visible forms of transmission tend to be more strongly censored and controlled.

It can immediately be seen that the link between economic and cultural capital is established through the mediation of the time needed for acquisition. Differences in the cultural capital possessed by the family imply differences first in the age at which the work of transmission and accumulation begins – the limiting case being full use of the time biologically available, with the maximum free time being harnessed to maximum cultural capital – and then in the capacity, thus defined, to satisfy the specifically cultural demands of a prolonged process of acquisition. Furthermore, and in correlation with this, the length of time for which a given individual can prolong his acquisition process depends on the length of time for which his family can provide him with the free time, i.e., time free from economic necessity, which is the precondition for the initial accumulation (time which can be evaluated as a handicap to be made up).

The objectified state

Cultural capital, in the objectified state, has a number of properties which are defined only in the relationship with cultural capital in its embodied form. The cultural capital objectified in material objects and media, such as writings, paintings, monuments, instruments, etc., is transmissible in its materiality. A collection of paintings, for example, can be transmitted as well as economic capital (if not better, because the capital transfer is more disguised). But what is transmissible is legal ownership and not (or not necessarily) what constitutes the precondition for specific appropriation, namely, the possession of the means of "consuming" a painting or using a machine, which, being nothing other than embodied capital, are subject to the same laws of transmission.[8]

Thus cultural goods can be appropriated both materially – which presupposes economic capital – and symbolically – which presupposes cultural capital. . . .

The institutionalized state

The objectification of cultural capital in the form of academic qualifications is one way of neutralizing some of the properties it derives from the fact that, being embodied, it has the same biological limits as its bearer. This objectification is what makes the difference between the capital of the autodidact, which may be called into question at any time, or even the cultural capital of the courtier, which can yield only ill-defined profits, of fluctuating value, in the market of high-society exchanges, and the cultural capital academically sanctioned by legally guaranteed qualifications, formally independent of the person of their bearer. With the academic qualification, a certificate of cultural competence which confers on its holder a conventional, constant, legally guaranteed value with respect to culture, social alchemy produces a form of cultural capital which has a relative autonomy vis-à-vis its bearer and even vis-à-vis the cultural capital he effectively possesses at a given moment in time. It institutes cultural capital by collective magic, just as, according to Merleau-Ponty, the living institute their dead through the ritual of mourning. One has only to think of the *concours* (competitive recruitment examination) which, out of the continuum of infinitesimal differences between performances, produces sharp, absolute, lasting differences, such as that which separates the last successful candidate from the first unsuccessful one, and institutes an essential difference between the officially recognized, guaranteed competence and simple cultural capital, which is constantly required to prove itself. In this case, one sees clearly the performative magic of the power of instituting, the power to show forth and secure belief or, in a word, to impose recognition.

By conferring institutional recognition on the cultural capital possessed by any given agent, the academic qualification also makes it possible to compare qualification holders and even to exchange them (by substituting one for another in succession). Furthermore, it makes it possible to establish conversion rates between cultural capital and economic capital by guaranteeing the monetary value of a given academic capital.[9] This product of the conversion of economic capital into cultural capital establishes the value, in terms of cultural capital, of the holder of a given qualification relative to other qualification holders and, by the same token, the

monetary value for which it can be exchanged on the labor market (academic investment has no meaning unless a minimum degree of reversibility of the conversion it
implies is objectively guaranteed). Because the material and symbolic profits which
the academic qualification guarantees also depend on its scarcity, the investments
made (in time and effort) may turn out to be less profitable than was anticipated
when they were made (there having been a *de facto* change in the conversion rate
between academic capital and economic capital). The strategies for converting
economic capital into cultural capital, which are among the short-term factors of
the schooling explosion and the inflation of qualifications, are governed by changes
in the structure of the chances of profit offered by the different types of capital.

Social Capital

Social capital is the aggregate of the actual or potential resources which are linked
to possession of a durable network of more or less institutionalized relationships of
mutual acquaintance and recognition – or in other words, to membership in a group[10]
– which provides each of its members with the backing of the collectivity-owned
capital, a "credential" which entitles them to credit, in the various senses of the word.
These relationships may exist only in the practical state, in material and/or symbolic
exchanges which help to maintain them. They may also be socially instituted and
guaranteed by the application of a common name (the name of a family, a class, or
a tribe or of a school, a party, etc.) and by a whole set of instituting acts designed
simultaneously to form and inform those who undergo them; in this case, they are
more or less really enacted and so maintained and reinforced, in exchanges. Being
based on indissolubly material and symbolic exchanges, the establishment and maintenance of which presuppose reacknowledgment of proximity, they are also partially
irreducible to objective relations of proximity in physical (geographical) space or even
in economic and social space.[11]

The volume of the social capital possessed by a given agent thus depends on the
size of the network of connections he can effectively mobilize and on the volume of
the capital (economic, cultural or symbolic) possessed in his own right by each of
those to whom he is connected.[12] This means that, although it is relatively irreducible
to the economic and cultural capital possessed by a given agent, or even by the whole
set of agents to whom he is connected, social capital is never completely independent of it because the exchanges instituting mutual acknowledgment presuppose the
reacknowledgment of a minimum of objective homogeneity, and because it exerts
a multiplier effect on the capital he possesses in his own right.

The profits which accrue from membership in a group are the basis of the solidarity which makes them possible.[13] This does not mean that they are consciously
pursued as such, even in the case of groups like select clubs, which are deliberately
organized in order to concentrate social capital and so to derive full benefit from
the multiplier effect implied in concentration and to secure the profits of membership – material profits, such as all the types of services accruing from useful relationships, and symbolic profits, such as those derived from association with a rare,
prestigious group.

The existence of a network of connections is not a natural given, or even a social
given, constituted once and for all by an initial act of institution, represented, in the

case of the family group, by the genealogical definition of kinship relations, which is the characteristic of a social formation. It is the product of an endless effort at institution, of which institution rites – often wrongly described as rites of passage – mark the essential moments and which is necessary in order to produce and reproduce lasting, useful relationships that can secure material or symbolic profits (see Bourdieu, 1982). In other words, the network of relationships is the product of investment strategies, individual or collective, consciously or unconsciously aimed at establishing or reproducing social relationships that are directly usable in the short or long term, i.e., at transforming contingent relations, such as those of neighborhood, the workplace, or even kinship, into relationships that are at once necessary and elective, implying durable obligations subjectively felt (feelings of gratitude, respect, friendship, etc.) or institutionally guaranteed (rights). This is done through the alchemy of *consecration*, the symbolic constitution produced by social institution (institution as a relative – bother, sister, cousin, etc. – or as a knight, an heir, an elder, etc.) and endlessly reproduced in and through the exchange (of gifts, words, women, etc.) which it encourages and which presupposes and produces mutual knowledge and recognition. Exchange transforms the things exchanged into signs of recognition and, through the mutual recognition and the recognition of group membership which it implies, re-produces the group. By the same token, it reaffirms the limits of the group, i.e., the limits beyond which the constitutive exchange – trade, commensality, or marriage – cannot take place. Each member of the group is thus instituted as a custodian of the limits of the group: because the definition of the criteria of entry is at stake in each new entry, he can modify the group by modifying the limits of legitimate exchange through some form of misalliance. It is quite logical that, in most societies, the preparation and conclusion of marriages should be the business of the whole group, and not of the agents directly concerned. Through the introduction of new members into a family, a clan, or a club, the whole definition of the group, i.e., its fines, its boundaries, and its identity, is put at stake, exposed to redefinition, alteration, adulteration. When, as in modern societies, families lose the monopoly of the establishment of exchanges which can lead to lasting relationships, whether socially sanctioned (like marriage) or not, they may continue to control these exchanges, while remaining within the logic of laissez-faire, through all the institutions which are designed to favor legitimate exchanges and exclude illegitimate ones by producing occasions (rallies, cruises, hunts, parties, receptions, etc.), places (smart neighborhoods, select schools, clubs, etc.), or practices (smart sports, parlor games, cultural ceremonies, etc.) which bring together, in a seemingly fortuitous way, individuals as homogeneous as possible in all the pertinent respects in terms of the existence and persistence of the group. . . .

Conversions

The different types of capital can be derived from *economic capital*, but only at the cost of a more or less great effort of transformation, which is needed to produce the type of power effective in the field in question. For example, there are some goods and services to which economic capital gives immediate access, without secondary costs; others can be obtained only by virtue of a social capital of relationships (or social obligations) which cannot act instantaneously, at the appropriate moment, unless they have been established and maintained for a long time, as if for their own sake, and therefore outside their period of use, i.e., at the cost of an investment in sociability which is necessarily long-term because the time lag is one of the factors of the transmutation of a pure and simple debt into that recognition of nonspecific indebtedness which is called gratitude.[14] In contrast to the cynical but also economical transparency of economic exchange, in which equivalents change hands in the same instant, the essential ambiguity of social exchange, which presupposes misrecognition, in other words, a form of faith and of bad faith (in the sense of self-deception), presupposes a much more subtle economy of time.

So it has to be posited simultaneously that economic capital is at the root of all the other types of capital and that these transformed, disguised forms of economic capital, never entirely reducible to that definition, produce their most specific effects only to the extent that they conceal (not least from their possessors) the fact that economic capital is at their root, in other words – but only in the last analysis – at the root of their effects. The real logic of the functioning of capital, the conversions from one type to another, and the law of conservation which governs them cannot be understood unless two opposing but equally partial views are superseded: on the one hand, economism, which, on the grounds that every type of capital is reducible in the last analysis to economic capital, ignores what makes the specific efficacy of the other types of capital, and on the other hand, semiologism (nowadays represented by structuralism, symbolic interactionism, or ethnomethodology), which reduces social exchanges to phenomena of communication and ignores the brutal fact of universal reducibility to economics.[15]. . .

Notes

1   This inertia, entailed by the tendency of the structures of capital to reproduce themselves in institutions or in dispositions adapted to the structures of which they are the product, is, of course, reinforced by a specifically political action of concerted conservation, i.e., of demobilization and depoliticization. The latter tends to keep the dominated agents in the state of a practical group, united only by the orchestration of their dispositions and condemned to function as an aggregate repeatedly performing discrete, individual acts (such as consumer or electoral choices).

2   This is true of all exchanges between members of different fractions of the dominant class, possessing different types of capital. These range from sales of expertise, treatment, or other services which take the form of gift exchange and dignify themselves with the most decorous names that can be found (honoraria, emoluments, etc.) to matrimonial exchanges, the prime example of a transaction that can only take place insofar as it is not perceived or defined as such by the contracting parties. It is remarkable that the apparent extensions of economic theory beyond the limits constituting the discipline have left intact the asylum of the sacred, apart from a few sacrilegious incursions. Gary S. Becker, for example, who was one of the first to take explicit account of the types of capital that are usually ignored, never considers anything other than monetary costs and profits, forgetting the nonmonetary investments (*inter alia*, the affective ones) and the material and symbolic profits that education provides in a deferred, indirect way, such as the added value which the dispositions produced or reinforced by schooling (bodily or verbal manners, tastes, etc.) or the relationships established with fellow students can yield in the matrimonial market (Becker, 1964a).

3   *Symbolic capital*, that is to say, capital – in whatever form – insofar as it is represented, i.e., apprehended symbolically, in a relationship of knowledge or, more precisely, of misrecognition and recognition, presupposes the intervention of the habitus, as a socially constituted cognitive capacity.

4   When talking about concepts for their own sake, as I do here, rather than using them in research, one always runs the risk of being both schematic and formal, i.e., theoretical in the most usual and most usually approved sense of the word.

5   This proposition implies no recognition of the value of scholastic verdicts; it merely registers the relationship which exists in reality between a certain cultural capital and the laws of the educational market. Dispositions that are given a negative value in the educational market may receive very high value in other markets – not least, of course, in the relationships internal to the class.

6   In a relatively undifferentiated society, in which access to the means of appropriating the cultural heritage is very equally distributed, embodied culture does not function as cultural capital, i.e., as a means of acquiring exclusive advantages.

7   What I call the generalized Arrow effect, i.e., the fact that all cultural goods – paintings, monuments, machines, and any objects shaped by man, particularly all those which belong to the childhood environment – exert an educative effect by their mere existence, is no doubt one of the structural factors behind the "schooling explosion," in the sense that a growth in the quantity of cultural capital accumulated in the objectified state increases the educative effect automatically exerted by the environment. If one adds to this the fact that embodied cultural capital is constantly increasing, it can be seen that, in each generation, the educational system can take more for granted. The fact that the same educational investment is increasingly productive is one of the structural factors of the inflation of qualifications (together with cyclical factors linked to effects of capital conversion).

8   The cultural object, as a living social institution, is, simultaneously, a socially instituted material object and a particular class of habitus, to which it is addressed. The material object – for example, a work of art in its materiality – may be separated by space (e.g., a Dogon statue) or by time (e.g., a Simone Martini painting) from the habitus for which it was intended. This leads to one of the most fundamental biases of art history. Understanding the effect (not to be confused with the function) which the work tended to produce – for example, the form of belief it tended to induce – and which is the true basis of the conscious or unconscious choice of the means used (technique, colors, etc.), and therefore of the form itself, is possible only if one at least raises the question of the habitus on which it "operated."

9   This is particularly true in France, where in many occupations (particularly the civil service) there is a very strict relationship between qualification, rank, and remuneration (translator's note).

10 Here, too, the notion of cultural capital did not spring from pure theoretical work, still less from an analogical extension of economic concepts. It arose from the need to identify the principle of social effects which, although they can be seen clearly at the level of singular agents – where statistical inquiry inevitably operates – cannot be reduced to the set of properties individually possessed by a given agent. These effects, in which spontaneous sociology readily perceives the work of "connections," are particularly visible in all cases in which different individuals obtain very unequal profits from virtually equivalent (economic or cultural) capital, depending on the extent to which they can mobilize by proxy the capital of a group (a family, the alumni of an elite school, a select club, the aristocracy, etc.) that is more or less constituted as such and more or less rich in capital.

11 Neighborhood relationships may, of course, receive an elementary form of institutionalization, as in the Bearn – or the Basque region – where neighbors, *lous besis* (a word which, in old texts, is applied to the legitimate inhabitants of the village, the rightful

members of the assembly), are explicitly designated, in accordance with fairly codified rules, and are assigned functions which are differentiated according to their rank (there is a "first neighbor," a "second neighbor," and so on), particularly for the major social ceremonies (funerals, marriages, etc.). But even in this case, the relationships actually used by no means always coincide with the relationships socially instituted.

12 Manners (bearing, pronunciation, etc.) may be included in social capital insofar as, through the mode of acquisition they point to, they indicate initial membership of a more or less prestigious group.

13 National liberation movements or nationalist ideologies cannot be accounted for solely by reference to strictly economic profits, i.e., anticipation of the profits which may be derived from redistribution of a proportion of wealth to the advantage of the nationals (nationalization) and the recovery of highly paid jobs (see Breton, 1962). To these specifically economic anticipated profits, which would only explain the nationalism of the privileged classes, must be added the very real and very immediate profits derived from membership (social capital) which are proportionately greater for those who are lower down the social hierarchy ("poor whites") or, more precisely, more threatened by economic and social decline.

14 It should be made clear, to dispel a likely misunderstanding, that the investment in question here is not necessarily conceived as a calculated pursuit of gain, but that it has every likelihood of being experienced in terms of the logic of emotional investment, i.e., as an involvement which is both necessary and disinterested. This has not always been appreciated by historians, who (even when they are as alert to symbolic effects as E. P. Thompson) tend to conceive symbolic practices – powdered wigs and the whole paraphernalia of office – as explicit strategies of domination, intended to be seen (from below), and to interpret generous or charitable conduct as "calculated acts of class appeasement." This naively Machiavellian view forgets that the most sincerely disinterested acts may be those best corresponding to objective interest. A number of fields, particularly those which most tend to deny interest and every sort of calculation, like the fields of cultural production, grant full recognition, and with it the consecration which guarantees success, only to those who distinguish themselves by the immediate conformity of their investments, a token of sincerity and attachment to the essential principles of the field. It would be thoroughly erroneous to describe the choices of the habitus which lead an artist, writer, or researcher toward his natural place (a subject, style, manner, etc.) in terms of rational strategy and cynical calculation. This is despite the fact that, for example, shifts from one genre, school, or speciality to another, quasi-religious conversions that are performed "in all sincerity," can be understood as capital conversions, the direction and moment of which (on which their success often depends) are determined by a "sense of investment" which is the less likely to be seen as such the more skillful it is. Innocence is the privilege of those who move in their field of activity like fish in water.

15 To understand the attractiveness of this pair of antagonistic positions which serve as each other's alibi, one would need to analyze the unconscious profits and the profits of unconsciousness which they procure for intellectuals. While some find in economism a means of exempting themselves by excluding the cultural capital and all the specific profits which place them on the side of the dominant, others can abandon the detestable terrain of the economic, where everything reminds them that they can be evaluated, in the last analysis, in economic terms, for that of the symbolic. (The latter merely reproduce, in the realm of the symbolic, the strategy whereby intellectuals and artists endeavor to impose the recognition of their values, i.e., their value, by inverting the law of the market in which what one has or what one earns completely defines what one is worth and what one is – as is shown by the practice of banks which, with techniques such as the personalization of credit, tend to subordinate the granting of loans and the fixing of interest rates to an exhaustive inquiry into the borrower's present and future resources.)

References

Becker, Gary S. (1964a) *A Theoretical and Empirical Analysis with Special Reference to Education*, New York: National Bureau of Economic Research.

Becker, Gary S. (1964b) *Human Capital*, New York: Columbia University Press.

Bourdieu, Pierre (1982) "Les rites d'institution," *Actes de la recherche en sciences sociales* 43: 58–63.

Breton, A. (1962) "The Economics of Nationalism," *Journal of Political Economy* 72: 376–86.

Grassby, Richard (1970) "English Merchant Capitalism in the Late Seventeenth Century: The Composition of Business Fortunes," *Past and Present* 46: 87–107.

16 Money, Meaning, and Morality

Bruce G. Carruthers and Wendy Nelson Espeland

Titus complained of the tax which Vespasian had imposed on the contents of the city urinals. Vespasian handed him a coin which had been part of the first day's proceeds: "Does it smell bad?" he asked. When Titus said "No," he went on: "Yet it comes from urine."

Suetonius (1957, pp. 290–91)

Cecil Graham. What is a cynic?
Lord Darlington. A man who knows the price of everything and the value of nothing.
Cecil Graham. And a sentimentalist, my dear Darlington, is a man who sees an absurd value in everything, and doesn't know the market price of any single thing.

Oscar Wilde (1980, p. 67)

On 25 July 1996, Ada Louise Huxtable, a noted architecture critic and historian, was honored by the Museum of the City of New York. That evening, Mayor Rudolph W. Giuliani presented Huxtable with the $24 award that is bestowed on people who have made important contributions to improving the quality of life for city residents. Named for the cash value of the goods that the Dutch offered to Native American inhabitants in exchange for Manhattan Island, previous recipients of this award included such wealthy and notable people as Brooke Astor, Felix Rohatyn, and Joseph Papp (see New York Times, 1996).

Clearly, the $24 that Huxtable received was, in Viviana Zelizer's (1994, pp. 21–24) terms, "special money" – money that was richly symbolic in ways that marked it and made it incommensurate with other money. But just how and by whom was this distinctiveness accomplished? What accounts for the specialness of Huxtable's money? And how, more generally, should we analyze the varied ways that monies become inscribed with meanings? Is it possible or even desirable to devise more systematic strategies for understanding the meaning of money?

We will argue that the meaning of money, like other forms of meaning, is enacted in use and that our understanding of how these processes unfold can be improved by systematically attending to some general features of the pragmatics of money. Before we tackle broader questions about the meanings of money, let us begin by unpacking the meanings of Huxtable's "special" $24.

One way that the symbolic significance of this money was signaled was the context in which it was presented. As the centrepiece of a public, ritualized event, the occasion marked the money. The food served, the clothing worn, the speeches made, and the photos taken all attested to the importance of what this particular money

Original publication: Carruthers, Bruce G. and Espeland, Wendy Nelson, "Money, Meaning, and Morality," *American Behavioral Scientist* (vol. 41, no. 10, August 1998): 1384–408.

stood for. The participants and the witnesses to this exchange also mattered for its meaning. The prominent people in the audience added their luster, as did the cultural institution that initiated the award, the mayor who conveyed it, and the accomplished woman who received it.

But all this portent and weight was in stark and calculated contrast to the trivial sum that Huxtable received. Twenty-four dollars in Manhattan might buy you a decent breakfast at a downtown hotel, a few hours of parking, or a cab ride from Wall Street to the Upper East Side, hardly a sum that would normally warrant the presence of the mayor of New York. We often think of the meaning of money as depending on what it can be exchanged for. Although we do not know if or how Huxtable spent this money, this sum signals to us that we should appreciate its symbolic value rather than its exchange value. Here, the amount matters not for what it can do for Huxtable but for what it says about her. And one of the things it does say about her is that she does not really need this money. If she or her projects needed money, its symbolic message would be compromised. In contrast, presenting $24 to someone like Mother Teresa would seem wildly inappropriate.

The significance of the prize money stemmed partly from a series of symbolic juxtapositions. The size of the award inverts one common pattern of equating price with value, where things of great value or significance are often represented by large sums of money. Some awards, like the Nobel Prize or the MacArthur Foundation "genius" grant that Huxtable received some years earlier, include sizable sums of money that reinforce the significance of the accomplishments being honored. This meager sum emphasizes the discrepancy between the amount of money that was awarded and the value of what was being honored – Huxtable's accomplishments. This discrepancy, by highlighting the inappropriateness of $24 as an estimate of her civic contributions, problematizes the commensurative capacity of money that we take for granted in routine economic exchange. The name of this prize, and no doubt the accompanying speeches, draws attention to this intentional mismatch, making it playful and funny rather than something to be reproached. Thus, a small sum of money symbolizes, in ironic fashion, a large civic contribution.

Another way to symbolize important values is to define them as intrinsically valuable, as incommensurate. This logic rejects money as an appropriate way to express or reward certain values, and their meaning is marked by removal or separation from the realm of money. Other awards, such as the Congressional Medal of Honor or the Presidential Medal, explicitly do not provide any money to recipients; cash would seem an inappropriate expression, as if money's profane associations would taint the sacredness of what is being honored. The creators of the $24 award rejected these alternative logics of valuing, instead adopting a form that makes explicit and plays off the disjunctures implicit in them. This "compromise" strategy pits contradictory symbolic logics against one another. In violating the assumptions underlying both, it evokes a rich semiotic space.

Of course, the meaning of Huxtable's prize derived not only from the small sum she received but from its specific magnitude. It mattered that it was not $23 or $25 she received but exactly $24. The meaning of this money depended on its historical associations with an earlier exchange that became notorious for its gross undervaluation. This interpretation reinforces the value of Huxtable's accomplishments by associating these with the value of contemporary Manhattan compared with its "purchase" price. But one could imagine that this association would mean something different if the recipient or members of the audience were Native American.

The meaning of Huxtable's prize money depended on its designation as an award, who was bestowing it, the occasion on which it was presented, to whom it was presented, its sum, and its historical associations; on assumptions about how these associations would be interpreted; and on the audience that witnessed this event and those who learned of it through various media. These aspects of its "context" made this money special, incommensurable with other monies. And although it is rare for money to be so elaborately marked, as Zelizar (1998) argues, people are ingenious at finding ways to transform the meanings of money in ways that render it personal, cultural, incommensurable, and moral.

Like all other social objects, money has meaning that depends on its use and context. Such uses are not, however, idiosyncratic. Nor is context ad hoc. Both are socially structured in patterned ways we can discern. In this article, we propose a set of categories and analytical distinctions that help us to interpret context and use. These should help us to think more systematically about the meaning, significance, and legitimacy of money.[1]

In a highly monetarized economy, money penetrates and participates in almost every economic exchange. Its social meanings pervasively influence the economic life of a society, and vice versa.[2] But money is so widespread, it has become almost invisible, a taken-for-granted, "natural," and easily overlooked feature of the economic landscape. We try to reestablish analytic distance to appreciate the profound effects of money.

Our efforts draw on Wittgenstein's (1958) pragmatic theory of language. Following Wittgenstein, we consider the meaning of money as something accomplished and revealed in its use. Wittgenstein rejects any theory of language that posits a constant relationship between words, their meaning, and how these correspond to the empirical world. Words are not simply the names of things, and their meanings cannot be reduced to the objects to which they refer; there are no rules and no precise relationships that govern the way we use and understand language in daily life. We believe that Wittgenstein's general argument can usefully inform the analysis of money. The meaning of money, like the meaning of words, cannot be reduced to that which it represents. Thus, it is misguided to try and identify universally representational properties of money and to link these to its meaning. The meaning of money does not depend on some characteristic that is common to all money. Instead, its meaning depends on what people in a particular context do with it.

Wittgenstein's (1958) analogies for understanding language suggest useful questions for thinking about how to understand the meaning of money in practical contexts. Wittgenstein uses two simplified models of language to ground his analysis: language as a tool and language as a game. In likening language to a tool, Wittgenstein wants us to appreciate that language shares many of the same characteristics as tools. Words are actions as well as symbols; we use words, like we use tools, to do things. Wittgenstein urges us to ask "On what occasion, for what purpose, do we say this? What kind of action accompanies these words?" (par. 489). Although the same tool can have diverse functions (think of all the things you can do with a hammer or a screwdriver), it is important to notice when we use certain tools and when we do not. Not all uses or occasions are appropriate. What cannot we do with this tool?

According to Wittgenstein, we should not be deceived by the superficial similarity of some tools. Even though cranks may look alike, they produce very different effects, and the meaning depends heavily on the particularity of these effects.

Different kinds of money, like tools, can look superficially alike although they do and mean very different things. The same piece of currency, like the same tool, can be used in a dazzling array of contexts to do very different things. There are some places where money does not or should not go and some functions for which it is inappropriate. What action does money engender? When and from where is its use prevented?

Wittgenstein's (1958) conception of the language game, which he describes as "consisting of language and the actions into which it is woven" (par. 7), helps us appreciate both the multiplicity of meaning in language and how meanings are constrained and defined by contexts. Meanings may be ambiguous, but they are not arbitrary. Although he argues that there is no universal relationship between words and their referent, there are constraints around meaning, and these are defined by the contours of their particular language game. Whether it is "poetry" or "following orders" or "telling a joke," it is possible for those engaged in a particular game to understand the meaning of words, to see some word as nonsensical or inappropriate. Language games provide a system of references, the necessary linguistic context for meaning. Their parameters are established internally, by loose, improvisational, and collective "rules" about how to use language in this particular game.

The meaning of money, like the meaning of language, is diverse, practical, and local but not completely malleable. Money is not merely a label or a symbol for something. Both analogies of language, as tools and as games, firmly ground the meaning of language in what people do with language, point to the diversity of meanings that emerge in use, and show how appropriateness is grounded in the loose, proximate rules that bound particular contexts or "games."

Markets share some of the characteristics of language games. As Zelizer (1996) argues, there are many markets that are distinguished by the particular systems of meaning that become attached to them. Markets proliferate, and people in markets are inventive. But like the variety of language games, the variety of markets need not compromise their connectedness. For Zelizer, diversity does not contradict uniformity. These are two aspects of the same transactions. The transformative potential of money derives partly from the tension between these two aspects: The universalism of money enables it to penetrate into, and link together, multiple contexts, each with its own particular meanings and relations. The semiotic power of the 24-dollar award results from a deliberate play on the tension between money's universalistic ability to represent value, on one hand, and its particularistic meanings, on the other.

What do people do with money? How does it function? Consider the standard economics textbook definition of modern money: Money functions as a medium of exchange, measure and store of value, means of payment and unit of account.[3] Because many things can perform these functions, it is more accurate to speak of monies rather than to assume that money is a singular, unitary thing.

Money is used to evaluate, to assess the magnitude of value possessed by some good or service. As such, it attaches a precise and often public number to represent the worth of something, a numerical price that "condenses" and summarizes value

(Simmel, 1978, p. 196). Money is also used as a numeraire to commensurate among alternatives faced by a decision maker (Espeland, 1998; Orléan, 1992, p. 140). Using money as a common denominator, a decision maker can make tradeoffs and comparisons and, in effect, choose between apples and oranges. Money also serves as a general resource, as the means to any end, that allows activities to proceed. Money is empowering, for it allows its possessor to do what she wants. Finally, money facilitates economic exchange, and in so doing it circulates, moving from one set of hands to another and connecting distinctive market transactions in a long monetary chain. In fulfilling this last function, money has long served as a hallmark of market or capitalist society.[4]

Each of these uses represents a way for money to acquire meanings, to bestow them, to shift and to transform them. Furthermore, although modern money is characterized by most scholars as anonymous, homogeneous, fungible, and universal,[5] in fact money itself varies in several different ways that relate to its meaning. As we elaborate below, money varies in its impersonality, ranging from highly anonymous to highly individualized. It can also differ in its scope, with general-purpose money at one end of the continuum and specialized or restricted money at the other (Douglas, 1967). Money can vary depending on how "natural" or "artificial" it seems. None of these characteristics is immutable or incontestable. In fact, the dynamism of money, and how its place in a society changes, depends very much on the kinds of conflicts, divergent understandings, and disagreements that arise over its proper role (Guyer, 1995, pp. 25–26).

Money in Exchange: How Flow Affects Meaning

Some of the different meanings that money can acquire depend on its universalistic potential: Money circulates – it flows from one place to another as people use it in successive exchanges and different contexts. The direction of these flows, and the social meaning of the places through which money moves, affects the meaning of money: Money itself can become morally tainted or purified. Terms like *dirty money* and the salience of money *laundering* suggest that money may not come through such exchanges unscathed. Yet, whether money gets colored by where it has been (or where it goes) is not a foregone conclusion. In fact, as the discussion between the Roman Emperor Vespasian and his son Titus suggests, this question, like many other moral questions, is subject to debate. Vespasian argues that money from urine smells no different than money derived from other, more reputable, tax sources. And yet, in Titus's mind, such money is somehow unclean, tarnished, or polluted. Furthermore, these meanings adhere to money as it performs one of its primary functions: facilitating exchange. They are not attached "extrinsically" or "artificially" but as part of money's normal role in the functioning of markets.

The status of money can be influenced by its place in a network of monetary flows. Money is affected by its *proximate source*, its *"ultimate" source*, and by its *future direction*. The status of where money comes from, and where it goes, matters. Consider first the proximate source of money. Where does particular money come from? If the source involves some kind of inappropriate, socially sanctioned, or morally problematic activity (theft, sale of illegal drugs, bodily functions), or if it involves illegitimate individuals (crooks, thieves, sinners), then it may become dirty money or be defined as "ill-gotten gains." Of course, fungible and homogeneous money is hard to track, and it is hard to determine where the money came from. But, frequently, monetary sources can be traced, and so the nature of the source becomes an issue.

The Kenyan Luo, a group of Christianized East African farmers, distinguish between good and bad money.[6] The latter is termed *bitter money*, and its moral status depends on its source. Money obtained through theft, as a reward for killing or hurting someone else, or through unearned gain (winning a lottery or finding someone else's lost money) becomes bitter. The sale of certain commodities like land, gold, tobacco, and cannabis also generates bitter money. Such money is dangerous – it threatens both the holder and the holder's family and must be kept strictly separate from transactions involving livestock or bridewealth. Its status as bitter is not permanent, however, for it can be converted into good money through a purification ceremony.

In a different cultural context, money derived from the sale of blood plasma also bears a cultural stigma (Espeland, 1984). Selling plasma comes dangerously close to violating American normative prohibitions on the sale of one's body parts or even, because blood is symbolic of life, of "selling life." Although legal, such market transactions are morally problematic. Sellers often distinguish between the money obtained from plasma sales and other money, earmarking the former for particular uses and purposes.[7]

The problem of how to mitigate the stigma of dirty money is a familiar one to state governments that depend on legalized gambling. Although gambling and lottery dollars look (and smell) the same as other dollars, their association with a highly disreputable activity taints them. State governments often "launder" this dirty money by earmarking it for noble purposes. Education is often a favored target for stigmatized revenues.

People distinguish money based on its source. In particular, earned money (of which the recipient is somehow morally deserving) gets differentiated from unearned money (derived from some kind of windfall). Whether the recipient saves or spends her money, and on what she spends it, depends on how the money is categorized (Lea, Tarpy, and Webley, 1988, pp. 230–31; Thaler, 1992, pp. 112–14).

Consider the example of Ms. Willis, a tenant leader and council member of a large public housing complex in a midwestern city. Her decision about whether to accept dirty money from gang leaders was a complex moral dilemma, one that reflected the inability of mainstream groups to provide for the basic needs of her community. Charged with raising money for a community party, she had been turned down by housing authority officials and had few other potential sources. "Guess I'll go back to Ottie [a gang leader] again," she concluded. "I just don't like takin' 'dirty money' if I can avoid it. You know?! But whatcha gonna do?" As drug money offered by gang members, its source tainted this money, however badly it was needed. Its meaning was mobilized – symbolically and materially – in the conflict over the moral standing of gangs as legitimate community members, their capacity to "buy" legitimacy with drug money, and conflict over who could rightfully represent and effectively serve the community (Venkatesh, 1997, pp. 96–97).

Money also derives meaning from what we might term its *ultimate* source (as opposed to proximate source). Who (or what) created and disseminated the money? Is the money issued by a sovereign government, by a private bank, by a local community, or by a single individual? Because money symbolizes or represents its issuer (whose specialized marks of authenticity and authority are frequently inscribed on it), the characteristics of the latter affect how the money is viewed and treated. Furthermore, the value of money depends on the issuer.

Money has had a historical connection with political sovereignty (Klinck, 1991, p. 3; Shipton, 1989, p. 6; Spufford, 1988, p. 83). To document their independence from former colonial masters, newly sovereign African countries frequently issued their own currency, following a fairly standardized iconography (paper money is usually stamped with numbers, pictures of political leaders, and signatures).[8] Money represents nationhood.[9] Kings and rulers put their faces or silhouettes on coins and often monopolized the right to mint new money (Geva, 1987, p. 139).[10]

One of the reasons sovereign rulers put their stamp on money (literally and figuratively) is that it can serve as an instrument of control. For example, sovereigns mobilize resources from the territories they govern in the form of taxes and tribute. To do so effectively, they try to track economic productivity and activity (Hart, 1986, p. 641). Tracing money, which is involved in most economic transactions in a monetarized economy, is much easier than directly monitoring the economic transactions themselves.[11] Consider the African colonial government's insistence on the collection of hut or capitation taxes in cash rather than in kind. The need for money forced many native Africans into the cash economy and particularly into wage labor (Arhin, 1976, p. 460; Shipton, 1989, p. 22).

A standardized currency helps sovereigns to monitor the economic base, but it also can enlarge that base. Uniform money encourages trade and economic development within national boundaries. This was one reason, for example, why the U.S. Constitution granted the power to regulate money to the federal government rather than to the individual states (Hurst, 1973, p. 18). Thirteen states could well have established 13 different currencies, which would have made interstate commerce much more difficult.

Tensions inhere in the connection between money and sovereignty. The scale of sovereignty has changed over time, but so has money. Even as governments try to control money, its evolution and growing liquidity threaten to undermine such control. These tensions are exemplified by the struggles to regulate an ever-innovating financial sector (which generated new forms of money) during the period from the 1960s to the 1990s in advanced capitalist countries.[12] Financial innovation undercut the economic sovereignty of nation states (Leyshon and Thrift, 1997).

The strong relationship between money and sovereignty has not been uncontroversial. In the early United States, for example, people were deeply concerned about the danger that the national government might get too much control over the coinage and become tempted to abuse, clip, or depreciate its value (Hurst, 1973, pp. 8–10). Later on, post-Civil War bullionists celebrated the autonomous value that specie (allegedly) possessed as a protection against politically driven inflation. Paper money, according to their analysis, was too easily controlled and abused by governments (Carruthers and Babb, 1996).[13]

Local units of government can also issue monetary tokens. These function as money within a small community and represent an attempt to bolster the local economy by restricting expenditures. Such money can only be spent locally, and so, rather than buy goods from outside, money holders must reinvest their purchasing power internally.[14] Acceptance of such currency symbolizes confidence in the community and support for one's neighbors.

Nongovernmental units can issue money. Before the Civil War, private banks, not the U.S. government, issued paper money. The multitude of banks meant that each type of money had a value that depended on the financial standing and reputation of the issuing bank (Myers, 1970, p. 121).[15] Dollar bills were not generic or homogeneous but were differentiated according to the issuer. No one in the United States imagined leaving the supply of money entirely up to market forces, although by granting private banks the right to issue bank notes, the supply of money was dispersed and "privatized" to a significant extent (Hurst, 1973, p. 31). Money can have individual as well as organizational sources. Personal checks function like money (and demand deposits are part of the official money supply), but their value depends on the individual who writes them.[16]

Money creation by nongovernment agents, either individuals or organizations, contributes to the idiosyncrasy of money and counteracts attempts by governments to try to standardize money. Even modern money remains heterogeneous. Of course, official, standardized, unitary money – the kind of currency issued by a central government – is what people have in mind when they first think of money. But one can shift attention to near monies, special monies, and quasi-monies: things that function (almost) like money and that may even be a part of the official money supply but that were not issued by the central government. Such things include personal or business credit, promissory notes, negotiable paper, demand deposits, and notes issued by private banks.[17] Alternative monies get produced privately in domestic households, as Zelizer (1994) has amply documented. But, they are also produced publicly, as part of standard commercial practices.

Personal credit is a kind of personal money. Unlike official money, it is non-anonymous – its value depends on a particular individual (the debtor or issuer). The example of 18th-century Paris bakers (Kaplan, 1996) suggests that the extension of credit establishes or constitutes a personal relationship between lender and borrower. It is a personal form of money, eventually to be exchanged for impersonal money (when the customer pays off his account) or offset against personal money going in the opposite direction (when two parties cancel offsetting claims and only settle the net balance). As Mary Douglas (1967) points out, credit often precedes money and so facilitates exchange even in economies where there is no generalized money supply (p. 121).

In early modern economies, credit was crucial for commerce (Earle, 1989; Hunt, 1996).[18] Early business handbooks (e.g., Defoe, 1987 [1745]) stressed the importance of credit for the success of business. No one could operate a trading firm, bakery, brewery, or textile mill if he could not obtain credit from his suppliers. Such handbooks underscored the necessity of credit and also advised on how to be creditworthy. The latter feature was conceived at the time to be a particular and deeply personal characteristic of the individual businessman. Credit was based on a man's personal character – his moral standing, ethical rectitude, and trustworthiness (Hoppit, 1990; Muldrew, 1993). Handbooks advised on which individual features reflected or signaled high moral standing (for example, the orderliness of one's accounts and the use of double-entry books were interpreted as good indicators of character and hence of creditworthiness).[19]

In the late 19th century, at the origin of today's credit-rating agencies (e.g., Dun and Bradstreet), creditworthiness was still a matter that rested on the personal characteristics of the borrower. In the textile trade of 19th-century Buffalo, New York, credit raters put considerable emphasis on the ethnicity of the borrower, sharply distinguishing, for example, between Jews and non-Jews (Gerber, 1982). Their assumption was that ethnic identity served as an indicator of character and trustworthiness.

Cash money differs from credit money by shifting and reducing the problem of trust. In credit relations, creditors have to determine the trustworthiness of a specific debtor in relation to the creditor (i.e., will so-and-so repay me?). If cash is used to consummate the transaction, the seller/creditor only has to know if the money is trustworthy, and she can forget about the other party. If the money is "green," so to speak, then it does not matter who the other person is.

Money's meanings depend on its future direction of flow as well as its proximate and ultimate sources. When dealing with fungible money, it is always hard to know exactly where it goes.[20] But earmarking and other techniques for differentiating money can be used to track it and discern what future transactions it enters into. The moral purity of a future use of money can help counterbalance the immorality of its source (as governments that "purify" gambling revenues by earmarking them well know).[21] Money that goes to a "good cause" becomes good money.[22] As well, idiosyncratic money (credit, commercial paper) often acquires the characteristics of its issuer, ensuring that money brings a reputation with it. Such money is definitely not anonymous.

Money and Nonexchange: Limits on Liquidity

Money's meaning is also a function of where it does not flow and why it does not flow. From what social spheres, activities, or exchanges is money excluded? How is its flow restricted? Douglas (1967) points out that even modern money is restricted to within national boundaries: Its purchasing power may be almost limitless within a country, but try to spend it elsewhere and serious problems arise. Restricted "spheres of exchange" are an anthropological truism (Bohannan, 1955, p. 1959) that reflect, among other things, social boundaries placed on the set of possible exchanges: Some things cannot be traded for others no matter what the terms of trade (Parry, 1989, p. 88). Generalized all-purpose money cannot function as such in an economy composed of separate spheres of exchange (Douglas, 1967).

Modern money may not be completely excluded from certain social domains or types of exchange, but its use is nevertheless highly constrained and restricted. Perhaps the best example of this concerns money's relationship to gift exchange. Money characterizes the exchange of commodities in markets, which is quite different from gift exchange. Although gift giving is universal, its pattern and meaning vary cross-culturally (Bloch and Parry, 1989, p. 9). In modern, Western society, gift exchange tends to be personal and altruistic, as compared with the impersonality and self-interestedness of commodity exchange. Gregory (1982) poses the difference sharply: "Commodity exchange is an exchange of alienable things between transactors who are in a state of reciprocal independence. . . . Non-commodity (gift) exchange is an exchange of inalienable things between transactors who are in a state of reciprocal dependence" (p. 12). Gift exchange establishes (or maintains) a social relationship between giver and recipient, whereas commodity exchange tends not to.[23] A gift invokes an obligation – a relationship of indebtedness, status difference, or even subordination. Consequently, the meaning of the gift must be appropriate to the relationship.[24]

Most exchanges in modern society occur in markets and, thus, are mediated by money.[25] Goods circulate as commodities purchased for money. Normatively, markets are distinctive institutions: "The norms structuring market relations . . . have five features . . . they are impersonal, egoistic, exclusive, want-regarding, and oriented to exit rather than voice" (Anderson, 1993, pp. 144–45). Yet, some exchanges are protected from monetarization and commodification because of their inappropriate ethos. Money in our society is so strongly identified with market exchange that its attachment to something brings with it strong "economic" connotations that may be deemed unsuitable. In many situations, the use of money violates and endangers the spirit of gift giving. Consequently, money is generally inappropriate as a gift, and even when it is used as such, all kinds of restrictions, framings, markings, and reinterpretations come into play.[26]

The ethos of the gift is strong enough to influence some market transactions. In the contemporary West, much cultural work has gone into defining blood donation as an instance of gift giving (Titmuss, 1971). Thus, to donate blood confers status on the donor, status that would not accrue if the person sold their blood. Furthermore, transplantable body parts (like kidneys, hearts, livers, etc.) are not for sale. But, in the United States, certain blood components can be legally exchanged for money. Nevertheless, given that selling blood transgresses sensibilities about the integrity (both physical and moral) of the human body, the exchange of blood plasma for money is enormously problematic. The meaning of money is deemed inappropriate to a context of gift giving, and so plasma selling is stigmatized. As Espeland (1984) shows, blood plasma centers devote considerable effort to managing and ameliorating this stigma.

Of course, the difference between gifts and commodities has little or nothing to do with the objects themselves but rather with the role that they play and how they are perceived. Things can be transformed from commodities into gifts (and vice versa) through their insertion into different types of exchange – the book that one buys at Barnes and Noble becomes a birthday gift for a friend as its price is removed and it is "personalized" through wrapping, the addition of an inscription, or the attachment of a card (Carrier, 1990, p. 30). Things are not intrinsically gifts or commodities – that status is bestowed on them depending on how they are used.

Even though things can be transformed from commodities into gifts, many gift exchanges remain separate from the monetarized economy. A guest who receives the gift of an invitation to dinner becomes indebted and may reciprocate later on by having the host over for a meal (thus extinguishing the debt). But polite guests would never dream of offering money in return. Nor would they treat such a social debt like a monetary debt: as a negotiable or transferable obligation.[27] The debt is personal and direct and cannot be shifted to others.

Such restrictions on the use of money in exchange are not immutably grounded in timeless and unchanging cultural categories. Norms of exchange evolve, and what may have been deemed inappropriate at one point in time can become acceptable later on. Those who Barth (1966) calls "entrepreneurs" attempt, with mixed success, to break down the barriers that separate spheres of exchange: "Innovation for an entrepreneur must involve the initiation of transactions which make commensurable some forms of value which were previously not directly connected" (p. 18). Entrepreneurs contest what is deemed an illegitimate exchange and try to redefine the boundaries of exchange. Others may resist their attempts.

In societies in which the monetarized economy is sharply distinguished from other social spheres, the presence of money in noneconomic exchanges can become highly problematic. Money brings with it a lot of moral baggage, and so members of the society (although not the entrepreneurs) will endeavor to keep money out of some exchanges. But the problematic nature of money is certainly not a universal phenomenon. As Bloch and Parry (1989) point out,

> The problem seems to be that for us money signifies a sphere of "economic" relationships which are inherently impersonal, transitory, amoral and calculating. There is therefore something profoundly awkward about offering it as a gift expressive of relationships which are supposed to be personal, enduring, moral and altruistic. But, clearly, this awkwardness derives from the fact that here money's natural environment – the "economy" – is held to constitute an autonomous domain to which general moral precepts do not apply. Where it is not seen as a separate and amoral domain, where the economy is "embedded" in society and subject to its moral laws, monetary relations are rather unlikely to be represented as the antithesis of bonds of kinship and friendship, and there is consequently nothing inappropriate about making gifts of money to cement such bonds.   *(p. 9)*

Gerriets (1985) offers a good example of this in her discussion of money in early Christian Ireland. Money was crucial in the management and maintenance of social ties but played little role in anything like a separate or autonomous economic sphere.[28]

How money gets used in exchange, and also how it is not used, both reflect and constitute meaningfulness. By virtue of its inclusions and exclusions in a social network of exchanges, and how it flows from one activity to another, money can become good or bad, appropriate or inappropriate, legitimate or illegitimate. As an economy and society evolve, not only does the network of monetary flows change, but so do the meanings that money acquires. Yet, exchange is not the only determinant of monetary meaning, for other factors matter as well.

Monetary Media

Over time, it seems that money has become less material.[29] From pieces of precious metal, to pieces of paper that represent (or are convertible into) metal, to inconvertible pieces of paper, to numerical entries in electronic accounts, money is becoming increasingly intangible. Cross-culturally, everything from cowrie shells to iron bars and cattle has functioned as money. Yet, the materiality of money mattered enormously in the past and even today still makes a difference. The extent of historical and cultural variation in monetary media suggests that what serves as the material for money is an arbitrary issue or at most a matter of convenience. Within societies at specific points in time, however, the matter of media has seemed anything but arbitrary.

Postbellum U.S. politics were dominated by monetary controversies (Carruthers and Babb, 1996; Ritter, 1997). Before the Civil War, the U.S. money supply consisted of coins (predominantly gold but also some silver) and banknotes convertible into specie. During the war, the United States went off the gold standard, and inconvertible paper currency (greenbacks) circulated as money. After the war ended, a widespread and protracted political conflict broke out concerning the choice between two monetary alternatives: gold (and gold-backed paper currency) versus greenbacks (inconvertible paper currency). Although this monetary controversy connected to many other conflicts (partisan, regional, class, ideological, etc.), much of the debate focused on the merits and liabilities of different monetary media. Bullionists – those who advocated a return to the gold standard – celebrated the intrinsic and natural value of gold and its traditional place as the basis for money. Inconvertible paper money, in their eyes, lacked substantial worth, and it devalued so easily that inflation was an ever-present danger. Greenbackers argued in response that value was conferred by law and that it did not inhere in the material out of which money was fashioned. Later on in the 19th century, Populists claimed that silver could function "as good as gold" and supported the monetarization of silver. Like the bullionists, silver advocates believed that the medium for money mattered.

The connotations of monetary media continue to resonate, long after the end of the Populist era. Consider a World Gold Council advertisement in the June 24, 1993, *New York Times* that states, "No one has ever said of gold, It's not worth the paper it's printed on," and that "gold has intrinsic value." Gold remains a powerful symbol. Although most people today rely on immaterial money (e.g., credit cards) for their market transactions, the traditional materiality of money still possesses an aura of solidity, beauty, and trustworthiness.[30]

Meaning and Monetarization

To monetarize means to attach monetary value to something. Another way that money acquires and bestows meaning relates to the consequences of monetarization. Sometimes, these consequences are deeply symbolic. Progressive-era women's reform organizations signaled their seriousness, their civic maturity, and their character as modern organizations by substituting cash contributions for personal service. The president of the General Federation of Women's Clubs chided her members, "As soon as women get big enough to spend money impersonally, then the story is told" (Clemens, 1997, p. 209). Elisabeth Clemens (1997) argues that these women understood that "cash was a criterion of citizenship" (pp. 208–10). This shift to a cash economy and the adoption of business practices, in turn, helped to displace the familiar models of sisterhood and maternalism that shaped how American women understood their organizations in the 19th century.[31]

Among other outcomes, monetarization involves affixing precise numerical values (the amount of money something is worth) to things. It also entails a distinctive type of valuation, quite different from and potentially inconsistent with other modes of valuation. Money can be "Procrustean" in its effects, as social values are stretched or trimmed to fit into quantitative monetary categories. Finally, by facilitating exchange, money can induce a set of equivalences across objects and activities that were previously considered incomparable or incommensurable. Because meaning is partly a matter of what something is like, creating new equivalences changes meaning.

In our society, it is considered wrong to value some activities using money as a metric (to do so would be cynical, in Oscar Wilde's sense). For instance, many domestic or familial relationships and activities are highly valued but not in monetary terms. Most mothers would not wish their children to attach a dollar value to the mothering they receive (see Firth, 1967, p. 19). Such a valuation would violate the normal meaning of motherhood, even though many of the activities that comprise mothering (e.g., baby-sitting, feeding, cleaning) can easily be purchased for cash.[32]

Some 19th-century reformers, as well as later feminists (Oakley, 1976), have devised estimates of the market value of women's unpaid labor as one strategy for publicizing and criticizing inequities.[33] But, many women remain leery of efforts to commodify domestic work. As Judith Stacey (1990) points out, "modern-traditional" conceptions of the family emphasize family relations as fundamentally different from market relations. For some, the family is crucial precisely because they believe it is a "haven" from the self-interested calculations that characterize economic behavior (Lasch, 1977). For women who embrace traditional roles, efforts to commodify their work are deeply threatening to their investments and identities (Stevens, 1996).

Different societies value different things in nonmonetary terms, but nonmonetary valuation is itself almost a universal feature.[34] The majority of contemporary Americans comfortably put a money value on land and will view such a monetary assessment as legitimate. The Yavapai Indian tribe of Arizona, in sharp contrast, has refused to put a dollar value on their ancestral lands (despite considerable political pressure to do so). Such a valuation violates their cultural heritage and insults their collective self-identity (Espeland, 1994, 1998).[35] In the past, widespread monetarization has altered people's perceptions of some quite ordinary things:

> Just as cultivable land ceased to be regarded simply as a source of immediately consumable produce and came to be seen as a source of money, so other resources came to be judged in terms of the money that they would produce. Forests ceased to be seen merely in terms of hunting for pleasure or food and were valued in monetary terms.
> *(Spufford, 1988, p. 245)*[36]

Even the monetarization of things that are now ordinarily exchanged in markets can be consequential. The monetary valuation of economic investments seems valid almost by definition (most people understand capital as a stock of money). Yet, as Baldwin and Clark (1994) argue, the use of money as a measure of value focuses attention almost exclusively on the most quantifiable aspects of a situation and necessarily overlooks the unquantified. According to their analysis, U.S. companies after World War II adopted the discounted cash flow methodology to assess capital-budgeting projects. They evaluated their investment alternatives in purely monetary terms, and in so doing, failed to develop various organizational capabilities that had a discernible effect on performance but that were almost impossible to cast in monetary terms.

Much the same problem applies to labor. Workers now routinely exchange their labor for wages, and so, in effect, a money value gets attached to their labor. Yet, the establishment of wage labor was hardly an uncontroversial or inconsequential process. In the French textile industry,

> they [workers] resisted trading off money for certain categories of things, especially limited control over their own bodies and routines and a coherent structure for the family life cycle. They resisted trading off money for these things because these things had an importance they did not wish to quantify.   *(Reddy, 1984, p. 334)*

The monetarization of labor was no uniform process, for the attachment of money to labor varied considerably, even within the same industry. In the 19th century, workers were paid using a piece-rate system in both the British and German wool-weaving industries. Yet, these monetary compensation schemes measured the product (length of cloth manufactured) in the case of Britain and the labor expended (number of "shots," or trips of the shuttle across the warp) in the case of Germany as the basis for wages (Biernacki, 1995). Multiple monetary measures of labor were possible.[37]

Valuation in general is a kind of assessment or estimation – a form of measurement. Some kinds of valuation simply put objects into different classes: This is good, that is bad; this is male, that is female. One can take a set of objects and determine which are similar (by virtue of belonging to the same class) and which are different. A different valuation might place the objects into classes that are ordered along some dimension (as in small, medium, and large). Valuations vary in terms of what psychometricians call the "level of measurement" (Fraser, 1980; Lea, Tarpy, and Webley, 1988, pp. 336–37). When things are valued monetarily, one knows about much more than just similarities and differences. Money allows for, and in fact compels, the precise specification of magnitudes of value (i.e., this is worth exactly $100), differences between value (as in, this is worth $50 more than that), and relative values (this is worth twice as much as that).

The numerical precision of monetary price renders exchange much less ambiguous than before. Thanks to standardized money, it becomes absolutely clear what something is worth, and the magnitude of equivalences set up in exchange are rendered unambiguous. Of course, for many types of exchanges, undertakings, and relationships, ambiguity has its virtues.[38] Gift givers normally take the price tag off a gift because knowledge of an exact monetary value encourages the recipient to draw conclusions ("Our friendship is only worth a $10 gift?") and make comparisons ("Samuel's gift is worth twice as much as Esther's, therefore I must mean more to Samuel") that violate the ethos of gift giving. In such a context, price provides too much inappropriate information. In other respects, price can provide too little information, as it offers only a one-dimensional assessment of value. The complexity of things with multiple dimensions may simply be ignored in a price.

Monetarization also encourages the belief that the arithmetic operations that can be applied to numbers (addition, division, subtraction, etc.) accurately represent real qualities of the things to which monetary value has been attached.[39] For example, to value jointly two assets, one might sum their individual monetary values, but such an operation would ignore the kind of asset specificities and synergies that make wholes sometimes more, and sometimes less, than the sum of their parts. Nonmonetary values may not conform with the laws of arithmetic, but widespread monetarization of value enforces such conformity (Ferreira, 1997). The monetarization and, consequently, arithmetization of the economy also encourages and privileges numerical skills. Numeracy becomes almost as valuable as literacy (Thomas, 1987).

Finally, the spread of monetarization inserts local transactions into larger circuits of exchange. Implicitly, all bilateral exchanges become multilateral (because money provides a common denominator, it makes all two-way comparisons possible), and so money creates equivalences between unlike things (Strathern, 1992). For example, suppose in some society object A did not equal and was not comparable with object B and, therefore, could never be exchanged for B. But with money, if A = x and B = x, then by the transitivity of an equivalence relation, A = B. This is another way of saying that generalized money threatens to break down spheres of exchange (Bohannan, 1959) and to commensurate incommensurables (Espeland, 1998).

Even in situations in which monetary valuation occurs and is deemed appropriate, moral sensibilities can still make a difference. It may be "right" to attach prices to things, but the question of the right price remains open. E. P. Thompson (1971) argued that the 18th-century English crowd used standard forms of collective action, in particular the bread riot, to enforce moral standards about what was a "fair" price for bread or flour. Although one might dismiss such normative standards as early-modern holdovers from precapitalist society, Kahneman, Knetsch, and Thaler (1986a, 1986b) present strong evidence that similar standards apply today.[40] Some mechanisms for market allocation in situations of excess demand are considered more fair than others (for example, queues seem much fairer to people than do auctions). People bring to economic exchange a reference transaction (often a previous price or market price) that helps to define what is fair. The circumstances of a price change dictate whether it seems fair (i.e., it is more legitimate to raise a price if costs have gone up than if demand for the final product has risen).

The perceived distinction between natural and artificial applies to prices as well as to monetary media (e.g., gold vs. paper). A market price has a natural or inevitable quality to it that administered prices do not, and so the latter are more vulnerable to contestation. Valuation of assets in bankruptcy court frequently involves the derivation of prices in situations in which the market provides little guidance (Delaney, 1994; Fortgang and Mayer, 1985). Consequently, bankruptcy valuation can involve a very political and conflictual series of negotiations among interested parties. The transfer prices used by large firms to account for their internal transactions also often lack market benchmarks. Without the legitimacy of a seemingly natural reference point, organizational political interests weigh heavily as these artificial prices get negotiated and administered (Eccles, 1985).

Conclusion

Money derives meaning and transfers it both in the course of facilitating exchange and outside of exchange. Money creates meaning pragmatically, that is, through use. Money is not a neutral or meaningless social object, and its meanings are consequential. People treat money differently depending on what it means – good or bad, appropriate or inappropriate, right or wrong, dirty or clean. Such meanings change over time, as "entrepreneurs" propose new exchanges, comparisons, and equivalences that transform preexisting categories and distinctions. The monetarization of economic life has led to the penetration of money into many (but certainly not all) spheres of exchange. Considerable effort goes into the protection of certain relationships and exchanges from money and into modifying, attenuating, or distinguishing money so that it becomes less dangerous. In our society, gift giving and money coexist uneasily.

Multiple monies exist in a structure with a core of official money (usually supplied by the national government) surrounded by a penumbra of quasi- and near monies that get supplied by banks, organizations, corporations, and individuals. If the core is standardized and anonymous, the penumbra is neither. Official money represents the sovereignty of government and, flowing easily from one transaction to the next, links them in a monetary chain that can transfer meaning from one site to another (e.g., dirty money comes from a disreputable source and must be treated differently). Quasi-monies are often less liquid and, by not flowing easily, cannot transfer meaning so readily. Yet, by virtue of who (or what) issued it, quasi-money acquires a distinctive meaning as the representation of the issuer. General monies also raise the issue of power more acutely than do special monies. The latter are not the kind of generalized resource that empowers money holders in a threatening way.

Those who use money to value the world see it through more quantitative eyes. The ability to apply mathematical operations to value has clearly been understood as a considerable economic advantage (witness the number of numerically based financial techniques that monetary valuation has generated). But it discounts, downplays, or even ignores those aspects of value that cannot be reduced to a single number. Although such a claim may seem fairly obvious in the case of pricing priceless heirlooms, it applies even to basic factors of production like capital and labor.

In addition to where it does and does not flow, who issues it, and how it values, money derives meaning from its medium. The tangibility of gold still weighs heavily on the public imagination, connoting intrinsic worth, natural value, solid tradition, and economic security. To gain marketing cachet, even plastic credit cards turn to gold.

This article lays out some of the dimensions of monetary meaning: proximate and ultimate source, future flow, mode of valuation, and monetary media. These dimensions undergird much of the variation in money we have surveyed: homogeneous versus differentiated money, general versus specialized money, material versus immaterial money, anonymous versus personal money. The next step is to demonstrate the usefulness of this framework in a sustained empirical analysis of money and monetary change – something we hope to undertake soon.

Notes

1 Our goal in this article is to begin devising a general analytic framework for analyzing the meaning of money. Here, we use examples drawn promiscuously from different historical periods and societies. We unfortunately must relegate to future work our efforts to enlist this framework in a more sustained, detailed, and historically responsible analysis of money.

2 For this reason, we draw distinctions between economy and society, or between the economic and the social, for analytical purposes only. In reality, of course, both influence and interpenetrate each other in variable ways that call for explanation (see Carruthers, 1996).

3 See, for example, Stiglitz (1993, pp. 880–83).
4 "A market system requires for its existence the full and free convertibility of all objects of human desire into money equivalents and the full and free operation of a separate economic sphere of social life" (Reddy, 1987, p. 154).
5 See the summary in Zelizer (1994, pp. 6–12).
6 This discussion relies on Shipton (1989).
7 Earmarking money involves setting it aside, in reserve or for some special purpose (Zelizer, 1994, pp. 21–25).
8 Such iconographic conventions are very old. Procopius (the Byzantine chronicler) notes that as Franks and other tribes conquered regions of the western Roman Empire, they also took over the mints and started to issue coins. Procopius thought it fine that barbarian rulers should put their likenesses on silver coins but thought it a travesty that such undistinguished and inaugust people would also put it on gold coins (Spufford, 1988, pp. 12–14). These conventions of symbolism even apply to paper money, as Marco Polo's description of Kublai Khan's paper money suggests:

> And all these papers are sealed with the seal of the Great Khan. The procedure of issue is as formal and as authoritative as if they were made of pure gold or silver. On each piece of money several specially appointed officials write their names, each setting his own stamp. When it is completed in due form, the chief of the officials deputed by the Khan dips in cinnabar the seal or bull assigned to him and stamps it on the top of the piece of money so that the shape of the seal in vermilion remains impressed upon it. And then the money is authentic. And if anyone were to forge it, he would suffer the extreme penalty.   *(Polo, 1958, p. 147)*

In 1792, the U.S. Congress asserted national sovereignty by defining the gold content of a dollar so as to distinguish it from the other foreign coins then in circulation (see Hurst, 1973, p. 32).
9 Consider Israel's switch in its currency units from pounds (borrowed from the British monetary system) to lira to shekels (a unit with rich historical connotations and cultural resonances).
10 Minting coins was a prerogative that engaged rulers personally. Numerous 16th-century Italian city rulers vied for the services of the famous goldsmith Benvenuto Cellini in designing their coinage. Rulers competed to have their portraits cast on the most beautiful money.
11 Thus, one way to evade taxes is to exit the money economy and exchange via barter.
12 For instance, the euro-dollar market that emerged in the 1960s escaped U.S. financial and banking regulations.
13 Hurst (1973) suggests why monetary controversies were so intense:

> But, regulation of the money supply made itself felt among the people with a sharpness and breadth of impact which did not characterize uses of most fiscal or regulatory law. Money was part of the form and substance of almost all economic transactions and entered into the calculations and expectations by which men structured much of their lives and behavior outside the market.   *(p. 91)*

14 Such local money tokens are issued in places like Ithaca, New York; Madison, Wisconsin; and Waldo County, Maine and are legal. See *Wall Street Journal*, June 27, 1996 (thanks to Marc Ventresca for calling this article to our attention).
15 For example, the real (as opposed to nominal) value of a one-dollar bill issued by an insolvent bank was less than that of a dollar issued by a healthy bank.

16 For some time, demand deposits have constituted a large proportion of the total money supply. The resurgence of state banks after the Civil War, despite a prohibitive tax on state bank notes instituted by Congress, attested to the growing importance of demand deposits as a proportion of the total U.S. money supply (West, 1977, p. 25).

17 A question we do not treat here concerns the large number of quasi- and near monies. Given the existence of standardized official money, why are there so many of the others? Two reasons might help explain this: First, the supply of official money is frequently insufficient to support all of the economic transactions that people wish to undertake (and so they develop substitutes). Second, money is not qualitatively superior to the alternatives. Money is usually justified by economists as a solution to the nontrivial problem of barter (which requires a "double coincidence of wants"). In fact, however, actual barter is quite a bit easier than this suggests (Humphrey and Hugh-Jones, 1992, pp. 4–6).

18 Freyer (1982) and Weinberg (1982) discuss the importance of commercial paper, another quasi-money, in the 19th-century U.S. economy. The value of commercial paper depended on the initial issuer but also on the reputations of those who endorsed it as it changed hands.

19 See Addison (1965 [1711]) and Carruthers and Espeland (1991).

20 This is partly why money is an exception to the common law rule that a seller can transfer no better title than she herself has. Someone who in good faith unknowingly takes money from a thief gets to keep the money, even though the thief did not legally own it (see Geva, 1987, pp. 117–18).

21 The proportion of state tax revenues that are earmarked for specific purposes is surprisingly high. In 1993, the average proportion across all U.S. states was 24%, and the distribution ranged from 4% (in Kentucky) all the way to 87% (in Alabama). Many states earmark questionable revenues from tobacco and alcoholic beverage sales (see General Accounting Office, 1995).

22 In early 19th-century United States, corporations were legitimized by generating tax revenues that could be put to legitimate public purposes like funding public education (see Freyer, 1994, pp. 92–95).

23 Appadurai (1986) elaborates the contrast:

> Gifts, and the spirit of reciprocity, sociability, and spontaneity in which they are typically exchanged, usually are starkly opposed to the profit-oriented, self-centered, and calculated spirit that fires the circulation of commodities. Further, where gifts link things to persons and embed the flow of things in the flow of social relations, commodities are held to represent the drive – largely free of more or cultural constraints – of goods for one another, a drive mediated by money and not by sociality.   *(pp. 11–12)*

For an analysis of gift giving in contemporary societies, see Cheal (1988) and Caplow (1982). In anthropological societies, gift giving manages relations among not only individuals but also groups, tribes, and villages (see Strathern, 1971, pp. 10–11; Mauss, 1990, p. 5).

24 For example, silk undergarments are considered highly inappropriate as a gift from a man to a woman unless they are in an intimate relationship. To give a Christmas ham to a good friend who is Muslim suggests that the insensitive gift giver is not really a very good friend (see Carrier, 1990).

25 Although commodity exchange predominates now, in the past gift exchange was much more important, precisely because it was so much more effective for the manipulation of social and political relationships. On Europe in the Middle Ages, see Grierson (1959), Geary (1986), and Spufford (1988, p. 17).

26 A friendly neighbor who does a favor usually gets repaid with a small gift, not with cash. Money's impersonality means that those who wish to give it as a gift must frequently personalize it (see Anderson, 1993, p. 152; Lea, Tarpy, and Webley, 1988, pp. 322–33; Webley and Wilson, 1989; Zelizer, 1994, pp. 77–91).

27 By virtue of their negotiability, financial debts can function like money in the following way. Suppose A owes B a sum and gives to B a promissory note. If B also owes money to someone else, C, B can give the promissory note to C in satisfaction of the debt. Thus, A's debt can circulate and function like money. In contrast, consider a similar pattern of social debts. A owes B dinner, and B owes C dinner. Social debts are not negotiable, and so B would not transfer A's debt to satisfy the obligation to C. Negotiability would violate the meaning of the social obligation.

28 The early medieval wergild system, which attached monetary "prices" to an elaborate list of wrongs, did not represent an immoral intrusion of mammon into the resolution of interpersonal disputes. Rather, it was a system of monetary compensation. Consistent with Bloch and Parry's (1989) argument, the economy did not constitute a separate, autonomous social realm (see Grierson, 1977; Spufford, 1988, pp. 9, 17).

29 In Simmel's (1978) terms, money has shifted from substance to function (pp. 168–69).

30 Even plastic money is given a metallic sheen. An American Express credit card with a higher credit limit gets labeled a *gold* or even *platinum* card and is colored appropriately. Regular cards are colored green, just like cash.

31 These reformers also recognized that the source of their money mattered symbolically. Fund-raising that capitalized on women's traditional roles was common, but some saw it as threatening women's claims to full citizenship. For example, a leader in Wisconsin's Political Equality League threatened to retire to a "cool spot near Lake Superior" rather than to resort to selling cookbooks or postcards to raise campaign funds (Clemens, 1997, p. 209).

32 Similar strictures constrain the valuation of children. Although children are considered highly valuable, valuation of them in monetary terms is considered wrong. This is why Landes and Posner's (1978) proposal for market governance of child adoptions generated such a vehement response (see Cohen, 1987; Landes and Posner, 1978; and, more generally, Zelizer, 1985).

33 See Siegel (1994).

34 Weiner (1992) proposes that a fundamental social and cultural distinction exists between alienable and inalienable things: "What makes a possession inalienable is its exclusive and cumulative identity with a particular series of owners through time" (p. 33). Such objects can be transferred, just not bought and sold (i.e., exchanged for money). In fact, to ensure their physical preservation and the maintenance of their special significance over time, they must be passed down from one owner to the next, as successive owners die (e.g., the British Crown jewels, hereditary landed estates).

35 On a more personal level, one can consider family "treasures" and "heirlooms" as the kinds of objects for which monetary valuation is inappropriate, at least for the family members.

36 Arhin (1976) notes that the introduction by the British of cash into the Asante economy changed social and political relationships.

37 Biernacki (1995) explains the difference in the monetarization of labor in terms of national cultural understandings of labor. Different meanings of labor entailed different monetarizations of labor.

38 For more on the political and economic uses of ambiguity, see Padgett and Ansell (1993) and Pollard (1983).

39 As Reddy (1984) puts it, "Unlike similar categories originating in earlier periods – noble and common, sacred and profane – the categories of market culture may all be expressed

in numerical form, representing a real or potential exchange price, and, therefore, they may be added and subtracted, substituted, or canceled out" (p. 12).
40   See also Alexander and Alexander (1991).

References

Addison, J. (1965 [1711]) *The Spectator*, vol. 2, Oxford: Clarendon.
Alexander, J. and Alexander, P. (1991) "What's a Fair Price? Price-Setting and Trading Partnerships in Javanese Markets," *Man* 26: 493–512.
Anderson, E. (1993) *Value in Ethics and Economics*, Cambridge, MA: Harvard University Press.
Appadurai, A. (1986) "Introduction," in A. Appadurai (ed.), *The Social Life of Things*, Cambridge: Cambridge University Press.
Arhin, K. (1976) "The Pressure of Cash and its Political Consequences in Asante in the Colonial Period, 1900–1940," *Journal of African Studies* 3: 453–68.
Baldwin, C. Y. and Clark, K. B. (1994) "Capital-Budgeting Systems and Capabilities Investments in U.S. Companies after the Second World War," *Business History Review* 68: 73–109.
Barth, F. (1966) *Models of Social Organization*, London: Royal Anthropological Institute of Great Britain and Ireland.
Biernacki, R. (1995) *The Fabrication of Labor: Germany and Britain, 1640–1914*, Berkeley, CA: University of California Press.
Bloch, M. and Parry, J. (1989) "Introduction," in J. Parry and M. Bloch (eds), *Money and the Morality of Exchange*, Cambridge: Cambridge University Press.
Bohannan, P. (1955) "Some Principles of Exchange and Investment among the Tiv," *American Anthropologist* 57, 60–67.
Bohannan, P. (1959) "The Impact of Money on an African Subsistence Economy," *Journal of Economic History* 19: 491–503.
Caplow, T. (1982) "Christmas Gifts and Kin Networks," *American Sociological Review* 47: 383–92.
Carrier, J. (1990) "Gifts in a World of Commodities," *Social Analysis* 29: 19–37.
Carruthers, B. G. (1996) *City of Capital: Politics and Markets in the English Financial Revolution*, Princeton, NJ: Princeton University Press.
Carruthers, B. G. and Babb, S. (1996) "The Color of Money and the Nature of Value: Greenbacks and Gold in Postbellum America," *American Journal of Sociology* 101: 1556–91.
Carruthers, B. G. and Espeland, W. (1991) "Accounting for Rationality: Double-Entry Bookkeeping and the Rhetoric of Economic Rationality," *American Journal of Sociology* 97: 31–69.
Cheal, D. (1988) *The Gift Economy*, London: Routledge.
Clemens, E. S. (1997) *The People's Lobby: Organizational Innovation and the Rise of Interest Group Politics, 1890–1925*, Chicago, IL: University of Chicago Press.
Cohen, J. M. (1987) "Posnerism, Pluralism, Pessimism," *Boston University Law Review* 67: 105–75.
Defoe, D. (1987 [1745]) *The Complete English Tradesman*, London: Alan Sutton.
Delaney, K. J. (1994) "The Organizational Construction of the 'Bottom Line,'" *Social Problems* 41: 201–22.
Douglas, M. (1967) "Primitive Rationing," in R. Firth (ed.), *Themes in Economic Anthropology*, London: Tavistock.
Earle, P. (1989) *The Making of the English Middle Class*, Berkeley, CA: University of California Press.
Eccles, R. G. (1985) *The Transfer Pricing Problem*, Lexington, MA: Lexington Books.

Espeland, W. (1984) "Blood and Money: Exploiting the Embodied Self," in J. A. Kotarba and A. Fontana (eds), *The Existential Self in Society*, Chicago, IL: University of Chicago Press.

Espeland, W. (1994) "Legally Mediated Identity: The National Environmental Policy Act and the Bureaucratic Construction of Interests," *Law and Society Review* 28: 1149–79.

Espeland, W. (1998) *The Struggle for Water: Politics, Rationality and Identity in the American Southwest*, Chicago, IL: University of Chicago Press.

Ferreira, M. K. L. (1997) "When 1 + 1√2: Making Mathematics in Central Brazil," *American Ethnologist* 24: 132–47.

Firth, R. (1967) "Themes in Economic Anthropology: A General Comment," in R. Firth (ed.), *Themes in Economic Anthropology*, London: Tavistock.

Fortgang, C. J. and Mayer, T. (1985) "Valuation in Bankruptcy," *UCLA Law Review* 32: 1061–1132.

Fraser, C. O. (1980) "Measurement in Psychology," *British Journal of Psychology* 71: 23–34.

Freyer, T. A. (1982) "Antebellum Commercial Law: Common Law Approaches to Secured Transactions," *Kentucky Law Journal* 70: 593–608.

Freyer, T. A. (1994) *Producers versus Capitalists: Constitutional Conflict in Antebellum America*, Charlottesville, VA: University Press of Virginia.

Geary, P. (1986) "Sacred Commodities: The Circulation of Medieval Relics," in A. Appadurai (ed.), *The Social Life of Things*, Cambridge: Cambridge University Press.

General Accounting Office (1995) *Budget Issues: Earmarking in the Federal Government* (GAO Report No. GAO/AIMD-95-216FS), Washington DC: U.S. Government Printing Office.

Gerber, D. (1982) "Cutting out Shylock: Elite Anti-Semitism and the Quest for Moral Order in the Mid-Nineteenth-Century American Market Place," *Journal of American History* 69(3): 615–37.

Gerriets, M. (1985) "Money in Early Christian Ireland According to the Irish Laws," *Comparative Studies in Society and History* 27: 323–39.

Geva, B. (1987) "From Commodity to Currency in Ancient History – On Commerce, Tyranny, and the Modern Law of Money," *Osgoode Hall Law Journal* 25: 115–57.

Gregory, C. A. (1982) *Gifts and Commodities*, London: Academic Press.

Grierson, P. (1959) "Commerce in the Dark Ages," *Transactions of the Royal Historical Society* 9: 123–40.

Grierson, P. (1977) *The Origins of Money*, London: Athlone Press.

Guyer, J. I. (1995) "Introduction: The Currency Interface and its Dynamics," in J. I. Guyer (ed.), *Money Matters: Instability, Values and Social Payments in the Modern History of West African Communities*, Portsmouth, NH: Heinemann.

Hart, K. (1986) "Heads or Tails? Two Sides of the Coin," *Man* 21: 637–56.

Hoppit, J. (1990) "Attitudes to Credit in Britain," *The Historical Journal* 33: 305–22.

Humphrey, C. and Hugh-Jones, S. (1992) "Introduction," in C. Humphrey and S. Hugh-Jones (eds), *Barter, Exchange and Value: An Anthropological Approach*, Cambridge: Cambridge University Press.

Hunt, M. R. (1996) *The Middling Sort: Commerce, Gender, and the Family in England 1680–1780*, Berkeley, CA: University of California Press.

Hurst, J. W. (1973) *A Legal History of Money in the United States, 1774–1970*, Lincoln, NE: University of Nebraska Press.

Kahneman, D., Knetsch, J. L., and Thaler, R. (1986a) "Fairness as a Constraint on Profit Seeking," *American Economic Review* 76: 728–41.

Kahneman, D., Knetsch, J. L. and Thaler, R. (1986b) "Fairness and the Assumptions of Economics," *Journal of Business* 59: 285–300.

Kaplan, S. L. (1996) *The Bakers of Paris and the Bread Question 1700–1775*, Durham, NC: Duke University Press.

Klinck, D. R. (1991) "Tracing a Trace: The Identity of Money in a Legal Doctrine," *Semiotica* 83: 1–31.

Landes, E. M. and Posner, R. A. (1978) "The Economics of the Baby Shortage," *Journal of Legal Studies* 7: 323–48.

Lasch, C. (1977) *Haven in a Heartless World*, New York: Pantheon.

Lea, S. E. G., Tarpy, R. M. and Webley, P. (1988) *The Individual in the Economy*, Cambridge: Cambridge University Press.

Leyshon, A. and Thrift, N. (1997) *Money/Space: Geographies of Monetary Transformation*, London: Routledge.

Mauss, M. (1990) *The Gift*, trans. W. D. Halls, New York: Norton.

Muldrew, C. (1993) "Interpreting the Market: The Ethics of Credit and Community Relations in Early Modern England," *Social History* 18: 163–83.

Myers, M. G. (1970) *A Financial History of the United States*, New York: Columbia University Press.

New York Times (1996) "Ada Louise Huxtable Receives Award," *New York Times*, July 25: B3.

Oakley, A. (1976) *Women's Work: The Housewife, Past and Present*, New York: Vintage.

Orléan, André (1992) "The Origin of Money," in F. J. Varela and J. P. Dupuy (eds), *Understanding Origins: Contemporary Views on the Origin of Life, Mind and Society*, Dordrecht: Kluwer.

Padgett, J. F. and Ansell, C. K. (1993) "Robust Action and the Rise of the Medici, 1400–1434," *American Journal of Sociology* 98: 1259–1319.

Parry, J. (1989) "On the Moral Perils of Exchange," in J. Parry and M. Bloch (eds), *Money and the Morality of Exchange*, Cambridge: Cambridge University Press.

Pollard, S. (1983) "Capitalism and Rationality: A Study of Measurements in British Coal Mining, ca. 1750–1850," *Explorations in Economic History* 20: 110–29.

Polo, M. (1958) *The Travels*, trans. R. E. Latham, London: Penguin.

Reddy, W. (1984) *The Rise of Market Culture: The Textile Trade and French Society, 1750–1900*, Cambridge: Cambridge University Press.

Reddy, W. (1987) *Money and Liberty in Modern Europe*, New York: Cambridge University Press.

Ritter, G. (1997) *Goldbugs and Greenbacks: The Antimonopoly Tradition and the Politics of Finance in America, 1865–1896*, Cambridge: Cambridge University Press.

Shipton, P. (1989) *Bitter Money: Cultural Economy and Some African Meanings of Forbidden Commodities*, Washington, DC: American Anthropological Association.

Siegel, R. (1994) "Home as Work: The First Women's Right Claims Concerning Wives' Household Labor, 1850–1880," *Yale Law Journal* 103: 1073–1217.

Simmel, G. (1978), *The Philosophy of Money*, trans. T. Bottomore and D. Frisby, Boston, MA: Routledge Kegan Paul.

Spufford, P. (1988) *Money and its Use in Medieval Europe*, Cambridge: Cambridge University Press.

Stacey, J. (1990) *Brave New Families: Stories of Domestic Upheaval in Late Twentieth Century America*, New York: Basic Books.

Stevens, M. L. (1996) "Kingdom and Coalition: Hierarchy and Autonomy in the Home Education Movement," unpublished doctoral dissertation, Northwestern University, Evanston, IL.

Stiglitz, J. E. (1993) *Economics*, New York: Norton.

Strathern, A. (1971) *The Rope of Moka: Big-Men and Ceremonial Exchange in Mount Hagen New Guinea*, Cambridge: Cambridge University Press.

Strathern, M. (1992) "Qualified Value: The Perspective of Gift Exchange," in C. Humphrey and S. Hugh-Jones (eds), *Barter, Exchange and Value: An Anthropological Approach*, Cambridge: Cambridge University Press.

Suetonius (1957) *The Twelve Caesars*, trans. R. Graves, London: Penguin.

Thaler, R. H. (1992) *The Winner's Curse: Paradoxes and Anomalies of Economic Life*, Princeton, NJ: Princeton University Press.

Thomas, K. (1987) "Numeracy in Early Modern England," *Transactions of the Royal Historical Society* 37: 103–32.

Thompson, E. P. (1971) "The Moral Economy of the English Crowd in the Eighteenth Century," *Past and Present* 50: 76–136.

Titmuss, R. M. (1971) *The Gift Relationship*, New York: Pantheon.

Venkatesh, S. (1997) "The Social Organization of Street Gang Activity in an Urban Ghetto," *American Journal of Sociology* 103(1): 82–111.

Webley, P. and Wilson, R. (1989) "Social Relationships and the Unacceptability of Money as a Gift," *Journal of Social Psychology* 129: 85–91.

Weinberg, H. R. (1982) "Commercial Paper in Economic Theory and Legal History," *Kentucky Law Journal* 70: 567–92.

Weiner, A. B. (1992) *Inalienable Possessions: The Paradox of Keeping-While-Giving*, Berkeley, CA: University of California Press.

West, R. C. (1977) *Banking Reform and the Federal Reserve, 1863–1923*, Ithaca, NY: Cornell University Press.

Wilde, O. (1980) *Lady Windermere's Fan*, New York: Norton.

Wittgenstein, L. (1958) *Philosophical Investigations*, 3rd edn, trans. G. E. M. Anscombe, New York: Macmillan.

Zelizer, V. A. (1985) *Pricing the Priceless Child: The Changing Social Value of Children*, New York: Basic Books.

Zelizer, V. A. (1994) *The Social Meaning of Money: Pin Money, Paychecks, Poor Relief and Other Currencies*, New York: Basic Books.

Zelizer, V. A. (1996) "Multiple Markets: Multiple Cultures," paper presented at the *Conference on Common Values, Social Diversity, and Cultural Conflict*, Center for Advanced Study in the Behavioral Sciences, October.

Zelizer, V. A. (1998) "The Proliferation of Social Currencies," in M. Callon (ed.), *The Law of Markets*, Oxford: Blackwell.

17 The Social Meaning of Money

Viviana A. Zelizer

The Domestic Production of Monies

Allowance versus a Joint Account: The Allowance as "Bad" Money

In February 1925, Reverend Howard Melish, rector of the Holy Trinity church in Brooklyn, addressing the New York Women's City Club on the importance of a wife's economic independence, related the following anecdote: "Yesterday," Melish told his audience, "I asked an old lady . . . what her idea was of a happy marriage. Without an instant's hesitation she replied 'An allowance.' " But the anecdote backfired. The next day, in an editorial entitled "They Want More Than That," the *New York Times* expressed the new, critical view of allowances: "Admitting . . . the equality of service rendered by wife and husband in . . . the family unit, why should the one rather than the other have an 'allowance' and . . . why should the 'allowance' be determined by the husband and be granted as a favor?" Allowances, concluded the editorial, "are for inferiors from superiors," and therefore an inappropriate currency for the modern woman.[1]

In the 1920s, even as popular support for allowances intensified, there was also a growing criticism of the allowance system from those who saw it as an inequitable and even degrading form of domestic money. Christine Frederick proclaimed it a "relic of some past time when women were supposed to be too inexperienced to handle money." Frederick, a leader of the popular household-efficiency movement, rejected the allowance as an "unbusinesslike" scheme that undermined the modern goal of running the home as rationally as a factory or an office. Benjamin R. Andrews, a noted authority in home economics, explained that a housewife's "compensation as worker is of the same kind as that of all workers – it is the living that she enjoys." That her wages were not "in the form of money income as is the pay envelope of her husband for his outside employment" hardly mattered. The wife received "real wages," meaning her "food, clothing, shelter and cultural satisfactions of all kinds," which were equal to her husband's benefits after his cash income was "transmuted by family expenditure into food, clothing," and the like. "His pay and her pay," Andrews concluded, "are ordinarily identical."[2]

Most "anti-allowance" advocates, however, did not press for domestic salaries but supported a democratic "joint control of the purse." The modern "good husband," according to a playful definition in the *American Magazine*, was a "fifty-fifty" man who "takes his wife into his confidence as a real partner and plays fair with her in every detail . . . (hardly ever) short-changing her." "Bad" husbands were

Original publication: Extracts from Zelizer, Viviana A., "The Domestic Production of Monies," chapter 2 in *The Social Meaning of Money* (Basic Books, New York, 1994).

either "fog throwers" who "never let their wives in on a thing. . . . They take their wives 'to have, to hold, and to baffle' "; or they were "dime tossers" who concealed their finances but told their wives they make "barely enough to live on. He gives her a dollar on Monday with the air of a philanthropist, and asks her on Friday where and how she squandered it." The "holdout," on the other hand, pretended to allow his wife to handle their family funds but "always holds out a substantial part of it through various misrepresentations."[3]

The new, improved domestic money was to be shared, designed to minimize gender as well as age inequality. Families were urged to "hold a periodic council around a table, with frank and courteous discussion of its ways and means, and with due consideration of how, and how much, each member can contribute in work, in money, in cooperation, toward . . . this whole business of the home." The father and mother would act as a family board of directors, allocating money according to its diverse needs. The new financial system would also include a specified sum for each family member's personal expenses, to be considered a budgetary entitlement and not a gift. The "personal purse" was not just a man's privilege: As the *Ladies' Home Journal* explained, "whether it be in the few pennies of childhood or the . . . many dollars of maturity, [personal money] seems to be a sacred possession. . . . There is no liberty without some money that belongs to us and not to a budget." Husbands were reminded that it was "dishonesty" to claim, "'I will keep this much or that much for myself and the rest belongs to the home.'" If the "family purse" was to become a true "partnership fund," according to the new financial agenda, then "all belongs to the home and the man's share for personal spending cannot . . . take precedence over the shares of other members of the family."[4]

But how many couples actually adopted the new domestic dollar? The 1928 *Harper's* study "Marriage and Money" found that, of 200 respondents, only 54 had what the magazine described as the more "feminist" financial arrangement: a joint bank account or common purse. In 1929, in *Middletown*, the Lynds reported that most couples depended on "all manner of provisional, more or less bickering" financial arrangements. And some two decades later, *Crestwood Heights*, a study of suburban life, discovered that despite democratic norms dictating cooperative spending of the husband's income, "the wife does not know, even roughly, how much her husband earns." Wives still had to "manipulate their household allowances" in order to obtain "unreported" personal funds. Tellingly, vaudeville comedians of the 1920s continued to get laughs by joking about women's domestic strategies: "Oh, how she always liked to clean my clothes; she often used to take spots out of my clothes. One night she took three spots out of my trousers – a five, ten, and a twenty spot." If women wore trousers, went another standard joke, a wife "would get up in the middle of the night and steal money from herself."[5] Although the actual finances of housewives may not have significantly improved, by 1930 the symbolic meaning of a wife's allowance was changing from a sign of independence and domestic control to a form of financial submissiveness.

A Husband's Allowance: Domestic Money in the Working Class

Domestic money was not defined only by gender, but also by the social class of the household. The working-class wife, suggested one home-economics textbook, could well be envied by wealthier women. Although the latter seldom have "ready money in hand," the wife of a workingman often "determines the . . . financial policy of the family and has control of the necessary funds." Indeed, in her 1917 study, the social investigator and settlement house activist Mary K. Simkhovitch found that as a family's income increased, "the proportion controlled by the wife diminishes till often she becomes simply a beneficiary of the husband." Paradoxically, class – in most ethnic groups – seemed to be inversely related to gender in the power structure of domestic money. In her 1910 study of Homestead, Pennsylvania, Margaret F. Byington discovered that the men "are inclined to trust all financial matters to their wives." On payday, workmen turned over their wages to their wives, asking "no questions as to what it goes for."[6] In working-class families, the allowance usually was designated for husbands and children, not wives. The social investigator Louise B. More's analysis of wage earners' budgets found that an allowance for "spending money" was made in 108 out of the 200 families she investigated: 94 men received all or part of the amount given; and in 29 families one or two children had an allowance. In most working-class families, it seems to have been the wife who "doles out spending money according to the needs and the earnings of each." The historian Leslie Tentler's study of working-class women from 1900 to 1930 concludes that this financial arrangement of working-class families granted a great deal of economic power to wives, making the home "their fief." Indeed, to contemporary middle-class observers, it appeared that husbands "who accept a daily dole from their purse-keeping wives are usually subject beings."[7]

But these studies and observations may have idealized, and thus overestimated, the economic clout of working-class wives. To be sure, administering the family income involved women actively in domestic finances, allowing them a degree of managerial control. What remains unclear, however, is their actual discretionary power. In the first place, money management in families with limited money incomes was an arduous task. Although working-class standards of living improved at the turn of the century, family budget studies show the precariousness of their financial lives. Husbands' and children's wages went almost exclusively to food, clothing, shelter, and insurance. And being the cashier put a heavy burden of responsibility on wives: household money troubles could be conveniently blamed (by family members as well as outsiders) on female mismanagement rather than on a tight budget or an irregular labor market.[8]

More important, as soon as there was any surplus income, a wife's apparent grip over the purse strings quickly loosened. Although the ideal good husband was indeed expected to turn over all his wages intact to his wife, receiving one or two dollars a week for his personal use, many did not. Studies of New York's West Side conducted in 1914 found that while "there is a current belief that the American workingman turns his wages over to his wife on Saturday night and allows her to apportion all expenditures," how much the wife actually received from the husband's wages and what he kept back "depends on the personal adjustment between them and not on a recognized rule." Evidence on precisely how the money was allocated is very limited. But the West Side study suggests that the outcome was usually rigged in favor of the husband. As one Italian wife explained: "Of course they don't give all they make. They're men and you never know their ways." The settlement-house worker Elsa Herzfeld's 1905 investigation of New York's West Side families found that while some husbands gave their wives their entire wages, receiving back their carfare and "beer money," other men gave "as much as 'he feels like' or 'as much as he has left after Saturday night.'" One husband deposited most of his earnings in the bank and put the amount "he thinks necessary for the household in the glass on the mantel." Sometimes, noted Herzfeld, "the husband does not tell the wife the amount of his wages."[9] Similarly, a later study of unskilled Chicago wage earners in 1924 found that, when asked about their husbands' weekly earnings, over two-thirds of the wives gave lesser amounts than the actual earnings found on the pay-roll. The investigator concluded that the man "may not give his entire earnings to his wife, but may simply give her the amount he thinks she should spend for the family."[10]

Thus, the idealized view of a solidary family economy coordinated and controlled by the wife concealed competing claims for money within the family. The husband's pay envelope was not always intact on arrival. Neither were the children's. Tantalized by the attractions of a consumer culture, children increasingly withheld or manipulated their earnings. David Nasaw found that, in the early part of the twentieth century, wage-earning children "who were obedient in every other regard did what they had to to preserve some part of their earnings for themselves. They lied, they cheated, they hid away their nickels and dimes, they doctored their pay envelopes." Indeed, according to one report, mothers did not like it when their sons worked in places where they were tipped "because it is then impossible to know how much money is rightfully his." Unlike the wage, a child's tip was considered "his own." While working girls were more likely than their brothers to hand their wages over intact, not all of them did. Italian working girls on the New York West Side told investigators how easy it was to "knock down" a paycheck when they made overtime: "Whatever you make is written outside in pencil. . . . That's easy to fix – you have only to rub it out, put on whatever it usually is, and pocket the change."[11]

Even the portion of money that the wife did receive and control was limited to housekeeping money. As with wealthier women, the working-class wife had no right, and much less access, to a personal fund. Pocket money for personal expenses was a male prerogative, or a working child's right. The working-class husband's allowance was thus a very different kind of money than the allowance of middle-class wives. Although partly allocated for useful expenses, food or clothing or transportation, it was also a legitimate fund for personal pleasures. Indeed, the historian Kathy Peiss's study of leisure among working-class women in turn-of-the-century New York clearly shows that men could afford to pay for their amusements – drinking in saloons, attending movies and the theater, or buying tobacco – but their wives had no money left for personal recreation. Looking back to the life of his parents in the early twentieth century, sixty-four-year-old Monsignor Lorenzo Lacasse recalled: "When my father brought his pay home, he'd lay his envelope on the corner of the table, to the last penny. My mother handled it. For a few extra cents, he sold chocolate bars in the mills." The extra "little money," however, was "for his expenses, for a glass of beer once in a while."[12] Thus, women's money retained a collective identity, whereas men's and children's money was differentiated and individualized. If a working-class wife needed more money, her options were limited. With little access to credit accounts, she turned to kin or neighbors, but often also to pawnbrokers and moneylenders. Sometimes women relied on their younger children for extra cash. During a government investigation of industrial home-work conducted in 1918, one mother explained that her little boy helped her to wire rosary beads at home because she needed "some money of her own." Another mother needed false teeth and "thought the children might just as well help to buy them."[13]

Novelists captured some of the contest, confusion, and pain involved in the ear-marking of working-class domestic monies. Take, for instance, Maisie's indignation – in John Dos Passos's *The 42nd Parallel* – when she went to the savings bank to deposit, in the children's schooling account, her baby's five-dollar "birthday money" sent by her brother Bill only to discover that her husband Mac had secretly withdrawn $53.75. When Mac comes home that evening, she angrily confronts him for "stealing money from your own children" to surely squander it "on drink or on some other woman." She did not know that Mac had needed the money to pay for his Uncle Tim's funeral. When Mac promises to replace the money, she ridicules him for not being "man enough to make a decent living for your wife and children so you have to take it out of your poor little innocent children's bank account." The incident ends with Mac walking out on his family.[14] In Anzia Yezierska's 1925 *Bread Givers*, a semi-autobiographical account of growing up in New York's Lower East Side, the popular – and recently rediscovered – narrator of Jewish immigrant life tells of her parents' disputes over their children's earnings. Her father insisted that a tenth of the children's wages be donated to charity (as prescribed by Orthodox Jewish law); "and he belonged to so many societies and lodges that even without our ever getting anything we wanted for ourselves, the money didn't stretch enough to pay for all the charities Father had to have." When his wife reminded him that the children needed money for clothes, accusing him of giving charity with the "blood money of your children's wages," the father countered that to "stop my charities . . . It's like stopping the breath of God in me."[15]

As home-economics experts began to encourage joint control of the domestic dollar, the working-class financial system lost its legitimacy. Studies of English working-class families suggest that there was a shift to the middle-class system of housekeeping allowance for wives. Limited data make it difficult to determine whether the same was true for the United States. During the 1920s, when the Lynds studied Muncie, Indiana, they reported that it was rare for a husband to turn over his paycheck and allow his wife control over the household economy. But class differences seem to have persisted: by 1938, according to the *Ladies' Home Journal* national survey on money, only 38 percent of women in income groups under $1,500 received an allowance, compared to 62 percent of those in families earning more than $1,500.[16]

Pin Money versus Real Money: Defining Women's Earnings

What happened when women's money did not come from their husbands' paychecks? When women worked for nonrelatives, whether at home or for wages, the boundary between that income and serious money was still preserved, only in different ways. In the working class, for instance, a married woman's income, usually earned by caring for boarders, taking in sewing or laundry, or, among farm families, by selling butter, eggs, or poultry, did not have the same visibility as her husband's paycheck.[17] Since her labor was part of a woman's traditional repertoire of domestic tasks, the money she made was merged into the family's housekeeping money and usually spent on home and family, for clothing or food. Legally, in fact, until the early decades of the twentieth century, those domestic earnings belonged to the husband. And the courts staunchly opposed converting a wife's money into her tangible property. In a growing number of personal-injury cases, where the law had to decide whether the husband or the wife was entitled to recover for a woman's inability to work, as well as in claims brought up by creditors, the courts insisted on distinguishing between the domestic dollar and an earned wage. If a wife worked at home, even if her labor was performed for strangers, caring for a boarder or nursing a neighbor, that money was not a real earning and therefore belonged to her husband. Ironically, but significantly, in some states a wife's domestic earnings could become her property but only as her husband's gift.[18]

Earned domestic money, much like the allowance, thus retained a separate identity as a gift, not as real money. Money earned by married women in the labor force was also special and different. It even had its own name. The term "pin money," which in seventeenth-century England had meant a separate, independent income for a wife's personal use – and was included as a formal clause in upper-class marriage contracts – lost its elitist British origins in turn-of-the-century America, and now meant the supplementary household income earned by wives. Still it was treated as a more frivolous, less serious earning than the husband's. As a 1903 article in *Harper's Bazar* aptly remarked: "No man works for pin money. The very idea makes one smile."[19]

The boundary between women's earned income and the husband's salary was also marked by their different uses. Historian John Modell, for instance, suggests that among late nineteenth-century, native-born American families, "all dollars were not equal," and women's income (as well as children's) was spent differently and less freely than the husband's. Among farm families, women's egg money and butter money were distinguished from husbands' wheat money or corn money. The historian Joan Jensen suggests there existed a dual economy, with women and children providing for living expenses while husbands paid for mortgages and new machinery. An Illinois farmer's wife, who enjoyed writing and kept a large correspondence, explained that despite her husband's complaints about the costs of her writing materials, "as a matter of course, I pay for it out of my own scanty income." Her neighbors, however, criticized her unprofitable pastime, while they proudly bragged about "how many . . . eggs and old hens they have sold." For urban middle-class women, discreet forms of earning pin money at home (making preserves, pickles, or poundcake; knitting shawls or sweaters; or raising poultry or Angora cats) were approved, but, again, only for certain types of expenses – charity, for example, or "a daughter's lessons in music or art." A "little stream of silver will flow into her exchequer," observed an article in *Woman's Home Companion*, "and at a pinch buy a new bonnet or provide a treat for a birthday, subscribe to a magazine or take tickets for a concert."[20]

During the 1920s and 1930s, as more married women entered the labor force, their earnings, regardless of the sums involved, were still defined as pin money, categorized as supplementary income, and used for the family's extra expenses or earmarked by more affluent couples as discretionary "fun" money. For instance, in 1928 one woman told an *Outlook* reporter that she reserved her income exclusively to buy clothes. Another explained, "We blow my money on extra trips abroad, antiques, anything extravagant." Others used their salary to pay the maid's wages and saved the rest. A story in the *Saturday Evening Post*, four years later, reported on the persistent "wife-keeps-all-theory" of wives' earnings. Couples in which the wife was employed were asked what her money was used for: "Keeps it all for herself . . . saves it, spends it, just as she likes," was a common response: "the important thing [is] . . . she mustn't help her husband out."[21]

Keeping Money Domestic

Domestic money is thus a very special kind of currency. It would be difficult to understand its changing meanings, allocation, and uses in the United States between the 1870s and 1930s without an awareness of the new cultural "code" and accompanying social changes. In the case of married women, their money was routinely set apart from serious money by a complex mixture of ideas about family life, by a changing power structure within the family, and by social class. Conventional expectations of the family as a special, noncommercial sphere made any overt form of market intrusion in domestic affairs not only distasteful but a direct threat to family solidarity. Thus, regardless of its sources, once money had entered the household, its allocation, calculation, and uses were subject to a set of domestic rules distinct from the rules of the market. Family money was nonfungible; social barriers prevented its conversion into ordinary wages.

But family culture did not affect its members equally. Gender introduced a further type of nonmarket distinction in the domestic flow of funds: a wife's money was not the same kind of money as her husband's. When a wife did not earn wages, gender shaped many things:

1. *The allocation of her money.* In the hierarchically structured family, husbands gave wives part of their income as a gift or, more rarely, as an entitlement. To obtain additional money, wives were restricted to asking and cajoling, or else stealing.
2. *The timing of this allocation.* It either had no prescribed timing (dole method), so that to obtain money a wife had to ask each time; or it followed a weekly or monthly pattern (allowance).
3. *The uses of her money.* Wives' money meant housekeeping money, a necessary allotment restricted to family expenses and excluding personal spending money. Pocket money was a budgetary expectation for husbands and children, but not for wives.
4. *The quantity of her money.* Wives usually received small sums of money. The amount of an allowance was not determined by the efficiency or even the quantity of a wife's domestic contributions, but by prevalent beliefs about what was a proper amount for a wife to receive. Therefore, a larger paycheck for the husband did not need to translate into a rise in the housekeeping allowance. On the basis of gender economics, it might in fact simply increase a husband's personal money.[22]

Changes in gender roles and family structure influenced the meaning and methods of allocation of married women's money. The traditional dole or "asking" method became, as the consumer role of women expanded, not only inefficient but also inappropriate in increasingly egalitarian marriages. The allowance, praised as a more equitable method of allocation in the early part of the century, was in turn condemned by home-efficiency experts of the 1920s and 1930s as an unsatisfactory payment for modern wives. The joint account emerged as the new cultural ideal. What about the uses of married women's money? In contrast to the variety of allocation methods, the earmarking of a wife's housekeeping income for collective consumption remained remarkably persistent. Despite the increasing individualization of consumption patterns and the encouragement by home-economics experts to allot personal funds for each family member in the domestic budget, personal spending money for wives still was obtained by subterfuge or spent with guilt.

Gender influenced women's money even when their income was earned. A wife's wages or pin money, regardless of its quantity and even when it brought the family a needed income, remained a less fundamental kind of money than her husband's wages. It was either collectivized or trivialized, merged into the housekeeping fund and thus undifferentiated from collective income, or else treated as a supplementary earning designated either for family expenses (a child's education or a vacation) or for frivolous purposes (clothing or jewelry). The trivialization of women's earnings extended beyond the private domestic economy. For the opponents of women's labor, pin money was a socially irresponsible currency, a luxury income that threatened the wages of the real provider. Thus, despite strong evidence that pin money was often in fact a "family coupling pin, the only means of holding the family together and of making ends meet," women's earnings were systematically stigmatized as "money for trinkets and trifles."[23]

The circulation of domestic money was not shaped by gender alone, however. Social class added an additional set of restrictions on the liquidity of money. The middle-class method of allocating household money was reversed in the working class, where wives handed out allowances instead of receiving them. The working-class wife's managerial power was thus greater than her middle-class counterpart, although her discretionary power may not have differed significantly. The complex cultural and social "life" of domestic money thus shows the limits of a purely instrumental, rationalized model of market money that conceals qualitative differences among kinds of money in the modern world.[24] Domestic monies are distinct transfers; not simply a sanitized, impersonal type of economic exchange, they are meaningful, socially constructed currencies, shaped by the domestic sphere in which they circulate and by the gender and social class of domestic "money handlers."

Children also handled domestic money. In fact, between the 1870s and 1930s, children's money became the subject of enormous controversy within families and among educational experts. Children, like their mothers, were caught in the predicament of practicing consumerism without having income of their own. As child labor laws put most children out of work, the dilemma involved children of all social classes. Authorities agreed that money should not be doled to the child: such gifts from parents, relatives, and friends made "a beggar of the child." Nor was a domestic wage appropriate: such payments threatened the boundaries between home and marketplace. The allowance – as the child's rightful portion of the family income – emerged as the proper income for children. But it had a different meaning, method of allocation, and uses than the allowance of middle-class wives or working-class men. Closely supervised by parents, the allowance was defined primarily as educational money, teaching children proper social and moral, as well as consumer, skills.[25]

To be sure, Marx and Engels were partly correct when they accused the bourgeoisie of reducing family relations "to a mere money relation." As we saw, money concerns did increasingly permeate the American household. In fact, in the 1920s some observers ironically predicted that the national enthusiasm for rationalized housekeeping and budgeting would turn "Home, Sweet Home," into "Home, Solvent Home," with "Ma and Pa a couple of cash registers, and the kiddies little adding machines."[26] Yet, such nightmare visions of a commercialized world failed to capture the complexity, and reciprocity, of the monetization phenomenon. Money came into American homes, but it was transformed in the process, becoming part of the structure of social relations and meanings of the family.

As we reach the turn of the twenty-first century, this domestication of legal tender still remains somewhat of a mystery. As households are being revolutionized by high divorce rates, as remarriage creates new kin networks, as single-parent units dramatically multiply while unmarried heterosexual or homosexual couples form new families, as women's paid employment expands and as home-based employment reappears, we barely know how it all shapes domestic monies.[27]

Although work such as the cognitive anthropologist Jean Lave's indicates that domestic earmarking is alive and well today, researchers have been primarily concerned with how the relative earnings of a couple modify the domestic power structure, in particular, the effect of a wife's increased earnings. And they find that indeed a married woman's higher income will generally increase her financial autonomy and domestic influence. But as they probe further, scholars of family life uncover some puzzling patterns. Take, for instance, the findings of *American Couples*, an extensive survey of contemporary households, that sometimes a wife's paycheck – even when she earns more than her husband – makes little difference to her domestic power: she still "places her financial destiny in his hands, granting him ultimate control over their money." A financial adviser reports similar cases, such as the client who "used to fight tooth and nail to win commissions at work, then would return home and obligingly hand her checks over to her husband. He would then determine the amount of her monthly allowance."[28]

When it comes to the division of household labor, a woman's income also works in unexpected ways. Although her money does have some impact on how much her husband will participate in domestic duties, the effect is remarkably small, and sometimes paradoxical. When sociologist Arlie Hochschild – as part of her study of dual-career families – looked at husbands who earned *less* than their wives, she discovered that none of them shared the housework.[29] What Hochschild calls the "logic of the pocketbook" also fails when it comes to the uses of women's wages. Especially in cases where wives provide the secondary income, her earnings are often earmarked for particular expenses, such as children's education, mortgage payments, baby-sitting and housecleaning expenses, or luxuries. The authors of *American Couples* point to the "interesting accounting system" in which the husband's money is defined as family money but "the wife may think that the money she earns is outside the joint account." Significantly, however, despite the prevalent assumption that her money is for personal frills while his money is communal property, in fact the wife's extra income is more likely than her husband's to be spent for family needs than on her personal needs. An important British study of money and marriage provides further evidence of how the differential use of money by women works; it appears that when wives control household finances, a higher proportion of the collective income is apt to be spent on food and daily living expenses than when husbands are in charge. It seems that husbands are still more likely than their wives to retain personal spending money.[30]

As they try to explain contemporary domestic transfers, researchers have begun to examine more closely what happens to income as it becomes part of the household. Most analysts conclude that the meanings, allocation, and uses of domestic money depend primarily on the relative persistence of the "male-provider" ideology. As long as couples adhere to the notion of the husband as the primary earner of income, it does not really matter how much a woman earns; her income will be treated as different, less significant, and ultimately dispensable. For Arlie Hochschild, it is the couple's beliefs about the relative power of men and women that shape the household's "moral accounting system"; wives who earned more than their husbands actually "balanced" their greater power by doing more housework.[31] Other scholars focus on the effects of accounting systems in the household, suggesting that separate accounting systems for husband and wife produce more equitable and rationally allocated household finances, while pooled incomes lead to unequal domestic arrangements. In the end, however, as two experts in contemporary couples have argued, the effect of separate incomes is tied to gender ideology: If couples reject the male-provider role, then a separate accounting system will increase wives' domestic power; yet in traditional households a woman's separate income is marginalized as pin money, bringing her no additional power.[32]

The sociologist Kathleen Gerson's recent research moves a step beyond these findings. Her look at variations in the family participation of American men shows that wives' earnings help shape the domestic economy, although not in the expected ways. The wife's share of earned income does not translate directly into power within the household, but the combination of her income and long-term career prospects may redefine the social relations of some couples as well as the husband's identity, shifting away from that of a traditional breadwinner to the more equal arrangements of what Gerson calls "involved fathers." And while traditional husbands continue to treat their wives' income as – in the words of one of her respondents – extra "gravy," the more egalitarian couples, albeit still a minority, pooled their monies, treating all dollars as equal.[33] From one perspective, this interpretation corresponds closely to my observations on the changing organization of money in American households. Contrary to the simple equation of money with power and rationality, amounts of income do not in themselves determine their uses or control; the allocation of household money always depends on complex, subtle understandings about relations among household members. Furthermore, an ideological explanation looks quite incomplete: in situation after situation, we have seen ideologies themselves changing in interaction with existing practices and social relations: remember how the exigencies of managing increasingly commercialized consumption undermined the view of a wife's domestic funds as her husband's gift. It would be surprising not to find a similar interaction among ideology, practice, and social relations operating today.

In addition, ties to third parties – employers, relatives, authorities, and, of course, children – strongly affect the ways that household members organize their use of money. . . . It seems likely that those kinds of ties affect household monetary practices today. For example, a recent study documents children's access to family income, estimating that, on average, a child receives about 40 percent of an adult share of that income. Clearly, in this and in other ways, the presence of children significantly affects the allocation of household income.[34] If a wife's share of the household income is no longer defined as a gift from her husband, the same is true, to some extent, of the children's share. However, this does not mean at all that gift transfers – monetary or otherwise – are disappearing in favor of some market-driven neutrality.

Notes

1   *New York Times*, March 2 and 3, 1925.
2   Christine Frederick, *Household Engineering* (Chicago: American School of Home Economics, 1919), p. 269; Benjamin Richard Andrews, *Economics of the Household; Its Administration and Finance* (New York: Macmillan Company, 1935), p. 398.
3   Hazel Kyrk, *Economic Problems of the Family* (New York: Harper and Brothers, 1933), pp. 182–83; H. I. Phillips, "My Adventures as a Bold, Bad Budgeteer," *American Magazine* 97 (January 1924): 64.
4   Alice Ames Winter, "The Family Purse," *Ladies' Home Journal* 42 (May 1925): 185; Mata R. Friend, *Earning and Spending Family Income* (New York: Appleton, 1930), p. 112; Andrews, *Economics of the Household*, p. 554.
5   Hamilton and MacGowan, "Marriage and Money," p. 440; Robert S. Lynd and Helen Merrell Lynd, *Middletown* (New York: Harcourt Brace Jovanovich, 1956), p. 127, n. 24; John R. Seeley, R. Alexander Sim, and Elizabeth W. Loosley, *Crestwood Heights* (New York: Wiley, 1956), pp. 184–85; W. M. McNally, "A New Monologue on Marriage," *McNally's Bulletin: Periodical of Sketches and Jokes*, No. 8, 1922, p. 4.
6   Mary Hinman Abel, *Successful Family Life on the Moderate Income, its Foundation in a Fair Start. The Man's Earnings. The Woman's Contribution. The Cooperation of the Community.* (Philadelphia, London: J. B. Lippincott Company, 1927), p. 5; Mary K. Simkhovitch, *The City Worker's World in America* (New York: Macmillan, 1917); Margaret E. Byington, *Homestead* (New York: Charities Publication Committee, 1910), p. 10. The available evidence suggests that a similar domestic financial arrangement applied to different ethnic groups. See, for example, Ruth S. True, *The Neglected Girl* (New York: Survey, 1914); Micaela di Leonardo, *The Varieties of Ethnic Experience* (Ithaca, NY: Cornell University Press, 1984); John Bodnar, *The Transplanted* (Bloomington, IN: Indiana University Press, 1987); research material from Ewa Morawska, 1985 (personal communication). However, Louise Lamphere, in "From Working Daughters to Working Mothers: Production and Reproduction in an Industrial Community," *American Ethnologist* 13 (1986): 118–30, suggests possible ethnic variations. On Jewish families, see Andrew R. Heinze, *Adapting to Abundance* (New York: Columbia University Press, 1990), chap. 6. Further research should better illuminate the impact of ethnicity as well as race on domestic money.
7   Louise Bolard More, *Wage-Earners' Budgets* (New York: Henry Holt, 1907); True, *The Neglected Girl*, p. 48; Leslie W. Tentler, *Wage-Earning Women* (New York: Oxford University Press, 1982), p. 177; *New York Times*, January 30, 1923.
8   See Daniel Horowitz, *The Morality of Spending* (Baltimore, MD: Johns Hopkins University Press, 1985), p. 60. Determining the impact of a particular household

financial arrangement on the relative power of family members is a difficult task. Not only can power be measured in a number of ways, but each dimension of monetary power within the family – whether consuming, saving, investment, or managing – has very special meanings that are culturally and socially constructed. More research is needed to define and understand the relative degree of power of the "cashier" working-class wife.

9 Katherine Anthony, *Mothers Who Must Earn* (New York: Survey Associates, 1914), pp. 135–36; Louise C. Odencrantz, *Italian Women in Industry* (New York: Russell Sage, 1919), p. 176; Elsa Herzfeld, *Family Monographs* (New York: James Kempster Printing Co., 1905), p. 50.

10 Leila Houghteling, *Income and Standard of Living of Unskilled Laborers in Chicago* (Chicago, IL: University of Chicago Press, 1927), p. 37.

11 David Nasaw, *Children of the City* (New York: Anchor, 1985), pp. 131–32; *Boyhood and Lawlessness* (New York: Survey, 1914), p. 69; True, *The Neglected Girl*, p. 49. See also Viviana A. Zelizer, *Pricing the Priceless Child: The Changing Social Value of Children* (New York: Basic Books, 1987), pp. 97–112. On the increased individualization of children's income, especially after the 1920s, see Judith E. Smith, *Family Connections* (Albany: State University of New York Press, 1985); Elizabeth Ewen, *Immigrant Women in the Land of Dollars* (New York: Monthly Review, 1985).

12 Kathy Peiss, *Cheap Amusements* (Philadelphia, PA: Temple University Press, 1986), pp. 23–24; Tamara K. Hareven and Randolph Langenbach, *Amoskeag* (New York: Pantheon, 1978), p. 258.

13 "Industrial Home Work of Children," U.S. Department of Labor, Children's Bureau Publication no. 100 (Washington, DC: Government Printing Office, 1924), p. 22. On women's alternative sources of income, see Kathryn M. Neckerman, "The Emergence of 'Underclass' Family Patterns, 1900–1940," in Michael B. Katz (ed.), *The "Underclass" Debate* (Princeton: Princeton University Press, 1993), pp. 202–3; Ellen Ross, " 'Fierce Questions and Taunts': Married Life in Working-Class London, 1870–1914," *Feminist Studies* 8 (Fall 1982): 590; Melanie Tebbutt, *Making Ends Meet: Pawnbroking and Working-Class Credit* (New York: St. Martin's, 1983); Pat Ayers and Jan Lambertz, "Marriage Relations, Money, and Domestic Violence in Working-Class Liverpool, 1919–39," in Jane Lewis (ed.), *Labour & Love: Women's Experiences of Home and Family, 1850–1940* (Oxford: Blackwell, 1986), pp. 203–4.

14 John Dos Passos, *The 42nd Parallel* (New York: New American Library, 1979 [1930]), pp. 140–41.

15 Anzia Yezierska, *Bread Givers* (New York: Persea Books, 1975 [1925]), pp. 89–90.

16 Lynd and Lynd, *Middletown*, p. 127 n. 24. Henry F. Pringle, "What Do the Women of America Think about Money?," *Ladies' Home Journal* 55 (April 1938): 102. See also Friend, *Earning and Spending Family Income*, p. 108. On English families, see Laura Oren, "The Welfare of Women in Laboring Families: England, 1860–1950," *Feminist Studies* 1 (Winter–Spring 1973): 115; Peter N. Stearns, "Working-Class Women in Britain, 1890–1914," in Martha Vicinus (ed.), *Suffer and Be Still* (Bloomington, IN: Indiana University Press, 1972), p. 116; Jan Pahl, "Patterns of Money Management Within Marriage," *Journal of Social Policy* 9 (1980): 332–33.

17 Joan M. Jensen, "Cloth, Butter, and Boarders: Women's Household Production for the Market," *Review of Radical Political Economics* 12 (1980): 14–24; Laurel Thatcher Ulrich, *Good Wives* (New York: Oxford University Press, 1983), pp. 45–47; Ewa Morawska, *For Bread with Butter* (New York: Cambridge University Press, 1985), pp. 134–35.

18 W. W. Thornton, "Personal Services Rendered by Wife to Husband under Contract," *Central Law Journal* 183 (1900); Helen Z. M. Rodgers, "Married Women's Earnings," 64 *Albany Law Journal* 384 (1902); Joseph Warren, "Husband's Right to Wife's Services,"

38 *Harvard Law Review* 421 (1925). Starting in the mid-nineteenth century, Married Women's Property Acts granted wives the right to own and control their property but focused primarily on inherited property. Married women's right to their earnings were excluded by the acts and were incorporated only slowly and with much resistance by amendments or later statutes. See Percy Edwards, "Is the Husband Entitled to His Wife's Earnings?," *Canadian Law Times* 13 (1893): 159–76; Rodgers, "Married Women's Earnings"; Warren, "Husband's Right to Wife's Services"; Crozier, "Marital Support," pp. 37–41; Carole Shammas, Marylynn Salmon, and Michael Dahlin, *Inheritance in America* (New Brunswick, NJ: Rutgers University Press, 1987), pp. 88–89, 96–97, 163.

19 Priscilla Leonard, "Pin Money versus Moral Obligations," *Harper's Bazar* 37 (November 1903): 1060. On England, see Lawrence Stone, *The Family, Sex, and Marriage* (New York: Harper and Row, 1977), p. 244, and Susan Staves, "Pin Money," in O. M. Brack, Jr. (ed.), *Studies in Eighteenth-Century Culture* 14, (Madison, WI: University of Wisconsin Press, 1985), pp. 47–77. See also Catherine Gore, *Pin-Money* (Boston: Allen and Ticknor, 1834), a popular early-nineteenth-century British "silver-fork" novel.

20 John Modell, "Patterns of Consumption, Acculturation, and Family Income: Strategies in Late Nineteenth-Century America," in Tamara K. Hareven and Maris A. Vinovskis (eds), *Family and Population in Nineteenth-Century America* (Princeton, NJ: Princeton University Press, 1978), p. 225; Joan M. Jensen, "Cloth, Butter, and Boarders: Women's Household Production for the Market," *Review of Radical Political Economics* 12 (1980): 14–24; "Story of a Farmer's Wife," in Holt, *The Life Stories*, p. 99; Sangster, "Shall Wives Earn Money?," p. 32. See also Thornton, "Personal Services Rendered by Wife," p. 188; Mary M. Atkeson, "Women in Farm Life and Rural Economy," *Annals of the American Academy of Political and Social Science* 143 (1929): 188–94; Ann Whitehead, " 'I'm Hungry, Mum,' " in Kate Young, Carol Wolkowitz, and Roslyn McCullagh (eds), *Of Marriage and the Market* (London: Routledge and Kegan Paul, 1984), p. 112. An investigation by the U.S. Department of Agriculture reported extensive conflict between farm wives and their husbands over the earmarking of monies. "Economic Needs of Farm Women," Report No. 106 (Washington, DC: Government Printing Office, 1915). For this reference I am grateful to Kathleen R. Babbitt, whose doctoral dissertation at SUNY Binghamton deals with this issue in greater detail. The relative importance of gender versus source of income in distinguishing between the two kinds of money remains unclear. For instance, W. I. Thomas and Florian Znaniecki, in *The Polish Peasant in Europe and America* (New York: Dover, 1958 [1918–20]), p. 165, suggested that the qualitative difference between the money a peasant got from selling a cow and the money his wife obtained from selling eggs and milk was not marked by gender but by the "different sort of value" represented by each type of money: the cow was property, while eggs and milk were income. Each type of money was set aside for different types of expenses. However, since property, within the peasant economy, belonged to a "higher economic class" than income, it is clear that gender did intervene in the social marking of the two monies; lower-value money was assigned to women.

21 Helena Huntington Smith, "Husbands, Wives, and Pocketbooks," *Outlook* (March 28, 1928): 500; Mary Beynon Ray, "It's Not Always the Woman Who Pays," *Saturday Evening Post* 205 (September 3, 1932): 11.

22 Laura Oren, "The Welfare of Women in Laboring Families: England, 1860–1950," *Feminist Studies* 1 (1973): 110; Hilary Land, "Inequalities in Large Families: More of the Same or Different?," in Robert Chester and John Peel (eds), *Equalities and Inequalities in Family Life* (New York: Academic Press, 1977), pp. 163–76.

23 Mary Anderson, *United States Daily*, September 23, 1929. Cited in editorial, *Journal of Home Economics* 21 (December 1929): 921. See also Alice Kessler-Harris, *Out of Work* (New York: Oxford University Press, 1982), pp. 100–101.

24   Ironically, Max Weber's own family provided evidence against his rational conception of money. According to Marianne Weber, in *Max Weber: A Biography* (New York: Wiley, 1975), p. 141, Weber's father "was typical of the husbands of the time [1860s] . . . who needed to determine by themselves how the family income was to be used and left their wives and children in the dark as to how high the income was." Helene, Weber's mother, had no housekeeping allowance "nor a special fund for her personal needs." I thank Cecilia Marta Gil-Swedberg for this reference.

25   Elwood Lloyd IV, *How to Finance Home Life* (New York: B.C. Forbes Publishing Co., 1927), p. 82. For an extended discussion of the emergence of the allowance, see Zelizer, *Pricing the Priceless Child*, 1987.

26   Karl Marx and Friedrich Engels, *The Communist Manifesto* (New York: International, 1971 [1848]), p. 11; Philips, "My Adventures as a Bold, Bad Budgeter," p. 15.

27   There is, however, an emerging interdisciplinary and cross-national literature – by sociologists, historians, economists, and anthropologists – that is contesting traditional unified models of domestic economies. For sociological critiques, see, for example, Philip Blumstein and Pepper Schwartz, *American Couples* (New York: Pocket Books, 1985); David Cheal, "Strategies of Resource Management in Household Economies: Moral Economy or Political Economy?," in Richard R. Wilk (ed.), *The Household Economy: Reconsidering the Domestic Mode of Production* (Boulder: Westview, 1989), pp. 11–22; Rae Lesser Blumberg (ed.), *Gender, Family, and Economy: The Triple Overlap*, (Newbury Park, Calif.: Sage, 1991); Marcia Millman, *Warm Hearts & Cold Cash: The Intimate Dynamics of Families and Money* (New York: Free Press, 1991). For the position of economists, see Robert A. Pollak, "A Transaction Cost Approach to Families and Households," *Journal of Economic Literature* 23 (June 1985): 581–608; Nancy Folbre, "The Black Four of Hearts: Toward a New Paradigm of Household Economics," in Daisy Dwyer and Judith Bruce (eds), *A Home Divided: Women and Income in the Third World* (Stanford: Stanford University Press, 1988), pp. 248–62; Edward P. Lazear and Robert T. Michael, *Allocation of Income within the Household* (Chicago, IL: University of Chicago Press, 1988). For anthropological studies see Daisy Dwyer and Judith Bruce (eds), *A Home Divided*; Marilyn Strathern, "Self-Interest and the Social Good: Some Implications of Hagen Gender Imagery," in Sherry B. Ortner and Harriet Whitehead (eds), *Sexual Meanings: The Cultural Construction of Gender and Sexuality* (Cambridge: Cambridge University Press, 1981), pp. 166–91; R. L. Stirrat, "Money, Men, and Women," and Janet Carsten, "Cooking Money: Gender and the Symbolic Transformation of Means of Exchange in a Malay Fishing Community," in J. Parry and M. Bloch (eds), *Money & the Morality of Exchange* (Cambridge: Cambridge University Press, 1989), pp. 94–116; 117–41; Marion Benedict and Burton Benedict, *Men, Women, and Money in Seychelles* (Berkeley, CA: University of California Press, 1982). For cross-national contemporary and historical studies of intra-family accounting systems in English households, see Ross, " 'Fierce Questions and Taunts' "; Laura Oren, "The Welfare of Women in Laboring Families: England, 1860–1950," *Feminist Studies* 1 (1973): 107–23; Peter N. Stearns, "Working-Class Women in Britain, 1890–1914," in Martha Vicinus (ed.), *Suffer and Be Still*, pp. 100–20; Elizabeth Roberts, *A Woman's Place* (New York: Basil Blackwell, 1984); Patricia Branca, *Silent Sisterhood* (London: Croom Helm, 1975); Gail Wilson, *Money in the Family* (Vermont: Gower, 1987); Jan Pahl, *Money & Marriage* (New York: St. Martin's Press, 1989); Whitehead, " 'I'm Hungry, Mum'"; Ayers and Lambertz, "Marriage Relations." For France, see Evelyne Sullerot, "Les femmes et l'argent," *Janus* 10 (1966): 33–39; Marie-Françoise Hans, *Les femmes et l'argent* (Paris: Grasset, 1988); for French and English working-class households, see Louise Tilly and Joan Scott, *Women, work, and Family* (New York: Holt, Rinehart and Winston, 1978). Marianne Gullestad, *Kitchen-Table Society* (New York: Columbia University Press,

1984), provides some wonderful data on working-class mothers in urban Norway, and Meg Luxton, *More Than a Labour of Love* (Toronto: Women's Press, 1980). For Canada, see David Cheal, "Family Finances: Money Management in Breadwinner/ Homemaker Families, Dual Earner Families, and Dual Career Families," *Winnipeg Area Study Research Reports*, no. 38. For Israel, see Dafna N. Izraeli, "Money Matters: Spousal Incomes and Family/Work Relations Among Physician Couples in Israel," *Sociological Quarterly*, 35 (1): 69 (16 pages). And for Argentina, see Clara Coria, *El Dinero en la Pareja Algunas Desnudeces Sobre El Poder* (Buenos Aires: Grupo Editor Latino-americano, 1989).

28 Blumstein and Schwartz, *American Couples*, p. 56; Victoria Felton-Collins, with Suzanne Blair Brown, *Couples and Money* (New York: Bantam, 1990), p. 147. See Jean Lave, *Cognition In Practice* (Berkeley, CA: University of California Press, 1988), pp. 131–41. On the relationship between gender, class, money and the distribution of family power, see also Robert O. Blood, Jr. and Donald M. Wolfe, *Husbands and Wives* (New York: Free Press, 1965); Mirra Komarovsky, "Class Differences in Family Decision-Making on Expenditures," in *Household Decision-Making*, vol. 4 of Nelson N. Foote (ed.), *Consumer Behavior* (New York: New York University Press, 1961), pp. 255–65; Mirra Komarovsky, *Blue-Collar Marriage* (New York: Vintage, 1967); Constantina Safilios-Rothschild, "The Study of Family Power Structure," *Journal of Marriage and the Family* 32 (1970): 539–52; Lillian B. Rubin, *Worlds of Pain* (New York: Basic Books, 1976); Susan A. Ostrander, *Women of the Upper Class* (Philadelphia: Temple University Press, 1984); Rosanna Hertz, *More Equal than Others* (Berkeley, CA: University of California Press, 1986); John Mirowsky, "Depression and Marital Power: An Equity Model," *American Journal of Sociology* 91 (1985): 557–92. See also Phyllis Chesler and Emily Jane Goodman's *Women, Money and Power* (New York: Morrow, 1976) for an early statement on women's relationship to money; and for a recent study of women's socialization to money, see Jerome Rabow, Michelle Charness, Arlene E. Aguilar, and Jeanne Toomajian, "Women and Money: Cultural Contrasts," *Sociological Studies of Child Development* (JAI Press, 1992), vol. 5, pp. 191–291.

29 Arlie Hochschild, *The Second Shift* (New York: Avon, 1990), p. 221.

30 Blumstein and Schwartz, *American Couples*, p. 101. See also Jane Hood. *Becoming a Two-Job Family* (New York: Praeger, 1983), pp. 6–71. For England, see Pahl, *Money & Marriage*, pp. 128–31; also Wilson, *Money in the Family*. For other cross-cultural comparisons, see Rae Lesser Blumberg, "Income under Female versus Male Control: Hypotheses from a Theory of Gender Stratification and Data from the Third World," in Rae L. Blumberg (ed.), *Gender, Family, and Economy: The Triple Overlap*, pp. 97–127.

31 See Blumstein and Schwartz, *American Couples*, p. 56; Hochschild, *The Second Shift*, p. 222. Blumstein and Schwartz also discuss how variations in the male-provider ideology as well as the social relations of gay male and lesbian couples and of cohabiting heterosexual couples modify the effect of money on couples' power structure; see *American Couples*, pp. 53–111. On some ethnic and racial variations in the relation between paid labor and household labor, see Beth Anne Shelton and Daphne John, "Ethnicity, Race, and Difference: A Comparison of White, Black, and Hispanic Men's Household Labor Time," and Scott Coltrane and Elsa O. Valdez, "Reluctant Compliance: Work-Family Role Allocation in Dual-Earner Chicano Families," in Jane C. Hood (ed.), *Men, Work, and Family* (Newbury Park, CA: Sage, 1993), pp. 131–50, 151–75.

32 See Philip Blumstein and Pepper Schwartz, "Money and Ideology: Their Impact on Power and the Division of Household Labor," in Blumberg, *Gender, Family, and Economy*, pp. 261–88. On the significance of accounting systems, see Hertz, *More Equal than Others*, pp. 84–113. Using a national sample of respondents, Judith Treas concludes that the

choice of domestic accounting systems depends primarily on considerations of efficiency (despite her data's indication that a wife's higher education promotes segregation of funds and that even in pooling couples, wives are more likely to withhold some of their income), "Money in the Bank: Transaction Costs and the Economic Organization of Marriage," *American Sociological Review* 58 (October 1993): 723–34.

33 Kathleen Gerson, *No Man's Land: Men's Changing Commitments to Family and Work* (New York: Basic Books, 1993), p. 192.

34 Lazear and Michael, *Allocation of Income within the Household*, p. 147. See also Joanne Miller and Susan Yung, "The Role of Allowances in Adolescent Socialization," *Youth & Society* 22 (December 1990): 137–59, on how adolescents define their allowances either as an entitlement or earned household income. On the effect of kin networks on domestic money transfers, see Carol Stack, *All Our Kin* (New York: Harper and Row, 1975); Elizabeth Bott, *Family and Social Networks* (London: Tavistock, 1957).

18 Opposing Ambitions: Gender and Identity in an Alternative Organization

Sherryl Kleinman

Money as Moral Currency

In a capitalist society, "money is often equated with goodness, ability, talent, drive, even moral uprightness" (Blumstein and Schwartz, 1983, p. 69) We may criticize how people spend their money, especially the conspicuous consumption of the nouveau riche, but making money is something we expect adults to do. Poor kids and rich kids know this, though they have different expectations about the likelihood that they'll succeed (Sennett and Cobb, 1972). Not making enough money, particularly for men in this society, often indicates to others a failure of character (Liebow, 1967; Newman, 1988). This isn't surprising in a society in which people believe that upward mobility is a real and likely possibility for those who work hard enough.

Yet along with the idea that money brings prestige and even happiness is the notion that money corrupts and poverty builds character. Some upper-middle-class parents worry about spoiling their children and make them work for their allowance or get jobs to pay for their cars. Popular sitcoms, such as *Good Times*, depict poor black families as happy despite their poverty. The TV version of poverty says: they ain't got money, but they got love.

Although participants in the youth movements of the 1960s and 1970s might have seen through the romanticized portrayal of poverty on television, they nevertheless took to the idea that living with less builds character. Because they hadn't been born into poverty, they couldn't claim that they had struggled and suffered their way to character. But they could do one better – refuse to accept their middle-class privileges. They criticized the consumption of the middle class and rejected careers that might have made them rich. Although disparaged as "slumming" by those who criticized them, some youths chose a lifestyle of simplicity, living in communes (Berger, 1981) or in low-rent districts, working in alternative organizations, such as free schools (Swidler, 1979), progressive newspapers, or food co-ops (Rothschild and Whitt, 1986). Thus, they added a dimension to poverty that built their own moral identity – they *chose* to live with less.

Original publication: Kleinman, Sherryl, "Money as Moral Currency," chapter 2 of *Opposing Ambitions: Gender and Identity in an Alternative Organization* (University of Chicago Press, Chicago, IL, 1996).

From the countercultural perspective, then, money is tainted and leads to corruption and co-optation. Understandably, then, members at Renewal (a free clinic) told me that they disliked talking about money, even though they talked about money-related matters about 90 percent of the time at their board meetings. At first I assumed that they *had to* talk about money. In a capitalist context most organizations, even alternatives, must deal with money. And Renewal had financial problems: when I first came to Renewal I learned that the organization was in the red and owed two staff members two thousand dollars in back pay. Given these stark material conditions, how could they avoid talking about money?

Thus, I initially thought of Renewal's poverty as a social fact and their money-talk as a necessary consequence of their unstable financial position. This chapter turns that analysis on its head: I conceive of poverty – in the case of Renewal – as a social construction rather than as a plain fact. If we understand members' poverty in the light of the identity they desired, it becomes something they *wanted* rather than something imposed on them from the outside. Their alternative identity was based on the idea that they had sacrificed middle-class privileges. Their belief in themselves as alternative actors and as an alternative organization depended on "objective" indicators of financial struggle.

As I will show, members used money – this potentially tainted substance – for their own *moral enhancement*. Their discussions about making money built up their alternative identity. But unlike their predecessors in alternative organizations of the 1960s, members of Renewal also wanted to think of themselves as responsible organizational actors. I will show how their talk about money reinforced their image of themselves as unconventional yet allowed them to feel they were doing the serious work of a conventional organization. This was a difficult feat, because admitting that they cared about conventional legitimacy would have put their alternative identity into question. By believing that they had to talk about money all the time, members masked the fact that they also valued the legitimacy that came from engaging in money-talk.

In addition to living simply, members of nontraditional organizations in the sixties and seventies took the idea of equality, especially with regard to pay, as a serious matter. They rotated tasks and received equal pay for both routine and more interesting work. Members of Renewal paid their workers unequally. Also, staff members received their pay from the poor, nonprofit part of the organization and consequently often received no pay. The practitioners were paid directly by their clients and then paid part of their income to Renewal for rent and services.

Given these arrangements, how could members claim an alternative identity? By generating the sense that they had a chronic survival crisis, members maintained the fiction that all of them – practitioners and staff – were *in the same boat*. They believed they shared a mission: fighting to keep Renewal alive despite the conventional environment on the "outside." The solidarity that this crisis produced made it difficult for them to recognize unequal divisions *within* the organization. Hence, their focus on the "survival crisis" masked inequalities in distribution of money within the organization.

Board members discussed three main ways of increasing Renewal's income: raising fees for classes and practitioners' services, having fund-raisers, and hiring a physician. As I will show, their talk about these money matters helped them manage their contradictory identity as a legitimate alternative.

A Physician's Reflected Glory

After long discussions about the current money crisis, someone would say, with a sigh, "Oh, if only we had a physician." Initially, that suggestion surprised me. How did members come to feel that the ultimate solution to their problem was to hire someone from the medical establishment?

Members believed that having a physician would solve their money problems. One board member pointed out that a physician could get clients' services covered through third-party payments. For example, if a physician approved a client's need for massage, then his or her health insurance might cover it. Presumably, more people would become clients at Renewal if their health insurance covered the costs. But since the practitioners only gave a percentage of their earnings to Renewal, a physician's recommendations wouldn't bring in much money.

Having a physician on the board or in practice at Renewal might have added legitimacy to the organization and thus brought in more clients. Then again, those who turned to holistic therapies as a reaction *against* the field of medicine might have assumed that Renewal wasn't alternative enough and gone elsewhere. But members didn't weigh these different hypotheses. Rather, they talked as if a physician would be a cure-all for their financial problems.

I could have concluded that members were inept or unrealistic. But I think they avoided figuring out the details of what a physician would bring to Renewal in dollars because these details were irrelevant for their purposes. Members wanted a physician primarily for *symbolic* reasons – having someone with an MD willing to work at Renewal made them feel they were part of a legitimate health center. Whether a physician attracted or turned off potential clients, members *themselves* wanted some association with a practitioner who had an MD.

Members couldn't have admitted that they cared about the reflected glory that a physician would bring to Renewal because this would have challenged their alternative identity. Board members who suggested hiring a physician always did so with deep sighs, as if to say, "I wish this weren't necessary." But *believing* it was necessary helped them build their alternative identity. "Needing" a physician meant that they were indeed poor and thus an authentic alternative. If they were successful in conventional terms they wouldn't have to rely on a physician – someone in a conventional profession – to help them stay afloat. Thus, members could look for a physician while maintaining an image of themselves as people who questioned the legitimacy of the medical profession.

Members talked at length about the *kind* of person and practice they'd find acceptable from someone with an MD. Not just any physician would do. Such talk made members feel they were engaging in the kind of conversation that should go on in an alternative organization. By turning their desire for a physician into a morally tinged issue they could look for a physician and yet build up their alternative identity in the process.

Participants came in contact with a family physician, Frank Sampson, who first became a board member and later practiced at Renewal about six hours a week:

> At a practitioner meeting Ron said, "This should remain confidential. I don't want people to get all rah-rah about this and then it doesn't work out. But I've just had talks

with Frank Sampson and he's interested in becoming more involved with Renewal. He'll be running for the board." Karen and Jack looked pleased. Karen said, "Neat." Ron added, "I value his services a lot, and I think he'd be excellent."

I never heard participants sound as excited over any other potential board member. (Since the turnover rate was high, I heard a lot of talk about people who might join the board.) Members sighed when they talked about needing a physician in the abstract, but displayed only enthusiasm about bringing in Frank Sampson. Here was a physician who thought highly enough of them to be on the board of their alternative center.

Frank had a position of honor at Renewal. One indicator of his high status was the level of excitement generated over his possible board membership. But there was other compelling evidence: members let Frank off the hook for actions they didn't accept from each other. For example, after he was elected, Frank missed the first board meeting. In all cases but Frank's, members treated attendance at meetings as a critical sign of organizational commitment. Board members always expressed concern about those who missed meetings early on in their tenure. Why someone missed a board meeting mattered; the acceptable excuses I heard included severe illness (not a cold or a chronic backache), a partner losing a child in childbirth, and a parent dying.

What happened in Frank's case? Jack, the Chair of the Board, announced with pride that Frank wasn't at the meeting because he was running in a marathon, "which shows you the kind of person he is." Everyone looked pleased. They understood that Jack's comment meant that Frank was the *right* kind of person for Renewal. Running in a marathon rather than coming to a meeting showed members that Frank was an atypical doctor and thus someone who suited their needs. A *physician* who chose to run in a race rather than attend a business meeting demonstrated appropriate distance from his conventional role. No one else who offered such healthy reasons for missing a meeting was so cheerfully excused.

Frank's membership in a high-status, *conventional* occupation enabled him to occupy a position of honor in an organization whose members prided themselves on being *alternative*. Members thought that Frank's association with Renewal might taint his reputation in the medical community. Hence, they thought of him as taking a risk and making a sacrifice. Soon after he became a board member, Frank worked a few hours a week at Renewal, which members also saw as a sacrifice. Since most members didn't have Frank's "capital," they couldn't give it up and gain special points in the process.

How else might members have reacted to Frank? Since Frank was a physician, members might have put him through extra hoops to prove that he was truly alternative. Or they might have treated his behavior in the same way they treated their own. Yet they did the opposite, complimenting him for acting in ways they disapproved of in each other. We interpret behavior as generous when it comes from people in higher-status positions, as in the case of fathers who do childcare and, because they are male, receive applause for their efforts while mothers do not. If we accepted that status as equal rather than better, then we'd also give that behavior equal weight.

What members *didn't* talk about, even after Frank started practicing part-time at Renewal, was the discrepancy between what physicians and holistic practitioners usually charged for their services. A physician would probably charge for fifteen or twenty minutes what a holistic practitioner charged for an hour or longer. Yet members failed to talk about this matter. In the case of other practitioners, "what to charge" at times became a hot issue, as I discuss in the next section. A holistic practitioner had to justify that his or her service was worth a big fee, but a physician did not. Members' unacknowledged sense that a serious health organization must have a physician was so strong that they failed to recognize the different standards they judged him by.

Members found in Frank a person who could make them feel legitimate without them having to recognize that they cared about his legitimacy. By playing up the ways that Frank violated the stereotype of the physician, they convinced themselves that they weren't hiring a typical doctor, but a holistic healer who happened to have an MD. Thus, they were acting as responsible *alternative* actors. Yet Frank the "un-physician" still had an MD, a family practice outside Renewal, and a university affiliation. Thus, he could make them feel they were members of a *legitimate* health center by his willingness to support them. In this convoluted fashion, hiring someone from the very profession members were distinguishing their services from became the best solution to their problems of identity.

Money-talk as Moral Currency

Members often talked about raising fees for classes, workshops, and practitioners' services or increasing membership dues. Board members were ambivalent about raising fees, particularly for classes and practitioners' services. For example, at one board meeting

> Someone mentioned fee hikes. Karen (practitioner) said, "I don't know about that. I think we'll put clients off that way." Bob said, "Look, we need to do this to survive. Everything's inflated these days, and our fees should come up, too." Carla (staff) said, "I don't know. I don't want us to become another middle-class commodity." Manny (practitioner) said, "But we'll still use a sliding scale."

This discussion was typical. Members always talked about whether *any* raise in fees was morally acceptable. After much talk, they'd agree to increase their fees. This then led to a long negotiation about the acceptability of a particular amount. Members spent hours considering whether a small increase in charges for services – even one dollar – was acceptable. Occasionally, members spent so much time agonizing over the raise that they'd discover only much later in the evening that the increase would bring in a negligible amount of money and thus wouldn't get them through their immediate financial problem.

For example, after two hours of discussion about a raise in workshop fees, Bob pointed out that since workshop leaders get 65 percent of the fees (and the rest went to Renewal), raising fees the proposed amount would bring in only a small amount of money. Similarly, allowing clients to "work off" their class fees by volunteering (proposed as a way to offset increases in fees) also didn't increase Renewal's income. Nor did a sliding scale, which someone always proposed. Yet members talked about such proposals at length and usually adopted them.

For a few months, I felt uneasy, anxious, and frustrated during these discussions. Surely members could come up with a better solution to this chronic financial crisis. But the board members didn't feel as I did. As I listened to their voices, scrutinized their faces, and watched them make points with their hands, they seemed anything *but* bored, uncomfortable, or exasperated. This surprised me: hadn't Karen told me, that first day, that their discussions about money bored her? Yet Karen, along with the others, seemed fully *engaged* in the process. Members looked tired, but not dispirited, by the end of board meetings. Rather, they showed the kind of fatigue that follows meaningful, hard work rather than repetitive, alienated labor.

How could members approach each discussion with renewed vigor? Couldn't they see that their discussions were patterned and predictable? It took me a long time to figure out that members' talk about money had *value*. By talking about money as a moral issue, worrying about whether they had compromised their principles, and finding temporary solutions to their immediate problem, they felt they were doing what members of alternative organizations are supposed to do. *I* found their discussions frustrating, and eventually routine, because I wasn't a member, I didn't participate in the discussions, and thus I couldn't reap the (moral) identity benefits of such talk.

Members' organizational poverty ennobled them. Although no one spoke these words, their endless discussions seemed to say: "The fact that we always need money to stay alive means that we must be doing something right. If we were making a profit, that could mean we'd sold out." As I argued earlier, members' moral identity hinged on their belief that they had sacrificed conventional middle-class privileges, especially money, to work for a cause. Their ongoing financial crisis proved to them that they were indeed an alternative; they *continued* to sacrifice middle-class financial stability.

What if they had treated money as a neutral object? Then they would have asked these questions: How much should we raise fees to get the money we need? How much will people pay? What is the market out there? But such questions would have robbed participants of a source of their esteem as members of an alternative organization – their belief that they are something *more* than a regular establishment.

Although members didn't purposely keep Renewal in debt, their financial problems made it necessary for them to talk often about their plight, to seek "solutions," and thus to have further discussion about the morality of making money. Members' poverty, then, was functional. If they had solved their financial problems, they would have exhausted a resource for maintaining their alternative identity.

There were rules for talking about money. You could only suggest raising fees a small amount; suggesting a big increase meant that you had ignored the needs of the poor. (In addition, by raising fees only a little, they failed to solve their problem and found themselves talking about another raise not long afterwards, thus ensuring more moral negotiation.) You had to express ambivalence about the raise; sounding neutral meant that you didn't care about the poor. You also had to suggest alternative forms of payment, such as volunteering at Renewal. Finally, if you proposed an increase in your rates as a practitioner, you were also expected to discuss the implications of the raise for the collective.

When someone broke a rule, others jumped in to correct him or her. Intermittent rule-breaking seemed only to reinforce their alternative identity because it heated up the discussion. What happened when a member challenged the belief that lay at the core of their identity – that it was important to sacrifice middle-class privileges? I saw the centrality of poverty to their moral identity when Manny, a well-respected practitioner and one of the three remaining founders of Renewal, broke the rules. For a few months, Manny had expressed an interest in making more money as a practitioner. After missing several practitioner meetings, Manny turned up with the following announcement:

> "I'm raising my rates to forty-five dollars a session [from thirty dollars a session]. I'll still have a sliding scale – I don't turn anyone away – but my base rate will be forty-five dollars." . . . Jack looked upset and said, "I have problems with the inflated rates of psychotherapists. Also, that's a big jump in rate." Karen said, "I feel uncomfortable having anyone charge that much for what we're trying to do." Manny replied, "I don't think poverty consciousness is the way to go." Ron said, "The other side is greed."

Manny announced rather than requested a fee hike, something that upset others. He saved face a little by saying that he would use a sliding scale and "wouldn't turn anyone away." Claiming that he was worth forty-five dollars (while other practitioners charged up to thirty-five dollars) suggested to the other practitioners that he thought his service, which was similar to Jack's, was worth more. Although the gap in pay between staff and practitioners shows that members had conventional ideas about which jobs deserve more money, no one was supposed to hint at the connection between individual worth and money.

Others bristled when he said, "I don't think poverty consciousness is the way to go." He explained that he wanted more financial stability in his life and wanted to buy a house. He made his statements clearly, directly, and in an even tone; he neither apologized for his change of heart nor tried to convince others to feel the same way. His lack of angst and passion also violated one of the board members' rules: you couldn't be matter-of-fact about money. Neutrality in tone meant coldness in heart.

The practitioners came down hard on Manny. They did so for two reasons. First, he questioned the basis of their alternative identity by rejecting chosen poverty (what he called "poverty consciousness"). Second, Manny also threatened the other, hidden part of their identity – members' desire to see themselves as responsible organizational actors. For example, at an earlier meeting, when the practitioners talked about filling vacancies on the board, Manny said, "I think we should get consumers on the board. If we still need people who set up Renewal to work on the board then I think it's stillborn." His statement shocked members. At another meeting, he said that an organization that couldn't pay its staff was "dead."

Manny intimated that Renewal's financial problems were a product of members' organizational ineptness rather than their lofty ideals. He more than hinted that Renewal was a bogus alternative *and* an ineffective organization. Thus, he made it difficult for members to claim either frame of reference. Despite Manny's popularity and his high status as a practitioner and founder of Renewal, he became too big a threat to members' self-images.

The practitioners discussed Manny's proposal with each other and with board members informally over the next two weeks. Consistent with their discussions about all raises, they discussed whether Manny's proposal would challenge Renewal's identity as an alternative, especially if all the practitioners charged similar fees. Manny failed to show up at the next practitioner meeting. Ron had this to say:

> Two weeks ago when this came up I thought it was only Manny's business. I've given it a lot of thought and talked to a number of people in Renewal and in the community, and now I feel differently. I *do* want to have some input into this and to do what's moral . . . I think there are a number of reasons for not letting him increase his fees. The first is that this decision affects me, us, our image. Second, it's a big increase, a big jump. Third, most of his clients can't afford it, like maybe 80 percent of them. Personally, I feel he's doing it for status reasons, status quo reasons . . . Phew! I said it. That's how I feel.

More discussion followed. Jack said:

> If we approve Manny's raise, then I'll have a problem with my own professional identity. On the one hand, it's none of our business. On the other, Manny isn't here, and he didn't call to say he wouldn't be here. I think that's indicative of his participation. I don't support the raise.

Manny quit working at Renewal soon after that. The practitioners reported to the board what had happened. This incident gave practitioners the opportunity to prove to other board members that their commitment to alternative ideals was more important than keeping "one of their own." The practitioners *didn't* tell other board members about their worry, expressed at practitioner meetings, that if Manny charged considerably more than they did, then clients might assume that his services were better than theirs. They also failed to mention that their clients probably wouldn't pay forty-five dollars for their services. As Ron had said, "charging that much would run me out of business."

I don't think the practitioners purposely omitted these concerns. But if the practitioners had revealed their concerns about losing clients or denting their professional reputations, other board members might have seen them as self-interested or insecure.

The practitioners, by focusing mostly on Manny's violation of alternative ideals, reinforced their moral identity and showed that they were committed to resisting conventionality. By bringing select elements of the incident to the board and giving their conclusion – to refuse the raise – the practitioners built solidarity with other board members, and maintained those members' trust in them. The discussion of the event at the board meeting reinforced board members' image of themselves, and the organization, as alternative. Because members defined what had transpired as a crisis that involved an agonizing decision, their actions became an opportunity for *moral renewal*.

We have seen, then, that members framed money-talk in ways that made them feel they were an authentic alternative. In the case of raising fees for services, it is more difficult to provide evidence for my second argument – that members liked talking about money because it also made them feel they were doing the hard work of a legitimate health organization. This is especially difficult to support because members were invested in distancing themselves from the business model; to acknowledge an interest in conventional legitimacy was to put their alternative identity into question. Yet it's plausible to suggest that members spent so much time on money because it helped them feel good about themselves from both alternative and conventional perspectives. They could believe they were doing the "real work" of a serious organization but in ways that fit their alternative ideals. As we saw in the case of hiring a physician, members valued the conventional. In the next section about fund-raisers, I will show other signs of the value they placed on conventional legitimacy.

Fund-Raising as Failure

Members' attitudes toward fund-raisers puzzled me at first. Although they found fund-raising events – such as festivals in which practitioners and teachers gave short workshops – valuable and fun, they seemed edgy, then lethargic, when someone suggested that they plan a fund-raising event to make money.

Why did members discuss other ways to make money (in fact, less acceptable ways) with great interest, but have little energy, let alone zeal, when discussing fund-raisers? Fund-raising events, I thought, were morally clean and thus should have reinforced members' collective identity as alternative. What an easy way, it seemed to me, for members to feel good about themselves. Why was it easier for them to use "tainted" means – such as raising fees – to make themselves believe they were living up to alternative ideals?

Fund-raisers were a problem from both the alternative and conventional frames of reference. First, talking about fund-raisers didn't provide members with meaningful opportunities to live out their alternative identity. Second, fund-raisers threatened members' image of themselves as competent organizational actors.

As I expected, members thought of fund-raising as an ethical way to make money. Although raising fees for services was morally questionable for them, fund-raising was not. Members defined fund-raising events as qualitatively different from regular services offered at Renewal. They thought of fund-raisers as voluntary, involving a participant's choice of activity; using a regular health service at Renewal was seen as less voluntary, involving a participant's need. Members, then, regarded participants in fund-raisers as customers or consumers rather than as clients. Fund-raisers were also "clean" because those who put the fund-raiser together usually received little or no pay for their time and effort and charged participants minimal fees.

Eventually I understood that the moral *acceptability* of fund-raisers made them *uninteresting*. Since fund-raisers were clean, participants had trouble fashioning moral dilemmas out of them. Moral dilemmas over money made money interesting. Because fund-raisers were "good" and didn't violate their image as an alternative organization, members found nothing of value to debate about.

Unlike the charged atmosphere in which members discussed other money matters, the air hung heavy in the room during discussions about fund-raisers. Participants spent little time (often no time) figuring out the morally acceptable fee to charge for fund-raisers. Rather, they treated money as neutral, asking largely technical questions: What would the organizing expenses amount to? What would people pay for the event? How much money would Renewal make? Would that amount take care of the immediate money problem? Because fund-raisers were clean, members didn't engage in moral struggles about what to charge. Discussing fund-raisers, then, denied members the opportunity to become impassioned in ways that reinforced their moral identity.

Members became particularly disheartened when someone suggested they put together a fund-raiser as a desperate solution to an immediate financial problem. Why? In the wider culture, fund-raisers are associated with causes rather than business (hence rendering them morally acceptable). But having fund-raisers made it difficult for members to feel that they resembled a legitimate organization. From a conventional, business point of view, fund-raisers are a sign of *failure*. Finding a physician and discussing raises in fees made members feel they were involved in a legitimate organization, but discussing fund-raisers did not. Fund-raising, especially during crises, was the equivalent of bankruptcy.

Why didn't members use the "need" for fund-raisers to reinforce their moral identity? Couldn't they have told themselves that they had to have fund-raisers in order to survive as an alternative organization in a conventional environment? Members' feelings of failure as a business that must "resort to" fund-raisers made it difficult for them to call upon poverty as the moral basis for engaging in money-talk. When they discussed *other* money matters, such as raising fees for services, poverty "beautified" – the moral discussions reinforced their alternative identity while also building up their view of themselves as responsible professionals. In the case of fund-raisers, poverty became a sign of organizational failure and thus brought them down.

Fund-raisers allowed me to see the value members placed on both alternative and conventional legitimacy. If members' only reaction to these discussions had been boredom, this would have supported the hypothesis that members found fund-raisers morally uninteresting and thus valued the alternative perspective *exclusively*. Because members became disheartened and discouraged rather than merely bored, I took this to mean that they lacked a conventional source of legitimacy. In fact, fund-raisers threatened their image of themselves as competent board members. Fund-raisers offered neither interesting moral possibilities nor conventional legitimacy. Their lack of value to members made them valuable to me as I tried to make sense of their reactions. Fund-raisers provided the "deviant case" that supported the more general point that members valued *both* alternative and conventional frames of reference.

Wrong and Right Ways to Talk about Money

Since some board members told me that talking about money was "boring" or "awful," I expected them to apologize when they talked about money at board meetings. Members spent 90 percent of their time at board meetings discussing money or money-related matters, so I expected to hear lots of apologies. Yet when I reread my fieldnotes, I was struck by the *absence* of disclaimers about money-talk at meetings. And those who apologized made others uncomfortable.

Who made disclaimers, how did they make them, and what did these signify to members? Those who had spent little time at Renewal before becoming involved in it tended to talk about money in inappropriate ways. They picked up on the idea that it was unacceptable to *want* to talk about money, but didn't yet understand that *talking* about money also served positive functions for members. In trying to fit in, these newcomers apologized for talking about money. For example, Alicia, who became Director of Renewal for a short time, always began her reports with an apology. At one board meeting she said:

> I want to apologize, but we're not going to have an organization without money. I apologize for being so uptight about it, but without money we won't have an organization.

Alicia suggested that Renewal, by needing money, was indeed poor and hence a true alternative. She seemed to be justifying members' use of a tainted activity (making money) in an alternative organization. Wasn't she doing what other, more experienced members, did?

Apparently not. In these few comments, Alicia turned members off because she suggested that they were failures, both as a legitimate organization and as an alternative. Her statement "We're not going to have an organization without money" insulted those who secretly took pride in Renewal as a serious organization. She implied that being poor is not only organizationally irresponsible but is also the very thing that will stop them from living out their alternative ideals – "without money we won't have an organization." Thus, she had unwittingly made them feel like double failures.

This deviant case highlights why others rarely apologized for talking about money. The plaintive cry that began such discussions – "We really need more money"– differed from Alicia's disclaimer. The lament said to members that they had to talk about money because they were poor, but this poverty resulted from the ideals they embraced, not from disorganization. Presumably they were poor *because* they were doing good.

Alicia paid lip service to the idea that money could corrupt by framing it as a necessary evil. Mostly she treated money as something that responsible organizational members must learn to deal with, an instrumental means to the moral end of maintaining an alternative organization. She followed her introductory statements with proposals for making money. Doing so kept members from feeling that they were engaged in the kind of talk participants at alternatives were supposed to participate in. Treating money as mundane deprived them of collective experiences that could have reinforced their moral identity. Alicia's words, then, put members' contradictory identity into jeopardy – they were neither truly alternative nor organizationally competent. Board members' *usual* practices buttressed their view of themselves as a legitimate alternative – their moral discussions about money made them feel they were doing serious business within an alternative framework.

Debra, a part-time staff member and board member, volunteered to be on the budget committee. Debra treated Renewal's financial problems as practical matters. She worked hard on the budget but found that others didn't take her suggestions seriously. In an interview after she quit the board, she spoke to me in an exasperated tone:

> Nobody had cared diddly-squat about finances. They felt like it was going to get taken care of somehow, and they didn't worry about anything. And the amazing thing is that they did as well as they did . . . We were spending 13 percent more than we were taking in, so we [the Budget Committee] just cut across the board 13 percent except

things we couldn't cut like the rent, utilities. And still people weren't paying much attention to the budget. Then the next time I gave the budget report I felt like I really wasn't getting through to people very well.

She eventually became angry about members' handling of money and other matters:

Lately, particularly, I get real mad at hippies. When Margaret [an outspoken alternative woman] was on the Board I would just get, uuuh [she shuddered]. I've just got to investigate why I feel this way. Partly I think it's their idea that being businesslike is not humanitarian.

Other members also wanted to be both "businesslike" and "humanitarian." But since members thought that seeking conventional legitimacy contradicted their alternative ideals, they couldn't acknowledge their interest in maintaining a conventional face. The difference, then, between Debra and most other members was this: she didn't see a discrepancy between conventional and alternative ideals. For her, there was no dilemma. Debra's statements, like Alicia's, intimated that members were immature, and thus incapable of running a "real" organization. The term "immature" is apt, for Debra was twenty years older than most members. And, like Alicia, her assumption that money was an instrumental means to a moral end threatened to rob members of the chance to use money to feel like moral actors; at the same time, she made them feel like relative failures at business.

Members approved of Debra's proposals, but they disliked her presentation of them as exclusively technical. It was possible to make budget cuts morally satisfying and organizationally legitimate. When Mike headed the Budget Committee and presented one of his reports, members not only felt satisfied, but were visibly moved. Mike told the board that his committee decided to consult the *I Ching* for answers to Renewal's financial problems. This got members' attention. By consulting the *I Ching*, he implied that money problems are not merely practical matters that require mathematical skills, but cosmic problems that require spiritual guidance. He gave an elaborate description of what the *I Ching* had indicated and how he had interpreted it.

Mike's *conclusion* was the same as Debra's: members needed to make cuts across the board. But the differences between Mike's and Debra's presentations led to dramatically different responses. At the end of his report, Mike gave members a handout with sixty-two ways to "tighten up." He passed around a typed report, with each suggestion numbered from one to sixty-two, thereby giving members an organizational document that they could refer to as a "solution." Thus, he not only made money into a spiritual and thus alternative issue, he also presented his report in a way that legitimated them as a serious organization. Mike legitimated Renewal as an alternative and a "real" organization in a way that kept members from recognizing that they valued the organizational rhetoric of the document – the "spiritualizing" of the document masked the conventional value of it. At the end of the report Frank, the physician referred to earlier, said that of all the board meetings he had attended in his career, none had been as beautiful as that one. Members glowed. The physician had offered his seal of approval – they were indeed a legitimate alternative.

Keeping Things the Same

Members talked about money in ways that maintained their identity as a legitimate alternative. Being in the red proved to them that Renewal was a true alternative. If their resources were greater, members believed, they wouldn't have to resort to such unappealing solutions as hiring a physician or raising fees. The despair and moral negotiation that characterized their money-talk made them feel all the more alternative. At the same time, their serious attitude about money matters built their image of themselves as legit.

Members acknowledged that they were committing a conventional act by raising fees at all. But this was a *safe* confession of conventionality; presumably, they needed to raise fees because they were poor, and their poverty meant that they were indeed living out alternative ideals. Because members' money problems made them feel poor and thus virtuous, talking about their financial crisis at board meetings produced solidarity, especially among central members – the staff and practitioners who served on the board. These feelings of solidarity, however, masked inequalities in the *distribution* of money within the organization. By saying "we are poor," members spoke as if each of them was equally affected by how much money came into Renewal. But only the *staff members'* pay depended on revenues generated by "the organization." Practitioners were paid directly by their clients, and their rent remained low. Thus, the staff and the practitioners were *un*equally poor within Renewal.

The dual nature of the structure made it possible for members to see those who held the most power – the practitioners – as altruistic. Structurally, practitioners were both inside and outside the organization. As private practitioners who collected fees directly from clients and then paid rent to Renewal, they were on the outside. As board members, teachers, and occasional volunteers, they were on the inside. When Renewal "needed more money," members treated practitioners' fees as one possible source. They discussed this as a moral matter with regard to how much a practitioner should charge a client (recall Manny) and how much a practitioner should reasonably pay Renewal for rent and services. In these discussions, then, board members treated the practitioners as another source of "external income" rather than as *part of the organization*. By being financially autonomous in relation to the organization, the practitioners were perceived as benefactors – those who *contributed* to Renewal – rather than as insiders who received the most rewards. From this perspective, it makes sense that the practitioners were seen, and saw themselves, as generous; they "donated" time, energy, and money to Renewal.

The practitioners, especially Ron and Jack, had a privileged position. As the two founding members of Renewal, they were thought of as synonymous with the organization. Yet Ron and Jack had a quasi-outsider position when it came to financial matters, a position they benefited from. Ron and Jack became the patrons who could bestow gifts – status, charisma, time, money – on the organization. In contrast to the "breadwinning" practitioners, the staff members, by being "paid," were seen as draining Renewal's resources.

Ron and Jack's privileged positions were also buttressed by their gender and class. Board members, especially the staff, thought these practitioners could have lucrative, conventional careers, but chose otherwise. Members assumed that Ron and Jack had sacrificed the privileges of professional, middle-class men so that they could do alternative work and act as benefactors for Renewal.

Staff women, on the other hand, had no privileges to sacrifice. As women in womanly jobs, they were expected to do lower-status work without complaining and to feel lucky to receive the "generous gifts" of the male practitioners. The staff women often received no pay for their labor and paid Renewal's bills rather than themselves, but their acts were *not* recognized as sacrifices. The practitioners' incomes were untouched by the poverty of the nonprofit part of the organization, but they had the ability to feed the image of Renewal as poor and thus alternative. Thus, those whose organization-related income depended the *least* on the poor, nonprofit part of Renewal had the *most* opportunity to earn others' respect by making "sacrifices" to it.

Members' denial of these inequalities was embedded in their apolitical and individualistic notions of equality. They believed that each individual is special and thus deserves equal respect. Hence, they believed that structural or financial arrangements – who got paid what and how – weren't important. Each person, they felt, already *had* equal respect. Believing they had taken care of the problem of inequality by positing that each person is "special," they denied their assumptions about which categories of persons deserve more – or less – at Renewal. Yet such ideas were implicit in their monetary arrangements; staff didn't "need" to be paid much or often, practitioners "needed" to be paid more and shouldn't have to depend on this poor organization to pay them. As in the conventional world, they assumed that the "professionals" of the organization should get more rewards than the staff. By remaining unaware of these assumptions, members could build solidarity around their moral identity.

Because members attributed their poverty to their alternative status, their solutions to their financial problems were always conventional, such as raising fees or hiring a physician. Because they believed they were *already* alternative – indicated by their poverty and their need to discuss making money – the possibility of organizing themselves in more radical ways didn't come up. For example, members didn't discuss whether an egalitarian or communal structure would have worked just as well or better for their "survival problem." Instead, they continued to complain about their financial problems and seek solutions that safely kept alive their identity as a legitimate alternative.

References

Berger, Bennett (1981) *The Survival of a Counterculture: Ideological Work and Everyday Life among Rural Communards*, Berkeley, CA: University of California Press.

Blumstein, Phillip, and Schwartz, Pepper (1983) *American Couples*, New York: William Morrow.

Liebow, Elliott (1967) *Tally's Corner: A Study of Negro Street Corner Men*, Boston, MA: Little, Brown.

Newman, Katherine S. (1988) *Falling from Grace: The Experience of Downward Mobility in the American Middle Class*, New York: Free Press.

Rothschild, Joyce, and Whitt, J. Allen (1986) *The Cooperative Workplace: Potentials and Dilemmas of Organizational Democracy and Participation*, New York: Cambridge University Press.

Sennett, Richard, and Cobb, Jonathan (1972) *The Hidden Injuries of Class*, New York: Random House.

Swidler, Ann (1979) *Organization without Authority: Dilemmas of Social Control in Free Schools*, Cambridge, MA: Harvard University Press.

19 Greening the Economy from the Bottom up? Lessons in Consumption from the Energy Case

Loren Lutzenhiser

Economy and the Environment

Considered strictly in environmental terms, modern societies leave much to be desired. They are large and growing in both population and sheer mass of activity. They have spread into nearly every ecosystem and linked themselves tightly together with flows of materials, products and ideas. As George Monbiot (2000) puts it:

> The modern industrial economy works like this: resources are dug from a hole in the ground on one side of the planet, used for a few weeks, then dumped in a hole on the other side of the planet. This is known as the "creation of value".

We might add that, in the process, resources are exhausted, there are fewer places to dig the second hole, and everywhere in between becomes increasingly crowded with people, things, and wastes.

The relationship of the United States to the global environment is particularly problematic. The US dwarfs other societies in its sheer volumes of consumption, production, and pollution. It dominates international investment and demand, serves as a role model for an expansive consumer culture, and shapes global standards for goods and services. At the same time, its stance on global environmental problems is often not helpful (Lutzenhiser, 2001).

The impact of economy on the environment has been theorized in a variety of both pessimistic and optimistic ways by economists and sociologists – from Malthus's (1798) predictions of inevitable famine, to Simon's (1981) faith in technology and human creativity, to Schnaiberg's (1980) observations about capitalism's self-destructive "treadmill of production." Ecological economists (e.g., Daly, 1997; Norgaard, 1994) and sociologists interested in "ecological modernization" (e.g., Mol and Sonnenfeld, 2000) see a middle ground. In their view, businesses, in conjunction with progressive governments and environmental organizations, can come to recognize that "sustainable" production requires a healthy ecological base – and that significant profits can be realized by cleaning up manufacturing processes, developing more environmentally friendly technologies, and creating new markets for environmental restoration.

This chapter was specifically commissioned for this volume.

Greening Business?

This "environmental stewardship is good business" view has gained some adherents among business writers, with the promotion of an "ecology of commerce" (Hawken, 1993), "the natural step," (Nattrass and Altomare, 1999), "natural capitalism" (Hawken, Lovins, and Lovins, 1999), and "earth's company" (Frankel, 1998). There is also some evidence of a "green turn" by some large US corporations.[1] But any ecological gains made to date through voluntary business action are tiny in comparison with America's global "environmental footprint" (Wackernagel and Rees, 1996). And US firms continue to support aggressively a wide range of anti-environmental groups and legislative agendas (Beder, 1997; Switzer, 1997).

It has been argued that any hope for fundamental change in the economy–environment relation (particularly in the US) might hinge on *consumer demands* for environmental improvements by business – in essence, a greening of the economy from the "bottom up" (Durning, 1992; Elgin, 1993). In the past, citizen/consumer support has led to environmental protection laws, as well as to niche markets for environmentally friendly goods (e.g., organic food and fiber, personal care products, green building materials). But any consumer-led greening of the economy on a large scale would also seem to depend upon consumers' willingness to make strong environmental demands, and their ability to do so.

How can we judge whether this is a realistic expectation? One strategy would be to look at evidence from ongoing efforts to "green" consumer choice and market demands. The conservation of *energy* is one area in which there has been a considerable amount of interest in influencing consumer choice over the past three decades. We also have a good deal of information about the efficacy of consumer-led economic change in the energy arena. And because energy use is the single most important source of global environmental damage, it is an important illustrative case.

Meet Joe Blaugh

In the following discussion, we consider the experiences of a fictional consumer named Joe Blaugh. As *Homo economicus*, Joe is interested in getting the most from his purchases, and he is loath to spend more than necessary. He keeps track of his income and expenses, and thinks about the future when saving, investing, and making charitable contributions. He's a model of sensible consumption, and he's also quite concerned about the natural environment and future generations of Blaughs. As a result, he does his best to behave like *Homo economicus ecologicus* – a savvy environmental consumer. In this, he's probably not unlike a majority of American consumers who don't have money to throw away, and who for decades have strongly supported environmental protection.[2]

The Energy System in Change

Before considering how Joe and the other Blaughs (his spouse, Liz, and their two children, Zoe and Zed) approach their energy use and conservation, it is useful to have an image of the energy system on which they depend. Energy flows are required for *all* human activities – from the smallest movement of the hand to the launching of rockets – and they take many forms.[3] These include food grown, prepared, and consumed; natural gas burned in furnaces; the operation of coal-fired and nuclear power plants; the ubiquity of electric lighting; refrigeration in stores; and petroleum used in commuting and shipping goods around the world. Electricity, gas, and oil networks crisscross the country, with giant converting stations located at their intersections, and a vast array of equipment and appliances in homes and businesses connected at hundreds of millions of outlet points. North American energy use is massive. It is greater in total volume and amount used per capita than any other society in the world and it is rapidly growing (DOE/EIA, 2001).

Historically, this growth in energy use was taken as an indicator of social and economic progress. However, energy crises in the 1970s problematized energy, and by the 1980s it had become an object of serious public policy attention. In the 1990s, concerns about greenhouse gas emissions from the energy system and global warming established energy as a significant long-term social, economic, and environmental problem.

The 1970s energy crises raised concerns about the effects of energy shortage and rising prices (on national security, unemployment, the poor, and the elderly), and they required quick conservation responses from consumers. Joe and Liz reduced their energy use by turning down their thermostat and taking shorter showers. However, as the crises passed, concern shifted to longer-term energy problems and the concept of "energy efficiency." Advocates argued that the more *efficient use* of energy through improved technologies could produce a variety of benefits to consumers, the environment, and the economy.[4] For example, a wide range of technical improvements to cars, houses, refrigerators, furnaces, air conditioners, motors, lights, and so on were demonstrated to produce significant energy savings. These were also shown to be *wise investments*, since any initial higher costs of more efficient equipment would quickly be recovered through lower energy bills, with pure savings following for years after.[5]

From the point of view of policymakers, a system-wide "efficiency gap" existed between the "technical potential" for a much more energy-efficient society and the actual state of affairs (Lovins, 1977; Nadel et al., 1998). So to promote the adoption of these improved technologies, utilities and governments mounted "demand-side management" (DSM) programs to market energy efficiency to consumers and businesses as cost-saving investments. They also offered *incentives* in the form of low-interest loans, tax credits, rebates, and even grants for buying and using more energy-efficient equipment.[6]

Consumers were assumed by DSM policymakers to act as *rational individuals* who are conscious of their energy use, informed about better technologies, and interested in making smart efficiency investments with fairly quick returns. Self-interest and system interest could be served by the same choices. As motivation to consumers, energy prices were high, and the media reported dwindling reserves of natural gas, as well as growing environmental problems related to acid rain from electric power plant emissions. Consumers were also subjected to a stream of public service announcements, newspaper ads, appliance labels, and efficiency information enclosed in utility bills. And if they remained uncertain about economic benefits, they were offered free "energy audits" to help calculate the value of promised energy savings.

Why Don't People Conserve When it's Economically Rational to Do so?

The system-level gains of DSM were sometimes respectable, although often modest, and regularly frustrated by "human factors" in program design, delivery, and participation (Vine, 1994). Consumer opinion surveys showed strong support in principle for conservation and renewable energy (Farhar, 1993), but researchers found that pro-conservation attitudes rarely resulted in *action* (e.g., Costanzo et al., 1986; Ester, 1985). The effects of financial incentives were also found to be limited (Stern et al., 1986). Even with subsidies, Joe and others didn't buy into many DSM deals.

Consumer economic rationality, the primary assumption of DSM, was called into question by behavioral researchers (Archer et al., 1984; Stern, 1986). Some concluded that consumers were defective (e.g., suffering from "energy illiteracy," Ester, 1985). Others suggested that the puzzle involved processes that economics and psychology were not easily able to explain (Black, Stern, and Elworth, 1985; Stern and Oskamp, 1987; see Lutzenhiser, 1993 for a detailed discussion of the controversy).

The DSM story is one of best intentions too often foiled and a confounding of policymakers who expected people to make obviously rational efficiency investments. However, the error was fairly simple. The fact that Joe and Liz are *social* actors had largely been ignored. Their everyday world is full of economic choices, to be sure. But it is a social world in which choices appear in many guises, and constraint rather than choice is usually the order of the day (Shove et al., 1998). The resulting "failure" of consumer rationality and pro-environmental attitudes to produce concrete change can be traced to three sources that are discussed in some detail below. These are energy invisibility, the social nature of everyday consumption, and the constraints imposed by macro-social systems.

Energy Invisibility

Energy is invisible in part because, as we have noted, all of social life is inherently energetic. Because energy flows are ubiquitous, they are ordinarily taken for granted and ignored. Although we routinely speak of "energy" in a variety of senses (e.g., "lacking energy" or "energizing the team"), our utter dependence upon energy becomes noticeable only when the power is off or a surprising utility bill arrives. As a result, Joe's understanding of his own energy use is captive to what anthropologists have termed "folk models" – understandings of how the material world works that are ordinarily quite different from those of engineers and physicists (Kempton and Montgomery, 1982).

Joe and the rest of us tend to experience "energy" *indirectly* and *physically*: as warm air from wall registers, light from the ceiling, hot water at the sink, a refrigerator that keeps milk and eggs cold. While adequate under ordinary circumstances, our resulting understandings are not useful in analyzing invisible energy flows or evaluating conservation potentials. These are such a challenge that even consumers who believe themselves to be well informed about energy and try to act in rational ways can be badly mistaken (Kempton, 1984). Researchers have found little evidence that consumers, working with common-sense paradigms and ordinary information on prices and technologies, possess the "minimal necessary information indispensable to even gross cost calculation" (Archer et al., 1984; also see Kempton and Layne, 1988).

Invisibility and misunderstandings about energy are not surprising, since most evidence of energy flows is actively *concealed* in modern societies. Power plants, wells, and mines are ordinarily located far from the points of end-use (in Joe's case, an average of 200 miles). The mechanics of system management are also kept at a distance: in utility headquarters, regulatory agency offices, industry compounds, scientific research establishments. Except for rare energy crises, these goings-on are not noteworthy.

And the elements of energy systems nearer to the points of use in the urban fabric are concealed as well: hidden in industrial areas, fringe neighborhoods, and behind fences and foliage. Within the dwelling itself, electricity, gas, and other utility systems lie behind walls, under floors, and above ceilings. In the suburbs, all outside connections to the house are usually buried. In Joe's case, the lone trace of the energy system is his meter panel, which is hidden behind shrubs and seen only by furtive utility employees. It is the same with his neighbors. Whatever any of them might be doing with energy – whether ordinary, innovative, conservative, or extravagant – is thoroughly concealed from view.

The invisibility of energy can also be traced to the fact that most social action in the household setting is routine and, therefore, *habitual*. Habits are the ordinary, unexceptional actions that people take without consciously thinking about them. They are the bedrock of social life – competent performances mastered through past encounters with people and things in the social world. As such, habits are not "dumb," but skillfully incorporate our expectations of how the world will behave (James, 1890; Peirce, 1878). In terms of energy use, Joe and Zoe habitually take long showers, Liz automatically turns on all the lights when she gets home from work, and Zed leaves his computer and stereo on most of the time. All of their social routines involve habitual forms of energy use – from quick trips in the car to pick up the *Sunday New York Times*, to leaving the porch light on in the evening. The fact that energy is being used at all is lost in the deep background of unreflected practice.

Collective Action and Social Roles

Just as economic action itself is "embedded" in social relations (Granovetter, 1985), energy use is buried in the social goings-on of everyday life. Here, the logics of home making, child rearing, cooking and cleaning, relaxing, or entertaining ordinarily have little to do with the energy flows that enable them. Even if energy were to be taken into account (Joe wants the thermostat set to a fairly low level on winter evenings), it is easily trumped by the social norms governing the appropriate and expected ways that things ought to be done in the culture (e.g., "don't subject your dinner guests to temperatures that are too cool," "keep your house clean," "own a car," "the children should each have their own room"). Any action to conserve has to make sense in terms of the shared cultural meanings. Joe's new windows weren't considered an odd investment by the neighbors, because the rationale wasn't purely environmental. As part of the "kitchen remodel," their legitimacy was secured by powerful status and "nest-building" norms (Wilk and Wilhite, 1984).

To say that energy use is *social* is not simply to say that individuals are influenced by social norms or that they have learned to incorporate other people's expectations into their routines. These are both true, but it is also the case that *groups* – not individual actors – are usually the consumers of energy. Joe, Liz, Zoe, and Zed gather in common areas to eat and watch television. They also have a social division of labor in washing, cleaning, shopping, and maintaining the house, one that is likely quite similar to those of their neighbors with whom they share values and under-standings (Kempton and Krebacher, 1984). Nonfamily members also contribute to the Blaughs' consumption. Liz likes to entertain, so they often have guests and co-workers over for dinner. Zoe's friends are there every day after school. As a result, Joe simply cannot act as a "self-interested decision maker." He must continually take into account the actions of others with whom his life is enmeshed.

These social relations are not reinvented by every Joe. They are largely inherited in the form of social roles. Only certain persons in households are *supposed* to be interested in matters such as energy use and conservation. Energy-using devices and systems are "technical" objects about which whole classes of people – the young, the elderly, professionals, women – are expected to know little or nothing. Joe *might* have some knowledge of furnaces, but since he is a career manager he is also exempt from this requirement in a way that his cousin, the factory foreman, is not. So it is likely that no one in the Blaugh household will be expected to really understand the inner workings of the family's energy use, and it would be considered somewhat odd if they did.

Status Arrangements

Social identities and statuses are at stake whenever we talk about consuming less of anything. To "have to conserve" is an indicator of poverty. To voluntarily conserve risks being stigmatized as poor, or, at best, miserly. Conservation also poses a risk of loss of normal comforts, along with convenience, cleanliness, pleasure, and the social costs incurred if these losses are noticed. Joe liked the idea of a more efficient front-loading washing machine, but Liz (who actually *does* the wash) recoiled at the thought of having to bend over all the time and fish around inside the machine for clothes.

Some of these sorts of choices certainly involve individual preferences, but few are lacking status considerations. And there are some striking differences in con-sumption across social class lines (Lutzenhiser and Hackett, 1993; Lutzenhiser, 1997). This is because, in addition to *conformity*, social *distinction* is an important aspect of consumer culture (Bourdieu, 1984). Joe and Liz are somewhat different from their neighbors (e.g., as a concerned environmentalist, he contributes to a variety of green causes and buys paper with recycled content). But their consumption patterns are more like those of their neighbors than those of nearby Pinnacle Estates or across town in Old Trackside.

The differences in energy consumption between the Blaughs and those who occupy higher and lower positions in the status ordering are the result of carefully cultivated lifestyle distinctions. Greater wealth needn't always be associated with higher rates of consumption and, in fact, items are often prized that are longer lasting and better performing. In American society, however, the lack of an old and well-accepted class structure means that status differentials have to be clearly *displayed* in order to be noticed (Veblen, 1927; Packard, 1959; Fussell, 1992).

Often, the items chosen for display have high energy requirements, e.g., trophy houses, sport-utility vehicles, large appliances, opulent bathing arrangements, "commercial" kitchen appliances, swimming pools, and so on. In fact, high rates of consumption are sometimes directly *celebrated*. Joe's neighbor Tom knows that his 15-mile-per-gallon monster SUV is understood by all to be expensive to operate, signifying that he's well off. Other times, highly consumptive items signal the possibility of privileged social goings-on (the pool "for the grandchildren," the guest room "for frequent visitors," the chef's range "for gourmet entertaining"). Regardless of whether the hoped-for events take place frequently or at all, the value of their sign-work dwarfs the (largely invisible) resource costs involved (Wilhite and Lutzenhiser, 1999).

Particularly in the US, all of this status signaling and lifestyle cultivation means that high rates of consumption are *assumed* in the social matrix within which actor and equipment are embedded (Lutzenhiser and Gossard, 2000). By overlooking this fact, efficiency advocates have often asked people to make changes in their lives that are culturally discordant, potentially stigmatizing, and contradictory to the "more is better" status logic that generally governs the terms of engagement in the US class system.

Adventures in Supply and Demand

However, Joe realizes that there is room for pro-environmental improvement in his lifestyle. And he has the good sense to consult experts: the utility company, environmental interest groups, various websites and publications. In the process, he wrestles with sketchy information and a bewildering array of options and claims – the world of high "transaction costs" (Williamson and Masten, 1999) that deters many consumers. Nevertheless, Joe is persistent and puts in the time required to become well informed. He then discovers that, in many ways, he's *stuck* with his present consumption patterns. He can't just insulate or willy-nilly order new windows or a new furnace. He and his remodeling contractor, Lance, find themselves constrained by the house at hand, its existing layout and internal systems, its mature landscaping, its orientation to the sun. A new refrigerator has to fit into the existing space in the kitchen (or the cabinetry has to be replaced). A new condensing furnace needs access to plumbing. The old air conditioner has a porch built over it. The windows are classics that are no longer manufactured and can only be upgraded at great cost.

In short, the built environment and settlement form – the historical creations of other Joes and Lances – significantly constrain their possible choices. Even though Joe has many more conservation options than renters and poorer people in his community, his improvements have to be "fit into" a pre-existing infrastructure created under quite different social, economic, and environmental conditions (e.g., when houses were built for families of seven, electricity was inexpensive, and smog hadn't yet appeared in the suburbs).

What's more, Joe would be lucky indeed if he found a contractor who really understood energy flows in buildings. Most do not. As a result, conservation fixes can be poorly executed and fail to provide imagined savings. Certain improvements may actually result in degraded performance elsewhere in the system through interactions between lighting, cooling, and ventilating subsystems. Do it wrong, and indoor air quality could take a dangerous turn. While the aggregate "efficiency gap" can be dramatic on paper, there is actually a good deal of uncertainty about just how much that gap can be narrowed in any specific case.

And even with high-quality design assistance (which comes at a price), Joe can only adopt innovations that are allowed under code and understood by code officials. The utility has to agree to connect his solar photo voltaic array to the grid, and the commercial supply chains he deals with have actually to be able and willing to supply him with what he wants. Joe can only choose something that's in stock (or that can be ordered and delivered in a timely way) and that can be readily installed and maintained. He happens to have located the newest high-efficiency hot-water heater on a website, but no one in the metropolitan area sells it, and his plumber is concerned about how long a special order will take. It turns out that tradesmen have little enthusiasm for innovation and are usually allied closely with particular manufacturers and distributors, who are also likely to be uninterested in energy conservation and the environment. Local businesses are resistant to stocking unusual parts, they probably don't understand the most advanced systems, and they are unwilling to sell things that aren't easily repaired. Vendors and installers are quick to perceive risks in technologies and potential threats to their social and commercial identities. Joe is told about the water heater: "We've never heard of such a thing," "Our wholesaler can't get it," and (ominously) "There have been some problems with those."

Maneuvering in the background of the supply system are countless other actors and interests of which Joe is only vaguely aware: the utility, state, and federal regulators; large energy suppliers; manufacturers of energy-using equipment (and their trade groups, ancillary industries, and lobbyists). Their interactions shape technological trajectories, fuels taxes and subsidies, and product offerings. They organize the supply worlds that Joe and Lance inhabit, and their structuring and restructuring of the energy system create uncertainties and constraints that further muddy Joe's already less than satisfactory conservation choices.

The Market Beckons

If Joe is very persistent – and lucky – he may be able to get the latest, greatest furnace, water heater, refrigerator, and windows installed and working. But if he is not vigilant, his hard-fought improvements can be subverted by Zoe, Zed, their friends, and their growing appetites. Also, Joe and Liz will contribute to their own undoing if, satisfied with their savings, they become more casual about heating or decide to buy a hot tub and a mega-screen television.

And chances are good that they *will* add new forms of consumption. On a societal level, despite its energy efficiency gains, the US has over the past two decades experienced a continuous growth in consumption that has outstripped population growth and marched in lock-step with growth in GDP (DOE/EIA, 2001). Joe and Liz, and soon Zoe and Zed on their own, will be buffeted by advertising appeals stressing the value of newness, bigness, speed, and power. They will be told that they should "super size" their purchases and that "shop until you drop" is an activity around which an acceptable identity can be built.

Media representations will show them that their lifestyles don't really measure up to the emerging standard of success, with "product placement" allowing manufacturers to display new consumption items as normal elements of the lives of characters and stars that they admire. Clever retail merchandising will encourage new consumption (Joe joins a cluster of other guys at the mall media mega-store to watch the new, giant-sized, digital, high-definition home theater set up; it's only a half month's salary, with no payments due for a year). Artful merchandising, coordinated with marketing and media, will, in the hands of skilled agents, be woven together to expand consumption and counter concerns about conservation.

Also, it's unlikely that Joe and Liz will be subjected to any real impetus to conserve from environmental groups, governments, or utilities. Pro-conservation efforts are handicapped by limited paradigms (e.g., "efficiency gap" and "rational actor" models), by conflicts of interest (regardless of the logic of DSM, utility culture is built around selling more, rather than less, energy), and by fear of consumer/citizen backlash (the specter of Jimmy Carter in his sweater haunts every politician who might be tempted to deliver a conservation message). Common wisdom among pundits and policymakers holds that consumers don't care about the environment and are unwilling to curb their appetites (e.g., Ferrell, 2000). These myths inoculate the system against the possibility of any serious top-down conservation initiatives, and effectively rule out democratic debates about energy futures, equity, conservation, environment, and the respective responsibilities of business, government, and consumers.

A Consumption-Based Greening of Energy Systems?

While a pessimistic account of the social structuring of demand is likely warranted, we also have to recognize that energy conservation is now an institutional part of the social landscape. The various Energy Star™ initiatives have met with widespread public approval and a significant degree of industry acceptance. There is some evidence of a growing green consumer movement, along with the tentative greening of business noted above. And to provide motivation, recurring energy problems (even "crises") may be facts of life in the future. It is interesting to note that, in something as close to a public referendum on energy policy as has taken place for some time, offerings of "green power" (energy from renewable sources such as wind turbines, geothermal sources, hydropower) have been well received by consumers when offered the choice, even at premium prices.

In the end, the energy system may be a particularly difficult case for the greening of consumption and production – more difficult than, say, expanding the recycling industry or increasing the supply of organic food. But energy use is an important source of environmental damage, and a sphere of social life that must be changed in order to avoid serious, widespread environmental change on a global scale. The prospects of doing so through the best-intentioned consumer action alone – if the social interpretation of consumption sketched here is accurate – seem remote. State regulation, business initiatives, and social movement activity would all seem to be necessary complements.

Notes

1   E.g., the Business Leadership Council of the Pew Center On Global Climate Change (Pew, 2001), the US Green Building Council (USGBC, 2001).

2   See Dunlap and Scarce (1991) and Kempton, Boster, and Hartley (1995) for discussions of American environmental values and consistently high levels of environmentalism in the US.

3   See Cottrell (1955) and Rosa, Machlis, and Keating (1988) for theoretical discussions of the significance of energy in human ecology and the evolution of human societies.
4   Strong supporters of the energy efficiency movement included National Laboratory scientists, state regulators, environmental and consumer advocates, and the US Departments of Energy and Environmental Protection Agency. See Lovins (1977) for one of the earliest statements of the efficiency argument.
5   Many of these technologies now carry the Energy Star™ label, which is affixed only to equipment that meets the fairly stringent US Environmental Protection Agency and US Department of Energy standards for hardware energy efficiency.
6   This could be done because paying people not to use energy (or, more accurately, buying energy back from people who were presently using it by subsidizing more efficient equipment) resulted in the need for fewer power plants. In DSM parlance, the "avoided costs" were higher (often much higher) than the "costs of conserved energy." Utility companies, who had previously thought only about building more supply to meet growing demands, actually were able to mount conservation subsidy programs to *reduce consumption* – in essence creating a "conservation power plant" that produced "nega-Watts," as opposed to "mega-Watts" (Lovins, 1996).

References

Archer, Dane, Costanzo, Mark, Iritani, Bonita, Pettigrew, Thomas F., Walker, Iain, and White, Lawrence (1984) "Energy Conservation and Public Policy: The Mediation of Individual Behavior," pp. 69–92 in Willett Kempton and Max Neiman (eds), *Energy Efficiency: Perspectives on Individual Behavior*, Washington, DC: ACEEE Press.
Beder, Sharon (1997) *Global Spin: The Corporate Assault on Environmentalism*, White River Junction, VT: Chelsea Green.
Black, Stanley J., Stern, Paul C., and Elworth, Julie T. (1985) "Personal and Contextual Influences on Household Energy Adaptations," *Journal of Applied Psychology* 70: 3–21.
Bourdieu, Pierre (1984) *Distinction: A Social Critique of the Judgement of Taste*, trans. R. Nice, Cambridge, MA: Harvard University Press.
Costanzo, Mark, Archer, Dane, Aronson, Elliot, and Pettigrew, Thomas (1986) "Energy Conservation Behavior: The Difficult Path from Information to Action," *American Psychologist* 41: 521–28.
Cottrell, Fred (1955) *Energy and Society: The Relation Between Energy, Social Change and Economic Development*, New York: McGraw-Hill.
Daly, Herman (1997) *Beyond Growth: The Economics of Sustainable Development*, Boston, MA: Beacon Press.
DOE/EIA (2001) *Annual Energy Review*, Washington, DC: US Department of Energy, Energy Information Administration; http://www.eia.doe.gov/emeu/aer (2/1/01).
Dunlap, Riley and Scarce, Rik (1991) "The Polls – Poll Trends: Environmental Problems and Protection," *Public Opinion Quarterly* 55: 651–72.
Durning, Alan (1992) *How Much Is Enough? The Consumer Society and the Future of the Earth*, New York: W. W. Norton.
Elgin, Duane (1993) *Voluntary Simplicity: Toward a Way of Life that is Outwardly Simple, Inwardly Rich*, New York: Quill.
Ester, Peter (1985) *Consumer Behavior and Energy Conservation*, Dordrecht: Martinus Nijhoff.
Farhar, Barbara (1993) *Trends in Public Perceptions and Preferences on Energy and Environmental Policy*, report no. NREL/TP-461-4857, Washington, DC: National Renewable Energy Laboratory.

Ferrell, David (2000) "Electricity a Mystery to Many Consumers: Most Americans Take Power for Granted But Know Little About it. That May Be Why They Have Difficulty Conserving," *Los Angeles Times*, 28 December: 1.

Frankel, Carl (1998) *In Earth's Company: Business, Environment and the Challenge of Sustainability*, Gabrioa Island, BC: New Society.

Fussell, Paul (1992) *Class: A Guide Through the American Status System*, New York: Touchstone Books.

Granovetter, Mark (1985) "Economic Action and Social Structure: The Problem of Embeddedness," *American Journal of Sociology* 91: 481–510.

Hawken, Paul (1993) *The Ecology of Commerce: A Declaration of Sustainability*, New York: Harper Business.

Hawken, Paul, Lovins, Hunter and Lovins, Amory (1999) *Natural Capitalism: Creating the Next Industrial Revolution*, New York: Little, Brown.

James, William (1890) *The Principles of Psychology*, New York: H. Holt and Co.

Kempton, Willett (1984) "Residential Hot Water: A Behaviorally Driven System," pp. 229–44 in Willett Kempton and Max Neiman (eds), *Energy Efficiency: Perspectives on Individual Behavior*, Washington, DC: ACEEE Press.

Kempton, Willett, Boster, James, and Hartley, Jennifer (1995) *Environmental Values in American Culture*, Cambridge, MA: MIT Press.

Kempton, Willett and Krabacher, Shirlee (1984) "Thermostat Management: Intensive Interviewing Used to Interpret Instrumentation Data," pp. 245–62 in Willett Kempton and Max Neiman (eds), *Energy Efficiency: Perspectives on Individual Behavior*, Washington, DC: ACEEE Press.

Kempton, Willett and Layne, Linda (1988) "The Consumer's Energy Information Environment," pp. 50–66 in *Proceedings of the American Council for an Energy Efficient Economy 11*, Washington, DC: ACEEE Press.

Kempton, Willett and Montgomery, Laura (1982) "Folk Quantification of Energy," *Energy* 7: 817–27.

Lovins, Amory B. (1977) *Soft-Energy Paths: Toward a Durable Peace*, Cambridge, MA: Ballinger.

Lovins, Amory B. (1996) "Negawatts: Twelve Transitions, Eight Improvements, and One Distraction," *Energy Policy*, 24: 331–43.

Lutzenhiser, Loren (1993) "Social and Behavioral Aspects of Energy Use," *Annual Review of Energy and the Environment* 18: 247–89.

Lutzenhiser, Loren (1997) "Social Structure, Culture and Technology: Modeling the Driving Forces of Household Consumption," pp. 77–91 in Paul C. Stern, Thomas Dietz, Vernon W. Ruttan, Robert H. Socolow, and James Sweeney (eds), *Environmentally Significant Consumption: Research Directions*, Washington, DC: National Academy Press.

Lutzenhiser, Loren (2001) "The Contours of US Climate Non-Policy," *Society and Natural Resources* (in press).

Lutzenhiser, Loren and Gossard, Marcia Hill (2000) "Lifestyle, Status and Energy Consumption," pp. 207–28 in *Proceedings, American Council for an Energy Efficient Economy 8*, Washington, DC: ACEEE Press.

Lutzenhiser, Loren and Hackett, Bruce (1993) "Social Stratification and Environmental Degradation: Understanding Household CO_2 Production," *Social Problems* 40: 50–73.

Malthus, Thomas (1798) *Essay on the Principle of Population*, London: J. Johnson.

Mol, Arthur and Sonnenfeld, David (eds) (2000) *Ecological Modernisation Around the World: Perspectives and Critical Debates*, London: Frank Cass.

Monbiot, George (2000) "Dying of Consumption: The More We Spend, the Happier We Become. Probably," the *Guardian*, 28 December: 18.

Nadel, Steven, Rainer, Leo, Shepard, Michael, Suozzo, Margaret, and Thorne, Jennifer (1998) *Emerging Energy-Saving Technologies and Practices for the Buildings Sector*, report A985, Washington, DC: American Council for an Energy Efficient Economy.

Nattrass, Brian F. and Altomare, Mary (1999) *The Natural Step for Business: Wealth, Ecology, and the Evolutionary Corporation*, Gabrioa Island, BC: New Society.

Norgaard, Richard (1994) *Development Betrayed: The End of Progress and a Coevolutionary Revisioning of the Future*, London: Routledge.

Packard, Vance (1959) *The Status Seekers*, New York: Pocket Books.

Peirce, Charles Sanders (1878) "How to Make Our Ideas Clear," *Popular Science Monthly* 12: 286–302.

Pew (2001) "Working Together . . . Because Climate Change is Serious Business," Arlington, VA: Pew Center On Global Climate Change; http://www.pewclimate.org/ (2/1/01).

Rosa, Eugene A., Machlis, Gary E., and Keating, Kenneth M. (1988) "Energy," *Annual Review of Sociology* 14: 149–72.

Schnaiberg, Allan (1980) *The Environment, From Surplus to Scarcity*, New York: Oxford University Press.

Shove, Elizabeth, Lutzenhiser, Loren, Guy, Simon, Hackett, Bruce, and Wilhite, Harold (1998) "Energy and Social Systems," pp. 201–34 in Steve Rayner and Elizabeth Malon (eds), *Human Choice and Climate Change*, Columbus, OH: Battelle Press.

Simon, Julian (1981) *The Ultimate Resource*, Princeton, NJ: Princeton University Press.

Stern, Paul C. (1986) "Blind Spots in Policy Analysis: What Economics Doesn't Say About Energy Use," *Journal of Policy Analysis and Management* 5: 200–27.

Stern, Paul C., Aronson, Elliot, Darley, James, Hill, Daniel H., Hirst, Eric, Kempton, Willett, and Wilbanks, Thomas J. (1986) "The Effectiveness of Incentives for Residential Energy-Conservation," *Evaluation Review* 10: 147–76.

Stern, Paul C. and Oskamp, Stuart (1987) "Managing Scarce Environmental Resources," pp. 1043–88 in D. Stokols and I. Altman (eds), *Handbook of Environmental Psychology*, New York: John Wiley.

Switzer, Jacqueline Vaughn (1997) *Green Backlash: The History and Politics of Environmental Opposition in the United States*, Boulder, CO: Lynne Rienner Publishers.

USGBC (2001) "Our membership DOUBLED in 2000 with more than 300 new members joining the Council," Washington, DC: US Green Building Council; http://www.usgbc.org (2/1/01).

Veblen, Thorstein (1927) *The Theory of the Leisure Class: An Economic Study of Institutions*, New York, Vanguard Press.

Vine, Edward (1994) "The Human Dimension of Program Evaluation," *Energy – the International Journal* 19: 165–78.

Wackernagel, Mathis and Rees, William (1996) *Our Ecological Footprint: Reducing the Human Impact on the Earth*, Gabrioa Island, BC: New Society.

Wilhite, Harold and Lutzenhiser, Loren (1999) "Social Loading and Sustainable Consumption," *Advances in Consumer Research* 26: 281–87.

Wilk, Richard and Wilhite, Harold (1984) "Household Energy Decision Making in Santa Cruz County, California," pp. 449–58 in B. M. Morrison and W. Kempton (eds), *Families and Energy: Coping With Uncertainty*, East Lansing, MI: Michigan State University.

Williamson, Oliver and Masten, Scott E. (eds) (1999) *The Economics of Transaction Costs*, Cheltenham: Edward Elgar.

Index